THE AUSTRALIAN FILM YEARBOOK

2021 EDITION

ANDREW F. PEIRCE

THE CURB

The Australian Film Yearbook, 2021 Edition
Andrew F. Peirce

Interior and Typesetting: Carley Tillett
Cover Design: webuyyourkids
Editing: Nadine Whitney and Nisha-Anne

First Print Edition June 2022, Australia

ISBN: 978-0-6454296-0-2 (paperback)
ISBN: 978-0-6454296-1-9 (e-book)

Published by The Curb
www.thecurb.com.au

This book is dedicated to

Travis Akbar

You are such an inspiration.
A vision like yours will help shape the New Wave of Australian film.

ACKNOWLEDGEMENTS

The Australian Film Yearbook was written on the lands of the Whadjuk Noongar people of Boorloo (Perth) Western Australia. I pay respects to their elders past, present, and emerging. Sovereignty has never been ceded. This always was and always will be Aboriginal land.

This book is a work of passion and love for Australian films and filmmakers, and would not have been written without the support, enthusiasm, and drive from the Australian film industry for its existence. I am beyond grateful for everyone who has contributed to this book via interviews, or written contributions. Your words alone give me reason to continue this celebration of Australian film for as long as my fingers will keep up with typing.

To my parents, Lynn and Michael, thank you for nurturing my love for films. Sarah and Paul, I can't wait to introduce my niece and nephew into the world of Aussie cinema and share my passion with them. Emily, thank you for being awesome.

This book would not be possible without the support and counsel from my partner Carley Tillett. Your guidance, intelligence and enthusiasm has kept this project afloat. Words cannot cover how grateful I am. Thank you.

I am lucky to have the support and friendship of two of the smartest and kindest people I know, Nadine Whitney and Nisha-Anne, who have both read the reviews, listened to the interviews, and guided my critical voice like nobody else.

I couldn't have done this book without the enthusiasm from Aaron McCann, who when I emailed just as the project was getting off the ground asking if he would kindly write the foreword, immediately said 'yes!' Aaron is a filmmaker I greatly admire and enjoy watching build a filmography as the years continue, and his work on the series Hug the Sun is the exact level of comedy we all needed after a difficult year.

The cover art is created by my good friends Sonny Day and Biddy Maroney, the awesome duo who make up the brilliant webuyyourkids. It's been a dream of mine to have Sonny draw a shark for something of mine, and here we are with the legend Valerie Taylor and a shark on the cover of a book I've written. Your art is an inspiration to me every single day, and you are both the kindest people on this place we call earth. Thank you.

the box office in the back half of 2021. With their return also came the comments of "I wish I knew these films existed. Australian audiences crave their identity on screen, they yearn to hear an authentic Aussie accent, to have their homeland reflected back at them. They want to see themselves up there on the same silver screen that has seen all of Hollywood's Chrises play a superhero of some kind (yes, even the Aussie Chris).

As I interviewed Australian filmmakers throughout 2021, I found a constant drive and desire from each person to celebrate and champion Australian culture and its identity on screen. Simon McQuoid talked about the experience of giving Josh Lawson the chance to bring ocker slang to Hollywood with *Mortal Kombat*. Kylie Bracknell talked about the transformative experience she created alongside Professor Clint Bracknell with *Fist of Fury Noongar Daa*, where they dubbed one of Bruce Lee's iconic films into Noongar language. *High Ground* costume designer Erin Roche wondered what her trip to England at 21 years of age, wondering what her trip would have been like if she had in her mind the spiritual conviction that comes from living on a continent which has "the oldest living continuous culture community of artists in the world". For *Sparkles* writer and actor Tina Fielding, the desire to see herself on screen, a queer woman with Down Syndrome, pushed her to write one of the best scripts of the year, and create an iconic dance sequence in the process. For *The Greenhouse* director Thomas Wilson-White, his desire to show different queer stories on screen, personal stories drawn from his own life experiences, drives him as a filmmaker.

Sally Aitken talked about the honour of embracing icon Valerie Taylor with the documentary *Playing with Sharks*, and bringing Valerie's legacy to a wider audience who might not have known of her work as an environmental activist, or even the global film industry. In the act of shining a light on one legend, the history of Australia gleamed with sudden urgency and vitality.

These stories live within each of us. Collectively they make up who we are as a culture.

For each person in this book (author included), our Australian identity is a deeply personal aspect of who we are as people. We are proud, we are passionate, we look out for one another, and most importantly, we love being Australian. We are also conflicted over who we are, grappling with the devastation of colonisation that still threaten 60,000 years of continuous Indigenous culture, a political system that actively harms asylum seekers, and that continuing sense of cultural cringe.

ACKNOWLEDGEMENTS

The Australian Film Yearbook was written on the lands of the Whadjuk Noongar people of Boorloo (Perth) Western Australia. I pay respects to their elders past, present, and emerging. Sovereignty has never been ceded. This always was and always will be Aboriginal land.

This book is a work of passion and love for Australian films and film-makers, and would not have been written without the support, enthusiasm, and drive from the Australian film industry for its existence. I am beyond grateful for everyone who has contributed to this book via interviews, or written contributions. Your words alone give me reason to continue this celebration of Australian film for as long as my fingers will keep up with typing.

To my parents, Lynn and Michael, thank you for nurturing my love for films. Sarah and Paul, I can't wait to introduce my niece and nephew into the world of Aussie cinema and share my passion with them. Emily, thank you for being awesome.

This book would not be possible without the support and counsel from my partner Carley Tillett. Your guidance, intelligence and enthusiasm has kept this project afloat. Words cannot cover how grateful I am. Thank you.

I am lucky to have the support and friendship of two of the smartest and kindest people I know, Nadine Whitney and Nisha-Anne, who have both read the reviews, listened to the interviews, and guided my critical voice like nobody else.

I couldn't have done this book without the enthusiasm from Aaron McCann, who when I emailed just as the project was getting off the ground asking if he would kindly write the foreword, immediately said 'yes!' Aaron is a filmmaker I greatly admire and enjoy watching build a filmography as the years continue, and his work on the series Hug the Sun is the exact level of comedy we all needed after a difficult year.

The cover art is created by my good friends Sonny Day and Biddy Maroney, the awesome duo who make up the brilliant webuyyourkids. It's been a dream of mine to have Sonny draw a shark for something of mine, and here we are with the legend Valerie Taylor and a shark on the cover of a book I've written. Your art is an inspiration to me every single day, and you are both the kindest people on this place we call earth. Thank you.

Thank you to Karen De Souza whose email sparked an idea that turned into reality.

A wonderful group of friends have helped me along my journey and these are a few of the folks I would like to thank for sharing their wisdom and support: Dr Jonathan Messer, Travis Akbar, David Giannini, Tim Leggoe, Christopher Spencer, Matthew Eeles, Jose Pucella, Adriana Begovich, Lucy Gibson and Revelation Film Festival.

Finally, the support from the Kickstarter backers from around the globe has meant more than anything. After I accidentally pushed the 'launch' button early, and was slightly terrified that this whole project would fall flat, to see it not only blast through its crowd-funding goal in 36 hours, but exceed it immensely shows that there are just as many people out there excited to hear about Australian films as I am. Thank you to:

Abbie Walton, Adam Morris, Alex Lorian, Alli Kett, Andrew Roberts, Annie Armenian, Anthony Tran, Ashley Hobley, Bede Jermyn, Ben Chamberlain, Ben Wright, Benjamin Morton, Bianca Katawiria, Brian MacNamara, Brooke Silcox, Buddy Watson, Carley Tillett, Chris Elena, Christopher Conway, Christopher Waldock, Clare Brans, Colin Sharpe, Connor Dalton, Damian Nixey, Dan Miranda, Dario Llinares, Dave Horsley, Duncan Martin Sheridan, Dylan Blight, Elaine Davin, Emily Davin, Eron Wyngarde, Fiona Underhill, G.E. Newbegin, Grant Watson, Hagan Osborne, Hope St Productions, Jacob BC, Jacob Hugo, James Maloney, Jason Jones, Jim Lesses, Jonathan J. Spiroff, Joseph Pallas, Kaleb McKenna, Kate Separovich, Kristy Tillett, Lauren Henderson, Leon Huxtable, Lester Conway, Levon J Polinelli, Lynn Peirce, Lynnaire MacDonald, Maddie Purdon, Marcus Liddle, Matt "Valkian" Murphy, Matthew Gasteier, Matthew Walker, Melbourne Documentary Film Festival, Michael Facey, Michael Peirce, Mike Brook, Myrhat Eliot, Nadine Whitney, Nathan Fontyn, Paul Ryan, Phil Kane, Phil Sarich, Rachel Grierson-Johns, Robbie Studsor, Ruth Richards, Sam Lara, Samson Tangney, Scot, Shane Pinnegar, Shaun Heenan, Simon Blackburn, Stephen Morgan, Steven Illes, Ted McDonnell, Tenille Hands, Tim Hoar, Tim Leggoe, Tina Fielding, Tina Zhang and Adriaan Haasbroek, Travis Akbar, Travis Johnson, Tristan Fidler, and Vanessa Gudgeon

Finally, thank you to the filmmakers who work tirelessly to bring their stories to life. I want to thank everyone who has contributed to this book with interviews, written contributions, and most importantly for your work making Australian films. Without your work, this book would not exist.

FOREWORD

What you presently have in your hands – be it a physical book manufactured in a brick-and-mortar warehouse, or a collection of ones and zeros beaming around a touchscreen — is a time capsule of a year in Australian film

2021 was one hell of a year.

From sun-drenched neo-noirs to found-footage drug busts. From quirky romantic comedies to psychological character dissections on real-life spree killers. From hitting the country music circuit to hitting the surf or hitting the pool or even just hitting some politicians with the truth about lobbying and corruption, it's been an exceptional year for Australian cinema and an even better year for writing about Australian cinema. We love our unique take on the world, and this book is as loving and unique in its critique as any other...well, maybe I'm just a little biased, and you should be too.

When Andrew Peirce asked me to write a foreword to what you're about to dive into, I was a little nervous, because I'm not Australian (I live here, but I wasn't born here, I immigrated here from Ireland in the late 1980s). The films I make I never try to infuse with "Australiana", that's just not in my Celtic DNA, but it certainly seeps in anyway, it's all around me and I just can't escape it. Once you're in – then you're in for good. That's the story of so many that now call themselves 'Aussies' we're a melting pot of multiculturalism. This land is filled with stories from one of the oldest living cultures on the planet, and also one of the "youngest" colonial settlements – the latter still needs to reconcile with its horrid past, and the arts are attempting to open that conversation. So here I am, writing a foreword to a friend's book. The one in your hands. A book about Australian cinema in the plague year of 2021 (is "plague year" correct? Sure, why not?).

Australia is seen as "the lucky country" and, for some, that rings true. We're certainly lucky to have such a diverse collection of films released every single year, films and documentaries that are not afraid to confront dark and troubling subject matters. We also don't shy away from making pure entertainment either -- hell, let's just say it: Mortal Kombat and Shang-Chi and the Legend of the Ten Rings are as Australian as meat pies (in that they both originated abroad, but when produced locally they excel).

Within these pages, or digital code, you'll find interviews, essays, reviews, and commentary on the year that was, plus an overwhelming love for Australian cinema from Andrew and his incredible team at The Curb. The site has been a huge supporter of Aussie cinema since its inception, and every single time I have had the pleasure of sitting down with Andrew, he's been nothing but gracious with his insight and his carefully written commentary.

I'll also say this: Andrew is a much better writer than I am, so please don't let this rambling foreword stop you from appreciating the myriad of opinions within. Just turn the page, or click 'next' or the arrow key, or swipe in a direction that lets you keep moving on, and dive into the year that was: 2021.

Enjoy.

Aaron McCann
Filmmaker and Australian taxpayer

INTRODUCTION

When it comes to the art of Australian film, the term 'cultural cringe' often hangs around its neck like a bad stench. That ungainly phrase was coined in 1950 by Melbourne critic and social commentator A. A. Phillips in an essay titled 'On the Cultural Cringe', published in the fourth issue of Meanjin, about the Australian tendency to denigrate our art and literature as being inferior to the works produced overseas, especially from Western countries like the United Kingdom and the United States.

Over seventy years later, audiences and filmmakers are still holding Aussie films up to the quality of overseas productions and battling the urges towards cultural cringe. Quality frustrations and box office struggles of Australian cinema have become such a frequent point of concern that it has become an annual event amongst Australian critics to herald 'the death of Australian cinema' and mourn its passing. Complaints of Aussie films being predominantly stacked with kitchen sink dramas hold some truth, given the high percentage of drama productions made in Australia. But it's a complaint that also hides the reality that modern Australian cinema is a multifaceted entity, embracing all genres, formats, and more.

What you hold in your hands is a book that aims to be the first of many that gives Australian filmmakers a platform to discuss their work, to help disrupt the flow of the cultural cringe we find ourselves wading against. With interviews across the board, reviews for films of all genres, and written contributions from filmmakers, The Australian Film Yearbook is an annual reminder of the creative abundance in this country.

As we saw during the 2020/21 season that Screen Australia dubbed "Our Summer of Cinema", there is an appetite for Australian films. Over one weekend, Robert Connolly's *The Dry*, Glendyn Ivin's *Penguin Bloom,* and Stephen Johnson's *High Ground* scored a trifecta and topped the Australian box office. Granted this success came during the perfect storm conjured by the pandemic, where Hollywood blockbusters moved releases to vague future dates or were shuttled online, leaving countries of low COVID-19 community transmissions struggling to run new films in cinemas.

By omission, these films succeeded.

Australian audiences saw Australian films in cinemas because that was almost exclusively what was on offer. This situation was fleeting, with Hollywood films eventually returning to cinemas and dominating the box office in the back half of 2021. With their return also came the comments of "I wish I knew these films existed. Australian audiences crave their identity on screen, they yearn to hear an authentic Aussie accent, to have their homeland reflected back at them. They want to see themselves up there on the same silver screen that has seen all of Hollywood's Chrises play a superhero of some kind (yes, even the Aussie Chris).

As I interviewed Australian filmmakers throughout 2021, I found a constant drive and desire from each person to celebrate and champion Australian culture and its identity on screen. Simon McQuoid talked about the experience of giving Josh Lawson the chance to bring ocker slang to Hollywood with *Mortal Kombat*. Kylie Bracknell talked about the transformative experience she created alongside Professor Clint Bracknell with *Fist of Fury Noongar Daa*, where they dubbed one of Bruce Lee's iconic films into Noongar language. *High Ground* costume designer Erin Roche wondered what her trip to England at 21 years of age, wondering what her trip would have been like if she had in her mind the spiritual conviction that comes from living on a continent which has "the oldest living continuous culture community of artists in the world". For *Sparkles* writer and actor Tina Fielding, the desire to see herself on screen, a queer woman with Down Syndrome, pushed her to write one of the best scripts of the year, and create an iconic dance sequence in the process. For *The Greenhouse* director Thomas Wilson-White, his desire to show different queer stories on screen, personal stories drawn from his own life experiences, drives him as a filmmaker.

Sally Aitken talked about the honour of embracing icon Valerie Taylor with the documentary *Playing with Sharks*, and bringing Valerie's legacy to a wider audience who might not have known of her work as an environmental activist, or even the global film industry. In the act of shining a light on one legend, the history of Australia gleamed with sudden urgency and vitality.

These stories live within each of us. Collectively they make up who we are as a culture.

For each person in this book (author included), our Australian identity is a deeply personal aspect of who we are as people. We are proud, we are passionate, we look out for one another, and most importantly, we love being Australian. We are also conflicted over who we are, grappling with the devastation of colonisation that still threaten 60,000 years of continuous Indigenous culture, a political system that actively harms asylum seekers, and that continuing sense of cultural cringe.

For many Australian film critics established and emerging, we have been fighting against that cringe since 1950. For Australian artists, the conflict of constructing an Australian identity in their work is equally fraught.

Over the following pages, you will read of more than 130 Australian films released during 2021. While all efforts have been made to include every feature and documentary that was released, alongside a wealth of short films, there will naturally be some accidental omissions. Additionally, the release of Australian films is fluid, with some making their debuts at film festivals and a wider release to come in the following year. As such, some films that may have initially appeared at festivals in 2020 will appear in this book, and many festival films that launched in 2021 will find themselves in the 2022 Yearbook.

It was a privilege to interview these filmmakers, and it is my privilege to be able to share these stories with the world. I hope that with each iteration of The Australian Film Yearbook, we can tear down that feeling of cultural cringe, and in its place foster a united sense of pride for the Australian film industry. We make some genuinely great films here.

Thank you for walking with me on this journey to celebrate Australian film.

CONTENTS

THEATRICAL
RELEASES

▶▷▶ **1** ◀◁◀

O ver these pandemic years, the cinema and film industry has had to duck, swerve, and adjust rapidly to a deadly landscape. With cinemas across Australia and the globe closed for most of 2020, there was a sense of hope and salvation as 2021 rolled around and cinemas prepared to welcome audiences back. With most of Hollywood fare pushed out of their lucrative holiday release dates to some amorphous time in the future, Australian cinemas were left craving something to give audiences.

In February 2021, Australian film history was made with Robert Connolly's *The Dry*, Glendyn Ivin's *Penguin Bloom*, and Stephen Maxwell Johnson's *High Ground* taking home the trifecta at the Australian box office; the first time ever that three Australian films had topped the rankings. Based on Jane Harper's bestselling novel, *The Dry* resonated with Australian audiences in a way that helped push it into the top twenty highest grossing Australian films of all time. To do this during a global pandemic is equally impressive.

The success of *The Dry*, *Penguin Bloom*, and *High Ground* showed that there was a clear appetite for Australian stories; a truth already clearly indicated with the positive audience reception to 2020 releases of Roderick MacKay's *The Furnace* and Jeremy Sims' *Rams*, both of which continued their box office success into 2021. Collectively, all of these films went on to be honoured at the 2021 AACTA awards with nominations in the Best Film category, alongside Justin Kurzel's eventual winner, the haunting *Nitram*.

Following in their footsteps were JJ Winlove's *June Again* and Josh Lawson's *Long Story Short*, both presenting lighter, audience-friendly tales about family, love, and life. Indie film *Unsound* was shifted from a 2020 release into a limited release during early 2021. The Hollywood-import sequel *Peter Rabbit 2: The Runaway* managed to capture the family audience, whilst the adult focused *Mortal Kombat* made a rare R-rated triumph at the box office, topping the takings in its release week. A rare cinema outing for Aussie genre films saw Luke Sparke's *Occupation: Rainfall* arrive at a time just as cinemas around the country went into lockdown, while Antaine Furlong's *Ascendant* disappeared without a trace. Powerhouse production house The Steve Jaggi Company helped bring countless Australian stories to screens of all sizes, with the Queensland-made rom-com *This Little Love of Mine* receiving a cinema release before finding a global audience on Netflix. In the documentary field, *My Name is Gulpilil, Girls Can't Surf, Firestarter: The Story of Bangarra, I'm Wanita, Love in Bright Landscapes*, and more all received varying audience attention, showing that it's not just fiction storytelling that audiences crave.

The early box office success of Australian film and its monopoly of cinemas was sadly fleeting, with lockdowns in NSW, Victoria, and Queensland further impacting the industry. Films that were bound to receive a cinema run, albeit a limited one, were scuttled off to streaming services, straight to physical media, or pushed into the next year. Both the Melbourne International Film Festival and Sydney Film Festival pivoted online, providing an in-home experience for all Australians, with the [delayed] Sydney Film Festival managing to present a run of reduced capacity screenings. Both festivals provided retrospective screenings of lost Australian classics like *Vacant Possession, Radiance*, and *Floating Life*, all of which joined the 21st Anniversary re-release of Andrew Dominik's debut feature *Chopper* in celebrating Australian film history. This is just a small slice of the Australian films that received a theatrical release, as countless indie films and festival films also found a home in cinemas across the land.

In the following pages, we explore the political impact of *The Dry*, discuss directing and costuming *High Ground* with director Stephen Maxwell Johnson and costume designer Erin Roache, Stephen Curry and JJ Winlove talk about working with Noni Hazlehurst in *June Again*, while also taking a look back at Eric Bana's career launching role in *Chopper*, and we close with an interview with *Unsound* director Ian Watson.

REVIEW
THE DRY

A DAMNING CONDEMNATION OF
SCOTT MORRISON'S AUSTRALIA

Co-writers Robert Connolly and Harry Cripps transfer Jane Harper's best-selling novel *The Dry* to the silver screen with great ease and jaw-dropping power, creating a masterful and iconic thriller. Eric Bana's federal cop Aaron Falk returns to the fictional rural hometown of Kiewarra, Victoria to attend the funeral of childhood friend Luke who died in an apparent murder-suicide that also claimed the life of his partner Karen, and son Billy. Yet not everything is as it seems - neither Aaron nor Luke's friends and family believe him capable of such an act against his family.

As with the novel, Aaron's past is revived, forcing him to revisit the tragedy that caused his expulsion from his hometown. The tense uncertainty that lingers over every scene is heightened by the flashbacks to the younger versions of Aaron (Joe Klocek), Luke (Sam Corlett), and their girlfriends, Gretchen (Claude Scott-Mitchell), and Ellie (BeBe Bettencourt). The jovial friendship the four share is tinged with toxic masculinity when Luke pushes 'play' too far by holding Ellie under water against her will when they visit a local swimming hole. While Gretchen, Ellie, and Aaron voice their anger at his actions, there's little change in Luke's behaviour. His behaviour is typical of what is often defended as 'boys being boys', a misguided statement that condones reckless behaviour. Luke's noxious roughhousing is shaded with a lingering darkness when we learn of Ellie's death by drowning, suggesting that Luke is capable of great violence and that he may have in fact taken the life of his own family decades on. Steeped in real tragedies that are all too frequent in our society, *The Dry* excels in peeling back layer upon layer of complexity around its central mysteries. If Luke did kill his family, then why did he do it? If he didn't, then what drove the heinous person who did?

Unlike American cinema, Australian films are surprisingly free from pointed commentary directed at the political climate they are made in. Where Spike Lee's *BlackKklansman* exposed the tyrannical and destructive impact of the 45th American President's administration, in Australia we were still playing catch-up with the devastation of colonisation and systemic injustice with films like *Sweet Country* and *The Nightingale*. When it comes to *The Dry*, the explicit manner in which Connolly and co-writer Harry Cripps transform the page-turning tension of Harper's text into a condemnation of the overarching political machinations of the Abbott/Turnbull/Morrison governments is one driven with a fury and desperation rarely seen in modern Australian narratives.

We see the weight of grief that hangs over an aching town gradually buckling under the weight of unceasing trauma. The remote town of Kiewarra is a farming community brought to its knees by incremental acts of devastation, and this excoriating act of violence only amplifies that pain, forever changing everyone in the town.

At once, an askew drone shot of a drought-stricken paddock reminds the audience of the continued governmental inaction on climate change. Later, we see the once vibrant river, full of water and brimming with life, transformed into a dusty ravine that swallows a stunned Eric Bana. Echoes of the devastation wrought upon the essential life source that is the Murray-Darling basin haunt our minds. The sound of chatter in the local pub is drowned out by the incessant artificial chimes of the fluoro-soaked pokie machines that drain any and all savings from the pockets of the townsfolk. To stay alive, the local school has to fight for funding opportunities, battling for essential improvements to keep the only school for kilometres alive.

Eric Bana
Photo Credit: Made Up Stories

Robert Connolly is working at his peak, taking care to paint the reality of every struggling Aussie outback town in the image of Kiewarra. Each stroke shows another aspect of government inaction and distancing from our elected leaders. We can hear a faint "I don't hold a hose mate, and I don't sit in the control room" (Scott Morrison) on the wind, carried upon the smoky breeze from the distant fires that loom perennially on the horizon. Connolly doesn't need to direct a pointed criticism of the Coalition government; the world he creates presents enough condemnation to fill a furious tome.

While the 'problem in a small town' trope has become tired and overdone, Connolly finds freshness and vitality within this drought-stricken landscape where the inhabitants are increasingly pushed to their limits, sizing up whatever way they can stay alive. The fallout of the crime haunts the town, lingering in the shadows of key characters' and circling their possible motive for murder. From the monetary to the vengeful to the eradication of a farming neighbour to purchase their now- abandoned property, each red herring has a logical undercurrent for wanting Luke and his family dead, evoking the continued belief that anyone is capable of killing in cold blood.

Yet while the mystery is investigated by the weathered Aaron, the lingering possibility that Luke might have actually killed his family hangs in the air. The potential violence that hides within each man is exposed completely here as moments of potential aggression simmers underneath the surface of almost each male figure. The towering Eddie Baroo maintains a semblance of civility in his bar, keeping the local blokes visiting the watering hole in some kind of order, even though it's a location that eternally feels like a powder keg on the edge of going off.

Performances across the board are stellar, with Eric Bana affirming his status as one of the most versatile Aussie actors. As Aaron Falk, he manages to slip between charm and concern, all the while presenting an unsettling air of untrustworthiness in his dedication to a lie he told as a young man. As the city-dweller returned home, he feels suitably out of place, disoriented and disorientating.

He's is supported by an impressive cast, a who's who of Aussie cinema showing why they're the respected professionals that they are. As the linchpin in the B-mystery, BeBe Bettencourt is superb as Ellie Deacon, imbuing her with a warmth and depth that proves why the town would be mourning her death years later. Matt Nable carries on his impressive filmography with a broken and unhinged man of the land who feels continually on the same precipice that everyone suspects Luke was on. Eddie Baroo brings a comedic touch to the film with his charming bar owner. Miranda Tapsell as Rita who worries about her police officer husband, Greg (Keir O'Donnell), once again reminds audiences why she's a great force on Australian film and television. Genevieve O'Reilly, James Frecheville, and Joe Klocek additionally bring their unique presence to this complex narrative.

But if *The Dry* belongs to one person, it would be Keir O'Donnell's overstretched police officer Greg Raco. As Kiewarra's sole law official, Greg is the first on the crime scene, where the lingering smoke of the shotgun hangs in the air. The toll this takes on Greg is visible in the eyes of Keir O'Donnell, traumatised and stressed. In a pivotal early scene, Greg takes Aaron through the house, describing what he saw when he arrived. The cries of the surviving baby reverberate in our mind as Greg struggles in the hallway with the weight of what will never escape his mind's eye. Aaron coaches him on receiving counselling and support, and Greg offhandedly says that he's getting the prescribed care, but the tone of his voice suggests that no amount of counselling will make the night sleep any easier to endure.

A criticism of *The Dry* would be the length that Robert Connolly pushes the depiction of the violence in the revealing third act. We have sat with the knowledge of the tragedy throughout the film, having seen the blood-spattered walls, watched the funeral take place, and witnessed the weight upon the minds of the townsfolk, and, most importantly, seen through the eyes of Greg the impact this has had on everyone. In a moment where Connolly could have exercised restraint, we see the family, including a wife and son who are defined by their death, murdered again. We already know what went on in the house on that fateful day and have endured so much that it feels excessive to push the audience and the characters through the images of the crime as it happened.

While in the moment I felt frustration, I also understand Connolly's creative choice here to depict the act, noting as it escalates out of control that the perpetrator is a familiar face, one who could be your friend, your neighbour, your family member. In this chaos of bloody terror, *The Dry* connects a taut line between government decisions and the manner that they inform our own personal choices. We are all responsible for our own actions, but the decisions we make are influenced by the world we live in, creating a feedback loop that is hard to break.

This is Scott Morrison's Australia reflected back at him in a venue that he would never dare set foot in, and if he ever did so, he would see an Australia that is distinctly foreign to him. At its quaking conclusion, *The Dry* left me shaken and devastated. It is a work of monumental importance – a towering achievement of Australian cinema, with the affirmation as the credits roll that Robert Connolly is one of the great Australian directors working today.

REVIEW
HIGH GROUND
A FRIGHTFULLY TENSE MEAT PIE WESTERN
STEEPED IN INDIGENOUS AUSTRALIAN HISTORY

The emerging Indigenous Australian New Wave film movement has seen two monumental films about Indigenous Australian history written and told from non-Indigenous perspectives: Jennifer Kent's soul shaking *The Nightingale* (2018), and Stephen Maxwell Johnson's *High Ground*. Filmed on Arnhem Land in the Northern Territory, *High Ground* is a frightfully tense meat pie Western that is as consistently breathtaking in its natural vistas as it is deeply unsettling in its traumatic depiction of white-inflicted tragedy upon Indigenous Australians. Just like *The Nightingale*, this is an undeniable benchmark for Australian cinema.

High Ground's pedigree precedes it with an exceptional cast of Australian screen icons: the legendary Jack Thompson, the always impressive Ryan Corr, the emerging brilliance of Caren Pistorius, a stunning performance from Simon Baker, who is confidently supported by Callan Mulvey, and newcomer Jacob Junior Nayinggul.

Baker takes co-lead as Travis, an ANZAC sniper turned policeman of the outback who is entrusted with implementing the law of the white man on Indigenous country – a land operated by its own laws and traditions for thousands of years. Travis is part of a troop of bullish and cocksure white policemen who are pursuing an Indigenous person who has stolen a cow. From the high ground above the Aboriginal camp, Travis watches as his fellow policemen brutally slaughter the Indigenous tribe. There was never any chance of a vocalised civility playing out, these men always intended to kill the tribe, acting on the feverishly genocidal mindset that wants to rid Australia of all Indigenous folk.

Skipping forward twelve years after the massacre, *High Ground* picks up with the narrative of the massacre's two survivors. Gutjuk (Nayinggul), who was a boy at the time of the assault, is now a young man in a Christian mission. He is deeply sceptical of the white man who calls him 'boy' and 'friend,' yet he is tethered to their camp by oppression. Then there's Baywara (Sean Munung-gurr), Gutjuk's uncle, a vengeful man who has forged a new tribe that seeks out to eradicate the white settlements from Arnhem land, and infuriates Moran (Jack Thompson) and his soldier brethren in the process. A war emerges between the two parties, fuelled by racism on one side and self-preservation on the other. *High Ground* moves at a breakneck speed through intense sequence after intense sequence, denying the audience a moment to catch their breath.

The landscape erupts from the soil into a work of overwhelming beauty. It is the picture-postcard image of Australia that we send to our international friends and family, leading them to believe that this is what all of our grand continent looks like. The cinematography from Andrew Commis manages to capture the grandeur of the land in a breathtaking manner, contrasting the unsteady shaky-cam during the white-knuckle violent battle sequences. The camerawork is struggles at times as it often pulls attention to itself rather than allowing the film to wash over the viewer; but when it's at its best, it's some of the finest in modern Australian cinema. A notable sequence where Travis shows Gutjuk how to shoot a gun presents the endless horizon of Arnhem Land as a wondrous Eden, untouched by civilisation and disrupted by the trauma of modernity.

Jacob Junior Nayinggul grounds the film with a searing performance that confirms his place as a powerful actor on the rise. Where *High Ground* teases out its moral complexities is within the relationship between Gutjuk and Travis. Gutjuk is a man driven by horrifying circumstance, thrust into a reality that he is almost powerless to escape. Travis, on the other hand, is a man driven by a moral code and a respect for the Indigenous people living on the land. Through Simon Baker's ever-observant eyes, we see a figure who wishes to mediate a harmonious relationship between the two worlds. Because of the catastrophic mindset of the Crown-led police force, that unity will never come.

As the white audience entry point, Travis is a relatable figure, especially in his well-intentioned desire to work alongside Gutjuk and his tribe to create a united 'civilisation'. Yet he is also a damning reflection, highlighting the clouded perspective of authority that white Australian culture is rife with. As is consistently the case, we cannot see an Australia without our presence in it, especially one where Anglocentric culture is not the dominant force, and it's this mindset that shows that Travis will never be a harmonious presence within the Indigenous culture of Arnhem Land.

Writer Chris Anastassiades meticulously weaves in a sub-narrative of communal Christianity, presenting a silently damning depiction of the manner that Christian missions across Australia employed religion to effectively whitewash Indigenous culture out of the children's lives. The ever-brilliant Caren Pistorius once again asserts herself as a star on the rise with a subdued performance as Claire, an optimistic and caustically collaborative force who, alongside her priest brother Braddock (Ryan Corr), sees herself as the essential glue to bond the two cultures together. Claire has at least taken the steps to understanding and learning the language of the land and, while it's never explicit, Pistorius does imbue Claire with a sense that she carries a level of guilt and ownership for her role in the transformation of Indigenous culture.

This active erasure of 60,000 years of continuous culture is presented in a matter-of-fact fashion as stolen tribes are commuted into the Christian camp. Body shame visibly descends on each person as they're adorned in 'civilian' clothing that covers and removes their Indigenous identity, applying a homogenous white identity to each of them. As they are taught English and scripture in a makeshift church that will eventually burn with the fury of a thousand lost souls, *High Ground* paints out a picture of the trauma to come with the Stolen Generations.

High Ground is a desperately essential film to witness and internalise. This is a film steeped in historical relevance, with its multiple fictionalised versions of the genocidal massacres inflicted upon the First Nations people of this land we call Australia, making it one of the relatively few Australian films to depict the heinous actions of white Australians in such unflinching manner. There is something to be said for exploring this history on film, especially given how many massacres occurred around Australia[1], but there's no denying that director Stephen Maxwell Johnson's taut and violent film arrives at an interesting point in the Australian film landscape.

Johnson's previous effort, the superb *Yolngu Boy* (2001), honoured his formative years in the Northern Territory. The film presented a considered story of Indigenous kids growing up in a world of duality, modern white Australia and traditional Indigenous Australia. His keen interest in the Australian history is further evidenced in *High Ground* where he echoes the groundwork of iconic Indigenous filmmaker Warwick Thornton and his masterpiece, *Sweet Country* (2017). In many ways, *High Ground* is the natural evolution of the filmic output of Bunya Productions (arguably Australia's finest production company), where lead producers David Jowsey and Greer Simpkin and their team continually bring together some of the finest talents in the Australian film industry to make iconic Australian films and television.

While masters like Rachel Perkins, Tracey Moffatt, and Ivan Sen had all been consistently working in Australian cinema for years prior to *Samson and Delilah*, it was Warwick Thornton's 2009 film winning Camera d'Or Award for Best First Film at the Cannes Film Festival that effectively kickstarted the Indigenous Australian New Wave of film. *Samson and Delilah*'s overwhelming success and market penetration came alongside Rachel Perkins' *Bran Nue Dae* (2009), and together they helped usher in the arrival of films like *The Sapphires* (2012), *Mystery Road* (2013), and *Top End Wedding* (2019), all showcasing the breadth of talent that exist in Australian Indigenous directors.

As such, *High Ground* comes at a time where the Indigenous Australian New Wave is at a turning point. As more Indigenous filmmakers are emerging, we're witnessing a change in the Indigenous stories that are being told, depicting lives that are no longer confined to the tragic narrative that has so often become synonymous in the public eye of what it means to be an Indigenous Australian. And for those narratives that do explore the rampant inequality and injustice that thrives within Australia's present and history, they are being told with Indigenous filmmakers and writers behind the screen, guiding and navigating these stories from a lived-in perspective, stripping away the approach of a maudlin emotional-tourist trip through a different culture, and replacing that with an informed perspective of what centuries of persecution looks like. While *High Ground* was made with extensive community consultation and the guidance and approval of countless Indigenous voices, it is still one written and directed from a non-Indigenous perspective.

This is not to discount the work of non-Indigenous directors crafting stellar Indigenous focused stories – after all, films like *Mad Bastards* (2010) and *Charlie's Country* (2013) have shown how deeply empathetic and reflective of the Indigenous experience narratives written or directed from a non-Indigenous perspective can be – but rather to highlight that Australia is currently witnessing a boom of creativity from Indigenous filmmakers. I'm well aware of the optics of a white writer critiquing an Indigenous narrative film and highlighting the non-Indigenous creative team behind it, but I want to stress that I'm doing so to question that if the Australian film industry is serious about seeking out greater diversity amongst the creative teams on films and television, then they also need to strengthen the ability for Indigenous voices to tell their own stories onscreen.

In one of the many memorable moments in *High Ground*, Callan Mulvey's haunting Eddy spits the phrase "You can't share a country", a hate-filled barb intending to further divide the land. It's that line that rings through my mind as I write this review, with white critics and filmmakers often being the town-criers bemoaning the reality that "Anyone should be able to write a story," or as in the case of transgender stories, "It's called acting," all the while neglecting the need for community consultation and input to create authentic and respectful narratives. Eddy's perspective highlights how dominant the white voice is in Western society, a point that is echoed by Jack Thompson's royalist police officer as he utters a prophetic line while he sits for a photograph alongside the Indigenous men that he so eagerly wishes to remove from the land: "It is a responsibility of those who make history to record it."

The legacy of white Australia is akin to that of an introduced species like the cane toad, brought to correct something upon the land that never needed correcting in the first place. Australia's history has been documented by these same Australians, the narrative controlled through a white lens. What sets *High Ground* apart from films that have tokenistic portrayals of Indigenous Australians is that community informed approach to the narrative. Writer Chris Anastassiades excels at crafting a respectful narrative that honours the legacy of the cruelly slain First Nations people, even going so far as to critique the white-saviour trope with Simon Baker's Travis (allowing Baker to give a career best performance).

And yet I can't help but ask whether non-Indigenous filmmakers are the right voices to tell these stories.

As Australian cinema seeks to diversify its creative forces, and as the demand for Indigenous stories naturally increases, there needs to be a grander choice applied when it comes to deciding who gets to tell Indigenous stories. Yes, *High Ground* is a stunning film that deserves every accolade it gets, and Stephen Maxwell Johnson's direction carries the echoes of Western-genre greats like John Ford and, from a modern stance, the Coen Brothers. But given how much of Australian cinema has been driven by non-Indigenous voices, isn't it time that they are able to tell their history onscreen?

Additionally, why is it that narratives or genres that are steeped in trauma celebrated more than those that skew away from the tragic past of Indigenous Australia? While *The Nightingale* has its place in Australian cinema as a harrowing work of brilliance, I want to ask why a more empathetic and progressive film like *Top End Wedding* is relegated to 'basic genre fare'? Miranda Tapsell and Wayne Blair's raucous delight of a film displayed an urgent sense of revitalisation for a dormant genre: the Australian romantic comedy. This feel-good film is focused on love and hope rather than the increasingly tropey tragedy of other Indigenous films. On the television front, Elaine Crombie and Nakkiah Lui's uproarious *Kiki and Kitty* sits comfortably alongside Steven Oliver's iconic droll delivery of the word 'slut' in *Black Comedy* as some of the finest Indigenous comedy in Australia. These Indigenous artists are presenting a future for Australian culture that is a hopeful one, and they ought to be celebrated and encouraged to make more.

And yet, as I write this, a line from Meyne Wyatt's powerful Q&A monologue from his 2020 play *City of Gold* rings through my mind:

> *"How are we to move forward if we dwell on the past?" That's your privilege.*[2]

That is my privilege, and one that shows that I rightly do not have the lived-in experience to comment on how and what Indigenous stories are told on-screen. Again, I recognise the problematic nature of a white Australian like myself discussing this in a review for a film as good as *High Ground*, especially given the extreme lack of diversity within the Australian film criticism circles. However it's a point that I would urge you, the reader, to examine: Elevate Indigenous Australian artists telling their own stories, whatever they may be.

I close this piece by reminding you that *High Ground* is an overwhelming achievement of cinematic brilliance. It continues the legacy of *Sweet Country* by exposing the horrifying actions of white Australians, reminding viewers that these devastating massacres took place right here on Australian land. For white Australians, it is important that we recognise that sovereignty has never been ceded, the scars of the past are still open and stinging with pain for Indigenous Australians today. While it is easy to sit there and watch these films and feel like you've made a difference by the mere act of witnessing it on screen, that in itself is an aspect of white privilege, and it is clearly not enough. It is equally important to seek out and listen to Indigenous voices and hear their calls for change and diversity in Australia, and to assist in implementing said change through organisations like Pay the Rent[3] or IndigenousX[4].

INTERVIEW
HIGH GROUND - DIRECTOR
STEPHEN MAXWELL JOHNSON

Stephen Maxwell Johnson's connection to Indigenous culture with a filmography that begins with directing Yothu Yindi video clips for 'Treaty' and 'Djäpana', and then progressing to his first feature film *Yongu Boy* in 2001. Made in collaboration with Yothu Yindi band member Witiyana Marika, Johnson's second feature *High Ground* embraces a 'both ways' style of filmmaking, namely, bridging two cultures together – blackfellas and whitefellas to tell one story.

High Ground was both a critical and commercial success, receiving a swag of industry award nominations and wins, and sweeping the board with wins in major categories at the Film Critics Circle of Australia 2022 awards.

Interview conducted January 2021

▶▷▶

Thank you for giving me your time to have a chat about your fantastic film.

Stephen Maxwell Johnson: That's an absolute pleasure, Andrew. Thank you for what I thought was a remarkably well written review. I thought it was great. I appreciate that.

It was a a difficult review to write because I approached it in a very— I asked questions which I'm not sure I should be the right person asking or not.

SJM: That's all right, mate.

But I did. And I'm glad that your film provoked those things in my mind.

SJM: But none of us want that angst get in the way of listening and learning and opening our hearts to everything that's out there to be sorted out with our history, because it's all of our reckoning, really, mate. And it's a tricky one. You know, I've been grappling with it all my life.

You've got a deep history with the Indigenous folks of the Arnhem Land and of Australia as a whole. You are definitely a lot more learned than I am. You come from a lot more of an understanding and educated history than most white folks in Australia do. How do you approach that?

SJM: Well, look, I'm very fortunate to have lived in the same life world as a lot of Indigenous people. I grew up in the Bahamas and Africa before I came out to the Australia and obviously Northern Territory and Arnhem Land. So all my life has really been about having wonderful friendships and adventures with Indigenous people. And I've never known anything different in my life, it's been my experience, and my world. And I struggled with the whole idea of black and white because so many of my friends - for example, Dr Mandawuy Yunupingu [lead singer of Yothu Yindi] was a very, very dear friend, and he was always about both ways sharing ideas, creating a bridge of understanding between two cultures, two people. And it's always been my conversation, that two-way conversation about being human in that way and what that means, and I've been very fortunate to have had a beautiful immersion in Indigenous culture here in Australia, particularly.

I find that relationship that you're talking about that that bridge between black culture and white culture is so brilliantly portrayed with such great complexity with Simon Baker's character, Travis. Can you talk about how you went about realising that character?

SJM: Chris [Anastassiades] and I, we grappled with this story for years as did Manduwuy, Witiyana [Marika], all the families. It's not an easy thing to do. There's no perfect or right way to do a thing, how clear could you be about having a crack at telling a story like this. You just navigate the idea of it, you do the very best you can collectively. We had this whole thing about dual protagonists in the film. People go, "You can't do that, you can't do it." Well, why not? Who set the rules here?

It was interesting just picking up on what you're saying about Indigenous stories, but it's a both ways story. It's offering up insights from different perspectives. We've tried to come up with something that really can be immersive and inclusive of all people in its storytelling. And that was always where we wanted to come from.

Simon's character Travis, and all the characters in the film are really based on true life people who we've learned about in our history, been inspired by true events and happenings and characters. Yes, it's a fiction in order to tell a deeper truth. That's what we went for; to create an exciting action-packed film that really would resonate with a very wide audience. At its heart is a lot of truth-telling. It was about trying to really connect with the real life and reality of men and women who were out on country at that time and had had the experiences that they had.

For example, Travis (was) from the war, those men came back so shell-shocked and so fucked up. They had to try and remove themselves away from society, and there they were at the interface of dealing with the world's oldest living culture. That's not a great set of ingredients to start with. It's complex and we were trying to find that truth and that edge and that reality for all of the characters in the film, really.

The beautiful thing about working with the Indigenous players was that that they have that connection to history in the sense where their grandfathers or grandmothers either survived or were in a massacre. That history is all very immediate. All of the Indigenous players in the film, the actors had never acted before, but that history, there is a connection there to country, to their grandfather, their great grandfather or grandmother who could have been in a massacre or witnessed a massacre. All of those stories are real and accessible for them. It was very much about finding that truth and those connections as we worked through the story and the scenes and the moments.

Really, Jacob, Esmerelda, Witiyana were putting themselves in almost a real-life story for their own selves that they've heard about and grown up with. It was a very primal connection that everybody found with the story in the film and their own true worlds. That stacks up. We've got to find that understanding of history in ourselves really.

One of the films that came to mind as well after watching this was Maya Newell's documentary In My Blood It Runs. And she talks at the end of that film how it was a collaborative process. While her name may be on the IMDb page, it's really a collaborative process of multiple different directors, multiple different voices all creating the film itself. I get the impression that's what you're talking about with High Ground as well. While your name and Chris' name are the two prominent names here, as you're saying, it's not just you two. It's been decades of work on this script. Is that the case?

SJM: Yes, mate, definitely. Look, it's been a bit of a lifer for me in a lot of ways. Witiyana was right there by my side, as was Manda previously. But Witiyana is a very, very dear friend. And as I have lots of friends right across Arnhem Land, Yolngu, all of these men and women as well. We sat down for years and years and years and talked all of this through, and we're all grappling with history. As a nation, we're all still learning, we're all trying to understand how we can approach this and tell stories and put stuff out there to help us all on our journeys.

High Ground was a part of that process for all of us. Have we got it right? I don't know. We've given it our best shot. And we've all had a wonderful experience making it and have been on a learning journey just by making the film and putting this thing out there ourselves, all of us, Black and white.

What's your experience so far with it, having traveled around the world?

SJM: It had its world premiere in Berlin. And that was wonderful. I mean, the German people obviously have an incredibly harrowing history themselves that they grapple with and they're dealing with, and obviously it's not that long ago. There's a wonderful audience there for the film and the story and a lot of deep connections to thematically what the film is about. It went down a bomb in Berlin, it went down very well. It was immensely well received. And I think people were incredibly moved and connected to the story in the ways that they were.

I want to talk about the visual style of High Ground. One of the things which I found really fascinating was how, when we're looking at the vistas of Arnhem Land, it's nice and peaceful and calm. And then when the tragedy and the trauma strikes, the camerawork really immerses you in there and becomes almost like you're in there with the action as it's happening. What decisions were made as to what camera work to use? What was it like filming on that land?

SJM: I did [clips] for Yothu Yindi, Treaty and all that kind of stuff. I've always been a proponent for believing that the camera is very much an eye. And the eye flicks around and moves and creeps its way through a scene and takes so many shots in a very short space of time in order to give you an impression of something.

And I've always believed in the idea that we went for this division format of 1.66 [ratio] to try and give height as well as width. It's not a CinemaScope kind of aspect because I don't think that's what we see when we look with our eyes, so it was trying to replicate that idea of the human eye and how it sees things and for the audience to be immersed through that perspective and that idea. I've always done that. I've had the camera on my shoulder myself most of the time, shooting most of the stuff I've done.

Obviously, Andy Commis, the DOP on this film, is an incredibly creative and talented man. And we connected early on talking about the style and the feel of this film and wanting it to be immersive and connective and affected by what we were seeing. I've tried to encapsulate that connective feeling with the action or the observation of something.

It's really impressive. We're such a broad country here that it feels like there's still so much untapped and unshown, and the new [image of this] land feels so vital and vibrant. It's opened up a whole different part of Australia that I knew existed, but I haven't gotten to see, and I'm grateful for that, thank you.

SJM: That's a pleasure, mate. Look, this thing's been on the burn for twenty odd years. It's been a work in progress for me in lots of ways. But we're all very, very clear about the story we wanted to tell. And it's been interesting seeing other films come out and comparing them with this one. And I think the timing's great. There's a point of difference with what we've done. I'm thrilled and feel so honoured to have worked with so many wonderful people to create it. And there's this beautiful sense of ownership in Arnhem Land of this story. And I'm very, very proud that we've done this together. It's a good feeling.

I want to talk about Jacob [Junior Nayinggul]'s performance as well. As you're saying, there's a dual lead quality to High Ground, we've got Simon's role as Travis and then we've got Jacob as well as Gutjuk. They both bounce off each other perfectly. They deliver some really searing performances. What was it like working with Jacob, and how did you find him as well?

SJM: Oh, he's a beautiful man. He's a ranger out on Arnhem Land. When I screen-tested him, I said, "Look, I'm a white fellow. I've just killed your family. Here's a spear, deal with me. How do you feel?" And he had an instant connection to that story, because he knows about massacres within his own family history. The look in his eye and the instant moment of being a warrior and going, "My job here is to defend my family and protect my land." It was just this instant pure connection and I said, "This guy's got it all."

And the beautiful thing [was] what happened onset was that he got very close with Simon. And it was almost like the two of them were living out an on-screen off-screen truth and reality because there you were with this mission kid in the film and he's looking at this white sniper heroic character. And they're working stuff out between them and a friendship forms and he begins to discover himself and all that sort of stuff where we're at with the film.

However, off camera, it was a similar sort of thing. Here was this Hollywood superstar, and there was Jacob, he knew who Simon was and he was in awe of him. [Simon had] done all this acting, and [Jacob had] never acted in his life. And Simon really took Jacob under his wings, he made Jacob feel safe and confident on set, he relaxed him. He connected with him quietly and beautifully on and off camera, and that carried through into the film. It was really lovely to watch and it was a thing that we hoped to achieve. And we did. And it's a credit to the two of them how well they settled with each other in each other's presence. Simon would just take it to him and give it back. And they were right there in the moment together because that was real in every sense of the word if you know what I mean.

The cast here is absolutely stacked. Everyone from John Brumpton who of course is a seasoned professional...

SJM: Legend.

All the way through to Jack Thompson, another legend, and Callan Mulvey and Ryan Corr and Caren Pistorius.

SJM: Beautiful, mate. Jack - he's always been a mentor of mine in my life as well. He's very passionate about Indigenous affairs, and culture. He's stood by my side for the time as well. I've had some amazing people working and helping and realising this with me.

What was it like reconnecting to the process of directing a film? I know you've done some TV work, but it's been a long time since Yolngu Boy. I loved that, but I was left asking, "When is he going to make another film?" And thankfully, you come out with this.

SJM: Hopefully, it won't take as long. That's for sure.

Fingers crossed.

SJM: This was a very particular project, there were particular complexities, and I'm very much one for process and taking the time to sit with family and really work things through and make sure we're all on the same page with things. It's been a long time coming, making this film. I've got some other very strong ideas that are in early research and development. We'll see how we go.

One of the things that I've been really, really grateful to see is that Australian audiences are resonating with Indigenous stories and there is an appetite for them.

SJM: As you talk about Indigenous films and Indigenous filmmakers, all that sort of stuff, I'm a massive supporter of supporting and working with Together Apart, Indigenous filmmakers getting out there and doing [their] thing. I have the right from the beginning of the time of my days on Treaty when people like Warwick [Thornton] and Rachel [Perkins] were all learning as well. We were all out there, young, vibrant, passionate about what we all wanted to say, and how we knew each other and not knew each other and all this kind of stuff.

I think it's exciting. I mean, who's got all the answers? Nobody. I think the coming together of spirits is good. The separation of things at times is good. I think each project, each story will be different, it'll be made differently. It'll be a different collective of people. And I don't think there's any rules, and there doesn't have to be. It needs absolute respect for the story and how it's being told and what ultimately that story is trying to say. And I think if that truth is there, then all the other things stack up, come together to make it happen.

I'm a big supporter of young Indigenous people learning the art of cinema and camera and sound and lights and action and all that, because there's some amazing talent out there in the bush, and I've worked together with those people and it's just brilliant. It's exciting as you could possibly hope for.

I think that's a perfect way to wrap up. I really appreciate you taking the time to have a chat with me about your film and your history as well.

SJM: With your story, it's not about correcting or anything.

It's just Bunya [Productions] came in on this later in the piece. This is very much a Maxo production. It was something that was born out of my life and history that pre-dates all of that. And so, I've been doing this a long time, and the people I've done this film with are lifelong friends. It's been a big journey, really, and it's exciting. It's really exciting. Jonathan Nadji and Alfred Nayinggul are coming to Darwin for the premiere and they're mentally proud of it all. It's a good thing.

You write beautifully, and I appreciate where you're coming from. I thank you for being passionate yourself and interested and wanting to learn and listen and understand more because it's all of our reckoning and our history in this country, and we all got to be brave and put ourselves out there and be heard.

INTERVIEW
HIGH GROUND - COSTUME DESIGNER
ERIN ROCHE

Erin Roche is an AACTA award winning costume designer who has over a decade of experience working in Australian film and TV. Her work includes the acclaimed series *The Beautiful Lie* (2015) for which she received her first AACTA nomination, the indie hit *Boys in the Trees* (2016), the 2021 indie drama *Disclosure*, and the NBC Universal production *La Brea* (2021). Erin won the AACTA award for Best Costume Design in a Film for *High Ground*.

Erin is a Doctor of Creative Industries, having graduated from the Queensland University of Technology in 2018. Her focus as a costume designer is on the triangulation of embodiment of character, voice of the designer and collaboration. Erin was awarded the Churchill Fellowship in 2016, allowing her to work with costume designers and production companies around the world on a seven-week professional development course.

Interview conducted December 2021

▶▷▶

Where do you start with a film like High Ground? Is it with the script? Is it with the concept?

Erin Roche: The initial part of the process was pretty traditional. Producers reached out to my agent, I was sent a script, we had a meeting to see how we felt. We talked to experiences that could help me understand the film, but it really started to mean something to me [when] Stephen Johnson took me on a recce for a week up to Arnhem Land. And usually, it's pretty rare I get to go on the recces just because of how production falls. But this was a couple of months before and it just really hit home.

We helicoptered across Arnhem Land to meet with traditional weavers and just the different people I met on that and experienced that part of the country; like I've spent quite a lot of time in western remote Queensland as a kid, and, certainly travelled various parts of Australia, but I've never spent time in Northern Territory, and it's just such a gobsmacking country, you're breathless. And you feel that as soon as you get there. For me, the connection with country really had an instant impact on my connection with the script.

I imagine from there you had the visuals of the Northern Territory in your mind for months as you're in preparation stage. Where do you start to prepare for how the costumes are going to inform the characters?

ER: You know, I dabble in academia. And really thorough research is where I start all projects, whatever they are. For me, it was really about unpacking the era and the difference in the two eras, and also trying to tap into what exists. If you're doing a Seventies film, you might be able to hire certain costumes. But the sad truth of it is in Australia, we don't have a Museum of Anthropology like they do in Canada which champions traditional dress, we just don't have those resources. I was not surprised but disappointed to find that there was no 'go to' resource centre or information of traditional dress from that era.

That opened up a different sort of approach to researching, you really have to embrace traditional oral cultures when you're working with traditional cultures. I really wanted to open up a dialogue with the locals in the area of Arnhem Land and Kakadu. And then when you're looking at the colonial costumes, all photographs from that era are black and white. And without doing any research, I was like, "Oh, yeah, they're the Navy uniformed police officers that I've seen in old Australian films." But when you actually start researching that and reach out to places like the Police Historical Society in the Northern Territory, you realise that actually they were mostly left-over World War One uniforms. And that they're khaki in colour.

There's lots of information that's costume-relative you miss out on in black and white photography. Those kinds of assumptions I've made without doing any research really proved me wrong pretty quickly. And then just the slight variations in the two eras that the film covers, and also thinking about the remoteness of the location and the impact that would have had on traditional dress. If we look at Caren Pistorius' character Claire, it's not high fashion of the era. And it's a really subtle thing but later on in the film, she's actually wearing the same skirt from the earlier period, it's just hemmed and she's actually made it work. I think that era-specificness of her costumes is incredibly subtle, but it's not like new fashions would have been coming through the middle of Oenpelli [Mission name, Gunbalanya traditional name] at the time. So that's pretty delicate.

Where do you start with building costumes for the cast? Do you start with that research and then pinpoint on, say, on Caren's character? Do you spend days focusing on her and then move on to the next character? Or you're seeing it all at once for each of the different characters?

ER: It's pretty much a broad collage. You go down a rabbit hole, it's a bit like Googling something and suddenly you're somewhere else. It's really hard to confine it to "Oh, today's my Baker day." It's really interesting where you start picking up ideas from when you're on that search. The film's not a documentary either, so there are certain aspects that we really pushed and cheated because to the modern eye, some of those period accurate ideas would be kind of ridiculous, like the hats of the era. True period correct hats were really extreme to our modern eye, for example, we really went with what suited Simon's physique and action as opposed to what was period accurate at the time. Because to my modern eye and anyone born in the last three decades, four decades, five decades, the sort of height of the hats of the era are almost comical. So you cheat stuff like that. But there's no way of narrowing it down to "Oh, I've got two hours, I'll do some Travis research." It's really broad.

With that in mind, do you then look at a character as menacing and powerful as Jack Thompson's Moran as being somebody who you can then use those eccentric stylings, that certain style of hat to really amplify who he is as a character?

ER: At a really basic level, as a costume designer, I see the body as my canvas, and the medium is cloth and clothing. I'm working with the body to help embody character. And it's really important that that body can carry off the actual garment. For example, with Jack in that outfit, Jack brought so much to the Moran character and the design process. I really had some great times with Jack and really appreciated the time he put into the research behind Moran. And just with his hat, for example, we went through a lot of hats to get to the hat that worked and wasn't comical and ridiculous. But you need a performer who can carry off that with confidence and not be worn by the hat, so to speak.

It really depends on the performer and that crossover of collaboration. And I can have all the research in the world and all the references, but until I actually meet the body, there's no guarantee that any of it works or makes sense. Until I meet the person and we work our way through our shared ideas and visions for the character, it's all just theory.

Can you talk about your initial interactions with the different actors? What was the difference between meeting with Simon and Jack as meeting with newer actors like Jacob, Sean, or Esmerelda?

ER: The main difference is level of experience as opposed to anything else. Simon, Jack, they are seasoned performers who understand the costume design process and their own experience, understand how their bodies fit within that equation, and also understand their relationship to the viewer more so than a new actor. With a new actor, you're really having to explain how the costume is a transformative tool and it's there to help them. It's not to hinder them.

The last thing I want to do as a costume designer is force someone into a costume that makes them feel uncomfortable or doesn't agree with their cultural beliefs because I think it's what's best for the story. And then in the end, that comes around to making their performance compromised because they can't deliver because they're distracted by whatever it is they're wearing. When you talk about Esmerelda, for example, we worked really hard to find a way to obviously embrace traditional dress but also make it appropriate for her as a woman representing her community now and the variations of what that might mean.

Esmerelda Marimowa
Photo Credit: Sarah Enticknap. Used with permission.

If you think about the centuries of shame that has been brought about [by] the idea of bodies and decades of mission culture and if you think of intergenerational - and also family hierarchies and networks. The appropriateness of her being topless, for example, which would have been very accurate just didn't really sit well with us and wasn't something we needed to do to deliver a really amazing strong Gulwirri character, although period accurate truth at the time would have been - she would have been topless, for example. So just navigating those delicate conversations is the difference, and that new performers don't really know about that process or even just the basics of fitting processes.

Initial fittings are really a space to play with character and search for character and have a conversation at an initial fitting, or any fitting isn't really a space for me to dictate to someone what they're going to wear and how they're going to feel in it. So being open to sharing how that can work for someone and trying to make them at ease with it, because it's quite a vulnerable thing; you're in a small room with someone you've never met, and I'm asking them to take their clothes off and put on something weird that they've never worn. It's a big ask.

And I think when you're dealing with really sensitive subject matter, we were filming massacres, and a lot of these people had never worn traditional dress and would talk about their ancestors when they looked in the mirror and that's a pretty intense thing to be experiencing in front of a total stranger. You really have to be sensitive to that.

What were the conversations like meeting with the First Nations people and talking about the importance of presenting their culture on screen?

ER: For me, the making of the traditional costumes in *High Ground* was life-changing. I spent probably six weeks working particularly with a group in Gunbalanya every day where I would drive across Cahills Crossing, count the crocodiles as I went, and we would go harvesting for the right bush fibres. I would drive across country. I just learnt so much - threw stones at crocodiles who looked at us for too long while we tried to find some native hibiscus. And I would sit with the women as they worked on the fibres and wove them and turned them into garments, and fail to ever split pandanus which is a real art form.

For me, that experience was second to none. And I could only relate it to sort of fieldwork I'd done for anthropology, studying in Oman in the Middle East working with traditional dress over there as opposed to costume experience. First Nations people have an oral history, so there's no written catalogues of what anyone was wearing. We really had to talk and discuss particular stitches.

If we look at the armbands, we took a few goes to find older stitches and for people to remember what their aunty had told them or to find ways to try and make it as authentically of the time as possible. It felt like we were breathing new life into some older ideas which is an incredible honour to be part of in those conversations and to be welcomed into a group like that was just a really rare and beautiful thing.

And if I think about - for example, Baywarra has this amazing medallion in the film, the sort of fierce warrior. I met with Connie Nayinggul, a traditional owner up there when I went on the recce with Stephen, and then I didn't see her for a month and I'd shown her a photograph of something I thought would be a good thing from an old photography collection. But we talked about the feeling we were after and then one day she just showed up in Gunbalanya with this thing months later, and it was amazing. And she dreamt about the character and got particular ochre from her country and hunted kangaroos with good shaped faces for their teeth for it. And just the presence of this medallion had a real power to it, you know? That's something you can't fake or repeat, you can't make that up and [I] didn't know that's how we would be making accessories. There are things like that that are just so unique and specific to this experience.

How would you usually source accessories and costumes? Would you make them yourself if you can't find them? Or is it a blend of existing costumes and then creating some?

ER: It's really varied. I come from a making background myself, studied fashion, pattern-making, worked my way up from a sculptural costume perspective. Making is my background, but certainly it depends on the size of the production, to be honest. I just finished a TV series called *La Brea* which was the biggest TV production in Australia for an age. And on that I had a whole art finishing team and a whole tailoring team. And the project was so big that I was creating the concepts and guiding people on how to do things, but I wasn't physically in there making.

So it's a real mix. On *High Ground*, Simon Baker's trousers got stuck in customs, so I was at the sewing machine the night before we started filming, sewing. It really depends on the circumstance as to what I'm doing. But often I will work with makers or as a last resort I will make but these days, I think my skills are somewhere else.

It sounds like you really have to pivot on the go quite a bit as well.

ER: Absolutely. Away jobs are always complex. In a way, remote jobs are more complex because you can't just whip off to the nearest shopping centre and get the thing. Going to Darwin was over a three hour round trip. One day, we'd had a runner buy something and they bought the wrong colour thread and I'm just, "Well, that will be perfect, thank you." If you run out of something up there, you can't just go replace it.

We had a whole conundrum with washing machines, and there was no one locally to fix washing machines. A broken washing machine's a week turnaround. A lot of the costumes are dyed with International Roast because that's what I could get locally. And time and time again, I bought the supermarket out of it. So yes, you have to be able to pivot. I feel very lucky that I have a skill base that comes from a making perspective because you know, having to make 1900s trousers requires tapping into pattern-making skills, production making skills that, not everyone has.

Do you have a favourite type of fabric textile?

ER: I would probably just say broadly natural fibres for art finishing, dyeing, wearability, movement. There's nothing like the beautiful drape of silk. A lot of Caren's costumes, the blouses were incredibly fine polished cotton. You can do a lot more with those natural fibres because when you're art-finishing and aging things up, you're working in other mediums that don't necessarily get absorbed very well when they're synthetic. But synthetic fabrics are coming a long way. It's just that's my preference.

With natural fibres, can you use them to imitate other styles of fabric and make it more comfortable for people to wear? I imagine it was quite hot or humid at least where you're filming?

ER: It was outrageously hot. And no, everyone was just royally uncomfortable. A big conversation was around the heat and how we wanted the heat to read and I had done Ben Hackworth's feature *Celeste* up in far north Queensland, Innisfail. And when I watched that film, it came up beautifully. But I was disappointed in how little the heat read because Innisfail, it was steamy tropical, some things don't read. And I really wanted to push that on *High Ground*, I wanted to have a read because some days it was 46 degrees. And I'd get up at 4am to go to location and it would be 99% humidity. It was next level, we were in the build-up to the wet season. So there was also that weird pressure that affects everyone up there.

Simon's such a good sport really because he was just hot the whole time. And, Caren was in a corset as well. So that was part of the performance. You can't fake that uncomfortable, itchy, clingy feeling and it's a real credit to those actors. Jack Thompson's sitting there in a white woollen suit in 44 degrees is next level dedication, because I think it adds to the storytelling. It's this Imperial ridiculousness determined to stick to their Imperial guns. And then you see the real contrast when Witiyana walks in. And the contrast between traditional dress particularly in that scene I just think is - it's one of my favourite visuals of the film - is the contrast there of the two leaders, and the ridiculousness of the Imperial white suit.

That is probably the most iconic scene of High Ground, the two groups sitting there meeting. What is it like, staging that type of scene and organising the costumes for people who are only going to be in that small scene?

ER: That scene was really powerful to be at. It was one of the bigger cast days we had, because there were a lot of two-hander, three-handers. And,

Witiyana did a welcome at the start of that day. It was a very powerful and emotional day, everyone was very charged and you really felt the conflict. Sometimes the making of something doesn't... you make a beautiful story, the making of it is not beautiful. Or you make cool, edgy fashion, but the making of it is not an edgy experience.

But, it was really confronting making a film about these massacres and at the same time, experiencing community for the first time and seeing the impacts of intergenerational trauma from these massacres, and experiencing country for the first time, in a sense. When you add all those really genuine emotions to a charged film crew who are exhausted, it's a really powerful thing. The actual coming together of that scene - and we filmed a lot of hours on it actually - was quite moving.

Callan Mulvey, Maximillian Johnson, Jack Thompson, Ryan Corr, Caren Pistorius
Photo Credit: Sarah Enticknap. Used with permission.

And certainly, having all those iconic leaders on both sides just standing there. The power is palpable. It really is. And it has immediately become one of the iconic scenes in Australian cinema. As you're talking about how the records of what existed back then don't really exist now, this in itself has become a living record of the past. And that's quite important because we don't get very many films like this in Australia. We don't get many films addressing the frontier wars, and the terrible aspects of the massacres that have taken place then. As you're saying, that's got to change - that's got to carry with you for quite a while. How does that inform what you're going to do forward? How does that inform your future projects?

ER: I would start by saying, Stephen Johnson had a real commitment to culture and tradition. There would have been ways that we could have cheated, making some of those traditional costumes, but Stephen Johnson had a real commitment to make things traditionally and to embrace the culture and include the community in the design process and the making process, which is something I really honour and respect. And combining my research background is something I'm very passionate about, particularly when it comes to working with oral histories and finding a way to visually honour those where there's no records before. It certainly sets a benchmark for a particular type of experience.

It was by no means an easy film to work on, apart from the subject matter of whatever you're working on oozes into your life, you become the project. And that's very hard when it's such an intense subject matter. Every job you learn something and you carry that forward. I think, obviously if I was working with community again, I would have some more ideas about how to approach that. But also it's a real benchmark for how I believe traditional dress should be approached in any representation.

I think it's done brilliantly. I wanted to gently move to talking about Disclosure, because that's another great film from this year. I'm curious what your role was in helping get that film made.

ER: *Disclosure,* a really interesting project, the script's really fantastic. And I think Michael the writer-director and Donna the producer, went about knowing that they had a micro budget, and the film as written for that doesn't necessarily come across as a low budget production. But working on something like that, you have to be particularly savvy. The way that Michael engages all main characters and how they are on screen the whole time almost in the same outfit was probably the main challenge. In a film like that, what's really important is balance. Essentially for me, the four characters have a visual weight, and my challenge was to get that weight pretty even across the screen. Whether they were all on screen together or if it was a two hander or one person that there wasn't a dominating factor visually when it comes to the costumes.

For some of the characters, at the start, they're in a state of undress. They're swimming or they're laying by the pool naked. There is that vulnerability there, and then they emerge into clothes and the power of how they manage the conversation that is being had changes visually with them. How did you manage that with them?

ER: Flesh, nudity, exposure, and vulnerability were all major themes and key points of discussion with development with Michael and the production designer as well, Juliet, and the cast. There's quite a mood tone to the costume design, and then working out small details that could play and help those. What comes to mind is when Emily [Matilda Ridgway] is getting dressed, and she finds her wedding ring or it's an accessory that she's playing with, that actually makes quite an important beat because she's really angry. And, that gives her an action but also reflects a pretty important part of their relationship as to what she's putting on. There are really small details there that added to the action that also really reflect character.

Subtlety is a really hard thing to push on camera or to get people to agree to because they like colour and movement. And I think there's something really beautiful and refined about how Juliet, the production designer, and I worked together and with the cast, I really feel like it's subtle and balanced. Period films do well at award ceremonies. I think it's a really incredible well-written script; and for a script to be able to hold interest for that long with that little movement going on is a real testament to the craft of writing. I think that's a real tribute to Michael.

Do you have a style in mind of what you want your body of work look like as you progress?

ER: I think everyone has a specific aesthetic. As an individual, I bring my whole life experience of travel, family, loves, hates, whatever, to what I do. I am very particular about the projects I will work on, because they become part of your life. If you're going to spend six months doing something or an away job is even a bigger ask of someone's life, then you really have to have a strong feel for it. And I need to know that I have a space to contribute and to be able to show my work. And that can be in a subtle way like on *Disclosure*; Michael was very open to my ideas and collaboration.

For me filmmaking is one of the greatest collaborative art forms, but within that, I need a voice. If I can't have a voice as a designer, then I'm not particularly interested. But also, in Australia, there isn't enough work around to say, "I'll only do period films" and "I'll only do *this*" - you really have to be able to switch between genres and styles. Because, unlike in the States or in England - I know designers over there who just go, "I only do this particular era", "1950s is my thing, I only do 1950s, maybe to 1970s films." But we don't have that amount of work happening here. You can't really be that specific.

But, more often than not, it comes down to my ability to contribute to a project. Really, it's the people. It's a long time to spend with people and I really need them to be nice. It's those things that really makes a big difference. And then just avoiding particular storylines. What I do gets seen by a lot of people and I want to make sure I'm putting good messages out there. I'm very conscious of how I represent women on screen or people of other genders. So, I just try and be particular and what I get out there through messaging in subtle ways.

Have American TV shows like La Brea, like Clickbait created a change in the Australian film and TV industry going forward because of that?

ER: We've had waves of American productions come and go before. It's pretty complex. At the moment we are in a really busy time and there's a crew shortage. And it's almost becoming a two-tiered industry where you have international productions where they're generally tied to an offshore agreement, which is pre-negotiated with the unions. And then you have Australian productions which in theory have better penalties but have much lower base rates. It's really hard to get crew on to an Australian production versus an American production. That's kind of what's happening. And it's a really tricky thing.

From my own experience having an opportunity to work on a show the size of *La Brea* is amazing. You get a really well-resourced team; you get to work with Hollywood filmmakers who know how to do great things. The budgets are phenomenal, the wages are well and truly above what you get offered on an Australian production. Voices land differently, I'll say that, but then the contrast to that is working on something like I've just started on *Crazy Fun Park* with Nick Verso, and it will be our third project together. And that is such a beautiful thing when you can enter a space with a collaborator you've worked for and you have an unspoken visual language. That's really amazing. And the skills I can bring from having done a really huge scale project to this is exciting, but it's really hard working within the financial restraints of an Australian project. And in that ideal dream world, I would get to be telling Australian stories with those Hollywood budgets. That would be the endgame.

Does that mean a lot to you, being able to tell Australian stories?

ER: Absolutely. I think it's so important for who we are. And that's something that really resonated in working on *High Ground*. I really became aware of how irrelevant the rest of the country was. As someone who checks the news all the time or Facebook or whatever, up there none of it mattered. Geographically, it's so removed, but also it is so irrelevant. There are people living in really horrible conditions. People are hungry. It's like another country. And when you have that, I just think the only way we can find ourselves as a country is to tell our stories and to see our stories.

When I was 21, I moved to London, I was so mad about British culture and I was gonna go meet the Queen and become a costume designer. I totally love that chapter of my life. But there was part of me that was really embarrassed about like Australia and coming from Brisbane and a cultural vacuum. And I just wonder who I would be if I'd gone over there thinking, "Yeah, I am from the oldest living continuous culture community of artists in the world, eat this, like Canterbury Cathedral with your dead priests." I just think if we tell those stories and we can all grow more confident as a nation. And we've got to get rid of this whole tall poppy syndrome. And it's all really interconnected. And I just think telling stories is the way we can do that.

Do you have any advice that you would give to emerging costume designers in Australia?

ER: Just keep moving. Just keep moving. Just find your people. Find a designer you like and track them down and try and work with them. Do all the short films, do the student films, do their music clips. All of that stuff adds up.

REVIEW
JUNE AGAIN AND LONG STORY SHORT
FILMS BECOME FRIENDS AND FAMILY WITH THESE
EMOTIONAL COMEDIES

JJ Winlove's *June Again* and Josh Lawson's *Long Story Short* shifted the dominant dramatic field of Australian cinema into lighter territory, while retaining their grounded relatable roots in these two family-focused dramedies. The question of what a modern affluent Australian family looks like is explored through the prism of a broken mind and the realm of reality torn apart by a magical and mysterious encounter in a cemetery. The two films are tied together by the presence of Australian screen legend, Noni Hazlehurst, creating a conversation between each other that forces viewers to reconcile with how they spend the precious and limited time we have on this earth.

In *June Again*, Noni plays the titular June, a matriarch who lives with dementia and due to her high level of care needs has been separated from her daughter, Ginny (Claudia Karvan), and son, Devon (Stephen Curry). The siblings Ginny and Devon, through life and circumstances, have themselves become estranged. In a period of lucidity, June embarks on a journey across Sydney to reunite and revive her struggling family and mend their fractured relationships by reminding them of the love they once shared.

Stephen Curry, Noni Hazlehurst, Claudia Karvan
Photo Credit: Ticket to Ride. Used with permission.

While Noni's presence in *Long Story Short* is fleeting, her lesson to Rafe Spall's Teddy feels as relevant to Ginny and Devon as it does to the audience at large; namely, we can make excuses for our own lives, pushing away major life events because of an ever-escalating, ever-avoided list of priorities that are neglected for a night of doom scrolling. The reality is we will never properly make gains in our own lives if we don't make the time for the things that are important, and to listen to those around us so we can become better people. We can snooze life events for as long as we want, but we never know when time will creep up on us and whisk away our minds in a devastating illness.

Using the cultural resonance of Noni Hazlehurst's intergenerational work on *Play School*, Claudia Karvan's work as everyone's friend on *The Secret Life of Us*, and Stephen Curry's cheeky and charming brother in *The Castle*, Aotearoa New Zealand director JJ Winlove has effectively constructed a makeshift version of Australia's family in his feature debut *June Again*. Together, these Australian screen icons bring a familiarity to the all-too-relatable tale of a mother living with dementia. Comedic flourishes appear in this deeply emotional drama, acting as a buffer for the heartbreaking conclusion.

Hazlehurst's calming presence as an all-knowing, all-understanding woman who has lived a lifetime in the space of a breath in *Long Story Short* acts as a shorthand for the wise elder figure in our lives. No stranger to taking relatable stories and filling them with unique Australian humour, Josh Lawson takes the high concept idea of a man, Rafe Spall, who wakes up after his wedding day to find that his life is jumping forward a whole year every few minutes. A novel notion like this runs the risk of falling off the tightrope, but thanks to the comfortable and enjoyable performances from Spall and onscreen partner Zahra Newman, as well as the delightful comedic presence of Ronny Chieng, *Long Story Short* acts as a feature-length reminder to not take life for granted, and frankly, to not be a dick. Fairly simple ideas, for sure, but ones that we all need reminding of every so often.

In both *June Again* and *Long Story Short*, we are reminded that films can be friends, providing companionship, and hard-hitting advice that we all need to hear sometimes. There's a comfort to the sentimentality here, as both films close on moments of earned emotionality, with both JJ Winlove and Josh Lawson never allowing the sweetness to tip over into saccharine. It's here that film can transcend friendship and turn into family, with Australia's Mum Noni Hazlehurst becoming our own mum in the closing moments of *June Again*, bringing a tissue box of tears along.

INTERVIEW
JUNE AGAIN - ACTOR STEPHEN CURRY
AND WRITER/DIRECTOR JJ WINLOVE

Within JJ Winlove's *June Again*, three Australian screen legends unite to tell a story of familial drama and comedy. Stephen Curry shares the screen with Noni Hazlehurst and Claudia Karvan, creating an organic representation of Australian families. His career spans decades with iconic films like *The Castle* (1997) and *Hounds of Love* (2016), and shows like *The Secret Life of Us* (2004-2005) and *Cloudstreet* (2011) making up his filmography. Curry received an AACTA Award nomination for his lead performance in Ben Young's *Hounds of Love*.

JJ Winlove made his feature film debut with *June Again*. He has pushed his creativity as a filmmaker, as seen in 2015 when he set out to write, produce, and direct twelve short films in twelve months, culminating in a project called *12:12*. *June Again* was released theatrically in 2021, while Winlove's other project, the audience inclusive experience *Crossing Paths* received a festival run.

In the following interviews, Stephen Curry and JJ Winlove talk about the creative process of making *June Again*, finding the comedy in drama, building Australia's family, and more.

Interview conducted March 2021.

▶▷▶

What's it like working with Noni Hazlehurst as your mum?

Stephen Curry: Equal parts exciting and daunting, I suppose. I felt like I've known her since I was three years old. That's something in itself. She's such a giant of the industry and she's just never put a foot wrong. She's one of those people that's so prepared. She makes it look easy. Claudia is the same as well. There's a real art form in working so hard that you make things look like they're easy, you know?

And with someone like Noni, to watch her in this film and you do sometimes, you feel like, even in a scene with her, you can't help but sit back occasionally and watch it and be blown away by her ability to absorb herself 100% with this character. She's playing June Walton, who's been suffering from dementia for five years, who has this period of lucidity. To see her performance and the way she has, the way she has fine-tuned that performance.

I keep getting asked by people, 'how do you get prepared for a role like this?' And it takes a lot of that work hard work out of it, because you can't help but be moved and be heartbroken by the performance that she gives. It's the same with Claudia. Noni has just been one of my heroes for a very long time, and she deserves her place as one of the doyennes of our game.

She's been Australia's mum for so long, but on the same hand, for a lot of people you have been Australia's brother. There's a real strong familial bond here, and it makes the film just soar. You've had so many different kinds of families on film, including one of the most iconic Australian families [Kerrigan family in The Castle]. What's it like creating this family?

SC: It's an interesting question. JJ Winlove who wrote *June Again*, and he's the director, he has researched this area [dementia] so completely, that he's written his piece where, again, half the work done for you in terms of knowing that this film is written with respect and his respect for sufferers of dementia, the respect for people who love sufferers of dementia. At its core is it's about and trying to understand the importance of family in the face of any sort of hardships. And this last year has been such a huge reminder to everyone, it's such a huge reset to everyone about what's important and what to hold on to, and to hold your loved ones close.

I like that word 'familial'. It's such a story about that. About stripping back to accepting people's foibles and accepting nobody's perfect. June herself has caused a lot of the fractures it within the family unit before she started to suffer from dementia. We all sat down that first day of the first read through and agreed that that keeping that respect and keeping that consideration for the reality of that piece, the moment people see that piece being presented as too comedic or not considered enough or anything like that we would have lost the point of the whole film.

It's really that thing where you just we just feel a shared sense of responsibility, and the end result is one of those things that you wish you could bottle this with films because it doesn't always happen. And I think that hugely is due to JJ's direction, but Noni and Claudia leading from the front. It's been a really great experience.

Has that been something that you have been trying to work away from, the shadow of The Castle? You've done some darker work over the years, and people might come to your films expecting comedic stuff all the time. This has comedy in it, but it's more grounded.

SC: I'm very, very cognisant of the fact that if it wasn't for *The Castle*, there's a red-hot chance I wouldn't be here talking to you now. That's one thing that attracted me to a lot of those darker things that I've ended up doing is because it's rather than distancing myself from... I think *The Castle* is one of the best films we've made in this country, the writing, the heart of it, and the skill of Working Dog and all of those things notwithstanding. For me I like to find things that are as challenging as possible. I love playing comedic dippy dudes, it's great fun, I love that. But I also loved playing the role I played in *Hounds of Love*, which is a completely different, which is basically a psychotic serial killer, the worst person in the world.

What this film is great for is it gives you a foot in both camps, about being able to actually just have a bit of fun with the stuff that is consciously co-medic. I really enjoy sinking my teeth into being able to take that dramatic challenge on, but all of that is being able to be wrapped up in a film where it's actually it's about the heart of this thing. That's what I want. I want characters that aren't caricature, that are well-rounded and interesting and human. Again, the moment people see on screen someone that's not human or recognisable as a real personality, I think you lose half your audience.

There's a personal aspect to that story for a lot of people who have gone through that same path with family members but having somebody like Noni Hazlehurst joining us along on that journey, who many of us grew up with on Play School, provides a comfort that also provides a flood of memories washing over them. It was that really nice communal aspect about June Again which is often missed sometimes with films. There is a nice recognition of the value of iconic figures like Noni. You've created a really interesting, community focused film that encourages discussion about a serious issue.

JJ Winlove: Thank you. With Noni, coming from New Zealand, I didn't appreciate just how iconic and how beloved she was with almost any age group. I tell anyone that I was making a film with Noni Hazlehurst in it, and they would just light up, and they just get so excited, whatever age they were. Everyone has a special memory of Noni, whether it's from *Play School*, or from more recent things. It was such a great facet of the film, and not just the production phase, but all the way through, because of what she brought to it just for that reason. She attached it to Australian culture and made it an Australian film, with Stephen Curry and Claudia Karvan, because both of those actors have their own cultural baggage in terms of what they've brought to Australian television and film.

REVIEW
CHOPPER
ANDREW DOMINIK'S MASTERPIECE

Australian culture can't help but make icons and heroes out of some of the most notorious criminals. The myth of Ned Kelly's anti-establishment, anti-police persona has forged a legacy that turned him into a celebrated man, a figure whose existence in Australian culture has endured as a beacon for people to believe whatever they choose to see in him. His anti-police role in society helped create his celebrity, and even with Kelly killing police officers who harmed his friends and family and causing all manner of damage to society as a bushranger, thousands signed petitions to stop him being hanged to death.

Justin Kurzel's *True History of the Kelly Gang* worked to slam the door shut on Kelly's legacy, suggesting that the applied importance of his 'final' words – "Such is life" – were misguided, with reports that he never actually said them, instead pushed into his history via the mouth of a politician. Kurzel's film examines the relationship Australia has with lionising criminals as celebrities, asking what the weight of fame built up throughout history does to our perception of their illegal exploits.

Ned Kelly didn't have the benefit of a broad media landscape in the 1800s to tell his side of the story, but given the cyclical nature of history, it seems fortuitous that Mark Brandon 'Chopper' Read would pick up Kelly's celebrated and iconic criminal legacy and use the avenues of television and writing to spawn the 'Cult of Chopper': a troupe of champions and supporters both domestically and internationally who saw the famed criminal as a champion for *them*.

Andrew Dominik's feature debut as writer and director, *Chopper*, masterfully collates the vibe and ethos of Chopper into a ninety-minute powder keg of a film. Utilising an overwhelming master of imitation, Eric Bana, to portray the mammoth violent figure, Dominik creates a film that's full of gut-twining tension, with tar black comedy, both working in parallel, making for a disturbing level of awareness of the height of celebrity within Australia.

This is not a birth to adult story, colouring in how Chopper became a crim. Instead, Dominik focuses on slightly fictionalised moments in Chopper's life, bookending the film with Chopper's life in prison. Pulled from Chopper's extensive bibliography and other reports about his criminal exploits, *Chopper* actively engages with the legend he became, admiring his art of storytelling, and reflecting on his impact in the criminal world of Victoria.

Bana's Chopper is entrancing, an enjoyably bleak and complex figure who creates an alluring air of ease, where one minute he's your best mate, and the next he's stabbing someone in the face. For those who grew up in the 1990s, Bana's move from comedy icon on *Full Frontal* and *Eric*, where he made a name as the mullet-wearing bogan Poida, to kung-fu boyfriend Con in *The Castle*, to playing Chopper felt like a natural transition.

Poida's uber-ocker story-weaving character came as a comfort to those who always felt like they were the brunt of the joke, the punching bag for elites who laughed at the tradies and workers of Australia. Bana was on the tradies' side, a stance that he's maintained throughout a career dedicated to Aussie culture, with his brilliant doco *Love the Beast* focusing on the thrill of car racing, or even his ability to drag St Kilda Football Club to the world of Adam Sandler with *Funny People*. He has, and always will be, a true-blue Aussie icon.

Chopper isn't your average bloke, he's a thug, a crim, a violent brute who stabs first and apologises later; but he still feels like 'one of us' with his larrikin vibe and a penchant for weaving an excellent, captivating story. He disarms with a false-relatability. Aussies love a good yarn, no matter how tall it is, and in the realm of Aussie story-tellers, there are few as captivating as Mark Read.

Bana's observant and calm portrayal of him is one of the great strengths of the film, making moments where he's stabbed by lifelong friend Jimmy Loughnan (a stunning Simon Lyndon) bleakly comedic and unsettling. He simply stands there, absorbing each knife impact with quiet shock, uttering the horrifically hilarious line, "Jimmy, if you keep stabbing me, you're going to kill me."

Elsewhere, Bana slithers his way through conversations, conniving and tricking his subjects into exposing their hidden agendas, helping unveil the truth within Chopper's simmering paranoia. As the film nears its conclusion, Chopper visits Jimmy at his home where he lives with his fiancé (pronounced with deft ockerisation brilliantly by Lyndon as 'fee-on-see') and kids in a smoke-filled apartment of grime and heroin. There's a hit out on Chopper's head, and he comes to Jimmy for some kind of atonement. As Chopper realises that Jimmy's in on the job, he pulls a gun on him, leading to the climax of the twelve-minute tense conversation, with Jimmy terrified for his life, screaming "Mark! You're being fucking paranoid!"

Chopper's response exposes who he is as a person completely – someone who is both right, but horrifyingly wrong: "Just because I'm being paranoid doesn't mean people aren't trying to kill me." It's telling that in the DVD commentary, Mark Read delivers a powerful line: Paranoia is the criminal equivalent of intelligence.

There's a balance with Chopper, a man who wants to be harnessing and taming the criminal world through the art of torture and violence. He'd rip off drug dealers, threaten them with death as he 'popped off' toes with secateurs, torturing them 'til they paid up, so he didn't have to kill them. Outwardly, Chopper stated he had killed anywhere from four to seven people, but in his books, he claimed he'd been involved with killing nineteen people and had an attempted murder record of eleven people. These figures are badges of honour to Chopper, statements of his criminal success that further accentuates his false-relatability.

It's fascinating then that the real-world actions of Chopper have been echoed in films like *Drive* to make their lead characters appear heroic. To be clear, Refn's film doesn't idolise the nameless lead character Ryan Gosling plays, but the audience certainly grows to applaud the hammer-wielding man who pashed 'the girl' after bashing the head in of a nameless goon. And yet, that same type of violence and brutality is what make both *Chopper* and its subject such unassailable icons in Australian culture.

There's an uneasy comfort to Chopper, especially as he talks about disrepute in the crime world, and how this is just crims being crims, having little impact on society as a whole. His perspective of Australia is that the world of regular society operates in a completely different landscape than that of the criminal world. He walked the same streets as everyone, but unlike cop-killing Ned Kelly, his actions only affected other crims. It's easy to see Robin Hood style allusions of grandeur from Chopper, an aspect of his myth that the media was all too keen to fuel.

When asked by Renée Brack's television interviewer how he sees himself, Bana's Chopper replies that he's "Just a bloke. Just a good bloke down on his luck." To Chopper, violence amongst friends is just that – friendly banter. A light stab here, a gunshot there, there's nothing to it, and it's easily forgotten. When Jimmy stabs Chopper in prison, after that $10K bounty is put on Chopper's head, and the screws ask Chopper about what went on, Chopper refuses to rat on him, saying another excellent line: "The bloke's been my best mate since 1975. We've had our fallouts from time to time. It's no big deal. It's like if your mum stabbed you," implying immediate forgiveness for a possibly death-inducing altercation.

Equally so, in that moment where Jimmy thinks he's nursing Chopper into death, the two embrace each other like the closest of friends. Faces close together, blood seeping out of Chopper's stab wounds (with immersive makeup effects by Deborah Lester, Rick Connelly, and Bob McCarron), this moment of intimacy exposes the off-kilter elements of bonding in the crime world. Later, when Chopper encounters the fictional character of Neville Bartos (Vince Colosimo in his finest performance), there's a moment of tension between the two, with Chopper unsure whether Bartos wants to do him in right there and then. The 'water under the bridge' exchange colours how outwardly remorseful Chopper could be about his actions, with Chopper stating "I don't know if you remember, Neville, but I had that bloody shotgun pointed at your head. I reconsidered and dropped it down to your kneecap." As if that moment of reconsideration is the grandest act of charity one could ever make.

The Chopper represented here is one that suffers immediate remorse. He stabs a man in the face, and apologises seconds later, offering a cigarette as atonement. On the commentary track, the real Chopper mentions his shared surprise with his on-screen doppelgänger that their victim would dare reject such a kind offer as a lit cigarette. Later, when he bashes his girlfriend Tanya (Kate Beahan) in the face, and then her mum (Pam Western) as well, he pushes the blame on Tanya for "Upsetting your mum."

We laugh through gritted teeth at moments of brutal horror, with Bana's delivery of the line being cruelly comedic, as are many other lines throughout the film. However, our laughter is reflected back on us - we're complicit in celebrating his rise to infamy, his journey into debauchery, and his illegal exploits.

The sound design by Frank Lipson and co amplifies this tension, with moments of violence like when Keithy George (David Field) is stabbed in the face while a barely distinguishable sports commentator blares on a radio. Later, a squealing kettle makes a gun in the face all the more unsettling.

Eric Bana
Photo © 2000 Australian Film Finance Corporation Ltd. Mushroom Pictures Pty. Ltd.
Pariah Films Pty. Ltd. All Rights Reserved. Used with permission.

These design elements could feel showy or performative in any other film, but in *Chopper*, each aspect adds to the tightrope tension. The climax of the film focuses on the death of Sammy the Turk (Serge Liistro) at Bojangles nightclub, a farcical moment that evolves into a farce of brilliance. For that moment, *Chopper* turns into pure theatre, with characters delivering rhyming couplets that detail the occurrence of that fateful night that put Chopper back behind bars. If Chopper himself weren't such a heightened bullshit artist, this scene wouldn't work as well as it does, but it's as apt as anything else here, a masterful creative decision that paid off brilliantly.

Again, in the commentary, Chopper talks about how he did bash down the door of partners but says that he'll neither 'confirm or deny the actions on screen', a strong hint of domestic violence. Decades later, Read took part in an anti-domestic violence advertising campaign in a pulled clip that featured a bizarre tirade[5] about the men who beat on women being weak and how they ought to be afraid because in gaol, rapists get the worst treatment. In the short thirty second clip, the threat of violence burns in his eyes. The keen desire to inflict some form of brutality on those who have done wrong, is a source of ecstasy. Yet, he's distinctly unaware that his own violence breeds further violence.

The bulldog threat that Chopper was to other thugs made the reality of a bounty on his head a permanent aspect of day-to-day life. It was expected for Chopper, a way of living, and his relationship with the police flourished because of this. Dominik's writing and direction plays this relationship as a joyful lark for Chopper, his recognition of their authority a source of comfort and safety for him. Between the age of twenty and thirty-eight, Chopper only spent thirteen months outside of prison, much of that time depicted in the film itself.

In the downbeat ending, backed by the chilling score by Mick Harvey, we see the tableau of Chopper alone in a cell, nothing but the blue cold light embracing him, a cigarette in his hand and finally devoid of an audience. It's a powerful image to finish on. We viewers see a pathetic figure existing by himself, his violence and exploits having gotten him nowhere in life. On the commentary track, Read mentions how that shot is supposed to be sad, but for him, that prison was home, a place of comfort.

The cinematography by Geoffrey Hall and Kevin Hayward goes a long way to illustrate the disturbing life of Chopper, with dulled neon lights of chilled red, frozen blues, and murky greens colouring each scene. If portrayed as a basic crime drama, *Chopper* would likely not have been as celebrated as it is, but the powerful aesthetic sets it apart from its genre counterparts. It's unlike any other Australian crime film, or by that reasoning, any other crime film in cinema history. *Chopper* is devilishly unique, reflecting the ethos of Mark Read in every frame, holding a mirror up to his conflicted soul. This is otherworldly, as if it's taking place out of time and history, like an anomaly in the world.

A decade later, David Michôd pulled crime back to the suburbs with *Animal Kingdom*, reminding audiences how close this criminal threat is to everyone. Ben Mendelsohn's charismatic 'Pope' is a crime lord pulled from the same realm that Chopper operates in. Downright terrifying but equally entrancing, the impact of Chopper, the master of tales, is inescapable. Furthermore, Dominik's direction clearly influenced its modern thematic counterpart, *Acute Misfortune*, Thomas M. Wright's anxiety-inducing film about Chopper's colleague and co-writer, Adam Cullen. The two co-wrote the book Hooky the Cripple, with Cullen drawing the imagery for Chopper's words.

Chopper's solitude in prison allowed him to write countless books, making him one of the highest selling authors in Australian history. From within the cold walls of prison, Read conjured a legend that infected society. This self-made authorial celebrity led to him being interviewed on TV, the pedigree of journalist Mike Willisee helping to extend the cult of a career criminal into the homes of Australia.

Yet, Chopper, the weaver of narratives about his own success, was always in control of his image. Heck, even Chopper bought into his own success, finding joy in mythologising and falsifying his own legacy. After all, what criminal was going to come forward and tell the other side of the story?

Dominik's film adds to that mythology, but at least from a critical stance that exposes the horrors of Chopper's criminality for what it was. 'Never let the truth get in the way of a good yarn' is the core mindset of Read and, given his eager support of the film and Bana's performance, it's clear that muddying the waters of mythology is okay by him.

Chopper lost to *Looking for Alibrandi* as the Best Film at the 2001 AFI Awards, a fact that Read finds amusing on the commentary track, stating 'comparing this film to *Alibrandi* is like comparing a rattlesnake to a Barbie doll.' *Chopper* was the highest grossing R-rated film in Australia, an honour it lost to Martin Scorsese's *The Wolf of Wall Street*. Its exceptionally quotable dialogue has become key to its enduring legacy, with many phrases entering common vernacular.

It's frustrating then that the film was unavailable for over a decade, with the DVD out-of-print and no streaming release. Receiving a belated 20th anniversary theatrical release in 2021 (thanks COVID), *Chopper* emerged anew from its own cinematic prison, with a pristine Bluray edition released later in the year. Included on the disc is a behind the scenes clip of Eric Bana meeting Chopper at his home in Tasmania. Seeing these two figures together amplifies how eerily close Bana was to portraying Chopper as he was. This is not an imitation, it's a full-blown possession.

In 2008, Read revealed he only had years left to live, and that he had been eligible to receive a liver transplant but in some skewed altruistic manner had rejected any possible organ donation. Detached from the mainland, he eventually died of liver cancer in 2013.

While this is a magnificent film, arguably one of the finest in the Australian film landscape, I can't help but wonder if this style of narrative helps further the 'Cult of Chopper.' Read lived long enough to see himself parodied by Heath Franklin, a comedian who essentially created a career around lampooning him. Read monopolised on his fame with speaking tours, ads about drunk driving and domestic violence, and even the odd comedy festival appearance. Later, his story was turned into a season of the massively successful true-crime series, *Underbelly*.

Is he the modern-day Ned Kelly? Is he a criminal hero? Does the fact that his victims were criminals themselves make the celebration and deification of his life all right?

Sitting in prison, Bana's Chopper flips through photos upon photo of fans who have sent him mail from around the world, some of scantily clad women with Chopper tattoos, others of people re-enacting the murder of Sammy the Turk. He jokes, "ol' Chop Chop doing his bit for Tourism Victoria", and horrifyingly, there's some truth to this statement.

Which is the irony of *Chopper* and its subject. The truth *is* there, but it's wrapped up in the beer-fuelled sardonic humour and wit that makes Chopper spin his own version of it into existence. Andrew Dominik is one of Australia's finest directors, and for this to be his first feature film is a testament to his skill and power as an artist. By lifting up Mark Brandon 'Chopper' Read to the height of a film icon, trapped in celluloid for generations to come, he both celebrates him and critiques him perfectly.

This is a masterpiece of a film, a sign that Australian cinema can reach monstrous heights of glory. Critically evaluating this film two decades on proves that its stature as an enduring classic will not wither with time. Just like the legacy of Ned Kelly, it will morph and change and transform as the legacy of Chopper continues to grow and morph and change alongside it.

INTERVIEW
UNSOUND - DIRECTOR
IAN WATSON

Unsound arrived in cinemas in early 2021 as a keen celebration of under-represented communities on film, following Finn (Yiana Pandelis), a deaf transgender man in Sydney, who meets Noah (Reece Noi), a gay musician who falls for Finn. Together, they discover the comfort of their own identities, while also finding love and a community within each other.

Seasoned television director Ian Watson makes his feature film debut here, with a script written by Ally Burnham. Ian came on board *Unsound* with over thirty years of experience in the industry working in television and short films. His notable work includes working on series like *Neighbours, Heartbreak High, SeaChange*, and *Love My Way*.

Interview conducted February 2021.

▶▷▶

How did you come about this script in and where did you learn about this story?

Ian Watson: I came onto the script and the production relatively late. Producer, Tsu Shan Chambers, and the writer Ally Burnham had been working on it for several years, and got two or three weeks out of production, and they lost their director. I was working with a producer Tsu Shan Chambers, we were doing short work at film school, and she asked me whether I – because of my TV experience -, could step across to read and direct it. I thought it was fantastic. I loved the script. I thought it plays right into my sense of where drama should be and how it should be done. It was a wonderful opportunity for me to get jump across and do a film which I hadn't done before.

Unsound had already been cast. We had a lot of time in rehearsal, where we workshopped the film, where we workshopped the script. We had consultants with us, the AUSLAN consultants and the trans consultants were there with us through the process, so it was just keeping them in an environment where they could work together. And the work is beautiful. They have beautiful connectivity. They're great as actors, they're both great listeners, it was an opportunity for us to just develop that core heart of the film, because for me, it was it's a really complex series of issues that come with the film.

And rather than laying the politics of the film there, what we decided to do is just allow it to be treated as the story of a love story. And in that way, we could tell this beautiful heartfelt story that allow the politics to exist within that. And then it fell into place.

Noah and Finn are not defined by who they are; being trans or deaf just happens to be part of who they are as people.

IW: Absolutely, that's the beauty of the script that we don't treat them separately, we treat them as part of the community. And for me, *Unsound* is essentially about community and identity. And it doesn't matter what's your community, it doesn't matter what your identity is, as long as the two line up and you find your place in the world. And I thought that the script exemplified that and made that clear, so that we could tell this story without politicising it too much, because that's not the point of the story. The point of the story is to show how simple and unique their lives are.

Can you talk about what type of discussions took place in making sure that the deaf representation was presented properly and respectfully on screen as well?

IW: In the writing process, we had consultants from the trans community and the deaf community working with the scripts. And then when we went into rehearsal, we follow that through so we had cast members that were AUSLAN only speakers, so all the time we had AUSLAN translator with us in rehearsal and on set. We had trans consultants with us in rehearsal and on set so for me, it made it much more of a collaborative process.

My roots go back to being a theatre director. I love to work in that collaborative space. It was quite an easy transition, but it was also how easily the consultants fell in into the process and how much they absorbed. It was a film about a community made by a community, and in many ways, it's a community film.

We kept that process through shooting and kept through into the edit as well, where we had the consultants back, just so we could acknowledge ourselves that we told the truth and told the story in the right way. I personally don't identify with any of those communities, but it doesn't stop me being able to empathise and tell that story and enable those people to have that story told. That's quite a hot topic at the moment, this notion of do we have to be of that community to tell the stories of those communities and I felt with my experience and the way this process had been set up by Tsu Shan, the producer, that we had permission to do this.

For a lot of people, it's a window to worlds they don't necessarily understand or have contact with. The more that we normalise diversity, the more that a film *Unsound* can be seen by people, and they understand that they have a lived-in life as well. They're just not part of a diversity of segments within the community.

I want to talk about the dance and nightclub sequences, they are such beautiful presentations of the deaf community. I was aware that there were these sorts of dances and events that deaf people could go to to experience music, but the way you presented here is so wonderfully informative and educational.

IW: I am aware that in places like in London, for example, they have deaf raves that might have up to 500 people, they're all in this room. With the speakers turned up, the bass turned up, and the speakers on the floor. We have a lot of people from the deaf community who came along to the shooting. These dance parties can work because a lot of people are dancing, and other people are just standing around talking and signing with each other because they're there for the community, they're there for the catch up, rather than for the dancing. The dance sequences became the core of what initially cements these people together. Out of that, we see that it's just the place for where the community can meet and can celebrate themselves.

A film like Unsound encourages the casting directors in Australia to think outside the box a little bit and go, 'gosh, there are great actors in the deaf and trans community, why haven't we been looking there in the first place?'

IW: I hope so. We love our cast diversity. A lot has changed over the years. I think now if we can start looking at the deaf and transgender actors, we can make up the distance lost. We don't have to politicise their community; we just have to have them as part of the film and television community. I remember from *The Secret Life of Us*, Deb Mailman was in season one, it was wasn't until season three or four that they actually started talking about her Aboriginality. And I think that type of casting is what makes it so wonderful. If we could just have these under-represented people presented just as people.

As a director, what were the things that you learned as you were going along? And the changes that you might instil into your productions that you will go in to in the future?

IW: Oh, that's a fantastic question. I've been thinking about it a lot, because I learned to trust other people around me more. I realised that direction is not such a solo practice, it's about collaboration. And if you're clear enough and willing enough people share things with you, people will share their feelings and thoughts. Whatever it is, whatever the show is, that it's using the resources, the real resources of the people's spirit, as much as the economic resources or what they can supply for the right people for the production. That was my first big take out, there's other people who can help and make productions more informed.

In terms of how I shoot television, I'm trusting more that I can tell the story visually with less dialogue. And because there's great slabs of *Unsound* where characters are signing, and my TV director instinct was 'is there enough information per frame for it to hold an audience'. I had to trust that if they're signing, I don't have to put music with it, because we have subtitles, and to let the film sit and let it be rather than trying to push it along. That was the other big take out. It's just about how I can trust audiences more to just be there with the story. Television is fast and furious, and networks are frightened by silences, of not enough happening. It was to break my own television mould a little bit as a director, which I really loved.

It's good to remind audiences that Australian films are good. I mean, this is a window where Australian films can be seen, and they're doing good business. And what it's going to do is make people realise that, "Hey, Australian films are good, and we should get on to them, we should go and support them." Australians can be really loyal to the television. And they've just got to learn that same loyalty to the films that come out of here.

▶▷▶

STREAMING
AND
HOME VIDEO

▶▷▶ **2** ◀◁◀

S ome may say that COVID pushed the Australian film industry to focus predominantly on streaming, the reality is that the writing had been on the wall for a long time, with audiences either being completely unaware of Australian films arriving in cinemas due to lack of publicity or avoiding cinemas and opting for the streaming release down the line.

Australian-based streaming service Stan. has become a surrogate home for Australian films, with an impressive line-up ranging from the queer-focused dramas *My First Summer* (Katie Found) and *Under My Skin* (David O'Donnell), to the AACTA award winning *Nitram* (Justin Kurzel), to *Streamline* (Tyson Wade Johnson), and they've continued celebrating festive films with *Christmas at the Farm* (Christopher Weekes). For cinema-going faithfuls, thankfully some of these streaming films were given a limited theatrical run, making the experience of watching *Nitram* in a packed audience all the more unsettling. Additionally, the swimming-focused *Streamline* was appreciated by a small audience who sought similar Olympics-adjacent fare, a powerful family drama with a stellar central performance.

Netflix also delivered with a wide array of Australian films: the Western Australian-set film *I Met a Girl* (Luke Eve) skipped cinemas and premiered on the service early in 2021 alongside Seth Larney's eco-focused science-fiction yarn *2067*. Christopher Amos' documentary *Hating Peter Tatchell* launched to global audiences, and Rose Byrne's narration carried the kid-focused nature documentary *Puff: Wonders of the Reef*, joining the equally family-friendly animated creature feature *Back to the Outback*, directed by Harry Cripps and Claire Knight. The Steve Jaggi Company strengthened their relationship with the streamer by delivering *Romance on the Menu* (Rosie Lourde), *This Little Love of Mine* (Christine Luby), and the teen-focused series *Dive Club*. Netflix also received the streaming debut of the oft-delayed Paul Ireland and Damien Hill Shakespeare adaptation, *Measure for Measure*. Finally, Jane Campion's triumphant return to movie-making, *The Power of the Dog*, received a limited theatrical run before a worldwide release on the service.

Public broadcaster SBS became a go-to service for documentary or factual programming, often blurring the lines between feature length films and shorter documentary events. *The Bowraville Murders* (Allan Clarke) received a welcome theatrical release, portraying the utterly devastating true crime story about Australia's broken justice system and how it discriminates and perpetuates prejudice against Indigenous Australians, while the exceptional social-focused documentaries *Strong Female Lead* (Tosca Looby), *Incarceration Nation* (Dean Gibson), *Off Country* (Rhian Skirving, John Harvey), and *The Department* (Sascha Ettinger-Epstein) each received festival runs. These titles, alongside *The Truth About Anxiety with Celia Pacquola, Osher Günsberg: A Matter of Life and Death, Our African Roots* (Tony Jackson) and *The Children in the Pictures* (Simon Nasht, Akhim Dev) made up the acclaimed Australia Uncovered series on SBS. Additionally, SBS and ABC also screened *Bowled Over, Birdsville or Bust, History Bites Back* (Trisha Morton-Thomas), *Girl Like You* (Frances Elliott, Samantha Marlowe), *Jaimen Hudson: From Sky to Sea* (Leighton De Barros), and *Step into Paradise* (Amanda Blue).

Amazon Prime complemented their emerging range of episodic content when they turned to Oscar-winner Eva Orner to create a devastating essay of the 2019/20 bushfire season with the documentary *Burning*. While Amazon Prime stopped accepting unsolicited documentary submissions in 2021, they were still an attractive streaming service of choice for indie filmmakers, with micro-budget films like *Stuffings* (Mathew J Wilkinson) and *Night Shift* (Joey Menzel) seeking audiences.

While the dominance of streaming services hints at an easy audience reach for filmmakers, the truth is a crowded market left filmmakers with remaining options to release their films, with some trying to reach audiences via the ever-dwindling physical media market. As such, Michael Bentham's *Disclosure*, Kurt Martin's *Moon Rock for Monday*, Paul Meins *Chasing Wonders*, Ricard Cussó's *Daisy Quokka: World's Scariest Animal*, and Sam Curtain's *The Slaughterhouse Killer*, skirted past cinemas, streaming services and beyond, and found themselves in the on demand/physical media market with precious little attention given to their releases.

As with many of the films featured in this book, the lack of publicity and accessibility has made audience awareness of Australian films plunge to drastically low levels. Websites like Cinema Australia, Screenhub, and Pure Shit, alongside magazines like Metro and Inside Film, do their best to shine a light on emerging and established Australian filmmakers, the overwhelming nature of the evolving media market means that without a prominent publicity campaign, audiences are left in the dark about the existence of too many films.

That said, *Occupation: Rainfall*'s marketing campaign included targeted advertising on social media, trailers before films, a public transport advertising spread and beyond, and yet the film struggled to gain an audience.

While we can point to the Best Actor win for Caleb Landry Jones performance in *Nitram* at the Cannes Film Festival as being proof of recognition of international acclaim, that alone is not a litmus test for the global audience reach. Trying to fit the Australian film jigsaw piece into the global film puzzle is equally frustrating. In the past, Australian films would hope for greater returns from international audiences, but even without COVID, that audience reach was dwindling. Naturally, audiences were already transitioning to streaming services, making the Netflix release of *Penguin Bloom* and *Occupation: Rainfall* in international markets purely logical. Despite its box office success in Aus, and its recognisable cast, the on demand digital release of *The Dry* in America made sense in the era of COVID. The downside with streaming services is that the lack of open and transparent audience metrics - who is viewing what - makes understanding audience appetites complicated, leaving filmmakers stumbling in the dark, wondering whether their project had any audience reach at all.

For short films, their lifespan is often defined by a presence at film festivals. The reality is different in the digital world where Australian shorts are finding an audience reach like never before via YouTube channels like Omeleto and Alter, or via self-hosting on Vimeo. Chris Elena's 2019 film *Audio Guide* launched globally via Alter, racking up tens of thousands of views within days, while South Australian filmmakers Indianna Bell and Josiah Allen's electric short thriller *The Recordist* has amassed over 99,000 views at time of publication, and Nick Crowhurst's sci-fi leaning *Down to Earth* has reached over 50,000 viewers. For short film directors, reaching a global audience of over 3.34 million (Omeleto) and 2.05 million (Alter) subscribers is far wider and far reaching than many other streaming services could offer. The quality of some of the short films being made in Australia right matches and often exceeds the quality of the features being produced. The sooner Australian filmmakers embrace their film legacies by ensuring that their shorts are made available to the widest audience possible, the better. For Perth-based fest, Revelation Film Festival, the solution to festival-released short films comes in the form of RevStream, their own streaming service that provides countless Australian short films for free.

For many aspiring filmmakers, the goal of showing your film in a cinema to a paying audience is the end point, the ultimate dream, but in this ever-changing landscape the reality is quite different and expectations need to be adjusted completely. Now that dream might be being picked up by a streaming service, or reaching a potential audience of millions of viewers, or at the very least, reaching an audience via self-publishing online.

Over the following pages, we interrogate the impact of *Nitram*'s themes with discussions with editor Nick Fenton and sound designer James Ashton, look at the emotionality of *I Met a Girl*, get a glimpse into the creative process of Indianna Bell and Josiah Allen as they made *The Recordist*, talk with Mark

Leonard Winter about his work on *Disclosure* and *Measure for Measure,* dive into the family drama of *Streamline,* and hear from composer Angela Little as she discusses how she reflects emotion in a score.

REVIEW
NITRAM

THE UNBEARABLE TENSION OF BEING

Complicated cinema is a tricky beast. It moves in the shadows, questioning the darkest aspects of humanity, unveiling parts of society that have been morphed, contradicted, and falsely critiqued in mass media. It can often ask us to empathise, or at the very least reconcile, with some of the most heinous and cruel individuals to have erupted out of the gaping fissures of the world. We only know of their existence due to the havoc and destruction they wreak upon those they choose to hate. With their pain inflicted, a future in a cell or a coffin awaits.

Yet, a film of their lives or their acts can be seen to further their legacy, amplifying their trauma-inducing actions and beliefs. Healing is an ongoing process, and a film about a perpetrator can exacerbate that pain. Out of violent tragedy rises the possibility of exploitation and manipulation by those distantly removed from the event. Opportunistic filmmakers and storytellers emerge, looking to manipulate tragedy for their own gain. Ultimately, this leads to the eternal question when a film that details the life of a mass murderer is conjured into the world: why.

When it comes to Justin Kurzel's latest film, *Nitram*, the question why do we need a two-hour film following someone we know committed horrific events and scarred a country with the deaths of thirty-five people, with twenty-three left injured? For those who lived within the continual media coverage of the event twenty-five years ago, the memory lingers large and long. But, for a younger generation, they may be unaware of the reasoning behind why Australia has strict gun laws, and what event created such a drastic change.

Given the exploitative, horrific, and downright disgusting portrayal of true events in the actively cruel true crime horror, *Snowtown* (2011, Kurzel's feature debut), it's understandable why many (this reviewer included) would be apprehensive about Kurzel addressing one of Australia's most horrific and traumatic modern events: the Port Arthur massacre of 1996.

American actor Caleb Landry Jones comfortably steps into the role of the titular Australian perpetrator, all long blonde hair, freckles, and a wavering voice of nervousness. He crafted his pitch perfect Australian accent by watching reruns of *Hey, Hey, It's Saturday!, Neighbours* and *Home & Away*[6], creating an off-kilter and stilted familiarity to his vocal performance. It's inspired casting to have an American playing an Australian, acting as an extension of the delirium-level adoration that some pro-gun owners have made part of their personality in the US. Landry Jones performance carries the air of a hidden infection, emerging as a raging illness

Nitram evolves from being a domestic character study of a freefalling family, into a gripping, devastating, and ultimately respectful essay of tragedy writ large, with a coda that aims to bolster the anti-gun rhetoric around the world. Comfortably supporting Landry Jones as his parents are Judy Davis and Anthony LaPaglia.

Davis' Mother is a slender and weathered being, the effects of raising a turbulent, propulsive child wearing her down every second of the day. Haunting moments of introspection come from Davis sitting in what quiet refuge she can outside her house, staring into the middle distance, questioning how exactly she landed at this point in her life. It takes a rare kind of professional to exhibit such a deep well of introspective existence, but Davis embodies it with a frustration and fury that is unparalleled.

Matching Davis at every step is LaPaglia, almost unrecognisable as a sheepish father who doesn't know how to control or connect with his son. Weight gathers around his waist like a sinker he can't shake loose, building up over time as he realises that his hopes, dreams, and aspirations gradually slough away under the burden of his son, society, and plain old bad luck. Together, these struggling parents exist as beings that have fallen out of a non-existent safety net, left adrift in a world where they have no handhold to grab onto.

Kurzel and Grant pointedly avoid criticism of his parents, instead, laying bare a need for a societal support system that provides space for great mental health care. The cognitive dissonance that the man behind the gun and the fact that he may not be evil *all* the time is a difficult thing to sit with, yet in a complex decision, they also decide to never truly make Nitram an absolute villain. Set during the early nineties, Nitram works as a criticism of Howard-era politics. While his important and swift gun legislation managed to take thousands of dangerous weapons off the street, Howard's government failed to provide any systemic support for those who might find themselves straying towards this kind of dangerous life.

Rounding out this central trio is an equally unrecognisable Essie Davis, playing wealthy heiress, Helen Harvey. He arrives at Helen's house, seeking work mowing lawns to earn enough money to buy a surfboard to impress a stranger he has seen on the beach. Helen's abode is unkempt, the smell of a burgeoning pack of dogs emanating from the screen. High ceilings give freewheeling flies the space to escape certain death, not that the occupants try to extinguish them. Helen embraces her life of solitude, supported by a seemingly unending fortune, yet Landry Jones' presence appears to be the connection to humanity she craves.

Davis and Landry Jones share a delicate bond during *Nitram*'s most tender scenes where, for a moment, it feels like Kurzel and Grant are asking the audience to empathise with grand complicity for Nitram, yearning for a fruitful relationship between the two. The anxiety-provoking sound design by James Ashton, Steve Single, and Dean Ryan seeps into the soundscape, disrupting any sense of calm that may be seeking roots. *Nitram* amplifies the anxiety of existence that permeates our day to day lives, with the sound of an unceasing fly hovering in a room bleeding into the early morning vibrato of suburban lawnmowers, making way for clicking fingernails and fretting breaths. A moment where Helen tries to teach Landry Jones how to play the piano feels off-kilter in a way that resembles an oncoming panic attack. As minute after minute locks itself away in the past of our lives, the permeating feeling that oxygen is gradually being removed from the room is hard to escape. Working in fractured harmony with this sound design is Jed Kurzel's score that overwhelms and stifles like an oncoming panic attack.

The unbearable tension of being emanates directly from Landry Jones central performance, with his gangly physicality crafting a young man anxiously and apprehensively moving through life. Landry Jones avoids stereotypical anxious actions, allowing his mannerisms, physique, and guarded eyeline build him up as such. Clothes hang off Landry Jones like he's some kind of David Byrne knock-off, yet instead of being in on the guise, he wears them with like a cloak of protection, fingers hanging barely out of the sleeves as if that was how they were always intended to be worn. His face is shrouded in hair, peering out from the curtain of fringe that hangs over it.

Caleb Landry Jones
Picture © 2021 Good Thing Productions Company Pty Ltd, Filmfest Limited. Used with permission

In a pointed decision, Shaun Grant's script removes reference to the murderer's name, and crediting his parents as just 'Mother' and 'Father'. This is still a story about that man, with *Nitram* opening with actual footage of a youthful kid recovering in hospital with severe burns he received after playing with fireworks, admitting that even after sustaining serious injury, he would gladly play with them again. By de-identifying him and removing direct reference to his name throughout the film, it helps 'other' his story, while also making way for the core anti-gun message of the film.

The answer to the question as to 'why' this film exists is answered with gut churning power in a climactic scene where Landry Jones easily strolls into a gun store, purchases assault rifles and shotguns without a gun license, and walks out with a smile from the store owner. If there's a moral core to *Nitram*, it's as a defiantly anti-gun drama that's driven towards a maelstrom of hinted catastrophe at the films close. Kurzel wisely chooses to avoid the violence of the massacre, taking us to the precipice of the tragedy and denying the carnage a place to live on.

As the film closes, Kurzel and Grant inform us that there are more guns in Australia now than there were in 1996, an utterly terrifying realisation of how little has changed, even under the notion of progression. With members of parliament actively working to water down gun legislation, *Nitram reminds us how hard we have to work to keep our gun laws in place.*

Shaun Grant talked in an interview with Deadline[7] about how an 'evil ignored is evil repeated', and with continual mass shooting events taking place around the world, the notion of needing a film like *Nitram* feels all the more pressing and urgent than ever before. Twenty-five years on from the event, and twenty-two years removed from the Columbine school shooting, it becomes even more salient to remember why change needs to take place, and why that change needs to be protected at all costs.

Where Kurzel's *True History of the Kelly Gang* played with the art of mythology and mythmaking, *Nitram* is steeped in a grounded reality, eking an empathetic truth out of a story that could have otherwise rejected any notion of that taking place. There is a grand level of maturity to *Nitram that* feels surprising and unexpected, ultimately leading to the realisation that Kurzel and Grant have tried to honour those affected by the tragedy with as much consideration as possible. *Nitram* is vital, devastating, and leaves you with a weight of despair and anguish that precious few films can, ensuring that this is a film that you cannot shake off.

INTERVIEW
NITRAM - EDITOR
NICK FENTON

Nick Fenton's career as an editor started in the UK, helping bring some of the great British films to life, from Clio Barnard's genre-defying *The Arbor* (2010) and Richard Ayoade's coming of age drama *Submarine* (2010), to Bart Layton's equally genre-defying *American Animals* (2018) and Dominic Cooke's relationship drama *On Chesil Beach* (2017). In 2019, he shifted to Australia, working with Justin Kurzel on his Ned Kelly flick *True History of the Kelly Gang* (2019) and Francis Annan's prison drama *Escape to Pretoria* (2020).

In 2021, Nick won the AACTA Award for Best Editing in Film for his work on *Nitram*, a win he repeated at the Australian Screen Editors awards in 2022.

Interview conducted October 2021

▶▷▶

I'm really eager to be able to chat with you about your work. Thank you.

Nick Fenton: That's all right. We're the last in a long line of contributors. So, it's the final piece in the puzzle, isn't it?

It's the old adage that films are made in the edit room. For film critics and people who write about film like myself, we continue to forget that and just almost take it for granted in a way that what's on screen is the director's vision completely. Whereas there can hundreds of people who are contributing to the film.

NF: There was a documentary film editor, Dai Vaughan, there's very few books on editing, but he wrote a book called The Invisible Man. And that was about editing and acknowledging their craft and putting them forward as someone who is forgotten normally.

That's a good point to kick off on, that 'invisible man' aspect. For you as an editor, what does that mean to be the invisible man behind the scenes bringing it all together?

NF: Well, it's a very interesting position that obviously I take quite seriously. You are the sieve with which you've got to filter all the ideas and somehow crystallise them into their perfect form. And that's from the performances that the actors give, the production design, that you decide to show the makeup, the sound, the cinematography, of course, the most glamorous of all contributors. You need to be the person who is bringing all those elements together in the service of the story.

You've got to know what the story is and what the story the director and the writer are trying to get across, and then how all those contributors are putting in their piece, using their creativity to tell that story. The director is then the conduit of that. And it's all those conversations that occur that are so, so important in allowing you to bring all those elements together. You're being left alone for long periods of time to work it out, to express yourself in your way. More often than not, it does involve an awful lot of chats, talking around the subject and the scenes and the story and how the final phase is going to do it all justice. And sometimes that can be very close to the original script. And sometimes it can be very, very different and change the whole expectation of everyone involved. It's very different from film to film.

I'm somebody who first became aware of your work as an editor with Clio Barnard's documentary The Arbor. I found that a really fascinating film and the editing sticks out so completely with that one because of the way that the dialogue is implemented in the film there. I was hoping you might be able to talk about how you came to work on that film, and what your discussions were with Clio on that film.

NF: *The Arbor* - that goes back to 2010. It was made by Clio Barnard who is someone I've worked with a great deal prior to coming to Australia. We've had a very long collaboration spanning about twenty years. The relationship with Clio was one of those great things where you're able to come back to the cutting room together and there's a great deal of trust and understanding in there. That's one element of that story. Her background was much more experimentation. She's since moved more into traditional feature filmmaking.

Most recently, there's a film that hopefully will come to Australia called *Ali & Ava*. Going full circle is what she is calling the third in her Bradford trilogy, of which *The Arbor* would be the first one, and *The Selfish Giant* was the second. There are people in *Ali & Ava* who she met through *The Arbor* through the story of Andrea Dunbar - who *The Arbor* is about - the Bradford playwright who was very young when she started writing plays for the theatre in London called the Royal Court. She was championed as this great voice of the working class in the north but of course her life was tragic in that that she struggled with alcoholism and struggled bringing up her kids and didn't know quite how to cope with all this attention. And almost in parallel to her story was Lorraine, her daughter, who also struggled with drugs and alcoholism, and she is the parallel story within *The Arbor*.

Now, what you're referring to the lip-synching idea which is something that Clio is very preoccupied in terms of documentary always being manipulated in some way and manipulating truths. There is always an element of construction or manipulation or point of view. And to make this idea very much in the foreground, she basically is using separate sound and image recording at different times. The visual is actors and the real audio of the real people involved in the story of Andrea's and Lorraine's life is what you hear coming out of their mouth, the real people being interviewed. Clio is someone who feels enormous responsibility for the contributors in her films. And it was another way of protecting them, by not seeing them.

I found it a really powerful film. And everything that you're mentioning there about the commitment to the truth and how truth is presented in documentary is so superbly realised there. But it was something that I couldn't escape thinking about when, bringing us forward a whole decade effectively, with both True History of The Kelly Gang and Nitram where Justin directs both of those films with this interesting perspective of the truth. I wonder if you could talk about the discussions that you had with Justin about how the narratives were going to be presented with these two very iconic and powerful moments in Australian history?

NF: I have felt that responsibility massively, certainly, in *True History of the Kelly Gang* because obviously there's descendants of Ned Kelly and descendants of the people he was the perpetrator of horrible crimes against still around, not too far in generational terms. And then, obviously, with Port Arthur, that's a massive scar on Australia's recent history. I trust audiences to be very sophisticated. And I think they know the difference between something that is artifice and presented as actuality and truth to what actually happened in the world of a documentary and the world of drama, dramatised fiction. I trust an audience in that respect to make that differentiation. And that's not to diminish the responsibility that we as filmmakers have towards the stories that we're depicting as well, and that's not to diminish the striving towards an authenticity in reflecting what if is a true story.

With *True History of the Kelly Gang*, that film is based on a novel which is dealing with the ideas of truths and myths and the clue is there in the title. It was very interesting hearing some reviews in Australia that claimed it to be hogwash. "That never happened." Well of course it didn't happen because it was a re-versioning of events from a novel, and playing with that exact idea of memory and myth-making and hero-worshipping and how history can be reinvented depending on the points of views that you want to take on it. It can be very selective.

Nitram is another way of trying to look at history from a different perspective with completely different intentions as well and presented with the utmost respect, I hope. It's obviously a very difficult subject to try and portray. My contribution was really trying to focus on the innocent people around Martin Bryant who struggled with him as a boy, as a teenager, as a young man who was very difficult to cope with. I really wanted the audience to be invested in that situation of what it must have been like for his father, for his mother. And for Helen who's no longer around, to a certain degree. What it must have been like for them to cope with someone who had the kind of mental health issues that he has.

Caleb Landry Jones, Judy Davis, Anthony LaPaglia
Picture © 2021 Good Thing Productions Company Pty Ltd, Filmfest Limited. Used with permission

How do you create empathy in an edit? How do you conjure the sympathy for those characters, for his parents this way? Watching the film, it is such a powerful film, and you're left feeling emotionally wrecked for his parents, for what they've tried to do for him, and for the situation that they're in as well.

NF: That's so hard to describe because so much of that is to do with the selection of the choices the writer has made, the choices the actors are making. And often when you're making a film, they're giving you a variety of choices and intensity and character. What they're doing is an interpretation of the character that they're trying to seek some sort of truth. It's really hard. I'm trying to find a consistency, a journey that is authentic and believable, that feeds into the whole experience that is logical as well. That does fit into that overall vision that Justin, in this case has for the story.

Again, it's down to lots of discussions. And one key thing is discovering the point of view within the film. With *Nitram*, there has been an awful lot of discussion about how you can't have empathy for a character that has been the perpetrator of such an atrocity. But I would say that there is. Whoever you're depicting, you have to have some sort of investment in their situation, in their point of view, in that moment in time in their life that you are putting across. It's just a point of emphasis within a scene. When someone is reacting to something someone else said, you are getting across a certain amount of empathy for that person who is reacting. Now, for the person who's trying to say whatever they're saying in their dialogue, you are also representing a point of view from them. It's all about finding the balance and the nuance within moment to moment that isn't just getting across facts or plot points, but imbuing emotion as well. That's the key thing. If it's not feeling, then it's just story. And the key thing is to get emotion in there as well.

It comes across so strong. It's a complicated film, for sure. One of the things which I was really impressed by was this is a film that is free from explicit violence in the film. And yet the feeling of it being a violent story is there. How do you manage to create a threat of violence in a cut, in an edit?

NF: See, I think there is quite a lot of violence in it, actually, in that there's an awful lot of potential violence. Now that's certainly to do with what actually happens from scene to scene and how that evolves. That scene on the couch with his father, the scene at the door trying to hand the money over when he's trying to buy the house off the old couple. When he's just shooting a gun. There's an awful lot of unseen mental turmoil which you could describe as violence, I think. And that's certainly to do with what we know he goes on to do; it is hidden.

We can't do it, but it would be amazing to show the film to people with no knowledge of what happened, and see if that's still there, but we only can bring our own experiences to it and we all come as individuals [with] different points of view to watching it so it's going to be different to everyone. I think it's one of the unsaid things that is in the film and certainly in Caleb's performance. And it would have been easy to portray a character that was just difficult and almost like a horror film, of a beast from the very start, but Caleb nuanced the performance so much that there was such a variety of humanity in some places even in there, which I think takes people by surprise, which I think is very interesting.

Very much so. The screening that I saw it at, you could feel the tension in the air, you could feel the conflicted feelings. And one of the things which I felt was quite surprising was the manner that the audience that I watched it in didn't entirely know how to react at times, and found some of the scenes quite amusing. And that certainly was a surprise for me. I imagine there's that nervousness of not knowing what's going to happen.

NF: That is important, I feel, because I think in order to introduce and invite people into a family, you've got to feel like you are there and part of them and understand them. And humour is a brilliant disabler of allowing people into a situation and liking them. That is entirely reasonable, that reaction, and observation from your point of view. And [it's] intentional. I'll say it. Yes, it's totally intentional.

What conversations did you have about those intentional moments?

NF: I think it's important that there is an element of mystique about the process. And it was a very small production. And I think on every level, there was an intimacy in the crew and in the cutting room where there's a sanctuary. I think it just comes from a place of trust, and that's Justin trusting his collaborators and then responding to that. It's important to discuss everything and anything so that's where it comes from, that place of trust. Exploring what it is that's the story that everyone's trying to tell.

This is your second film with Justin, with True History of the Kelly Gang being your first in Australia. What's been the difference of working in the UK versus working here?

NF: Well, it's warmer here. I think every film is different, and so you're always forging these relationships and trying to find your way and do what's best for the film. That continues wherever you are. You just want to keep going really, and hopefully find the best people and the best projects - that's your desire - that are always interesting and not straightforward. That's all I'd love to continue doing. I was very lucky to land on Justin's lap, when he gave me the call if I was interested in doing *True History of the Kelly Gang*, I was finishing up a film in London, and my family had already arrived in Australia. He had no idea that I was actually moving to Australia, so it was a very great serendipitous occurrence for me. [I] landed on my feet, I think.

There's an outsider perspective to this as well, because you're dealing with two very deeply Australian stories. Were you familiar with them before coming to both the Kelly Gang and Nitram?

NF: I knew about Ned Kelly, and I knew about Peter Carey's book. So, I absolutely was aware. And also, the Sidney Nolan paintings. And, Port Arthur was also a world-wide event that I could remember. I was aware of those stories. I wasn't quite aware of how divided Australia is and on their perspective of these events. In some ways, that there's been quite a shock, actually in terms of the loud voices that you hear.

They can be very outspoken as well.

NF: Yeah. They can.

How does that affect you as a creative person?

NF: Well, I actually think about it quite a lot. Because, Australia has this sense of... people's view of Australia is often very friendly, happy go lucky folk. But really, it's actually much more multicultural than people expect as well, which I think is great. It's amazing. But those minorities don't necessarily have a voice here as much as they might, say, in London or elsewhere. In the UK, having lived there fifty odd years, you're aware of the difference and so it doesn't surprise you when it comes up. Because it could be class, it could be culture, it could be anything and so you're never shocked by it. It's part of the discussion, whereas here, sometimes it certainly shocks me because it's new and you don't necessarily expect it. I think that's the difference, if that makes sense.

It does. I want to lead to closing up the discussion with talking about maybe one of the best climaxes in Australian film history which is in True History of the Kelly Gang and that shootout and the choice of the visual style there. I wonder if you can talk through editing that particular sequence and choosing the shots that would amplify the tension and anxiety and the fear that was in the Kelly gang as they're being shot at?

NF: Ari Wegner and Justin shot it, [with] Karen [Murphy], the production designer. It was shot in a very particular way, in a very claustrophobic close way, a lot of small cameras in that Glenrowan pub. They were working in a really intimate way again where point of view was very much from them, in that claustrophobic world. There was a real mystery, it wasn't like a high budget where the police, the cops were coming at you in their thousands. There was a real mystery to them and where they were. So that was certainly the starting point. I think you're talking about within the bar, are you? As opposed to when Ned steps out?

Yes.

NF: All of it?

All of it, and together because it is a sequence of two halves where they're in the bar, and then of course they step out and there's that searing night-time vision of these oncoming police officers and being highlighted by their gunshots. The tension that is there is palpable. It comes from the visuals, but I think it comes even more from the editing itself.

NF: Well, that's great. I think it's a combination of all those things, because the performances - and it's always abstract, what's going on - you're so disorientated and you're not using the normal rules of a dialogue scene when they're all just bathed in blood and the scene, it was actually shot much, much longer and it ended up being really trimmed down so that it escalated like a crescendo. And that certainly did happen in the edit.

We can't talk about it without mentioning the amazing sound work and Jed's music. I think it is that whole collection of contributors pulling in to that crazy spiral of hell. Going to the climax of him getting shot and the burning building which is almost sort of a release. You're almost glad it's over really when that building's burning down. I do often think there was some amazing beautiful footage, a scene shot where there was this ash just floating in the air, this was cut out. But that was like something from Tarkovsky, it was just incredible. But it was not about Ned and we couldn't justify it. It's amazing what doesn't end up in that you may have loved.

How do you approach a director when there is a moment that you feel needs to be excised that they love?

NF: Well, with sensitivity and caution, and it's important to back all that reasoning up with a good argument that feeds into the whole picture, the whole story. There are always those moments when you feel this hard-fought scene that was impossible to get suddenly doesn't have its place.

I can only imagine the number of moments of beauty or tranquillity that are left on the cutting room floor. And we always think it's sad because of what we might have lost. But then when we see the final edit, we realise, okay, it needed to go because of creating something that was brilliant, as in the case of both Kelly Gang and Nitram, which you should be proud of as an editor. They are really astounding pieces of work, and I think they're really modern classics of Australian cinema. I'm excited to see where you continue going as an editor here in Australia.

NF: That's very kind, Andrew. That makes me feel a bit more at home.

INTERVIEW
NITRAM AND MORTAL KOMBAT - SOUND DESIGNER JAMES ASHTON

James Ashton has worked in the world of sound for over twenty years across Australia, China, and the UK. His work can be seen as a sound designer on films like Wong Kar Wai's *The Grandmaster* (2013) and as a supervising dialogue editor on Zhang Yimou's *The Flowers of War*, through to working as a sound editor on Garth Davis' *Lion* (2016) and *Mary Magdalene* (2018). He has been recognised with AACTA nominations for his work on *Tanna* (2015), *Paper Planes* (2014), and *Nitram* (2021), and won for his work on *Lion* and *Mortal Kombat* (2021).

Interview conducted September 2021

▶▷▶

When did you get a moment to sit down and just absorb Nitram before starting work on it?

James Ashton: When you're working on the film, for every film or TV show that I work on, I'll always watch it through from the very start, from beginning to end, so that you can understand what you're working on, and to try and get in the director's head and just appreciate it for what it is, before you start dissecting it and breaking it down. I think I watched *Nitram* the day before I met with Justin to talk about the film. You need to understand what you're working on before you talk about what you're working on with the director obviously. And then you usually won't watch it again continuously until the very end of the process so that you can see how it's all come together.

There is some confusion of late about the distinction between sound design and sound editing. For you, how do you describe the role of being a sound designer to people?

JA: Being a sound designer, broadly speaking, is finding a sonic voice for the director's story. I'm trying to breathe sonic life into what the director is trying to realise. I'm not a fan of the distinction necessarily between sound editors and sound designers, because fundamentally, when you're editing sound, you're making creative choices about what sounds you're going to use and what sounds you're going to exclude. And that by its very nature is designed. There is creative intent there, even with the mundane, sonic things like doors opening and closing, everybody will make choices about what door sound is right, and what door sound is wrong. And that, fundamentally, is design.

I don't think it's necessarily fair to have this very broad distinction between a sound editor and a sound designer. It comes more with responsibility; who involved in the sound team is going to be responsible for really finding a voice for a film? Or, perhaps with regards to an action film, working on key action moments that are imperative to the storytelling, versus who's going to be responsible for the more A to B sounds like doors opening and closing, cars passing in the background. So, the sound designer has more responsibility in terms of driving the story forward.

When you head out into the world and hear different things, do you collect sounds and think 'oh, I've got to keep that in mind for something later on'?

JA: I never switch my ears off, they're always listening and what my ears are hearing, I have no doubt, are very different to what most other people's ears are hearing out in the everyday world. I find that in reality that there's not that much that I see in the real world that makes me go, 'oh, I've got to have that in this in this project that I'm working on'. That happens sometimes from time to time, but I don't generally find that inspiration comes to me from the real world.

Maybe that's because what we do, fundamentally, is not the real world. We're trying to hide reality and craft something that it's not necessarily real. Or maybe that my brain just sort of is happy to switch off, and be a little bit detached. My ears are particularly tuned in when I watch other people's work, like after dinner, when we sit down on the sofa and watch a TV show of an evening. I can't watch a TV show without thinking about the craftsmanship that's gone into the soundtrack, whether it's low budget, high budget, American, Australian, whatever. I can never switch that that sort of analytical sort of always going.

And going back to the first thing we spoke about, the first time you watch a film, I think that's really indicative. When we first watch a film, it's before the post-production has been completed, so there are a lot of warts. The film feels very unpolished when we first get to watch them, and so when you lose yourself to a story on that first viewing, you know that you're going to be working on a great film. When you forget about work, you forget about analysing 'what do I need to do here?' 'What will I need to talk to the director about there?' When you just completely get lost in the story on that first viewing, that's when you know that you're going to be working on a cracker.

Nitram was one of those films and particularly, Garth Davis' *Lion*, I just completely switched off to the sort of mechanics of what I was there for, and just lost myself in the film. And, I think the way that that film was critically received is a good reflection of that initial reaction to it.

Lion is a really powerful film. I love that film a lot. And I think there is a real distinct difference between how India sounds and how Tasmania sounds in that film, too.

JA: Vastly. It goes without saying that we worked pretty hard. We didn't have to work hard to create that difference, because they fundamentally sound sonically completely different. But we did, it was definitely conscious that we had to sonically create a strong contrast between the two locations of the film. It was so much fun to work on that film, just the sonic chaos of India versus the tranquillity of Tasmania and to have pieces of both of those to work on was a lot of fun.

In the case of Lion, what was it like working with a first-time feature filmmaker?

JA: Every director is different in terms of what their expectations from the sound department is. And it goes without saying that the less experience the director has, the more they rely on you to guide them as to what's appropriate or not appropriate, and what might be possible or not possible. And that's great, because when you present stuff to them, their response is naturally just an emotional response. "What you've presented triggers the right emotions"; or "No, no, that's not my intention, the creative intent is not right there, how do we go back to the drawing board and re-address that."

Whereas the more experienced directors who have been through the process multiple times, because they understand the process, they can let themselves get more involved in the mechanics of the process a bit more, and they're a bit more comfortable deconstructing things and pulling things apart. Which is not necessarily helpful, sometimes it's better for the mechanics not to be pulled apart. And you either respond well emotionally to something or you don't, and you say why in either case, and then you take stock and move on and move forward from there.

Garth was great to work with, because I think most things that were presented to him exceeded his expectations that went beyond what he felt was necessary or required or what he'd imagined. It was a pleasure to work with him, because he was just so positive in the feedback that he gave.

And he's gone on to have a really stunning career. It's really something to have your film nominated for Best Picture.

JA: He's a great guy, he's a lovely, lovely human being, and hats off to him for just being such a wonderful human being. And that is part of why he's got to where he is, I think, because he's just such a great guy. To an extent, Justin Kurzel is not dissimilar in that regard. He's the sort of guy that you'd be very happy to sit down at the pub with, and have a beer with to talk about something that's got nothing to do with film. But then when you do talk about something to do with film, there's clarity and focus and a real purpose to what he has to say. So that's why his career has gone quite successfully for an Australian director. He's had a pretty strong career as well.

What was the conversation like with Justin coming to Nitram? What did what did he say to you about the themes of the film?

JA: It was really interesting working with Justin. I don't recall ever going to a sound brief, where you just talk about the voice that you want the film to have, in that initial sort of conversation. I don't think I've ever been to a sound brief where there has been so much clarity as to what the expectations were. He was very, very clear and very, very precise about what he wanted. And I was a bit blown away. Some of the things that he asked for, which he was so particular about, quite a few of them didn't end up in the final film, because they just didn't work, but his ideas were so clear that I was taken aback with just how much force that he put into what he wanted this film to sound like.

Caleb Landry Jones, Essie Davis
Picture © 2021 Good Thing Productions Company Pty Ltd, Filmfest Limited. Used with permission

Thematically he wanted a distinction between the suburbs of Tasmania, where Martin and his family resided, versus the tranquillity of the property where Helen lived. He wanted there to be a sonic distinction. He wanted the suburbs to sound suburban, mundane, familiar, but boring, like it was uninteresting in terms of where these people were at in their lives.

Whereas Helen's place needed to be pure and free, and uninhibited. It was done very, very deliberately, that whenever we're at Helen's place, there is never the sound of any sort of machinery there. No cars, no planes, nothing mechanical at Helen's place. Whereas the suburbs of Tasmania the suburbs of Hobart are the opposite to that; there's lots of dull cars in the background, lawn mowers, garbage trucks, dogs barking, all that kind of stuff.

The most challenging place sonically to work on was Seascape, where the first murders took place. Justin wasn't as clear with what he wanted there. He didn't know what was required there. And so, we stumbled across the sound for that place by accident. A lot of the shots that we had there, it's quite windy, and that's just the nature of what the weather was doing on the day that they shot. I thought, 'well, if we're going to try and give a voice to this place, we'll find something that can work with the wind'. And so, I started playing with wind chimes, and they went in and Justin just loved that. He thought that was kind of appropriate for whatever reason. And the wind chimes became a became a theme throughout the Seascape. And so, in that regard, these three different locations have three separate sonic identities that keep recurring each time we go back to them in the film.

One of the notes I've written down was the tension that is built from that suburban life there. One of the sounds that lingers in my mind was the sound of the lawnmower. It's a sound that we're also familiar with, the sound of a Sunday morning, but there's something that is really tense and unnerving about the way that the lawnmower sound is presented here, it cuts through in a way that I didn't expect. Can you talk about how you build anxiety or tension through a sound? How do you design a sound to sound tense?

JA: That's an excellent question, which I can't really answer. The lawnmower is... that's a completely mundane sound. And that wasn't designed in terms of the way it was sonically presented. It's just the sound of a lawnmower, there's no trickery going on there. The design is in the choice, the choice that's made when to have the lawn mower. Why, for how long, and also particularly what you've pointed out is how obvious it is. That lawn mower played with the drama of what was happening in that room very, very well.

That was an example of how ideas bounce backwards and forwards. Justin hadn't specifically said that he wanted that lawn mower there in that scene, he had generally said that he wanted 'suburbia'. And he gave the example of a lawn mower being a part of suburbia. So, I laid it into that scene. But I didn't put it in the scene as loud as it played in the film, but Justin heard it, and he's like, "That lawn mower is great. What if the sound of that lawnmower was like cutting up Martin's mental state of mind inside his head." We really played with pushing that more and more to the point where you couldn't even hear the dialogue anymore. And obviously, everybody agreed that that was too much. But the balance that was struck was where it plays in the final film.

The manner that the direction, the acting, the script, and then the sound design, all adds to this level of tension, the feeling of the unexpected, there's something that's going to happen. And it all plays like an orchestra.

JA: It was such a great film to work on. One of the reasons that was really great, from a sound designers' point of view, is how little music there is in the film. There's almost no music and Justin toyed for a long time with the idea of not having any music at all, right up to the second last day of the sound mix, he was still playing with not having any music in the film at all. And I was an advocate of that, not because I thought the sound design was so good that it didn't need music. What I loved about the way Justin made this film, was that the film doesn't tell you how to think or feel the way most films do. It doesn't dictate to you what you should be thinking at a certain moment, it presents everything in a very Through the Looking Glass vibe.

And I felt, which I expressed to Justin, as soon as the music comes in, you spoil that Through the Looking Glass feeling because immediately you're starting to tell people how they should be feeling, which I don't think this film needs. I said, "I think you should trust yourself. You trust yourself that the story is strong enough to tell itself without trying to tell people how to feel about the film emotionally; just let people sit and watch it. And they'll respond to it naturally for what it is." I think, given the sensitivity of the subject matter, that was a really relevant point to raise.

But it was great to be involved in crafting something that could tell the story in this Through the Looking Glass vibe. It felt very, very non-manipulative. The reality was that we were making some very clear choices to steer the emotion, just not overtly the way music does. I think the reality is that the soundtrack came up very well, it ended up becoming quite a strong and when I say soundtrack, I'm talking about the sound of the film as a whole, not just the music per se. It really has a voice.

With the piano sequences where Martin and Helen are playing chopsticks, is that part of sound design? Or is that part of something else?

JA: All that stuff had nothing to do with the sound department. All that stuff was shot on location, so there's no trickery. Jed Kurzel who did the music, he didn't have any involvement in any of that either. It was all shot on camera, by the actors and woven into the film by Nick Fenton, the editor. We didn't play any tricks. No tomfoolery. It just it literally plays as they shot it.

Because that's equally unsettling too. It sounds like a torture.

JA: And it was interesting working with Justin because he likes to let quite a lot of randomness into his film. A film like this, every everything is scripted and pre-planned, everything is pre-planned. And so it was kind of unusual to work with Justin because he embraced the randomness that happened as part of the shoot and as part of the locations of the shoot. And I can't recall off the top of my head, but it wouldn't surprise me if the piano was not written into the script at all, it was there on the location, and the actors started playing with it, and he embraced that.

There were a lot of things where he heard sounds on the location that had nothing to do with the story itself, but he latched on to them emotionally and requested that they become part of the soundtrack. And a key one of those is the geese at Seascape. He said, there were geese on the location, and he just felt that that was just such a wonderful sound to weave into the story. Most directors would be like, "Well, these don't have anything to do with the message that I'm trying to communicate, so let's remove them, let's get rid of them." Whereas Justin was the opposite. He's like, "I want to embrace this, I want to explore an idea here, let's push it forwards."

There were several ideas like that. I don't know if you noticed. I mean, you probably did notice because it was pretty overt in the in the gun shop—

—that was literally the next thing I was going to ask you about.

JA: —haunting wind in the gun shop. That was part of the location sound. Justin liked it, he liked that it had this haunting vibe to it, and from a technical point of view, that wasn't a sound that we could remove, if Justin wanted to remove that wind sound, we would have had to call the actors in for ADR, which is, quite rightly, something directors are very hesitant to do. And so instead of trying to hide the wind sound, we actually embellished it, and I went into my sound library to find more dramatic winds to help push that along. And so that happy accident that was part of the filming of the film that had nothing to do with the storytelling in the first place, actually became a fundamental part of the soundtrack.

That gun shop scene, when I watched it in the cinema you could just feel the oxygen in the room just disappear. It's such a powerful scene. Besides the wind, was there much that you could bring to that to amplify the sound of the guns being loaded and checked?

JA: That's really where you start getting more legitimate sound design, not that it's more or less legitimate, for all those gun sounds, once they go into that secondary room of the gun shop, those gun sounds are very, very hardened. Guns don't naturally sound like that. Although in film, we think that they do. What you hear in *Nitram* is what you'd expect a gun to sound like in the cinema. But I worked very, very hard because Justin specifically requested it, he said, "I want the sound of these guns to scare the fuck out of you." He said "People should be scared, scared shitless when they hear these guns being cocked."

And I'm like, "Okay, great, that's what we're gonna do." A lot of those sounds, the hammers being cocked and uncocked, they're not gun sounds at all. They're big metal bars being slammed against each other that had been pitched down to give them a real, real ballsy weight and depth because sonically, guns just don't have that, they sound thin and clunky and light when you listen to them at face value.

Do you enjoy that creation of sound? Obviously, you would do because it's part of your job, but the building a sound library, it seems like a really extensive, difficult thing to do, but it also sounds like a pretty enjoyable thing to do as well.

JA: Yeah, I love it. I mean, one of the one of the things I have most fun with is finding sounds that have nothing to do at face value with that you're trying to put a sound to. Something that's completely unrelated. How do you weave that in to the scene that you're making? And sometimes you have to do things because the real-life sound isn't dramatic enough. A gun cocking is a classic example of that.

Other times you have to do it because the sound in the real world doesn't exist. Last week I had to make the sound of somebody passing through a big wave of cobwebs. A cobweb doesn't make a sound, but the director wanted it to have a sound. And so I was asked to find a sound for the cobwebs, and that I just think it's so cool. What do you put in there for something that doesn't actually have a sound at all? That's super, super exciting. And I enjoy that a lot.

I can imagine. With the films that you've done, it must be pretty exciting to come up with some iconic sounds that really stick in your mind. Mortal Kombat is a film that is full of the sound design that adds to the character of the film, and without it, it's a little flat. Is that the exciting part of sound design?

JA: Oh, absolutely. 100%. *Mortal Kombat* was a sound designers paradise, because you don't have to stick to a rulebook that's based in reality. With something like *Nitram*, the choices that you make have to be rooted in reality, because if you start to make things too hyper real, it will break the facade, and the audience will become consciously aware that what they're what they're watching is not real, that it's been manipulated. And you don't want to do that with a film like *Nitram*, but with a film like *Mortal Kombat*, you have to do it, because there's this expectation that everything is so much larger than life. It's aliens from another world going into battle against each other, it has to be way over the top. There's no limit as a sound designer to how wacky you can get with sounds for a film like that. And it's great when you come up with something that you think is really wacky, and you play it to the director, and they're like, "No, I think we can work a little bit harder." You're like, "Whoa, okay, yeah, strap in guys, we're going for a ride."

For younger Australians who are looking at getting into the work of sound design, do you have any suggestions or tips that they might be interested in knowing?

JA: To anybody who's interested in or who is considering work in the industry, it is rewarding to work in the film industry, in a creative space, and if that sort of creative reward is something that you'd like to pursue, then definitely get in touch with local practitioners, local designers, local studios, and make inquiries about doing internships, or sitting in full time work experience. That's how I started. I did work experience at a studio when I was in my last year of high school, and one thing just turned into another thing, and here I am, many, many years later. Follow your nose, follow your dreams. If you want it, go out there and get it.

When you zoom right out and look at the big picture, nothing is going to stop people's appetite for content. There is a very, very strong desire for content on our screens. And so, as long as broadly speaking, that continues to be embraced and nurtured, I think there is hope for a strong ongoing industry, because I don't see that appetite waning anytime soon.

REVIEW
I MET A GIRL

BRENTON THWAITES IMPRESSES WITH A GROUNDED
AND DEEPLY EMPATHETIC PERFORMANCE

Within the first five minutes of the tender Aussie romance-drama, *I Met a Girl*, a sense of deception slides over you. Our lead, Devon (Brenton Thwaites), has disrupted his brother's wedding, stabbed himself in the chest with a broken bottle, and received electro-shock therapy. And that's before he tries to take his own life.

Director Luke Eve and writer Glen Dolman have delivered a grounded human experience with *I Met a Girl* that lingers longer in your mind than what the film premise would suggest. After his initial life stumbles, Devon meets the girl of his dreams, Lucy (Lily Sullivan), and spends the day with her, basking in the warmth of love and romance. After he arranges a dinner to introduce Lucy to his brother, Nick (Joel Jackson), and she doesn't turn up, the reality starts to set in that maybe Lucy doesn't exist, revealing the difficulties of mental illness that Devon lives with.

With an impressive performance from Brenton Thwaites, *I Met a Girl* presents the internal struggle of people who live with the various skewed realities that mental illnesses can conjure up. Devon lives with schizophrenia and does so with understanding and compassion from Nick and Nick's wife Olivia (Zahra Newman) who provide him with a home and food. On paper, alongside mental health support, it seems Devon has all he needs to live a steady life.

However, as is the case for many folks who live with mental illnesses, finding the right balance of medications and societal support can be difficult. For Devon, the daily toll of literally mind-numbing medications wears upon him, allowing the hallucinations of various entities to distort his reality. Dolman's script is keenly aware of the complexities of medication, with a notable line about one antipsychotic medication working against another antipsychotic medication, highlighting how hard the search for some semblance of ballast in the mind can be.

Thwaites echoes Sam Worthington's performance in *Paper Planes*, where an actor who has 'made it' in Hollywood is able to return to Australia to stretch their creative muscles and remind us why they were successful in the first place. He navigates the role of Devon brilliantly, playing him as someone keenly aware of his illness, almost overcorrecting to be the kindest and most caring person he can be, to a fault. While I'm personally not able to talk of the authenticity of Thwaites' portrayal of the illness, it's clear that there's a deep level of empathy from Thwaites, eager to honour those who live with schizophrenia as best as possible.

Supporting turns from Joel Jackson, Zahra Newman, and Lily Sullivan elevate Thwaites at every turn. Jackson and Newman respectfully show how important supportive family members can be, while also exploring the difficulties that come with being a carer. Lily Sullivan masters the role of a character who simply isn't there, neatly presenting the trick of a man learning to love himself through a woman he's made up, yet equally feeling like her own entity. While *I Met a Girl* feels a little bloated in the third act, it's Thwaites and Sullivan's chemistry that deliver a satisfying emotional conclusion.

Films about mental illnesses run the risk of being inauthentic, disrespectful, or highly performative, and it's a blessing that *I Met a Girl* is none of these things. Luke Eve's direction is caring, creating a piece that seeks to strip away the destructive and harmful depictions of schizophrenia on film. While Brenton Thwaites' Hollywood career appears to be continuing indefinitely, hopefully he's afforded the chance to deliver performances like this in the future.

CONTRIBUTION
THE RECORDIST - WRITER/DIRECTOR
INDIANNA BELL

Co-directors Indianna Bell and Josiah Allen are quickly proving to be one of the most exciting up-and-coming filmmakers in Australia, with their 2019 film *Call Connect.* receiving worldwide acclaim. Their 2021 short film *The Recordist* was nominated for Best Drama, Best Directing, Best Editing, Best Performance, Best Sound Design, and Best Score at the 23rd South Australian Screen Awards.

The Recordist won the Narrative Short Jury Award at the 2020 Austin Film Festival, and subsequently took home the Australian Cinematographers Society Gold Award for Sam Twiddale at the 2020 ceremony. While *The Recordist* made its Australian premiere at the 2020 Adelaide Film Festival, it's on You-Tube channel Omeleto where the short has found a receptive audience, with over 98,000 views at time of publication.

Writer and co-director of *The Recordist*, Indianna Bell, writes about her experience as a filmmaker below.

►▷►

The genesis of this idea came at the beginning of 2019 when Josiah Allen and I (co-directors of *The Recordist*) were in Sydney taking part in Tropfest's Masterclass Program. During this whirlwind experience we were also being filmed as part of a behind the scenes documentary. For this reason, for the first time in our lives, Jo and I were fitted with lapel microphones. The sound recordist warned us to not forget that we were wearing them throughout the day and proceeded to tell us about some cringe-worthy stories of crew members who had forgotten that all their words were being transmitted via a tiny mic taped to their chest. During this conversation, it struck me that a sound recordist holds an incredible amount of power in this way. I was inspired to write a story that takes this often-overlooked occupation into a dark and twisted place, placing it against the backdrop of the 'Me Too' movement in the Film Industry.

Considering that our first film, *Call Connect*, was a one-character, one-location and one-take conversation piece, *The Recordist* was a huge step up for us as filmmakers. It presented us with a whole set of new challenges (locations, extras, set building...) that we needed to somehow make work on our tiny budget. We also faced some unexpected hurdles, with our shooting period nestled neatly between the black summer bushfires and the beginning of the COVID pandemic. All of our post production was completely indoors- with everyone involved working remotely throughout the entire process.

Myself and Josiah graduated from Flinders University's Screen Production program in 2016 and, along with our creative partner John Chataway, banded together to form the young filmmaking collective 'Stakeout Films.' Since forming, we have always strived to make each project bigger than the next in an effort to push ourselves, upskill and make a horrendous amount of new mistakes.

Josiah Allen and Indianna Bell
Photo © Stakeout Films. Used with permission

Brendan Rock
Photo © Stakeout Films. Used with permission

After *The Recordist*, we quickly went into pre-production for our first feature project, a micro-budget thriller that we just recently wrapped shooting. With each project we learn some new and difficult lessons, but there are a few really key ones that we have found have helped us so far. Firstly, we've learned the importance of writing with budget in mind. Simplify, simplify, simplify... because even the most basic ideas, with minimal cast and locations, always seem to find a way of growing bigger. So starting small is really the only way to avoid disappointment down the track. The other most consistent thing that we have found is that no amount of study or work experience beats just going and making your own stuff. Regardless of the budget or scale, the only way to get better is by just doing and doing it yourself.

Indianna Bell and Josiah Allen with the Crew of The Recordist
Photo © Stakeout Films. Used with permission

INTERVIEW
DISCLOSURE & MEASURE FOR MEASURE -
ACTOR MARK LEONARD WINTER

A ctor Mark Leonard Winter honours the late Dame Hill with a masterful performance in Paul Ireland's *Measure for Measure*, taking over the role that the late actor was due to play. His turn as Angelo contrasts against his performance in Michael Bentham's *Disclosure* impressively, showcasing the diversity of roles that Mark can easily tackle. In *Disclosure*, Mark plays Danny Bowman, husband to Matilda Ridgway's Emily, friend to Geraldine Hakewill's Bek and Tom Wren's politician Joel. The four friends collide as Danny and Emily 4-year-old daughter alleges that Bek and Joel's 9-year-old son sexually assaulted her. The film focuses on the heated and turbulent discussion the four friends have with each other as they try to resolve this traumatic event. Bentham's film arrives at a charged time in the global atmosphere, where discussions about sexual assault and abuse are becoming more frequent.

Paul Ireland arrived on the Aussie film scene in 2015 with *Pawno*, a microbudget feature made with proud confidence alongside mate Damian Hill. Their follow up, *Measure for Measure* is a Melbourne set Shakespeare adaptation, scripted by Hill and featuring a jam-packed cast of Aussie titans. Dame's script swings for the fences and brings strine to Shakespeare with ease, in turn giving Hugo Weaving a villainous lead to sink his teeth into. Where *Pawno* highlighted two stars on the rise, *Measure for Measure* cements Megan Smart as a force to be reckoned with. Her performance as Jaiwara imbues the film with the emotional undercurrent it requires, with Smart showing accents of strength and vulnerability, often in the same scene. Supporting turns from Daniel Henshall and Fayssal Bazzi all help make each act of violence carry its intended weight. *Measure for Measure* triumphs in a grand manner, it reaches for the skies and has the spirit to get there.

Within both *Measure for Measure* and *Disclosure*, Mark Leonard Winter cements himself as one of Australia's most exciting and promising actors, building on the success of his 2016 Helpmann Award win for his performance in Simon Stephens' *Birdland*. With over a decade of experience in both film and TV, Mark has made a name for himself in notable films like Robert Connolly's *Balibo* (2009), Jonathan auf der Heide's *Van Diemen's Land* (2009), Craig Monahan's *Healing* (2014) and Jocelyn Moorhouse's *The Dressmaker* (2015), amongst others. His career continues to shine with a role in Baz Luhrmann's *Elvis* (2022) on the cards.

Interview conducted September 2021

How was the making of Disclosure? Have you watched it back and experienced it again?

Mark Leonard Winter: I've only watched it a couple of times. I get really excited by films like that, by people getting together outside of their usual channels of making a film, and I find it so exciting to be around that energy. There's a sense of urgency of 'we've got to make this thing and we've got to find a way to make this thing,' and I thought Michael, the director, did just such a beautiful job creating this chamber piece of this mess of a situation that all these people are in. It was really interesting.

As an actor watching it, it was quite a challenge, in a sense with the style that Michael wanted to shoot it. They were very long, for the most part, locked off takes and heavy, heavy dialogue. And, usually you work in the camera, work in the edit a bit when you're shooting that sort of stuff. "Okay, I'll get that in the close-up and we'll get that in the wide." Whereas this was just... the whole thing was very exposed and very vulnerable with the place that the characters are in. I thought it was beautiful to see [the] vision come together in the finished product. It was really cool.

That opening is confronting in a lot of ways because you don't expect it to start off with [a sex scene].

MLW: No.

It's really personal as well. What's it like knowing that that's how the film is going to start?

MLW: Well, I think we were fortunate in a way. When you read the script, there's always those scenes where you're like, "Oh, okay. All right. Well, that one's coming up." And they sort of sit there and they're in the back of your mind about 'when's that gonna happen?' And we got quite lucky when we were filming in that on our first day of filming essentially, it rained. And so that was Plan B, that scene.

So it was like, "Okay, Mark, Matilda, we're going to do this now." In a sense, it worked out well because it was like ripping off the band aid. And, you don't really have time to overthink it. You're just there. You're just doing it. It worked out all right.

The relationship that you have with Matilda feels like you've lived a life together. What's it like building that kind of relationship on screen?

MLW: I think for a start the four of us it was very much a quartet. We're all very close. I'm actually engaged to Geraldine who played Bek-

Congratulations.

MLW: -in the film. Thanks, I'm still in shock. So, in that sense, we had that sitting underneath us, that there was a lot of trust, there was a sort of intimacy between us as friends anyway so it allowed us to settle into those relationships and allowed us to be vulnerable within them, and will each other on to explore this material. The challenge, playing that character and establishing that relationship with Matilda, was really what the piece was trying to ask; "How do you respond as a father to this, the thing that's most precious to you, has been through something that you can't begin to wrap your head around?"

You can't actually understand it. It was just trying to be very real with the crisis that they're in. And yet I felt that that family had that relationship. That couple were strong together, and they made each other stronger whilst challenging each other and supporting each other. And I think that that's what the film starts to open up so well is the truth of this event. They're just desperate to not acknowledge the truth of it. They're there to find the truth and work out, but the more the truth comes to light, the harder it is for them all individually. I think it was just really trying to cement that this was a loving family just like any other that is dealing with something inconceivable to all of them.

Mark Leonard Winter
Photo © Michael Bentham. Used with permission.

It's not just a loving family, it's a loving friendship as well. These are two close friends that have effectively been separated by a traumatic instance that nobody expected. There's a really powerful moment later on where you're talking with Joel in the forest and there's that fallen tree, and the moment is very complex because you've both got this thing sitting between each other. And yet you're still friends and you want to talk about "Jeez, what do I do about this tree? How do I deal with that?" That feels like such a morally complex moment there. How did you navigate the friendship and addressing the seriousness of the situation?

MLW: Well, I think that that was the word that I used before, the mess of it. They're just in this mess and they're all scrambling to try to find a foothold with how they can deal with this and process this. And in terms of thinking about it as a quartet, the note that the character that I play is that I sincerely think that he believes that they can come out of this, putting the care of the children foremost and work out a way to deal with this crisis. And I think that he's incredibly shocked at the de-evolution, he's shocked by where they all end up and where he ends up personally.

It's just so complex. They're all dealing with something so complex, and the fact that he admires this man and respects him as a friend and then [they're] in a situation where it's like, 'are we going to be ostracised from the community? Am I going to lose my career?' And as an actor, you're looking for those things of like 'this piece is posing big questions and not offering any answers'. It's people in free-fall, trying to grab onto whatever they can on the way down and trying to find a way to make themselves feel better. Slowly the welfare of the children gets further and further away, they become more selfish and more self-involved, desperate to avoid the truths of themselves and the part that they may have played in contributing to this catastrophe that they're stuck in.

What I really loved about the script is how it manages to encompass so many different societal issues that are going on. The things that we personally have influenced on the kids that are in our lives, whether they're our own kids or nieces, nephews or friends' kids. And I found it's a really complex script, but it's keenly informed. What was the rehearsal process for the film?

MLW: Well, Michael, the director, had some friends who he was connected to with this, so he felt like he knew it quite intimately. I love the way the script managed to capture so much of the societal complexity that these people could be run out of the community. The complexity of the event that the film is built on, and how do you wrap your head around that?

And then something else that became really interesting was we shot this sort of before the MeToo explosion and women not being believed, and Bek who Gerry plays, she was in that initial read of the script, she was sort of unlikable. Seeing the film now and her journey - obviously, Michael and Gerry did a lot of work on it, and Gerry's an incredible actress - but suddenly it's about a woman who's never been believed her whole life, and it just has exploded in this new light from the zeitgeist. And suddenly your sympathies are quite with her even though she's such a difficult character, in a sense. It was a very raw and brave performance that I thought that she delivered, just fantastic.

The script is just such a testament to Michael that there was so much contained in this essentially single location pressure cooker, what it manages to open up and explore. It's quite extraordinary and quite an achievement

Tom Wren, Matilda Ridgway, Mark Leonard Winter, Geraldine Hakewill
Photo © Michael Bentham. Used with permission.

For her, she's trying to stand by herself but also stand by her politically inclined husband and do the right thing by him. She is both a wife and a secretary at the same time. And yet the relationship is this loving relationship that has tenderness and support. The other relationship there is this a bond as they swim together naked in the pool. They have openness in their relationship, also with their sexual interests. It's interesting to see how relationships open up in different ways. Was that an interesting point for you? Did that point of difference set them apart in an interesting way for you?

MLW: Yeah, I think so. And I think it was really interesting that the couple that I was in, they're so loving and so open. Not without their challenges, but they're not necessarily a powerful couple, you know? And then it's so interesting looking at what would be deemed a perhaps more success-ful partnership in the eyes of the world and there's so many little hidden doors and problems that they're trying to overcome and you see again the quartet aspect of it. You're just trying to find these different notes, these different voices within the four of us.

I really loved the feel of those two couples coming together and you've got this organic loving exploratory unashamed couple, in a sense. And then it feels like you're dealing with another couple on the other side separate to the event - that's the catalyst for the film - that is dealing with quite a lot of shame internally within their relationship and quite a lot to negotiate. I thought they were great counterpoints to each other.

I'm curious about the political stance in the film, too, because it feels pointed that one of the characters is essentially a right leaning person, a Liberal member, though it's not explicitly stated that he's a Liberal person. But there is a difference between the two left-leaning folks and a Liberal stance there as well. Was that something that was discussed at length or a pointed discussion of how the two different sides of the polit-ical spectrum might deal with this kind of situation?

MLW: Look, we didn't get into it so much in terms of the discussion around politics. But I think it opened up what the pressures are. What the added pressure that it puts on him that he's the Minister for Family Affairs, that it just makes the situation impossible. I thought of Danny, the guy I played, as this sort of Guardian type journalist, you know? Quite well-meaning in a sense, but in another sense slightly naive about the goodwill of people.

We never spoke directly about [politics], but I think it was just inherent in the writing that this adds such a burden to do each character individually with how they're going to handle this and process this. And of course, the terrifying thing that this is a high-profile couple. And if this goes public, that has massive implications for all of them and their children. And that's fundamentally what they're trying to protect.

It seems like a pointed decision to not have the children in the film. How was that to be parents to children that you don't meet? The daughter is there at the end, but there's no direct engagement with them.

MLW: I thought it was very clever on Michael's behalf because what was something that I found so interesting about the film was that they become children by the end of the film. Logic, reason, compassion, generosity, they've gone. They're just in this absurd state of hatred and not understanding and so I think, in a sense, the children are there in a way because they become them. And I think in a way the film is looking at the parents. That's what it's exploring, it's trying to explore. How can people deal with a truth that is just inconceivable?

As an actor, you've done a lot of films that have had morally complex tales in them. Is that something that you seek out?

MLW: I think so. You're always looking for something that you don't necessarily understand in a way that feels interesting, that's asking more questions than answers. And they're often the most interesting works because they're trying to get into something that's elusive. It's messy. I am really attracted to those types of roles. It's exciting because you don't know what's going to happen. I'm always hunting for that sort of stuff.

I know we're talking about Disclosure, and it's a really brilliant film. But I'd be remiss if I didn't ask you about Measure for Measure. I love your performance in it. It's a great film all round. What was it like working on that film, given the history in there, and working with Damian's script who was a great man, really great man?

MLW: Dame was a real hero of mine. And he was in third year at VCA [Victorian College of the Arts] when I was in first at the acting school, and he was just really good to me, and he took me under his wing in a way, and he just had a really great perspective on working. And when he made *Pawno*, I was just like, "Man, this is just brilliant." He just managed to take his career into his own hands and find his voice and find his agency. He called me up and said, "Do you want to come and be in my next film? You could play my offsider." And I was like, "Of course, man." I just respected his work so much and just thought he had this singular quality that no one else can come near, and such a beautiful artist.

It was, I think, the Friday before we were due to start on the Monday when Paul, the director of the piece, called me and said that he had passed away. Any film is a miracle, you know. The creation of any film is a miracle. But the fact that we managed to get that one into the world, I think, is something a little bit extra special.

What happened was that they had Hugo to play the Duke, but they only had him for a specific amount of time. And Paul thought like, "All right, well, I think we should keep going." And he said, "Would you be open to stepping into Dame's role and we push the shooting back a week?" and I said, "Okay, let's try." Paul kept the ship together. And Hugo was just like a bald eagle hovering over the whole thing, taking everyone under his wing in a way. And I thought that the film came together really well. And, it was hard to walk in what were Dame's shoes.

I can imagine.

MLW: I hope that he wasn't disappointed.

I don't think he would be. He was a great guy. I had interviewed him, and he was just such a kind soul. And I think that I think you did a great job of honouring him and his work and his performance what would have been in there. I feel like you you've delivered something that was really next level and astounding.

MLW: Thanks, man. I really appreciate that because it was a big undertaking and it's still emotional to think about it. He was just so real man. Dame was just— he didn't act. He was just real. He was just there, no one else can do it. You know, no one. I miss him. I miss him a lot.

Same here. Gosh, I wish he was still around.

MLW: That's the thing and that's part of the tragedy was this guy was just in bloom, man. You know, he was just... it was just all unfolding. But I feel grateful that I had a chance to be in his life and learn as much as I could from him. Not only with his artistic world, but just the way he carried himself, you know?

Oh, yeah.

MLW: I think he fought hard for what he wanted to do. And, I really respect that.

I'm just a guy who writes about films and talks about films, and I got to know him online, and I went through a divorce, and he sent me a message one night just saying, "Hey, mate, I saw that you're going through a divorce. If you need to chat. I'm right here." I'm like, "You're an AACTA nominated actor and writer." That's what kind of person he was. Hats off to him. I'm just so touched by his presence and I continually think about him all the time.

MLW: Yeah, man. He just really cared about people. And he really cared about people going through hard things. I think he could just really empathise with that. What a guy.

Mark, I really appreciate being able to talk to you. I have one last question which might be a big one. I like to focus on Australian film because we do a lot of great work and highlighting films like Disclosure and Measure for Measure, I think is really important because on a global scale, I think that people tend to forget that they exist.

MLW: Well, it's hard.

What does it mean to be an Australian actor working today?

MLW: For me, I think I'm really proud of it. And I'm really proud of the work that we're doing. And you mentioned those two films, and [with] *Disclosure* I just loved being a part of that work where you just say, "Let's get together and just do it," because it's so energising and exciting. Because they're massive operations to get a film off the ground. People doing this stuff and putting their voice out there. And I just feel like we're in a really exciting spot with it. Look, I just feel proud to be part of it. And I think the industry is pretty amazing. And, I feel like we have to fight for every inch we get, and it'd be great to punch through where these things start resonating globally, but there's a lot of things in the way of that.

But the creativity that we have here, it's been so interesting with the pandemic because just everyone's back, man. Everyone's here, you know. No one's in LA or in the UK. Everyone's back in Australia, and people are popping up in odd roles and go "Oh, they must be home." But I think we make awesome shit. I just think it's exciting people here doing such exciting things.

And I feel like we've got nothing to lose, you know? The riskier we are, the more dangerous it can all become, and the more exciting the films are. I feel excited about it. And, obviously digital has just changed everything where you can just try to get some people together and just be creative with making things. To hark back to Dame, he just laid out the breadcrumbs of "All right, this is how you do it. This is how you find your voice and find your people."

It feels like a lot of the great films and TV have been made in Australia is in the indie scene. I watched a fantastic SBS show the other week which was just made here in Perth, and it's like they just appear and it's fantastic. There are so many great people using what limited budget they might have to make fantastic films just like this one.

MLW: What was that? Was that *Iggy and Ace*?

Iggy and Ace. Yeah.

MLW: My friend Monica Zanetti directed some of that. I haven't seen it yet, but I'm looking forward to it.

I really liked it.

MLW: Nice. It's great. And she just did something before that, a lesbian rom-com [*Ellie & Abbie (& Ellies Dead Aunt)*]. You're just like, "Ahh, it's terrific!" And then it's indie now, but then everyone grows and their experience grows and their creativity and their voices will grow and then that just keeps expanding. And I think it's just really exciting.

Well, as somebody who loves your work and loves Geraldine's work, I'm really excited to see what you both continue to do and where your careers go from here and grow because you've got long careers ahead of you and some exciting work coming up. I'm certain of it and I'm looking forward to it.

MLW: Fingers crossed, man, and thanks for chatting with me about the movie though. I really appreciate your time. And, it just helps a lot trying to get these things out in the world somehow.

REVIEW
STREAMLINE

A MASTERFUL DRAMA FEATURING A CAREER-DEFINING
PERFORMANCE FROM LEVI MILLER

This piece contains discussions of domestic violence and sexual violence.

There's a welcome familiarity to Tyson Wade Johnston's feature debut film, *Streamline*. It drips with Australiana, positively drenched in the history of Australian drama, steeped in the early morning legacies of thousands of youthful sportspeople who yearn for athletic greatness. In an assured and confident manner, Johnston contributes a timely statement to the enduring conversation about Australian masculinity, circling out the swimming scene for its pervasive toxicity.

We follow Benjamin Lane, played with a lived-in quality by Levi Miller, a fifteen-year-old Olympic swimming hopeful pushed to his limits by the death-rattle of puberty, 3am training starts with a lead-heavy coach, and a fractured family relationship further strained by the re-emergence of his father (Jason Isaacs) from prison. With an all-too-familiar confluence of life events piling on top of each other, Ben has to navigate some kind of path to adulthood. His mother, Kim (Laura Gordon), is equally exhausted by the weighted daily routine that Ben goes through, and while she eagerly supports his growth, the constant push that she has to muster takes its toll.

As the focal point of *Streamline*, Levi Miller delivers a performance that is a certified career-defining moment for the already exemplary actor. Over the past decade, Miller has stunned with lead performances in *Red Dog: True Blue*, *Jasper Jones*, and a solid supporting turn in *A Wrinkle in Time*, but it's here as Ben that he is pointedly making the transition from a youthful great into becoming one of the most impressive young adult stars in Australia. Miller's Ben is realised with a proudly internal performance where all the simmering rage, conflict, and whirling chaos of being a teen ripples under his tense and tired muscles day in, day out.

Miller's informed acting is deftly elevated by a supporting cast that consistently works to enrich a particularly relevant narrative about toxic masculinity. Laura Gordon's mother, Kim, feels like a continuation of her stunning performance in *Undertow*, a film which exposed the horrifying sexual violence in the sports scene. Gordon is one of the great modern actresses working in Australia today, and her work here adds to an impressive career.

Equally impressive is the always watchable Jason Isaacs as Ben's absent, once-violent father, Rob. Isaacs presence is strewn throughout *Streamline*, but the impact of Rob's violence against both Ben and Kim looms over every frame. We meet him as a weathered and broken man seeking to atone for the pain he inflicted upon his family, and later as a shell of a human hidden in the washroom of a small restaurant. The toll of prison has clearly changed him, and Isaacs sorrow-filled performance leaves an enduring question in our minds: if prison and the act of losing one's family needs to occur to change a violent man, then where does the necessary break in the violent familial cycle come from?

Throughout *Streamline,* we witness the constant dehumanisation of Ben. In all aspects, he's called 'boy', not Ben. He's rarely seen as a solitary person, instead he's a tool, a muscle designed and crafted to do one thing: swim. In turn, Ben becomes almost mute, rarely speaking, as if he's been routinely beaten into submission and is now afraid to exist as himself. A rare point of comfort comes from his girlfriend, Patti (Tasia Zalar), but even in that sanctuary-like relationship, the pressure of training and success intrudes. The question of whether Ben actually ever wants to become an Olympian, let alone be a swimmer, feels decidedly absent.

As the looming Olympic qualification trials hang over Ben's head the sound of his coach, Glenn (a domineering performance from Robert Morgan), saying "If you screw this up, then it's a four year wait til the next trials," rings through his mind. That stress and the reappearance of Rob pushes Ben into boiling point territory, leading him to the brotherly home of his estranged siblings, Dave (Jake Ryan), and Nick (Sam Parsonson), both of whom have been moulded by Rob's violence. In a masterful shorthand, we get an immediate understanding of what kind of brother Dave is, with his muscled shoulder emblazoned with a Southern Cross tattoo. Jake Ryan's performance balances the tension of tenderness and terror expertly, highlighting how easy it is for violent father figures to be both endearing and traumatising at the same time.

Streamline shines a light into the shadow of abuse, with Sam Parsonson's brilliant turn as Nick, the brother trapped by Dave's exacerbated violence which turns him into a dual victim of domestic abuse. When Ben emerges in his life, Nick does what he can to try and steer him away from the path of turning into their father once again, as Dave has. Ben is just another young boy who was born a blank slate that his father sought to slather all of his own parent-inflicted pain onto, even though they had promised to themselves that they'd be the ones to 'break the cycle'. As each man manoeuvres himself into Ben's life, he's pushed further and further to the devastating moment that lingers in the mind of this child of abuse, the one where he is left to ask his abusive father: "What did I do to you?"

The film tears apart the natures of brutal men in society, exposing the lineage of noxious father figures who use abuse and cruelty to 'raise' their kids, or in the case of Glenn, 'train' them. Glenn pushes Ben to his limits, demanding that he break that one hundredth of a second gap between failure and success, even if it takes all night. It's hard to shake the feeling that Glenn is less concerned with Ben's wellbeing and more with the prestige and accolades that he will receive as the person who discovered the 'next Ian Thorpe'.

Visually, *Streamline is* marked by the reflective and evocative cinematography from the great Michael Latham. Arguably one of the modern masters of the screen, Latham's camera continually highlights the thematic depths of the narratives he explores. Here, the piercing cold of a winter swim hangs over the film, permeating each frame with its muted blue and grey palette, only to be separated by the lung-consuming haze of the burn-off season. Latham evokes the feeling of pressure, anxiety, and the stress of being trapped with a stunning awareness that will surely become a template for future cinematography hopefuls. Scaffolding the film is the emotional score by Angela Little that soars and drops as the narrative demands.

If there's a complaint about *Streamline*, it comes in a finale that feels all too neat and comfortable, given the dramatic heft that has come before it. At its core, *Streamline* is a sports film, and unfortunately it leans in on the trope of sports films: answering the question of winning or losing. The climax cheats Ben's emotional arc of its logical conclusion, instead relying on whether he becomes an Olympian or not. A more confident completion would be Ben's emotional acceptance of the trauma he has lived with all his life, but the ending that exists does not rob Streamline of its brilliance.

Streamline is an impressive and towering achievement from Tyson Wade Johnston, one that will be distinguished as a turning point in Levi Miller's enduring career, a pivot that will likely guide him towards more mature performances. There's a glimmer of Nicholas Hoult or Jamie Bell within Levi Miller, and given the legacy those two actors have crafted, one can only hope Miller will be afforded the career to do the same.

INTERVIEW
STREAMLINE - COMPOSER
ANGELA LITTLE

Angela Little is a screen composer and vocalist who received her first big break composing additional music for Baz Luhrmann's *Australia* for which she shared an AFI award nomination. Her work has spanned genres and narratives, from Alex Proyas *Gods of Egypt* (2015) to *Zach's Ceremony* (2017). In 2021 alone, music she had composed featured in the Netflix series *Dive Club*, Gabriela Loza's short film *Erased*, and the Stan. sports drama *Streamline*.

In 2018, Angela completed her Master of Music in Screen Scoring at the University of Southern California, where she was the recipient of the Sandra & Alan Silvestri Scholarship. During her time at USC, Angela was mentored by Academy Award nominated composer Thomas Newman. In 2019, Angela won the APRA-AGSC Screen Music Award for Best Music for a Short Film for Rebekah Jackson's *For the Girl in the Coffee Shop*. Her music can be heard in Sasha Hadden's 2022 drama *A Stitch in Time*.

Interview conducted November 2021

Angela Little: I think with music, often it's something that someone watching a film doesn't even consciously think about for the most part. It's interesting. That's why I was really delighted when you mentioned the music in your review of *Streamline*. When film music does its job well, you actually don't want an audience member sitting there and thinking, "Oh the music, the music, the music." Because if they're consciously observing and focusing on it too much, then you're kind of taking away from the drama. The job of the film composer is really to support what's on-screen rather than to try and overtly draw attention to what they're doing.

But at the same time, it's one of those symbiotic things. When film music is doing its job well, supporting everything and melding with the other elements of the film in a way that makes it feel like it's an integral part of the story, that's one of the very things that helps make an audience member who's not specifically focused on the music to go, "Oh yeah, I thought that was a great film!'

I am always on the lookout for new scores that when I'm sitting here writing reviews or interviews, I can have on in the background. And if it can reflect what I'm writing about, it helps even more and it draws out a bit of emotion in a way that I can then put into my review which is nice. I'm sure that not very many other people are like that.

AL: Oh no, you'd be surprised. I've had so many writers tell me that they write to music - screenwriters, journalists, novelists. I think it's actually pretty common, because it brings a different perspective and energy to things, not even just emotionally but physically. There's a reason people exercise to music, for example! On an energetic level that's so much easier when you're listening to something that's upbeat and has a lot of rhythm. On the other hand, if you hear a melancholy piece of music, or a song that's somehow associated with a sad memory for you, it's really going to bring you back to that instantaneously. Music affects the way people feel and think on a fundamental level, it's quite primal. And that's why I think it's really effective for writers, because they need to put themselves fully in that moment they're creating, and it's a lot easier to do that when you can use music to transport your mind and your body and your emotions there in a very visceral and immediate way.

You'll be glad to hear that we've released a soundtrack to *Streamline* [on streaming platforms]. We felt like it was something we wanted to do because it was an interesting score - in some ways very melodic, in others very textural, there was a lot of contrast. The mastering engineer said, "Wow, this has got so much dynamic range and it really oscillates between quiet, lush and beautiful, and very dark, deep and dark." And when I heard it mastered, I was like, "Yes! This is really exciting!"

Awesome. I'm very much looking forward to hearing it. I think with Australian films, we don't tend to get the scores to listen to very often.

AL: No, we don't.

That market feels like an afterthought, in a way. Like "Oh, is anybody going to pay attention to this?" Yes!

AL: I know, I love releasing soundtracks because I feel like it gives a nice insight into the music, to be able to listen to it on its own. When it's in context in the film, of course you're hearing it with the scene, but out of the context of the film, there's so much more that you can pick up when you just listen to it as a standalone thing, which is a great experience for people that are interested in that.

Your work is so kind of varied in a lot of ways.

AL: Thank you! The short film *Erased* I wrote the music for, that's been going around festivals all over the world. It's a sci-fi film. It's great to have written the music for a sci-fi film made by a woman. It's a fantastic story. I think it's interesting that historically women have very much been pigeon-holed into a certain type of genre that they end up scoring, and it's great that's changing now. Hildur Guðnadóttir winning the Oscar for *Joker*, that was incredible and really showed me, and I think a lot of other female composers, that that perception is changing. Which is important, because it was a very limiting thing.

That was something I found brilliant about *Streamline*. I was able to really connect into a story about the coming of age of a teenage boy. The things that he was trying to overcome in the story – the pain of figuring out who he is and what he really wants, self-doubt, family trauma - they're very universal issues. And that's something that's historically been missing from the idea that what we're capable of scoring shouldn't be a matter of gender, because there is a universal element to every story. And to connect to that is really the key, regardless of who you are. You've got to find that connection point.

What makes films really connect and hit home might not be your story, it's never going to be your exact story. But even if it's far far away from your story, it's still those connection points that cause you to feel something for that story. For example, in the case of *Streamline*, we haven't all been Olympic hopefuls. I definitely wasn't!

Certainly not me, either.

AL: But we've all been teenagers. We've all had issues with our parents and questions about who we are and who we're going to become. And a lot of people have had traumatic relationships with their relatives that have manifested as they're growing up and have defined who they are. And they've had to try and break free of that, or they've had to try and heal that.

As a composer and as someone that's part of creating that, that's what I look for, to find those points of thematic connection, because that's where the connection points are for the audience too. And then the question becomes, how do you find a way into this that will allow the audience's empathy to kick in, which is at the heart of feeling something for a piece of art, really? There's cerebral appreciation and then there's a resonance that's much more intuitive and emotional. Music can fulfill both of those functions. So, I'm always looking for, what's at the heart of this scene, this story?

Is that what makes an Angela Little score an Angela Little score? When you look at your body of work and going forward as well, is that what you want people to resonate with when they listen to your scores?

AL: Well, that's an interesting question, because I used to be a singer-songwriter in the earlier days of my career. I was always writing music. One of the things that really made it meaningful to me was - I remember doing shows, we would play festivals, we played a lot of folk festivals in Australia, like Woodford and Port Fairy - and I remember I'd do gigs, and people would come up to me at the end of the gig, really emotional, sometimes crying. Whatever it was, could be they had broken up with someone, someone they loved had passed away, it had triggered a memory. Somehow, something in the music really helped them process it. It was cathartic. And that, for me, has always been the meaning for me and the purpose in creating.

To me, film is a medium that can really wow people and leave them thinking, "Oh, that was a really cool experience." And that's completely valid. But I've always found a lot of meaning in helping people connect to their own sense of empathy and humanity. Good stories do that, they leave you quite deeply affected. That's something I keep at the centre of my scoring, whatever the project.

I'm very lucky to have the expressive medium of music. There are times where I'm in the studio and I find myself so in the moment and feeling something for what I'm doing, and that's incredibly fulfilling, it connects me to my emotional core, I would say. But for a lot of people who maybe don't have that mode of expression, how do you do it? Well, you do it by watching or reading stories. Listening to music, especially combined with a story the way it is in film, gives people a way into that. And that's always been something that I find incredibly rewarding about it.

Very much so. And it shows in the work as well, that connection really shows in the score. In Streamline in particular which feels like a complete work. It's brilliant in all different ways. But that score really elevates those dramatic scenes in ways that I had hoped. When you are approached to do a film, where does the scoring aspect start for you? Is it the script? Is it having seen the film? Or at what kind of point do you come on and are immediately thinking of what kind of music fits with the film?

AL: It really depends from film to film, because they're all different. You tend to come on at a different point in every production. Sometimes it's at a really early stage, and you'll see a script. To be honest, when you see a script, sometimes the film ends up being so different from that. You could have all the ideas in the world from the script, but when it comes to seeing the finished cut, it's very, very different.

I think what's valuable in coming on early is that you grow with the project, like you actually have time to research and experiment and conceptualise, whereas what's quite common is that the composer gets brought on when the edit is finished, with a very tight turnaround time for the score, which is of course doable because any film composer needs to be able to write music really quickly - but you miss that time to let it seep into your bones. And I love having that time, because often the time when you're not feeling stressed about it, and you're able to just sit with it, and maybe read the script or watch an early cut is the time when the best ideas come. Even if the film is going to go through changes from there, you get a sense of it.

To me, that sense of the project is really valuable. I'm one of those fairly intuitive creative people who sometimes has ideas come to me really quickly and as if they're almost fully formed. For example, there's a film I'm working on at the moment, a documentary called *Everybody's Oma*. I'd seen an early cut of the film and I had plenty of time to think about it, and I'd spoken to the director and got a really good sense of the project and what we were trying to do. One day I just sat down at the keyboard to come up with the main theme. And within five minutes, it was there. I just had to quickly switch on a preamp and start singing into the microphone to get it down because it was just right there, right away. I worked with the team during their edit and wrote a lot of thematic material that the editor placed through the film, so when it came time to complete the score, we were already very close, because they'd used my music to temp the film and they'd identified areas where some of the themes I'd written could be developed further and in different ways. That was a wonderful way to work.

It's ironic that often when you have more time and more leeway, that's when the immediacy happens, because you've got time to enjoy and experiment and let it all bubble away in the subconscious. I'm a big believer in the value of that. Honestly, the number of times I've gone to sleep of a night thinking about whatever I'm creatively working on at the time, and in the morning, I'll sit down, and there's the solution. I very much believe in the power of having time to let my subconscious tackle some of that stuff, because it does it very well - sometimes better than my conscious mind does!

So, there's a beauty in coming onto a project early. But as I said, frequently, what also happens is you come on quite late and you've got a very limited time-frame. And you need to just make it work in that time-frame. Again, that's a particular way of working that yields its own rewards, because you don't have too much time to ponder, you just have to do it, and so you do it. And you come out the other end and what's there is something you can be proud of. But personally, I love to have more time.

Sometimes you come on when it's a rough cut, as I did with *Everybody's Oma*, and that's also great. You can get a sense of the film and start to develop thematic ideas and put together sounds because you know, each film has its own palette of sounds. I think of it like the artist's palette, the sound palette for a score. Each score has its own unique set of ideas and sounds behind it. And that's something that I always take the time to develop. It was a very big feature of the *Streamline* score, actually. That was very intentional, all the sounds that were used there and how they were used.

It sounds like you're really able to work in kind of very different states, under strong pressure and then with the brevity or the length of production allowing your mind to think. It's a hard thing to be able to do, to kind of push your creativity in a short period of time and also a long period of time because that can get away from you in a lot of ways.

AL: Yes, they're quite different skill sets, in a way! I had a conversation with a friend a while back about the creative muse and getting inspiration, it was an interview for her PhD thesis. In talking about my process, I realised I've gotten used to having to adopt the mentality when there's no time, of not waiting for inspiration and instead just getting something, anything down. Because the worst fear is always the empty page in front of you. It's the same as a writer when there is a blank page. You're like, "How do I start?" Or "I put these first few bits down, and they sound terrible!"

But once you get going, you never end up where you started, and something that sounds terrible at the beginning of the day, more often than not by the end of the day will sound good. And if it doesn't, you just start again! Often in the beginning I don't know where I'm going, I'm experimenting, trying to find a thread to follow. Once I get further along into it, it all comes together. You can't be too paralysed to just start. I think it's taken me a long time to learn that overcoming that paralysis is part of the process too. You have to start somewhere. If you have that determination to have something done by the end of the day, you will have something done by the end of the day.

Generally speaking, there are pieces I've written that I listen back to that I remember at the time were just so painful getting them out. At the time I kept thinking, "Oh, this is terrible, this is terrible." When I listen back to it now, the only thing I can compare it to is that it's a bit like having a baby. You forget about the pain of it and just look at the end result and go, "Oh, that's nice!"

Having talked to a few people about composing, about creating music, there is a mystery to it, because it feels so almost ethereal in a way. I know the irritating question is, "How do you come up with the music?" You've explained it really well there. But I know that a lot of people are like, "I don't understand how you can just sit down and create something." But then I've had people say to me, "I don't understand how you can sit down and write this." But it's the building up of experience, it's a building up of skills and talent and recognising and focusing and honing in on those skills which is really important. And it's clear that's something that you've done over a long period of time and again, it shows in your work, it shows in how the very styles and strength of different music works. You've done Zach's Ceremony, which I remember being a really brilliant score as well. And then we've got Dive Club and then we've got Streamline. It's like three completely different things.

AL: And also *Never Too Late* as well, which I did recently, and which was very different to all of those you've mentioned too, lush strings and piano.

Of course. Yes.

AL: I think when you write for film, it's very much, what does the project need? And, what's interesting about that is that sometimes it's a little bit outside of your body of experience. Musically, I mean. I'll give you an example: in *Zach's Ceremony*, I really wanted to incorporate Indigenous elements into the score. There was a fantastic didge player who contributed to the score, he brought so much to it. And there was a lot of guitar in that score because, I was thinking [of] teenage boys going through this period of growing up, and I was thinking back to when you're a teenager, sitting around and playing songs on guitar, every teenage boy wants to learn guitar and express his feelings through guitar. But then there's also the earthy beauty of the acoustic guitar, and for a film that featured country and landscape almost as another character in itself, it felt very right. I don't play guitar, so to create a score that was almost completely guitar-based was a great challenge for me. But for lots of reasons that just felt like the right sort of palette for that film.

Dive Club is another good example. The brief and the idea of the score was for it to be an adventure on the high seas. I named the main theme, 'Call to Adventure'. We talked a bit about *Pirates of the Caribbean,* and a sea shanty sort of idea really took hold. I have a background in Celtic music, and of course a lot of sea shanties came from Celtic origins, so that was another layer of understanding I could bring to that music. And I play the low whistle, which I ended up playing live and featuring on the main titles.

That's what I love about screen composing. There's a real openness in terms of the direction things can go. And it's a process of talking to the collaborators: directors, producers, other collaborators on the score, to find what is that musical language we're going to use to tell the story. Yes, they're all very different scores, but at the same time, there's my own voice that comes through. It's a real joy to be able to use that in different ways for different projects that need different approaches.

Talking about Streamline, when you're doing research for that, what kind of research do you do? Obviously Australian film has a great history of making sports films, particularly swimming-focused films, we've got a lot of them. But did you go back and re-watch them? Or was it a matter of looking at coming-of-age stories?

AL: For me, *Streamline* I saw it much less as a sports film and much more as a coming-of-age personal odyssey film. Boy goes into the darkness and has to figure out how to come back out of it, he has to find what's going to heal his wounds and the trauma of the past. With *Streamline* I was really focused on Boy's perspective and how the events of the film were affecting him, and that was where the music was coming from much more than any attempt to make it like a sports movie in terms of the music score.

It's so dark in ways.

AL: It's really dark. I mean, Boy has experienced serious physical and emotional abuse. When you look at those scenes of his father nearly drowning him in the bath as a child, it's just so traumatic. I watched those and just thought, "Oh my God." When I watch something like that, I put myself in the place of whatever is happening. How would I feel if that were me? How would I feel if that were happening to my child? The pain of even contemplating that experience is terrible.

Why would his dad do that to him? Boy has never been able to answer that question. For years, he's tried to answer it, and he can't answer it, and it's destroying him, completely destroying him. In many ways, he blames himself. And he goes looking for answers in the wrong places. He goes looking for answers with his older brothers. And Dave, his older brother, is starting to exhibit similar abusive tendencies towards his family members, including Boy.

I get emotional even talking about it now. It would be a really a painful question that any child who hasn't felt love from a parent, or who has suffered any kind of abuse at the hands of their parent in particular, but really anyone that they love and who is supposed to protect them, is going to be struggling with for the rest of their life. It's tragic that the bond between parent and child could go so wrong. That was where I was coming from with that music because it was all about Boy's pain, and he couldn't resolve and he couldn't overcome [that], so how could he live the life he wanted to live until he could resolve that question that had always been there since his childhood, since those things happened to him.

There is so much that resonates with searching for the love of a parent. But on the same hand, Jason Isaacs' character, Boy's father, has clearly grown up and realises that he's made massive mistakes with his sons. And that in itself is equally painful because he sees what he was as a person and is trying to make amends. How do you reflect that in the score too, that kind of conflicted character?

AL: That was really interesting. The scene where Boy & his father finally have the conversation that begins to resolve their past, on the soundtrack I've called that cue 'We Are Made by Our Mistakes'. The line that Jason Isaacs [the actor who plays Boy's father] actually uses in the film is, "Men are made by their mistakes." But I called the cue, 'We Are Made by Our Mistakes,' because it seemed to me it's true of everybody, to be honest. Or perhaps it's more true to say, we're made by what we learn from our mistakes. But that's too long a title!

And yes, Jason Isaacs' character made some terrible mistakes. You could even say unforgiveable mistakes, but at the same time, you're right, he has grown up and he's realised how terrible that was and the damage that he did, and he's trying to atone. With the score, there are a whole bunch of linked cues. There's this whole sequence of events where Boy, Dave, and their father are linked musically in this story.

So, first we have the scenes where Boy flashes back to when his father was almost drowning him in the bathtub as a child. Score-wise, those scenes were written with the idea that it was almost as if we went underwater with Boy. Everything became very disorientated and distant and echo chamber-y. And there were these really low frequency sounds that I put in there to increase the feeling of sinking to the bottom.

When Boy's father first gets out of jail and surprises Boy by coming to his race meet, the music cue that follows their encounter recalls the bath scene, because I wanted the viewer to understand that this unexpected meeting with his dad would send Boy uncontrollably back into that trauma, mentally and emotionally. I wrote the bath scene first because I realised that the bath incident is the thing that keeps coming back, it's the inciting incident that led to all these echoes and ripples that are still happening in Boy's psyche now. And so at the race meet after seeing his father, the real world around Boy fades away, and suddenly getting into the water becomes an absolutely fearful experience, which is a disaster, because he's about to swim a really important race. That was a great example of collaboration between myself and the sound designer on the film, Nigel Christensen, we worked together using both sound and music to create that sense of Boy entering into a very disturbed psychological state.

Then when we get further into the film, another scene that again uses those similar sounds and ideas is when Dave physically abuses their father in the restaurant. The reason for that being that each time we're seeing these echoes of abuse and the ripples of the abuse through the years, that's where that music happens. It's never explicitly stated, but you're going to assume that Dave was also abused by his father and that that is now leading Dave to become abusive in turn. And we are musically in Boy's head watching that play out in front of him. You can see the shock and trauma reflected in Boy's face when he's watching it happen. And then later in the film again, there's another flashback where Boy has another memory of the bath. All of these scenes are linked musically because psychologically for Boy, all these events are a direct result of that trauma.

Levi Miller
Photo used with permission

Then there's another theme that comes in when boy leaves Kim [his mother] and runs away to Dave's place. That's a music cue called 'Broken Dreams'. There are a lot of treated strings in that cue, and there's a particular melody played on distorted electric violin. The idea behind that theme is that Boy at this point has rejected everything that mattered to him in his life [his relationship with his mother, and swimming] and he tries to solve his problems by running away from them. And he's running from one person to another, but not finding the answers he needs. And so later in the film, when it comes to the scene where Boy drives to his girlfriend Patty's house and there's an altercation between Boy and Patty's brother, Dave arrives on the scene [having chased Boy down] and Dave takes the rap for assault and gets arrested, and Boy again runs away. At that moment, we hear that same musical theme writ large.

I decided to name that cue on the soundtrack 'Nowhere to Run,' because in lots of ways, that scene is very pivotal to the triangle of Boy, Dave, and their father, because Dave finally, I think, sees the possibility of breaking the cycle of abuse for Boy, and makes a decision to sacrifice himself for Boy to be able to go free. So that's a moment where you see Dave step up and tacitly acknowledge that what he has been doing is damaging, and he wants to try and save Boy from going down the same path. That's a really pivotal moment.

One thing I love about that cue is there are these sounds in the background almost like howling wolves, like Boy is being chased by his demons, and no matter where he runs, he can't escape them. Those sounds were created through a combo of various effects on the strings. Of course, although at first Boy just seems to be running without knowing where he's headed, he ends up at the restaurant where his father works, because psychologically he has reached the end of the road, and now he has to answer the question – *why did you do this to me*? When Boy finally confronts his father, at the final point of release and healing in their conversation, the Broken Dreams/Nowhere to Run theme comes back very differently, very warm and emotional, very beautiful, because finally Boy understands that what happened to him in his childhood wasn't his fault, and that his courage in confronting it head-on has led to the chance to heal. This is the moment where that question is finally answered. And through that conversation his father also opens the way for Boy to reconcile with his mother.

That's really fascinating. And, again, it makes me want to revisit the whole thing once more. Because getting to hear and see these things in new lights, it helps inform A) how it was created; and B) how the plot is reinforced throughout different manners, the cinematography, the visual style of the film reinforces everything too, and the performances, the direction and the score and editing - it's all this one complex complete thing.

AL: I could write down the musical themes to show… there are these particular intervals that are in the melody in all those cues. It's an example of a motif, it's in those two cues I was talking about where boy is running ['Broken Dreams' / 'Nowhere to Run']. That melodic motif is the same in the scene where Boy and his father finally have that conversation ['We Are Made by Our Mistakes'], but it's treated so very differently.

And that's what's beautiful about music. Music is a series of notes when it comes down to it, but how you work with that series of notes and the different things that you can do with them to create very different ideas and interpretations and feelings and moods is really pretty amazing.

This is the other thing about film composers; what you're doing, to the naked ear, is probably totally incomprehensible for most people. But you're creating these very nuanced, interlinked ideas. And there's something rewarding about that too. A composer for film is very much part of the storytelling. Using a different language, yes, but still very much a storyteller.

Does it feel like you're creating magic in a way because of the way that the audience might not be completely aware of what you're doing to them?

AL: Yeah, I know. There's something a bit Machiavellian!

It's good. Of course. [laughs]

AL: [laughs] I'm just kidding. Or am I? Like I said, the function of music is quite a subconscious thing for most people, unless you're musically trained. Most people are not going to pick up on those intricacies. Not consciously at least, but there's no denying that if someone hears a series of notes or a melody enough times, they're going to remember it and perhaps most importantly in the case of film, associate it with something. It's why people can hum pop songs, and why people have songs they've heard a bunch of times just pop into their head unannounced, because it does get stuck.

So undoubtedly the music in a film is affecting people more than they realise, and that's where good musical design comes to be very important when it comes to composing for a film or a series, because you have got to put all those building blocks in place to shape the arc of the score. One of my friends calls it musical architecture. And this concept of musical design or architecture is also fantastic because it helps you as the composer to make decisions about why you're putting a certain musical theme or palette with a certain scene, and how that will musically develop over multiple linked scenes and story arcs. I'm always very much about the 'why' - 'Why is music here? What function is it performing?' We don't just put a piece of music on there for the heck of it. It's never about just, "Oh yeah, we might as well throw something on there."

For me, it's always, what's music doing in this scene? Which character are we with? What's going on below the surface with that character? For example, often times music is much more effective when it's expressing subtext. Music has almost endless different angles it can take in a scene. So, I think there's a bit of a weighty responsibility there as the composer, because we can really affect the way someone interprets what they're watching.

Very much so. You compose predominantly for Australian films. How important is that for you, to create the aural landscape of an Australian film?

AL: Music is a universal language. But I also think we really need representations of our culture and the people that we are. So Australian film is very important to me because there's an identity there. To be able to use my creative skills to form part of that body of work that expresses our identity is really important to me. It always has been.

I think that it really helps create, to use those words again, the aural landscape of Australia on film. It reflects who we are as people, and that's something that we need to both celebrate and hold up a little bit more, I think.

AL: Totally.

As you're explaining how the different motifs work in Streamline, I'm curious how you document all this down as you're creating it. Is it all in your head? Or do you record it as music? Or do you write the notes down? Or do you have a script and you want to write, "I need this feeling to be reflected here"?

AL: What I do is a spotting session. I sit down with the various collaborators on the film, which could include the director, producer, sometimes the editor, depending on the project. Sometimes it's just the director, it really depends. But we'll sit down, and we'll do a spotting session where we'll go through the film, bit by bit, and talk about the scenes and where we're going to put music. Some films have a very tightly edited temp music track, which can sometimes inform the in- and out- points, for example, and various other musical aspects, like the pace or the tempo that they're looking for. So sometimes there's temp music on the film which gives you a little bit of that information.

I'm someone that really believes in detailed spotting. Spotting sessions normally take a bit of time with me because we don't just go, "Yeah, music starts there, music ends there." I find it's helpful to really interrogate what each scene is about. And I take the time to understand what my collaborators, whoever it is I'm spotting with, what is their intention here? How do they see music working or functioning in the scene? What is the director aiming for emotionally with that scene, for example? How do we feel about the characters in the scene? We talk about all of that in a lot of detail. For me, understanding the drama that's playing out in a detailed way is essential to being able to write the right music for the scene.

An example from *Streamline* that we've already talked about, is the scene where Boy runs away from his mother, Kim, and goes to his brother Dave's home. On-screen is a teenage boy riding a bike. He's just riding. He's just left his mum and he's riding a bike and he's upset and he's going to his brother's house. When it's down to literal interpretation and brass tacks, that's what's happening in front of us. But we know because of what we've seen previously in the film, that what's actually happening is Boy is rebelling against his mother's discipline and the path in life that she has mapped out for him. He feels out of control of his own life and he's trying to take that control back. He's trying to come to terms with his father re-entering his life and his past trauma, but he's not able to, and his mum can't help him do that, no matter how hard she tries, because she's also traumatised by it. He's trying to run away from his problems because he doesn't know how to deal with them, and they feel like truly insurmountable problems to Boy at this point. He's completely lost. These are all the meta themes that are in play at the time that we're witnessing that action on screen. So, the music is much less about a Boy riding a bike from his Mum's to his brother's, and it's much more about expressing Boy's psychological state, and all those bigger things going on that are going to then get explored and unpacked and unravelled in the rest of the film. No words are being spoken, and music is largely responsible for conveying all this in that scene. So, no pressure! [laughs]

But seriously, the way I tend to keep track of these sorts of thematic links is that when we do the spotting session, I write notes on all this sort of stuff. And as I do, I'll always start to see patterns emerge. Something that's very helpful as a film composer is to really understand writing and drama. You have to understand how drama works. Protagonists and antagonists, conflict and intention and opposition. I've just been watching Aaron Sorkin's Masterclass. It's fascinating, it's fantastic. Because you have to understand all of those fundamentals of storytelling, of drama, of writing, when you're composing film music, because so much of the artform is, as I've said, being an effective storyteller in my particular language, which is music.

I keep track of it all in a cue sheet. I will have notes about how one thing is connected to another from a storytelling perspective, so I can keep track of threads that go through the story, and I can be calling on similar musical or sonic material for those scenes that share common threads. To that end, I often don't work chronologically, either. Instead, I'll work in sections of [musical] themes. So that I can conceptualise how that dramatic thread will run through the whole film.

The difference in the joyfulness of Dive Club, then the sombre homelife of Streamline, is juxtaposed perfectly with Erased. It's interesting hearing you play with the different instruments that have become linked with each genre. When you're composing, do you compose with instruments in mind, or does the motif come first?

Absolutely, I always work with instruments in mind. Sometimes, the use of a particular instrument is the key to finding the essence of a music cue. Being a film composer requires understanding combinations of sounds just as much as it requires creating combinations of notes. The choice of instruments immediately gives such a strong sense of what music is trying to convey.

For example, as I mentioned earlier, the use of Irish whistle in the Dive Club theme immediately gives the music a very different sense than if I had used any other instrument on the melody. It's a wind instrument, so has a real feeling of life to it, it's an instrument you can carry around in your pocket that a sailor could pull out and play on deck, it's an instrument that's used extensively in Celtic and sea shanty traditions. The whistle is also associated with the sea and boats [ship's whistle etc].

In the case of *Erased*, that story follows the unravelling of a relationship that takes place on a barren, sterile, alien planet. So, I wanted to create juxtaposition in the choice of instruments – I chose a palette of quite bare, clinical synths and then combined them, in moments where the characters turn inward or attempt to resolve their human pain, with traditional musical instruments like piano, to help the audience understand the big divide between the cold and alien landscape, and the human suffering and emotion that was happening within it.

With *Streamline,* just as much as it was about the instruments I chose, it was the way I treated those instruments and sounds. I made extensive use of reverbs and delays, and other interesting effects, to give otherwise traditional sounds a different feeling and association, for example to create the illusion of being underwater. The amount of reverb added to the sound is literally called 'wetness', and using extremely reverbed sounds creates a distant, muted, blurry quality that was perfect to capture a sense of both the literal world of the film [the pool, the bath, the recurring theme of being underwater] and the troubled state of Boy's mind, where important truths seem unclear, illusory and always just out of reach.

The themes of Erased involve the balance of emotions, the seeking of a baseline emotional state. Yet, there is a tension to the film that feels like the world is off kilter. How do you balance the line of being calm and peaceful, yet equally like the narrative is on the precipice of something breaking?

Again, it's a combination of instruments, sounds, and harmonies. The story is set on a planet where everything seems calm and serene, but it's all a façade, it's all artificial. There are harmonic combinations that create a sense of something being a bit off-kilter, and I make use of those in this score. It's just a very subtle shift of notes, so the music shifts from calm to feeling slightly off-kilter sometimes with the adjustment even just of a single note in the drone. The music needed to be very restrained, because that's the nature of the characters and their relationship. They're carrying a lot of hidden pain just below the surface that they can't talk about, can't express to each other.

When it comes to the use of sounds, one example is introducing elements like low frequency pulses, which build gradually to give a sense of unease in a different way. Low frequencies tend to make people feel uneasy. It's a primal response that comes from, I guess, the fact that we've evolved to know that a low frequency increasing in volume in the natural world means an imminent disaster is approaching, like an earthquake or a landslide or a tsunami. So, it triggers a very uncomfortable physical and emotional response, which is perfect in this context, because that's exactly what the main characters in the film are also experiencing. I'm excited that all that came through in your reading of the music!

FILM FESTIVALS AND INDIES

3

Once upon a time, film festivals were a place for new films to test audience appeal, build a profile, and then launch to a wider platform six to eighteen months down the line. Now, a film festival can often be the only place a film may receive a theatrical or online release. While the general consensus amongst film critics is that you should only include films in end of year lists that have been made available to a wide audience, the reality is a little bit different when it comes to film festivals, and as such, films that were made available to a wider audience online, or may have had a limited festival run, are considered for this Australian Film yearbook edition.

The impact of COVID meant that festivals like the Sydney Film Festival, Melbourne International Film Festival, Revelation Film Festival, the Melbourne Documentary Film Festival, the Sydney Underground Film Festival, the Sydney Science Fiction Film Festival, and more, had to pivot some of their line-up online, making sections available to a wider, national audience via on demand streaming options. Elsewhere, the WA Made Film Festival, Cinefest Oz and the Brisbane International Film Festival, and more, retained their in person, cinema-based festival presence, playing as launchpads for films receiving wider releases in the 2022.

Time reinforced its fluidity, with many independent films finding themselves in a stilted release pattern, like Parish Malfitano's *Bloodshot Heart,* Jayden Stevens Ukrainian/Australian co-pro *A Family,* and Joseph London's epic Fremantle cult-focused documentary *The Beloved* each finding releases that crossed from 2020 into 2021. Elsewhere, films like *Here Out West, River,* and *The Drover's Wife: The Legend of Molly Johnson* received festival attention in 2021, with their wide theatrical releases secured for 2022.

Indie films also established their presence on the festival circuit. These include Tom Danger's teen comedy *Sweethurt*, Kyle Davis' *Dry Winter*, James Vaughan's *Friends and Strangers*, the pandemic-focused *Neon Across the Ocean*, tweaker-flick *We're Not Here to Fuck Spiders*, the micro-budget, almost-lost horror *Everybody Gets Stabbed*, Thomas Wilson-White's personal queer fairy tale *The Greenhouse*, and JJ Winlove played with the format of cinema with *Crossing Paths*.

Outside of the festival circuit, indie filmmakers utilised impressive groundwork and community fundraising to organise screenings via platforms like Demand Films and Fan Force, often highlighting social issues that need greater attention. Here we find Catherine Hill's day-in-the-life drama *Some Happy Day*, about a homeless woman and her social worker; elsewhere Perth based production company HALO films launched with a socially-conscious line-up of films from *The Xrossing*, to *Greenfield*, and *The Last Horns of Africa*; Jo Hunter, Zoe Naylor, and Jerusha Sutton, alongside a troupe of inspiring women and men, revealed a hidden story in Australia's maternity system in the documentary *Birth Time*; finally, experimental rock band Tropical Fuck Storm stared down the dormant live-gig scene in Australia and turned their anger into a concert film like no other with *Goody Goody Gumdrops*.

Genre films also sought the comfort of localised, limited screenings, making appointment viewing for horror and sci-fi fans alike. Martin Wilson's animals attack thriller, *Great White*, ran limited theatrical screenings before launching on demand; Genna Chanelle Hayes refugee focused drama *Akoni* navigated closed borders to provide limited Q&A screenings; and indie horror director Chris Sun unleashed *The Possessed* on select audiences. Gorehounds and horror freaks were catered for in Melbourne with the tenth anniversary of MonsterFest, which screened the documentary about one of Australia's great indie success stories: *The Tunnel: The Other Side of Darkness*, Josh Conn's debut bloodbath *Crow Valley*, Samuel Galloway's white knuckle illegal dogfighting underworld flick *Mutt*, Martin Copping's psychological thriller *The Dunes*, Cameron McCulloch's long lost thriller *Scam* re-emerged, showcasing Kestie Morassi's feature debut, and closed with the 2022 zombie-fest *Wyrmwood: Apocalypse*.

If there's one thing that's been made abundantly clear during the writing and researching of this book, it's the wealth of Australian short films that exist in the world. From Chris Elena's provocative *Refused Classification*, to Jon Bell's soul shaking horror *The Moogai,* to the refugee focused *Two Sands* and *Freedom Swimmer*, to the explosive and violent school room short *Reptile*, to Nash Edgerton's closing film in his animal trilogy, *Shark*, to the powerful sister drama *You and Me, Before and After*, to Sharnya Yates exploring the transgender experience from a lived-in perspective as a mother whose daughter comes out as trans with *Choice*, and it's bringing an audience to tears in two minutes with *While (Alive) {}*, the spread of genres and styles covered in these varied short films should remind film lovers that the length of a film should never indicate its quality.

Flickerfest continued to celebrate home-grown talent as one of the prominent Academy Award qualifying festivals in Australia, with world premieres of Nate Gothard's whimsical and charming caper *Saving Daylight*, Sophie Hawkshaw's coming of age drama *Spark*, Ruby Challenger's allegorical *Hyde*, James Weir's father son drama *Julia*, Alisha Hnatjuk's fraught and tense personal drama *Jean*, Gabriel Morrison's homeless fable *Joy*, Madison Novak's mental health teen drama *Ella*, Ruby Lennon's glimpse into the secrets of women's bathrooms with *Occupied*, D.C. Fairhurst's pickpocket tale *This Town Ain't Big Enough for the Both of Us*, Angus Wilkinson's future-focused film *The Exit Plan*, Eddie Diamandi's chaotic funeral film *The Wake*, Lydia Rui's imposter syndrome short *Prom Night*, Jasmin Tarasin's tale of 1920s Australia through the eyes of a young Chinese woman with *The Story of Lee Ping*, Radheya Jegatheva's epiphany from a portrait with *Painting by Numbers*, and Stephen Lance's identity drama *Torch Song*. Flickerfest remains one of the strongest festivals in Australia that supports and champions short films.

Molly Reynolds and Shekhar Bassi's mixed drama and documentary in the London shot *ShoPaapaa*, becoming the first Australian feature film to explore what the COVID lockdown experience was like on film, albeit through the eyes of creative artist. Here, Shekhar plays to an audience of no one, with co-producer Rolf de Heer stating:

> "*Locked down, shielded and isolated, ShoPaapaa hobbles around his tiny universe. In a monologue that has no audience, he rails against racism and bullies, he ponders his existence lying fallen on the floor, and he makes his bed...slowly, miserably, painfully. And he never loses hope.*"[8]

That connection to hope, and the yearning for an audience is one constant that links all Australian filmmakers together. Where we go from here in a COVID world is leaving the Australian film industry moderately perplexed. Does reducing audience figures for wide release Australian films mean that the emerging presence of Australian films at film festivals will increase? As dedicated Australian film festivals continue to be a rarity, with only WA Made Film Festival taking the stake as being a purely Australian film focused festival, it seems that the opportunity for an emerging film festival which focuses solely on Australian films is sitting there for the taking. Film festivals naturally bring audiences in, providing a communal aspect of film going that we all crave and love, it's just finding a safe way for audiences to feel comfortable enough to attend in the future to allow for the varied film festivals across the land to survive.

Across the next entries, director Joshua Reed talks about the journey to make *We're Not Here to Fuck Spiders*, outback poverty is exposed in *Dry Winter*, Poppy van Oorde-Grainger talks about bringing South Sudan to Australia in *Two Sands*, James Vaughan's *Friends and Strangers* explores Australian culture through millennial ennui, filmmakers Brooke Silcox and Olivia Martin McGuire discuss the creation of *Freedom Swimmer*, our pandemic life is captured in *Neon Across the Ocean*, JJ Winlove discusses changing cinema with *Crossing Paths*, Perth distributor HALO Films and one of their 2021 features *The Xrossing* gets a look in, while Perth co-directors Cody Cameron-Brown and Ziggy O'Reilly explore emotions and robots with *While (Alive) {}*, we take a sojourn into the country with the music doc *Goody Goody Gumdrops*, hear Perth based filmmaker Sharnya Yates on her short film *Choice*, take a look at Nash Edgerton's economy in storytelling with his short film *Shark*, before closing with filmmaker Alexander Lorian's *Good for Nothing Blues*.

REVIEW
WE'RE NOT HERE TO FUCK SPIDERS
A GRITTY AND GRIMY FEATURE
THAT SHAKES WITH TENSION

Set within a rundown gothic house in some nondescript suburb in Sydney, *We're Not Here to Fuck Spiders* is a found footage film that follows the illegal exploits of its inhabitants after a stranger breaks in and installs surveillance cameras throughout the house. In a title card, we're told the footage made its way online, and what we're about to watch will detail the going-ons of the inhabitants throughout the summer of 2017. Copious amounts of alcohol is consumed, crack pipes are given a fair workout, the house falls into further disrepair alongside the excessive amount of violence that erupts.

Spiders initiates itself as a mood-piece, starting off as an observational glimpse at the drug scene that permeates throughout Aussie suburbs, with director Josh Reed letting you wallow in the wasted lives on display before teasing out the somewhat familiar narrative of police corruption, bikies, and home invasions. What sets *Spiders* apart from other 'drugs are bad' films is the observational style that feeds into the feeling that anything could happen at any moment, amplifying the knife edge tension and anxiety within walls that feel like they will collapse at any moment from stress and anger.

This is helped by the impressive performances that feel almost a little too real and lived-in. If it weren't for the familiar faces of Fayssal Bazzi, Lindsay Farris, and Stephanie King, I would have been absolutely convinced that Reed had managed to observe a genuine drug house for months to make the film. Farris' frenetic Anton is the head of the house, with his reluctant 'partner' Effs (King) being routinely submitted to his abuse and aggression. In the opening shot, we see Effs escaping the house, with the housemates setting off to drag her kicking and screaming back. As the house is empty, the neighbour across the road, Jimmy (Max Brown), slips in to install his security cameras.

While *Spiders* boasts stellar performances, it carries few genuine characters. Instead, Reed allows the house and the circumstances of its occupants to become the character. A sword on a mantle, the ever-growing pile of beer bottles, the gradually degrading couch, the varied graffiti on the walls, a stolen goldfish, and the ever-simmering beat of pulse-racing house music. With each minute spent in the house, you need to keep reminding yourself to have a shower when the film is over, so permeating is the filth.

As the dealers relationship with the drug-providing bikies shows who has the upper hand, the ethics of Anton and co is revealed, as he tries to push against their kitchen becoming a meth lab, stating that he just wants to be a dealer and "That's it." It's fruitless though, with the lab being installed in a barely used kitchen that hasn't seen a wholesome meal being made for an eternity. The obligatory fridge resides with the weathered presence of misuse built up over time as person after person comes to its door in search of food to complement their diet of ice and weed, only to be presented with a harsh unwelcome light illuminating emptiness.

The lingering question of 'why' Jimmy's capturing everything hangs over every frame. Is he an undercover cop? Is he creating something lurid for sadistic online viewers? Or, does he have a deeper connection to the occupants of the house? Answers are gradually revealed throughout the ninety-minute runtime, leading to a gut-churning climax that feels like you've slammed your fingers in the car door, ensuring it throbs inside your mind long after you've finished watching.

Max Brown
Photo Credit: Josh Reed. Used with permission.

It feels like Reed enjoys toying with his audience, making them trudge through the deliberately unpalatable events occurring in the gross and gritty house during a heat laden summer where the worst people are in the worst situations doing horrible things to each other. At times, it feels like *Spiders* is treading water, spending just a little too long on scenes that carry little consequence. Instead of leaving the viewer gasping for air, they're left having a hard time breathing and just getting bored by the situation waiting for it to move on.

As slow and tedious as some of the early scenes can be, it does subvert the definition of the title: *We're Not Here to Fuck Spiders*, i.e.: we're not here to waste time. Literally all these characters are doing is wasting time, expending the possibilities of their lives on drugs and alcohol until it kills them. That sense of possibility permeates through the air, with Effs being the character that shows the greatest amount of promise of a life outside of this drug-den. Early on, we see her reading *The Handmaid's Tale*, and it's not long before we realise that she's as trapped as the characters of that famed novel. Stephanie King is impressive in a taxing role that demands she be the recipient for Anton's rising cruelty, with assault upon assault becoming the most nauseating experience within *Spiders*.

I'm finding it increasingly difficult to stomach scenes of violence against women, and it is necessary to warn potential viewers that these sequences are difficult to stomach. Reed does present them in a horrifying manner, especially in one genuinely unsettling sequence where the bass of the music causes the camera to rattle and shake like it is trying to push itself out of its tethered shell and stop the violence occurring. It's creative moments like this that highlight how far Reed is working to condemn the actions on screen and the world of drug dealers.

There's an echo of Aussie film history ringing within *We're Not Here to Fuck Spiders*, and Josh Reed well and truly earns his place alongside the greats. There's a passed-on communal crack pipe feel borrowed from Bert Deling's *Pure Shit*, which loans its eagerly provocative vibe to *Spiders*. (It's worthwhile noting that *Pure Shit* was nominated for Best Picture at the AFI Awards in 1975, a comparison you wouldn't see with todays AACTA's.) Reed's heritage is also proudly on display, with a poster for his fathers (Colin Eggleston) film, *Fantasm Comes Again*, hanging in the living room alongside a poster for Reed's debut feature, *Primal*.

Filmed in 2018, and finally arriving in 2021, *We're Not Here to Fuck Spiders* is proudly low-fi, inventively indie, and devoutly Australian. It shakes with tension, ensuring it will be a favourite with lovers of gritty and grimy features.

CONTRIBUTION
WE'RE NOT HERE TO FUCK SPIDERS -
WRITER/DIRECTOR JOSHUA REED

Australia's no country for genre filmmakers. The relative success overseas of my first film, *Primal*, was met here with deafening disinterest, and for reasons I won't bore you with I was unable to move to LA, which would have been the sensible thing to do. I persevered though, because I'm not a quick learner, and tried to get up various projects, but by 2015 it was clear if I wanted to make another film, I was going to have to do it on any fumes I could coax from an oily rag.

Found footage has always interested me. There's something about the footage the film is edited from being part of the film's narrative that's rich thematic terrain, adding character intent to the capturing of every image and potentially creating a higher level of voyeurism, and therefore complicity, on behalf of the audience.

Narratively, the idea of a dead man's switch (spoiler, sorry) came first, because it made the filming not just part of the narrative, but central to it. I've always been interested in group dynamics, the way we subjugate ourselves to a collective hierarchy, potentially condoning (or turning a blind eye to) things we would never do or accept as an individual, so an abusive household came next. The drugs came third, because they isolate the household from the rest of the world, create a contained microcosm that can be documented on a limited number of hidden cameras.

Once we'd decided to do it, I sat down to write a script, but every constructed dialogue exchange felt artificial when I filtered it through the prism of found footage, so I pretty quickly decided it had to be improvised. The chief advantage of making a film for no money is that you can be experimental in ways a budget would never allow, and I felt it'd be interesting to push the improvisation to the point where the actors would know everything about their characters, and how they interrelated with the other characters, but wouldn't know anything outside of that. They'd be discovering the story as they activated it and it unfolded, with us shooting the film in sequence.

So instead, I wrote a very detailed scene breakdown and varyingly complex character profiles, and we set about finding cast and crew. Some of the cast fell into place easily, because they were actors who knew and trusted me or they were excited by the process, but the role of Anton proved very difficult. As the dominant, and most malevolent, force in the house, he was a risky character to commit to without knowing where the story was going to go. Added to that was the fact that I did tell everyone that the film would involve sexual assault, and that Anton would be the perpetrator, because that was information everyone needed to be able to factor in when deciding if they wanted to be involved.

offers no sign of encouraging any sense of rejuvenation, let alone catering for a diverse range of romance options.

As *Dry Winter* closes, we see how the great expanse of nothing offers little for the plenty. Prior to the agricultural industries transformation of the land, it would have been a magnificent, vibrant landscape, but now it's devoid of its soul, and the shadow of that soul has long faded out. A post credits scene shows the future of the town, a group of kids, building a bonfire, with the barely audible dialogue of one kid saying "I get it now", hinting at the notion that they should just burn it all down and start again. But with what? And if they did, what would it turn into?

Kyle Davis and Bridget McDonald have crafted a curious film here, one that has me keen to see their future efforts. It feels like it should be a depressing affair, but instead it plays in a respectful and tender tone that supports this existence, never condemning or fetishising the life folks in small towns just like this are almost forced into living. *Dry Winter* will suit fans of quiet, contemplative fare, even if it is similar to other films of its ilk, like *Strange Colours* and *Watch the Sunset*.

CONTRIBUTION
TWO SANDS - WRITER/DIRECTOR
POPPY VAN OORDE-GRAINGER

Written by Kook Manuer and Poppy van Oorde-Grainger, *Two Sands* is based on an incredible true story from Kook's childhood in South Sudan as well as the writers' shared experience of being teenage new arrivals in Perth.

Two Sands cast and crew
Photo Credit: Drew Kendall. Used with permission.

Kook and I met in 2012 at Aranmore Catholic College's Intensive English Centre where Kook was a student and I was teaching animation. During that time Kook told me an incredible true story about when he got lost in the wilderness in South Sudan as a boy. We made a short animation about it and I always thought it would make a great live action short, if we could afford to film in South Sudan!

Three years later I was working in France with homeless refugees and Kook's childhood story of being lost kept playing on my mind. As people told me about their refugee experiences, the image of Kook as a child separated from his tribe felt very resonant. This gave birth to the idea of weaving flashbacks of Kook's offers no sign of encouraging any sense of rejuvenation, let alone catering for a diverse range of romance options.

As *Dry Winter* closes, we see how the great expanse of nothing offers little for the plenty. Prior to the agricultural industries transformation of the land, it would have been a magnificent, vibrant landscape, but now it's devoid of its soul, and the shadow of that soul has long faded out. A post credits scene shows the future of the town, a group of kids, building a bonfire, with the barely audible dialogue of one kid saying "I get it now", hinting at the notion that they should just burn it all down and start again. But with what? And if they did, what would it turn into?

Kyle Davis and Bridget McDonald have crafted a curious film here, one that has me keen to see their future efforts. It feels like it should be a depressing affair, but instead it plays in a respectful and tender tone that supports this existence, never condemning or fetishising the life folks in small towns just like this are almost forced into living. *Dry Winter* will suit fans of quiet, contemplative fare, even if it is similar to other films of its ilk, like *Strange Colours* and *Watch the Sunset*.

CONTRIBUTION
TWO SANDS - WRITER/DIRECTOR
POPPY VAN OORDE-GRAINGER

Written by Kook Manuer and Poppy van Oorde-Grainger, *Two Sands* is based on an incredible true story from Kook's childhood in South Sudan as well as the writers' shared experience of being teenage new arrivals in Perth.

Two Sands cast and crew
Photo Credit: Drew Kendall. Used with permission.

Kook and I met in 2012 at Aranmore Catholic College's Intensive English Centre where Kook was a student and I was teaching animation. During that time Kook told me an incredible true story about when he got lost in the wilderness in South Sudan as a boy. We made a short animation about it and I always thought it would make a great live action short, if we could afford to film in South Sudan!

Three years later I was working in France with homeless refugees and Kook's childhood story of being lost kept playing on my mind. As people told me about their refugee experiences, the image of Kook as a child separated from his tribe felt very resonant. This gave birth to the idea of weaving flashbacks of Kook's

A number of actors had considered the role before ultimately declining, and one had committed then dropped out three weeks later, ten days before we were due to shoot. Lindsay Farris hadn't immediately struck me as a natural fit for Anton, but he'd been so good in *Primal*, and was such a strong and committed actor that I decided he'd make the role his own, and I rang him. He was home for Christmas and was about to fly back to LA, but agreed to do it. He postponed his flight, came down to Sydney and threw himself into preparing for it. I now can't imagine the film without him.

We sourced an abandoned house I'd had my eye on for years as an interesting location, and rigged it with Blackmagic pocket cameras I sourced from a bunch of friends. We cabled the cameras to a spare room on the second floor where we set up our video village to be the base of operations. Every room was also wired for sound, as was every actor. Because we never quite knew where the improv would take us, all contingencies had to be catered for, which was a massive technical and logistical task.

The bones of the story has a damsel in distress structure, a woman trapped in a castle by a monster and being rescued by a knight, but we were inverting that, making Effs the agent of her own salvation. This created a complex double bluff for Steph, who played Effs, because she was playing a character who was playing the role within the house of the compliant girlfriend, but was actually carefully sowing the seeds for her escape. Max, as Jimmy, her accomplice, was also playing a double role, both of them not only keeping their real intentions secret from the audience, but also from the other actors.

Lindsay Farris, Stephanie King
Photo Credit: Josh Reed. Used with permission.

To build on those damsel-in-distress narrative bones I introduced a sword, which also gave Anton a focal point for a certain grandiosity his megalomania engendered, and I based the bikie gang that supplies Anton with Meth on a

14th Century French chivalric order, Emprise de L'Escu Vert a la Dame Blanche (the Enterprise of the Green Shield with the White Lady), which dedicated itself to rescuing damsels in distress. They became the Green Shield MC, with their colours drawn from the chivalric order's coat of arms. I liked the idea that their initial good intentions had degenerated to base money making, as systems mostly seem to. The cops in the film have also degenerated to this level, as cops mostly seem to.

We shot for a week, moving fast but always running the scene as often as we needed to to get it right. It was a week of heatwave, and the house was sweltering, and derelict, but Steph and Linds moved into it for the duration of rehearsal and shoot in order to fully immerse themselves in the world we were building. It was intense, and inevitably the actors all began to formulate their own ideas about where the story was going.

We shot right up to the last few minutes of the film, but the final denouement was complex so we'd decided the only way to make it work was to tell the actors where we were at, and bring them up to speed on everything that they didn't know in order to deliver the best end we could. So after lunch on the last day I sat everyone down and spilled the beans.

It was awful. God, it was awful. We only had about five hours left of daylight to get it in the can, and they hated it. I hadn't considered that they'd have their own ideas about where it was going, and that they'd initially feel their ideas were better. So, we spent the next two hours going over it, explaining how all the pieces fit together, and when they'd finally absorbed the complexity of it and come around, we started blocking out the final beats. By the time we were shooting again, the sun was sinking rapidly and we were racing against the clock. But we got it done.

Post production was a whole other ordeal. We'd planned to get a first cut done then approach Screen Australia for finishing funds. We figured we'd be a shoo in, given what we had and the pittance we were asking for, but Scroz said no. Words to the effect of "Interesting, but not something we can support", and contained in those seven words is everything you need to know about how gutting 10BA at the end of the 80's and setting up the Film Bank decimated the Australian film industry.

After that, post took three and a half years, and a lot of begged favours to get it over the line, but we got it there in the end. It's a difficult film, and obviously not to everyone's taste. Abuse and sexual assault are finally being acknowledged and addressed by the cultural centre, but this wasn't the case when we shot the film, in January of 2017, nine months before the Harvey Weinstein story broke. If we'd shot a year later maybe we'd have chosen a different thematic core. But then again, maybe not.

REVIEW
DRY WINTER
A SUBDUED LOOK AT LIFE IN THE DUST BOWLS OF
AUSTRALIA

Illegal fireworks explode with the feeling of boredom busting in the opening of the low-fi, low-budget *Dry Winter*, disrupting the night in a remote, unnamed dust bowl town in South Australia. Cheap thrills flow into ultra-low socio-economic living, with a dirt patch for a garden, backyard dog breeding to pay the bills, and home haircuts to save bucks where possible. Director Kyle Davis finds life in the lifeless town, breathing energy to Bridge McDonald's keenly informed script.

The narrative, for what it is, follows a couple living together as a pair of not-quite-teens, not-quite-adults. They're on the cusp of desolation, waiting for their inevitable collapse into the physical labour of rural life. Jake (Andrew Phillips) works odd jobs here and there, with recreational drug use and cheap beer filling in the gaps in the days. Kelly (Courtney Kelly) works at the local servo, tending to the same regular customers who keep it alive. A night out consists of Kelly watching Jake play the pokies at the pub to earn a few extra bob to pay for drinks and dinner, not exactly riveting or romantic for a young couple.

Money and luxuries are in short supply, with finances being scrawled on bedroom cupboard walls in texta, wringing each last cent out of cost of the rent, puppies, car, and utilities. An opportune find of an ok condition couch helps add some casual comfort to an abode lacking the accoutrements of comfortable living. Later, that same couch becomes a makeshift tattoo parlour with a backyard ink-session further proving that these are the lives of the casual DIY'ers. Big ticket items are perpetually out of reach, but that doesn't stop the lifestyle being sought out.

For the most part, *Dry Winter* never condemns or mourns the life these characters live. Instead, it lets us become comfortable with these lives, with Jake feeling as if this is the height of lifestyle that he is perfectly comfortable with attaining. It's not until late in the film that we realise that this desolation is having a major impact on Kelly's life, with a mundane routine of wake, work, sleep, wake, pushing her forward in life, even if it's just in a well-trod circle. Eventually, the familiar narrative of needing to break away from the rural small-town life creeps in, as Kelly seeks a life away from this world.

Like many of these indie films, the atmosphere of *Dry Winter* drives the plot, with the mood permeating through each frame, building upon itself, layer by layer, hoping to reach some kind of resonance with the viewer. Instead, the vibe that Kyle Davis' direction conjures feels less like a guiding force, and more like the result of a 'shoot and sort it out in the edit.'

Depending on your tolerance or appreciation of these kinds of films, that's either a compliment or a complaint. Personally, these kinds of quiet, meditative affairs, the sort that request the audience glean the narrative and character motivations from continued lingering shots, are exactly in my wheelhouse. With that said, even I found my patience wearing thin as shots lingered on objects without any real purpose, like a static shot of a service station squeegee bucket and water can for twenty seconds. The cinematography from Gere Fuss is frank and impressive, capturing the bleakness of the dust bowl town masterfully, but the lack of context for some shots became a little frustrating.

In those moments, I wondered what kind of empathy was trying to be evoked for this small-town rural experience. Davis' lack of objectivity makes this feel like more of a documentary than a work of fiction, as if the crew just walked into a drought-stricken town and filmed for a couple of weeks. By the nature of their circumstances, Kelly and Jake are naturally reserved, holding back their internal minds and merely just sitting with the boredom they have to live with. This doesn't make them the most engaging characters, but thanks to the solid, informed performances from Courtney Kelly and Andrew Phillips they do become easy to spend time with.

While *Dry Winter* may not challenge the notion of small town living in a substantial way, it does at least set itself apart from its thematic brethren by being absent of any pronounced drama or threat. There is precious little focus on destruction of any kind that these kinds of stories about small towns have so often become typified by. Gone is the distinct crime narrative, missing are the murders. Sure, there's the occasional petty crime, with the Friday night wind down recreational drug use, but for many living this kind of life, it is reality. These aren't characters looking to destroy society or tear down the world they live in, screaming to break out, they just *exist*. It isn't easy living, but it certainly has become a comfortable kind of normal, at least for Jake and his friend Liam (Michael Harpas).

Drought has stunned the town into an existence that feels like it's one dust storm away from blowing away. A highway lingers nearby, skirting the town and disrupting the remaining natural beauty of the land with its cement pylons erupting out of the otherwise serene river; a likely governmental decision from above to 'cut out the chaff' and help tourists get to their desired destinations quicker. Like so many small Australian towns, their lifeblood of a natural flow of people driving through is removed, effectively nullifying the connection to the rest of civilisation that the town may have.

For the men of *Dry Winter*, dodgy drinking games and fishing by the roadside are enough for them, but for the women, it's clear their existence in this world is a fractured one. The work, what exists of it, is mostly skewed towards the men, with physical hard labour coming in the form of shearing and building fences. For the women, it's bar work and servo work, and that's it. It doesn't take much to realise why young women are leaving rural towns[9] at a higher rate than young men, there's simply no future life for them here. Here, the town story of *being* lost into a film about *feeling* lost in a new country. By keeping flashbacks short and abstract, I felt we could use places in Perth to stand in for the South Sudan locations.

When I got back to Australia I asked Kook, now in his 20s, if he'd like to make that film together. Kook said "Yes, I'm excited to have the vision of what I went through in front of me on screen, so it will make me and other people from Sudan feel truly welcome in Australia. It's something I survived and learnt from and I want to share with people."

From there we applied for funding from Screenwest and teamed up with producers Lauren Brunswick and David Kucha and co-producer Dan Thom who helped us pull together an amazing cast and crew including some incredible first-time actors from the South Sudanese Australian community in Perth.

I'm drawn to stories about trying to make a home in Australia because that was a big part of my life when I moved here aged 13. Obviously my experience was very different to Kook's, but even though I spoke English and had both parents with me, I will never forget how lost I felt at the time.

When I asked Kook why he thought the film had been successful he said "The emotion of the kid who got lost in the bush and the journey itself touches people's heart, and I reckon that's why people are responding to it. It's a true story as well, it's not something that's been made up, it's based on a true story. When I showed it to my boss at work, he cried. I never talk to him about me, so I told him if he sees the film he will understand me. After he saw it, he said he never realised I came this far to be where I am."

Garang John Deng
Photo Credit: Drew Kendall. Used with permission.

REVIEW
FRIENDS AND STRANGERS
A EUROPEAN-ESQUE TAKE ON MILLENNIAL AUSSIE
ENNUI AND MALAISE

It's pointed that James Vaughan's debut feature film, *Friends and Strangers*, held the prestigious honour of being the only Australian film mentioned in the annual influential Sight and Sound '50 Best Films of the Year' list. Sitting snuggly at number 46 between Paolo Sorrentino's latest and a comedy about migration, *Friends and Strangers* echoes its list-based siblings with its decidedly European tone and style. The European-adjacent vibe is a key creative choice with *Friends and Strangers*, with the heft of European cinema helping inform the critical-of-modern-Australia vibe that Vaughan's film is going for.

Friends and Strangers was made with the blood force of similar Australian indie-filmmakers, with Amiel Courtin-Wilson (*Hail*) and Ted Wilson (*Under the Cover of Clouds*) working on the crew – both of whom have crafted micro-budget indies that have subverted what Australian cinema can be. Vaughan's addition to the Australian film canon shakes at the rafters of Screen Australia, attempting to tear that institution down, as if Vaughan and co are saying "You're part of the problem here." For a pertinently quiet and subdued film, *Friends and Strangers* has a substantial lot to articulate.

The plot follows Ray (Fergus Wilson), a guy going on a road trip with Alice (Emma Diaz) to deliver a car. It then flows and tumbles into motifs and scenes that feel disconnected as Ray returns as a man-sized waif floating through Sydney for something to tether himself to. At times, *Friends and Strangers* feels aimless as it focuses on empty alleyways and far-off strangers, but Vaughan's layering of imagery, tone, and complex themes comes together like a magnificent papier-mâché art piece.

At its core, *Friends and Strangers* is about art, it's about culture, and most importantly, it's about Australian history. *Friends and Strangers* eschews traditional Australian film structure and modality, at times leaning towards parody with the presence of pan pipes ringing through time from Peter Weir's *Picnic at Hanging Rock*. Vaughan delights in exploring Australian culture with the almost monotonal Ray, utilising this unwieldy figure of millennial apathy who is continually searching for some kind of identity (it's pointed that Ray is continually swallowed whole by his clothing) as a comparison for the stagnant, absent presence of Australian culture as a whole. Here, that culture dissolves like an expired aspirin in a glass of tepid water – it may as well not be there at all.

Vaughan envelopes the film in the smothering nature of colonial Australia, opening with watercolours by William Bradley, an 18th century cartographer who was on the First Fleet that took convicts to Australia, delicately tying that artwork to modern art, showing that the foundations of Australia's art are built on the work of violent invaders who disregarded and destroyed 60,000 years of continuous culture. Vaughan closes *Friends and Strangers* with the ultimate reminder that this film was made on the lands of the Eora and Ngunnawal people, a pointed remark that isn't there just for cultural accuracy and respect. It's there to remind viewers that this sojourn through white malaise drapes the possibilities of a nation in a noxious haze that smothers any sense of progress and healing for a fractured nation.

Yes, *Friends and Strangers* is pointedly focused on white protagonists, but Vaughan does so in a manner that highlights the fruitless results of generations of white invaders. It's as if he's saying, "You have ruined a culture, and yet, you have no culture of your own to claim." Vaughan's writing and direction, paired with Dimitri Zaunders observational cinematography, quietly exposes the absurdity of white Australian culture proudly existing on a continent that should be proud of Aboriginal and Torres Strait Islander culture, yet equally proudly denies that cultures existence, smothering it underneath layers of banal artwork with manufactured meaning. A late scene leans heavily into absurdist comedy, seeing Ray traipse through the house of a wealthy harboursider who fails to understand the context or meaning behind the expensive art that adorns his walls. When Ray accidentally slips and punches a hole in the house's thin walls, the impression that he's just created a knock-off Jackson Pollock piece, almost mocking the art that surrounds it, hovers there in the air.

Friends and Strangers leans into being a grand analogy, reminding Australian viewers that we are all connected by a shared history of living on stolen land; and due to the failure to properly embark on conciliation with the traditional custodians of this land we call Australia, future generations will struggle to feel truly Australian, truly at one with this country. The inaction of consecutive governments for Aboriginal and Torres Strait Islander rights is accentuated by their failure to unite a country through a treaty, stilting everyone.

While *Friends and Strangers* meanders through deliberately dull motifs, it manages to weave its way to a conclusion that suggests that this too shall pass into history, like a once shiny dollar coin, neglected and forgotten on a riverbed. Images of the Crown and statues of invaders stand triumphantly on once pristine landscapes, and each time they appear, the observance from a young girl early in the film re-emerges, all she sees as she travels around Australia with her father is weeds and trash, introduced chaos and carnage.

It makes absolute sense then that *Friends and Strangers* has found a dedicated audience in Europe, a region where this kind of introspective fillum is commonplace, where the questioning of culture is encouraged. Only time will tell whether Australian audiences will come around to appreciate the complexity at play here as we witness one of the more intriguing and thought-provoking new filmmakers to emerge right now.

INTERVIEW
FREEDOM SWIMMER - DIRECTOR
OLIVIA MARTIN MCGUIRE AND
PRODUCER BROOKE SILCOX

Each year brings new short films that push the format of filmmaking into powerful, important directions. Alongside *The Moogai*, *The Recordist*, and *Two Sands*, is the searing and devastating documentary short film *Freedom Swimmer*. Utilising animation to re-enact the story of a grandfather making the dangerous and deadly swim from China to Hong Kong in search for his granddaughter's freedom, *Freedom Swimmer* manages to utilise the language of cinema to tell a truly human and timely story.

Director Olivia Martin McGuire and legendary producer Brooke Silcox talk about the making of this award winning short below. *Olivia, Brooke, No Thing Productions, and Sacrebleu Productions collectively* won the prestigious Yoram Gross Animation Award at the 2021 Sydney Film Festival where *Freedom Swimmer* also received a nomination for the Dendy Award for Best Short Fiction. It also won the Best Short Form Documentary at the 2022 AIDC, and received nominations at both the Melbourne International Film Festival and Slamdance Film Festival.

Interview conducted November 2021.

▶▷▶

Freedom Swimmer is a masterful short film, following the life-saving journey of a grandfather, swimming through treacherous conditions with his daughter from mainland China to Hong Kong, in turn bringing about the life of his granddaughter, who now also finds herself in a similar situation. This a powerful film that highlights how history lives within us all, often within the scarring nature of intergenerational trauma. Can you talk about the value of history to you, and what it meant to bring this story to life?

Olivia Martin McGuire: I think all too often we look at immediate events and make quick judgements from these. Our social media culture seems to exacerbate this with even faster stories swamping us which we are encouraged to like or dislike within seconds.

Having lived in China and spent time interviewing lots of families for my previous film *China Love*, I came to really focus on the unbelievable recent history of China and how this has shaped so much of where it is heading now.

I guess on a microcosmic level – I have a personal interest in how we can understand ourselves and the people around us by listening to the stories of our lineage.

The film ebbs and flows between filmic styles, with documentary footage slipping comfortably in with animated sequences, and enactments. Each blend together so gently, culminating in a deeply emotional experience. How did you come to the creative decision to use three different types of filmmaking techniques here?

OMM: The pandemic really set some significant limitations. Also, we worked really hard to make sure all Hong Kong voices and collaborators were kept anonymous. Originally it was going to all be shot in Hong Kong and literally within a week or two of flying there the pandemic hit. We were really lucky to find Agnes and the team at Sacrebleu in France to help us animate the stories of the grandfather's past. The documentary material demonstrates the parallels and poetry of the story from past to present but ties it to truth. The journey to find the right documentary material of past and present was extensive and involved many months of searching and refinement.

Freedom Swimmer talks about a massive societal upheaval happening right now in the world. While the China and Hong Kong of the past may appear different, the cyclical nature of oppression is still there. Can you talk about the desire to reflect the past with the present to tell this story?

OMM: I guess maybe that has been a motivation in my projects to date. To look at what is behind events. When I started chatting to people around me in Hong Kong, as the building of the protests began in 2019, I noticed parallel language used from the youth around me as the elderly freedom swimmers. There is a weight to the concept of freedom in Hong Kong that is hard to understand without putting it in perspective with the history of the city.

One of the most powerful and enduring aspects of Freedom Swimmer is the manner that you give the freedom swimmers, protestors, and the production team and crew, anonymity. How did you organise the interviews and blend them together into one unified narrative?

OMM: This was really important to achieve for us. The people who told us the stories in the film wanted to tell their stories but feared the consequences. So, this was a way that the stories could be circulated without retribution. After the interviews were conducted there was a process of refinement for clarity and impact, which took months. We also had a very patient and talented editor and we worked hard at finding ways to connect the different mediums together.

Freedom Swimmer
Copyright Olivia Martin-McGuire & Brooke Silcox. Used with permission.

Agnès Patron's animation is stunning, with the moving narrative emerging out of the depths of darkness of the black background. Can you talk about the creative choices that were made with the animation, and how did you implement aspects of the interviews into these visuals?

OMM: Agnes is such a talented artist. I saw her film "And the Bear" and was immediately taken with the way she paints her work out of the darkness rather than from a white page. A lot of the stories we were dealing with were journeys in the dark. China didn't have much electricity at that time, and they were moving in darkness – following the neon lights across the water of Hong Kong. Also, the protestors dressed in black – so they could be masked in a sea of black. We had a script that Agnes worked to and provided Agnes with a lot of historical reference imagery and information for elements of the story to be captured in her animation. We also had determined what the archive footage would be before Agnes commenced the animation, in this way she could draw from it to unify the story.

Brooke, your work from RocKabul, to Judas Collar, and now with Freedom Swimmer, as a producer has continually sought out narratives about the changing world around us and the impact of humanity on transforming societies, fractured nature, and fringe culture. What draws you to these narratives and filmmakers' stories?

Brooke Silcox: As a producer the stories that grab me are universal, unique, authentic and ones that I consider will resonate not just in the short term but also over time. I have been fortunate enough to work with passionate directors who are on the forefront of some of the most important topics of our generation and bring with them not just the stories but also a connection to them that runs deep. Also, for me, my background in Fine Arts, Theatre Arts, Cultural Studies and Law has helped me to take a big picture perspective of where we are as a society and consider what may be the changing paradigms of existence as we move forward. This in turn informs the stories that I think are relevant to humanity's development.

Given the coda at the end about the threat to Hong Kong protestors around the world, the realisation that this was a global production made me recognise even more how important the fight for Hong Kong is. You both worked hard to create Freedom Swimmer across different continents, and within an emerging pandemic. I'm hoping you can both talk about your own personal perspectives when it comes to creating this story at such a vital point in history.

BS: I suppose the potential extraterritoriality of the law is demonstrative of our current global culture and is reflected in the making of the production itself. It was truly a global production with collaborators across Hong Kong, Australia, France and the UK. We were connecting daily using Skype, Zoom or email while some were about to go to bed and others just waking. As storytellers we want to be at the forefront of history and our experience.

In 2019 and 2020 the situation in Hong Kong was the headline. Both of us know that what you see on the news is one perspective, there is a lot of subtlety and nuance to a lot of the global situations we see play out in front of us. For us, we wanted to understand what is behind the news headlines, what the human truth and experience is. We specifically created this story for a Western audience because we understood that there are a lot of unknowns about the situation.

There were voices from Hong Kong who really wanted to share their story, not just of what was going on in the immediate time but how the situation now was informed over generations. In making it known to a Western audience (or an audience generally), there can be more empathy and understanding which in turn we would hope leads to more unification rather than division.

In one of the most heartbreaking moments, during the swim from China to Hong Kong, the grandfather says in voice over when asked if he was afraid, 'there is no fear, when there is no hope'. This is a line that will ring in my mind for a long time. What does hearing a line like that say to you about the strength of human spirit for survival?

OMM: I am glad that stood out to you because it was a line I heard a few times during the interviews – and felt we had to get it in the film. I felt it gave some insight into what it takes to flee your home. The next thing he said (which we had to cut) was "The more you have the more afraid you are." I think it is really hard for us to empathise with people who are displaced and perhaps he is right – those of us who are more privileged also live with a lot more fear and because of that, less empathy.

The story being told is presented in a gentle, considerate manner, with the camera focusing mostly on the set of the kitchen that the discussion between Grandfather and Granddaughter is taking place. I'm hoping you can talk about the production design choices here, and the steps taken to make this feel like an authentic, lived-in homely environment.

OMM: We had a wonderful production designer who really researched and tried to replicate the rooms we had been sitting in – in Hong Kong. We were not able to go back to Hong Kong but we tried to rebuild that world. The colour palette and the objects in the room came from the props and costume designer's family (who had emigrated from Hong Kong). The green that was used was emblematic of the houses we knew in Hong Kong but also had a touch of the palette of the film Amélie. We considered, given the French connection in making the film, that the use of the green was something we were comfortable leaning into.

Finally, as the world finds itself in the depths of an enduring global humanitarian crisis, with some 82.4 million people being forcibly displaced around the world, what do you hope that viewers will take away from watching Freedom Swimmer?

OMM: I think to empathise and think about what it takes to flee your country. For those I spoke to –they said that living in the place they were was the same as dying – so swimming across the night sea was the best option, even though so many didn't make it.

How can we find ways of circumventing our fears, empathising and finding better solutions for this crisis?

REVIEW
NEON ACROSS THE OCEAN
A QUIET AND CONTEMPLATIVE GLIMPSE INTO THE
ISOLATION OF A PANDEMIC

As I'm sitting here writing this piece, I stare out at a vacant suburban street. Australia is in the midst of yet another lockdown, trapping us in our homes, making us all the more aware of the silence of the world when we're removed from it. Cars infrequently make their presence known, usually being a sign of normalcy, now becoming an aspect of irritation. Local public ovals that once filled the air with the sound of growing athletes finessing their chosen sport now have socially distanced pedestrians taking themselves and their overjoyed dogs for their prescribed 'one hour' of exercise.

After watching *Neon Across the Ocean* on a dreary, wet winter day, I listened to director Matthew Victor Pastor's interview with Maridel Martinez on SBS Filipino[10], where he mentioned the joy of knowing that someone, *somewhere*, was going to see his film in a cinema. I'm writing this review for Perth's upcoming July 2021 Revelation Film Festival where it will screen. The festival has already had to cull its opening night and second day of screenings due to Perth's lockdown, with the looming threat of more days of lockdown on the horizon.

All of this familiar isolation lingers over every frame of *Neon Across the Ocean*, a film made during the 2020 stretch of the COVID-19 pandemic in Melbourne. Pastor's camera focuses on Mandy (Waiyee Rivera), a 17-year-old Filipino Australian who is trapped in the crux of the fallout of the pandemic, with her final year of high school looming, alongside the separation and eventual divorce of her parents, her desire to travel back to her mother's homeland of the Philippines acts as a possible tether to pull her loose from this societal malaise.

Neon Across the Ocean opens appropriately, with the rain-soaked streets of Manila embracing the reflection of the sugar-soaked glimmer from the neon signs of the convenience shops, bars, and bordellos, highlighting the beauty of the manufactured world around us. Here, we meet a youthful Gerald (Gregory Pakis), an Aussie bloke perusing the bars of Manila and searching for someone to take home with him. Pastor casually moves us forward in time, picking up with Mandy's story and teasing the relationship between her younger father and the divorce that has separated her family.

Waiyee Rivera's subdued performance as Mandy helps carry the thematic heft of *Neon Across the Ocean*, with her internal conflict writ large over an empty city. Like all the characters in the film, Mandy sits on the precipice of her emotions. They equally hold back from truly engaging with their emotions for fear of it spilling over and drowning their lives. Mandy's own life issues and concerns are amplified by the pressing detritus of the catastrophe that has changed the world. Yet, at 17, she's clearly awaiting the moment that she is free to change into the person she should be, free from an enforced world of education and isolation that has been holding her back.

Mandy yearns to reconnect with Manila, a place where positive memories that linger grew from, a possible home, whatever that may be. In her birthplace, Australia, she is continually othered, made not to feel like she is Australian. She talks about walking over a crosswalk, where white Australians expect her to move out of her way, but Mandy pushes back, making sure that she will move out of the way for nobody.

Later, Mandy comments: "My dad sleeps a lot, I think he's depressed", with her friend replying, "All adults are", in a manner that suggests that depression is an inevitability when it comes to the ageing process. Through Gerald, we see the impact of the pandemic on the already financially-strained. Mandy lives with her father who has seemingly collapsed into a state of disrepair. He complains about her lack of eating, all the while his diet consists of beer upon beer upon beer. The sound of a microwave heating upon yet another frozen meal is accentuated by the sight of a kitchen bench draped with quick-eat food wrappers and a pile of oranges that are destined to never be eaten. Within this home, life has given up on living.

Mandy's brother, Marc (Corey Reason), has moved into his own apartment. The pandemic has allowed him time to comfortably stretch into the creative energy within him, as he finds his voice through rap. For Marc, moving in with his partner has allowed his own personal freedom to be who he wants to be. While we don't spend much time with Marc, his presence helps highlight how much Mandy wishes to grow into who she feels she wants to be.

Pastor masterfully uses each setting to inform his characters. Within Marc's home, we see the reflection of Manila in a neon lit cross, strung up safely in his rented apartment. On his windowsill, a house plant sits awaiting its full potential. The quick-removal hooks remind us of how renting in Australia has changed over the decades. Underneath the same bleak hog bristle white sheen that covers rental property after rental property, lies the feature walls of freedom that renters once had. They were free to live in a home that reflected their personalities, but now, they're restrained by property owners who are terrified that their investment properties will be tarnished by a misplaced hook, or an off-beat paint choice.

Quietly, Pastor makes us ask ourselves: what is a home?

Is it the land our parents came from? Or is it, as the saying goes, 'what we make it'? Or, is it the people we surround ourselves with?

For much of the film, Mandy's mother, Anna (Rachel Javier), is absent. Mandy yearns for her presence, and for her support. With Gerald failing to give Mandy the support she needs, Mandy finds comfort with her tutor, Serena (Chi Nguyen), who helps guide Mandy through the difficult final months of her high school studies. To Mandy, her comfort and companionship becomes its own pseudo-home in a way, with the two visiting a makeshift hut on the docks of Melbourne. In a moment of nurturing and care, Mandy and Serena share a meal with one another, looking over the waters and contemplating a future that may swerve and change at any moment.

Matthew Victor Pastor's writing and direction is restrained and reserved, almost to a fault. He allows the quiet and the languid pace to permeate into the themes, reflect it into his narrative, and then to become and embrace his characters. *Neon Across the Ocean* has a calming vibe, that is powerfully accentuated by the stunning digital cinematography that captures the blazing neon at night, and the mundane dreariness of the Melbourne weather perfectly. While it is a comfortable watch, it also asks a lot from its audience to weave together the themes and narrative, often making it feel like work to glean what Pastor is saying or working towards, rather than giving enough to allow the audience to feel like they're participating in teamwork.

I do find comfort in films that make you work, that ask you to invest in their narrative and motifs and question what the grander theme or meaning of the piece is, but with a film like *Neon Across the Ocean*, while I found myself absorbed with its ideas after the film concluded, I often felt myself feeling despondent with the whole endeavour in the midst of it occurring. This may be Pastor's direction reflecting how easily detached and shocked many of us were left – and still are – after the pandemic, with the oncoming gradual trudge to 'normalcy' allowing us to finally sift through our Facebook posts, group messages, and desperate diary entries to truly examine what we all went through.

In that regard, this is a film that thrives in my mind post-credits, and for that experience alone, I'm eager to absorb myself in the filmography of Matthew Victor Pastor, which is deep and rapidly amassing into a catalogue of varied films. *Neon Across the Ocean* is itself the first of a trilogy of films that will address the emotional resolutions of the pandemic, with *A Pencil to the Jugular* soon to come.

Neon Across the Ocean is explicitly a film about solitude, and as such, it finds itself alongside a deep brethren of Australian films that exist and live in isolation. These are festival films like James Newitt's *I Go Further Under* or Alena Lodkina's *Strange Colours*, equally quiet in tone, and also profoundly isolated in narrative and themes. There's an acquired audience for these kinds of films, ones that require an audience that will sit with the film and ruminate on the silence, not allowing themselves to be overwhelmed by the boredom that may arise. Many audience members may feel that to be bored by a film is a death sentence blow for the film itself, yet, in *Neon Across the Ocean*, boredom helps accentuate Mandy's journey, allowing the audience to truly feel what she is going through.

Neon Across the Ocean requires the necessary patience that comes with quiet and slow cinema, a patience that many of us had to exercise as we waited in lockdown after lockdown during 'our pandemic year', where we either grew to resent that enforced quiet, or embrace it, letting it change us and morph us into new people. It's the same patience that I'm exercising right now, as I write this review in hope that it is not in vain. That Matthew Victor Pastor, and the Revelation Film Festival, are able to screen *Neon Across the Ocean*, and countless other films that cater towards a varied audience group who will devour these kinds of meditative fares this coming weekend. As news of each lockdown takes place, it's hard not to feel as if we will forever be trapped, denied the chance and freedom to change into the people we should be, or once were.

Neon Across the Ocean doesn't deliver hope of change, but it does provide familiarity and a recognition that we weren't alone with feeling the way we did, and for that, I'm grateful it exists.

INTERVIEW
CROSSING PATHS - WRITER/DIRECTOR
JJ WINLOVE

Innovation in storytelling and filmmaking is great way to receive different audience interactions, as director JJ Winlove explored with his interactive feature film *Crossing Paths*. Screening at the Sydney Film Festival in 2021 to sold out audiences, *Crossing Paths* put the story telling decisions in the audiences' hands, quite literally, with an app that allowed them to decide which narrative path to follow next. With twelve characters and countless possible narrative presentations, *Crossing Paths* sought to engage audiences in a new, and unique manner.

Each screening began with one of the twelve characters being chosen at random, their narrative sees them encountering another character, and at the close of their scene, that's when the audience decides which one to follow. Intending to create discussion after the film, and change the way that viewers interact with cinema, *Crossing Paths* saw an emerging filmmaker push himself into new fields. JJ Winlove is something of a rarity in Australian film, having had the good fortune of having two films released in the same year, with *Crossing Paths* following up on the critically and commercially acclaimed *June Again*.

Interview conducted October 2021

I take it The Crossing Paths came first before June Again.

JJ Winlove: I put *Crossing Paths* together in the middle of the process of making *June Again*, because there were some big, big empty periods where we were waiting for things to happen. And I was getting a bit... I don't like waiting for other people to make decisions. I thought, "Okay, well, I'll use this time to do something else." And so that's when I launched into *Crossing Paths*. But of course, as soon as I committed to that, that's when *June Again* started happening, so then I had the two things happening simultaneously for a little bit, which was tricky.

Where did the idea come for Crossing Paths?

JJW: Someone sent me a link to a thing in the US where if you pitch an interactive short film, there was a grant for $10,000 for making an interactive film. I've never made anything interactive before. I did a bit of research and for a week I just watched every interactive short film I could find and at the end of the week, I decided that actually this wasn't for me. I found that the medium, for me, it was too much halfway in between a game and a traditional movie. A movie is very passive, you can lean back, and a game is very active, and you're very involved, whereas an interactive short film felt stuck in between those two things. I feel like that's why the medium has never really taken off in an ongoing way.

So, I decided not to submit for that grant. But I had in the process of doing that this idea lodged in my head that I just couldn't stop thinking about and that was what if what if it wasn't a game, what if it was just a way to explore a group of characters and the way they interacted and so there was no right or wrong, there's no winning or losing it was just more of a tool for exploring, rather than trying to solve the mystery or win some challenge.

There is a great film, one of my favourite films when I was a student and it's one of Richard Linklater's first films called *Slacker*. The basic premise is that it follows one character. It's set in Austin and that character will run into a couple of other people and have a conversation, and when they separate, the camera will stay with the people that that character has just met and then they'll meet some people and then it will stay with those people and on and on, and once you realise that's the format of the film you just settle in and really enjoy just this constant parade of all these crazy, interesting characters and I've always loved that film. That tied in with, well, what if there was an interactive version of that where you can decide whether you stay with the same character or you can switch to this new character that just came along and I just got really excited by that idea and I couldn't stop thinking about. So eventually I just thought, the only way I can get it on my head is to just make it.

How important is it for you to reflect Australia as a whole?

JJW: What's interesting, because I'm a New Zealander, I moved over here in my early 20s. I have a slight remove in my take of Australian people and culture, which I think is actually a good thing. I've always noticed that a lot of the best photography that happens in a country is often taken by people from outside that country because there's a sense of remove that helps you to see what's unique about that country or that culture. New Zealand and Australia, obviously, we are quite similar culturally I think but there are differences; differences in the sense of humour and there's differences in the way we talk and the general personality so that's always been fascinating to me. The differences I think with *Crossing Paths*, it was a chance to explore some of those different types of Aussie characters that I've met along the way.

How do you go about writing Crossing Paths? Do you have a pinboard with string hanging up connecting people together?

JJW: That was one of the trickiest phases of working it all out. The way I ended up doing it was I had a spreadsheet. Actually, I'm not much of a spreadsheet person but I ended up using Excel or whatever it was and building this very complicated matrix of different characters and settings at different points because I wanted to make sure that each character ran into the right number of other characters and that no character didn't run into anyone or ran into too many people. I was constantly moving pieces around the spreadsheet for weeks before I finally got everything fitting in, and a way that felt natural rather than forced.

And then when I wrote the scripts, I had a similar problem with, how do I actually write? Because it's not a linear story, how do I write a non-linear script? I ended up creating these interactive PDFs where each time a character met, you could click on that, and that part of the script, and it would open up a different PDF that would let you know about 40 different scripts that were all interconnected through this matrix that I built. It was a real headache. But once I worked out the system, it was actually kind of fun.

Do you think it's something that you'll do again?

JJW: I'd love to actually find some time. After I finished the project, I was like, "Okay, I'm not going to do that", we just want to do something completely different. But I think it's such a versatile engine that the system, it could be applied to so many different types of stories, and so many different genres. And, it could even be applied to an existing property, a one-off interactive version of a show that people know really well. I'm very excited about trying to use that system of interacting characters in it, and applying it to a different kind of story. And I think that'd be a really interesting,

What excites you about the upcoming Sydney Film Festival? Most filmmakers will want audiences to not look at their phone, but that's an integral part of this, with audiences voting on character choices.

JJW: It was interesting that the whole way that this came about in terms of the audience voting was accidental in a way because when I first made it, it was designed to just be on a computer with a single user. And then we were planning on cast and crew screening and we were thinking, "Well, how's this going to work?" And we had this idea, and we had an app built, a very simple app where you tilt your phone left or right and that will register on your website that the host has, to see which way the story should go. It was just a very basic little thing. And when we got everyone in the audience, all the cast and crew downloaded it onto their phones. And then I was the emcee, standing beside the screen with my laptop and the controls, and I was watching the numbers come in. And we didn't know how it would play out.

But it ended up being absolutely hilarious, because I ended up staring out the audience when it was when it was neck and neck, when it's the same number of votes each way, I kind of prompt the audience to change their mind. The audience got very involved, they got quite vocal, and they start to argue which way this should go. And it became more of a show, than the normal dark room cinema experience, and I got such great feedback afterwards. There was a real energy that it created, as people got really invested in different characters. That just happened as an accidental way of trying to work out how we show this to a group of people.

Is that something that drives you as a filmmaker to reinvigorate the cinematic experience? We're so used to going to the cinema, watching a film and then going home, and that's about it. Whereas this feels like it is designed to encourage that discussion afterwards.

JJW: It fascinates me. I always think it's a shame when you watch a great movie with a group of friends, and then you sit around and say "Alright, I'm going home, see you later." And you want to go and discuss the film, especially if it's a good film. And that is to me as much fun as the film itself, that level of discussion. This process of voting actually kind of made it happen in the room as the film was showing. It really does add the level of another layer to the experience. I don't know how that could happen with a more linear type of films. Whether I spend more of my time developing interactive kind of films, I'm not sure because I still love that linear filmmaking process. If there was a way of bringing some of that into traditional filmmaking, I'd love to explore that.

How did you go about casting for Crossing Paths? What was the pitch that you gave to actors when they were given the script?

JJW: The good thing about it was that it was such an unusual proposition, and I think that's what fascinated people about it. When I told them what I was trying to do, and I approached it very much as an experiment, I said, "Look, I don't know if this is going to work, but if it does, I think it will be exciting." Because it's so character driven, there's twelve characters, and I think in most stories, you have a protagonist or a main character who has most of the focus of the film, but with this, it was every one of the twelve characters act as if they have their own film that then crosses into other people's films. There are no central characters, they're all completely even in terms of their presence and story. I think that was also a healing practice as well, that they had their own character that they could own throughout the whole piece.

Everybody has a moment to shine. And it's quite interesting to see how your interaction with one character flows into the next, because of the way that it's set up, that the narrative will flow into one another, and how you feel about these characters the first time you meet them, it might be completely different.

JJW: That's one of the things I got excited about. The whole idea of first impressions; if you meet somebody, if they came up to you on the street and start talking to you, you have one impression of them, whereas if you meet them through a friend, you will have a completely different first impression of them. And so, with this story, it randomly picks a different character to start with. Each time the story starts, the audience will have a different impression of each of the characters based on how they encountered them, whether it was beginning or halfway through the story. And that mirrored my experience of encountering people.

What discussions did you have with the actors about that? Usually, they would get a script that is beginning middle and end, but how did you how did you discuss that with them that the audience's perception of the character now might be different later on?

JJW: That was something that was inherent in the in the way it was set up. For me it seemed like this very complicated mosaic of different characters or meaning, but I think for them they were able to just focus on their character and just follow that half a day of story. They start off in the bedroom and they go down they catch a bus and then they're in the street, so I think for them it wasn't as complicated as it was for the rest of us. It was more just a 'day in the life' story for the characters and the actors.

One thing that we did talk about was perspective because that's something we play around with in *Crossing Paths*. There's one part in particular where I really push that, where one of the male characters Poe [Johnny Lahoud] walks past another character Bella [Chantelle Jamieson], and we shot it like a romantic comedy where he sees her and his eyes light up and he's just fallen in love, like those old impulse deodorant commercials from the 90s and he follows her and he's kind of dancing, walking on air. He floats after her down this alleyway and knows he's going to find her and tell her how beautiful she is. We shot that very much like romantic comedies are with saturated colours and all that kind of thing.

Then for her story she's walking down the street and this guy is just staring at her and it's really creepy and he's just not taking his eyes off her and she's going "Okay, this is this is weird" and she notices that he's still watching her as she walks away so she ducks down an alleyway to get away from him and he starts following her. And she started to get really worried. We shot that more like a thriller, we desaturated the colours, we used ominous music. We borrowed all the tropes from romantic comedies and thrillers and used them to push those two storylines apart to show that the same experience or the same activity can be two completely different experiences for two different people. And so that was a really fun thing to discuss with the actors and how we shot it was really fun, even composing the music, the whole way through. That was probably the most interesting in terms of those discussions with the actors.

You're playing with so many different genres as well, you've got the thriller, you've got the romantic comedy, you've got the stoner comedy, the relationship drama as well. Was that something you really enjoyed dabbling in the different genres?

JJW: Yes, definitely. Because often when you're running a normal, traditional linear story, you've got to be so careful with tone and staying consistent the tone. Of course, you can introduce different types of tone at different points, but you have to be so mindful of that. Whereas with this, it was it was really fun just to have each character could have their own tone. There's one character who is asking everyone for money in the story. And if you don't start with her story, she just seems like someone who is asking for money because maybe she's trying to get some booze or drugs.

The way we shot it was that on the comedic characters, she just seems like this throwaway character that the other characters laugh about, or fob off. But when we follow her story, it's much more serious. And when you learn the reason that she's asking for money is because she's in a lot of trouble. And so that was a deliberate case of introducing two completely different tones and seeing what happens when they interact, because you might switch from the comedy version to her story, and then back again. I didn't know if that was going to work. I didn't know if that was going to jar and that was part of why I was interested in trying this to see what would happen.

REVIEW
THE XROSSING

DISTRIBUTOR HALO FILMS CHAMPIONS WESTERN
AUSTRALIAN MADE INDIE FILMS WITH ITS 2021 SLATE

With over 25 years of industry experience, Perth based producer and local film champion Ian Hale launched the all-embracing Western Australia distribution company HALO Films in 2020. The idea of HALO Films originated during the COVID lockdowns which saw the local industry shuttered and brought to a halt. With the first films rolling off the rank in 2021, HALO Films immediately signposted a promising future for local Perth independent cinema. Starting off with Julius Telmer & Jevgeni Jevsikov's *Greenfield*, and moving onto Steven J. Mihaljevich's *The Xrossing*, HALO Films then brought on board their first documentary, De Bruno Austin Garth's *The Last Horns of Africa*. With an award-winning feature already under the HALO Films banner (Adam Elliott's 2022 film *Edward and Isabella*), the future is looking bright for this independent distributor from WA.

Right across Australia, emerging filmmakers are finding their voices through microbudget feature films. From Lucy Coleman's masterful weaving of three thousand bucks into the stellar feature, *Hot Mess*, but that style of indie drama is almost built to be economical. When it comes to genre-heavy fare, like the thriller Robbie Studsor's *Burning Kiss* or the horror Robert Woods' *An Ideal Host* or Zack Inglis' *The Light*, the reality is much different, with each dollar being spent needing to look ten times its worth. Proudly asserting itself into the indie film scene is *The Xrossing*.

A young girl is dead. Her body lays behind the house of moderately reclusive Indigenous man, Bobby (Kelton Pell). His outsider status has him being racially profiled by a trio of young blokes, who are convinced he's the murderer, and as such, they set about disrupting Bobby's life over a series of unsettling events. One of the guys is Chris (Luke J. Morgan), a student at TAFE learning about film production, and hoping to find a path away from the crime-adjacent world of the Perth Eastern Hills. Chris is the moral center point of *The Xrossing*, someone who initially engages in the acts of bullying and vandalism, and yet, through the assistance of fellow student, Abbey (Georgia Eyers), he comes to recognise the cost of his and his friends' actions on Bobby.

Leader of the trio is Shane (Jacob O'Neill), an impressionable young guy who looks up to his criminal leader brother Phoenix (Steven J. Mihaljevich) as the beacon to which he should follow. Phoenix is a short-fused, meth dealing crim who slams fists before thinking and has a posse of equally nefarious thugs behind him to cheer him on. Suitable role model, Phoenix is not. It's Shane's desires to be like his older brother that causes the majority of the angst directed at Bobby, even though there's precious little evidence that he's the killer of the young girl.

Made for $80,000 over three years, with a lot of sweat and tears, this Perth made socially-conscious thriller is Steven J. Mihaljevich's first feature, is a little shaggy around the edges, but like all the other microbudget features mentioned, asserts Mihaljevich as a strong creative talent to keep an eye on. It's this energy and filmmaker vision that is setting HALO Films apart from other areas of the film industry. Ian Hale's ability to pinpoint emerging talents and nurture their vision both during production and post-production shows that with HALO Films he has established a place for independent films to amplify their voices.

As is often the case with microbudget films, Mihaljevich takes control of multiple aspects of *The Xrossing*, wearing a director, producer, editor, actor, and co-writer (alongside Carl Maiorana) hat throughout the production. With extensive shots of the Perth skyline and the Metro area, alongside shots of iconic locations like Northbridge TAFE, plus the undercurrent of bikies and gangsters that exist on the fringes of Perth, *The Xrossing* feels apt with its reflective modernity.

Yet, while *The Xrossing* is frequently tense and engaging, it does struggle to create an in-depth exploration of the impact of prejudice and social division that thrives within society. What hampers the relatable narrative of tolerance and acceptance is an arms-reach distanced B-plot narrative focused around generic drug dealing criminals. If there's one aspect of microbudget filmmaking that I'm eager to see modified, it's the continued interest from young filmmakers into the world of gangsters and crims. The old adage 'write what you know' is most applicable to green filmmakers, cutting their teeth on narrative storytelling for the first time, so while I'm sure the machete-wielding illegal exploits of crime figures is entrancing on page, its presence in a grounded film like *The Xrossing* only hampers the overall plot and themes that the film is trying to touch upon.

Which is no major slight on the film as it does carry truly impressive elements. Luke J. Morgan continues his impressive work, as first witnessed in the equally micro-budget short film, *Residue* (Kori Reay-Mackey, 2019). The chemistry that Luke. J Morgan shares with Georgia Eyers (who carries the same screen presence as a young Teresa Palmer throughout each of her scenes) is tangible, and highlights the fact that these two actors are names that you'll grow to become familiar with over time. Their work here hints at grander careers to come.

Equally impressive is Kelton Pell. To fans of *The Heights* and *Three Summers* (Ben Elton, 2017), this is no surprise, as Pell is a seasoned actor who carries an impressive impact on screen, assuring the audience that his place in a story becomes a seal of approval. His Bobby is a conflicted character, one who has his own reasons for staying isolated from society. As we get to know him, we see his tender interactions with his friendly Pink and Grey Galah, and watch him craft guitars out of gardening tools. It's the scenes between Bobby, Chris, and Abbey, that resonate the strongest in *The Xrossing*, making me wish that the crime aspect was stripped out completely and that we were given more time with this trio.

It's also worth highlighting the great score by Desmond W. Richardson and James Leadbitter that is reflective of the sundrenched landscape of Perth and all the harshness that thrives within it. Cinematography by Shane Piggot is also commendable, even though there is an overt over reliance on drone shots.

With *The Xrossing* and the library of films distributed by HALO Films, the ingenuity and ability of indie filmmakers to craft compelling narrative arcs with minimal financial backing is clear. This is a new distribution company to keep an eye on.

CONTRIBUTION
WHILE (ALIVE) {} - DIRECTORS
CODY CAMERON-BROWN
AND ZIGGY O'REILLY

Co-directors Cody Cameron Brown and Ziggy O'Reilly have created an impressive stop motion animation blended with live action film that spans the entirety of a human life within its short runtime of just over two minutes. It is an impressive feat to be able to pull on the heart strings in such a short period of time, but together, Cody and Ziggy have sought to blend art and science in a way that provokes thought and discussion long after it has finished.

While (Alive) {} screened at the 12 Films Heart short film festival at Perth's 2021 Fringe Festival, as well as at the Revelation Film Festival, and internationally at the Cyborg Film Festival in Perugia, Italy.

▶▷▶

CODY CAMERON-BROWN (DIRECTOR)

I was raised on *Wallace & Gromit, Pingu, Plasmo* and Tim Burton, so the art of stop motion has always been a major inspiration to me as a creative. I had my first crack at animating with plasticine when I was 10; I made an innocent figure wave his hand at the camera until his arm ripped from the bone, leaving him screaming in pain - (I of course provided the scream).

I kept making weird shit throughout the years, so it was written in stone that one day I would contribute to the animation medium as a grown-up filmmaker. At 28, I joined forces with my dear friend, Ziggy who works in social robotics. How many people can say they have a friend who does that? I've always loved robots from a pop culture standpoint, whether it's Terminator or Data from *Star Trek*, but only since learning about Ziggy's profession did I start thinking about the moral implications that come with bringing robots into our world.

While (Alive){} is the result of curious minds from art and science coming together to tell a story of connection between a human and a robot, who must face the tragic inevitability of biological mortality.

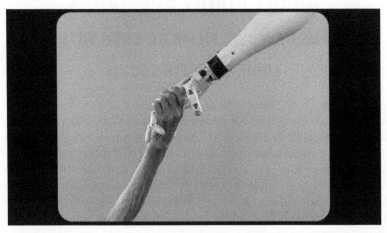

While Alive
Copyright Ziggy O'Reilly & Cody Cameron Brown. Used with permission.

ZIGGY O'REILLY (DIRECTOR)

I watched *Ex Machina* in 2016 and became so interested in androids that I made the rational decision to quit my job and travel to an artificial intelligence conference in New York. Thankfully, it all worked out and I got deeper into Social Robotics (not dumpsters)...

Later, in conversation with my cherished friend Cody, we discovered a parallel between social robots and stop-motion puppets; both can be physically manipulated to appear as if they have thoughts and feelings. So together, we created a robot character that audiences could emotionally respond to.

This project began as an exploration into the future of human-robot interaction, but during post-production it became something more personally meaningful. On boxing day, I received the news that my Nan passed away. Tragically, due to border closures, I could not process my grief within the warm embraces of my family.

While(Alive){} then became a reflection on the importance of physical affection when confronting the fragility of existence.

Can this need for physical touch be provided by a robot, in a world where human interaction comes with more risk than ever before?

REVIEW
GOODY GOODY GUMDROPS
AUSSIE MUSIC FILMS GO BUSH WITH
TROPICAL FUCK STORM

Industries across the board were shattered by the all-obliterating force that was COVID-19, but no industry was greater devastated than the live arts industry. With theatres shows skittled, live music soon followed as music festival upon music festival, band upon band, postponed tours and gigs to vague dates in the future that were also inevitably postponed. Some bands resorted to streaming live gigs online from empty auditoriums or their living rooms, with the hope of recouping funds from dedicated fans while the mythical $200 million competitive art grants fund from the Federal government hung out of reach like a carrot on the line.

Tropical Fuck Storm's ability to pivot and make the best out of a horrid situation has pushed them into a rarefied place in Australian film history: the concert film. With a new album and a planned tour (rescheduled twice, eventually moving into 2022), best hard rock/heavy metal ARIA award winners Tropical Fuck Storm decided to enlist co-director Nina Renee to make a concert film like no other: *Goody Goody Gumdrops*. Billed as a flick inspired by *Wake in Fright*, *The Cars That Ate Paris*, and *Picnic Hanging Rock*, *Goody Goody Gumdrops* is more like an unhinged outback music event, replete with countless wayward canines, copious amounts of booze, and the occasional campfire sing.

Given Tropical Fuck Storm couldn't officially launch their third album, *Deep States*, this manic film makes all the sense in the world, with it being beamed into living rooms and cinemas over a few days in December. For fans, the sight of the visually expressive group (Gareth Liddiard, Fiona Kitschin, Erica Dunn, and Lauren Hammel) blasting out their raucous tunes to a crowd of pissing dogs, oblivious to the bacchanalia going on around them, made for a thrilling event. For the uninitiated, this downward spiral into absurdity might reflect the experience of the madness of isolation that much of Australia experienced throughout 2021 in an all too familiar fashion.

As the band find a calm spot by the Goulburn River to harmonise, they find manage to distil the depression and despair of the pandemic with mournful lines like the opening of Maria 63, with Gareth pulling his heart out as he sings with the knowing tone of a broken man: "It took me years, but then we finally had a time and place to meet." Nature joins in the chorus as bugs fly around and branches fall off, crashing into the dried-out leaf litter. The quiet solitude is momentary, as the band breaks the silence with a round of skeet shooting with clay pigeons replaced by golden records. There's no metaphor here, just unbridled absurdity.

In between tunes, Helena Rose Holmes gives a tarot reading, the band makes cocktails, and they try to resurrect a broken-down bus, and as they do so, they manage to conjure the grandest representation of their iconic band name. In the midst of the Victorian outback, they manage to truly become Tropical Fuck Storm. As with any great storm, it is destructive, wreaking all manner of sonic havoc on the mind of the viewer, ensuring that this limited experience will linger in the air of each gradually diminishing breath with ultimate ferocity. There's a level of fever dream delirium at play here, but that's a commonality with all Tropical Fuck Storm albums and gigs. At least now it's captured on film so you know that what you experienced actually happened.

While God gave germs their dominion, it was artists a found a path to continued existence. *Goody Goody Gumdrops* could never replace the feeling of a live gig, the stench of a stranger thriving to the music besides you as you precariously hug your flailing pint to your chest as you all communally shout out of tune "This was supposed to be a summer banger // but now it's just another bummer sanga", but as a decimated arts scene tries to crawl its way back to normalcy, it showed a path to maintaining a captive audience, all the while performing in one of the most unique settings around. In the realm of concert films, *Goody Goody Gumdrops* stands proud as a fine Australian entry into the sub-sub-genre.

INTERVIEW
CHOICE - ACTOR, DIRECTOR, PRODUCER, AND WRITER SHARNYA YATES

Multi-hyphenate filmmaker Sharnya Yates tells the story of a daughter coming out as transgender to her family in the short film *Choice*. Written, directed, and performed from an informed perspective, with Sharnya and her daughter Saffy playing mother and daughter in the film, *Choice* aims to be a supportive tool for parents and teens going through similar experiences.

Choice had a successful festival run throughout 2021, with screenings at the Revelation Film Festival, Cinefest Oz, the Sydney Women's International Film Festival, Lift Off Global Network in Los Angeles, and the Female Voices Rock Film Festival in the US.

Interview conducted June 2021.

▶▷▶

Let's talk about your wonderful short film Choice. It's really beautiful. It's really well made.

Sharnya Yates: Thank you very much. Filming (was in the) Southwest, we wanted to showcase the Southwest, and we wanted to give it a real West Australian feel, hence the FIFO dad. The mum's a real mum. She's tired, she's exhausted. Looking at her running, she's not an athlete. And she's not looking like a model on screen. We wanted to have it come across as quite raw and real so people could instantly relate in some way.

It was about raising awareness for transgender youth suicide prevention, but in doing so, it's less about the actual transgender child focus, and more about how the parents affect what happens once their child comes out. It's directed at parents and teachers and caregivers and the community in general. And it's a film that's going to trigger some people, especially in the younger generation. One young person that saw it felt quite triggered because she has a transgender sibling. And just seeing for instance, this scene where Jesse/Sophie has the tissues in the toilet, that really, really spoke to her and she was like, "Wow, I feel guilty just being born female when my now sister couldn't develop those kinds of things, never had that experience." And she was really sad about it, and it was really good to get her perspective on it.

There's a balance between showing the difficulty of Sophie being open about the life that she's living, but also highlighting the difficulty that parents are going through, and it never villainises them or victimises them. It shows two people who live a weathered life. And while she loves her kids, there was a palpable feeling of "Oh, this is just one more thing I have to worry about." And it wasn't a derogatory "I can't believe my kid's trans", it was that she's got a lot to work out. How was it creating this particular story?

SY: There's a lot of what we've experienced as a family with my transgender daughter, Saffy, who actually plays Jesse/Sophie in the film, which wasn't actually planned. Towards the end of the casting process where we were struggling to find transgender actors that had some acting experience and then there were those that we did find who were like, "Oh, we're just not sure." And then Saffy piped up and said, "Well, you know..." She was happy the film was being made and very supportive, but she didn't want to be in it and didn't want to put herself in that position. Obviously, she had to go back pre-coming out and she's further along in her transition so this was really quite difficult for her in the filming process to do that mentally.

When she said "I want to audition," I was like, "Oh okay, wow, this changes things," because I'm going, "That means I'm going to be directing you part of the time." But I also thought, "Wow, this is a bit too close to home." I said, "You need to do an audition tape." Because at that time, COVID was still active, and we were doing self-tapes. I said, "I'll send it to Claire [Leach] and a few other people. I'll get their opinions, and I'll step back a bit."

She was made to do this, she's lived it. It just seemed so right, and she really brought it to life on camera. It was using some of the experiences from our own life, there's definitely a lot of that in this film. But I also spoke to families across Australia and just through my research with Telethon Kids Institute as well, got a feel for what other families are going through. We've mixed the different things up.

There's a lot of us in it. But then we changed things around. I was quite accepting, when she came out, although probably very similar to Nina in the film in being overwhelmed with so much going on, another little child and just a million things happening. And also, Saffy does have a stepfather, although not modelled on Paul in the film at all, although he is FIFO. We've taken the FIFO side of it but we switched the roles of the parents a bit. We wanted to appeal to men in general. We wanted them to be able to relate as not always being like the baddie. Because a lot of the time in a lot of families, quite often it will be the dad that struggles more, especially if it's a male to female transition. They will struggle a little bit more sometimes than the mother. But we wanted to switch that round so we could show that this isn't always the case and really speak to our audience, the men in our audience as well.

A lot of families in Australia have it lot worse than what we have portrayed. A lot of transgender youth don't have support from either parent or they're kicked out on the street or there's just that lack of understanding, so we didn't go as far to that point. We wanted to keep it similar to our story, but enough to show that the parents' decisions really have such a big impact on the children. When I did my research with Telethon Kids Institute, they did a trans pathway[11] survey, and that found that if transgender children have just one supportive adult in their life, that reduces some of the mental health issues associated (with coming out). Just having one supportive person at home in your home base where you feel safe is so important. That's why we're really speaking to parents here, saying you can be that person. It's all about tolerance, it's about acceptance. A lot of people I know - friends, family - they've struggled with the idea of it, but when you're left with the tats showing one in two transgender youth will have attempted suicide, that's horrendous. That's not okay. Very, very scary. That's why these kinds of conversations are so important.

The figures that you put at the end of the film are quite a gut punch. Gay and lesbian stories on film were often steeped in tragedy, and now since there are more stories being told, there is a lot of warmth and happiness in them. But trans stories are often still steeped in tragedy. And that's what I found so refreshing about this is you're saying it's so important to be able to see a narrative where it's not distinguished by a tragedy. It's not distinguished by the people who have lost their lives.

SY: We wanted to show that it could so easily go that way. And we want to show people watching it that it's very easy for people on the outside that haven't done any research into transgender youth or don't have any understanding about it whatsoever - for them to look at a family and then judge. But they have no idea what's going on behind closed doors. And what we have portrayed is something very, very common. That narrative of what's going on between the parents and then what's going on with the child is so, so common in the teenage years, if not a lot worse. For me, it needed to feel authentic, and it needed to be as raw as we could make it, to an extent.

The title of the film leans into the conversation that the two parents have with each other. How did you go about scripting and getting the right wording to be used there?

SY: It's funny, because I did have a couple people review the script originally and there were there were a few comments of "There's bits of cliche in it." I said, "Yes, but this is how it is. This is life. Life is cliche, sometimes."

Cliches are steeped in truth.

SY: Exactly. When writing that scene in particular, I took myself back to the times I was really struggling with exhaustion and struggling to deal with the mental load of seeing what my daughter was going through and I can't fix it for her. And I'm in a world of pain over here and she's in a world of pain over there. And in the conversations I've had with my husband and Saffy's father - my husband is not Saffy's father - and with other people, and it just came onto the page. It just kind of came out. But I had to refine it quite a lot. I went through it and I'd be like, "No, I wouldn't have said it like that, or I feel like Nina" - because obviously, it's not about me, I am quite different to Nina. But there is a bit of a mix in there. I had to really pull myself out of that as well.

And Nina, when she walked out and she's having a cigarette, she's making it about herself. But that's what parents often do. Especially when they're exhausted and they're tired, it becomes about them. And I think that's what we wanted Paul to show - was to snap her out of it, to go, "Look, I know you're going through this." I also wanted to show the dynamic between a FIFO husband and wife. Even with my husband we have those arguments about who does it harder at home and who does it harder at work. That struggle with coming home and dealing emotional, explosive children sometimes, I feel like that scene encapsulates so many different things for me.

I want to commend you; Paul's discussion surprised me in a way which I didn't expect. You so often see the typified FIFO man as being this gruff bloke, and sure that exists, but there are nice tender caring people. And I think the thing that I felt was really important was it highlighted the depth of his character so well, it's clear that he's been having discussions with the people that he works with, about their lives and his life in particular. And when he says, "Look, one of my mates had a trans kid and this is what happened," there's an acceptance there.

SY: I really have to commend Claire Leach my co-director. When we were workshopping this, she was really pushing for that. 'Let's make the dad more understanding.' Because then when we have these gruff FIFO workers out there watching this, they will be able to go "Oh, yeah," and can take it on board a bit more and relate to a bit more. Because they don't want to be seen as the bad guy. As soon as you show them as the bad guy in a film, they're going to push back and go, "Well, that's not me." And then they've disconnected from it.

But instead showing them that there's other ways of being. I would say the majority are gruff and perhaps less understanding in a lot of situations, but we really wanted to switch it around and go, "No, not everyone is like that." And maybe this could help tell the story to a wider audience if we make it like that. My husband's probably way closer to Paul in terms of sensitivities in a way, but certainly not modelled on him. They're very different people, but he's probably able to be a little bit more sensitive than your standard gruff guy.

These kinds of stories help break down the assumed normality of life. I really appreciated that it helps break down the mentality around teenagers going through a transition. Please don't answer this if you feel it's too personal, but for you, what was your transition journey?

SY: The change in my daughter when she came out and wanted to be called - she didn't come out and say, "Hey Mum, I'm transgender" - she said, "I want to be called *this* name," and then just walked off. All right, so we're left to go, what does this mean? And then we had a parent call up and say, "I'm just letting you know that" - I won't say her previous name because that's [deadnaming] - "But such and such is now saying that they're called this. Is that the way it is?" So that was a bit of a shock to us because we'd only just heard briefly, she hadn't really talked to us but she started talking to other people first, which is another sign.

Then I thought, "Wow, this is something we need to take note of." Once I was like, "Okay, well, if that's something that you feel, we'll be supportive." And the change in that child coming from a sadder place to a happier place, and seeing her smile more and seeing her come into herself; that's what made me realise this is here to stay. And then it made sense. There weren't any real signs when she was younger in terms of what people would generally talk about - 'was she wearing female clothes, was she into playing with more girlier things'. She wasn't doing any of that. But she did have more female friends. And she did have a lot of emotional struggles on the playground and I think it's because she had that struggle within herself. She didn't know where she was fitting. So that made sense. Once you see your child start to shine a little bit and find themselves, it's quite obvious that it's not a phase and this is who they are.

Was that a conscious choice to film in that location in the Southwest?

SY: It was. Because I wrote it down here. And because Saffy has experienced some of her turmoil down here. A lot of it was in Perth, a lot of the mental health had gone downhill a bit more in Perth. But when we moved here, nature has been part of our lives for a long time. And when I originally wrote the script, Nina was going to be running, but she was running in a forest. And then I decided to move it to the ocean. And then looking back at our own experiences of Saffy, it just worked beautifully. It definitely was a conscious choice. But the direction changed a little bit as we started to understand and write the characters a little bit with more depth.

Because I raised the money myself, I decided not to go to Screenwest because I missed out on a couple of the closing dates when I was organising all of this. I thought, "I'm going to take full creative control of this." I did two Australian Cultural Fund campaigns and then I also did presentations to the Rotary Club and Lions Club of Margaret River, and the shire down who gave us a $2,000 arts grant. When you start involving people down here as well, we wanted to showcase that community. We would have filmed the entire thing down here if we could have, but we had to cheat it and use a house in Fremantle to make it look like it could potentially be down here. Because of COVID, the cost of having everyone down here - and when we were shooting, it was pretty much holiday time - it was just gonna be a nightmare and way over our budget so.

And thankfully Fremantle's got a lot of places that look like places from down south. So where to now for you?

SY: I'm not sure. It was such an intense journey. And because I've worn so many hats in this production - co-producer, co-director, acted in it - I've done so much work that it's taken a lot out of me. But at the same time really, it's given me a life. It's kind of where I'm at - I think Saffy as well - we're at that point where a lot of the hard work has been done. We want to sit back and enjoy it a bit. We want to enjoy and see where this can go. But obviously, the whole idea behind the film was that after the festival route, we would be able to give it to institutions to be able to help (others). So hopefully it can go further and help more families. That's the plan. We want to keep it going for as long as we can. As far as more productions, I don't know. I don't know where it's going at the moment.

I just need to take some time and enjoy it and see where it goes. But I know Saffy enjoyed the process, although it was very difficult for her, each day pulling her back out of that mental space that isn't so pleasant. I had to pull her out of that. I'd direct her a couple of days and then Claire would help on the day she was directing, when I was acting and whatnot. I think that was exhausting for her. But seeing the end-product - although it's hard for her to watch herself like that. And even for most actors, watching themselves on film is pretty hard - I think she's proud and really happy about where it's going.

You've made a wonderful film. The passion and the heart and the humanity is clear in every single shot and frame and the performances, the script and direction is wonderful. It's the type of narratives that we need to hear and need to see.

SY: I think we need more of that. We need more stories that have an impact. I think we need more rawness, if you like, on the screen, more authenticity. We're very, very excited. We're so passionate about that.

REVIEW
SHARK

NASH EDGERTON'S BLACK COMEDY OPUS HEADS TO THE HIGH SEAS FOR RELATIONSHIP MAYHEM

Over connected short films, *Spider* (2007), *Bear* (2011), and *Shark* (2021), Nash Edgerton and co-writer David Michôd delight in creating a trio of ever-delicious pitch-black comedies. In the space of a swift fourteen minutes in the third entry, Nash Edgerton creates a truly sublime punchline to the relationships of his oafish boyfriend character Jack. After his first girlfriend was hit by a car, and his second fell off a cliff, here Jack's wife Sofie (played with perfect repartee by Rose Byrne) is prepared for whatever hijinks of mishaps may come her way, including a fateful diving trip into the middle of the ocean.

Riffing off the established prankster who simply does not learn from his mistakes, and always takes things one step too far, *Shark* sees Edgerton masterfully conquering the short film format once again, working alongside Michôd like two school kids having fun with one-upping each other. These shorts have become a playground for Australian actors and crew to dig into something a little bit off-beat and kooky, with talents like Greig Fraser, Mirrah Foulkes, Warwick Thornton, Teresa Palmer, Ben Lee, Ione Skye, and Rose Byrne all jumping in to have a go at laughing alongside the mishaps of this bumbling boyfriend.

There's a naughtiness to pranking people that usually ends up with the prankster laughing at the pranked individual, delighting in their screams of shock and laughing at their terror-riddled faces. But with this trilogy, Edgerton ensures that Jack continually gets his comeuppance, often in a brutal and unexpected manner. In *Shark*, Byrne's Sofie is Jack's equal, with her utter delight at surprising Jack making it feel like he's true match. The film meets these two characters on their level, and ratchets up the surprises and pranks over its swift run time to the point of giddy delight.

It's feels like a rarity to see feature filmmakers return to the world of shorts, but it's clear that Edgerton and co are left unbridled here, able to enjoy the fun of storytelling without restraints. Hopefully this trilogy of films shows that filmmakers can swing between features and shorts comfortably, reaching a receptive audience with both formats. Screening at the Sydney Film Festival and Toronto Film Festival in 2021, and subsequently screening on Hulu in the US, *Shark* was celebrated with nominations at both festivals, and around the world at various international short film festivals.

CONTRIBUTION
GOOD FOR NOTHING BLUES - WRITER/
DIRECTOR ALEXANDER LORIAN

I first had the concept of *Good for Nothing Blues* in late 2015. It was after a bad period of my life, mentally, for various reasons. Unemployment in WA was over 6%, and between studying, I had been through several years of struggling to find a job, both due to my own faults and inexperience and the huge amount of competition. My early adult years had been full of severe anxiety and depression. This milieu of uselessness and unbelonging became the basis for the central story of Calvin, although as often happens, the story quickly grew much broader and more complicated, which was partly intentional, as I wanted to focus on the dry irony and comedy and make it fun rather than bog the viewer down in the lethargy of depression. Calvin's friends became as complex and nuanced as himself (I can't help but feel the group dynamic was subconsciously influenced by *Daria*'s "Fashion Club") and the crime elements developed into a twisted web of panicked bogans, obsessive cops and vengeful mob members.

I didn't finish writing the script until 2018, but when I did, I was confident that would be the best thing I had made. The script came in at a whopping 138 pages. It was going to be a huge project. We ran auditions and selected a cast. All unknown actors, but good. Very good. A few had to leave due to difficulties in scheduling but the ones who came in to replace them ended up being better than I could have hoped and now I can't see the characters without them! It was an ensemble cast and we had a heavy focus on rehearsals to nail the chemistry and flow.

I was inspired by the comedic yet natural and free flowing dialogue of films like *The Big Lebowski*, and we had a strong focus on creating a believable and relatable chemistry between the characters, focusing on getting, whenever appropriate, long single take shots where a number of characters share the screen simultaneously, and their little reactions and interactions all play off each other in real time. This was not something that could be covered up with cutting to closeups all the time. It was a risky move, but one that, for the most part, really paid off.

Funding the film was tough. We shot on a meagre $12,000 budget, when we had originally planned for $20,000. We got $4k from an investor, $4k from extended family and friends, and $4k of my personal funds. An earlier Kickstarter campaign had failed, but the cast and I were determined, united by a passion for what we knew was a film unlike anything produced locally before.

Half the budget went towards paying people what little we could and the rest mostly into production design and locations on our 28-day shoot.

Bryce Myles Fenwick, who played Gary in the film, really stepped up when our production designer soft-pulled-out, taking on almost all art department work, and that basically saved the film. In post-production, Diego Espinoza stepped up as sound editor and gave the film the amazing 5.1 surround sound track that it has today. This was a project of scrambling, struggling, re-re-planning, and a fair bit of guerilla filmmaking, to make $12,000 look like $50,000.

I had high hopes for the film, but was filled with fear that nobody would care, that nobody would watch it, and that nobody would like it. And while it was certainly true that local media did not care at all (we got zero coverage despite repeated efforts), the audiences responded as excellently as I could have hoped. The premiere and subsequent screenings were a laugh riot. Despite coming in at over two hours, nobody seems to be bothered by the length, as the pacing keeps people engaged.

We've been to a few festivals, less than I'd hoped but not surprising for a film this long, but the reaction from real people has been astounding. Now with six local screenings and seen by almost 1,000 people, I have strong confidence in the film gaining a following on home and digital release. I'm immensely proud of this project, that I kept it true to the original vision, of all the incredible work the cast and crew put in, and of the development it shows in our respective skillsets.

I long to see a new wave in Western Australian filmmaking, one that is unique, idiosyncratic, challenging and not bound by popular convention or the general limitations of our government funded productions. I know a number of people around me who are up for the challenge, and I hope I can be part of that too. Even if I don't manage to fund larger projects in the future, I'll always have *Good for Nothing Blues*, and that's something that nobody can take away from me, or, for that matter, any of the amazing, wonderful people who were a part of it.

DOCUMENTARY FILMS

D ocumentaries outnumbered feature films released in 2021, with a vast array of diverse films finding audiences in cinemas, at festivals, and online. By their nature, docs often run with lower budgets, with many high-end feature documentaries costing around $600,000[12] to make.

In 2020/21, the Gallipoli Clause that allows for productions to claim expenditures made in countries other than Australia under the Producer Offset was at threat from being removed by the Federal Arts Minister Paul Fletcher, causing genuine fear and anger within the film industry. Thankfully, just before the close of the 2021 parliamentary year, parliament voted to retain the $500,000 producer offset[13], meaning that documentaries like Sally Aitken's *Playing with Sharks*, Matthew Walker's *I'm Wanita*, Yaara Bou Melhem's *Unseen Skies*, and Cathy Henkel and Sam Lara's *Laura's Choice* could all continue to claim the Producer Offset for their international legs of production if they qualified.

The lower budget requirements of documentaries has seen a huge variety of features emerge, with everything from the immediate and socially conscious group of features that created a multifaceted narrative approach to the traumatic 2019/20 bushfires (Eva Orner's *Burning*, Justin Krook & Luke Mazzaferro's *A Fire Inside*, Sandrine Charruyer & Sophie Lepowic's *Inferno Without Borders*, and Anthony Ash Brennan's *We Are Conjola*), to the COVID-responsive documentaries like Nicole Miller's *This is Port Adelaide*, to a wonderful array of documentaries that focus on various aspects of the arts (from country music with *I'm Wanita* to Hollywood with *John Farrow: Hollywood's Man in the Shadows* to theatre with *Firestarter: The Story of Bangarra* and beyond).

Given the nature of documentaries, their production cycle can vary greatly, with some taking years to create (the six-year journey of Frances Elliott & Samantha Marlowe's *Girl Like You* immerses you in the core relationship, while *Meet the Wallers* twenty-year filming journey carries you along one family's journey), and others taking mere months, like *Inferno Without Borders*.

It's within documentaries that real voices are able to talk about criminal injustices against the First Nations families in Allan Clarke's *The Bowraville Murders*, or to allow athletes from all sports codes to openly discuss the daily racism they endure in Peter Dickson's *The Ripple Effect*, or to have Australian film history shifted monumentally with Alec Morgan and Tiriki Onus' *Ablaze*.

Australian cinema is best when it reflects on Australia as a whole, highlighting this country's strengths and weaknesses, its cultural uniqueness, and its historical failures, using the medium of film to encourage some kind of growth or change within our world. Narrative features operating under the blanket label 'Feature Drama' (as per Screen Australia) are often risk-averse, terrified of upsetting someone (this is partly why *Nitram* had to establish production outside of the Screen Australia funding model), making documentaries the prime area to present the ugliness and beauty of Australia in the same reflection.

Screen Australia's[14] Gender Matters initiative states that for the 2018/19–2020/21 period, 41% of directors on feature dramas were women, while for documentaries they made up 45% of the successful Screen Australia applications. These, of course, are growing percentages that represent only Screen Australia successful productions, but if we look industry-wide, we can see that women are further underrepresented in the directing field of feature films, with their presence during the 2015-2020 period hovering around a depressing 20%, but in the documentary field, they make up 37% of the total productions over the same period.

These figures aren't perfectly comparable due to clashing time periods and the emergence of the Gender Matters campaign, but when we take 2021 as a whole, in comparison to feature films, documentary filmmaking is where women directors are making a name for themselves as either directors in their own right or co-directors. With screen veterans like Sally Aitken, Eva Orner, and Cathy Henkel, all ushering in new works, alongside emerging filmmakers like Sam Lara, Yaara Bou Melhem, Madeleine Martiniello, and Sonia Bible, it's clear that within the arena of documentaries, women are currently creating some of the greatest cinema that Australia has been fortunate enough to witness.

Across the following pages, we take a look into the world of documentaries via realms of different themes: socially conscious narratives, the environment, the arts, films about films, music, and sports.

SOCIAL ACTIVISM

While all documentaries are keenly interested in bringing their subjects narratives to the attention of the viewer, a socially conscious documentary often carries a greater urgency at showcasing the important and pressing social issues from around the world.

These move from the intensely political with Tosca Looby's archival documentary about ex-Prime Minister Julia Gillard's term in *Strong Female Lead*, or Craig Reucassel's swing from political comedy to activist filmmaking with *Big Deal*. It's here where we find the political activist tales of a queer icon in Christopher Amos' *Hating Peter Tatchell*, or the familial activism for the right to access voluntary assisted dying in Cathy Henkel and Sam Lara's *Laura's Choice*. A socially conscious documentary can highlight the dramatic changes in our world, as we see with Catherine Dwyer's Women's Liberation Movement story *Brazen Hussies* and Sally Ingleton's environmental activist film *Wild Things*.

But it can also highlight how the shifts of the foundations of society can carry a racist tone, with Allan Clarke's furious *The Bowraville Murders* working alongside Dean Gibson's unsettling *Incarceration Nation* to highlight how the Australian justice system consistently lets down and destroys the lives of Indigenous Australians. Rhian Skirving & John Harvey's *Off Country* further examined the racial divides within Australia, focusing on Indigenous students moving from their home to boarding life at a school far away from their home. Then there's Trisha Morton-Thomas' *History Bites Back* where Trisha, Elaine Crombie, and Steven Oliver join up to comedically tear apart social media comments about Indigenous Australians, providing a historical context for the truth along the way.

History informs the present with Adrian Francis' anti-war film *Paper City*, which sees the survivors of a US attack on eastern Tokyo seeking reparations decades after the wartime tragedy that claimed over 100,000 lives. Barat Ali Batoor shares his own story of survival and seeking asylum in the documentary *Batoor: A Refugee Journey*.

As we look into the past, we're encouraged to look into the future with Yaara Bou Melhem's activism-by-way-of-art story *Unseen Skies*, where artist Trevor Paglen utilises the footprints of artificial intelligence and mass surveillance to reveal just how much we are being observed through his stunning art pieces.

The heinous and cruel possibilities of technology is examined in Simon Nasht & Akhim Dev's unsettling *The Children in the Pictures*, which tells the story of Task Force Argos, an investigative team who rescue children being sexually abused by highly organised dark web networks. Complementing that film is Sascha Ettinger-Epstein's *The Department*, an intimate and supportive story of the workers of NSW's child protection system, as well as the families they become involved with.

Families are the core narratives of Läwurrpa Maypilama & Patrick Josse's *Djäkamirr*, the story of childbirth from the perspective of Yolngu women in

Galiwin'ku, and their role as caretakers of pregnancies, as well as Jerusha Sutton, Jo Hunter, & Zoe Naylor's *Birth Time*, which explores the birthing practices used within Australia, asking questions about how the birthing experience could become a less traumatising process in the modern world.

Socially conscious documentaries are ultimately about the relationship a subject has with the world around them, and what changes they wish to see in the world. With Frances Elliott & Samantha Marlowe's *Girl Like You*, the relationship of trans woman Eloise and her partner Lauren becomes the socially conscious narrative about the complexities of realising identities within queer relationships. And finally, Matthew Salleh's *We Don't Deserve Dogs* examines one of the oldest enduring relationships, how people relate to canine companions, and how they influence our day to day lives.

Socially conscious documentaries are represented with pieces on *Strong Female Lead*, *Big Deal*, *Laura's Choice*, *The Bowraville Murders*, *Unseen Skies*, *Girl Like You*, and *Batoor: A Refugee Story*.

REVIEW
STRONG FEMALE LEAD
A HORRIFYING SLICE OF MISOGYNISTIC AUSTRALIA AND
ITS ETERNAL LIFEFORCE IN POLITICS

Documentaries are often made in the editing room, where the point of view and directorial intentions are honed, finessed, and corralled into the final product that we call a 'complete movie'. In the case of a film like *Strong Female Lead*, the narrative intentions are divined and curated from a deep well of archival footage, focusing on the rampant misogyny and toxic masculinity that erupted to the surface of politics, mainstream media, and society during the tenure of Australia's first woman Prime Minister Julia Gillard.

Following in the monumental impact of the devastating Adam Goodes documentary, *The Final Quarter*, *Strong Female Lead* curates Australian history in a manner that throws the words of the lecherous back at them as pointed barbs. Here, the hate-filled rhetoric of Alan Jones, Tony Abbott, and the plethora of mouth-breathers that thrive on the internet are left out to dry, with their noxious words lingering in the air like a foul stench. Like Adam Goodes, Julia Gillard is presented here as a gradually weathered person, someone whom a fair proportion of society decided was worthy to have the failings of a country thrown at, like a vaudeville show and a basket of rotten fruit.

Strong Female Lead is a scathing indictment of Australian politics, arriving at a time when the people's house is already smouldering from the accusations of sexual assault occurring within its walls. Tosca Looby's direction carries us from Gillard's entrance into the role of becoming Australia's first, and only, female Prime Minister, through her time being pilloried, berated, and abused in Parliament by the leader of the opposition and his equally disturbing followers, to her ejection by ex-Prime Minister Kevin Rudd who sought the role of leader of the country.

The images of future PM Tony Abbott, future Speaker of the House of Representatives Bronwyn Bishop, former MP Sophie Mirabella, and other notable Liberal Party figures, standing on the grounds of Parliament House with repulsive and offensive signs about the leader of the country linger throughout the film, with the realisation that what should have been a career-ending moment for Abbott instead turned into a firestarter for the country further stoking rampant misogyny on the airwaves, in the newspapers, and in Parliament itself.

These kinds of moments are aplenty, and in a creative choice that stands *Strong Female Lead* apart from *The Final Quarter*, a choral chime of phrases plays in the background, amplifying the Grecian level tragedy and operatic notion of politics as a whole. As the main stage footage plays out the loud and furious drama that stirs the anger within us all, the chorus erupts with chants of 'big arse' and 'first female PM', with the impact of the words (both negative and positive) lingering in your mind throughout the film. It's a creative choice that may either distance the viewer or further draw them in to the tragedy of the piece.

As a destruction of the toxic masculinity and misogyny that thrived during Gillard's run as Prime Minister, *Strong Female Lead* does stray a little too close to lionising and celebrating Gillard as a leader. She is, like all world leaders, fallible, with broken politics and harmful ideology that further lead to the Australian Labor Party being indistinguishable from the Liberal/National coalition. But, as is clearly depicted here, the impact of Gillard's decisions about asylum seekers is overshadowed by the misogyny she suffered through her tenure, to the point where Abbott, arguably one of the most Machiavellian opposition leaders in Australian political history, drove the conversation surrounding the price on carbon (which was never a tax), forcing Gillard onto a backfoot that she was never able to recover from.

This continued attack is witnessed time and time again, with a late moment where ex-MP Christopher Pine talks over ex-Labor MP Kate Ellis, striking the point of what misogyny in politics looks like. This culminates in one of the most important moments in Australian political history, Gillard's significant speech attacking Tony Abbott, with the words "I will not be lectured about sexism and misogyny by this man, I will not" ringing through your mind endlessly. Gillard's fury is contrasted in footage of newsreaders comparing the viral nature of her speech to a video of a skate boarding dog getting 20 million views on YouTube, effectively adding to the misogyny of society by comparing the first female PM to a dog.

What stuns the most about *Strong Female Lead* is how clearly it lays bare the reality of what it means to be a woman working in Australian Parliament. Moment upon moment, with horrifying hate speech being eagerly thrust onto the Australian public branded as 'news', we see a reality that makes it even more unbelievable that Prime Minister, Scott Morrison, and his equally noxious cohorts, were left surprised by the level of misogyny in Parliament. If they truly believe this is a surprise, then it's clear they were not paying attention, for it was there all along.

Alongside Annabel Crabb's ABC series, *Ms Represented*, the continued activism from Australian of the Year Grace Tame, and the emerging stories from ex-MPs like former federal Liberal member Julia Banks[15] and Senator Concetta Fierravanti-Wells[16], as well as the work of Greens Senator Sarah Hanson-Young, *Strong Female Lead* works in unison with the wealth of material in Australian society in 2021 that worked to expose the foundations of Parliament House for what they are: a 'Canberra bubble' where men feel they have the right to act however they please, demean women, and disrespect the Australian public with behaviour that we would condemn our friends and family for.

It was then unsurprising to see federal politics disregard the public opinion in wanting women in leadership positions, when the other preferred prime minister Julie Bishop[17] lost to Scott Morrison, when a leadership spill occurred in 2018 turfing then PM Malcolm Turnbull from the top job. The enduring nature of misogyny ensures that men will always consider themselves the best person for the job and will vote for each other to keep themselves in power. It's hard to not walk away from *Strong Female Lead* feeling that misogyny is not just part of the woodwork of Parliament House, but it is also a core party ethos for the Liberals.

At the close of *Strong Female Lead*, the footage of the lineage of strong female leads around the world, from Angela Merkel to Alexandria Ocasio-Cortez, and Jacinda Ardern, figures of great inspiration and hope. It's worthwhile noting that post-politics, Julia Gillard has become a major champion for women leaders around the world, with books like *Women and Leadership: Real Lives, Real Lessons* being co-written by another great woman leader Ngozi Okonjo-Iweala, encouraging young women to get into politics and enact change around the world for women everywhere. *Strong Female Lead* is keenly of the moment, with the film closing with Amanda Gorman's powerful poetry reading at Joe Biden's inauguration, supporting yet another strong female lead, the first female and first African-American and first Asian-American Vice President, Kamala Harris.

While these closing moments are powerful in their own right, they do feel exclusive from the main narrative about Julia Gillard's time in politics. This doesn't detract from their presence, but rather highlights the need to close a dark film with an aspect of hope. Julia Gillard will stand as one of the great leaders in Australian political history, and Tosca Looby, alongside producer Karina Holden, and editor Rachel Grierson-Johns, have clearly pulled together a film that honours her legacy and the horrifying slice of misogyny that Gillard and her fellow women MPs, as well as her colleagues in the Senate, had to suffer through.

INTERVIEW
STRONG FEMALE LEAD - EDITOR
RACHEL GRIERSON-JOHNS

B y collating media images, news footage, parliamentary question time, and social media reactions, editor Rachel Grierson-Johns worked alongside director Tosca Looby to create *Strong Female Lead*'s power in depicting the systemic attacks of misogyny and sexism that Julia Gillard endured through her tenure as Prime Minister of Australia.

Rachel has worked in television and film for over twenty years, working in the UK, USA, and Australia. She shared the Australian Screen Editors award for Best Editing in Factual Entertainment for her work on *Love on the Spectrum* with co-editor Simon Callow-Wright in 2020. Rachel's work has included the critically and commercially acclaimed series *Employable Me* and *Love on the Spectrum*. Rachel discusses the editing process of *Strong Female Lead*, while also exploring the films influences, the difficulties of editing during a pandemic, and the future of editing in this interview.

Interview conducted September 2021.

Readers should be advised that this interview includes discussions of sexual abuse.

▶▷▶

How did working on Strong Female Lead come about for you?

Rachel Grierson-Johns: I'm a freelancer and I do quite a lot of work for Northern Pictures. I have done *Love on the Spectrum*, *See What You Made Me Do*, and *Employable Me* so I've done quite a lot. And I saw *The Final Quarter* and I just remember going "Oh my God everyone, this film *The Final Quarter* (Ian Darling's documentary about footballer Adam Goodes) was amazing." I'd really love to do that film but about sexism and Julia Gillard, because I'm obsessed with that sort of style of archive-only style. I love *Amy*, I love *Senna*. I love all the films from Asif Kapadia.

Tosca heard me and she said, "Oh, I want to do that too. I've been wanting to do a film like that for ages." It was just a tearoom chat, but next thing I know Tosca is on it. There's funding for a trailer, then I'm cutting a trailer in my spare time. That was the end of 2019, cutting a trailer and I thought, these films, half of them never get off the ground. And you just think, even if it does, it's going to take a couple of years, so I just didn't really think too much of it.

As I'm cutting it, I was going "Okay, this is good. But, is there enough material to make a whole film like this?" We were always questioning and not quite sure if there's enough material, "How long is it going to be?" "Oh probably going to just be an hour or maybe 40 minutes." We just didn't really know. So that's where it began and then we got funding from SBS.

We weren't meant to start cutting it till later on in 2020, because I was doing *See What You Made Me Do* with Tosca as well. It's a SBS show about domestic violence. Then the pandemic happens, and stuffed up all the shooting. We had a little bit in the can to edit, but then we had to stop shooting. Then we went, "Well, we've got this archived film that we've sort of got funding for and we were gonna plan to do later on in the year," and then suddenly it's like, "Right, yes, keep everyone working." And so we were able to start working end of May in 2020.

What draws you to this archival style of documentary filmmaking?

RGJ: I feel like sometimes talking head interviews take you out of the moment for me, and brings you back to the present. And sometimes it's nice not to have that feeling to be broken. And with important films like *The Final Quarter* which is about racism, and *Strong Female Lead* which is about sexism, it's hard. A lot of people are going to have opinions about it. I always knew that there was going to be a reaction to it. And it has been overwhelmingly positive, but there's been negative reactions.

I think the beauty about films — and I'm going to keep going on about *The Final Quarter*, because I love that film — it wasn't people talking in interview about their own experience, they weren't putting their agenda forward. It was things that actually happened and you can't just think that they happened. It was what was said at the time. And I just felt that was so much more powerful to me than having someone interviewed saying, "Well, when I remember when that person said that, and it made me feel that," it just takes you out of the moment. You needed to feel that moment and feel the shame of what was said.

To me it was the reason why we went with this kind of style, because there were so many horrible things that were said and it's not like there hasn't been discussion about the sexism that Julia Gillard faced. I just didn't feel that it would benefit to make another film where people discuss it. It was just like: this is the pattern of it.

I think that's the thing like [racism in] *The Final Quarter,* it's like you saw a pattern of sexism through the media through Parliament through the way that she was discussed and the differences of how her clothing was discussed, how her relationship and her childlessness was discussed, which would never happen to a male leader, in my opinion, and never has happened to a male leader.

That was why I really like that style. I just think it's much more truthful. Not to say that those kinds of films are unimportant or don't have their place or that I don't like making films with talking head interviews. I just feel like when you're trying to show a pattern of behaviour for something like sexism or racism, then I think that style is better.

Both films are absolutely powerful. The Final Quarter and Strong Female Lead, they're coming at times where it feels essential to now. It feels kind of like kismet in a way that this film has come out in the year that it has. How has that been for you as somebody who's worked on the film to have it released in a year where so many stories about sexual assault, abuse, and the misogyny within Parliament House has been amplified this year. How does that feel for you?

RGJ: Well, it was just so bizarre. I'm not a person that believes in spirituality or anything, but they did feel like there was this unforeseen, invisible force pushing this film to get made. Like the pandemic helped us because it made us do it earlier. But when that stuff started happening around us, I think it was the end of 2020 was that *Four Corners* report (*Inside the Canberra Bubble*) about the stuff that goes on in Parliament House, the prayer rooms are all the extramarital affairs, all of that sort of stuff.

And we thought, 'oh, okay, this is this is the time for it come out.' We heard about *Ms Represented* (Annabel Crabb's show about politics from the female perspective) that ABC show that was getting made, which it was good for us, but also bad because, like, "Oh, we could be saying the same thing." I think that series is amazing. And it's almost a companion piece to *Strong Female Lead.* But once Grace Tame and Brittany Higgins and all that stuff came out, and then the wanking on the desks and all that, we were like, 'holy shit.' Wow, the timing just seemed insane.

I think SBS wanted us to even put it on the air earlier, they wanted us to do it in the height of all that, and we didn't want to have our air date too close to *Ms Represented.* And I'm glad that we waited because I felt Julia Gillard would bring enough to the table to have it discussed. And we didn't have to be on the back of the storm. It did create its own storm, hopefully. We couldn't believe what was happening. And I think it's amazing and positive, really, that these things are being shown and being discussed.

For us, we lived through what went on with the Gillard government and the rampant misogyny that occurred during that era, yet collating it all into a film and seeing it [at once], instead of experiencing it over the years, it's a damning thing to experience. How did you go about collating the images and editing it into something that carried weight? And was there anything that you had to leave on the cutting room floor?

RGJ: There was so much we left on the cutting room floor. So much. That was part of the edit: just taking stuff out, because the pattern of her clothing was something that just went on throughout, but it just became relentless and boring. Some of the feedback on earlier cuts, we had a two-hour cut at one point, it was like, some people just went, "I want to vomit."

We just had to pull back on it. I think she announced the election at the end of 2013, and then the Murdoch papers were like, 'Oh, she's got a new haircut.' 'Wow, look at those glasses.' 'Oh, my God, look at those glasses.' You look and it always just took away from whatever she was trying to say. And there's endless things about her shoes.

We had to simplify complicated things with Parliament, because very early on we're trying to explain things, but we didn't want to make a film that was too isolating for people that weren't really into politics. We're trying to do film that was about politics, but not too much. It was trying to simplify the political things, but also be truthful to that.

I've never done anything like this before. I was just looking through hours [of footage], I mean, we had over 300 hours of archives. Tosca, she had an Avid as well at her house, because we did this all remote. We were just looking through [clips]. Each and every week I'd have a drive arrive. And so for a week, I was just collating clips.

I just organised it into years: the end of 2010, into 11, 12, and then 2013, which was ultimately the government's demise. And we went through that way and I cut down years and then went from there. I could start cutting things that you knew were going to be in the edit: the misogyny speech, obviously, the carbon tax rally, and tried to work out what was around that area and what led to that area.

It was just the process of going through all these archives. "There is a news piece here, there's a clip of a press conference in this news, what went out on ABC? Is this the whole press conference that exists?" It was constantly just ordering footage and waiting, I always have to put that scene down because I'm waiting for that press conference to come through or that footage to come through. Because not everything is archived properly. I was just hoping that the footage you want is still around and that rushes still exists. It was a weird process of media wrangling in the beginning very early stages of the edit for months.

I worked on the edit from the end of May 2020. We worked from the end of May, and then we downed tools in September, because I had a baby, and that gave us eight weeks off, and then I took to it whenever I could and did it part time. And then from January, February, March, April, I had a friend help out like a nanny a couple of days a week. I was doing it much more of the time. But that's when the film got really refined, because it was just — gosh when we first did a rough cut, it was so long! And didn't have the emotion. It's the sort of film that takes time. It's not a six week edit, or an eight week edit that I'm used to doing so.

When you're getting the images and the clips, do you get in contact with the media organisation and say we need this? Or is there a different archive storage of this kind of material?

RGJ: We had someone in our team that was in charge of getting all the archival ordering for us. Laura Grace is amazing. And she became very good friends with Charles at ABC. She was constantly ordering stuff from him and he would also say "If you ask for that, then this great bit is available." And because Parliament closed during the pandemic, we were able to get lots of Parliament footage quickly as well, which doesn't normally happen. We ordered reams of that. And from all the other sources as well, radio, all that kind of stuff. It was a constant process of going through our emails, going to the archive, and [adding it] all into the system.

It seemed it's really overwhelming. That's the thing with The Final Quarter too, when it's presented in an hour and a half kind of experience. You just think "how did we let this happen?" I'm curious for you, as somebody who sat there watching all this, how do you grapple with what you're watching? How do you deal with that mentally, and stay on focus?

RGJ: There was a lot of late-night Zoom calls to Tosca going, "You'll never guess what I just found out." There are the things that just went under the radar. For example, some of that Charles Wooley interview about, "Do you love your partner," "Does your partner love you?" I watched it and went, "Oh." And then I went, "Hang on a second." Sometimes things needed a couple of watches, because no one would ask Scott Morrison if he'd love his wife. And it was these little subtle moments that were more 'the penny drops' to me, because I went "Hang on a second what, what am I watching here?"

We all knew that, for a certain extent, the whole thing with Tony Abbott was he had a problem with women, but it was just more surprising to me was the subtleness or the insidiousness of how the media treated her. It was just quite shocking, actually.

When you put it all together, you think, "Oh, there was that moment." And then there was that *At Home with Julia* thing, which I remember watching and thinking "What? This is awkward." You see prime ministers get satirised all the time, and it's funny and whatever, but this is a personal relationship getting satirised while the Prime Minister is still in government, and they're pretending to have sex. I just went "That would never happen with a man." Those sorts of moments where you had to just do a double take and go, "Am I seeing this right?"

Prime Minister Julia Gillard
Photo Credit: Phil Hillyard. Used with permission.

I remember when that was on, and I just thought this is utterly absurd. It's disgusting and absurd. It doesn't make any sense why they made or screened it.

RGJ: And that was the ABC! We've seen some reviews where people are like, "Oh, this is just SBS bias or blah, blah," I'm going "No, no, it was all media." It wasn't just Murdoch or right-wing people; it was the ABC that did that. This wasn't something that it was just a certain section of society. This is all of society really, I thought. And that, to me, was more shocking than just lots of Murdoch papers. I mean, obviously, they were involved as well, but, yeah, there was just lots and lots of late-night phone calls to Tosca.

The film is really of the moment as well, in the sense that it wraps up with events from earlier this year. And it feels a bit like a baton handing off in a way where it's like, Julia Gillard is a strong female leader, and here are the next generation of leaders coming up. What was the decision behind showing some of those clips here? Especially the poetry from Biden's inauguration [by youth poet laureate Amanda Gorman], which is beautiful.

RGJ: Earlier cuts — the feedback was that it was truly negative. "Why would women watching this ever want to go into politics or leadership or in business roles or anything like that." We'd always thought that this is the kind of film that more than anything we wanted young women and girls to see and think "Hey, I want to be different, we're not going to let this happen again. And I'm going to change this." We didn't want to leave it negative.

And for a long time, it was just in the edit as a title thing, 'epilogue' and I'll deal with that later. But, because of all the things that happened with Brittany Higgins[18], and then the march happened too. I remember reading just going, "Oh, my God, there is this march happening. We've got to get footage of that." And then Kamala Harris was Vice President. It all just seems to be happening around us.

And we would collate it at the time. And it felt like, "Well, that's the end." We needed to say, "Look, girls, there is change happening around the world. And it's happened here, and we'll get another female leader later on, we've just got to make sure that this doesn't happen again." We just wanted to leave it positive. Even though it's a hard film to watch.

The feedback I've gotten, lots of women have gotten very angry. And I think that's a good thing to get angry, we should all get angry, and men got angry too, I should say. But we shouldn't just let that anger go to waste, we should channel that energy into change.

How important is it for you as an editor to work on projects like Strong Female Lead and Love on the Spectrum, which brings a different view of society to the world in a wonderful way. I mean, everybody loves that show, as they should do, it's a beautiful show.

RGJ: Look it's my dream. I think every editor will tell you they want to work on something they care about. And in a way, I always feel very sad that *Strong Female Lead* ended, because it was like a drug. It's like a drug Andrew. I did this in the midst of pregnancy, lockdown, having a baby, and I was tired and but I just had to do it.

I just became obsessed with things. And you think "I've got to see this through." It was a dream of mine, like anything like this, where your core values are being able to [be] expressed through an edit. It's a dream come true. I'm very, very, very privileged and lucky to being able to work on a film like that. And I don't know if I'll ever get the chance to again, so I'm a bit sad about that. It's just exactly why you do these jobs. It'll definitely be one of my favourites, for sure.

Where do you see the future of editing going in Australia? It's interesting with the Australian industry at the moment with changes. I'm curious for you, somebody who's working in both film and television and episodes, where do you see the future of editing going from here for Australia in particular.

RGJ: As far as the lockdown, the pandemic, it's really helped. It's being able to work remotely and I think that's helped me tremendously with the young family. And that seemed very empowering as a woman to be able to still have a career and still have a family and not feel like either one of those has been ignored, because I've got the flexibility that I didn't have previously.

I think a lot of editors are working remotely at the moment, and I think that will be something that won't go away. I hope it doesn't. And I think there's merit to working remotely and working with the director together [in person]. In a perfect world, there'll be a mix of both. I'd like to see that in future of editing.

Working on these archives feels like you're very much a co-director. That's why really, I don't care about credits. I like going under the radar if I'm honest. It was very nice at the beginning of the film that we did a film by her [Tosca] and me, because we were very much just partners in crime. The edit was the filmmaking itself. There was no shoot. It was all about the edit really.

Hopefully, Screen Australia and people come up with more archive ideas, and we'll keep looking at history through this lens. I'm sure that there's probably people now looking at this going, right, this one, let's make one about how First Australians are treated and how refugees are treated. I'm sure there's lots of ideas popping around. And I'd love to see those sorts of films.

What does it mean to you to have immense creative choices in a particular film?

RGJ: There's lots of different types of editors. And I like watching rushes. I like forensically watching them. Being a documentary editor, it's almost like a bit of detective work, you sometimes have to find a story. The story is there, there's a billion ways to tell the story. It's not like a drama where there's a script in store, you can deviate from the script, a little bit in drama, but in documentary you can tell this story in so many different ways to tell it, and I think that that's when you feel — you feel the power of it. For example, I've done a lot of true crime, the order matters so much. "How do I tell this?" How you drip feed information to the audience helps them come to the right conclusion at the right time, or give them that emotion at that time.

And in a way Strong Female Lead is its own kind of crime investigation.

RGJ: I suppose. Yeah. I suppose it is.

I have felt like that going through that many rushes. Sometimes there'd be days where I'll be like 'oh', you think you're watching the most amazing thing, here's this debate between Tony Abbott and Julia Gillard during the election where 'the worm'... it's like there's like a blue line for men and the pink line for women and they respond to whatever they're saying. You think that sounds amazing and then you watch and go "Oh my God, that was the most boring thing," and then you go "Oh just watch this Charles Wooley thing, whatever" and then you're "Oh my God this is *what*?" It is like that sometimes. It's also like you're just watching lots of detective footage.

A point I should make is that it really drove home to me as well how the different networks report things in different ways. Some of the coverage of things, how SBS would cover something is very different to how Channel Nine would cover something and then you start to think these disparities matter, because it shapes people's opinions and their world-view. That really interests me.

It's very easy for a lot of people, I imagine, that they have a news channel of choice that they watch and then probably don't stray into other territories all that much and it's interesting to see what we're blind to in different ways.

RGJ: Definitely. Especially the whole carbon tax thing, that was honestly night and day, I was like 'wow this should be like taught in school'. I just found that really, really fascinating.

Do you have any suggestions for up and coming or emerging editors in any tips as to what to do in the industry?

RGJ: My advice would be to edit anything. It doesn't matter what it is. I see some really great up and coming junior editors and I think, "They're going to be very successful," and then I do see their mentality like 'this is not what

I want to do, I want to edit this amazing documentary it's going to change the world', and you think 'well, you've just got to work your way up there'.

Edit anything.

It's always a step forward and it's always about stories, always about telling a story, story is key. Whether you're editing a corporate video about concrete, which I have done before, you've got to figure out what shots am I going to use to tell this story? What were the things are going to go in this? What you have to learn, the conceptual side, whether you're editing a music video, what effects make someone feel something, it's all relevant, even reality TV. I've done reality TV, that is more like cutting to story and cutting quick, learning quickly, and be able to identify how to cut a conversation down to make sense. And to hit the right story points, get the point across, but also get the emotion across. It's something that comes with time.

Do you find your voice growing as an editor as you go along?

RGJ: Of course. It's sort of 'been there, done that' and you kind of go "Okay, well, I think this could work because I've sort of done something like that before." And you get a bit more confident. "Well, I like the sound of that music, but I don't know if that's going to fit but we'll give it a go and then hang on, I've got this idea in mind." I'm always up to trying what directors want to do and then giving my feedback, what I think will work, because it's always a collaboration. I'm very often wrong, and sometimes I'm right. And I guess that's the beauty of it.

REVIEW
THE BOWRAVILLE MURDERS
A DOCUMENT OF AN UNJUST AND
ACTIVELY RACIST SOCIETY

Readers are advised that this article contains the names of Aboriginal people who have died.

There's a certain level of expectation that comes with true crime documentaries. With the echo of the tone set by Errol Morris' *The Thin Blue Line* ringing through the years carrying on with films like the *Paradise Lost* trilogy and *The Jinx*, there's an understanding that a true crime documentary should close with the actual perpetrator being caught, giving some kind of closure for the victims and the family. With a slew of searing and powerful revelations being made along the way, these films made an undeniable, significant impact on their subjects' lives.

Yet, it's hard to shake the obvious racial aspect that's missing from them: they're all about white victims. Sitting alongside devastating and essential documentaries like *Murder on a Sunday Morning* and *The Tall Man* is the heartbreaking and anger-inducing *The Bowraville Murders*. Where these films focused on the perpetrators, falsely accused or otherwise, *The Bowraville Murders* engages with the enduring, decades long search for justice for three young Aboriginal kids from small rural town of Bowraville, NSW, who were murdered over a five-month period in 1990-1991, and whose killer still remains at large: 16-year-old Colleen Walker, four-year-old Evelyn Greenup, and 16-year-old Clinton Speedy-Duroux.

Directed by Muruwari investigative journalist, Allan Clarke, *The Bowraville Murders* further exposes the already crippling structural and institutional racism that forms part of the foundational aspect of Australian society. In complex and painful detail, *The Bowraville Murders* meticulously documents the past thirty years of a judicial system that failed three young victims before they even had a chance at justice.

Importantly, Clarke details how family and community focused the Aboriginal population of Bowraville is, highlighting how close each of the victim's families were, living together on the same street, joining in celebrating the oncoming new year and Christmas as a community. The tragic events play fresh in the minds of many of the residents who talk about their fight for justice throughout the film, with family members and close relatives each speaking with distinct clarity about what occurred, while also fairly criticising the manner that the police who failed in their duty of care simply because the victims were Aboriginal.

Victim-blaming carries across the decades, with application upon application for retrial being denied amidst a complex and labyrinthine legal system that actively obfuscates and shuts off any path of justice for Aboriginal folks in Australia. If this were an isolated case, it would be frustrating and upsetting, and ideally be used as a signpost for a moment of change in Australia, but this is modern Australia, and it doesn't take much to realise how stagnant and actively cruel the justice system is for Aboriginal folks. Amplifying that depressing realisation is Clinton's nephew, a man fighting for justice for his murdered uncle, saying the "Wheels of justice move slow, but only for Blackfellas."

In a moment of hope, ex-Detective Gary Jubelin is drawn into the case, immediately becoming furious at the shoddy and careless police work at the time of the crimes taking place, and seeking to rectify the harmful and wilful errors of his police force colleagues by supporting the Bowraville community. But that hope is fleeting, as his years of support comes with disappointment as appeal after appeal is denied. In a damning moment of causation, Jubelin's vocal disgust at the way the police force and the judicial system treat the victims and the Aboriginal community leads to a loss of work by way of complaint. The message is clear from the police: by standing up for 'them' and not defending 'us', you are not welcome here.

In a film that's already packed with compelling and anger-inducing narrative beats, it is almost extraneous to have Stan Grant appear, sitting in a vacant theatre, further explaining the significance of the lack of criminal charges associated with this murder. His presence is valuable and integral to outlining how this is not an isolated case, highlighting how, when discussed alongside the overwhelming number of deaths in custody, horrifying victim-blaming, and cultural erasure, 'Australia is a crime scene.'

As such, *The Bowraville Murders* paints a damning picture of a racist system that actively shuts off the path for justice for Aboriginal folks, year after year after year. If you couldn't see that we live in a racist society that is structurally designed to denigrate and deny the traditional owners of this land we call 'Australia' safe lives, then this film will slam that notion home powerfully. True crime documentaries often conclude in a tidy and resolute manner, but there is nothing neat about the story within *The Bowraville Murders*, with the lack of closure leaving you as angry as the families who are still seeking justice. As a document of an unjust society, this is heavy work, but utterly vital viewing.

INTERVIEW
THE BOWRAVILLE MURDERS - DIRECTOR
ALLAN CLARKE

A llan Clarke is a Muruwari and Gomeroi man who has made a career as an investigative journalist. His work on the podcast series *Blood on the Tracks* won him a Walkley Award alongside Yale Macgillivray. Allan's work can be found on SBS, ABC, and Buzzfeed. His work has spanned across TV, print, podcasts, and with his highly acclaimed 2021 film, *The Bowraville Murders*, he transitions to the world of documentary filmmaking.

Interview conducted April 2022.

Warning: Aboriginal and Torres Strait Islander readers are warned that the following story contains references to deceased persons.

▶▷▶

I watched The Bowraville Murders last year and was just quite stunned by it, and really impressed by how emotional it was as a film. Congratulations on bringing this story to life. It must have been a very difficult journey to begin with.

Allan Clarke: Well, thank you. Yes, it was a difficult period to get the film up, first of all, and also to ensure that the families were prepared to talk about the worst time in their lives, the loss of their children. And so it was important for me to ensure that they were first of all comfortable, but also they felt like they had a platform to speak openly and honestly, and to be in a safe space where they could be emotional. And so before we ever started filming, it was important that I spoke with all of the families and we would form a bond. We would speak a lot about what are some of the things that they wanted to say in the film.

It was interesting, because I didn't have any preconceived notions of what the film would look like in terms of narrative or even having a shooting script that we would religiously follow. It organically happened after those conversations with the families. And, looking back at the media over the last thirty years, I think a lot of the times their voices were erased from a lot of the media coverage. And so essentially, this became an opportunity for them, at the end of thirty years, in this enormous legal battle to be able to speak in an unfiltered and raw way.

I felt it was really important that Australians and the world could see how the impact of not only having your child murdered, but also facing racism from the police and authorities in those early days of the first investigation, how that actually impacts these families, and they have to live with it every day, and what kind of grief and trauma comes with that. So it was important that we made a film that made people bear witness to what this and the police response has done to that community.

There has been this proliferation and real interest over the past decade in true crime stories. And one of the things which I noted was that unlike a film like The Thin Blue Line or Paradise Lost trilogy or The Jinx where there is this sense of closure for the people in those stories, all of those subjects are white. Whereas there is no sense of closure here for the families, for the victims. How do you manage the balance of knowing that there is no real closure within this particular story and trying to deliver what is really becoming quite a popular format of filmmaking of storytelling in true crime stories?

AC: I mean, true crime is such a broad term now and there is such a proliferation of it. Some of it is exploitative and some of it is very nuanced, it's such a large spectrum. But also you want people to be engaged when they're watching a film. Basically, I go through to pick some of the stronger elements of the essence of the true crime narrative to keep people engaged. Some of that is the forensic investigation, some of it is the whodunnit [aspect]. There are small cliff-hangers along the way, utilising that to keep people engaged. Also then, through the backdoor, having the audience actually bear witness to their grief and trauma is a really a powerful combination.

I've spent most of my career working on the intersection between Indigenous people and the justice system, and I found that being able to subvert the true crime genre to get people interested in an issue or issues within the Aboriginal community that they might not necessarily seek out has been a very powerful way to tell those stories and actually engage the public. And with this, I wasn't interested in creating something that looked at the case forensically or the cases — calling Clinton and Evelyn's cases forensically — because that had been done. There is a book, *The Bowraville Murders* by Dan Box, and Dan appears in the film. And there was some great work done before this film around the ins and outs of the cases, the kind of evidence-based stuff, the court cases.

I wanted to punctuate the film with that obviously, because people need to know what happened. But I think this is unique in that there is this raw emotion that is often left out of true crime genres because often there's a focus on the salacious or the investigative stuff. We followed [the families] over the last two court cases up to the highest court in the country, and then they were rejected. There was this real sense of 'Do we matter in this country?' There's a bigger issue here, a bigger question. The highest court in the country has just rejected us, basically denied us justice. What does that do to not only the parents of Colleen, Clinton, and Evelyn, but their families, their community? intergenerationally, how does that affect the younger people within those families? They're the kind of themes I wanted to explore.

Before these children were murdered, the families were already facing issues within Australia, issues with the police, segregation. The parents of the murdered children all grew up on Bowraville Mission which was run by the government. They couldn't even leave without facing potential violence or verbal assaults from the white community in that town, and that racial line is still very much alive. These are big ideas and concepts that we wanted to infuse in there, and why historically the justice system is like this with Aboriginal victims of crime.

I think in a way, we've been able to blend these two worlds in filmmaking or documentary-making, in terms of taking that true crime genre which is so popular and people really get invested in, taking the best aspects of that and interweaving it with this kind of raw emotional material that often is left out of that genre. So, hook them with the true crime stuff and then give them an entree into a world that they would never enter into, which is look, these people — they're parents just like everyone else, but they've had to face these extraordinary battles.

That needing to tie up those thirty years — was that part of the decision of having somebody as prominent as Stan Grant there to help clarify the history in the film?

AC: That was kind of the most daunting thing: how do you sum up thirty years of this constant legal battle, David and Goliath battle really, between these three families and the Australian justice system? How do we do that justice? I think we did it in the film. But yes, there were a lot of things to consider, going into it.

And just going to your last question, yes, there is no sense of closure. I want the audience to feel like they actually went on that journey for thirty years. And this is where the families were really vocal with me in terms of what was in the film. They really wanted people to see the raw pain of it all, the grief, the trauma, the struggle just to fight this kind of battle, and then for it to be for nothing at the end. I wanted the audience to feel like they went through that, all of those highs and lows, it's a real rollercoaster. And then at the end, the families are sitting at home and of course, they're questioning what was it all for? Are our kids important?

And so the point that there is no closure at the end is a reality, not only for these families, but particularly for many Aboriginal families in many different ways. There is always a sense in the Aboriginal community that "Yes, we're never going to get the justice or recognition we deserve." And so I wanted people to feel unsettled at the end.

Because there are moments towards the end of film where it looks like that this is going to go their way and everyone is sort of exhilarated until they get to the High Court, because it looks like this man is going to be retried. And then it all just collapses, and that's been happening since the early 90s when this took place, when the kids were murdered. So up, down, up, down. And so at the end, I think it was important that people felt unsettled, and that there was no closure. I wanted people to feel that so they could feel the way these families have felt. That was a really important thing for me.

You've been covering these kinds of stories for years and years and years. I understand there was a point where you decided to take a break from reporting the stories of Aboriginal deaths. What was the personal jour-ney that you went on that you said, "Okay, this is a film that I want to make, and this is a story that I want to be able to tell?"

AC: Yeah, you're right. I did take a break, I was very public about it. I did a piece for Background Briefing[19] about why I took a break. To be honest, I hadn't really thought about it until the George Floyd stuff had happened. I had moved to France with my French partner, and I felt like I was taking a break from reporting but in fact I was actually really depressed, if I'm being honest. Because there were these things that I was just ignoring, I barely could get out of bed, no motivation. I just had nothing. I was cutting people off.

And then the George Floyd stuff happened in the States and I was watching a video of it and it sort of triggered something. I realised all this kind of emotion bubbled to the surface. I was kind of traumatised. I wasn't dealing with the emotion that some of the work I do brings to me.

So I wrote, it was sort of a stream of consciousness. And yes, I realised in that writing, which I decided to publish, particularly for other people in my situation to understand that it's normal. But yes, it's hard to deal with this stuff, you have to have a self-care plan, you have to have a support network around you, because vicarious trauma does affect you.

After this, *Bowraville* had come along, and it was the first project after all of this mental health stuff happened, and I'd had a break. And so I felt like it was the right time, and I felt like I was able to recognise some issues. Like how can I mitigate that? Can I tell this story clearly? Because when you're doing these stories, it's not about you, so you have to be able to compartmentalise some of the trauma that is coming your way. Because it is about the families, you're there for them, doing a feature documentary and having the time to spend with them.

It felt very empowering actually, to give them the agency about what was going in this, and we worked together. Their strength was so empowering. We had a safe environment to work with, we had a mental health nurse for people who were interviewing them. We made sure that everyone was having adequate breaks, because those interviews were kind of gruelling. And just spending time with them without cameras as well. All of that stuff helped me reset my boundaries in a way and how I approach these stories and work with communities to ensure that they have the best platform they can have to clearly tell their story. It's interesting because it is something that often filmmakers or journalists or people in the industry don't talk about, those impacts on the team that are covering these stories. This was a great way to show how it can be done where everyone is cared for.

I interviewed Yaara Bou Melhem about her documentary Unseen Skies and she's a lot like you, a Walkley Award winning journalist, and I was fascinated then about her decision to transition from being a journalist to a filmmaker, because that's not something that tends to happen often, not just in Australia but around the world. And here I am talking to you, another Walkley Award winning journalist who's transitioned to being a filmmaker. The relationship between being an investigative journalist and a documentarian — how do you find the difference between the two? Is there much of a difference? How do you bridge that divide?

AC: Yaara is brilliant, and she inspires me no end. In fact, we worked together at SBS many years ago. Her tenacity is incredible. For me, being a news reporter, that kind of daily news reporter really didn't satisfy me for many years. The goal was always to be more investigative and have space to tell stories properly. I feel like going from that into film wasn't such a leap because it felt like the kind of investigative work I'd done for television or for podcast because we had ample space to tell those stories.

At my heart and soul, I'm a visual storyteller. I started in television, it's the bulk of my work, and I love being able to visually tell these stories. So it was really appealing for me to go into a documentary that potentially would be seen by a different audience as well in a different way. Also, there is a freedom in film or documentary, because often there are these parameters as a journalist, particularly working for outlets, in terms of what you can and can't say in your work because it is journalistic by its nature. I started to get frustrated with that because I want to be able to go into something where I'm not constrained by that. And film does that.

I also feel like journalists do make great documentary filmmakers. Because we bring a journalistic rigour to the process, one that maybe a filmmaker who has just been trained as a filmmaker and has never been a journalist might not have. Often with my work, you'll see it's infused with that journalistic eye in certain parts, particularly around ensuring that that things are fact-checked to the nth degree, et cetera, that we're talking to all possible angles.

But the fact is with Bowraville, I could never have done that as a journalist because people would have said, "Oh this is giving too much credence to the families, there is not enough objectivity here." But for me, I was like, well, the families are the story, and people should bear witness to what they're saying. And what they're saying is completely truthful because first of all, we checked everything to ensure that what they were saying was correct in terms of what happened in the beginning.

But then, being able to make the leap from journalist to filmmaker and call out the racism so bluntly, because, you know, if it looks like racism and smells like racism, it is racism. In the beginning, to be that bold as a journalist, I would never have gotten past producers. So there is a freedom to working in documentary. While it is still high pressure, it's a different pressure and one that I enjoy. Whereas as a journalist, it can be incredibly exhausting. It can be a different type of pressure.

I was doing a television series before this one for NITV called *Cold Justice* which is a series based on four different cold cases. So I think making the leap from television to film was kind of where I feel most comfortable now. It's not to say that I don't dip my toes back in it. At the moment, I'm working on a podcast and also writing some feature articles. I feel like I'm the type of person [who has] worked pretty much on all platforms. And some stories just suit certain platforms.

You're talking about these different stories and storytelling methods. What does it mean to be able to tell these different stories as an Australian filmmaker, as a journalist? What does that mean for your identity as a storyteller?

AC: Look, I feel incredibly privileged to do it. For me as a storyteller, I feel it's important that people are agile in terms of utilising all of the kinds of platforms that that we have. Long gone are the days where people would say, "I'm just a radio news journalist, I'm just a podcaster, I'm just et cetera, et cetera." I just have a hunger to tell people's stories and I'll take whatever platform I can get, to be honest.

I feel like over the years, I've evolved to be able to go, "Okay, well, this story I don't see as a feature documentary, I see it as television series or I see it as a podcast, so we're going to do it." Even though I've sort of dipped in and out of in the early years Indigenous affairs, most of my career has been around Aboriginal issues. The public apathy towards Indigenous and Torres Strait Islander affairs is insane in Australia, because there is a real silence around it. People just aren't interested.

So over the years, I guess my goal has been to work hard to capture that audience of Australians who don't seek out Indigenous affairs issues. And to do that, I've had to kind of evolve my storytelling into "How do I utilise the mainstream things that are popular and have people engage with these stories." That's why I think working across multi-platforms, utilising something like the true crime genre means that I'm accessing a huge audience within Australia who are just kind of blown away by the fact that these things are happening in their own country and they don't know if it's happening. The response has been incredible. For me as a storyteller, it's been incredible because that's all I want to do. As a storyteller, you need people to be listening and watching and reading your stuff. That's the whole point.

One of the things which I was struck by is just how immersive and urgent Nathan Barlow's cinematography is. I was hoping you might be able to talk about the guidance or the work that you did with Nathan on creating the visual language or style for this particular film.

AC: So we had Nathan and we also had Tyson Perkins, and they were co-DoPs. They both had a very particular style which I loved. Nathan is great at being on the go and being able to capture actuality. Nathan's like a ghost. He can be there and you'll not notice which is great because he captures that urgency, that real life actuality that you need.

And Tyson is an incredible young Indigenous up and coming cinematographer. His early work was in commercials, he did a lot of stuff with incredible production value. There are moments with this film [where] we want to do this kind of recreation feel, so we want to light it in a certain way. I was really particular about having these almost beautiful vignettes throughout the story that were high production quality, which is really hard when you're working with real people on real schedules — you're not working with actors or anything — in hard conditions, because you're on location in a community. But it was worth it.

With Tyson, there were some recreations. We were shooting in the middle of the night, he's lighting it correctly in the middle of the road. We had one witness in the truck re-creating what he saw with someone lying on the road, things like that. And it looks incredibly cinematic, and Tyson, that's his wheelhouse.

They both brought these two styles that meshed really well together. I don't like to dictate in terms of being really stringent about "Okay, this is the shot list, this is absolutely what we need right now." I would have a set list of shots I wanted, and then the rest would be up to them to capture what they wanted. I think that's the best way to be so it's a real collaborative process.

And then during the day, when we were capturing people just doing their everyday things naturally, or conversations that were happening organically, Nathan was incredible at being really nimble, to get around and get these beautiful shots but at the same time capture that actuality that you've seen in the film that allows the audience to come into Bowraville Mission, into these people's homes and feel like they're a fly on the wall. So yeah, it was an interesting dynamic, but in the end, the results were amazing.

I didn't realise that Tyson was involved with this, and I love his work quite a lot. He, alongside Dylan River, has really proven to be one of the best cinematographers working today. It's really immersive stuff. That's a perfect way to wrap up as well, leading into a question about working alongside Rachel Perkins. I understand that she's been a bit of a figure in your life growing up as somebody to look up to. Can you talk about how much she has been an influence on you as a journalist and now as a filmmaker as well?

AC: Rachel is a kind of trailblazer in Australia, and not just as an Aboriginal woman and filmmaker, but also as an Australian filmmaker, Black or white. Her work is impeccable. I've always been inspired by her. When I was quite young and first moved to Sydney, I can remember sort of saying, "I really want to meet Rachel." In my head, I would have these lists of people that I wanted to meet. Sometimes I wonder where that kind of gumption has gone. Because back then, I would just crash parties and talk to people and I remember Rachel was one of the first people to graciously talk to me when I was maybe, what nineteen. And from there, she's been nothing but incredibly kind to me. I think her work speaks to me because it cuts through into a mainstream audience, and people are then engaged with these stories that at their heart are kind of Black or Aboriginal, but they're universal themes.

Also, the way she is able to empathetically portray Aboriginal people and their issues and our grief and our trauma — you know, these all resonate with me growing up in a small Aboriginal community, these issues. I love the way she's able to do that so respectfully. I do take inspiration from filmmakers like Rachel. Even as a journalist when I was doing television stuff, long form television, I really kind of baulked against doing traditional television shots and narratives. I wanted to utilise how filmmakers were telling their stories and infuse that into my journalism. Rachel is amazing. She has inspired so many people, and I'm just one of her biggest fans.

I'd read that story about you wanting to seek her out when you're nineteen. I've been doing interviews with filmmakers like yourself for almost ten years now. And when I started doing this, I had a whole list of people I wanted to meet and talk to, and I guess it's the same kind of thing for you as well. It's that trying to discover that gumption. Sometimes there's still a bit of nervousness. I'm sure you probably still get that at times.

AC: All the time! And I still do, I don't think it ever goes away. I think you need a raw ambition if you're going to go into this industry, whether it's journalism or whether it's film. You really need to put yourself out there. Now obviously, I don't do that. But when I work with people or meet them, I'm just so in awe or there is a nervousness, I'm constantly nervous. Yeah, it's hard not to then feel like "Oh wow, like these people have done this, this and this, and how can I possibly ever work with them or be in the same room with them even?" You pinch yourself when you get to that point.

At the time, I had no ambitions of when I first met Rachel to be a filmmaker or work in documentaries. For me, it was about journalism. The way she wasn't pigeon-holed really appealed to me. She wasn't just a filmmaker, she didn't just make scripted film, but she had made documentaries, she'd worked on all of these incredibly important subjects through documentary. And I thought that's great. That's where I'd like to be at some point, which would be able to work across different genres and different platforms and different mediums.

You've done such a great job and are such an inspiration as well. Listening to you talk about the approaching people and stuff, it's funny how even having accolades and winning awards — they are important, they mean a lot, but it still doesn't take away that feeling.

AC: Absolutely. I constantly feel that kind of imposter syndrome. Even the year I won the Walkley with Yale [Macgillvray] who did an incredible job working with me on *Blood On The Tracks*. You know, you're in the room and you just kind of constantly going "Why am I here? Like I should just let go." And I was smoking back then so I'd be outside every fifteen minutes, having a cigarette, just going "I can't be in there." And then someone would come up and talk to you and you'd be like, "Oh my god, this is insane. Like what am I doing? Nothing's real."

I still get that nervousness, but there are still people I seek out because I think sharing knowledge or just asking the questions [is important]. I don't think you should ever stop learning, and these people hold incredible vast amounts of knowledge and practical skills. I think that's really important, to be able to talk to these people and keep learning.

REVIEW
BIG DEAL

A CLEAR-EYED HOLISTIC EXPLORATION OF THE
BROKEN AUSTRALIAN POLITICAL SYSTEM

On September 15th 2021[20], former attorney general Christian Porter revealed that part of his defamation legal fees had been paid by the Legal Services Trust with funds from an unknown source. On the episode of The Party Room podcast[21], *7:30*'s chief political correspondent Laura Tingle comments that we will likely never know how much of Porter's legal fees were paid, with the notion that Porter will merely 'slip away' from politics scot-free and with little accountability. This feels like an anger-inducing act of normalcy from the so called 'Canberra-bubble', pulling one Jenga brick away from an already teetering tower of hypocrisy from our elected officials. While Prime Minister Scott Morrison created a wealth of hot air about being 'surprised' about Porter's actions, the reality is that this happens all the time in politics.

Director Craig Reucassel (of *Chaser* fame) and Christiaan Van Vuuren (of *Bondi Hipsters* fame) decide to head to Canberra to take a look at the broken system of politics and how much influence big money has on Australian politics in *Big Deal*. Like many Aussies, Christiaan incorrectly believes that Australian politics is in a better position than our American friends, and it doesn't take long for him to realise that just like America, the influence of big money in Australia is drastically swaying the direction of this country in horrifying ways. The big difference is that in America, they are open with who is spending the money to fund politics, whereas Australia's political system is rife with manipulation, as any donations under $14,000 can be made anonymously.

Documentaries like *Big Deal* work with an agenda: they are clearly trying to sway the viewers opinion and world view, leaving them with a call to action (*Big Deal* closes with a link to their website[22]). They often come with a feeling that they're skewing towards either side of the political spectrum, but *Big Deal* is not that film. Christiaan delivers his interviews with apolitical questions, showing alarm and surprise when he engages with both major parties and hears how open they are about money exchanging hands. As ex-politician Sam Dastyari explains, "It's not corruption if you don't ask for anything to be done, you just assume it'll happen." In an all too relatable moment, Christiaan distils this frank political manipulation in a 'pub test' scene where he compares buying a politician to buying a round of beer. We all know that the next round is on us after our mates shout, we just don't need to say it out loud.

With a young family and a terrifying future of inaction against climate change on the horizon, Christiaan embarks on a journey through the halls of Parliament House and the streets of Canberra to get to the bottom of how deep the influence of lobbyists and major corporations' wallets have on Australian politics. Along the way, Christiaan interviews an array of powerful figures in Australian politics, from ex-Prime Minister Malcolm Turnbull, to Senator Jacqui Lambie, Liberal MP Jason Falinski, former Lord Mayor Jeff McCloy, and Labor MP Linda Burney, with each expert bringing an eye-opening view of how easily money influences Australian politics behind closed doors, with precious little disclosure as to who it's come from.

What surprises the most about *Big Deal* is less about how easily politicians are bought but how Christiaan's perspective and presentation changes as the film progresses. Given Christiaan's roots as a YouTube celeb, *Big Deal* kicks off with a swathe of 'Aussie guy gives political opinion' style skits, varying from setting up a shared Google Doc spreadsheet to help the major parties track incoming donations easier, to delivering a giant cheque so they can take a photo and share it on social media when a donation comes in. Mileage may vary with these kinds of clips, but given the popularity and cut-through they have with a wider populace, it's understandable why they're implemented here.

Then, as the gravity of what is taking place in Canberra sinks in, Christiaan's skits make way for a wide-opened, rug-pulling realisation of just how difficult of a beast big money is to tackle, especially for the regular folks in the world who don't have access to a cool $100k. Right at the point that you feel that this is all too overwhelming and you're starting to ask yourself "What the bloody hell can I do to stop this?" *Big Deal* reveals the work of grassroot activists and communities who get behind independent Canberra-hopefuls like Independent MP Dr. Helen Haines, who followed on from retiring Independent MP Cathy McGowan in the seat of Indi, Victoria. Alongside organising team members Amanda Aldous and Alana Johnson, Helen talks about how the community of Indi got together to keep a once-safe Liberal seat Independent, and provide a balance of power in politics.

Near its close, lead organiser of the Sydney Alliance, David Barrow, pulls one final rug from Christiaan and the audience, reminding us that the insurmountable fear and crippling apathy that Australians as a whole have when it comes to politics is the greatest tool for keeping status quo with the flow of big money through the corridors of parliament house. Politicians want us to feel like we can't change anything, and they want us to grow even further apathetic to the blatant movement of money from the wealthy to the law-makers. The term 'it's just politics' strengthens their movement, making us feel like we don't have the ability or power to influence change in our busy lives. *Big Deal* thankfully avoids a defeatist mentality, leaving us on a moment of hope and inspiration.

Christian Porter has now left politics, moving into a cushy private sector job, just like ex-MPs Christopher Pyne, Julie Bishop, and state MP Ben Wyatt did. We may never know who his mysterious benefactor was, continuing this charade of corruption in plain sight. *Big Deal* plays as a clear-eyed holistic exploration of the broken Australian political system, let's hope it one day become a record of the past.

INTERVIEW
UNSEEN SKIES - DIRECTOR
YAARA BOU MELHEM

A ward-winning journalist turned director Yaara Bou Melhem turns her attention to the skies with the work of visionary American artist Trevor Paglen. As an author-artist-activist-musician, Trevor Paglen is known for his work documenting black op sites used for government surveillance and data collection around the world. Moving through the Nevada desert, Paglen captures satellite movements, while Yaara Bou Melhem and cinematographer Tom Bannigan follow his movements, documenting his view on mass surveillance, all the while initiating his most audacious project: launching a satellite into orbit. *Unseen Skies* follows Paglen's journey, organically weaving in the work of the Kronos Quartet, surveillance states, and more.

Yaara Bou Melhem is a journalist and documentary filmmaker who has received five Walkley Awards, two UN Media Peace Awards, and two New York Film & Television Festival Awards. *Unseen Skies* is her debut feature-length documentary, and sees her continuing the style of journalism that she has undertaken as a foreign correspondent with Dateline, SBS TV and Al Jazeera English. In this interview, Yaara explores her work as a journalist, the distinction between being a documentarian and a journalist, and questioning the surveillance state.

Unseen Skies screened online via the Sydney Film Festival, and will receive further festival releases throughout 2022.

Interview conducted November 2021.

How did you come about Trevor Paglen's artwork and life?

Yaara Bou Melhem: I actually have been familiar with Trevor's works for perhaps ten years or so now. I first came across his work when I was actually at SBS at *Dateline*. And I had read that he was going out to remote parts of the Nevada desert, trying to photograph black sites or military bases that don't exist on the map, because authorities don't want you to know that they're there.

I loved his thinking on it. He's like, "Okay, well, what is it that they don't want to see? And how can I let people see what's there? How do I visualise this thing that's not on the map?" And then you go again, and there's another layer of meaning where he came of age as an artist at the time that 9/11 happened. And at that time, there was something that the geographer Derek Gregory called the 'Everywhere War' taking place. Trevor Paglen himself is also a geographer. He looks at the landscape and infrastructures very differently, as a geographer and as an artist, and he wanted to understand: what does the Everywhere War look like?

For him, that looks like all of these military bases that weren't on the map, these Cold War era relics that have been now appropriated for the War on Terror. It also looks like secret bases in Afghanistan which he went and photographed. He also wanted to look at secret sites via satellites that were being launched and that weren't officially being recorded as being spy satellites. And he would go out to remote parts of again the Nevada or California desert where there's little light pollution, and with the help of amateur astronomers, he would figure out which satellites that were passing through his frame at that particular moment was likely to be this particular spy satellite that these people had been tracking.

He made these incredible artworks out of these things that we're not supposed to see. He was trying to show us another way of seeing these infrastructures that are all around us, and that play a role in our lives and yet perhaps we're not that aware of exactly how it all works or what it looks like.

I was a bit overwhelmed at times by the enormity of it all. And then I kept on thinking about you sitting on the other side of the camera and I'm thinking, "What must it be like to experience that in person," to see him capturing all these images and knowing what he's capturing as well?

YBM: Trevor has such a long history and such an enormous process and enormous research process behind a lot of his works. And a lot of the time I spent trying to research the very same thing so that we could have meaningful conversations when I'm out there filming with him as he conducts his work. I think the really profound moment for me was when I saw the evolution of his work from just being about state surveillance to also being about corporate surveillance and the use of AI and computer vision software by big tech companies.

Trevor actually has this great line in the film where he says, "There was this time when I was looking at the NSA, and I realised there was this way bigger thing out there called Facebook and Google. And they have much more data on us than any of these state surveillance companies or state surveillance apparatus would ever have." I mean, some of these companies have such granular data on us that they'd know how we think, how we feel, our emotional state. They're in our private homes and we let them in.

There are all these apps on our phones, and they know our social networks from very close people to people we met on a bus. That was a penny drop moment for me during the filming process, and I knew very early on that that evolution from state to corporate surveillance as opposed to surveillance capitalism — because all these big tech companies are really operating for profit — that that became a major feature of the film.

And the collaboration with the Kronos Quartet, for me, that sort of collaboration and the meaning behind it was the essence of the film. Just to give you a sense of what that collaboration is, there's the Kronos Quartet, which is a famous San Francisco quartet, performing some music tracks. And at the same time, there's a screen above them where some computer vision software — AI, for want of a better word — is analysing these musicians as they play. And, some of the analyses are really quite off the mark. And sometimes it's a little bit funny and other times, it's just weird and strange.

And then the penny again dropped for me. The heart of that collaboration comes down to the very last track, I think, in that performance, and it's a piece by Steve Reich called *Different Trains*. And they play the first movement which is about the optimism that around trains and how this new technology has come in and it's going to make life better and it's going to make life more efficient, and it's going to connect people across vast distances, the synergies between that and the optimism around technology and how it's going to connect the world and how it's going to make our lives better.

But they don't play the second movement of that piece which is talking about the Holocaust and how trains were used in perhaps the biggest crime of the twentieth century. And Trevor makes the point [of] "Okay, what are the synergies between that optimism that we had about this new technology of the trains to the optimism that we now have with AI and that new technology?"

It is a really scary optimism as well. Of course, Facebook tracks us everywhere. And what Trevor does is manage to make that tracking system small and relatable. And that I think is really helpful for audiences and for myself in particular. Sometimes you wake up and you feel it's a bit too much. How do you deal with that yourself? I know that you've been a journalist for a while and have been tackling some pretty serious things and big issues or big topics in society. So how do you find the small in the big?

YBM: I think it's really interesting that you say that it's small, because to me, it didn't feel small. But we tried as much as possible to add to what's already out there with other films on this issue. I think a lot of them go into a more didactic kind of unravelling of how all of this works and perhaps even more in the activist-led space.

Whereas with this, I wanted it to be more of a visual exploration of the issue. Because for me, I can talk about this issue until I'm blue on the face. But I think I needed to be able to see what some of these technologies look like. What's sort of inside the black box, as it were, and how does that operate? What does that look like? Because I think knowing something is different to realising it or to seeing it. And I think that's the real beauty in Trevor's work. He does give you another way of seeing the world. He gives you another perspective through his artworks. And he has all the same meanings that we've been discussing and that other people discuss when we're talking about these issues. But it's just another view, another perspective that we might not otherwise get.

How much does that inform you as a filmmaker as opposed to how much it informs you as a journalist? Is there a difference between being a journalist and a documentarian? Do you see a polar difference in the two?

YBM: I don't think there's a polar difference between the two. I think there's a lot of correlations and crossovers. But at the same time, I think that I couldn't have done something like this as a journalist. There was, I suppose, creative licence that I had in making this film.

First of all, I'm working with an artist. And so that raises the bar of the visual language that we used and also the latitude that we have in terms of how we present this. We can take a more artistic approach. And also it allowed us to be a lot more poetic in how we approached this issue. It allowed us to be a lot more poetic in how we told Trevor's story and how he went about creating his artworks and following his process in a way which I think would have been really difficult in journalism, because there's a lot more of a factor of impurity in journalism which doesn't really allow you to deviate too much from the way you present that. There's a way of doing journalism. There are certain structures, and it can be inhibiting.

But I think for a story like this, I [had] wanted to do this as a journalism project a long time ago. But it wasn't going to work. And it was only when I could see this as a film where we followed this huge monumental project that Trevor Paglen was embarking on with the launch of a satellite artwork into lower earth orbit on a SpaceX rocket, and were able to tease out that narrative and tease out the narrative of his other works through the film. It was really only then that I could see this as a film.

What drew you to journalism in the first place?

YBM: There's so many answers to that question. So many things that drew me to journalism. I have a very strong interest in social justice and public interest issues. I'm very civic-minded. I also grew up around journalism, my dad was a journalist. Journalism for me was always something that was about the public interest, and about bringing stories that perhaps aren't popular into the mainstream. And I say that because my parents had to leave the Middle East during Lebanon's civil war, because journalists were being assassinated for telling the truth. And they obviously couldn't see a future there, doing what they do.

But they continued to practise their work here in Australia, and I grew up around that, I grew up around politics. I grew up around the internal machinations of Middle Eastern politics. And I grew up around asking questions and holding power to account. I was always encouraged to ask questions and be curious, and I think that really has made it inevitable that I was going to be in storytelling in one form or another. Journalism was the obvious choice for me at the time because that's what I knew, that's what I was around. And that has evolved now into also documentary filmmaking.

I was looking at how many documentarians had originally started from a journalistic background, and there are a whole bunch of film critics who have turned to filmmaking, but precious few journalists who have turned to documentary filmmaking. There's John Pilger of course who is a pinnacle of the art of documentary filmmaking in Australia in particular. But I couldn't really come up with too many names outside of that. The journey from journalism to filmmaking — it feels like a rarity. Was there a risk involved in in taking that choice? Or was there a comfort in knowing that because of your journalism heritage, you'll be able to tell a story is as powerful as you could here?

YBM: I think that there is this resistance between the two communities, which I've never really understood. You could bring the same sorts of skill sets, especially if you work in TV broadcast journalism which has been my background. From the journalism community, it's like documentarians are usually biased towards their subjects or towards the piece that they're doing. Whereas journalists, we're not supposed to be even though everyone has their own subjectivities and biases that they bring to the work that they do. That's another story and another issue altogether that we can unpack in a whole other interview. And I think with documentarians, there is this sense that journalists don't know how to craft a story. I don't agree with either of those summations. I think that it really is up to individuals in terms of how their creative process and what skill set they bring. I've never really understood that rift, and I'm not sure if how big it is either, and I don't know if we're overstating it.

*I don't know how big it is either because it's not something I've encoun-
tered all that often. And then watching Unseen Skies, there is a questioning of power, there is a questioning of what's going on here, there is that
journalists' strength there. But then again, if I didn't know that about you
as a filmmaker, I would have still gotten that knowing what I've got from
the film itself, if that makes sense. The questioning is still within there.
I don't need to have known that you have a journalist's background to
have made this, if that makes sense.*

YBM: That's really interesting, because one of the things that did draw me
to Trevor is his questioning of power or our assumptions of how the world
should work, and how he tries through some of his work to show us okay,
what about if the world wasn't like this? What about if it was like this instead? And I think that questioning of the status quo, that challenging of
power was something that really drew me to Trevor, and it's drawn me to
other protagonists in my films in the past too.

*What changed about you as you were making this film? Obviously, you
go into it with an idea of how this story might play out. And then at the
end, it might be something different or you've learned something. Did
you find that you had changed as a person?*

YBM: I suppose changing as an artist or storyteller would probably be the
more accurate thing for me. This whole process made me realise that you
can take certain risks in the way that you tell stories and that you don't have
to be didactic in the way that you tell it. I really enjoyed it as a filmmaker,
I enjoyed that creative process, I enjoyed the collaborative aspects of it.

You know, it really does take a village to make a film and there were some
fantastic people who worked on the film with me. We had a fantastic producer in Ivan O'Mahoney from In Films, we had Participant in the US, [a]
fantastic team out there. And our cinematographer Tom Bannigan who
was with me from the very beginning. Really, it was he and I who set the
visual tone for the piece from the very beginning. And having that continuity, I think, was really important for the film as a visual medium, but
also as a piece that's about an artist.

I had a fantastic editor, Francisco Forbes, who's got a philosophy film background. We had lots of debates during the edit because of it, which I loved.
I think I need someone to challenge, "Why are we doing it this way? Why
don't we do it this way?" Or really nutting out what layers of meaning are
we imbuing in this scene? And how should we do it? We had a fantastic
composer with Helena Czajka who took this idea I had of, "Hey let's use
NASA samples to another level." She scored whole music scores that are
composed completely of B-samples. You know, sounds from space, like

sounds from the International Space Station and Jupiter's moons. She managed to make this incredible score that really spoke to the themes of the film. It was a fantastic process, and there was a great team behind it.

Everything that you're saying about the sounds of the space station and finding art in the world in different ways really surprises me, because I have a very literal mind and I forget that we can use the sounds of machinery, we can use the sounds of space, we can use surveillance as art. And this film reminded me of that. There is a production company in the US, and their line is art and activism. And that is such a powerful way of describing what Unseen Skies is: art and activism. I love that it provokes my mind and says, "Think about this a little bit more."

YBM: I think the sorts of films that really draw me are at the intersection of art and the public interest, or art and social justice. And this was such a joy to work on because of that. Because the themes are just so important but at the same time, we're able to present them in a way that hopefully is relatable and also beautiful, so that the themes don't overwhelm you.

I think it is really beautiful. There is a shot where we're going through the gorges and the topography, and it's trying to make sense of the topography. These are things I've never seen before. I've never considered the world like this. And I like that, I like being having my life pushed back against me in some ways.

YBM: And that's what we were trying to do with the use of these algorithms. It's showing you an image, and you look at it, and you have your own interpretation of it. And then showing you what a machine is doing when they're looking at it and trying to interpret it. And then hopefully, that is a reminder that this is happening all the time. Our images are being analysed by machines for whatever the commercial application is, all the time.

Getting a sense of what that looks like, getting inside the black box, as it were, is important. And we're just trying to give you a taste of that. Because at the end of the day, if we're not critiquing these systems and we're not pushing for regulations to protect us from how our data is being used, then it'll just continue. Our data will continue to be collected. And what Frances Haugen said — the Facebook whistle-blower to US Congress — said about Facebook putting humans over profit. That will continue. And I think we need to start understanding and get a grasp of what is going on. Hopefully this film helps in some way to that end.

Is that where you see your filmmaking journey continuing, interrogating AI and computers and inside the black box?

YBM: I think there's a lot of correlations between the sort of work I do in terms of interrogating power and interrogating what the status quo is and what our assumptions are of that. And I think that's where my work will continue to head. One of my previous films was with Maria Ressa who won the Nobel Peace Prize, a Filipino journalist, and she does a lot of work against disinformation. She calls Facebook a frenemy. She's doing quite significant work globally in that space. And again, that's a woman who's interrogating power, a woman from the Global South no less, interrogating the power that is wielded from Silicon Valley. I think that's going to continue being the focus of my work, questioning power and our assumptions of how the world works.

REVIEW
LAURA'S CHOICE

ONE OF THE TOWERING ACHIEVEMENTS OF
AUSTRALIAN DOCUMENTARY FILMMAKING

In August 2006, I travelled with my grandfather to his home country of Scotland. Together, we drove across the land to almost all corners, catching up with his sisters and relatives, driving through the 'other' Perth, and even catching a glimpse of the ultra-Mel Gibson-looking William Wallace that carried a bemused look on its face that said "Yeah, I can't believe it too." We visited the Scottish Parliament House, and ate baked potatoes with haggis for lunch. In the streets of Edinburgh, my grandfather walked me to the point where my grandmother had slipped on the cobblestones and broke her hand years earlier, leading her to have countless surgical procedures that resulted in the removal of her middle finger.

My grandfather walked me through the history of his life in Scotland, visiting the town he grew up in. He told me of the troubles of growing up during World War II, where he was a few years too young to enlist, keeping him out the battles and leading to an immense frustration as buildings crumbled around his family under the bombing raids of attacking forces. It was a moment of bonding that you often read about happening to 'other' people, just like you're reading about it happening to me now.

The trip was a history lesson of Scotland, allowing me to fully appreciate how my grandparents found each other and started their life journey together. We discussed the pride he felt when he was able to explore the world, working under the Union Jack. Talking about Scotland led to exploring the complexity of Mary, Queen of Scots, and the lineage of the monarchy, and I grew to appreciate his world view even more.

It was clear to me how full a life my grandfather had lived, moving from Scotland to Australia, and raising a family in a foreign land. He delighted in telling stories of being chased by hippos in Tanzania, about disrupting an unruly troop of baboons. The joy he had from getting to see his grandchildren grow up was tangible.

Years later at a nondescript family event, after my grandmother passed away, my grandfather probed me and my ex-wife about the best way to end his life. There was little warning that that's what he would ask, with him springing the question when the rest of the family had gone inside to tend to other tasks. He'd grown tired of life, and as he lived alone, with no companions to while his time away with, he found himself contemplating a finality that escaped him. The signs of depression were there, and while discussing with him what he wanted from life, I ended up with the notion that maybe finding a canine companion to keep him company might lift his spirits. Sure enough, when a suitable pup came along, his life carried a purpose and he was encouraged to engage in activity. Outwardly, he had been given a boost, but it was merely a salve for the ensuing decade, as each of my discussions with him were tinged with that notion that he had lived a full life, and that he was finding it harder to shake the tiredness and oncoming degradation of body and mind.

We talked about wanting to visit Scotland again, which he did with family, and about the past and the future. It wasn't the only thing on his mind, but when I was with him, he felt comfortable enough to be open about his mental struggles. I'm grateful that I have been able to give him that kind of salvation, but now, in 2021, with my grandfather disappearing into the realm of dementia, I can't help but think of the farewell that he might have had if he were afforded the opportunity to engage in voluntary assisted dying.

If I'm being completely honest, I don't think my grandfather would ever have followed the path to engage in voluntary assisted dying, but I know that he would have found great comfort if the option were there. I know that he had researched how best to end his life if he so decided, and had discussed with me about what I thought. He often confided in me the desire to just pass away in his sleep, all the while lamenting the rarity of that occurring.

As a grandson, it was a complex situation to be in, but I felt the trust that my grandfather had in me had given him the space to discuss these difficult topics. I would never judge his thought pattern or the notion of ending his life. As time went on, my grandfather reduced the frequency he would talk about ending his life with me, something that I've now grown to realise was possibly due to his mind disappearing. At times, I felt alone in this deeply personal experience. While I brought up the subject with family, I'm not sure we ever had the toolset to actually approach what my grandfather was experiencing properly.

Then I watched *Laura's Choice*.

This beautiful, compassionate, funny, and life affirming documentary follows Laura Henkel, her daughter Cathy Henkel, and Laura's granddaughter, Sam Lara, as they share the journey of supporting Laura on the path of voluntary assisted dying. Laura is flanked by her family and friends who all support her journey, even if they initially struggle to reconcile with her decision. Additionally, we, the audience, are trusted by Laura to employ the empathy we all should carry, to understand and appreciate her choice, and to have our traditional notions of what death and dying means in our world of extended mortality.

Laura's Choice begins with Sam and Laura heading to Europe to embark on a cruise and visit destinations that Laura had long dreamed of visiting. Sam follows in her documentarian mother's footsteps with ease and comfort, immersing herself into the role of the eternal observer, capturing footage of Laura living a full life, exploring the sites, and making friends with everyone she meets. This was never intended to be the prelude to a story about a grandmother's voluntary assisted dying journey, but it feels like the most appropriate manner of introducing this narrative.

We get to experience the joy of Laura's life, with her living out the dream that we work our lives to achieve: overworking 40-plus hour weeks, just to have enough money to one day retire and travel the world, with energy-drained bodies and looming fragility. Sam's youthfulness buoys Laura's spirits and drive, and it's in these early moments that we get to see how supportive, inclusive, and all-embracing Laura is as a person. Each moment in her life is an opportunity to create a shared memory, an experience to remember.

The joy of a holiday together is fleeting, and in one of the most powerful moments of modern documentary cinema, we experience the lightness of unbridled joy as Sam puts the camera in Laura's hands, pushing her on her mobility aid walker, and running together with no worries in the world to bother them. Immediately, we're smiling, laughing, and full of every ounce of joy that life should bring, and then, in an instant, the camera falls, tumbling with Laura onto the pavement. Laura is injured. A tragic moment becomes one that is clearly difficult for Sam to grapple with as it brings an end to their trip, and hastens the ageing process for Laura.

Documentary filmmaking is rife with these kinds of scenes, where the unexpected occurs as the camera's rolling, and life-changing instances take place. These moments can't help but colour what comes after, and here, our anxiety and stress and concern for both Laura and Sam's health and mental state is elevated. Sam's ownership of the accident is painful to see, but the continued presence of Laura as the comforting grandmother eases some of that discomfort.

This resulting film is not the one that Sam intended to make, nor is it one that Cathy ever expected to make either. When Laura returns to her home in NSW, on the other side of the country from her daughter, she finds her life changed, and the reality of what's to come with the ageing process sinks in. She calls Cathy, asking her to come visit, with the intention of ending her life when she arrives. This discussion felt all too familiar to me, with Laura outlining what she would do, and Cathy, patiently and rationally talking her mother out of that decision.

The moments of my grandfather and I discussing what he had read, and talking about trying to acquire Philip Nitschke's contraband-adjacent book, *The Peaceful Pill Handbook*, in Australia, came flooding back. As Cathy assists Laura in exploring the possibility of voluntary assisted dying, I yearned for that kind of open discussion with my own grandfather. As shown in *Laura's Choice*, it is not about pushing a loved one down the path of voluntary assisted dying, but about opening up the discussion process to see if this is the path they truly wish to take.

Cathy and Sam frame the narrative of Laura's journey with scenes of a bonding session between mother and daughter on the family couch, reflecting on their shared experience of supporting Laura via a deep and meaningful discussion that gives each other the breathing space to decompress. I am beyond grateful for these scenes, especially in the manner that they each provide the other a judgement-free space to share their feelings. These moments are akin to a therapy session, but therapy sessions often come with the notion that they are private and enclosed, and of service to the patient alone. What these moments between Cathy and Sam do is encourage the viewer to find the space and empathy within their own family to discuss these difficult subjects without judgement. Naturally, this is not always possible, with each family member having their own lived-in journey that will inform how they engage with these topics, and additionally how they engage with their family members, but I would hope that through Cathy and Sam's combined compassion and empathy that viewers will be given some aspect of encouragement to approach these subjects within their own family and friend circles.

For Laura, the decision to enlist Cathy and Sam to document her story on film was clear: she intended *Laura's Choice* to be a firestarter, a call to action that would help bring about a much-needed discussion regarding end-of-life care in Australia. While many states have already implemented voluntary euthanasia laws, there are regions like the Northern Territory and the ACT where they are still waiting for the federal government to allow them to reinstate the right to make voluntary euthanasia laws. And even with these laws in place, there are reasonable arguments that they have not gone far enough in giving people the right to die.

We learn that for people who live in countries[23] where they have an end-of-life choice, they invariably choose to have a longer life, knowing that the option is there. Yet, for those living in Australia, the only choice regarding end-of-life decisions available in some states is in relation to how much 'suffering' the 'patient' is undergoing, and whether their life expectancy is less than six months or not.

During filming Sam and Cathy collectively took part in the protests at Western Australia's Parliament House, where hundreds of people made their voices heard about the need for the right to die. Voluntary assisted dying advocate and activist Belinda Teh appears, having reached the steps of Parliament House after walking 3,500 kilometres back to Perth in the name of her mother, who experienced agonising and painful final hours of her life[24]. Sam comments on the amount of older people there were at the rally, a vast difference compared to the often-youthful protests that have continued throughout the streets of Perth over the years. It's clear that for the ageing, the notion of a difficult, complicated, or traumatic death lingers on their mind.

I am loath to bring up this comparison, as I can understand the connotations of a person, or persons, being the deciding figure in whether someone lives or dies, something that *voluntary* assisted dying actively removes, but from my eight years as a veterinary nurse, I often heard from owners who had made the difficult decision to euthanise their animal companions, that they wished that we were able to have this option for ourselves. The term 'quality of life' is used across the board when it comes to deciding whether an animal has neared the end of their life or not, and while that differs from person to person, the reality is that the human companions are often pushed into a difficult position when deciding to release their animal companion from whatever ails them. In my eight years of nursing, I only encountered one animal, a twelve-year-old Cavalier King Charles Spaniel, who had passed away in their sleep. The rest were assisted along.

Yet, animals don't have the autonomy or agency that we do. We have to make the decision for them. For humans, we often don't have that luxury, which is why *Laura's Choice* is all the more powerful a film. For humans, we lament the fortune of people who pass away during their sleep, calling them 'lucky' for having a 'peaceful' death. We live in the 21st century, we shouldn't still be going through these immense struggles just to die with dignity.

While viewers may fear that the machinations of voluntary assisted dying might open up vulnerable people to exploitation, *Laura's Choice* seeks to assert the rules that are firmly in place to stop any possible nefarious manipulation of the process. We experience every step of Laura's journey, from the doctors' appointments to verify that Laura is of sound mind to make the decision to end her life, to the actual process of dying itself.

Much of the footage is captured by Cathy and Sam, with additional cinematography provided by Mahmudul Raz in Perth and Patrick Wally in Switzerland. Patrick Wally's drone shots are masterfully employed alongside the powerful score by Nicolette Boaz as we near Laura's final moments, with the aerial twilight shots of the Swiss countryside influencing the peaceful death that is soon to come. This is not a difficult or complex death, it is dying with dignity, and for this alone I am grateful that Laura trusted us with allowing to see her passing and for sharing her life with us.

Laura's dream of being an actress was sidelined throughout her life, and while she sought an audience in friends, family, and strangers, she was never truly encompassed by the title of being an 'actress'. In one of the most uplifting and inspirational moments in *Laura's Choice*, Sam gives Laura the celebration of the theatre that she so often craved in her life. With the looming date circled on the calendar, Sam organises a photo shoot with Laura, putting the spotlight on her and making her the star she should always have been. While there is frequent levity in *Laura's Choice*, this moment of celebration for Laura reminds us that we need to create moments and memories *now*, rather than when it's almost too late.

The same goes for the life celebration that takes place just before Laura embarks on her final journey abroad. It's almost become a trope how people talk about wanting to have a funeral before they die, a farewell party for the 'guest of honour', yet we rarely ever do it. In Kristen Johnson's essential documentary, *Dick Johnson is Dead (2020)*, Kristen presents a fictionalised funeral for her father, an act that has far too heavy an emotional toll for Dick's friends. Here, Cathy and Sam organise a Mad Hatter's tea party farewell for Laura, where the memories of her life can be celebrated with her there to experience it. Guests were given a book from Laura's collection to take home, and a photo of Laura, keeping a part of Laura's life with them always.

If you'll allow me a moment of introspection, I personally feel that the notion of having an event where my friends and family corral around a coffin and talk about my life in a past tense sounds, well, morbid. And it is morbid, but

I don't want my life to be defined by morbidity. I've lived a full life, and I've lived it with purpose and value and importance. Just as Laura lived a full life, and just as you have lived your own life. It's not egotistical or self-satisfying to say that I want to be celebrated while I'm here, and I want to be celebrated with my friends and family when I know that my time is coming to a close.

If there's one aspect of *Laura's Choice* that I hope all viewers take away with them and implement into their own lives, it's the celebration of a life lived with the person themselves there to bathe in the adoration, respect, love, and joy that they should be adorned with as their time come to a close. Seeing Laura's smile, and the warmth that emanates from her at her celebration, shows how important that moment was to her. It was the reminder of the greatness her life has brought, and the meaning that she brought to those around her. It's only human to desire that kind of affection from those we hold near to our hearts.

It's clear that for each moment in her life, and with each encounter she has, there is always an opportunity for Laura to make a new friend, and in many ways, when she calls on Cathy to document the voluntary assisted dying process, she is embarking on her final act of making new friends. Yet, this time, the friends she makes are ones she will never meet: us, the audience.

While everything I've written suggests that this is going to be a maudlin, depressing, and traumatic affair, the reality is the opposite. *Laura's Choice* is continually entertaining, occasionally hilarious, and deeply humanistic. This is one of the finest examples of empathetic filmmaking ever, and immediately stands as one of the towering achievements of Australian documentary filmmaking. I am quite certain that I will never see another film quite like *Laura's Choice*, and I'm forever grateful for having the experience of getting to know Laura Henkel.

I write this knowing full well that both Sam and Cathy will likely read this piece, and I take solace in knowing that this journey for them both, has been, and will likely continue to be, a difficult one. To have someone, a relative stranger, albeit one that they have both discussed the film at length with, sit here and critically assess their filmmaking, and conceivably, their 'life', presents a potentially unsettling prospect. Through *Laura's Choice*, we are invited into their family in a manner that feels wholly inclusive and all embracing, and I do hope that my words here have empowered the film and of Laura's invitation to experience the breadth and enormity of her choice.

Yet, I also write this knowing the immense gravity that comes with allowing an audience of strangers to experience a deeply personal journey, albeit one that is tinged with controversy, misinformation, and heightened community attention. And with that in my mind, I'm forced to turn to the form of dialogue I have with you, my trusted reader, a humble piece of film criticism.

I often hear from younger film critics that they struggle with reviewing or writing about documentaries, and I often wonder if it's that they might find difficulty in writing about, or critiquing, the 'real life' that's presented in a documentary. Yet, if I were to give some guidance in this piece, it would be for those writers, and for the viewers of films like *Laura's Choice*, to find that personal connection with the material, and to find themselves in the story. And then to also explore the directors' choices, as filmmakers, as people wanting to tell an empathetic and moving story.

I opened this review by talking about my grandfather, one Ian Jamieson, a person who I love deeply, and who has taught me more about life and living than I will ever truly understand. I know his time on this place we call Earth is getting shorter every day, and yet, I also know that he wouldn't want me to hang onto the sadness of his passing. Instead, I will hold onto those moments we spent together in Scotland, or when we would watch movies at the drive-in theatre in Busselton, or the subsequent enthusiasm that he had in retelling the absurdity and madness of Jim Carrey's *The Mask* for years after watching it, or listening to his passion for geography and the different landscapes around the world. This brilliant man, this kind soul, deserves celebration, and he also deserves dignity.

We all do.

Roger Ebert said "Movies are the most powerful empathy machine in all the arts"[25], and there's no deeper proof of that in action than with *Laura's Choice*. While this is a 'call to action' film, this is, oddly enough, a proudly entertaining experience. It feels odd, and possibly disrespectful, to say that, but the truth is, I know that I will be finding comfort in *Laura's Choice* again in the future. Comfort in knowing that Laura was able to die with dignity, and that she had the support and love of her family to do so. I will find comfort in the compassion, and the strength of Cathy Henkel and Sam Lara to tell this story. I will find comfort in knowing that there are people in the world who recognise the need to celebrate those we love, and to honour them with dignity.

This is not easy filmmaking, but nor should it be. Cathy is an established as an excellent filmmaker, and with her guidance and support, Sam is going to be an equally powerful filmmaker in her own right. It feels absurd to be talking about the quality of the direction here, especially at the close of this piece, but I do so in a way to say that this almost transcends the notion of what directing a documentary is. Together, Cathy Henkel and Sam Lara have created a powerful bond between one another as filmmakers, and as mother and daughter.

I want to thank them both for introducing us to the majestical Laura Henkel. I want to thank them both for their vulnerability, and for their strength. I want to thank Laura for trusting us with her story. And I want, for us all, to have the right to die with dignity.

INTERVIEW
LAURA'S CHOICE - DIRECTORS
CATHY HENKEL AND SAM LARA

Mother-daughter filmmaking team Cathy Henkel and Sam Lara united to tell the deeply personal story of Mother-Grandmother Laura Henkel in the documentary *Laura's Choice*. Throughout this powerful documentary, three generations of women navigate the path through to voluntary assisted dying.

Cathy Henkel is an award-winning filmmaker, having received the award for Best Documentary at the IF Awards in 2008 for her film *The Burning Season* (2008), as well as the Best Documentary Feature award at the 2004 Tribeca Film Festival for her film *The Man Who Stole My Mother's Face* (2003). Her other work includes *I Told You I Was Ill* (2005), about comedian Spike Milligan and *Rise of the Eco-Warriors* (2014), about protestors in the jungles of Borneo. Cathy shared an Australian Director's Guild nomination with Sam Lara for their work on *Laura's Choice*.

Sam Lara has been directing short films, music videos, and factual content for over ten years. She has been recognised with nominations at the Sydney Film Festival, Melbourne International Film Festival, Flickerfest International Film Festival, and the Byron Bay Film Festival, amongst others. Her previous work includes the short film *Featherweight* (2019), about a young boxer seeking her father's approval, as well as working in assistant directing capacity on acclaimed films like *Go!* (2020), *Below* (2020), *Three Summers* (2017), and *Top Knot Detective* (2017), amongst others. In 2020, Sam began serving as the Western Australian chapter head of the Australian Director's Guild.

Laura's Choice screened at the WA Made Film Festival in 2021, Perth's Revelation Film Festival in 2020, and screened via ABC over two nights during 2021.

Interview conducted February 2021.

I watched this last night. I was absolutely moved by it. Thank you so much. I found it beautiful. I want to thank you both for trusting the audience to tell your story and Laura's story. That's really hard. And I know it's hard because I've watched you both sit there on your couch, talking with each other. And that kind of openness has got to be really difficult. Thank you for being vulnerable for everybody else, because that's what this film feels like. As soon as I finished watching and I closed my laptop, I just wanted to say thank you and give you a hug. Because you've been through so much.

Cathy Henkel: Oh, that's really lovely.

Sam Lara: Thank you.

CH: Hug accepted.

SL: Social COVID-safe hug.

And thank you for trusting me to do an interview with you and talk to you about this. Because the first kind of thing is there is a button on this film. And the button is Laura's journey and Laura's story, in the sense that this is supposed to be a call to action, a spark. How do you deal with that emotional transference of carrying on this kind of story and this legacy for somebody who's so close to you both?

CH: Wow, okay, going straight to the hard stuff.

I'm really sorry. I am sorry.

CH: All right. Oh, look, this is a question we're grappling with.

My mum was very insistent that first of all we make the film. She has had a film made about her before [*The Man Whole Stole My Mother's Face*]. And she saw the power that that film had to create a conversation and an impact in the area of sexual assault and victim-blaming and so forth. She's the one who said, "I want you to make this film. But I want it not just to be my story, I want it to be about the bigger issue of how the elderly manage their last days and how they deal with death, and I want it to provoke a conversation." She was so insistent on that.

She went to the media herself, she went through the whole process of applying to the clinic herself, and she dragged us along, filming. And we came to see a huge amount of benefits from this way of dying, and we can talk about that separately. But in terms of the impact she wanted, really she just wanted us to start this conversation. And here we are doing it. We hope that the ABC broadcast will generate a lot of conversation. We're expecting some of it will be not particularly in favour of what my mum did and may even be a bit antagonistic or hostile. We don't know how that's going to happen or how we're going to deal with it. But that is the tricky part of this project — putting something out that is so personal at my mother's wishes and saying, "Let's have a conversation, bring it on."

And it is a really necessary and relevant conversation. I believe that the ABC audience will really appreciate this kind of story. And it's something that needs to be discussed for sure. Sam, I'm going to give you a bit of an easier question to launch off things. I've been a fan of your mum's work for a long period of time, I think that you're a fantastic and really brilliant documentarian, and thank you for your work there. Sam, what is it like learning from somebody like Cathy? What is it like growing and appreciating how to be a filmmaker?

SL: Historically, we've made very different films. Throughout my childhood, my parents were both documentary filmmakers, and I had absolutely no interest in filmmaking to begin with, and then absolutely no interest in documentary. I wanted to work purely in scripted, because I thought that's where all the fun happened. And sort of fell into making some short form factual stuff, but again quite different in content to my mum.

And then this came along, and Grandma set the challenge to both of us. And I had set out to make a film about our Euro trip. When we went on our 2016 adventure, I thought, a twenty-four-year-old and an eighty-six-year-old traveling Europe — this is going to be a hoot, it's going to be really light-hearted. And obviously, there were lots of obstacles that we didn't anticipate. I had come with this footage and with this idea in mind, and then when Grandma decided that she was ready to go and she asked us to make this film, I had a third of the film there ready. Cathy started filming the stuff that happened in the middle, and it just sort of organically happened, and Grandma set the challenge to us to work together and make this thing.

Look, it was challenging, it was really hard. Mum and I were both grieving and trying to deal with what Laura had asked us in our own way and also our own really complicated and different relationships. It was really difficult. But I think ultimately, when you've got a shared project with someone, it has a way of bringing you together, because you've got shared goals. I think it was quite an incredible thing to do with someone while you're both grieving. It brought out a lot of stuff that we might have suppressed otherwise. And it forced us to put our feelings into words for narration. We had to plot our characters' journeys. We were forced to talk about a lot of things. It was incredibly difficult. Being down in the trenches ultimately, I think, it's going to have made us stronger as a family.

In terms of what I learned about filmmaking: it was a baptism by fire. Don't ever put yourself in a film. Don't ever put yourself in a room while you're grieving. I mean, there's so many rules that we broke. I wouldn't recommend it to anyone. Cathy would come into the edit suite every Friday, and it was like having someone check your work. An incredibly experienced documentarian coming in, and Cathy's so good with story and structure and narration. It was so great having that kind of outside perspective to sort of stop me from drowning at the end of every week.

CH: I mean, the beautiful thing is we both learned things. I learned an enormous amount from Sam. I think she's a very gifted filmmaker, and I'm gonna say I think she's better than I am. I think she's got a real flair and a natural, instinctive talent that's just divine. I learned a lot as well and was able to pass on the odd thing I've learnt over my few years. It was really a mutually learning experience. As difficult as it was, there was underlying respect there that helped us through and that was there all the time and I think remains to this day, respectful of what we each bring to the project which was complementary and different. The end result is that combination of two very different filmmakers from different generations being sort of thrust together and having to make it work.

Laura Henkel
Image Credit: Sam Lara. Used with permission

And I guess in a way you have Laura as the backbone there as well, ensuring it's a request which would be hard to deny. I know that we see what your reactions are to start off with in the film, but what kind of headspace were you both in discussing at the time? When Laura says, "I want you to make this film," how did you both discuss that process?

CH: Well, at first when she asked me, I just thought, "Well, I will just humour her and we'll just make a little home movie that will be a tribute piece to mum." And Sam's got this beautiful footage of the Euro trip that may or may not be a separate film. At first I was really reluctant to see it as an ABC production, for example. But as we progressed and the story started to unfold and we both began to realise that our journeys were fascinating even to us, that we were learning so much about how families cope with this — and then also, we had support from our state agency — and an award that we won very early on, the Brian Beaton award — that was encouraging us to see this as a film, and that it was a film that there was a big audience for. So we came to that really quite late in the piece. Sam, you might have a different answer to that. But that's my answer.

SL: No, I think that's spot on. I think it was never one day we were just a normal family going through something, next day, we were going to make a big film about it. It happened really kind of slowly and it kind of crept up on us. I think we started filming things at her request. And then like Cathy said, we got some interest and some support. And I think we still sort of thought maybe it was just a smaller project. It just happened quite organically that it turned into an ABC commission and the product that you've seen.

CH: And I think when we got to Switzerland, those last four days which form about a quarter or a third of the film were just so extraordinary. The things that were happening and the way mum was dealing with it. We had this beautiful cinematography and sound team come down from Vienna to film it. I remember one scene one time, Patrick's [Wally] drone footage of Switzerland and I just [went] "Oh my god, this is a film. This is a beautiful film." And everything that happened in Switzerland was just really riveting to us. And we thought if we can capture this and put this in the film, I think it will be really interesting and very dramatic and compelling.

I really love the cinematography here. And I love the way that it accentuates the peacefulness of voluntary assisted dying. Because I think what this film does — if you don't mind me saying — is that this film strips away the mentality that a lot of people might have about the process that goes on. There's still quite a lot of archaic [expectations about] what actually happens in this process. And the beautiful cinematography paired with the footage of these final moments are just — it shows how peaceful it all actually is. And I really appreciate that, again coming back to that honesty.

I will say this is probably one of the hardest interviews I'll ever do because it is so personal. And it's not just personal for you, but it's personal for everybody who goes through this kind of thing. We all have family members, my grandfather is going through something very similar. And I recall having discussions with him about end-of-life care and he didn't feel confident enough to be able to actually have those discussions with anybody other than me. What your film does manages to allow, encourage, and support people to give their relative the space to have those discussions. That's a lot of words, I'm sorry.

SL: That's what we've found. No, no, I mean this is not unusual. I think what we've really found is when we've had screenings is that everybody has a story. And people feel really compelled to share it after they've watched the film. It's something that people really want to talk about, and this film gives them an opportunity to. I think that's quite magic.

In terms of showing what happened on the day that she died, I am an organiser, I like to know what's going to happen, I like to be able to plan for things, I have an Excel spreadsheet for everything. And I couldn't find anything anywhere that showed what actually happens when someone goes to Switzerland. It's always they go into a room, and they shut the door, and that's where the film ends.

First of all, showing someone passing away and showing that it can be quite peaceful is really important. But also just for other people who have a family member who's maybe going to go through this, showing them what happens in terms of you have time with the body, and then the police come, and then they are going to take the body away, and then you have the opportunity to go to the cremation. Just knowing the steps of what's going to happen for my brain was so helpful. For me, I felt I wanted to show that for the families' benefit, other families who are going to go through it.

Everything that you just said is what we hear when people come out of the screening. I think that's really positive that people want to share these stories and that they feel able to. We're actually in the process of building a website for *Laura's Choice*. It's going to have a part called Laura's Kitchen Table[26]. The idea is that conversations that change the world happen around a kitchen table. That's where they begin. It's a forum for people to come and have safe and respectful conversations about end-of-life choices. Because I think after the public screening, everyone can talk. But after an ABC broadcast, people are gonna want to talk about this with other people if they've watched it alone. And so we're hoping to give them an opportunity to do that.

Definitely.

SL: There you go. I word-vomited back at you.

That's good, thank you.

CL: I agree that everyone finds their own way into the story and makes it personal, and that's one of the unique factors about this. It's not a film that people walk away with a shrug. Everybody finds themselves or their family or someone they know somewhere in this film. For me, it was the opportunity to show a peaceful death, a beautiful death. I feel very privileged to have been able to say farewell to a parent in such a beautiful way, in such a profound way. And I think that seeing that, and that that's possible, and also that she wanted it to be joyful, and she wanted to be not sombre. She wanted fun, she wanted it to be a glorious celebration of her.

And how good is the music score as well? We're just so privileged to have had the wonderful music of Nicolette Boaz who composed some music that still brings goosebumps to me — to be able to add that and really bring out just how profound and beautiful death can be. I hope that people will embrace that and not feel always death is something to look away from or to avoid or just not even talk about. I really acknowledge you for doing this interview because even journalists are scared of the topic for some reason and yeah, so you've been bold to jump in.

Thank you. If there's one thing which I've noticed with the choice of subjects that you've chosen as a filmmaker, Cathy, they often — not all of them of course, but they have tackled subjects that are relatively considered taboo in our society as a whole. I feel like nowadays we can openly talk about sex and that's perfectly fine. That used to be a taboo, but now death is kind of being embraced as a major taboo that we don't talk about it, even though the world has gone through this major catastrophe and everybody has experienced it in some ways. And this film really takes us down that path. I'm curious for you as a director, is there a desire or a conscious drive to want to unveil the natural instincts and the nature of these taboos, that they shouldn't be taboo at all?

CH: Well, I think so. I mean, I am definitely my mother's daughter. She was very unconventional and very thinking outside the box and eccentric to a degree and definitely didn't conform to the rules of society. She was a really independent thinker, and she encouraged me to be independent, questioning things and tackling issues that aren't normally tackled.

I mean, with *The Man Who Stole My Mother's Face*, we dived into victim-blaming, which at that point hadn't really been much talked about, or the notion that rape is a men's issue was quite new. Mum was very, very keen on breaking those taboos. And then of course, she's done it with this topic. I also addressed with the Spike Milligan film the idea of comedians with manic depression or with depression that they often go hand in hand. And at that point, talking about mental health was again taboo. So I have done that.

And I guess it's partly — I have to credit my dear mother for planting that instinct in me, and maybe I've planted it in you, Sam. I don't know. Possibly.

SL: Time will tell.

Sam, where do you feel that your journey will go from here? I mean, this is a pretty big start.

SL: Yeah. I'm still so deep in this film, to be honest. There's still so much work. I'm one of the producers as well as the co-director. In the lead up to this ABC broadcast, it's pretty full on. We're also doing an exhibition to go along with the film which has been really a great outlet for my creativity after dealing with deliverables and paperwork for the past few months. So that's having its opening night two weeks from today. It'll be at the Spectrum gallery at Edith Cowan University, and it's called Conversations Around a Kitchen Table. There'll be a big kitchen table in the middle where you're encouraged to sit down and talk about death with your loved ones or with friends or strangers. There will also be interactive video displays and photos from the film. So that's where all my energy is going at the moment. It's really, really exciting to be playing in a different medium. And then watch this space.

With that in mind, do you think that the modern filmmaker needs to be tapped into different mediums nowadays to get the message and the film out? One of the things which I've noticed of late, especially with the documentaries in Australia, is that there is a post-platform release where there is the film, and then there is a podcast, or there's a discussion or there's a website. How important is that for you both as filmmakers to have that continued discussion point beyond the film itself?

SL: I think it's project-dependant. For this one, it makes a lot of sense. And there is some kind of multi-platform opportunities with it. It's not a temporary issue. Everyone will die, everyone has known someone who's died. It's totally universal and permanent, we can't escape it. And I think it makes sense for this film to have a life after the broadcast and for us to sort of nurture that. But I don't know if every project needs it. It depends if you have an impact strategy or not. I quite like these other elements of filmmaking. I like dipping my toe into other artforms. I think it's really exciting and it keeps things fresh. But yeah, I think it's totally project dependent. What do you think, Cathy?

CH: Well, I was going to say impact projects do require some kind of platform in place where people can have the conversation and where you can find out more. Probably about half of the films that I've made have had an impact campaign, so it's not new for me and it has quite a long history, and they've become now almost part and parcel with documentary. I just love the idea of trying new ways of engaging with your audience.

And this exhibition, as Sam said, is just so much fun and a really fresh way for us to put these ideas into a physical space and have people come in and, you know, I'm very excited for opening it and seeing how that plays. But yes, this film has a long life. It's not going to date, I think, and we need to set up something that will give it that permanence where it can continue. I mean, I'm keen to let it go and say, "There, Mum, we did it. Bye." But I think we need to have a place where people will continue to discover it. Of course, it has its international journey still to come. I think we're going to be living with this for some time. We just want to have a place for it to comfortably and safely and respectfully land and be managed.

With that in mind, there's two more questions that I want to touch on, and they blend into one another in a way. How do you both prepare yourself for that continued journey for this film? Not just the obvious things, going to see a therapist and talking about, but I'm hoping that you're both being kind to yourselves, because it's hard to approach this kind of film on a regular basis. I just want to know that you're both okay, is basically what I'm trying to say.

CH: Oh, that's very sweet. Therapy is a part of it. Yeah, it's taken its toll on my health, for sure. And I'm in a recovery phase. I didn't quite anticipate how rough it was going to be. So I'm in recovery now.

And yeah, how do we prepare for the next stage? I don't know. We're just doing still one day at a time really, aren't we, Sam? There's just such an endless list of things to do. You just really have to wake up every day and just get on with it. I hope that the ABC broadcast will bring some part of it to an end. But I don't know. It all depends on how people respond and what happens after which we really don't know, do we?

SL: No. I'm a big advocate for therapy, though. And I've been seeing a therapist since the trip with my grandma, specifically. I'm sure you remember the fall that happens quite early on in the film. So I had some EMDR therapy to recover from that which was transformative. I think preparing ourselves for other people's emotional responses — it brings up a lot in people, and there are going to be people who are very, very opposed to what my grandma did. I don't know how you prepare for that. I don't know if you probably can, other than going, "That person has their own life experiences and I have mine and we have differences and that's fine." And I guess we don't know what's going to happen after the broadcast. Sort of like there's a cliff there and we're not sure what the path goes up after that. So we'll see.

CH: We've got little parachutes though, haven't we, Sam? I don't know if they're going to hold up.

One of the things which I've gathered from the film is that you both have a really strong support network. And that's really helpful when dealing with the loss of a family member, when dealing with the release of a film, even the stresses and anxieties of day-to-day life. And I guess you both are in such a unique situation where it's all compounded into one kind of entity. Again, I hope that you've been kind to yourselves, because that leads me into my next question and the final thing that I want to talk about. The joy in this film, the positivity here — because, you read the description of what Laura's Choice is going to be, and the immediate reaction I'm sure for many people is "I'm going to be crying throughout this entire film." And you're not. There is something about this film that — I could put this on again right now and laugh and cry and feel warm and happy and all this kind of stuff. Because Laura is such a beautiful, joyous person and we're all lucky to have spent two hours with her and getting to know her and love her. I guess what I want to know is how do you both feel about sharing that kind of joy? How important was that for you both to share?

CH: We should have started with this!

I should have.

SL: Can we take that quote and put it on the website?

CH: It actually brought tears to my eyes when you were saying that. That joy is so important to the story and to us. She turns out to be very funny. I was quite surprised at just how cheeky and funny she was towards the end. She constantly surprised us. We had wonderful surprises like Dr. Christian who — when people see the film, this doctor who comes to assess her turns out to be really quite hilarious. And so the joy of it is terribly important, and I'm glad you picked up on it. The ABC are billing it as a joyous end of life story, and I think that's a really good way to present the film.

I think that's the best way of saying it. It is a joyous story. Sorry, Sam, you continue.

SL: No, I was just gonna say I think life is totally absurd. You have in your mind of how really big serious events are meant to go, and ridiculous stuff always ends up happening. Life is not sentimental at all. Dr Christian is the perfect example of that. That's not how we thought that day was going to go at all. And it's the same with Grandma, she was just full of surprises and she really set the tone that she wanted it to be joyous. You know, the photoshoot that I did with her in the theatre — that was such a joyous day, and I know that I wouldn't have done that if I didn't know the day that she was going to die. It's unexpected, but having a confirmed death approaching creates moments of joy and beauty that you wouldn't otherwise have.

CH: And I think for audiences, the idea of a farewell party to say goodbye to of family and community — it's not a celebration we normally have. One of the things I think that comes from the film [is] that it's a good way to end a life and to have a celebration of your life. While you're still there, people can say what they want to say and hear what they have to say. It was very beautiful. Of course, Mum chose to frame it as the Mad Hatter's Tea Party, so we had to dress up in ridiculous costumes and wear funny ears. But again, it added to the zany joyousness. And there's some things we added in the film that just makes Sam and I laugh and we left them in because we find it funny. We really did want to make sure that there was a good balance between what is quite profound and at the same time was very joyous.

I love this film. I'm grateful that you're both sharing this story and have each other, because I think that there are so much to take away from this film. And certainly for me at least, one of the things is I know I want to have a life celebration before I go. I want to have friends and family around to do that. And I think that that's something that we need to do more often. Because we don't know when we're going to go. Sometimes we do get a choice, sometimes we don't. We've got to make every moment count which sounds so silly. But this film shows that we need to make every moment count because, as you were saying, Sam, you wouldn't have done the photoshoot if you didn't have that date. And we need to do more photoshoots, we need to do more of those kooky things.

CH: The Buddhist in the film makes a comment [which] I think might be a nice way to leave this: "The more we focus on death, the more we appreciate the life that we have." And it's therefore not something to be avoided. Because knowing the date made us really get the best out of every bit of the last days with Mum. So I do think there's a value in thinking about death as it does deepen your appreciation of life.

Yes, I think that's a perfect way to wrap up.

SL: Thank you, Andrew.

Thank you, Sam.

INTERVIEW
GIRL LIKE YOU - DIRECTORS FRANCES ELLIOTT AND SAMANTHA MARLOWE

Co-directors Frances Elliott and Samantha Marlowe document the relationship of Lauren and Elle, a couple who experience the complexities of staying together as Elle transitions genders in *Girl Like You*. Filmed over six years, *Girl Like You* explores the fluidity of gender and sexual identity, while also embracing the pressures of love and companionship.

Frances has worked in film and TV for over ten years, and is known for the award nominated short film *The Beeman* (2018), about a conservationist an unwanted swarm of bees, as well as her work in different creative capacities as an editor, writer, and script supervisor on fellow Western Australian filmmakers work like *Sparkles* and *Featherweight*.

Samantha Marlowe is a documentary filmmaker who has worked as a writer and director in both TV and film. She has worked as an editor and writer on the acclaimed series, *Desert Collectors* (2020-22). Alongside fellow filmmaker France Elliott and producer Cody Greenwood, Samantha was nominated for her work on *The Beeman* at the 2018 ATOM Awards.

Alongside producer Cody Greenwood, Frances and Samantha won the award for Innovation in Feature Documentary/Non-Fiction at the West Australian Screen Culture Awards in 2021.

Interview conducted November 2021.

Readers are advised that the next interview contains discussions about dead-naming, supporters fatigue, and mental illness.

▶▷▶

If you could tell yourselves anything at the beginning of filming, what would you say?

Frances Elliott: Oh my god. I think the thing that I would probably tell myself — the biggest thing that Sam and I learnt in terms of documentary filmmaking is we started the process as very much that old-fashioned way of making documentaries, which is just sitting them down and just having really long conversations in sit-down interviews. And I guess what we realised throughout the evolution of telling the story is a better way to make documentaries and get your point across is actually just filming people in their natural state and just watching it happen.

Our documentary really evolved over time from being quite interview-heavy to be more cinema verité. And I think that's something that we'll definitely go on with in our next documentaries. Because you can tell so much about the couple and how they're going and where their relationship is at by just watching them interact with each other and being set in different settings with different people, rather than sitting down and asking them about it. That's definitely the biggest thing I learned from it.

Samantha Marlowe: Yeah, that was a huge one. And I think another one as well is if we had known that it's going to be a six-year timeframe at the beginning, I just don't know how we even would have processed that. I think Frances and I were really naive at the beginning. We thought we'll sit down, we'll film Elle's transition. It'd be a year, a year and a half, and then we'll pump out a documentary and we'll have this great piece of reference for the queer community and the trans community. But it just evolved from there.

We couldn't stop filming, we had to keep filming the story. And the road to getting it funded as well, it was a really, really long road to getting it funded. We had no concept of that as emerging filmmakers in our early 20s. We thought we would be able to do a couple of applications here and there... The story is so great, the story needs to be told. We were so passionate about the story that we thought that it was a shoo-in to get funding, but it turned out to be such a longer journey than that as well. That was a great question. If we could tell ourselves something back there, definitely the style aspect, and also just prepare yourself for the work that's to come.

FE: I'm almost glad that we didn't know that it was going to be six years at the beginning of it. Because as Sam said, we really thought that Elle would immediately start transitioning and we could cover it in a year. But the reality was that Elle didn't make the decision to transition until two years into our filming. And then she's still transitioning today. Transitioning takes a really, really long amount of time and we definitely didn't know that at the beginning.

One of the things which I'm really grateful for with films like Girl Like You existing is because the public consciousness of what it means to go through a transition is, "Oh you just start taking pills, and suddenly, you've got breasts and you're a woman," or, "Your breasts somehow disappear and you're a man." No, that's not how things work. It is a very long process. It's not just an overnight thing. And there is a mental health aspect to it too, which is all encompassed in the film in such a powerful, powerful man-

ner. You hinted at it in your response there before, but did you have an idea of the complexity of what you were engaging with when you started?

SM: Yeah, we definitely didn't. Like you said, I think Frances and I, we were really ignorant at the beginning of the filmmaking too. Even though Elle was a close friend of ours and we cared about her deeply and we had long conversations with her, it was really a journey of us learning all the complexities surrounding a gender transition — the time, the social, emotional, mental, financial factors that come into that.

The part of the film that we're proud that we covered is Elle's confusion on where she sat within the gender spectrum and coming to that conclusion in her own way. She went on a journey herself and learning what does it mean to be male or female? It's not just masculine or feminine qualities. There's so much more to that. I think all of us went through a journey of learning about all those complexities.

FE: And we really wanted to cover that aspect of Elle juggling because I feel like in a lot of transgender narratives that we saw, it's this thing that happens where transgender people often say, "I knew since I was four years old, and internally I knew exactly what I wanted to be, and it was just the outside who was pushing back. So I couldn't go on hormones until I did all these things." But we also wanted to normalise the fact that it's a big decision and it's okay not to be sure. And, I think Elle did it very responsibly in the way that she really didn't jump headfirst into it until she was sure. And we really liked that period of indecision and self-doubt in the film.

The film is not just about Elle's transition, but it's also about her relationship with Lauren as well. That's got to be such a difficult thing, to get them to be open and accept that the cameras are there and filming their lives. And there was an interesting moment where Lauren's at work and everybody's asking, "Why are these people stalking you? Why are they stalking you?" And the openness of A) why you're there filming her and B) what's going on in her personal life is really difficult for her to engage with, especially in working in the drag racing scene. What conversation did you have with both Elle and Lauren as the film was going along?

SM: I mean, it's interesting with us, we're in such a unique situation where, as filmmakers we're so lucky with Elle and Lauren because our friendship allowed them to trust us so much that there was no conversation had, they would just be as candid and as raw. It was like sitting on a couch with your friend and having a conversation. And I think that shows through on film because they're just saying how they feel in that moment, wearing their hearts on their sleeve. We never really had to have a conversation where we sat down and pitched to them, "We want you to just let the walls down" because the trust was already there with them. I think for us as well, Frances, you could probably speak more to when boundaries were crossed with Lauren.

FE: It was. They were really great with opening up to us. And I think that that was because we were such close friends with them that it was just like we were hanging out and filming. I remember Lauren saying at one point really early on, "Oh, I understand how the Kardashians feel now." Because after a while you just become so oblivious to the cameras because they're always there that you sort of ignore them, which I thought was really funny.

But there were definitely moments where we did push the boundaries a bit. And I know one of the conversations that we have with Lauren. There's a clip in the documentary which is really important. It's when we're at Heidi's, and Lauren's having a breakdown in the kitchen with Elle. And she's speaking about how she has compassion fatigue and supporters fatigue. I filmed that on my iPhone when we're at a party.

That was one of those things that we discussed on camera later when Lauren was like, "You know, I understand the importance of that being in the film because it represents so clearly where I was and was absolutely the bottom of what I went to. But you know, at a certain point, you're my friend, we're at a party. I don't want you to film me when I'm crying." I know that was one of her limits. But at the same time they both are very understanding of how those parts of the film were crucial to showing the audience really how bad things were for them at that time and what they were going through emotionally.

You were talking about trans narratives in films and documentaries before. Were there any particular films that you had looked at as a templates of what to follow, or what not to do with depicting trans stories on film, especially in documentaries?

SM: It was actually a really interesting thing, when we first started making the film, and we were searching around for reference films with transgender content and relationships. And there just wasn't any. There was nothing in Australia, and there was barely anything overseas. And that's why it became super crucial for us to tell the story.

You can see in the film that a really big part of Elle's journey to deciding whether or not to take hormones is her scouring the internet for answers, because there isn't any clear-cut bible for her to go to. She didn't have anyone really to relate to. So she's going on YouTube and looking for things here and there. And Frances and I found ourselves doing that as well, just trying to find content anywhere. I'd seen a couple of things which had really piqued my interest like Jazz Jennings. That was a YouTube series at the time, and we wanted to make something that was mainstream and accessible.

FE: One of the initial conversations that we had with Lauren and with Elle was that empathy for them, that they didn't have anything that reflected what they were going through. They couldn't talk to people around them in the same way that we could when we're in a cisgender relationship about what we were going through. And we really wanted this film to be something that transgender people could look at and see themselves represented properly on the big screen. And as well, trans people with transgender partners to reference their experience and feel seen and heard in this documentary. We really wanted this to be the point of reference for all those people.

That was one of the things which I've noticed throughout the years is that trans narratives have traditionally been shown either by cisgender actors or actresses like Eddie Redmayne. And, sure, they get Oscar nominations and awards, but there's no authenticity there. And they are often narrative films. Whereas in the documentary realm, I can only think of — outside of this film — there's It's Not Just Me (2017), Jonathan Messer's documentary, which screened at Revelation Film Festival a few years ago, and then Sam Feder's Disclosure (2020), and that's really about it. And both of those came out during the production of this.

FE: We even made a conscious choice that we wanted to put some really global and universal themes in this documentary. Themes of love and heartbreak and self-sacrifice, and things that pretty much everyone can relate to, because we didn't want this film to just be for the LGBTQI community. We wanted it to be for everyone, and hit a really mainstream audience. Because as well, we wanted it to be something that cis people could watch and take down their own biases that they have about transgender people and to normalise the transgender relationships that are going on around us.

I think a lot of times, a lot of cis people see transgender relationships and queer relationships as other to their own. But I think when you watch Elle and Lauren's story, you can connect to them on an innate human level, and I know a lot of people after the film were going, "Oh I relate to their relationship so much. And I had a partner who did this, and I had a partner who did that." So it's connecting people in a way that drops their own biases around transgender relationships. It's what we're really seeking to do.

With six years of footage, how do you pick what's the best thing to show that would represent and support the narrative as a whole?

SM: A lot of time in post-production. Frances and I spent a lot of time throughout the whole process, because as you said, it's classic indie film filmmaking where it really was just Fran and I. We would watch every shot, we would log it personally; this is before the days of putting it in, and getting spat out transcripts. But that was really valuable to us in a lot of ways because we knew all of these interviews back to front, and we knew everything that was discussed within them. So when it came to the writing process of finally piecing it together at the end, we spent a lot of time and thought into how we were going to structure this film. Frances can talk a little bit more to it, she comes from a background of writing, so it was super valuable for this process to just be able to follow the drama structure that Frances has followed in previous films that she's made.

FE: I come from a drama writing background, and I spend a lot of time in writers' rooms and conceptualising TV and film ideas and stuff like that. And Sam and I employed the three-act structure in this film that drama uses which basically follows the character's emotional journey. You have a flawed troubled character at the centre of it who goes through an emotional journey and a transformation on screen. And that helped us a lot in terms of putting this film together and making it as potent as we possibly could. Because we really followed the structural things in drama which make it as dramatic and engaging as possible.

It is supremely engaging. Where so you plan to go from here? Is this kind of the field that you aim to continue working with? And knowing that this one took six years, how will you address the next one?

FE: Our plan is to move forward in a very similar way. Sam and I want to keep co-directing everything. And we're working with our producer Cody [Greenwood] who played a really big role in getting *Girl Like You* financed, and helping us through that production. So we're going to move forward in a similar way.

We are in pre-production for our next feature documentary which follows Renee Gracie. She's one of Australia's first Supercars stars. She was the first female to race in Bathurst in seventeen years, and she got pushed out of the industry due to sexism and being sexualised because she's a young beautiful woman. She's now turned to OnlyFans and she's actually Australia's number one earner on OnlyFans. She is so interesting and so amazing. It explores a lot of similar themes that we are really interested in, which are sexuality, gender and feminism.

In terms of the six-year thing, I certainly hope it doesn't take us that long. The really good thing about *Girl Like You* is when we were trying to get it funded, we really didn't have anything to show as proof that we could do it. We had a couple of short documentaries that had done quite well on the festival circuit, but no proof we could make a feature film which is a completely different kettle of fish. I think now we do have *Girl Like You*, I'm hoping the funding process will be a bit easier in terms of getting it funded. And I think when money comes, it kicks things along enough in a faster gear. We had to do things with *Girl Like You* very differently because we just had no budget for five years. Everyone was making it. It's a passion project. But I think definitely Sam and I want to continue on the same route and put at the centre of filmmaking connection and empathy and discovery. And we want to keep doing that.

I think that's really important. I've talked to Cody Greenwood before, I love Cody's work. She's one of the most exciting producers that's working today, supporting projects like yourselves and Sparkles. What's it like working with Cody?

SM: Cody is a powerhouse. She's just born to be a producer. She's born to be a creative. We got really lucky with Cody because at the beginning of our *Girl Like You* journey, we were all emerging filmmakers, we're all roughly around the same age. We pitched the project to Cody and she was instantly on board. And to have her working on this project as a passion project, like Frances said, for five years, and just absolutely exhausting every avenue for us. Cody said to us early on, "I will get this film financed." And she was very serious about that. And she quite simply did not stop until she did. One of Cody's specialties is getting films financed, and she's very, very good at it. And we're just so lucky to have her. She's very across everything. She has great relationships with everyone and we love her. Shout out Cody.

It's nice when you get a producer like that. For me, as somebody who enjoys watching Australian films, there are so many emerging filmmakers like yourselves. And sometimes I don't know anything about the project. And I'm like, "Oh, I'll just pop this on, watch it and enjoy it." But then you see a name like Cody, and I'm like, "Yep, I can trust everything that is going on here."

FE: I think she would be very, very happy to hear that because she makes a lot of really conscious decisions about what films she wants to be putting into the world and really sort of selects them quite carefully, so I think she'd be really happy to hear that.

I think she does a great job supporting filmmakers like yourselves. How much does the identity of being a Western Australian play into being filmmakers for you? This film really embraces the WA art scene, both film and music. How important is that to you as filmmakers?

SM: It's hugely important to us. We're really lucky in WA because there is an exceptional amount of female documentary filmmakers within the WA industry which is really amazing. And it feels like we're in this new wave where, with all these female filmmakers which are all emerging and in the same space as us, we're all looking at things through a female lens which is something that Frances and I are super conscious with the films that we're making and the themes that we're exploring. I think in that sense, just having amazing filmmakers within this industry that are female peers is great as well.

FE: That was really important for Sam and I. We had a lot of female directing mentors and people that we could go to, to help us through it. That was really important. And also, for us the telling of this story, like you touched on before, our idea of what transitioning is comes from an American upper-class version of it, with people like Caitlyn Jenner who go behind closed doors for a couple of months and come out completely transformed. But the reality is Elle and Lauren were living in middle-class Western Australia. And they're musicians and they're artists, and the whole process of transitioning within that area is very, very different, because it means they don't have a lot of access to money, they can't afford to go to therapy. It's such a different journey.

Sam and I really wanted to make some conscious efforts within this film to really paint a picture of the landscape that they're going through this in. For example, we kept the characters quite contained, because what they were going through was very much behind closed doors and only shared with the people closest to them. At one point in the journey, we were like "we're going to talk to endocrinologists and doctors and surgeons and all that sort of stuff." And then we were like, 'no, that's not the reality of what they're doing and their experience.'

In WA and largely the world, the world around them is so gendered. We really wanted to represent that in the film. Really little things about the film are really conscious choices that Sam and I are making. Every cutaway in the film and B-roll, we've made sure to include gendered aspects of the world around them. When we do a wide shot of their house, we have a woman with a pram walking past and a nuclear family walking past to just show really what Elle and Lauren are up against.

One of the really powerful elements of Girl Like You is how those gender biases just slip into how we talk about things. And there's this transition from the dead-naming of Elle and calling her 'him' in the beginning when friends, family members and especially Lauren are dealing with the reality of what their future is like together. There's that really devastating moment where they're talking about proposing and Lauren, without a

conscious aspect says, "Oh, you know, Elle will be the one that will pro-
pose" and she says it in a joking way. And Elle understandably takes it
in a very heartbroken manner because "oh, it's the man's role to do that."
And so those gendered stereotypes really make you consider how we talk
and the language that we use.

FE: Thank you. There are so many little parts in that. It's so difficult for Lauren as well and for Elle because they were in certain roles at the beginning of the film, and then as Elle transitions, they're just constantly shifting. And for Lauren who's always identified as a straight woman, it was really difficult for her to know how to behave because she didn't really identify as a lesbian, and there's a lot of stuff that comes up from that as well. But then that also brought up some identity issues for Elle because obviously she wants her gender affirmed and she wants to be seen as a lesbian couple. I think they were both going through different gender role switches and they were both pulling against each other all the time.

SM: We see that with the other characters as well. Even with Peta, Elle's mum, you can see how she struggled with it all initially. And she's really honest about that, just being able to let go of the son that she gave birth to and accept Elle into her life and her resistance against that as well. When she says "I couldn't even change her on the phone. It takes me a long time to accept that," you just think how difficult that would have been for Elle as well.

I found the moment where Elle is saying "I am queer," and her mum says
"Don't use that word" and it feels like she is over-correcting. It feels like
there is so much complexity in that brief moment where you don't know if
she's trying to be an ally or is just afraid of that word and afraid of what
it contains. It's not for us to interrogate, it's for us to sit here and go, "This
journey is really difficult for everybody involved." And I think that's a re-
ally powerful thing: looking at the mum, the friends and all these kinds
of things and seeing how a transition affects everybody.

FE: Totally. I think that for Elle's mum as well, it's this thing that we wanted to paint a picture which is acceptance within your family is not black and white like we often think it is. I feel like we've seen the two extremes which is either just blind acceptance and welcoming their new child into the world, or "Get out on the streets, and I can't be associated with having a queer child." Where we wanted to represent Peta is somewhere in between. She can struggle with different aspects and still be loving and accepting Elle as a new identity. And it's a more difficult, more complex situation than is often painted in mainstream media.

How do you balance the line of being a director, a friend, and at times a therapist? There are certain points where it feels like you are being the support network for both Lauren and Elle.

SM: It was tricky. It was a tricky balancing act. And there were definitely times where throughout filming we would sit down with Elle and we'd have an hour and a half or a two-hour conversation, and we'd go into everything and it would have been a massive catch up in telling us all of her thoughts and feelings and where she believes that Lauren and her are in the relationship.

And then we'd go to the next room and do the same thing with Lauren. There were a lot of times they just were completely not on the same wavelength. They were both suffering in different ways. That was difficult for Frances and I, because obviously you want to either go to Elle and shake her and be like, "You don't realise that Lauren is suffering," or go to Lauren and be like, "You don't understand, Elle is having some really dark thoughts, and they're scaring us." As directors to see a window into her suicidal ideation that she had at the time, which was a really scary time for us all.

In terms of balancing that, we just tried to be really good friends to them independently from the film, and just be there for them and offer them as much support as we could as friends separately. We learned really early on in the process to not to mix our friendships with them too much, but to be there for them as individuals.

FE: I think we came up with a rule, which was anything that's spoken about on camera behind closed doors, we wouldn't bring up to the other one. There was a level of keeping their secrets for a while, which was a little bit complex, I think, and very complex when we eventually did show them the film because they obviously didn't really know what the other one was saying throughout and that was a bit shocking at times for them when they were watching the film back

What has the discussions been like with both Lauren and Elle?

FE: They're both really fantastic. I think before this they were quite apprehensive, of course, as you would be. It's such an intimate look into their lives. But I think for them, they both have really solid reasons for wanting to do this. And it's about helping people in a [similar] situation as them, and they still stand really strong to that. We've been doing a lot of press with them and talking about it, and they're both just fantastic and supportive, and we're still really close with them, and everything's all good. We're really lucky in that aspect.

What's the release strategy for it?

FE: We've done a festival run, and we're early on into our festival run; it's screened at CinefestOz here locally and it's also premiered at Raindance over in London. And the ABC are screening it, and they've also bought the international rights to it, so they'll go out and sell it to international sites, sale agents, because we definitely want it to have a global audience. They're going to go and sell this one-hour version, which is the one that's broadcasting on ABC, to international sales agents.

Is there a longer cut as well?

FE: Yes, there's actually three different cuts, believe it or not. How we actually got this funded was a hugely long process which took us five years. And we went through every single funding application we possibly could and got knocked back and knocked back and knocked back. Eventually, one of the ones that we did land was a 6 by 10 version. So there is a 6 by 10 version which was the first one that we cut. And then from there we cut the feature which is Sam and I's preferred version, the version that we always wanted it to be. And then there's a cut down version of that, which is 57 minutes which is the ABC version. So there's three different versions.

For readers, a 6 by 10 is an episodic one. Is that correct?

SM: Yeah. Intended for iView originally. That's how we actually pitched it to ABC was by showing them the 6 by 10. And they went, "We'll have a broadcast version." We went "Great." Look at that.

Is there anything specific that you need viewers to know about prior to watching Girl Like You?

SM: Go in with an open mind. I think people will be surprised with how much they relate to both Elle and Lauren at different times, and how easy they are to both love in different ways. I think if people go in with an open mind about all of their preconceived ideas about gender, sex, sexuality, all of those kinds of things, they'll surprise themselves.

INTERVIEW
BATOOR: A REFUGEE JOURNEY - DIRECTOR
BARAT ALI BATOOR

After already having embarked on a long asylum seeker route through three continents, Afghani photojournalist Barat Ali Batoor was then smuggled over multiple borders, surviving a shipwreck, before finally making it to Australia where he was granted refugee status. Once he established himself in Australia, Batoor retraced his 13-month long refugee boat journey, transferring the experience in his documentary *Batoor: A Refugee Journey*.

When he lived in Afghanistan, Batoor was one of the countries leading documentary photographers, receiving international recognition for his photo essay of the 'dancing boys[27]', imprisoned boys and men used for entertainment and prostitution. With death threats and the targeted killings of Batoor's own Hazara community, he had to flee for his safety. His story is presented in this film, aiming to bring the reality of the asylum seeker journey to a country that desperately needs to hear it.

Batoor: A Refugee Journey had sold out screenings at the 2021 Melbourne Documentary Film Festival, arriving just as the US and allied forces pulled out of Afghanistan, leaving it to be overtaken by the Taliban.

Interview conducted July 2021.

▶▷▶

Your history is quite a fascinating one. I want to touch on your photography first of all, because as we see in this documentary, you're quite a profound photographer. You make some really quite brilliant photos there. Did you always have any interest in getting into photography?

Barat Ali Batoor: Surprisingly when I was growing up, I never thought that I will become a photographer. Even in family settings or among friends, in those times — thirty years ago, twenty-five years ago — when we used to go for picnics or something like that, only point and shoot film cameras were popular and available within our communities. So even with that camera, I was not the photographer often, it was others. I never knew how to do that, the others used to take photos.

But I was always interested in art. Growing up I liked drawings and painting, and I participated in school plays, a couple of them. My most interest was there. I wanted to become an actor or model, and I wanted my fashion photos or portfolio to be taken by a photographer. Which I learned later on, "Oh there are professional photographers who take photos." But they were pretty expensive, I could not afford.

When the September 11 attack happened and I was around seventeen, eighteen years old, I had an opportunity to work with these journalists. And then often journalists were paired with a photographer, so I saw these photographers with giant lenses and big cameras. When I earned that money, I thought, "What should I do?" One of my friends, he bought a camera. He said, "Oh, I want to spend my money on a camera." And I said, "Okay, maybe yeah. That's a good idea. I will do it as well." (laughs) I took that. We started doing wedding photos and trial and error with film cameras. It was a slow process until I learned it. And then I used to do wedding photos and like some street photos as well. It was very expensive to buy roll of films and develop them.

And then in 2005, when I moved to Afghanistan, by then I had a digital camera. Then I explored documentary photography, and that was the history. My interest in art or fashion or acting or modelling brought me here. I came on the other side of the camera, I didn't get a chance to be in front, too.

There's a huge difference in documentary photography as opposed to taking wedding photos. How did you approach the difference between the two? Did you learn on the job or learn as you were taking the photos how best to take the most impactful photo?

BAB: I'm a self-taught photographer. It was trial and error, using and making mistakes, and then redoing it and looking at work of other photographers, especially in documentary. Initially, I didn't know many photographers, it was only one or two doco photographers who were renowned and I saw their documentaries on National Geographic, and they were the idols for me. I was trying to replicate their work or copy their style in the beginning. And it all came through trial and error until the later years when I was already in the field for seven, eight years when I had opportunity to join a couple of workshops, one in Afghanistan and two in Turkey. That was an eye-opener for me and opened me up towards documentary.

How important was that for you?

BAB: Of course, those workshops were very important and an eye-opener in my career, because before that I was mostly working on short term stories. But I learned more about the importance to work on long term projects as well. I was introduced to different styles of photography within documentary or photojournalism. So that was very good for me.

Before that, I was very inspired by Steve McCurry. He was probably the first photographer that I was introduced to and he was my inspiration. I was trying hard to kind of copy his work. If you see my early work, you might see that I have been trying to follow that path. But after those workshops, my work completely changed, my style completely changed, and they do not look like National Geographic or Steve McCurry's style anymore. It is very different.

Do you feel that you've created your own style? When people look at your photos, do you say, "This is who I am as a photographer"?

BAB: I think so. When you capture images, of course there are similarities, but I think my photos now I can say — even in the beginning as well, you might see inspiration but it is not completely a copy of a Steve McCurry, but I would call that inspiration. Lately, I can say that they are my signature photos, they are my style. I am very open and not afraid of experimenting and changing my style. But I think there is a foundation there which remains the same. I feel that it is there. Whatever I do, that is there.

How do you embrace a project like taking photos of the dancing boys which are so intense? There's so much history and narrative within the actual photo itself. How do you plan what you're going to do?

BAB: Oh, that was a completely different project than any other project. I mean, the actual documentation of photos didn't take that long. The research of that project and homework to reach these people took very long. I researched and tried to be introduced to these people for around eight months. My only struggle was how to find them, how to get permission to take photos. And the photos I took, they unfolded in a very short period of time, it was within a couple of days or maybe weeks. But it was a couple of months to prepare and reach different organisations in order to find these people.

It's quite eye-opening for me, because I wasn't aware of the stories that were coming out. And after watching your film, I've done a lot more reading and it's quite eye-opening and distressing in a lot of ways. Was there much pushback when you were doing your research and investigation? I imagine that would have been quite difficult.

BAB: This was very risky. I knew I could get killed for that. Those people involved are very powerful in countries like Afghanistan. They have their own private militias or they are powerful within the government settings, and I knew the risks there and I was afraid. But what I was surprised by [was] I was also pushed back or discouraged by people within the human rights settings like those who are champions and work within the human rights organisations and they are there to raise voices for those people whose rights are violated.

In particular, I want to mention that in order to find these people, I tried to reach Afghanistan's Independent Human Rights Commission. The deputy director — when I met him, he was a nice guy and he introduced me to one of his officials. This guy, he looked educated or maybe he spent some time in the West or somewhere, like from his attire. When I said "Okay, this is my project, I want to work on this," he was so rude to me. And he said, "Oh, you are getting funds or grants from the Western world and trying to bring a bad name and reputation to Afghanistan." I was surprised, you are the one who should be encouraging me to highlight this, that this should not be happening. These sorts of experiences were very surprising for me.

I can understand. How did you deal with that personally?

BAB: I felt very bad and devastated after listening to this. Because I had been trying very hard to find these people, to take photos and work to complete the story. But I was continuously unsuccessful, I did not get any help. I was hoping that these people would be helpful. But when I heard those remarks or comments from this gentleman, I was hopeless. I was thinking of giving up, because I had a six months period timeline to complete that project. I actually received a grant from Soros Foundation and they accepted [my proposal]. I was about to give up on that project and to return the grant money back to them.

It's good to see that the project was completed and that the stories are told. The broader narrative of your film here is a lot more than that. I want to talk about how you made this particular film. Because there is a lot of footage, there's a lot of photos of the very difficult journey that you went through. Was there ever a point in your mind of what this would become in the end? Or was it just a case of "I need to document everything because I don't know what's going to happen in the future"?

BAB: Because my background is not film — when I had to leave Afghanistan, I knew about this issue of migration because I belong to the Hazara community or ethnic group in Afghanistan. So my people were displaced when the Taliban in 1990s took over Afghanistan, in the massacre of the Hazaras in Mazar-i-Sharif in Kabul in central Afghanistan. A lot of people migrated to different countries and that was the first time a big number of Hazaras tried to come to Australia via sea.

I knew people who drowned in the sea and went missing. And to this day, their families are still hoping and waiting that they will return. They are not accepting the fact that they have gone. Now it is twenty-one years or twenty-two years. They are still waiting and hoping that one day they will hear something, receive a phone call or something.

When I was in that situation, I went to Pakistan. The initial thought was I will live in Pakistan where I was born. At that time, the targeted killings of the Hazara was on peak in Pakistan. Hazaras live in an area which is probably a three- or four-kilometer area radius, lesser than what we were allowed in Victoria in lockdown. We were allowed to go like five kilometers radius, we thought we were in jail. But that actual place [in Pakistan] is much smaller and surrounded by military check posts. And still, terrorists were carrying out suicide attacks and targeting Hazaras — the supermarkets, schools, colleges, the business centres and on public transport anywhere.

I thought maybe I will document that and I can live there. But the situation was so bad that we were not sure if I will be coming back alive when I was leaving home. It was so uncertain, and my family was very worried. A lot of people at that time were leaving, and a lot of people were working or operating in Quetta to arrange their trips to other countries without any documents. So I decided that I will leave and it was in my mind that I will document this story, because I knew what has happened. Already a lot of Hazaras at that time left, and some of my friends just before I left, some of my friends drowned en route to Australia just a couple of months before that.

I wanted to visualise this, how does it look like? That was a question for me as well, I never saw anything visual. Except the big billboards which was a fishing boat full of people by the Department of Immigration. They made all these billboards and put them in Quetta to discourage people not to come to Australia. '*You will not ever be settled here.*' But they were killing us. We have a very famous photo — like a bomb blast went off, and people are laying and dying, like they are dead on the ground. And in the background, you see that advertisement of Australian government. That was the only image, a reference for me. Other than that, there was nothing. So I decided that I will document it. If I'm lucky.

I did not have enough money to have backup cameras or enough memory cards or enough batteries to support. And I did not have memory cards or anything to store the images, so I was trying to be very limited with my shoot. Also, I was not sure if the smugglers will allow me to take photos because that is a different situation. I would be completely at the mercy of those people smugglers. But I was lucky. I didn't face problems while taking the photos. And the smugglers, they were okay. I was surprised by that. And I did document most of the journey.

I also borrowed a handycam camera. If you see the video footage of the boat, I filmed that with a small digital handycam camera that I borrowed from my sister. The film was not my idea. It all came afterwards when I travelled via sea. Our boat leaked and it was sinking, the memory card survived [with] some of those photos and images. I was interviewed by Mark Davis from SBS Dateline and he put together a half an hour documentary. I had access to those footages as well. And from there, this idea came in my mind that I can work on a longer version to cover the whole story.

The part where Mark Davis covered was mostly that trip, but what I was concerned with was more to document the stories, the reasons why these people are leaving and the other hardship that they face through the journey, and how do they go through — while they are in limbo — how their lives look. After I was resettled in Australia, I retraced my journey. I went back to Pakistan. Still the situation was very difficult and I found people who were related to my story and to find the reasons, and also travelled the way again to fill the gaps. "Okay, what parts of the film are missing?" This time I had proper gear and I created more footage and captured more stories of different people. I met a lot of people like you saw in the film. So those people who are with me in Indonesia or on the boat, I followed their story all the way towards the end.

It's a long journey that you've been on. When you look back on it, what's your reflection now, as you sitting in 2021, looking back on the decades that you've been through?

BAB: A lot of people ask me if I am traumatised by those experience, if those traumas trigger. But I don't know. Sometimes it does. But sometimes it feels like a dream.

Like it happened to somebody else.

BAB: An unreal thing, like how could I go through so much? Because now when you're comfortable, you don't think that you can be that strong, resilient, to go through and fight back. But for instance, now I think "Oh, I don't know how did I do that?" But sometimes it feels so unreal to me. How did I survive the first event in Afghanistan and then how did I cross the border there, and then I saw people being killed in front of me in Pakistan, and then I escaped from there. And then I almost drowned in in the sea. And still I survived and spent nights in jungle without food and water. Everything looks so dramatic to me now. Sometimes I feel like that was just a dream or, I don't know, a fiction probably. I think it feels completely different. Unreal.

How is it for you talking about your experiences? Now you've got this film out, you've done interviews. Is it easy for you to be able to talk about these events and to make people aware of what's going on and the history there? Easy is not the right word to use but I hope you understand what I mean by the question.

BAB: I know there are emotional attachments to it. So those emotional strings get attached. When I speak to these sometimes, I think like I'm gonna cry, but I try hard not to do. But, I think this is very important for people, not only in Australia but internationally to understand what is wrong, why these people leave. I also think there could never be the best time for this film to be released.

It's perfect timing.

BAB: The US is leaving, and the betrayal of that country to Afghanistan and to the people of Afghanistan is massive. I call that a betrayal.

It is, yes.

BAB: They have been so disloyal and untrue to their promises and to the commitments they made to the people of Afghanistan. And they just are leaving at the mercy of the terrorists that they have been fighting for two decades. And now they have just completely legitimised them overnight and have empowered them with more power. Those Taliban, they are coming back with more power. They are much scarier monsters than they were in the 1990s.

And the people in the districts that have fallen already to the Taliban have already suffered. They are being flogged for different reasons, for adultery, for anything. Women, minorities, children. They are the prime target of these monsters and terrorists. And I think it is the mistakes and failures of countries like the US and the NATO allies and unfortunately Australia is on that page as well. And they've left the people who have been helping them throughout those years, with their missions to their soldiers who have supported and provided their services to the diplomatic missions, to the aid missions. They are just left behind and their families and those people are just there and waiting for their time to be ended.

Your film helps humanise the people who we often only hear about in the news. And we know that they have been abandoned by Australian government, by American governments. It is a betrayal. These are people who have helped the US forces or the Australian forces to combat the Taliban, and yet they've been just abandoned, and which is terrible. As you were saying, with the Australian billboard "You will not be wel-

come here," what's the perspective of the Australian government from an international perspective, from people who are trying to seek asylum here? Is it known how difficult it is to actually seek asylum here or how xenophobic they are?

BAB: When you are in a situation that you're not sure that any second could be your last second, and you could be killed with a bullet or a bomb blast or it could be slit your throat, you will try hard for your survival. It doesn't matter how harsh policies [are], you're applying. But if it is not Australia, maybe some other country. The burdens are on the poor countries who are even not signatory to the Refugee Convention. But countries like Australia or America or the European countries, we have more obligation towards those people.

And in the case of Afghanistan, it is even greater responsibility because the mess created in that country is ours. We have done that, and we should take some responsibility. We have already destroyed that. And the hopes that were given to the people of Afghanistan, they were shattered overnight. The women rights, the slogans that you have given them, the human rights, the education — everything has been shattered overnight, and you are not taking any responsibility now. But there should be and there must be some moral and ethical responsibility for these countries to take and kind of help those people. But people will try hard if they could get to safety.

I'm really glad to see that your film has sold out its first screening. Congratulations. I'm hopeful that it reaches a broader audience and reaches an audience who are receptive. What does that mean for you to be able to reach a sold-out audience to be able to share your message this far?

BAB: I think that says that we have compassionate people in Australia who really care about this issue and probably who knows what is going wrong in our country. And we have 30,000 people living on bridging visas and shared visas and even on temporary protection. A lot of them, they do not have any type of support. And during pandemic, they didn't have any kind of support. They were just helped by communities, people, charity organisations. The government did not take any responsibility towards those people. And a lot of them, a majority of them are from Afghanistan, the country that we have made a mess in. We are not left with any ethical reason to keep these people in limbo anymore. We are torturing them, we are killing them everyday, psychologically. I guess that the session which is sold out tells me that there are people who are supportive of this. It is only within our political system and bureaucrats that are the problem, that needs to have some humanitarian and humanised elements.

I saw that Kon [Karapanagiotidis], the head of ASRC, the Asylum Seekers Resource Centre, had retweeted about the film as well, which is really fantastic to see. That's a great foundation that has given a lot of support to people in Victoria who need the support. I wonder if you could possibly talk about the fields that people have been able to get support? As you're saying, people on bridging visas and more were abandoned by the government here in Australia over the pandemic last year. Could you talk about the support systems that did come up in place?

BAB: First of all, I think Kon has kindly retweeted that. And he is also in the panel of the Q&A session which is great, so he can also shed some light on that issue. But during the pandemic, organisations like Asylum Seeker Resource Centre and other charities and community groups from within the communities — they were there to support these people who were left without jobs, without any financial support from the government, without any health support from the government, without anything. They were taking everything. In my personal capacity and professional capability, I'm in touch with the community and these organisations played a fantastic role in supporting these people who are left behind.

And I'm glad to hear that because as an Australian citizen, it is really sad to see our government fail daily on basic empathy, and fail a country which we're there to support. And I'm really grateful that your story is out there as well, because it's an important one. Thank you for sharing it, as difficult as it might be. Thank you for sharing your photography as well.

BAB: Thank you. This is very lovely to speak with you.

Have you continued on with your photography here in Australia?

BAB: I still do photography. A lot. Because Australia is a country — I have to fight on different fronts, I have to support myself, I have to support my family overseas, I have to also do photography. Like I [have] a proper full-time job, and I also do teaching rotations, and I also take photos. But now after my experience in video, I do a lot of videos as well. Maybe I'm not working on those sorts of very difficult stories that I used to do in Afghanistan or Pakistan, but it's still like stories I have done. I have been involved with refugees mostly, and not only what they are going through, but I also have highlighted their contributions back to the country. Because we always get negative news, so I've been trying to reuse my skills or energy to highlight some positive stories and to show the real picture, what is actually happening and who these people are. We are just like you and like anyone else living in this beautiful country. Our blood is of the red.

ENVIRONMENTAL DOCUMENTARIES

If there was a constant theme among the environmental documentaries of 2021, it was that of climate change and the enduring devastation being wrought upon this planet by the impact of decades of inaction. The horrifying and brutal bushfire season of 2019/2020 was explored from the local perspective with Anthony 'Ash' Brennan's community focused *We Are Conjola*, to the global with Sandrine Charruyer & Sophie Leopwic's *Inferno without Borders*. Complementing these two films, and further highlighting the array of stories that came out of the worst bushfire season Australia has seen in modern times, were Justin Krook & Luke Mazzaferro's volunteer firefighter focused *A Fire Inside*, and Eva Orner's furiously political *Burning*.

Each of these films told the stories of regular Australians battling the elements to keep their fellow Aussies safe. Harrowing images of houses, the bush, and animals harmed by the bushfires flow through each film, reminding viewers in every frame of what can happen when a bushfire strikes. Adding to the climate change theme is Douglas Watkin's *Alick and Albert*, a story of an unlikely bond between Prince Albert II of Monaco and Alick Tipoti of the Torres Strait, and the threat of rising seas on the island homes of the Torres Strait.

Sally Ingleton's *Wild Things* gave voice to the new generation of environmental activists across Australia, working together to combat forest destruction, and to help secure a cleaner future for all Australians. A similar energy thrived within Garth De Bruno Austin's *The Last Horns of Africa*, which told an internationally focused story of conservationists putting their lives on the line to protect African rhinoceros from a hidden rhino orphanage to the expansive Kruger National Park.

Yet, not all environmental documentaries need to be activist in tone, as witnessed with Leighton De Barros' visually stunning *Jaimen Hudson: From Sky to Sea*, which tells the inspiring story of cinematographer Jaimen Hudson who uses his drone to capture stunning footage of the aquatic wildlife on his doorstep in the Great Southern of Western Australia. Additionally, Nick Robinson's Netflix family-focused *Puff: Wonders of the Reef* anthropomorphised marine wildlife with narration by Rose Byrne, remining audiences of the millions of aquatic creatures that live on the coral reefs around the world.

Environmental documentaries are represented with pieces on *Burning*, *We Are Conjola, Inferno Without Borders, Alick and Albert, Wild Things*, and *Jaimen Hudson: From Sky to Sea*.

INTERVIEW
BURNING - DIRECTOR
EVA ORNER

*B*urning assesses the remnants of the horrifying Australian bushfires of 2019-2020, collectively known as 'Black Summer'. Director Eva Orner holistically approaches the disaster by asking how this event took place, what could have been done to prevent it, and championing the work of the firefighters, activists, survivors, and climate change experts along the way. Eva Orner's films are deeply political, with *Burning* holding the Scott Morrison Liberal-National Party to account for their inaction on climate change.

With complex and difficult-to-watch imagery, *Burning* is an up-to-the-moment realisation of the impact of climate change happening right now. Complete with unsettling footage of the damage that the bushfires had on animals, firefighters, houses, and more, *Burning* also looks at the health repercussions of these catastrophic events, including a story of a baby born after the bushfires with lungs full of soot. This is a harrowing film, but an essential film nonetheless.

Eva Orner is an Academy Award winning filmmaker for her work with Alex Gibney on *Taxi to the Dark Side* (2007), a film about America's torture and interrogation practices during the War in Afghanistan, an AACTA Award winner for *Chasing Asylum* (2016), a film that examined Australia's inhumane treatment of asylum seekers and refugees.

This interview took place in advance of Eva Orner's panel at the 2022 Australian International Documentary Conference, where she presented a panel about being an Agent for Change.

Interview conducted February 2022.

▶▷▶

I watched Burning last year via the Toronto Film Festival online. It was a bit of a surreal experience as well because I watched it — probably I shouldn't be telling the filmmaker this, I'm sorry, but I watched it on my phone just before I had to go to a press screening.

Eva Orner: It's okay.

And I was sitting in Luna Leederville and just had tears streaming down my face while I was watching it.

EA: Oh gosh. That's pretty good on a phone.

It was so good. And then I watched it again at home when it landed on Amazon Prime. This is the third time I've seen it, just re-watching it last night. And it's such an effective film.

EA: I've only seen it, I think, three times on a big screen like in a cinema. I don't think I can ever do that again. It's really painful.

It hits like a punch in the gut which is how it should do. It's got to be hard to make that kind of film, I imagine. Emotionally, you make some really devastating films. And I'm grateful for that because the stories need to be told. But I'm always concerned about your mental health and well-being after you make them.

EA: (laughs) I guess now that I've got a body of this kind of work, I get asked about that a lot. And I think ten years ago I was kind of hitting a wall and I didn't really know how to deal with it. And I had to get some therapy and it was a little bit of post-traumatic stress. There was a lot of guilt, a lot of pain, and I had to learn how to be able to do this and live with it. And I don't want to be at a point where I've distanced myself from it and don't feel. So it's more how you can also live a full life and not be consumed by guilt and pain.

I had a really great therapist, I text him every now and then or I'll send him an interview where I mention him. (laughs) I don't know how he did it. It's sort of magic to me how psychology works, but he managed to put me in a position where I can — it's not killing me. For a while it was starting to impact on my life in a really heavy way.

It's a good thing for a lot of us to go to therapy to get the support that we need. As we move forward into a climate change world, it's going to become even more pressing. One of the things that people have concerns about is climate change. And it's hard. "Go seek help, seek therapy" is what's often said, because it's something that is really difficult to maintain and grapple [with], especially since obviously bushfires become so more frequent and so prevalent. I'm in Western Australia and our beautiful South West is currently burning. It's terrifying.

EA: I saw that. And it's weird. It's like the beginning of February and I'm sitting at home in LA. And it's the tail end of winter here and today's 31 degrees Celsius in Los Angeles.

That's crazy.

EA: There are times in winter when it does get warm. I think 31's pretty out there for the middle of winter here.

Especially since it was 41 degrees last week for us. It shouldn't be the same temperature over there as it is here.

EA: Yeah, it's not good.

The urgency of the issues of the world, of the politics of the world, is really prevalent in your blood as a filmmaker. Where did that come from?

EA: Gosh, good question. I don't know. I think there's a bunch of things. I've always had a really curious nature. I've got a strong journalistic streak in me and I love storytelling but I also love storytelling that's significant and has consequences. When I moved to America, I worked with Alex Gibney who's one of the key documentarians working today. And he just made a film called *Enron,* and we got to make a whole bunch of films together. And I think I got a sense of it from him as well. I think I've got a real interest in giving voice to the underdog and the persecuted and people who don't have a voice. I think that's really important.

And I think it probably comes from my upbringing, from my family history, and I don't think I realised this until only a few years ago. My family's from Eastern Europe. My father is no longer with us but he was born in Poland, in Vilna, Jewish in 1937. Three of my four grandparents were murdered in the Holocaust. They came to Australia in the Fifties. My parents met in Melbourne where I'm from and had a great immigrant experience in a country that welcomed them, like many people who arrived in the Fifties. I grew up with parents of action, without grandparents or cousins or a big family because most of my family was killed in the Holocaust.

I think knowing that happened to your family because of who you were in terms of your religion at a very young age maybe put something in me that — a fire — that I wanted to give a voice to people who are voiceless. That's my amateur kind of sleuthing psychology, working out maybe where all this comes from. But I definitely had a — what's the word? I guess a brand. It's a terrible word to say. I mean, it'd be really nice to do something fun as a filmmaker. But I think I'm really attracted to stories that I think are really important for our time and for people who need voices.

And I do quite like to go up against the government.

I do get that impression throughout your films. Watching Chasing Asylum and Burning in particular, there is this real 'stick it to the government vibe' to them. Having seen your films multiple times, I continually sit there and I wonder, how do you manage to balance the activism and the storytelling and yet never feel like it's you standing on top of a soap-

box and preaching and pushing people away as can sometimes happen with those narratives? How do you manage that balance?

EA: That's nice to hear, thank you. I'd probably give that credit to my editors. (laughs) Because I think I do kind of get on a soapbox. Films like *Chasing Asylum* and *Burning* – I have to have a very clear opinion and point of view. A lot of films – pure vérité observational – even the most vérité film still has the filmmaker's imprint. I think I'm very clear on where I stand and what I believe and who my villains are. My two Australian films I've made since I moved to America, which is *Chasing Asylum* and *Burning*, I'm very comfortable pointing my finger at the government. Also in *Burning*, at the Murdoch media.

And I don't think there's anything wrong about that, I actually encourage that. I don't think it's propaganda. I think the people that I criticise are very comfortable saying it's propaganda because it's against them. But it's a thoughtful essayistic approach to filmmaking with proof and examples, and it's a visual storytelling. I hope they make compelling films, but I think it's okay to have an opinion in filmmaking and on subjects like the treatment of refugees and climate change. I think we need a lot more opinion, backed up by facts, and all of these films are all backed up by facts. If they weren't, I'd be sued.

The amount of people that you have in the film talking about what is currently going on [is impressive]. There is a point where Greg Mullins says, "If you're a climate denialist, I don't care about you anymore." The truth is there. We know what is going on.

EA: I think Greg is phenomenal. The film is a bit of a love letter to him and his career because he's done such a service to Australia. The governments tend to not listen to him and I think he's had a huge impact but also a really hard time. I have so much respect for him and I admire him so much and how he doesn't give up. I feel like that about all the people in the film. They're so extraordinary.

There are so many legends and icons here and people who clearly don't ever really expect to have been in the spotlight. Daisy [Jeffrey] talking later on in the film, "This is the most frustrating and difficult thing I've ever been associated with." I'm paraphrasing but you can just tell that she just wanted to have a life as a kid. And this has been pushed upon her just like it's been pushed upon so many other people in the film that they are forced into action.

EA: That's what I love about Daisy. She's so important in the film, because so many people, older people say, "Oh, you know, the younger generation will solve – it's their problem to fix even though we created it." And you really see what that means when you talk to Daisy, the amount of pressure that's on her shoulders and what she had to do from the age of like sixteen. I mean, she's now currently at university, I think she's eighteen or nineteen. She spent the last couple of high school years doing this as almost a full-time job, being a climate protester and a student activist, and that's fantastic. But at the same time, she laments the fact that she should just be being a kid. I've never really heard a young activist talk like that, and I thought it was really powerful and really fresh and something that should weigh heavy on our shoulders, the mess we've created for the younger generation. I have so much admiration and love for Daisy, I think she's quite extraordinary.

She really is. I remember attending protests here in Perth at the time and just feeling the country being united by this anger and frustration and just the despair for the younger generation because the older generation has in many ways abandoned them in the political leaning and stuff like that. It becomes so frustrating to have these political squabbles about something that is so real and so tangible and we can see it actually happening.

I think it was during the Q&As for Chasing Asylum, you'd mentioned about how 40% of people will go and watch this film and already be on board with the narrative and supporting asylum seekers, and then 20% will have their opinion changed, and then the other 40% will stay the same. Is that something that you've kind of brought to your films as you've made them with Chasing Asylum and with Burning as well? This idea that there is a percentage of people who are already on board with the story, and then there's a percentage who will be changed by what you're presenting? And then others who will just say, "This is a lie."

EA: I think probably forty on each side that have got their mind made up. It's the magic twenty – I mean, this is in my head – the magic sort of 20% in the middle who aren't sure who you could sway. But that 20% is enough to change the world. I mean, if you look at how tight the elections are in America or even Australia, it's that group in the middle that can go either way. I feel like that's your audience in terms of effecting change. And it's about getting them to see the films that you make.

That's one of the great things about being lucky enough to make films for the global streamers. My previous film was with Netflix and my current film is with Amazon. You're getting your film going out to over two hundred countries on the same day and tens or hundreds of millions of people. To me, that's what's great about working with such incredible platforms.

Probably the climate change figures are different in Australia now because I think more and more people are coming around to it because it's inevitable. Everyone's feeling it. Everyone's seeing it. And I'm assuming the amount of deniers is getting smaller and smaller. But we've got an election coming up and I have a horrible feeling — I tend to be a realist, not an optimist and I guess some people would call me a pessimist but I'm not. I'm incredibly concerned that the government's going to get re-elected. If a film like this can have an impact, that would be wonderful. I hope as many people as possible can see it.

I agree. And being on Amazon has made it so much easier to be able to point to people and say, "Here it is, watch this film."

EA: Exactly.

The voting public's mind is so easily swayed by the media cycles and things like that, and it can easily feel like, "Oh this happened a few years ago, it won't happen again for a while." That's a bit terrifying, especially [with] all the media things that I've been hearing. I'm a bit like you in the sense of being a realist, but everything's pointing to having a hung parliament of some sort. And that terrifies me because we need to have some kind of change. And yet we're sitting here talking about what kind of curry Scott Morrison's made. Let's focus on the world that's actually happening out there.

EA: It's very scary, and I feel like it's similar here. We're facing the inevitable here in America of losing both houses in November and then facing maybe the increasing inevitability that Trump will get in, in a couple of years. I feel like it's really up to us to vote out bad leadership, but we're not doing a very good job of that globally.

That's why I was appreciative of the focus on the Murdoch media as well in Burning because it is really pointing out the hypocrisy and the madness of it, especially when – I think it was at the end of last year when they started going on about "Oh, you know, climate change, we need to have some more action on climate change." And it's like, "Hang on. You didn't have that opinion years ago, and yet now you've woken up and decided to write something that says that we need to have some kind of action." It just doesn't make any sense.

EA: I think that's worth talking about because they've been the villain in climate change denial for decades, and it's been a company policy. And last year toward the COPS [Conference of the Parties] in Glasgow which was – I think it was November. We went there and showed the film there. It was just before that they came out with this press release saying they've decided to turn around their policy on being climate change deniers – is essentially what they said.

It's not fact-based journalism. It's not fact-based reporting. I wouldn't even call it journalism or reporting, I'd call them basic liars and spreaders of misinformation. I'm very comfortable doing that.

And that's what they've continued to do. It was very sloppy journalism that the press around the world picked up this pathetic press release where they said "We're not going to do this anymore," didn't take them to task enough for the damage they've done, and then just kind of left it out there hanging when they really did nothing to reverse their position. It was incredibly cynical and it's what they do best which is to spread misinformation.

The other thing that I think is really interesting is in my lifetime a fact used to be a fact, and science used to be a fact. And I find it so concerning and terrifying that science is now debatable. How did this happen? A lot of it's through religion, I think, and obviously rampant conservatism. But the fact that people can just say "I choose not to believe the science" and get away with it — to me, that's criminal.

It very much is. And that was part of the comfort of seeing Kevin Rudd's push to have a royal commission into Murdoch media. And of course, we've not seen that come about yet. But that's again the hope of having a change of government. Whether that happens or not, who knows.

EA: It's very easy for Kevin Rudd and Malcolm Turnbull to do that now because they're not prime ministers. But when they were prime ministers, they were pretty soft on Murdoch. And that honestly pisses me off. Because people now lionise them and say what a great job they're doing. And I understand politics is complicated and governments are made up of coalitions and you have to bow down to some conservatives and I get it. But at the same time, the power of standing up when you have the voice as the leader of the nation is very different from when you are the ex-leader of a nation. It's all very well for Malcolm Turnbull to be doing what he's doing now. But why wasn't he doing it when he was the Prime Minister?

Agreed. And it seems that now that they both out of being prime ministers, they've found a heart, they found a soul. It's like "Where was that when you were in"?

EA: It's great and I say fantastic. But let's just not forget who they were when they were in charge and what they did.

CONTRIBUTION
WE ARE CONJOLA - DIRECTOR
ANTHONY 'ASH' BRENNAN

NYE 2019 will never be forgotten for the people of Conjola on the NSW South Coast. On that day, the whole world found out about this little piece of paradise for all the wrong reasons.

In Conjola Park on the western edge of Lake Conjola, 89 houses were lost. One of those houses, was mine. But I wasn't there. My only solace was a video from my brother's family in a boat fleeing the flames.

A month after the fire, I was with my neighbour Adam. He told me he and his wife had lost their home plus all his life's work of sculpture, paintings and tools. Adam said "I need to start creating again so I can start to heal."

That was my light bulb moment.

One of my other neighbours, Stefo, started writing amazing poems on the recovery page, inspiring the community to write poetry to express their grief. Then local painters, other writers and musicians started creating with the same effect. It became apparent to me that locals were turning to their art to create and inspire a pathway to recovery. As a filmmaker, I felt I needed to document this process.

Once I started preproduction, the community said to me that I was the one they entrusted to tell their bushfire story. I felt an enormous responsibility to get it right. And to tell the community's story, not a story that necessarily aligned with a TV broadcaster's demographic.

The result is a 1 hour 46 min documentary *We Are Conjola. Our Fire. Our Story.*

With the help of a small crew and the community, I'm proud to say that this film is my greatest work to date. It's fair to say that's also been the most personal and emotional. What makes this film even more special is that it was funded mostly by people who lost their houses. The brave people of Conjola wanted their voices heard.

From the obvious questions of climate change and Indigenous land management to the not so obvious failures of emergency services, *We Are Conjola* puts the viewer in the line of fire and asks, "What would you do in this situation?"

More importantly, the film acts as an historical document from which government agencies can learn from their failures, to hopefully lessen the impact of such disasters in the future. As well, this film shows the importance and value of art in our community.

When the film was released in local cinemas exactly 12 months after the fire, I was concerned that it could possibly trigger those who were impacted.

In fact, their reaction was completely the opposite with the community unanimous that the film has helped them recover by giving them some closure.

All nine local cinema screenings of *We Are Conjola* sold out as quickly as they were announced and all were met with standing ovations. To sit amongst the locals in the cinema, and hearing their gasps, tears, and laughter was my highlight from this incredible journey.

The film has also been a hit on the festival circuit, winning awards in New York, Los Angeles and Edmonton, Canada. And at the 2021 Melbourne Documentary Film Festival, *We Are Conjola* was awarded the judges prize for best film and I was nominated for best director. The awards and accolades are obviously great reward for this massive task, but they are accepted on behalf of the Conjola community whose kind donations, support and insight made this film a reality.

INTERVIEW
INFERNO WITHOUT BORDERS - PRODUCER LAURA SIVIS, DIRECTORS SANDRINE CHARRUYER AND SOPHIE LEPOWIC

Inferno Without Borders answers the warning siren of the 2019-2020 Australian bushfires with an investigation into the impact that the fires had on a global capacity, with smoke impacting neighbouring countries like New Caledonia and New Zealand. It also seeks to listen and learn from Indigenous practices to ensure that the environment is respected and nurtured as a whole.

Sandrine Charruyer is a producer and director who has previously directed *PAMdemonium* (2018), a documentary about Vanuata's resilience and restoration after cyclone Pam hit in 2015. She works alongside a diverse team of filmmakers at the Sydney based production company Anphietom Productions.

Sophie Lepowic is a Belgian/Australian actress who has worked on both the stage and in feature films and TV. Sophie has also written and directed short films, and worked alongside Sandrine in the editorial department and as writer of *PAMdemonium*.

Laura Sivis is the Head of Production & Creative Affairs at Courage Films. She has worked on productions around the globe, including producing *PAMdemonium*, and various short and documentary films.

Inferno Without Borders screened online via the Melbourne Documentary Film Festival in 2021.

Interview conducted September 2021.

▶▷▶

Laura Sivis: I am the producer of this project. And my production company is Courage Films, and I've worked in tandem with Sandrine to help get this project together.

Sandrine Charruyer: I'm the director, producer, provider of *Inferno Without Borders* project, and I work with Laura Sivis and Sophie Lepowic who is a writer.

Sophie Lepowic: I am part of the team. And I've been co-directing and writing the project.

This is a really deep look at the impact of climate change, and also the importance of listening to First Nations peoples and their traditional fire practices. Could you talk about the broad scope of how this production started?

LS: We were essentially on the road to making another documentary and our broadcaster on that project, and with the fires unfolding in Australia, he turned around and said, "Hey, look, we'd be really interested if you could find us a documentary on the Australian bushfires." And in fact, rather than finding an existing documentary, we ended up doing a documentary on the fires. And rather than doing a documentary about the devastation, it was really about looking more broadly around cause and forest management. It all came together very, very fast.

We were just before Christmas in 2019, and we're getting these phone calls and we're really not focused on jumping to a completely new film, and there was no time to raise finances. But they offered a presale, and we went, "Okay, let's run with it." Sandrine pulled the crew together. They're a crew that worked together before, and they got filming. From the initial ask to actually being out there behind the cameras was less than a month. It was only a matter of a few weeks that they were out there and already on the field, filming and interviewing. It was pretty intense. That's how it all began, it was very, very fast.

Could you talk about the decision to cover the First Nations people's practices of fire?

SC: I can answer to that question. It came up because first of all, initially when I had been asked by the French broadcasters to shoot a story about a bushfire, there were certain things they didn't want. They didn't want the same story that we were seeing already, which was very much focused on animal victims, burned lands and so on. They asked me to dig it out as something different, something a little bit with a deeper meaning.

I had absolutely no idea what sort of story I was going to bring up because I was not there. My head was in the other project we were working on. However, I started to go to the climate change protests in January, and I met a few people there who moved me in many aspects. I met some victims from Cobargo who told me their story. And I met some Aboriginal people who explained to me why they were protesting and what should have been done if the government had listened to them. And that's where I heard for the first time the word 'cool burning'.

I started to investigate from there, and I started to have a look and watched some Q&As, and I discover the leader of the Mulong community group Victor Steffenson, and he run the Firesticks Alliance, and I started to listen to what he was saying. That was a big gong in my head, and I said, "Why don't I know about cool burning? I've been living here for twenty-one years, and I've never ever heard about cool burning." And I asked my husband who is Australian, "Did you hear anything other cool burning methods?" And he said, "No, I've never heard about it." It was interesting to see that there was some kind of ignorance, not only from the Australian audience, but also from the French audience of course. That's where this all started, basically.

I like to think that I know what's going on in Australia and what the practices are and what we should be doing, especially when it comes to climate change. But the practice of how to deal with bushfires and protect the landscape and nurture it in this manner was new to me. I didn't know it at all. And that's one of the strengths of this film, it's not just a look at what happened, but look at how we can protect the land going forward. I want to know from each of you, what drove you to want to tell this story?

LS: I live on the bush so I have fires in my backyard all the time. Even Sandrine pointing out the cool burning – I mean, our house is used as an outpost for the firemen to monitor the fires in the bushland because I live on the edge of the national park. And I've never heard of cool burning ever, and yet I've seen them go out and do back-burning and fight fires on a regular basis. It's quite a strong connection from my perspective of why is it important to learn a new way to manage fires.

The other thing is that we each have family and friends overseas, and they were all very, very invested in what was going down in Australia. All they could see was the maps where all the fires were, and all down the east coast of Australia was a continuous band of fire. It was about really looking at why Australia had come to this point. And with our eucalyptus forests being exported to other countries, they're actually beginning to have the same problems as what we have, but they don't have any Indigenous wisdom or knowledge of how to manage eucalyptus forests. I think that we've really felt that this story had a voice and a story to tell across the globe.

And it was really about showing how this knowledge needs to be extended to the wider community and also to the local community. Because as we pointed out, a lot of us had no idea what cool burning was, yet we've grown up in this country and we've been to school in this country and have worked with the local firemen, and yet we still don't know, which seems crazy.

SC: It became a big concern for everyone because in New Caledonia, they dropped the project we were working on and moved on to the next because they had the fumes coming here from Australia to New Caledonia, crossing the borders, and going out to South America and Peru. We had to tell the story about it. That's what influenced the name of the film: *Inferno Without Borders*, there is no borders anymore. And it's a big problem.

LS: The climate change issues obviously affects the whole globe, not just locally. And the spotlight really is on Australia and how poorly they've been managing climate change and investing in it in terms of trying to reduce emissions. That side was really important for us.

SL: I have to say that when we first went on the road, we actually had no story, we had no script, no narration built. We didn't know what we were going to tell. But what we knew is that we had a lot of questions, we needed to educate ourselves. We found lots of people that we could interview and we had all those experts in climate and cultural ecologists and firefighters and the Aboriginal community. And we knew that we had lots of questions. And we did educate ourselves.

When we gathered all this information, we realised that we were not the only one who didn't know anything about those different kinds of fires, how the land was managed. I tried to put the story in a way that it would be didactic, and all those little elements would be introduced one at a time. People would understand what's happening, what could have happened, why it's not happening.

And we were really giving definitions of what are the hazard reduction fires? What is that? It's a prevention fire. Okay, how is it being done? What about the cool fire? It's also the same, it's the prevention. And then we talk about back-burning. What is it? Oh, this is when the fire is already there. It's quite a challenging and complex topic to explain. We were lucky enough to meet all those people and come across success stories about when cool burning fires were done and did protect some areas and not others, because they were not managed right away.

Then I knew we had a story to tell and we wanted really to give a voice to the Aboriginal community and make sure that that knowledge would be shared. I hope that lots of people will learn from it. Because we did. I was just very, very, very happy to know that we really had a story to tell. Because when you live on the road and you got your camera, you got the car, you got all the gear, and you got to go and shoot, but you don't know what you're going to bring back.

We were building the questions and more and more questions between interviews. We were talking in the car, we were a small team of four. We had Sandrine, we had two cameras, and myself. And we were just like, "Okay, did you hear what the person said? Oh, we should ask more about this and that." And that's how we've actually managed to gather all this information to be able to deliver something hopefully that will bring a lot to everyone watching.

Let's talk about the actual shooting process, because you're shooting in some really difficult territories, and the demands and requests of you to shoot in really dangerous areas is quite intense.

LS: Well, for starters, Sophie is asthmatic too.

How did you manage that, Sophie? Hopefully you had all the right medical things that you needed to keep yourself safe.

SL: Absolutely. And, we couldn't really go to any area that would be dangerous, because you needed permits to shoot. If you want to shoot actual fires, you can't. We did go after, so we still had smoke everywhere, but most of everything was already burned, and it was really shocking to see that devastation. And as we were building the film, we had to gather lots of archive footage to show people how it was really happening and get that sense of emergency.

It was quite challenging and finding somewhere to stay. Because we were on the road for ten days and we were going up north and we had to change our plans because new fires were burning. We couldn't go that way anymore. We had to change direction and interview other people that we were supposed to meet three days later. It was very, very challenging.

SC: As Sophie mentioned, it's been quite organic and deciding intuitively what we do day by day. Plans changed all the times. And for example, we didn't have any firefighters and we were still shooting. Sophie knew someone who knew someone who was a firefighter, but she couldn't reach him. They were all busy still, it was almost at the end of the bushfire. But we were facing some [fires that were] blazing everywhere and the smoke was still around. In some specific areas, some roads were not accessible. Sophie was saying, "I can't reach him." And I said, "We cannot have a story if we don't have a firefighter." It was very stressful. And when Sophie came up and said, "I got him," it was like, "Oh my God."

SL: We've been very lucky because every person we've interviewed has told us, "Oh, if you want to know about this, you need to talk to this person." When we were on the road, we were calling, organising, writing questions. Everything was happening in the car on the spot. We didn't sleep much.

SC: I barely slept on this project. We were swinging between producing and directing. That was quite a thing because you have all this line of conduct as a producer, but you also have that creativity part of you who wants to emerge as a director. For me particularly, there was a balance between both, and it was really hard for me to keep the focus. But we did it.

And thanks to all the interviews we had, they were amazing and unexpected for some of them. They would not have been on my list and then they come up, they come on board, and they've been very brilliant. Everyone has been very honest, authentic, and useful. I was quite amazed to see that overall, everybody believed in Aboriginal traditional methods. Everybody, every single person we asked, they were all approving and they were saying, "We don't know why they are not allowed to do anything. They are the experts."

For each of you, how do you deal with the anger of the inaction of climate change?

SL: I think there is hope, because all the people we interviewed, even the firefighters, they said they do know it's the right way. And this is being introduced. It's too slow, but it's happening. We just need to make it happen faster.

LS: As Australians who have quite strong ties internationally, I feel embarrassed. You can see how much other countries are doing. And I feel incredibly embarrassed that we are perceived as a community of people that don't care about the environment. Australia has some of the world's greatest natural wonders, and we're perceived as a people that just don't give a damn, and we're letting our government do this. That's how we're perceived overseas. And for me, that is incredibly frustrating and it makes me angry and embarrassed, and you feel powerless to make a change.

Then you come up against people who don't believe in climate change or greenhouse warming or all those sorts of things. And you say, well, you might not believe in it, but you can't disagree that what we've been doing is adding to it. If there's some natural cycle that somehow the world goes through a cycle of ice ages and hot periods, fine. But we don't need to add to it. All the pollution that we spit out into the world doesn't need to be added.

SC: For me, it's frustration which comes with anger but frustration knowing that I raise my child here in Australia. My background is French but I love Australia, and Australia adopted me and I love Australia. Right? I was super surprised that these traditional methods is one of Australian patrimoine [heritage]. And why is it not part of the education here in Australia? Why is it not part of the history or part of the normal things to do to protect our land and animals? That was a big surprise to me.

Especially because we French people see Australia as a land that is highly protected by the government. Hyper ecologist. And this is what we see from outside. But when you live in the country, it's bizarre to not have that in place. It's an Aboriginal country, and we all live here on this land, and we should know the land better. And it should be part of the education. That's what we heard with the victims. They say that from the children's perspective, but also from adults' perspectives. They have a house, big land, and they don't know how to manage it, how to protect it. We hope this film will actually help educate people in that sense, and open minds for other perspective who are right here on this country and on this land.

As we wrap up this discussion, is there anything that you want people to know about prior to going into seeing this film?

LS: The main thing to say is that the film is released through the Melbourne Documentary Film Festival. It was delayed three times because of COVID. So it's finally going out now. For us, that's exciting.

The Melbourne Documentary Film Festival is going online, isn't it?

SC: Yes, for one month actually. So that's where we take a chance to really spread the word and make sure that everybody watches it, being aware that there will be quite a lot of topics about the bushfire. But what makes the difference with us is obviously we are the only one who really focuses on the cool burning and the Aboriginal community aspect. Which is a bonus for us. It will show a different perspective of that bushfire. So that's awesome. That is actually thanks to the team of Melbourne Documentary Film Festival, because they've pulled their hair all the time changing. It's a big work to organise a festival and they've done a great job to try to make everybody happy, and make the premiere for all the filmmakers and their films. It's been exhausting.

That's the life of the indie filmmaker though, isn't it?

LS: This is a little bit special. Indie filmmaking has always been hard, but you usually have a target and you're trying to hit the target with no resources. Whereas this time you're trying to hit a moving target several times with no resources, which is pretty challenging.

REVIEW
ALICK AND ALBERT
A ROYAL RELATIONSHIP INSPIRES
GLOBAL CHANGE THROUGH ARTWORK

Consider a message in a bottle.

There's something romantic about the notion of a note, slipped into a bottle, written to communicate with a stranger in a far-off land, sealed with the hope of connection, and tossed into the ocean where the wills of the waves spirit it away on a journey that could last weeks, months, or decades. It inspires mystery, intrigue, and the hope of connection with a far-off stranger sometime in the future.

Romanticism is wrapped up in the message itself, and it is less about the act of littering that comes with tossing a bottle into the ocean. When we do this, we consider that the bottle will eventually become someone else's problem, someone else's object to deal with, and as such, the message becomes a polite way of saying "Hello, here is a bottle you may now discard, I would like to meet you one day."

In Douglas Watkin's wonderful documentary *Alick and Albert*, the 'message in a bottle' is Alick Tipoti's artwork. Alick is a man who lives on the island of Badu in the Torres Strait utilising his artwork to tell the story of his culture, of the people of the islands he lives on, and the marine life that provide a connection to land and spirituality. When Alick visits Monaco to display his artwork, a powerful friendship is forged across the oceans with Prince Albert II from Monaco. At L'Institut Océanographique de Monaco where Alick's art is displayed, Alick gives an off-handed invitation to Albert to come and visit Badu. Alick doesn't truly believe that Albert would take him up on the offer, but sure enough with a chartered plane Albert visits Badu to see how the culture of the Torres Strait people lives and to also witness first-hand the impact of climate change on these small islands.

Thematic multitudes exist within *Alick and Albert*, paired with stunning visual imagery of the islands the dugongs and turtles that call the ocean home and of Monaco's grand architecture. Each shot reinforces the notion that art equals cultural preservation, an ethos and mindset that would be best kept in the front of the mind of many Aussie filmmakers.

"To be a good hunter, there needs to be a strong connection with the hunted." While Alick is referring to the dugongs here, the reverberations this statement carry recognition of Luis vas des Torres' travels through the strait in 1606, the impact of colonisation, and in turn, the impact of climate change and pollution on the islands. The 'good hunter' is the people of the Torres Strait, but also the pollution itself, arriving each dawn on the shores of Badu like an unwelcome visitor to be cleared away by the islanders. The turtles' migration and breeding cycles are disrupted by rising sea temperatures, the dugongs aren't migrating in the way they used to, and the main export for the Torres Strait – crayfish – is dwindling due to the impact of climate change on the reefs. Within Alick's artwork, gloriously translated to animated sequences throughout the film (one can only dream and hope for a feature animated film done in this style, documenting the Torres Strait Islander way of life, culture, and history), we see the past, present, and future of the Torres Strait, from the arrival of Luis vas des Torres, to the bond with the dugongs, and the impact of the rising tides.

While politicians in Canberra joke about the rising waters lapping at the doorstep of Pacific Islanders, the reality for the Badugal council of Badu is that they need to start considering a plan for the Islanders as the impacts of climate change come to their home. On Badu, while most of the village is on a higher ground, significant areas like the cemetery and the village waterfront areas are at risk of succumbing to rising tides and destructive storms. For neighbouring lower lying islands in the Torres Strait evacuation plans are being put in place as the reality of these islands disappearing completely is arriving sooner than expected.

Prince Albert of Monaco and Alick Tipoti
Photo Credit: Ariel Fuchs. © Monaco Expeditions. Used with permission.

Albert's journey to Badu is initially to experience the Torres Strait lifestyle, to see where Alick gleans his artistic sight from, but he soon realises that his presence and support can be felt further than a royal visit. For Albert the message in a bottle is shown with the countless bottles and plastics scooped up by locals. But, unlike the hopeful discarder, eager for contact, the people (you, me, everybody we know) who discard these plastic bottles do so with the belief that they will be recycled in the future. The truth is quite different.

The spirit of Alick and Albert's friendship thrives in the direction by Douglas Watkin which is light, and comforting. It gives space to the problems that the Torres Strait islander people face on a day-to-day basis but does so in a manner that is never leaden or exhausting. Instead, with a script by Douglas, Alick, and Trish Lake, Alick and Albert reminds audiences of the importance of culture and community. A pointed emotional moment has the women of Badu meeting Prince Albert and letting him know about their history of watching his mother, Grace Kelly, on screen in a segregated cinema on Thursday Island. Through the magic of film, a foreign culture was introduced to the Torres Strait paralleling how Alick's artwork has traversed the seas to be introduced as its own 'foreign' culture to Monaco. Equally, Alick and Albert works in harmony with many recent Australian documentaries like Maya Newell's collaborative *In My Blood it Runs* (2019), Aaron Petersen's *Zach's Ceremony* (2016), and even *Fist of Fury Noongar Daa* (2021), where the reminder that the preservation of language, and the education of Indigenous languages, means a continuation and support for the Indigenous people of Australia.

Language and art keep culture alive in a tangible way, and as such keeps the practices and processes of life alive too. Echoes of the Tim Cole's glorious documentary, *Small Island, Big Song* (2020), carry through here where the migration patterns of the Pacific Islanders helped bridge communities and share resources. It's here where science meets culture, and Alick informs Albert about the Aboriginal and Torres Strait Islander people being the original scientists (as an aside: a welcome shout out to Corey Tutt's excellent family friendly book, *The First Scientists*, also released in 2021, needs to be mentioned here, a vital addition to every growing kid's library). Through a bond, Albert brings the Oceanographic Society to the Torres Strait, working in unison with Australia to research the impact of climate change.

A grand and cruel irony is how the Liberal-led Australian government throughout the years has put their focus solely on the growing economy, favouring mining companies over other industries, in turn leaving local industries like the crayfish divers of the Torres Strait in jeopardy as their livelihood is threatened by the growing impact of the warming waters around the globe. This quiet condemnation is presented here less as a fist-shake to consecutive conservative governments, and more as a dour recognition that this is the worsening future that faces the world as a whole.

At its close, *Alick and Albert* reminds us that the bonds that we foster along our journeys come from unexpected places. Through Alick's art, he has created a modern 'message in a bottle' – a way of understanding our world in a holistic manner through the emotions that it conjures within us. Instead of a wishful throw into the ocean, Alick instead has launched his artistic net far and wide, embracing the world as a whole in a call to recognise the Torres Strait and the plight of the Badugal people who call the region home.

INTERVIEW
WILD THINGS - DIRECTOR
SALLY INGLETON

Wild Things follows the stories of a new generation of environmental activists, making their presence known around Australia to protest mining developments, destruction of threatened rainforests, and more. With social media at their fingertips, these eco-warriors utilise whatever they can to build awareness of the impact of climate change and stop further developments that might hasten its progress.

Director Sally Ingleton has built a career around producing and directing award winning documentaries, utilising her company 360 Degree Films to build awareness of what is going on in the worlds of environment, science, wildlife, and more. Sally was nominated for an AACTA Award for her work on *Jimmy Shu's Taste of the Territory* (2020), and for Best Documentary in 2006 at the AFI Awards for *Welcome 2 My Deaf World* (2005).

Wild Things received a theatrical release across Australia in 2021 with Q&A sessions taking place with guests like Dr Bob Brown, Dr Lisa Searle, and climate activists Harriet O'Shea Carre, Milou Albrecht, and Callum Neilson Bridgefoot.

Interview conducted January 2021.

►▷►

You've been making social documentaries for quite a while now, going back to Muddy Waters (2003) talking about the changes that would happen with the Great Barrier Reef and more. How do you manage when there's been little change politically and societally when we're not having much traction with action on climate change?

Sally Ingleton: I think as a filmmaker, you want to make stories that will have some impact and that obviously are about critical social issues or social justice issues of the time. I started making environment films back in about 2000. I did a film called *Dolphin Mania* that was looking at a family that ran a wild dolphin swim program in Port Philip Bay, and there were a lot of environmental issues that were tied into that film.

And then I started working on this terrific story called *Muddy Waters: Life and Death on The Great Barrier Reef.* That was really all about the impact that poor land management and particularly banana and sugarcane farming at the time was having on the Great Barrier Reef. The story followed a community of farmers as well as a team of marine scientists that were doing a very interesting study in all the inshore coral reefs. The scientists were showing that those inshore reefs were really suffering, and they just weren't recovering at the same rate. And they put that down to the regular impact of just constant flows of chemicals coming off the land. I guess what did start to happen in the process of making that film was that the farming community did start to become more aware that they did need to take responsibility, and certainly there was incremental change.

I'm not sure — that's nearly twenty years ago now — whether there is much better land management happening on the Great Barrier Reef now. This bigger looming problem has taken over and that's climate change, because a lot of the damage being caused to coral reefs is from these increased extreme weather events. Numerous cyclones that have really hammered the reefs, and a lot of cyclones don't actually reach the shore, and so people don't worry about them. But they do have a really severe impact on coral reefs, they break them up and smash the reefs. And cyclones [are] a natural weather event but if they're happening more and more regularly, the reefs just don't get a chance to recover. And that issue has been around for a long time now.

When I talk to the scientists, they are really frustrated that not enough is happening, not enough leadership from governments, not only in our particular government but governments around the world to reduce carbon emissions. And I think a lot of scientists — they don't know what they have to do in order to get the message through because the science has been clear, crystal clear for probably two decades now about the impacts of climate change. What's tragic is we've just wasted a huge amount of time. If we had a zero-emissions policy put in place much earlier, then we would have had a really good chance of reducing the temperature rises and reducing the amount of carbon emissions that we're putting in the air. But we're still arguing about it. There are still people arguing about, is there climate change or not? I mean, it's absurd, really.

We've now got a new president in the United States [Biden]. And one of the first things he did literally minutes after he took office was get the United States to re-join the Paris Agreement. That's a really good sign because it does send a message to many other countries around the world that he's going to take climate change seriously, and hopefully get a really good emissions policy in place. Fingers crossed.

Wild Things is about protesting and the power of protests. Do you see your film as an act of protesting itself or do you see it as a document of protesting?

SI: The reasons why I wanted to focus on frontline non-violent action was that, by and large, a lot of the protesters get a really bad rap. They're often criticised by governments. There's all sorts of rules and laws that are coming in constantly to try and stop people from protesting, and making it illegal. People do have a right to protest, because often the laws are not always right. Just because it's a law, it doesn't mean that it's necessarily right.

In the case of chopping down trees in these beautiful ancient rainforests, often the trees just go to woodchip. The bulldozers move in, they take selected trees. And often, they're only using a small percentage of the timber in that tree, and the rest of it just gets left on the forest floor. It's used for things like somebody's coffee table. There needs to be much more education around the importance of protecting these ancient rainforests and not using these wonderful old growth timbers for things like somebody's coffee table or a new ceiling.

It reminds me a bit about ivory: many years ago people would buy ivory products, and they would just see it as an ornament or a status symbol. They didn't realise that by buying that ivory, they were fuelling this trade in ivory and the killing of not only elephants but rhinos in Africa. Now I think there's a lot more education around that. A lot of countries have made the importation of ivory illegal. I think the same needs to happen with rainforest timber. And it's terrific to see that it is starting to happen, Andrew. I think Bunnings has put a ban on selling rainforest timber[28], and that's not just Australia, but particularly Asia, because a lot of the rainforest timber comes out of Asia. That's just basically destroying the habitat for many of the world's most wonderful creatures like the orangutan.

You only have to look back at a number of the big landmark campaigns that have happened over the last thirty or forty years such as the campaign and blockade to protect the Wild Franklin River. I mean, if protesters hadn't gone to that blockade and set it up and done those continual actions over the summer of 1983, that dam would have been built and that river would no longer be wild. And now forty years later, that river is now one of the top ten white-water rafting destinations in the world. It attracts lots and lots of tourists from all over the world who want to raft that river. It's actually making far more money for the local economy than if it had been turned into a dam. The Daintree Rainforest is another case where there were plans in the Eighties to build big roads through that area. And protesters got out and stood in front of the bulldozers and protected large tracts of that rainforest. There's still more that need protecting. At least some of those areas now are national parks, and the same with many rainforests in northern New South Wales.

In the Northern Territory, protesters formed a nine-month blockade to stop a uranium mine from being built in Kakadu National Park, and that mine was not built, the Jabiluka Mine was not built. And just recently, we had protesters down in Tasmania that went into where bulldozers were logging with the permission of the Tasmanian government, an area that is habitat to the swift parrot which is critically endangered. There's only three hundred of these beautiful birds left. Protesters locked on and basically stood their ground, and there's now been a logging reprieve. The logging has stopped and there's now a court case pending on protecting that area. But if the protesters hadn't gone and done that, then that area would have just been clear filled.

The film is really showing the value of frontline action. Especially at this time, so many people are fed up with the fact that governments aren't taking enough action and they've decided, "Well, okay, what can I do?" And one thing that people can do is join a group, get involved at a local level or see what sort of causes you're interested in supporting and see what you can do, see how you can participate. And in some cases, that means going to the frontline.

One of the things which I find really interesting is the choice of protests that you have used. They are three really major protests in Australia and covering three very different aspects of global destruction. How did you decide which ones to choose?

SI: It's a good question. I did a lot of research on current campaigns and met people involved in many campaigns that are currently taking place around Australia. In the end, I settled on following the people that were trying to stop the new coal mine going here in Central Queensland colloquially known as the Adani mine, the Carmichael coal mine. One of the reasons why I chose that particular campaign was that coal is an energy source of the past. It was terrific in its day but we no longer need coal. There are many other cleaner forms of energy that can be utilised that won't be producing the massive amount of carbon emissions that coal mining does. The price of coal has gone down right around the world. Many, many countries are phasing out coal because they know it's just dirty energy.

It's ridiculous that Australia is still supporting the mining of coal and still building new coal mines. And they're not putting enough effort into working out how they can transition the economies of a lot of those little country towns where people have relied on working in the coal industry in some cases for three generations of people working in coal. That story is told in *Wild Things* but not only from the white European perspective, but from the Indigenous perspective. Often, the Indigenous people are moved off their land, and people move in and start mining coal without getting any permissions, without any transfer of land or titles. The Aboriginal people from that country, they always knew that mining coal would potentially be dangerous, that it could be poisonous. That is certainly proving to be the case with the amount of carbon emission that has been produced by fossil fuels. But people need jobs, we fully appreciate that. It's just that what needs to happen is there needs to be a much more active transition to clean energy and a real commitment by governments to start building the necessary infrastructure that's needed in order to get that transition happening much faster than what is happening at the moment.

The other big campaign is the forests. Part of that is because forests are so important because they're carbon sinks, they draw down carbon from the atmosphere. But they're also really important sources of habitat and really important homes for many, many creatures. There's enormous biodiversity in forests. Australia, we're very lucky, we've got wonderful natural landscapes. And because we've got a small population in Australia, by and large, a lot of our landscapes are still intact. But we need to keep them intact. We can't just destroy them. And one of the potentials with those forests is if you can protect them and keep them as they are, then future generations will be able to visit those forests and see all the creatures, see the biodiversity that lives in those forests. Who wants to go and see a clear fill? There's nothing to see with a clear fill. It's just ridiculous that ancient old growth forests are largely being used for woodchip.

In Kalgoorlie they're talking about the super mining pit that's nearing the end of its life. And I've been there and it's a big hole. I know that they're talking about how to deal with that as a tourist attraction. Do people really want to travel that far to go and see a big hole? Is there any interest in that? I don't think so. There's no interest in seeing a place of massive destruction. It's devastating. You can't help but think of all the displaced animals and the destroyed aspect of it all, and the devastation that's been added to climate change.

SI: Now more than ever, as a species, we need to be able to go to wild places. If you go and walk in a park, or you go and walk by a river, you go into a forest and take a walk through that forest, then you feel good. You breathe in the fresh air, you can observe all the tiny little creatures, the birds, the insect life and so forth that live in those forests or live in those wild places, and you come out feeling relaxed. You feel better. They're healing environments. As a human species, there are so many stressors in our lives now, we all lead these really, really busy lives. We need to take care of ourselves. And one of the best ways we can take care of ourselves is by spending time in the wild.

I want to shift to talking about politics for a moment as well which is such a joyful discussion to have. President Biden is enacting some climate change actions and changes that need to be instigated from an American perspective, but in Australia, there seems to be a cross party approach of sitting on your hands and not doing anything. I was reading that there was pushback from the Labor MP Shane Broad[29] about the funding for Wild Things and how he was frustrated that there was some funding possibly put towards it. There seems to be from a political perspective antagonism towards both protesters and action on climate change. How do we change that particular perspective?

SI: One of the reasons why I wanted to make the film was to show that frontline action is really important and it is something that does work. And if it hadn't been for the efforts of protesters, a lot of the wonderful wild places in Australia would no longer exist, they just wouldn't be there anymore. There has been a political pushback and a clamp down on protesters. And there's an attitude that protesters are dole bludgers and you see this a lot in the film. People will drive past a protest and they're yelling out, "Dole bludgers, get a job" and so on. And it's really unfair because so many of those protesters do have jobs. The protesters that we focus on — particularly Lisa Searle — she will spend a certain amount of her time protecting the forests in Tasmania, but she's also a doctor. And she will take time out away from her work as a protester to go and run a hospital in Central Africa for Medicins Sans Frontieres. She's somebody who's incredibly busy and incredibly committed to her beliefs in terms of protecting those forests but also looking after the human beings on the planet, and often those that are more disadvantaged than others.

Particularly, I think the film will have a really important role to play with young people as well, because a lot of young people are despairing at the moment about their futures, about what's happening with climate change, the fact that there's such a lack of action. They don't know what to do, and they're suffering from a lot of anxiety. And I think to see the stories of the teenagers that were once like that, feeling really anxious and unsure about themselves and feeling depressed about their futures — they slowly started getting active and getting involved in school strikes or climate movement, it enabled them to start to feel like they've always mattered and that they actually got really empowered by that process. Hopefully, lots of young people will be inspired when they see the film to think, "Well, we can meet with other people, we can actually get active." It does matter.

I think if you just look back in history, that's the way change happens. It's through people power. Any revolution, it's been the uprising of people.

INTERVIEW
JAIMEN HUDSON: FROM SKY TO SEA -
CINEMATOGRAPHER AND SUBJECT
JAIMEN HUDSON

Drone cinematographer and wildlife enthusiast Jaimen Hudson has made a splash online with his videos of the South West of Western Australia. Pristine waters are embraced by an aerial eye that gleans the joy from dolphins leaping out of the waves, and with the warm motherly care of a whale and her calf. His videos have been seen by millions, and have opened up a slice of the world that many may never be able to visit.

He also is in a wheelchair, living a life with quadriplegia caused from an accident in his youth. With friend and documentarian Leighton Barros by his side, Jaimen embarked on the journey of his life: to enter the waters he so eagerly films, and to swim once again. In *From Sky to Sea*, Jaimen takes us through his day-to-day life, his drone work, and through the experience of swimming once again.

Interview conducted March 2021.

▶▷▶

This film covers quite a fair chunk of your life, so I imagine that Leighton [de Barros – director] was with you for a period of time making this film?

Jaimen Hudson: It's a bit surreal to be sharing your life in a documentary that's going to the movies, but it's something I'm extremely thankful and honoured to be a part of really.

We've known each other for a long time. Before I was ever into drone photography, when I was walking around, he actually used to hire my family's boat to go down and do some whale filming. And we just happened to cross paths again when we were doing our drone licences together just by fate. At that stage, some of my drone videos have been quite popular online, and he said, "I really love your story, we should catch up sometime," and then we got to chatting. Jodie, his wife, and he really believed in this story. And now it's a real thing.

I want to talk about the actual the drone footage and the cinematography and what drew you to that in the first place because there is beauty in WA's nature, in our aquatic life. And I want to know what you get from our nature.

JH: Absolutely, man. For me, it was at first just a means to a hobby, really, because I had a motorbike accident when I was seventeen and no longer could access surfing and skateboarding, diving, all those things I used to love. One day this guy came into our shop and he wanted to go to Lake Hillier the next day, which is that beautiful pink lake that is off Esperance, which you may have seen in some of my vision or photos. He wanted to go there the following day, and a lot of people don't realise it's about 130 kilometres away. It's about a five-hour boat ride in one direction, it takes quite a while to get there. But sure enough, he's like "I want to leave at 3am in the morning," and so he booked it all in.

Turns out he was the marketing officer for DJI. They're the drone manufacturing company. And this was back at the launch of the Phantom 2 I think, so very early on in the drone realm. And when he got back in, he showed me the footage, and I was completely blown away by the cool perspective it gave you. Immediately I thought maybe this is something I could do and started researching if I'll be able to use a remote controller. Eventually, my family, my now wife then girlfriend Jess, mum and dad just said, "Look, just buy one. And if you can't fly, then we'll just sell it."

So I bought one. And then I was hooked. Obviously, we've got beautiful beaches and everything down there, but the wildlife just fascinates me because it's right there. They lead this completely different life to what we do. They're always migrating, on the hunt to get food. And they're these ginormous creatures. Dolphins are so similar to us in the sense that they surf waves, and they jump out the back of it, and just look like [they're] having a grand old time.

Upon sharing my videos with people, I started to realise that not everyone has access to that because me personally, growing up with it, you take it for granted. Whereas a lot of people that comment on my videos, they've never even seen the ocean before in real life, so to see that is a whole other world. Now I'm addicted to trying to film wildlife really and share the photos that I get.

As you got into drone filming, did you teach yourself how to frame shots?

JH: I did. I practised and got slowly better at it. And then you start to watch your vision back and you realise what you don't like about it, jerky movements and everything like that. You're trying to get better at doing that.

And that's the one thing with wildlife, there's never another [take], you can't ask them to go do it again. You have one shot at trying to do it. I practised my flying so that when the time was right to film the wildlife, I just try and position the shot. And then over time, I'd play it on my laptop and everything would be going on down in the bottom left corner instead of in the centre of the screen, so then I got to make sure I get [the action] in the middle.

And it took time, but it's what it's like. It becomes an obsession, doesn't it? It's like a hobby, but I just love doing it. Now any bit of spare time is spent out droning really.

You are quite lucky to be living in one of the best places on Earth. We've got so much beautiful nature and just being part of it is nourishing. The main drive of this film is the journey to get you back in the ocean, getting you back out there into the sea and getting to experience that. What's that feeling like for you? As somebody who prior to your accident who did a lot of swimming, what was it like not being able to go into the ocean?

JH: I think the ocean, like you said, is very grounding. Really, you can have a tough day and you go to this beautiful place, like an amusement park for adults really, and you can really start to feel better about yourself. That's what I love about the ocean.

Growing up, we were very lucky, my mum and dad owned a house directly opposite West Beach, so it's a great location. But then it almost worked against me in a sense after my accident because I would sit there and I'd see everyone getting ready to go out surfing and I remember crying, just wishing that I had that access to it again.

Droning definitely filled that void.

That's what I loved about being out. And now that was my thing: I'd go out while everyone else was surfing, I'd be trying to film them surf or I'd go out and do a search for the wildlife, but being able to go back in the water was...

I honestly remember the moment that salt water hit my lips, it was this moment of euphoria. I was like, "Wow, it's just as I remembered it," even though it had been nearly thirteen years. It was just like I remembered it.

It's a really beautiful moment and I'm grateful that we got to experience it and to share your story and get to see it happen. How important is it for you, with a young family, to capture these stories, to capture your life events on film?

JH: That's a funny one. I'm very grateful to have people capture it, because obviously [my son is] not going to remember any of this stuff, so for him to hopefully see it, and not only for him, but I hope a lot of people get this out of it, that sometimes in life shit happens and you do get setbacks. And you can feel really down and out, and then I was only seventeen, but I was just lucky to just have a right mindset that I wanted to go out and still make something for my life.

I always wanted to do something great with my life. I'm not gonna let that stop just because I had my accident. And the fact that we can document that and now share it. The beauty is I'll be able to show my son when he is old enough to remember and he'll see all these great things we did. But I hope other people out there who have never met me before will see that every morning, it takes me an hour and a half with carers to get ready for the day.

And I still try and get out there and make the most of that day. I'm just grateful there's people that are willing to come and get me out of bed and assist me. I just hope people will maybe watch it and feel motivated, not necessarily inspired but motivated to make the most of their life while they still have their life because you never know what can come. Life can be unfair to people and it can be cut short, so try and get out there and make the most of that way you can.

If you don't mind me asking, how did you mentally deal with your accident? What hurdles did you go through to get to where you are today sitting here talking to me?

JH: I think a huge part of me being able to deal with it well was like I told my mum I wanted to hate going to work on Mondays just like everyone else. (laughs) And she would always remind me when I didn't want to go to work on Mondays, but I think working was a huge part of it. If every day is a day off, how are you going to appreciate the days off?

If you work, you appreciate the time you do get off. And it also gives you something to focus on getting into work and knowing that you have tasks ahead of you that day, you're contributing, and then also you're earning your money, so you can go out and treat yourself to different things, buy a drone, for example. I really do credit work massively for that.

And then also having great people around me that were willing to take me out and about. I was seventeen when I had my accident, I had my eighteenth birthday in hospital. Going out and still partying and doing all those things, like not coming [home] until late — my family would get up and put me to bed when I get home. I'm very grateful for that.

I have to wake up, but just trying to live as normal a life as possible. And there's this weird stigma, I think, almost in Western Australia or Australia that people are too hard on people with disabilities, but I've just never experienced anything like that. Everyone's just so overwhelmingly supportive. If you go out and you're trying to get up a step, someone will come over and give you a hand, and people are more than happy to help.

It's trying not sit at home all day. Just get out there. And even if you don't feel like it going, be a 'yes man'. You know that movie by Jim Carrey? *Yes Man*. And it's so true. You think like, "No, I don't want to go do that," but then you go and do it, you have such a good time, or you have a good experience. So just try and if people offer to assist you, go out and do it. If you're feeling down in the dumps, call a friend up and go catch up with them. Just surround yourself with people that are positive and happy.

As we see in the film, you've got a great social network, and you've got a great support network of people who are there helping you out and making your dream happen. There is a moment where one of the people [an unidentified doctor] says, "Look, we can't go ahead with doing the swim." But your determination there in that moment is so powerful. Your response is "I understand, I take on board what's going on, but I still want to do the swim." How did you deal with that hurdle?

JH: That was very frustrating to me, because that lady or gentleman, whoever it was, had never met me, but I get where they're coming from. They're just trying to cover their arse if something were to go wrong. Personally, I've dealt with so many hurdles. I think once you've had something like what has happened to me, there's no fixing me, you know what I mean? Unless there's some major advance in modern science. I can't even open and close my hands anymore. If someone goes and crashes my car, those things can be fixed. I've experienced the depths of loss and sadness. And everything above that is not as bad, to be honest with you. It doesn't seem that bad sometimes. Frustrating? Absolutely. In that scenario, I wasn't going to let it spoil the party, that's for sure.

Your videos have reached millions of people. How does that feel to have your work reach a wide array of people?

JH: It's amazing, surreal. I'm so grateful for social media. I know people give social media a bit of a bad rap. And it does have its downsides by all means, but for me, it's been just incredible.

It's helped me become the photographer that I am because I get to share, and it encourages me and inspires me to want to share more. I get comments from people all around the world. And once the World Surf League put up my video, it got more than 120 million views. And no one would know I filmed that other than the fact that they tagged me at the bottom of the page, but certainly, it's still their most viewed video of all time, and they're a surfing website! They're not a wildlife page.

It's surreal. And I'm truly grateful. I feel so grateful for all the positive feedback. I've only had a few experiences where people are negative, but in an online world there's always someone out there. But the majority of the feedback is overwhelmingly positive for me, so I'm just super grateful. And it only encourages me to want to do it more.

Part of the selling point of the film is getting to see you out in the ocean and seeing the joy in your face. It's so tangible. It's so real. Do you get out to go for swims all that often?

JH: Not as often as I might like. We filmed that up north in Exmouth and as you can imagine, that's a big trip so we had my mum and her partner Colin and my wife and then we had Leighton who was cameraman but also would help assist get me into my dry suit and everything. Chartering a boat is not cheap for several days to get out there. I haven't done anything crazy like that yet.

After that, we came home to Esperance and because we run a tourism business, it's just been pretty much seven days a week so I haven't had a chance to get in. The water in Esperance is a bit cooler and because I can't regulate my body temperature, I need it to be a good 30-degree day before I go splashing around in the ocean. Usually, we have a beach chair and we will be right down to the water's edge and let the water wash around my face and then my son can run around.

What kind of message do you want viewers to take going into the film?

JH: It's not like a 'poor me' disability film or anything like that. There's a lot of beautiful scenery in there, beautiful wildlife shots. And it's just telling the story about a guy who's got a high-level disability. I'm a quadriplegic, so limited mobility, and trying to get out there and capture these things. I hope people just go in there with a bit of an open mind, and come to see something cool and I hope they get out of it whatever they like. They might just watch it and think that was cool, or with a bit of luck, I want to motivate people.

I really am a firm believer that you only get one shot at this life. I feel like before I had my accident, I wasn't getting up early and going for runs. I remember, not long before my accident, my dad wanted to help me clean up some bricks in the backyard. And I was like, I can't be bothered doing that. Whereas now I'd love to help. It's one of those things that you don't appreciate what you got till it's gone. And I just hope people can maybe compare their lives to mine. Not saying I've got it worse by any means. But just my limited mobility may be different to what they have, and hopefully it'll inspire them to get out and go see and do some great things.

THE ARTS

In a year where the Australian arts scene was utterly devastated by a pandemic that caused reduced capacity events, shuttered theatres, and kept audiences driven away, it was comforting to see Aussie arts history being celebrated at length through documentaries.

Madeleine Martiniello's joyous *Palazzo Di Cozzo* told the story of Franco Cozzo, a man who brought a slice of Italian culture and grandeur to the homes of Australians with his extravagant baroque handmade furniture. With *Palazzo Di Cozzo*, Martiniello reminded the culture that thrives within our homes, a notion that was reflected in *Alick and Albert*, where the Pacific Ocean home of the Torres Strait informed the culture of Alick Tipoti's artwork. This marriage of art and culture was also masterfully documented in Wayne Blair & Nel Minchin's expansive and emotional *Firestarter: The Story of Bangarra*, following the lives of three brothers Stephen, David and Russell Page as they turned a dance group into a First Nations cultural landmark.

2021 saw Australian culture lose one of the greatest actors of all time, David Gulpilil AM. Within his close friend Molly Reynolds' stunning documentary *My Name is Gulpilil*, viewers were given one final chance to celebrate David's oeuvre and honour his legacy. David walked viewers through his life story, telling it in the manner that he wanted to tell it.

Legacies were a key aspect of many other arts-focused documentaries, with Bruce Beresford's short film, *An Improbable Collection*, taking the time to reassess two neglected European artists who have found their work in an unlikely place: Mildura, Victoria. Elsewhere, Academy Award winning writer/director, John Farrow, was remembered in the appropriately titled *John Farrow: Hollywood's Man in the Shadows*, which revived the Australian filmmaker's legacy in the Golden Age of Hollywood. Living legend cinematographer Christopher Doyle told his own story with all the frankness of someone who has nothing to hide in Ted McDonnell's insightful *Like the Wind*.

But it wasn't just screen legends who got the camera turned on them, it was also family members, as shown with Jim Stevens fascinating exploration into the lives of the Waller family over twenty years in *Meet the Wallers*. With family films making up the bulk of the runtime, *Meet the Wallers* creates a relatable picture of an Australian family living through struggles, hopes, depressions, and more. It's a tender film, one that would work comfortably as a companion piece to Jane Castle's history-exposing *When the Camera Stopped Rolling*. Here, Castle turns her camera towards her mother, Lilias Fraser, and her monumental role in Australian cinema, being a pioneer with over forty films to her name.

This exploration of Australian film history carried through many of the arts-focused documentaries of 2021, with Sally Aitken's celebration of conservationist and cinematographer legend Valerie Taylor in *Playing with Sharks* being one of the most prominent examples of the year. Aitken's embrace of a screen legend is felt through this fascinating journey through Valerie's history as a diver turned cinematographer. Valerie Taylor's impact on Australian cinema was as notable as her impact on international cinema as seen with her role in filming great white sharks for Steven Spielberg's industry-transforming *Jaws*.

On the small screen, it was 1983's *The Day After* that changed what made-for-TV movies could be, and within Jeff Daniel's deep-dive archive-based *Television Event*, viewers were taken through a step-by-step rundown of just how important film and TV can be – especially when politics gets involved. And closer to home, Jenny Kee and Linda Jackson explored their identity through clothes in Amanda Blue's *Step Into Paradise*.

Politics dictated how artist Rosaleen Norton lived her life in the 1950s, with director Sonia Bible bringing the controversial artist into the 21st century with *The Witch of Kings Cross*. Here, Rosaleen Norton's occult-focused, sexually provocative artwork is celebrated, while the highly conservative government of the time is criticised for their cruel, harsh treatment of Norton's lifestyle and artwork.

Music fans were given a wide array of genre stylings to appreciate with everything from the David McComb and The Triffids biography *Love in Bright Landscapes* (Jonathan Alley), to discovering the next country music legend in Matthew Walker's *I'm Wanita*. Producer Cody Greenwood continued bolstering her impressive filmography with great films like Gracie Otto's *Under the Volcano* which told the story of George Martin's AIR Studios Monserrat and the impact it had on music history. While concert halls across Australia remained empty and bands yearned to play in front of audiences once again, Aussie rock band Tropical Fuck Storm joined up with co-director Nina Renee and took off to the Victorian countryside to make *Goody Goody Gumdrops*, a concert film where the band played to a crowd of dogs wandering around in a paddock.

Arts-focused documentaries are represented with pieces on *Playing with Sharks, Palazzo Di Cozzo, Firestarter: The Story of Bangarra, My Name is Gulpilil, Like the Wind, An Improbable Collection, Love in Bright Landscapes*, and *I'm Wanita*.

INTERVIEW
PLAYING WITH SHARKS - DIRECTOR
SALLY AITKEN

Valerie Taylor is an Australian icon made famous for her fearless diving skills, underwater cinematography, and for her conservationist work alongside husband Ron Taylor. Director Sally Aitken explores Valerie's inspirational life within the Disney Original documentary *Playing with Sharks*, taking viewers from Valerie's early days as a competitive diver, to becoming shark bait and testing out a chain mail diving suit, to filming shark sequences for Steven Spielberg's iconic blockbuster *Jaws*.

Sally Aitken is a director who gives her subjects space to explore their own stories, telling them from an emotional place. With her AACTA Award nominated doc on film critic *David Stratton: A Cinematic Life*, Sally walked with David through his life history, and in turn, explored Australian film history at the same time. With *Playing with Sharks*, Sally heads out into open waters with Valerie, affording the living legend the time to step into the past and revisit memories, as well as catch up with some aquatic friends that she'd met along the way. By allowing her subjects to be free and comfortable, Sally Aitken reveals herself as a tender and empathetic director, forever allowing her subjects to feel free within the eye of the ever-observant camera.

Alongside *Playing with Sharks*, which Sally won the World Cinema – Documentary award at the 2021 Sundance Film Festival, her work in 2021 also included the Disney+ special *Shark Beach with Chris Hemsworth*. Sally was nominated for an AACTA award for Best Documentary alongside producer Bettina Dalton for *Playing with Sharks*, while editor Adrian Rostirolla was recognised with a nomination for his editing. Composer Caitlin Yeo had a terrific year at the 2021 AACTA Awards, winning for Best Original Score in a Documentary for *Playing with Sharks*, and for Best Original Score in Television for *New Gold Mountain*.

Playing With Sharks had a limited theatrical run in Australia prior to being exclusively released via the Disney+ streaming service.

Interview conducted December 2021.

▶▷▶

I just love Valerie Taylor with all that she's done. And I loved your work with David Stratton's documentary which was just equally brilliant. Playing With Sharks really was a pairing made in heaven.

Sally Aitken: Thank you on both counts, and so interesting because I had an email from a mutual friend of Tim Winton's just yesterday actually — I'm mentioning it because of the WA connection — and I had had the good fortune to meet Tim earlier this year on a on a different project. And he, like you, said "I'm desperate to see your film. You know, I just — Val Taylor." They've actually worked together in the past, especially around the constant protection of Ningaloo Reef and so on. She's one of those figures that's touched people in incalculable ways and across multiple generations.

Very much so.

SA: I'm so happy to have been part of something that means her story can be even more profoundly understood, because she's completely unique.

Very much so. That's what I've noticed with your work, you embrace people who are really monumental figures in their field of work. David with film criticism and film preservation in Australia, and then Valerie with both film and being an ecological activist, her support and care for the oceans and for the wildlife that lives there, it's really important. Is that what draws you to being a filmmaker to telling these stories?

SA: Oh, that's such an interesting question, because I thought you were going to put Frank Gehry also in there.

Yes, yeah, Frank Gehry as well.

SA: (laughs) No. And actually, I was gonna make a very flippant joke about just having a passion for seniors!

I didn't want to say it, I didn't want to say it.

SA: I'm obviously always humbled by the idea of the human capacity for greatness. But I wouldn't necessarily say that's what compels me as a filmmaker. I'm very, very interested in shedding light on stories that really can offer something – and particularly on stories that we think we know – but that you offer something new, a new lens on what you think you already know. That's very interesting to me.

It's the way of making those stories accessible. It's really important to me that it's not some indulgent filmmaker ego trip, that I really want the work to have some value in terms of a greater understanding of something, or cementing a legacy or shining a light in an area that has been underexposed. It's the stories and the people that compel me. Of course, I take the visual side very seriously, and I'm immensely passionate about the craft.

But some people feel that they themselves have really important things to say. I suppose my approach is I want to shine the light on the thing.

With Valerie, did you grow up knowing her work? What was your relationship over the years having experienced her and Ron's work?

SA: It's such an interesting question, because I didn't know Valerie's story. I didn't know her work necessarily. I grew up in New Zealand. Of course, their documentaries made it to New Zealand, but I was perhaps the generation just after the height of their popularity in terms of being a regular presence on Australian television.

Funnily enough, you always know you're interested and that there is something really interesting to say when you just hear a bit and you go, "Oh my god, I need to know more. What?" I knew that that was a really good sign because I was like, "Who is this woman who like literally makes herself shark bait? Sorry, who is this person?" I probably brought a freshness because of not knowing.

Bettina Dalton, who is the producer of the film, is a natural history filmmaker and is passionate, and has been passionately concerned with films about the ocean, and had herself been inspired. We were talking about people being influenced. As a young girl, Tina had seen that image of Valerie on the front cover of National Geographic with the shark and her arm, and said that in a very profound way, that inspired Tina to actually pursue a career in natural history. First as a ranger, and then as a storyteller.

That was quite an interesting combination, someone who knows the ins and outs of that story in a deep way and someone who's actually really freshly saying, "Okay, but stripping away these things, what do we want to hang on to?" and in an emotional way that's really interesting about this completely and utterly idiosyncratic character who has profoundly changed the course of conservation, if not the woman as well.

I think it's interesting that I didn't know Valerie, but I'm also a complete obsessive. So as soon I started, it's like, seriously, be careful what you wish for. Because she's kept a handwritten diary since the 1960s. So of course, I started with that. I just started reading like an insane person. And I don't even know if you can begin to imagine the volume of the archive alone. It really was a joy and a curse.

I can imagine. It's like that scene in A Cinematic Life where David has his filing cabinet and going through saying "This is what I've watched and when." I interviewed him when that came out and it is one of my most cherished moments. I had to interview him at about two o'clock in the afternoon. He flew across from Sydney that morning, and by that stage, he'd already watched two films. And I'm like "David, what?" And he's like, "I've got to write it down, I've got to document it." But that's how important these things are.

SA: I know. He's amazing. Actually, there was a gorgeous interview just about two days ago on the ABC. I was just in the car, and David was there. And he was talking about that crucible of his grandmother taking him to the cinema as this young child, and how he can still remember walking down the hill and going into the theatre and that they would go four days a week. I actually had never heard [that] from David, and I was as a story-teller like, "Can I go back and fix that, pop it back in?"

He told the story about how when he was at boarding school. If you recall, he was this young child who was being looked after by his grandmother because his father was away at war and his mother was quite involved in the Red Cross. And his grandmother would take him to the movies. It was really escapism in every way. He fell into this fantasy world as a way of pro-cessing what was going on, and loved it. And then his father came back, they left living with his grandmother, he was quite unmoored.

And then even more insult to injury, his parents decided to have another child. Well of course, because they're reunited after war and poor David was sent off to boarding school. And you know the kind of character that David is, personality wise. But he said that the boys in the dorm at night would ask David to tell them a story, and so he started to recount the sto-ries in the movies that he had absorbed and I was like, "Ah, we should have had that in the film." Because that makes so much sense to me that this early recounting — and then he said, "And I would add my own in-terpretation." And I thought, "Oh my god, there's the critic. There's the crucible of the critic."

That is a really good story. For me, that is a comfort film. I put that on quite frequently, and just experiencing his story is really quite comfort-ing. But then experiencing Valerie's story is also really quite comforting too. There's something your direction, it's not hagiographic or it's not an exuberant celebration of them. It is just "Here is their story." And there's something quite gentle about that. How do you go about deciding how to direct these kinds of stories?

SA: Oh, that's such a hard thing to qualify and quantify. Look, I appreci-ate you saying it's not hagiographic, because it definitely is not that. But I love the idea that people reveal themselves to you. Or that you can help them reveal themselves to the viewer. I also really believe in the power of anecdote and metaphor giving us a lot about who someone is, particularly somebody like Valerie.

Actually, weirdly they're both a bit similar. Not character wise, but neither were very keen on talking deeply about themselves. And it's hopefully a badge or something when people say, "Oh, that was so revealing." Good, okay. But I think that with somebody like Valerie, her whole life has been this kinetic energy. She's actually all about action. She does not dwell in the past, in the sense [that] some people are really very self-aware and introspective, and it's almost like emotions are a bit indulgent for Valerie.

That's not to make her heartless. It's actually to say that's the thing that makes her move forwards.

Jaws is a brilliant example of that. She's immensely proud of their involvement in the film. For a lot of people, I must say particularly the Americans, they're like "Oh my god, I can't even get my head around that." This sort of hand-wringing, it's very Australian. She's like, "Well, clearly more work needed to be done because clearly it was the stupid public who believed the craft of Steven Spielberg." I don't know how I tackled that other than try and tell the truth of who they are through what they've done and what they say. And look for the ways to let the audience make that connection themselves.

Ron Taylor, Valerie Taylor
Photo ©Bruno Vailati Filming. Used with permission.

Dealing with Ron's death in the film [was interesting]. The craft work of the editing in *Playing with Sharks* is brilliant; Adrian [Rostirolla - the same editor who edited *A Cinematic Life*] and I, we talked a lot about how we would deal with that death because of exactly what I've just said. She's not someone who spends a long time in an emotional place, and yet in an interview — as a director — I know how profound that loss is, and so very carefully approaching that and discussing that and letting that reveal itself and it's very slight in quantity, what she says.

Hopefully a lot of people find that very moving. I think it's that light touch, making sure it isn't untruthful in the way that you reveal something like that. It's not untruthful to how that person compartmentalises that part of their life. When she talks about the pillow, I mean, that says profound loss like nothing else to me.

I always wonder when coming to films like this where I've had a connection with the subjects throughout my life. I grew up watching them with their series Inner Space. My grandmother had this mythology of Jaws. She said, "Oh, you can't watch that film because it's too terrifying. But you can watch the series that the Taylor's did."

SA: Awesome.

And then I didn't watch Jaws until I was twenty, twenty-one. And I was like, "Okay, it is terrifying. Maybe not in the level that I should have been watching it [at] six, seven years of age." But I always wondered if my life connection would be too strong to have the emotional ties to that. But no, the way that Valerie's story is presented, and the stories in her face when she is talking about the friends, the creatures, that she meets in the ocean; it's not a silly thing, there is emotion there. These are genuine friends who she spends time with.

SA: Well, you're an acute reader of film, Andrew, because that whole set-up, the anticipation of going to see my friends, and that unorthodox pairing of this - "What, sorry, you're 85, and you're what, you're going swimming with sharks? Who is this person?" Again, it's that thing of trying to let the audience come to that. They both start out indestructible forces of nature, if you will. And by the end, we've got this profound awakening of the beauty and the fragility of all life. That's the idea anyway.

How was it traveling with her going to the dives?

SA: It was hilarious. She loves a drink in the evening, she's great company. No, it was amazing, actually. Because when we were travelling through the airport to go to Fiji, it was amazing, because every single Qantas staff member — so first of all, she slightly plays it up because she's in the wheelchair so we can get going through. She was streetwise. It was amazing because every single staffer was like "Are you Valerie Taylor?" It was that moment, for me, of seeing the recognition [that] was quite interesting, because until that point, I hadn't really realised the way she had really penetrated the Australian psyche. That was very affirming, actually.

It was very interesting because the film was made for an international distributor and also with the international film-going audience in mind. And we knew that we couldn't make a film that says, "Oh here's this person that everybody knows" because actually, for the rest of the world, she's a hidden figures character. In fact, that's actually how I approached the storytelling in some ways. You know about *Jaws*, you think you know about sharks. What you don't know is this character behind the scenes who's been not only influential in even the origin of *Jaws* — if you actually think about that, that's amazing.

The work that she and Ron were doing was so inspiring to Peter Gimbel for him to go in quest of the great white shark, make *Blue Water White Death*, which then galvanised Peter Benchley to finish writing the story. I love Wendy Benchley when she's like "Peter had this idea about a fish" and I was like "I don't know about that." That's hilarious, right, when you know about it in hindsight. And that movie in turn then came back and Valerie and Ron then responded. It's an amazing bit of both cinema history and also natural history.

Jaws put sharks literally on the cover of Time Magazine. It's not a binary *Jaws*: bad. There's a lot that came out of that film ultimately that has raised awareness in really profound ways. You have to be careful not to reduce the story down to simple good, bad. Not that.

Exactly. As you're saying, it's film history, it's natural history, there's so much tied there. What I find really fascinating is how an idea or how an image can inspire somebody who you never meet on the other side of the globe to do something that will influence your own life. That's a powerful confluence of events.

SA: It really is. And it was so, so interesting, because speaking about that power — in the film we have a section where we're talking about the impact of *Blue Water White Death* and the image and the actual idea of Valerie, this blonde hair under the water, and these giant oceanic white tip sharks – I mean, those scenes make the hairs on the back of my neck stand up – but that potent juxtaposition of this slight — not in spirit — but just physically slight female and this powerfully impressive creature with a mouthful of teeth swimming around without a cage. And then that in turn meant the policeman of a Welsh village had the poster. It's amazing.

Valerie's just been actually back in the States. The number of people who've just come out and said, "You know, I remember" or "I knew" — yeah, it is potent. And it's wonderful to be part of a film [like that]. She won the Jackson Wild Legacy award this year which is essentially the filmmaking and natural history equivalent of the Oscars. It's Jane Goodall, David Attenborough, Valerie Taylor, and it was just so humbling to feel like that might have happened because the film exists and people are now realising what she's done. It's one thing to make a film you feel really proud of it, but to be part of that part of it as well is amazing.

There is an element of selflessness to your filmmaking too that we're talking about here in allowing these stories to take place which is really quite wonderful. There's no ego or anything, it is purely the celebration of Valerie's tale. And that's really important. With the Shark Beach series with Chris Hemsworth, how was that continuation of Valerie's story through a series for you? How did that kind of come about?

SA: They're very different offerings, obviously. And it's very lovely to hear the response about the lack of ego because these films — these ones that we're talking about, Valerie and David — obviously they celebrate a person. But, very, very, very much not hagiographic. I'd use the word celebration and revelation. But it's across the board. It's just about having a curiosity. And it doesn't have to be a person, it can be any subject.

With Chris Hemsworth, I mean, look who wouldn't want to work with Chris Hemsworth? I mean, hello? You know? "Do you want to do another film about sharks?" I'm like, "Maybe?" I'm a curious person so I sort of feel like I had canvassed that area, actually. And then they're like, "And it's with Chris." I was like, "Yeah, yeah, my diary says I'm free." (laughs)

So that was probably more a curiosity on my behalf, if I'm being really honest about it, about the magnitude — not that that's what the film is about — but why I said yes was I'm interested to know what it's like to work with someone who carries that amount of aura and celebrity. Absolutely not in an egotistical way, I might say. Chris is a really, really hard-working, absolutely lovely guy. We got on really well. [He's] really funny. So Australian. Like he's carrying the boom kit, you know what I mean? I'm like, "What?" I'm the director that's like, "Yeah, we're on the smaller doc. Oh shoot, I'd really like you to walk twenty-five minutes now to the inland because it's gonna be worth it." And he was like, "Okay. Let's go!" My interest there was probably more in the experience of entering Chris' world and what that was really like. The story itself I put directorially speaking in a slightly different context.

I want to reach back and talk about the imagery of Valerie in this swim-suit in the ocean, and that Bond-esque figure is so iconic. It really is. And I rewatched Girls Can't Surf last week which is a brilliant documentary.

SA: Yeah. Isn't that a wonderful film? Oh my god, the energy in that film is just — I loved it so much.

And it's interesting to watch them so close together because they are about figures who are breaking into masculine dominant societies, places. What's it like telling that aspect of Valerie's story here?

SA: Well, we just channel the film industry, Andrew, because they're male-dominated spaces as well.

That's true. It is true.

SA: One of the most interesting things for me is I absolutely love the tex-ture in the film archive of Ron and Valerie's collection; the colour, the stock, just the extraordinary things that they've seen and captured over the years. Interestingly, for me personally, when I watched *Girls Can't Surf*, I was like, "Oh my god, I'm looking at my photo album." Because I'm more of that generation and I remember when Billabong shorts came in. I was wearing them [as a] teenager.

I think that what is really interesting about both of those films is that they do tackle that question of trailblazing in areas that were dominated — not exclusively male but certainly heavily dominated by, if you like, a mascu-line force. And we'd joke a little bit — because actually if you say the word feminist to Valerie, she bristles. She's like, "I was just doing my thing," you know, and we've had lots of really interesting conversations about "Maybe she was just underwater when second wave feminism happened."

But it's interesting because Valerie was quite singular in that world, and therefore it's not as threatening. You become this kind of curiosity. I would say for those surfers because there's more of them, there's more of a push-back, it's suddenly "Oh, they're a bit more of a threat." And that's true, I think, in all spheres of life for women. You look at the exceptionalism of a woman — Margaret Thatcher, and it's not somehow as threatening. But suddenly when there's more women in a space.

What's so interesting is there's heaps of room on that platform, if we just keep building extra bits of platform.

With someone like Valerie, she was a model. She loves pink. Nothing is really neatly categorised. It's not like you can't be those things. And I personally feel the more stories we have about women in all kinds of spheres, the less 'female diver' or 'female surfer' or 'female director' needs to be the qualifier at the beginning. It's the full range of the complexity of what it is to be a person. You know, we see all sorts of stories about men doing all sorts of things. And we don't say 'male diver'.

We just don't do that. Hopefully we'll get to that point. But we're fair ways off it at the minute.

There's a moment where Valerie gets told that she can't wear the pink swimsuit, and you can hear the sadness in her voice. "Well, I like that colour. It looks good on me."

SA: Yeah, exactly.

It just heightens how much of a character she is, and how exciting she is to spend time with.

SA: And constantly surprising, you know? We did a lot of media obviously, internationally and so on. It still goes on, it's wonderful. It's such a joy to speak about the film. When we might be on a Zoom and Valerie's there, and someone will ask something and I just sit back, "I haven't heard that story, that's amazing." And she's befriended my daughter. I have a thirteen-year-old daughter who's a really intelligent young woman, and Valerie has just really embraced Juliet. She's constantly open, Valerie.

You've got a good connection.

SA: We've got a great connection. Which is not to say that we didn't have our moments in the edit suite where she was saying, "Oh, do we have to put that shot in?" She feels pain when she sees the early slaughtering shots. And I was like, "Yeah, we do, actually. Sorry. We do." They're robust conversations, for sure.

And they are hard scenes to watch, for sure.

SA: Oh yeah.

I've watched the Becoming Cousteau doc as well—

SA: [by] Liz Garbus.

—and that has so many hard scenes to watch. But then it pays off in the end where you see the activism coming out of learning about the actions, learning that we shouldn't have done that. What I like about both of

*these films too is that you provide figures or you give a platform for fig-
ures who become inspirations for others. You're talking about Valerie's
relationship with your daughter and it reminds me of when I met Jane
Goodall years ago, and she talked about the Roots & Shoots organisation
that she's got, getting young people interested in activism in looking after
the environment. And then watching David's film, it's like getting people
excited about talking about Australian films again.*

*Is that something that you enjoy, getting to encourage people to be ex-
cited by the subjects?*

SA: The thing for David... this was not the driving force in the film but hopefully it means that it worked in some way because the number of people
who responded saying, "I now really want to go and see all these films." I
mean, he was so ecstatically happy with that response, I can't tell you. The
number of people who come in response to Valerie's film and say, "I didn't
know, and now I'm going to be much more conscious about the plastic" or
the whatever it is that they feel that they've taken away, just the awareness
of how few sharks there are. I mean, they're not made as earnest campaign
films, if you know what I mean. They're made as adventure stories or insightful history or whatever. But if they have that effect, then that's great.

*I want to touch on your work as a filmmaker. What do you want to achieve
as a filmmaker? When you look back over the years and you say, "This is
what I've done," do you have an end goal in place to be like "This is what
I want to have achieved"?*

SA: Oh my gosh.

It's a deep question, I'm sorry.

SA: No, no. It's a great question. I can tell you what I don't want, which is to
be boxed as one thing. I very much hope for many, many, many years over
the future that the work continues to evolve and people are surprised, and
that there's a very diverse range of subjects. I'm a curious person. I want
the work to reflect that curiosity. I really genuinely believe that the world is
absolutely full of stories just waiting to be uncovered. I hope it's in the line
of being visually exciting. The visual language is really important to me.

With that in mind, I'm passionate about moving into drama as well, narrative drama. I am always drawn, however, to the unusualness of human
life. I'm sure that whatever the work is, whether it is ultimately a narrative
or a documentary, that it will have some of that sense of wonder actually
at the world. And that the way that they're made is not conventional, that
the craft is interesting and surprising too.

Your voice does strike through there. And the editing is so wonderful in these films, too. It complements everything so perfectly. And I love the way that the modern shots counterbalance the brilliant cinematography that Ron does. It is gloriously presented here, which is so wonderful.

SA: That's so lovely. It's interesting, just to share one anecdote, you asked about travelling with Valerie. Very, very early on in the piece, we went to Fiji. And I'd already begun the deep dive into the archives. And we'd gone and we'd actually filmed those scenes of her cageless with the bull sharks. Actually, just bizarrely, that was one of the first things we shot. We shot the ending first. It was because the water temperature is good at that time of year and the sharks are plentiful.

We had obviously a brilliant day on the boat and we were coming back to shore. I was looking at Valerie, and she was looking off to the side. And I was like, "Oh my god, I've seen that same face." And that night, I pulled up the rushes from that day and put a frame grab of this face in repose looking out to the ocean. And I found the same shot from a reel from the 1960s, and I put them next to each other, and I was like, "That's the film." There's something in that juxtaposition.

That's the life. You don't know as a younger person where your life is going to go. And you don't necessarily have the privilege as an older person to look at yourself at that time. But in film, you're able to bridge that timespan in a way that becomes quite profound. And then that way, it's all about stories, you know. Your life is something that exists in all those planes. The past and present meeting was actually quite conscious and it came from that moment on the boat.

One of the things which is really striking is how the use of archival footage reminds us how important it is to — not document everything in our lives — but to actually make note of the important moments in our lives. Make note of the non-important moments in our lives. And those aspects are obviously what makes up a lot of the archival footage. It reminds how important it is to archive and document everything.

SA: Look, I agree. And you know, when you watch any film that's full of this extraordinary archive, you think, how did they have the presence of mind to document it there? I don't know if you've seen, there's a beautiful film *Secret Love* [by Chris Bolan] on Netflix. The love story of a lesbian couple whose relationship has been secret for seventy years, and oh my God, the archive! The archive is just incredible. Get snapping, Andrew. Get recording and snapping.

REVIEW

FIRESTARTER: THE STORY OF BANGARRA, MY NAME IS GULPILIL, AND LIKE THE WIND

THE LEGACY STORIES OF BANGARRA DANCE THEATRE, DAVID GULPILIL, AND CHRISTOPHER DOYLE

The legacy of some of Australia's finest creative icons were cemented in history with three powerful documentaries: Wayne Blair & Nel Minchin's *Firestarter: The Story of Bangarra*, Molly Reynolds *My Name is Gulpilil*, and Ted McDonnell's *Like the Wind*. Each film gives their subjects the space, time, and ease to be open about their life stories, placing their truth in the cinematic history books.

Within *Firestarter: The Story of Bangarra*, viewers are invited to learn the legacy of the Page brothers, Stephen, David, and Russell. Collectively, they make up the Bangarra Dance Theatre, and with Wayne Blair and Nel Minchin's considerate direction, the vitality of the dance company is given space to breathe on screen. With the establishment of the National Aboriginal Islander Skills Development Association (NAISDA) in 1975, the world renowned Bangarra Dance Theatre was created in 1989. With it came a venue to foster and grow Indigenous art, dance, and music, and break into mainstream stages across Australia, telling these deeply personal stories with each new event.

With the blend of archival footage, interviews, and captured dances, *Firestarter: The Story of Bangarra* becomes an ultimate collaboration between cinematographers, with Tyson Perkins, Andy Taylor, Ricky Schamburg, Peter Alton, and Luke Peterson all working together, across time, to honour the explosion of Indigenous culture across the decades. From the 1967 cultural referendums, through to the protests during the 1988 Australia Bicentenary, to Paul Keating's Redfern speech in 1992, through to the act of bringing First Nations culture to the world at the Sydney Olympics in 2000; each era is embraced with visual power.

Each shot reinforces the fight that the Page brothers had to push against the dominant white culture that continues to smother the oldest continuous culture in the world. Here, audiences crave 'tribal dances', applauding the act of traditional dance, only to criticise and question the move towards progressive, modern dance routines. For the Page brothers, the dance theatre is integral to their identity, to who they are, and as Aboriginal land continued to be away and Indigenous rights were continually denied, the weight of the trauma became unbearable.

Firestarter: The Story of Bangarra reminds that art is a political entity, and within it, intergenerational and residual trauma resides. For the dancers at

Bangarra, they have no choice but to push through that trauma to present their cultural identity to a wider audience. There is extreme power within artistic activism, as each new Bangarra production reveals in impressive detail. Wayne Blair and Nel Minchin ensure that each frame honours and celebrates one of the most iconic and important dance companies Australia has ever been fortunate enough to witness.

Firestarter: The Story of Bangarra received a wider audience, thanks in part to Screen Australia's 'Our Summer of Cinema' campaign that highlighted the variety of stellar Australian films on offer during the 2021 summer film going season.

Given an equally wide reception and audience was Molly Reynolds' emotional farewell to the Australian screen legend, David Gulpilil, with *My Name is Gulpilil*. Released into theatres, with a successful screening on ABC soon afterwards, *My Name is Gulpilil* was Reynolds second documentary made in collaboration with David after 2015's *Another Country*.

Trying to encompass the life and legacy of David Gulpilil over the space of 100 minutes is a difficult prospect for any filmmaker, but with tenderness, compassion, and keen awareness of the weight of time, Reynolds gives David's story the respect it deserves. Moving from archival footage, to past interviews and stage performances, to present day where David's health is failing, informs just how quickly life can slip by.

Made with the assistance of the Adelaide Film Festival, *My Name is Gulpilil* tells the story of an artist who knows the power of a story. Importantly, David's own life story. David is keenly aware of how his face, his voice, and his expressions can fill a frame, and in turn, is fully aware of the importance of his life story within Australian history. At one point, David says, "My acting is normal, I don't have to pretend. I just jump in and the camera sees me. Like this, like you're looking at me now." When David's self-awareness is paired with Reynolds' empathetic direction, and Maxx Corkindale & Miles Rowland's delicate camerawork, *My Name is Gulpilil* conjures the feeling of a grand investiture.

Nature and country play a vital role in David's life. An early shot sees David following an emu, walking together along a road. As David looks back at the camera, the place where we have come to know him, the emu follows. Later, as David's cancer diagnosis and treatment becomes clearer, David talks about how Yolngu lore says that he will become a fish while he awaits rebirth. Marrying his future with the present, we see a fish on the shore, gasping for breath, stuck between two worlds.

Removed from his homeland, David finds himself receiving treatment in suburbia, making the daily journey down the brick driveway to the mailbox, waiting for news that will never come. The mundane routine of suburban life smothers his connection to country, and with the medical treatment that exhausts and stilts David's energy, he starts to become a shadow of who he once was. It's when David returns to country that he's able to recall his past life, to envision his future.

Reynolds use of imagery in these moments is inspired, with shots where the galaxy transforms into the image of an MRI matching the emotional intensity of the film. Throughout the film, Reynolds' tries to find David's connection to country within the shot, like the now iconic image of David, draped in a golden yellow jacket, retelling his life stories like he has the dirt of the earth embracing him. It's here that the joy of tales of being introduced to 'ganja' by Bob Marley, or getting stoned with Dennis Hopper come through with David's cheekiness and charm.

Tania Nehme's masterful editing carries us through David's life, the past, the present, the future, allowing us to experience them all in unison, as if time doesn't exist. At once, the youthful David that danced for the Queen, who brought Aboriginal culture to a global audience with films like *Walkabout* and *Storm Boy*, sits alongside the David who yearns to be on his homeland, who talks of loneliness, who speaks of his own mortality.

Throughout *My Name is Gulpilil*, we're continually reminded by the power of storytelling. While the credits might state that Molly Reynolds is the director, this is clearly a collaborative piece, with Molly becoming the conduit to help David tell his story. By its close, the harmony of preservation and memorial works in unison to celebrate the legacy of Australia's finest actor.

Alongside countless other documentaries, *Firestarter: The Story of Bangarra* and *My Name is Gulpilil* show the importance of archiving and preserving the stories of artists, icons, and monumental figures while they are alive to tell their own story. Sometimes sitting the subject down directly in front of a camera, and recording the answers to their questions is all that needs to happen to secure their legacy on film.

This is what Ted McDonnell did with his film *Like the Wind*, which saw famed cinematographer Christopher Doyle open up about his creative process, working outside of Australia, and more in frank detail. Doyle is an artist who doesn't beat about the bush, calling a spade a spade, and through McDonnell's patient direction and questioning, he is able to explore his influences, the manner he works on set, all the while reinforcing the need to be clear with your creative ambitions with statements like "Do you have something to say? Because if you don't, who will listen?"

Interspersed between Doyle's dialogue with the camera are moments from films he has shot, like *Chungking Express* and *Ashes of Time*, as well as support from creative colleagues like Phillip Noyce who reminds viewers of the impact that Christopher Doyle has in filmmaking. In a moment of condemnation, Doyle laments that the Australian film model of financing simply isn't viable for his creative energy, acknowledging that under Australia's production schedule, he would be making one film every five or so years, rather than the rapid pace of projects that he takes on board. For Doyle, quality and quantity are synonymous. It doesn't matter what he is doing, just as long as he is creating *something*.

While *Like the Wind* feels at times disjointed, with its non-linear storytelling, it plays as if it's mirroring how Christopher Doyle is as a person; a little bit scattered, a little bit unfocused, but with all the energy in the world to just *create*. Just like *Firestarter: The Story of Bangarra* and *My Name is Gulpilil, Like the Wind* reinforces the need to honour, celebrate, and most importantly, reflect the subject's personality and life within the filmmaking itself. Together, these films celebrate the need for documenting the legacies of creative icons.

INTERVIEW
AN IMPROBABLE COLLECTION - DIRECTOR
BRUCE BERESFORD

AFI Award winning director Bruce Beresford has a career that ducks and swerves through different genres, from the Ozploitation flick, *Money Movers*, to war drama, *Breaker Morant*, to the Best Picture winning, *Driving Miss Daisy*, and now to his short documentary: *An Improbable Collection*.

Playing at the 2021 Melbourne Documentary Film Festival, *An Improbable Collection* follows the works of artists Frank Brangwyn (English) and William Orpen (Irish), both of whom have extensive works from their collection based in (of all places), Mildura.

Bruce talks about how the collection came to be there, the importance of embracing and respecting art, and how art and artists change throughout the years.

Interview conducted July 2021.

▶▷▶

You're really digging into the art history of Australia with this and At the Coliseum Deluxe [which Bruce provided narration for]. How did you come to this story?

Bruce Beresford: I'd always collected paintings by those two painters in England, because both of them fell from favour, [so] the paintings are very cheap. Even with my puny income, I could buy some. And I've got them because nobody wanted them. Even though they were two of the most famous artists in the world at one point. Nobody wants them now. I've been buying them for some years. I've only got two by Orpen, but I've got about 15 by Brangwyn. And someone said to me one day in London, "Oh, did you know there's a lot of Brangwyns and Orpens in Australia?" And I said, "No, where are they?" And they said "In this little town called Mildura." I said "No, impossible!" Anyway, when I came back to Australia, I drove down to Mildura, which is a long way from Sydney. And there they are. And I tell the story in the film about this guy who collected them and nobody wanted them, and when he died, he left them to the Mildura council.

So much art history, just sequestered in a place that is so far away from where it began.

BB: I think what's so extraordinary is that the two of them Brangwyn and Orpen, are two of the most famous artists. They were they weren't just sort of mildly talented, they were literally household names.

The paintings that you feature in the documentary are really very stunning.

BB: Oh they're fabulous.

I found it very informative. And it made me a bit sad actually. One of my main passions is film criticism and discussing film history, and yet one of the things highlighted in the film is how the critics of art at the time just pushed them aside.

BB: You've hit the nail on the head. That was one of the reasons I made the film because I was so intrigued by that. Just how famous you can be. Bang, you know?

What does that mean to you as a as an artist, as a director?

BB: Well, I don't lose any sleep over it. I mean, it's something that happens. It'd be interesting to see if either of those two painters ever make a comeback, because as I pointed out at the end of it, there've been other painters who have. Look at someone like Norman Lindsay. You could pick up pictures of his 20 to 25 years ago, you could get just about any Norman Lindsay picture for a few dollars. Literally a few dollars. Now they sell hundreds of thousands of dollars. So he came back.

Is it a matter of encouraging discussion about these artists?

BB: I think what happens is that art movements shift, tastes change. People fall out of fashion. When I was a student, there was a big swing towards abstract pictures. And anybody who did a picture with something recognisable in it was laughed at. Well, that's changed a lot now there's been a bit of a move back towards figurative painting.

I don't know if you've been watching the Rachel Griffiths series Finding the Archibald but I found that very interesting.

BB: Yes, well, looking for all those pictures is quite interesting.

Just the curiosity of seeing so much history — not lost as such, because some of these are in people's attics or people's living rooms and things like that. How do we keep this kind of history alive? How do we keep it relevant?

BB: I'm surprised at the number of famous Archibald pictures they can't find. I suppose they sold them off. Of course, there's a lot of paintings. Brangwyn and Orpen between them painted an enormous number of pictures. In London, there's a lot of Orpens in the Imperial War Museum, because he was a wartime artist in the First World War for four years. They have a lot of his best pictures. Of course, that's what they're interested in. They just want pictures of action at the front. Brangwyn lived so long, he lived until he was 88, and was incredibly prolific.

I find the war imagery was so dramatic and so powerful and striking. And yet the varied paintings just carry so much different emotions and drama and life to them that I was quite impressed by how broad the emotional scope was there.

BB: It's true. There were things in the film that struck me as very funny. I mean, look, he spent seven years painting those pictures for the House of Lords, and then they rejected them.

Which is a real shame.

BB: What a blow. But they're there. You can see them in Swansea in Wales.

What's the difference of seeing these kinds of paintings in person as opposed to a picture on your phone or the computer?

BB: Of course, when you see any great art for real, it does make a tremendous impact on you. I remember when I first went to Paris and I went to the Jeu de Pamme to look at the van Goghs. When you actually see them, it's quite frightening. You realise that no reproduction ever really reproduces them. The actual picture is more startling. I think that's true of the Brangywns and the Orpens too.

For me personally, a couple of years ago I went back to Canberra and got to see the Pollock's Blue Poles painting. And, I've watched documentaries on it and read so much about and have seen pictures of it, but then seeing it in person— it's overwhelming. As you're saying, you've got a couple in your home. What does that do to you as somebody living with such powerful art?

BB: Lots of people got pictures in their home. It's not as if I've spent a fortune buying these pictures. Remember, these were pictures nobody wanted. I didn't spend a lot of money on them. The investment's been incredibly modest.

But it's less about the investment and more about the art itself, isn't it? How you feel about it.

BB: I love having those pictures. We've also got a flat in London where some of the best pictures are there, and I find when I'm away, I really miss them. I've only got pictures in the house that I love to live with. In the room I'm talking to you now, there's a lot here. And the living room at the back the house is full of them. I've never had the money to spend a lot of money on art. I've never made that much money. It's all been fairly modest. And I've been lucky that I stumbled across Brangwyn and Orpen when they were out of fashion. I got them cheap. Well, they're still out of fashion.

Do you have to register that you've got them anywhere? Do you have to notify somebody that you've got them? There's no catalogue or anything?

BB: No, there's a lot of books about Brangwyn. There's only one ever published after 1935. All the books that I've got on Brangwyn, huge books, they're all mostly from the 20s and up to 35. And after that, there's none.

And then we've got this collection in Mildura.

BB: The collection in Mildura, they have a lot of pictures. Because that guy Elliot really, really went to town buying them.

Is that a permanent collection?

BB: Yes. They're not always all on display, but they frequently are. Because actually in Mildura, they haven't got much else. The Brangwyns and the Orpens, that's really what their collection is.

As you were saying before, there was a bit of a surprise in your voice when you were saying out of all places, Mildura has these paintings. In the middle of nowhere, effectively.

BB: People in England were amazed to find out they were there.

These paintings seem so tied to the history of England and Ireland in so many different ways. What does it mean to have them so far away from home?

BB: I think it's like any great art really, you can admire it anywhere. A lot of the galleries in Australia are full of medieval paintings, Renaissance paintings, 19th century paintings. They still make a big impact, because the artist had something to say when they did them. And I think the emotional appeal is universal.

That profound painting with the nude woman and the priest is just over-whelming. It really is.

BB: Oh yes, the Orpen, yes.

Did you get to see that one in person?

BB: Oh yes, that's in Mildura. Most of the pictures in the film are in Mildura. Not all, there was a section on some of the murals that Brangwyn did in America. The people who had those, I got them to send me images of them which we could use. And of course, then we went to Dublin and there's a statue of Orpen that's gone up now.

It's a beautiful statue.

BB: He's not forgotten in Dublin.

One of the things that is touched on is how you talk about the different artists have to use various different tools, and they create different things. It's not just paintings, there's furniture, there's sculptures. You have a fascinating and deep career in feature films and then moving to documentaries.

BB: Actually, when I was in England in the Seventies, I did a whole lot art documentaries.

Returning to roots in a way.

BB: I did about 10 of them for the Arts Council of Great Britain. They must still have them.

And what were they about?

BB: Oh, I did a great pile. I did one on Magritte. I did one on Lichtenstein, Poussin, Henry Moore, Barbara Hepworth, Giacometti, and two or three others. There was a great pile. I did them for the Arts Council. And then they presumably still got them all.

I would really hope so because your work is greatly important and just like talking about these artists, we don't want to lose these important cultural aspects of different artists careers, and it would be really something to be able to dig into those and to see your journey as a director throughout the years from these documentaries to modern day.

BB: Yes, I've not got copies of all those documentaries I did. I didn't have copies of any of them. And I assume the Arts Council in Britain still got them. I've never even looked up online, but I'm sure they've still got them. One of them about Magritte was actually shown it in the cinemas throughout Britain. The others were really for special screenings or television. But the one on Magritte was shown in the theatres.

What type of art got your eye immediately?

BB: The Arts Council ones were really ones where they would get in touch with me and say, "Look, Bruce, there's this special exhibition on Magritte or Lichtenstein. We want you to make a film about it." What I always tried to do was to make it interesting so that it told you a story about them. And I was usually working with some critic who was a specialist in that particular guy. They weren't just photographic records, they were documentaries with information. There wasn't everybody I was mad about. I thought Magritte was great, but there were others that I wasn't that crazy about their work, but I still made the films. I was very young.

How old would you have been when you're doing those?

BB: In my 20s.

And then you returned to Australia.

BB: I came back to Australia when I was about 30. I've still got a flat in London. So I go back and forth. And if it wasn't for the COVID thing, I'd be there now.

As you're making these films, do you branch across different countries? I know you've made some American films and British films.

BB: It's just where the script takes you. Whenever I get a script that excites me, it could be anywhere. I've made films in all sorts of strange places.

You certainly have a very varied and broad filmography that you've got. Do you think about that much?

BB: Not really, because I think if I come across a story, a script, or maybe I even write it myself, something that interests me and it could be anywhere. And also I don't like to repeat myself. I like to do a film on a subject, and I usually find by the time it's finished, I'm exhausted with it. And then I'd like to do something different.

I was thinking about this yesterday when I was watching this, we've had the the 40th anniversary Breaker Morant last year, and then the 40th anniversary of Puberty Blues. And now I'm watching An Improbable Collection, and I'm thinking, could you get any more diverse?

BB: (laughs) No, not from *Barry McKenzie* to *An Improbable Collection.*

It's crazy. It's great as an Australian film lover that people are given the chance to dig back into your filmography and see how diverse the films were. I think that a lot of people when they hear the name Bruce Beresford, I imagine they have a film that comes into their mind. And for me, it's Breaker Morant.

BB: Yes, it tends to be *Breaker Morant* or *Driving Miss Daisy.*

When you think of a Bruce Beresford film, what do you think of?

BB: You know, I don't know that I'd ever think about it really. Each film has been a story that fascinated me and usually a big struggle to get them made. If someone says to me, "Oh, after you've done all of those films, you must be able to do anything you want." I wish that was true! It's certainly not true. It's still very difficult. Every one of those films is a big effort involved to getting them off the ground.

I imagine that might have been something that would have been proposed to you after winning one of the most prestigious awards around which is Best Picture. I imagine that people would have assumed that the world is your oyster after that. What was that like after that?

BB: Well, it didn't really make a lot of difference, because I'd still say "I want to do this, I want to do that." And they'd say, "Oh I won't make any money Bruce, we can't finance that kind of stuff." It might have helped a little bit. It must have helped a bit because I've kept working.

You have, and you've done a great job. You've made a really impressive, important career. I want to touch on something raised earlier, which is the impact of critics. Who do you feel deems an artist to be minor? With the artists that are in An Improbable Collection, there were critics who said that they were minor, but is it also society as a whole who deems them to be minor?

BB: Well, it's the art critics really. They moved from trend to trend, and they're the ones who decide. And then of course as I said in the documentary, these positions are never fixed. A lot of these people, they're forgotten for hundreds of years, and then make comebacks. That's happened to a lot of Renaissance painters. They happen to people like Caravaggio, who was considered a hack for 200 years, and suddenly someone writes a big article and says, "Wait a minute, let's have another look at this." Next thing you know, his stuff, if it ever comes on the market, is going for millions and millions and millions of dollars. Certain art critics can be very, very influential. And they really control taste.

Do you feel that that's the same case for Australian film criticism as well?

BB: Not to the same extent, and not to the same extent these days. When I started making films, there were certain critics like Pauline Kael or David Denby in America, who, what they said about a film tended to make it a success or not. If Pauline Kael liked it, or Denby in the New York Times liked it you could think well, it would probably be a success. But now everybody's a critic, with all the stuff online. There's so many opinions floating around, that those people who used to be very dominant opinion formers don't have that power anymore. They're still influential, I think, but it's not as not as total as it was.

What about the changing aspect of the Australian film industry. How do you feel that it's changed over the years?

BB: I think it's been an incredible worldwide success, really. It's gone on and on and on with really first-class films never stopping. You think, "Who comes now?," and then someone else crops up and someone else crops up and someone else crops up, and of course, it never will stop. And there'll always be talented people who've got something to say which is new and original and fresh. I'm very optimistic about it.

With Puberty Blues it's nice to know that your film has been respected enough that people have made a TV show about it. What's your reflections on that film 40 years on?

BB: You know, I haven't seen it since we did it. I've never seen it again.

Do you revisit any of your films at all?

BB: No, never.

Why is that?

BB: Well, because by the time that you've finished them, and they're all ready to be watched, I've seen them so many times and worked so hard on them for so long that when they're finished, they're finished.

Even something like Breaker Morant?

BB: Yeah, I've never seen it again.

That kind of surprises me.

BB: Do you sit down and read your old articles?

No, no, that's true. That is true. Especially the older ones where you look at it and you go, "Why did I do that."

BB: I'd probably feel the same about the film.

REVIEW
PALAZZO DI COZZO

MELBOURNE LEGEND FRANCO COZZO IS PROUDLY
CELEBRATED IN THIS GRAND DOCUMENTARY

The old joke 'if it's baroque, don't fix it' is more apt than most when it comes to Sicilian homewares icon, Franco Cozzo. For decades, the Melbourne legend has filled television and the airwaves with his distinctive Italian accent, joyfully uttering his ultimate catch phrase 'grand sale, grand sale, grand sale', plus his proudly unique way of pronouncing 'Footscray'. In Madeleine Martiniello's life-affirming documentary, *Palazzo Di Cozzo*, Franco's legacy, and the impact he has had on generations of European migrants and the grander Australian community at large, is given a tender and comedic exposé in an utterly joyous manner.

One of the joys of documentary filmmaking is the way the format transports you into the lives of strangers, opening you up to a slice of the world that you didn't know existed. Additionally, a great documentary has the power to leave you feeling like you've learned something about yourself in the process too. As a Perth-born Aussie, I lived far out of the market reach for Franco Cozzo's impactful advertisements, missing a cultural landmark that clearly impacted Melbourne culture, and the Italian diaspora, in a way that enriched our diverse and proudly multicultural society.

Yet, having watched *Palazzo Di Cozzo*, and being invited into a world of cultural variance, I couldn't help but recall the ultimate 90s Perth TV advertisement icon: Luigi, from WA Salvage; a figure who sits safely in the array of 'only 90s kids will remember this' Perth memes with his own iconic catch phrase filling the airwaves 'we aint fancy, but we cheap'. While Luigi and WA Salvage may have disappeared into the history of time, living on in the memories an ageing generation, Franco Cozzo's legend endures through the ages, from his figurehead furniture stores, to his iconic, culture-enhancing advertisements, to his wall-busting smile and generosity, each standing as a testament to luxury furniture, Italian culture, and a changing society.

Martiniello interviews Franco as he sits on an ornate gold throne with plump white leather, draped in a glow of yellow paint, and swallowed in a cloud of cologne. He is a king in his own kingdom, surrounded by a self-made wealth, supported by a burgeoning family. Through archival footage, notably an exuberant interview on the Don Lane show, we see that time has not weathered Franco's vitality and joy for life, Italian culture, furniture, and most importantly of all, his family. Sure, he may have more white hair, and a few more wrinkles, but his heart beats as the same Franco Cozzo who arrived in Australia, bright-eyed and full of motivation. It's an infectious joy, rubbing off on fellow Melbournians, musicians, and artists alike, and ultimately rubbing off on the *Palazzo Di Cozzo* audience.

No greater is the realisation of the communal nature of cinema than in up-roarious moments of delight, warmth, and compassion, as Franco dances with his daughter on her wedding day to a song written in his honour. In my second viewing, I watched *Palazzo Di Cozzo* in a stacked auditorium, delighting in the feeling of laughter rolling throughout the room, while also soaking in the warmth of culture being respected, elevated, and adored. In many ways, it felt like the buzzing feeling of a busy, bustling shopping centre, where the tangible feel of money being exchanged, and the excitement of buying *something* takes place. For want of a better term, given the era we're currently in, it felt *contagious*.

While the exorbitant prices of Franco's furniture might cause alarm (with most having a five-digit figure attached), it's the connection to home and heritage that has many Italian, Greek, and other European expats keen to have a Franco Cozzo adorned home. Martiniello takes us into the homes of some of Franco's most dedicated customers, each of whom explain why they love the kind of 'statement' furniture that Franco sells. In isolation, the ornate couch or marble table might look garish, but in unison with its furniture brethren, there's a harmony that simply makes the room sing like choral angels from above. Amplifying the importance of continued culture is the presence of siblings who stand in their parents home, holding a receipt from decades ago, showing at $17,000 price tag for furniture. The siblings talk about how their parents couldn't afford a car, or luxury items, and lived an impoverished life, but if there was one thing the Italian expats needed to make their home feel like *home*, it was handmade, baroque, Franco Cozzo furniture.

There's never a feeling of Franco fleecing a community hungry for their own culture, but if that thought even enters your mind, a quick trip to Italy to watch these glorious couches and tables being constructed shows you why they fetch such a high price tag. For some, the furniture may be as eccentric as the salesman himself, but there's a warmth and humanity to each piece, crafted by hand, delicately structured out of glorious varieties of prestigious wood and materials. It is, quite simply, the most human furniture we have, and thanks to Martiniello's direction, we understand why it's the furniture for many.

Interspersed between scenes of Franco at work, his commercials, and interview footage, are shots of a magical gold and white Monopoly-esque map showing the outlay of the Melbourne suburbs, hinting at the wealth of Franco Cozzo furniture behind the closed doors of Footscray, North Melbourne, and beyond, while also echoing that glorious baroque style. With great pride and respect, Martiniello builds a grand story of luxury, embracing the values and importance of continued culture, and most pertinent to Australia as it stands today, *Palazzo Di Cozzo* shows the enduring importance and strength of our multicultural society as a whole.

As the interest in baroque furniture declines, so does the foot traffic for Franco's landmark Footscray store. Instead of being a buzzing shop of potential, it becomes a weathered storage facility for almost $5 million worth of furniture. The life and vibrancy still exists, because Franco still exists. *Palazzo Di Cozzo* closes on a note of hope, with Franco vowing to continue on regardless of how many people want to buy his furniture. Whether his children continue his store after he is gone is unclear, but even if Franco Cozzo's furniture stores follow in the footsteps of WA Salvage, at least we have this majestic, beautiful, and downright joyous documentary to help remind us all about the grand icon that is Franco Cozzo.

INTERVIEW
LOVE IN BRIGHT LANDSCAPES - DIRECTOR
JONATHAN ALLEY

Music writer and broadcaster Jonathan Alley embarked on a mammoth journey when he decided to tell the story of David McComb and The Triffids in his first feature-length documentary. With a production that spanned a decade, the resulting film *Love in Bright Landscapes* is as comprehensive and in-depth as any documentary could be about the Australian music legend. With interviews between Triffids band members, David's family members, and his fellow musicians who were inspired by David's work, *Love in Bright Landscapes* helps reflect the music legend in all his glory.

Jonathan Alley has been a music writer and broadcaster for over thirty years, working as a freelancer, producing music, and even presenting on the iconic Triple R FM and Radio National. Jonathan has also worked in film distribution at Madman Entertainment's marketing division, being involved in releasing iconic music documentaries like *DIG!*, *Be Here to Love Me: A Film About Townes Van Zandt*, and *Martin Scorsese presents The Blues*.

Love in Bright Landscapes received a limited theatrical run across Australia. Production of the film was supported by a live concert called Deep in a Dream which featured interpretations of David McComb's songs by Australian artists. Interview conducted September 2021.

What's the process been like over the time of making this?

Jonathan Alley: It's been a mixture of intuition and planning. That I think is probably only appropriate with someone like David. We had a list of people we knew we had to talk to: his parents, his brothers, obviously the other Triffids. But there were other people who were non-musical people that we discovered through speaking to people close to him. For example, we spent a couple of days on the New South Wales South Coast with The Triffids old manager, Sally Collins. We did two interview sessions with her, her sessions were great. Through talking to her, just casually, she mentioned people to us that you're only going to find out about through sitting down and having a chat with people who are sort of between the cracks. So non-musical friends who were very, very close to David, someone like Bill Dunbar in Sydney, who's not a music guy. But he was one of David's closest friends and gave us a great interview would be a good example of that.

I've encapsulated my entire approach to it as sort of intuitive and sort of gut instinct. Dave's own approach to his own writing was incredibly intuitive and about gut instinct. The Triffids' interpretations of his music were overtly intuitive and the songs are all the better for it. I spent a long time knowing what I didn't want, and that was a 'by the numbers' rock doc, sitting behind the studio desk, listening to a guy push a fader up and go, "Hey, listen to the drum sound we got on this track." I just did not want that. And I didn't want a lot of people describing things that had happened, just as talking heads on camera. I knew I didn't want that.

It took me a long time to intuit what I did want, because I didn't see that I had the tools, the aesthetic kind of assets in front of me to achieve that. When certain things coalesced in the last few years, I would say 2017 to 2020, those things would be the fact that we discovered a tranche of letters that John and David McComb had written to one another through the Eighties and Nineties that were a private correspondence, but they were released to us by the family. John has now sadly passed away as well. They were passed on to us by the family. And I think there's material in those letters that's quite personal and quite reflective of where David was at as a person.

On top of that, you had the publication of the poetry through Fremantle Arts Press. I knew that I had to involve the poems in the film in some way, but it would be lazy to lean on [them] too much, but it also would be quite remiss not to include them. I needed to find the best way. We were interviewing DBC Pierre for the film in England, and I was listening to his voice on my headphones, and a little voice just said, "This is the guy to read the poems." And he was into it, he spent one day of 2017 in Australia. And we fingered him for that one day, and he spent a day recording with us in Sydney before he took off again. He was the person to do it because he just had this incredible intuitive empathy to the work. Rather than wanting to sound like David would have sounded, we wanted someone who sounded completely different, and yet also somebody who could speak with empathy to the content of the letters and the poems. All those things basically coalesced to form the way to bring the film to a screen without it becoming what I didn't want, which was something very by the numbers.

It's not by the numbers at all: the archival footage, the slides, the footage of the music being filmed in concerts all just brings it to life and fills it with this energy. It's tangible. For people who aren't familiar with The Triffids, which, in today's day and age, it feels like a surprise that there are still people who are not familiar with The Triffids. One of the things which I found really surprising was how much people were not familiar with The Triffids when they were still around. Even though they were big, they weren't having the impact with band labels that they should have. What were the surprises that you found along the way?

JA: A lot. Inevitably, the deeper you delve into the person behind the work, you're not just analysing the work, you're finding out about what's really driving the person behind them. For someone who is enigmatic as David, then inevitably, there are surprises.

Personally, I think that my major surprise, really, my major revelation was that someone so driven and someone so determined ended up getting quite lost. He was on a certain trajectory, and that was to be successful with his song writing. And the vehicle for that success would be the work that the Triffids did on those songs. The last two records they made, as good as they are — and some of his best song writing is on those records, on *Calenture* and *The Black Swan* — in retrospect, and this probably didn't feel that way at the time, but in retrospect, there's a sort of feeling that things are starting to unravel.

After that, he spends time in London, trying to find this music publishing deal and trying to find a solo deal, spends two years doing that with no real success — a few good singles, some good demos, but didn't get a record out of it, he didn't get a record deal. Then he spent time recording as a satellite member of The Black Eyed Susans, and then he concentrated again on trying to make a success of a solo record. But again, that came unstuck because of the health issues that cropped up. After having this really golden run through the early-to-mid-80s, critically anyway, he really seemed to run up against a few walls through several circumstances, and he didn't seem to have the kind of tools to deal with those. It's quite saddening. Some of it's just happenstance, it's unfortunate circumstance, and some of it is to do with things like fashion, which is forever fickle. He was just so lucky, but he was also so unlucky in so many ways. The fact that he got quite lost was a surprise.

Also, the fact that he seemed to be so many different people to so many different people. In the first few minutes [of the film] is an interview where his childhood friend Julian Douglas-Smith says, "What is [the] real Dave McComb, that's an open door." And then Graham [Lee] says, "Well, he had to be about five different people to be happy." And I think there's really something to that, he had to be so many different people, to different people around him. That must have become quite wearing after a while. He put himself under an enormous amount of pressure to continue to work and I think that must have been, in ways, personally quite wearing.

I also found his humour really surprising. I knew he was funny and, having met him, I knew how black his sense of humour was. When he got ill, it was really black. It was deeply darkly black, and that element surprised me certainly.

There is an interview that you show where somebody asked David about The Triffids being nice people and his response is "What?" It's the realisation that doing an interview is completely different from who they are as a band. What was the difference between the person you interviewed and the person that you see as you're collating their life into a film?

JA: There's a lot to that. First off, I think in broad terms, the David you saw in interviews was at once completely different from the person himself, because when David is being interviewed in general, he, quite obviously and quite understandably, he tends to be talking about the record he's got out. "Well, The Triffids got a new album. David, tell us about this album *Born Sandy Devotional*." So he's gonna talk about the record, of course he is.

The other thing he does, very astutely, is talk about other people's work, the way it's influenced him. A lot of that's very surprising because his taste was so eclectic. This is somebody that read Flannery O'Connor and [Rainer Maria] Rilke, but also loved Roxanne Shanté, and Prince, and trashy late-night television. There's no highbrow, there's no lowbrow. There's just connection. And I think that's a really important element of how Dave saw things. He talked about a lot of external inspiration. And he talked a lot about his own music. It's very, very rare though that he talks about where he is personally. He's just a very private man. And that's totally fair.

But the one place where this does come up, I think he's being interviewed by 6UVS in Perth in the Eighties [now known as RTRFM]. And he just says, "Oh look, I'm sick to death of critics trying to sort of delve into my personal life to interpret how that is being played out on the songs. It's just gone too far. Because I realised that songs are actually just these constructions that can come from all manner of different places. But critics don't seem to understand that they seem to take everything too literally."

And I think that really annoyed him when people took his songs too literally, because let's face it, they're so enigmatic and kind of metaphorical. You'd be an idiot to take them literally. But it seems in the 80s of all eras, of course, if you were ever going to take something too literally, it was probably in the 80s. People obviously did. People thought *Wide Open Road* was actually about a road. So there's that side of him.

To come down to my own interview with him, it didn't very last long, because I was young. I was only 23, and it was for *Love of Will*, the solo album, and the record company hadn't sent me the record. I was out on a limb, trying to sort of fudge questions about things that I didn't really know as much about as I should have. And David, being the sharp individual that he was, picked that up just like that. By the end of the interview, we were a little more relaxed and we sort of found some common ground talking about hip hop music and Al Green, but he could tell that I hadn't heard the record barring maybe two tracks that I had heard because they were out as singles. I'm still annoyed that I still don't own *Love of Will*, and like a lot of people I'd really like to own *Love of Will*, and I don't. It's a pretty weird 20 minutes of our lives in that he meets this young guy who should have done his homework and hadn't, and I walk away going "Oh, gee, that should have gone better. I really respect that person. I could tell there was a lot more that I wanted to be able to ask him but couldn't." And he walks away off into the future, and I walk away off into the future.

Neither of us have got any idea that five years later, he's going to be gone. That I'm going to go and meet his parents. I'm going to go to the houses he lived in as a child. I'm going to meet his close friends. I'm going to read private postcards and letters that he sent to people. Neither of us had any idea of this. And that's really strange to me, that he just walked off and I never saw him again. And yet he's been this constant in my life for the last 13 years.

I literally hear his voice every day. It's like he's there, but of course, he's not.

That's something that I've experienced myself in doing interviews. I interviewed Damian Hill the actor about three weeks before he died, and that was a bit of a strange feeling for me. Especially because it's somebody who you look up to, you respect just like he did with David. If you don't mind me asking, how did you feel when he passed away? What was your experience knowing that you spent time talking with him?

JA: When he died, I hadn't seen him for a number of years. I didn't know Dave, I've met him. But I didn't know him. I'd seen him perform, but I certainly was not someone with a meaningful relationship with him in any way. But having said that, I did know that he had had these health challenges. And I also knew that I hadn't seen him either performing or around for a long time. I had wondered what had been going on, how he'd been travelling. A work colleague of mine rang me from downstairs at the office [and] went, "Oh my God, did you hear about David McComb?" And, of course, the first thing I said was, "Oh, did he die?" It was a shock that I'd anticipated. When I interviewed Allan 'Alsy' McDonald, when Jill Birt came home and told him the news in 1999, his first reaction was "Oh well, that was going to happen, wasn't it?"

It was awful. It was [a] terrible tragedy. Of course, it was, but it was something that I think some people saw coming. And yet to me, it was just very saddening. I think the great tragedy when someone like David dies is that you're never again gonna know what they thought. You're never going to read another poem. There's going to be no more poems, there's going to be no more songs, there's going to be no more opinions. There's going to be no more of that mind.

You've got lots of great stuff that he left, all the records. There's no bad record, which you can't say about most people. Whether it's Triffids or Black Eyed Susans, or David McComb solo, there's no bad record. You can't say that about a lot of people. And the poetry is another world of its own and deserves the recognition that it has been achieving. All power to Fremantle Arts Press for putting out that volume of poetry, and the work that Niall Lucy and Chris Coughran did to produce it.

But again, it's finite. It finishes in 1999.

Because after 1999, he's not here. That is the other thing I would say when you consider what he could have done that's really sad: could he have written a film screenplay? Yeah. Could he have written a novel? He probably would have done. He may have written a stage play. He definitely had a humorous book of letters in him, which I just think would have been uproarious. I think there's so many things he could have done that we'll now never see and that's another element of the tragedy.

I'm curious about living with his voice in your mind. I listen to The Triffids pretty much every week, they're in my rotation consistently, so the songs are in my mind consistently. My encounter with The Triffids was through Born Sandy Devotional, like a lot of people, and that helped frame my relationship with living in Perth, living in Western Australia. And understanding this state a little bit more. I've always had a bit of a conflicted relationship with Australia, with Western Australia, as I think that David did as well, and that feeds into his music. What is your experience of having his voice, having his music in your mind? What does that do to your day-to-day life?

JA: That's a very good question. You're probably the only interviewer who's asked me that question. I actually think it's the question. Because to me one of the reasons I wanted to make the film was to try and distil the ever-evolving relationship the human mind and the human heart can have with this body of work. Because it's ever changing, it's ever evolving. Once it's got you, it's got you for life, this canon of work. Because it's ever evolving, it's got something for you at every stage of your life, and your reaction to a piece of music or one of his pieces of music. You have to give The Triffids credit here too, because of the way that they interpreted his songs.

It's a world of ever opening doors. You open one door, there's five more doors. You go through one of them, there's ten more doors to the imagination. You will see different images and have different feelings a number of different ways with a number of different songs.

Stolen Property is a magnificent example of this. It's so powerful, and sometimes it can be so uplifting. Other times it can be so sad. And then you'll hear a little line in it every now and again. The classic one is when people listen to that song, they know that line 'an aphorism for every occasion'. And then you think, "Well, what's he really getting at? Who's got an aphorism for every occasion? And what's he really saying about that person?"

That's just one line in one song in a whole canon, and you can think about that line in so many different ways. That's just that tiny microcosmic example. Whereas other people, I think with [Bob] Dylan's writing, you can probably have that ever-evolving relationship, but it's generally a pretty rare thing. Maybe Leonard Coen's another one. But overall, it's a pretty rare thing in music.

I think one of the reasons that the work continues to have this renaissance is that we live in really fickle times. Culture doesn't have a shelf life anymore unless it's some mega-marketed binge watch thing you watch on Netflix. Art is really hard to find and latch on to and have a relationship with. It's there. It's being made, but you've got to go through all these different rabbit holes to find it. And music isn't a cultural event anymore, it's just more fucking content. "It's a stream." Next. "Oh, it's been synced to an ad." "Oh, it's the ad with the video with the guys on the exercise mill, look they're clever, aren't they." "They got synced to an underwear ad and there are women on roller skates." It's just sort of part of this fucking hurricane of content that whirls around your ears.

Whereas with something like David's canon, it speaks to people's deeper core of who they are as a person. And once you're hooked, you can't really dismiss that experience. And I think it's so at odds with the kind of cultural environment that we find ourselves in now that people latch onto it for the best reasons and that is that it makes them think about what it is to be a person.

I've been sitting with his music for about two decades now.

JA: Sometimes culture just makes complete sense in the moment it's in and then the culture moves on. Other things just stay forever. And David's stuff stays forever.

One of the great thrills has been able to be see The Triffids perform live with the rotating catalogue of different voices. Rob Snarski was just fan-

tastic in one of the concerts that I went to, and I'm kicking myself that didn't go to one that Gareth Liddiard was at.

JA: I saw Gareth sing *Stolen Property* and *Field of Glass*.

What does it do to you to hear The Triffids songs sung by somebody that's not David?

JA: There's a very specific sense of those songs really being free, brought to life like you could almost reach out and touch them. The *A Truckload of Sky* show was the same actually. Having only seen that show once and seeing The Triffids without Dave four times, I did have a similar feeling that they've been brought out and let into the air and they're sort of floating around and you can almost touch them. It's that same feeling. It's always interesting to hear other people's interpretations of the songs, and do them justice in their own way, like Gareth Liddiard doing *Stolen Property* or *Field of Glass*. It's an innately powerful experience. It's really interesting to hear other interpretations, like there's Black Eyed Susan song called *Ocean of You*, which Dave wrote for Rob Snarski to sing. And that's on their very first EP, and then it was on *Welcome Stranger*.

When I saw *A Truckload of Sky*, they did a completely different arrangement of that song, with Angie Hart singing it, who used to be in Frente, and it was like listening to Bruce Springsteen's *Nebraska* record with sort of smatterings of Suicide, Alan Vega, Martin Rev. It was really a late night, two in the morning, film noir, down on a lonely street atmosphere, and a totally different arrangement of that song. And it just worked superbly.

I really had to hand it to them, that they hadn't just gone through the motions. That's given that song a kind of extra life in a way that I think Dave would have just loved, because he loved Springsteen's *Nebraska* record and he loved Suicide. And the way Angie sang it was just sensational. But again, you have that atmosphere of that sort of late night film noir vibe to it that's not in the original recording. And you hear Angie singing, "I'm out of my depth in an ocean of you." You transpose that line onto the new atmosphere that they created in that song, it still works. There's a sense of dark yearning in the original, whereas with this one there was this utter resignation. It was a totally different experience of that song and yet the song still lived in that same way that you could almost reach out and touch it.

I've seen The Triffids do that show four times. I remember seeing Melanie Oxley in Sydney sing *I Want to Conquer You* from *The Love of Will* record and that was stunning. I remember seeing Mick Harvey did *Kelly's Blues* in Perth. And that was a real surprise. And also Mick's interpretation of *The Seabirds*. I think that is a really difficult song for anybody to sing, and I think it's one of David's greatest lyrics. As Graham says in the film, it's like a short story in three minutes of music, and there's nothing out of place in it. Absolutely every line, every piece of music that accompanies the words makes complete sense. And it's a really difficult song to sing phrasing wise as a vocalist. And Mick actually really nails it. If you go back and watch that one online, he really knows how to sing that song and get inside it.

It's a pretty big challenge to get up and sing those songs, and I think that the vocalists that really do it best are the ones that really know how to get inside what those songs are at this intuitive level. Mick nailing *The Seabirds* in the way that he did, and Melanie nailing *I Want to Conquer You* in the way that she did at Sydney are really good examples of that.

I like the song that you choose to close the film on, Tender is the Night, and The Diving Bell do a stunning cover of it. It just kind of broke me in a way which I didn't expect. That song is always a powerful song. But that particular cover in itself was just overwhelming. These songs will live on beyond our lives.

JA: The story behind that was that we own that recording. The Diving Bell was fronted by a lovely German woman named Claudia Snyder who we were working with. We used to work at a film distributor called Madman, and she was working at Madman as well. And we just got to know her, and we asked The Diving Bell to play our benefit show at The Corner Hotel here in Melbourne. And that song went down an absolute treat when they played. We selected several recordings from that show to be part of our *Deep in a Dream: An Evening with the Songs of David McComb* album, which you can still buy off our website and you can still get on Bandcamp. We had originally wanted to use *Save What You Can* as the credits, and for certain contractual record company related reasons, we weren't actually able to do that, although we used it elsewhere in the film. So it seemed a really logical way of finishing the film up. It was sort of a happy accident, the use of that song. It works an absolute treat.

We do have The Triffids version [with] Jill Birt as a kind of forerunner to it just a few minutes earlier at the end of the film, and then we hit the audience with it. Having done a friends and family screening of the film at ACMI here in Melbourne, the Australian Centre for Moving Image, and seeing the power of that with the full sound system and with the 5.1 mix, and seeing how it affected the audience, I'm quite happy to say that I think we got that right.

I think that people who aren't familiar with The Triffids will still get so much from this because it's more than just the music. It is about an art-

ist whose life was taken too soon, but it's also about the people who lift him up and support him.

JA: I think David was such a kind man, such a giving person that he actually really inspired people to help him. If Dave needed to borrow an amp or he needed a musician to fill in for a show, or he needed you to help him write a song, people wouldn't say no, because it was him. He had this network of people around him. In The Triffids family and the wider Triffids family, there's enormous amount of goodwill and generosity, they're really kind people. They're really decent people, and they're people you want to spend time with. It's been a real pleasure getting to know some of them. You learn a lot about a person by the company they keep. You really do. I think the fact that they're just such fundamentally decent, good people speaks volumes about him. I really do.

One of the things which I found really powerful is what he saw in people who were inexperienced in the instruments that he chose them for. And that in itself shows the trust and the vision that he had as an artist.

JA: Again, there's two sides to it in that he picked people like Jill who couldn't really play keyboards or Graham, who was a very advanced musician, but had been playing the pedal steel for not that long because he knew they could play intuitively. And that's what makes The Triffids great. And that's why when they come up against the kind of one-dimensional Muggle world, for want of a better term of the music industry, where [you] have a producer who says "No, you've got to do it this way," or a label that says "No, it has to sound like this, we have to have gated reverb on the drums or it won't get on the radio." That's where his kind of artistic approach ran up against problems, because the industry machine couldn't understand the sort of intuitive understanding he had of his own music and what those songs could do. He was just way ahead of everybody, basically. If someone couldn't hear something in 1989, well, maybe they can hear it now, and I hope they can.

REVIEW
I'M WANITA
A FULL-THROATED CELEBRATION OF
AN UNKNOWN LEGEND

K asey Chambers. Lee Kernigan. Slim Dusty. Wanita.
These are the many faces of Australian country music. Over the decades, figurehead after figurehead has emerged, breaking into the greater public consciousness in a way that most country music struggle to do. As a genre of music, country tunes sway in and out of favour with commercial stations, and each new artist gives listeners a glimpse into their soul, making the twang of a *geetar* feel personal.

But what of the artists that sing their hearts out to early crowds at country music festivals? The unknown legends that idolise Loretta Lynn and Hank Williams, laying their own legacy down on the ground at her altar and living a life shadowed by tragedy and illuminated by the hope that thrives within country music. With Matthew Walker's expressive, vibrant, and true-blue documentary, *I'm Wanita*, we are introduced to a slice of genuine country music stardom: Wanita Bahtiyar, aka Wanita, the self-proclaimed 'Queen of Honky Tonk.'

Wanita is a devout country musician and has been for twenty-five years. She's also a sex worker who lives with no compromises; her truth is the one that sings loudest of all. Wanita comes from a working-class background, an aspect of modern country music that seems to be absent from the stadium filling superstars like Keith Urban, or even (once upon a time) Taylor Swift. Through country music, Wanita finds her own holy gospel that speaks to the cultural truth that lives within her. In one of the many rip-roaring scenes, Wanita proclaims her love for her music idol by explaining succinctly why they, and by extension country music, matters the most for her: "Loretta Lynn was the greatest interpreter of the common man, the common person, the common woman, the common transexual, whoever, I don't give a fuck."

When you think of country music, the image of someone who has lived a full life opening their soul up through music conjures in your mind through a haze of whiskey and tears. Wanita's songs expose her as someone who has lived a life, pouring her emotions out tune after tune. She has a wonderful turn of phrase that delights with equal amounts of truth, vulgarity, and honesty, like when she spits out the words 'soft cockerism' with a knowing glint in her eyes.

Living in Tamworth, Wanita's life of music consists of belting out her stunning voice with ultimate passion to a half full pub of disinterested diners chowing down on dinner. Her Turkish husband, Baba, lives with growing agitation alongside her. His own story feels like one ripped from a classic country tune: he is the father of the man that Wanita was paid to marry so he could become an Australian citizen when she was in Turkey. Instead of returning with him, she fell in love with Baba, and the rest, as they say with a harmonica wailing in the background, is history.

At 46, Wanita realises her own full potential as an artist, yet she also knows that the time for local success in Australia has likely passed. The hope for some kind of fame and adoration in America sits in her future. With her close friend Gleny Rae Virus by her side, and despite the fact that money is hard to come by, Wanita journeys to the great land of Nashville, Tennessee to record an album and try her hand at making it big (also titled *I'm Wanita* and released in 2021).

I'm Wanita feels like the ultimate introduction to a legend we should all know. As we get deeper into Wanita's story, it's hard to shake the question: after twenty-five years of continued work as an artist, why hasn't Wanita been elevated into the realm of country music royalty in Australia? Regardless of her faults and foibles, it's clear Wanita is a legend in her own right. She›s also a walking talking archive of country music, as we see in a sorrow-tinged moment of joy, where Wanita binge drinks with young folks to teach them about Slim Dusty. In these moments, we realise that without country music, life means little at all to Wanita.

Leaning into a certain type of stereotype for country musicians, Wanita isn't without an amber ailment. With the dream that she's hoped for all her life in sight, frequent consumption of whiskey and other spirits almost scarpers Wanita's chance of recording an album in Nashville before it even begins, as it becomes harder to keep her focused in the studio. In these moments, a palpable feeling of attaining a lifelong dream permeates from the screen, with tangible anxiety and stress hanging on every breath showing why she might rely so much on the bottle.

Frustrations carry across from Wanita's friends and bandmates, to Baba, the husband who doesn't understand her English, who argues with her about car problems over the phone as she sits in Sun Studios, Nashville, a world away from home. Throw in a daughter who can't and won't talk to her, each instance of life-disturbances simply amplifies Wanita's passion and life force via country music.

In these moments, I was reminded of the multitude of music documentaries I've seen thar are often rote life stories delivered in a talking head fashion that fails to truly harness the energy or prowess of the artists they're documenting. They're often respectful and hagiographic to the point that they diminish why the musician or band became who they were. I realised fairly quickly that *I'm Wanita* is not that kind of film. It sweeps you up completely in her life. This is far from being a rose-tinted glasses documentary, instead, it's a full-bodied, full-throated passionate embrace of its subject, the genre they adore, and life itself.

This is thanks to the masterful direction from Matthew Walker, and the immaculate editing from Peter O'Donoghue and Nikki Stevens, that is both supportive and critical of Wanita. Each cut swerves and ducks alongside Wanita's trajectory to recording success, culminating in a grand and glorious staged performance with a full band helping amplify Wanita's celebrated grandeur.

A standout moment comes late in the film, where Wanita sits in the recording booth, conjuring her record in Nashville out of the ether. Here, we hear her voice by itself, stripped away from the backing music, getting a glimpse of its power entirely. It's alive with vitality, thriving with importance. It's spine-tingling stuff. It's here that we recognise that Wanita is an icon alive out of time. If she were around in the golden age of Slim Dusty, it would be Wanita that we hold high alongside that Aussie icon.

Wanita's hopes create a splashback, drenching the battlers and the street urchins with support and adoration. She leans in and gathers them up in a warm embrace, either literally, or metaphorically with her music, swooping in and making sure that everyone that soars in her orbit lives with as much comfort and care that she can muster. Instead of being the next Coal Miner's Daughter queen, Wanita ends up getting stuck in the world of reality, singing amongst the people she wants to sing about.

That kind of energy can be exhausting for those wanting to lift up and support Wanita, leading them to get worn down themselves. In that way, *I'm Wanita* isn't a hagiography. It works alongside Wanita's legacy, stating this is who I am, warts and all. Like it or leave. As mentioned in the film, people are continually challenged by Wanita's precarious existence.

There's a power to *I'm Wanita* that I didn't realise I was craving. The musicality of Wanita's life is intoxicating, joyfully so. Yet, as she sits outside Loretta Lynn's house, with Loretta Lynn's cat, Angel, we can't help but weep a little for the life she's lived in the shadow of greatness, hoping for a moment in the spotlight. Whether this film will help usher that in or not is another aspect altogether, but I sure do hope that like *Searching for Sugarman (2012)* did for Rodriguez, *I'm Wanita* ushers Wanita onto the mainstage in the prime spot, because she darn well deserves it.

INTERVIEW
I'M WANITA - DIRECTOR
MATTHEW WALKER

S elf-crowned 'Australia's Queen of Honky Tonk', Wanita Blanche is the exact kind of person you want to lose yourself in a documentary about. For
director Matthew Walker, meeting and filming Wanita Blanche opened up a
world of country music, sex work, and mental health stories, amongst many
other things. With the expressive documentary *I'm Wanita*, Walker supports
Wanita's journey to record an album in the country music Mecca that is Nashville, Tennessee.

Matthew Walker has worked predominantly as an editor in Australian film
and TV, with titles like *Not Suitable for Children* (2012), *After the Apology* (2017),
and *There Goes Our Neighbourhood* (2018) under his belt. As a director, he has
worked on the short films *The Verticals* (2010) and *Heart of the Queen* (2015)
before embarking on the feature-length documentary *I'm Wanita*.

He was nominated for Best Direction in a Documentary Feature at the 2021
Australian Directors Guild Awards, Best Documentary alongside Carolina So-
rensen, Clare Lewis, and Tait Brady at the 2021 AACTA Awards, and won the
Australian Documentary Prize at the 2021 Sydney Film Festival, as well as Best
Feature Documentary at the 2022 AIDC Awards.

Interview conducted December 2021.

►▷►

*I understand there was a short film, Heart of the Queen, that started off
this story. Was it a proof of concept in a way?*

Matthew Walker: It was eventually, yeah. The start of the short film was
how it really kicked off. I got a phone call from a high school friend [Na-
dine], who had been talking to someone up in Tamworth, this guy called
Gavin Butlin 'Butto', who had funded Wanita's last album, *The Original
Wanita*. He's not risk averse. He's running the Airlie Beach Music Festival, and he's run a lot of pubs, so he knows what he's doing. He threw out
this idea that someone should make a documentary about Wanita and he
said to her, "Do you know anyone?" and although I hadn't spoken to her
for quite a few years, she just gave me a call out of the blue, and said, "Do
you want to come up to Tamworth during the 2014 Country Music Festival and film a doco?" There was no description about what this doco was
or about this woman Wanita. I remember thinking at the time, this is the

kind of thing that just comes out of absolutely nowhere that can sometimes turn into turn into something, you hear about these stories and you read about these stories. So, I just went "Yeah, I think I can do that."

I went with Natalie van den Dungen, she's a director in her own right [*Persecution Blues: The Battle for the Tote, Bunny New Girl*], and Mat Govoni, who's now a film producer. They came up with me, and we met Wanita for like a minute before at a gig, and we just started filming straight away. We took this very Nick Broomfield-approach of just walking in filming and shoving the camera in people's faces.

This is the story Wanita likes, initially, we did a dolly shot of her car out the front, and she got pissed off with us, that we were being "soft cock, and get in amongst it," which I knew was what I wanted to do, but I was kind of playing along, "Yeah, let's just get this dolly shot." And so, when she said that, we just launched into it and she made a speech from her bed, "If you're real, you're going to end up like me, completely stuffed by the activities of the Country Music Festival." She laid down the gauntlet to for me to try to keep up with her. And then Baba (Wanita's husband) walked into the room and started talking in Turkish, quite enthusiastically and saying that he wanted to tell the real story of Australia's Queen of Honky Tonk, what it's like living with Australia's Queen of Honky Tonk.

This is five minutes after we started filming, (Baba) wants to give an alternate version of the story. He wants to undermine the promo aspect of the doco, which I assumed was what we were going to be making, a little promo film for some country music artists. Wanita said, "Yep, go and let Baba talk," and he sat down at the dining room table, and made a great big long speech in Turkish, about— well, I didn't know what it was about at the time, because I can't understand Turkish, but it was quite dramatic. Wanita let that through, and I could hear her on the other mic, freaking out about what he was saying, talking about how we're going to have to edit this out. And then she made a retort to that from the kitchen, which we came to call 'the kitchen address', about how difficult it has been being the 'Queen of Honky Tonk', autism, neurodivergence and whatnot.

And after that series of events, which was the first half hour of filming, I felt like it was a story that I could really get my teeth into, it really resonated with me this idea of a person who had such a big dream, and such a feeling of destiny as a youngster, and that here she was at 45 and she was still talking about the heartbreak of that, not being recognised as who she always felt she was. I was remember waking up the next day and flicking through all the elements to this story and thinking 'there's really something here, there's something very rich here'.

I get the impression from watching the film, one minute with Wanita feels like it's a lifetime, because she's larger than life, so full of life that you just get an idea of who she is immediately, and so I can understand completely why you'd want to run off and make a film about her.

MW: People don't usually talk about that stuff, they're guarded about things like that, and it might come out after a long time that they always wanted to be a rock star, or whatever it is, and that they feel like they are living a life that wasn't the one that they were meant to be living. But she had no filter about talking about that stuff, and actually talked about it very eloquently and dramatically, and the neurodivergent element of the story really interested me as well, because I've got a new neurodivergent son.

Also, that relationship between her and Baba is a really classic relationship of a practical person, and a more artistically minded person, and the clash when they don't understand each other, or what motivates each other, it's writ very large in their relationship, and further amplified by the fact that they speak a hybrid Turkish-English-German made up language that they've constructed themselves, apparently.

That's the magic of a documentary, that they present the truth, a truth that if it was presented as fiction, it would feel it would feel fake. There is so much that's genuine and authentic about both Wanita and Baba that is endearing, even when they're yelling at each other. What was your perspective, as you're sitting there watching this unfold?

MW: I empathise with both of them, that's what I found all the way through the edit as well. Whoever you are watching, you see their side of the story so well, that it becomes very difficult, because all sides of the story are valid. When I'm watching it, I was very aware of the comedic elements to what I was seeing, but also the real emotion behind it all the time. Over the years that kind of got played out and got more serious as things went along.

How do you balance the level of presenting the comedy and the seriousness? Of course, it's hard when it's playing out in front of you, but how you decide what is presented in the edit or in the script, as you're collating the film at the end? That's got to be quite difficult to navigate the tone to make sure that you're presenting things respectfully.

MW: Absolutely. There was never a script, we worked straight away and just started putting stuff together. Being respectful to all the people involved was a real pressure to try and get their stories right in a short period of time or try and tell their stories in a way that was true to the essence of them. I went for those scenes where I knew the conflict or the situation went to the heart of the thing, and so there were certain moments like that argument in the driveway where Wanita is talking about teaching Slim Dusty songs to the kids, and she had been out drinking and whatnot, and Baba is saying, "I'm not going to help you anymore." and she's talking about the harmonica, and it all comes to this moment where he's saying he's helped her all these years night, day cold, warm, and she comes back at him with "I fuck for 17 years."

That was a moment that really went to the heart of the conflict. As you say, you can almost not script it the way that unraveled before my eyes. And the coat hanger moment was another moment. [It] was really the metaphor of him cleaning up the mess of Wanita's coat hangers and trying to order them, the love in that act, but also what a small act that is, to try and rein in the chaos of Wanita. I went for those moments and cut them as scenes, and then built other stuff around them.

Archer Shepherd, Wanita Blanche, Matthew Walker, Kathryn Milliss
Courtesy of People Productions. Used with Permission.

Then the beautiful speech that Baba does, I didn't know what Baba was saying at any point during the whole thing, and I loved that aspect of it, because you just find out months later [what was being said]. During the short film, I got the kebab shop guy to come up to my bedroom and translate everything. That great speech where he talks about this "I'm no genius" in terms of Wanita's financial stuff, which was another key conflict in their relationship that she didn't care for money, she gave it away and he was all about money. We put those scenes together, and then we had those little islands of key scenes, and then it was a matter of building the story around them.

As you're talking, it's very personal, it's extremely personal, and then, as we go to Nashville, and those moments were some of the more tense moments, because I was so invested in what Wanita wanted in her life, and so keenly aware that who Wanita is as a person might threaten her own dreams. How do you manage that story as you're documenting this? Do you have an idea of where this narrative might go? Or are you sitting there opening up for the possibilities of anything occurring?

MW: I was totally open to the possibilities of anything occurring. As we pitched the film and wrote treatments and whatnot, there was a lot of people saying, "You know, she's not going to just go to Nashville and be picked up and become a star. It's not going to happen, that kind of thing doesn't happen anymore." Everyone kept saying this, and I never ever said that was what I was intending to happen. It was the zeitgeist of the filmy narrative world at that time, it was like it was expected that it will end in some kind of triumphant victory. Whereas that was never my intention at all. I was happy for whatever to happen. I tried not to influence events at all.

Having read some of the interviews that you've done for this film, there seems to be a pointed question of your relationship with country music like that is the prominent thing that you have to either respect or enjoy country music or have an understanding of the history of country music, but it's clear that the interest is Wanita herself. It feels like what you're saying about this judgment of what will happen with Wanita when she goes to Nashville, 'will she be a success?' and everybody's saying that she won't be, that there's this [perceived] judgement of country music as well. But you quite clearly as a director disregard that all together. How important was that for you to just focus on Wanita as a character and everything else will come organically together?

MW: It was very much about music as well, the fact that it was country music was neither here nor there to me. But the more I learned about country music as I went along, the more I understood Wanita's character, where she'd come from, and what it represented to her and what classic country music meant to people. It was definitely about music. Being an amateur muso myself through my 20s, and just knowing musicians and the amount of time and effort and hope and creativity that people put into it over years and years, and I think in this country, in particular, it's really, really hard to have your efforts recognised.

It's also that the magic, you keep going back to it because it's got this hold on you. And it does enter your life when you're 14 or whatever, and it's a very, very powerful thing that keeps drawing you back in. But a lot of people who don't succeed with it, learn to put it aside. Whereas someone like Wanita is true to that feeling, that magic feeling and lives her life by it. The music thing was important, but the character of Wanita, you can just see the elements playing out in her before your eyes. I loved her chaos, the way she celebrated chaos and became enlivened by it. How frustrated and bored she is with the idea of "You do this, and then you do this, and then you'll get to there"; like she just cannot stay on track, and I empathise with that.

On her in front of the camera, she's got Gleny and Archer helping her out. But on the other side of the camera, I've got Clare [Lewis] and Carolina [Sorensen] helping me out. I really relate to that enthusiast element that Wanita's got; when you have the idea, you act on it, you've got to act on it right now, before you start talking about and realise that so many things could go wrong if you do this, or it's not such a great idea, it's not that smart. You can talk yourself out of stuff, but if you act on it when that initial spark of enthusiasm comes through, amazing things can potentially happen or go seriously wrong as well. And so, in that way, Wanita's character resonated with me. She's a lot more extreme.

A lot of what you're saying applies to music, but I'm hearing a duality here where it could also apply to film too, where you throw your entire life into it, and it becomes part of who you are, and, especially in Australia, you have to fight for it in so many different ways. Where did your journey start with film? You are predominantly an editor and have moved into directing later on. Was that always your interest, or was it just the entity of film itself?

MW: Through my 20s, I fell in love with music, I played in a band, I wrote songs, it didn't go anywhere. I loved writing and I took a lot of photos, all that kind of stuff. I loved journalism and non-fiction writing. And I was in London briefly and I got this temp job at a post-production house and I had one of those epiphanies where there were all these edit suites; it was just as non-linear editing had taken over in 1998. There were these people in an edit suite downstairs and you just saw through the door occasionally, it was a BBC group, and they were doing a war documentary, and they had all their walls plastered with photos from the war, and they'd arrived before I got there, and they'd leave after I left. And at some point, I went, "Actually editing is the place where it all comes together: music and storytelling and writing and images" and I just had this sudden realisation that it might be a really good fit for me.

I asked one of the editors if I could borrow the edit suites at night to learn how to do it, and they said, "Yeah, sure." They gave me all these archives from the BBC and I started cutting some film clips for my band and my friends band and whatnot, just with archive stuff, random bits and pieces, and I just really took to it, I just loved it immediately.

I came back to Newcastle, where I was living at the time, and I found out that there was one Avid in Newcastle at Peach advertising, and I rang them up and said, "I want to be an editor." And they said, "Well, we've got an editor. So that's good. See you later." And then, two weeks later, they rang me up and said, "Our editor just quit, did you call up before?" They invited me and I didn't know what I was doing, but somehow, they ended up giving me a job, and I started working in this advertising agency that had some quite big accounts – they were punching above their weight. I had control of the Avid for three years, and then I realised that after those three years that AFTRS, which was a thing that I'd looked at in my early 20s, and visited and thought, "God, I'd love to come here one day," but you can't because you need an industry experience. And I suddenly went one day, "Oh shit, I've got industry experience! I could apply for AFTRS." I did that and got into drama editing. And that's when it all kicked off.

With editing, it's such a controlled environment. You don't need to deal with other people too much, in fact, you've got one thing that you're focusing on. So, I think at that point in my life it really appealed to me, that contained, controlled environment where you could just do that one thing that you loved. I always had that urge to make my own thing. I did make short films and whatnot over the years, fairly regularly. But when you're editing, it takes so much time, it stops everything, and it's very hard to get something going. And so finally when this thing came along, I just went "Okay, I'm just going to launch myself at this because this is actually moving and it's got a chance."

What's the collaborative aspect like? As you've mentioned, you've got Clare, you've got Carolina as producers and Tate [Brady] too, and then you've got Peter [O'Donoghue] and Nikki [Stevens] in editing. What discussions took place as I'm Wanita was being made?

MW: It was hilarious. I made the short film and then tried to put it in festivals, and finally went to Antenna. Margaret McHugh, who I always am very grateful for, selected it for Antenna, we had been going for two years, so it was at the end of its run as a short film, and it got this beautiful slot just before the intermission and really receptive audience and it went down really well, lots of laughs and everything. And someone came up to me afterwards and said, "You should take that for development for Screen Australia because it's the start of a world." And the thought hadn't occurred to me before, then a couple of months later, I did.

I was working with Michaela Perske as an editor on *After the Apology*, so she came in, we got development, we shot some more Wanita, she said the Nashville thing so that became the spine of the film, and then I was working with Clare and Carolina on Clare's doco, *There Goes Our Neigh-*

bourhood. And halfway through that I showed them the trailer that we'd made during development, and they both liked it.

After we finished the edit on Clare's film, Carolina rang me up the next day and said, "Right, this is how we can do it." And she had mocked up this whole budget and everything. And, so I just went, "Right, this is brilliant, let's go!" I never understood the whole funding thing, I've seen many people go through it, but I didn't actually know it. It seemed like this labyrinth. And she took me through it, "Now you got to do this, and now you've gotta do this, and now you've gotta do this." And we got Tait on board as our elder statesmen producer, and we eventually got funding. Clare was on the ground with me a lot, she filmed, she did sound, she's brilliant as a, what you'd call a field producer in television, she would just make things happen, she's just fearless and [has] boundless enthusiasm, won't take no for an answer, she's perfect like that. Carolina stays at home and manages everything from afar but has an incredible intuitive grasp of every problem and works out solutions to them very quickly. Throughout the edit, Carolina would call me every morning at about nine o'clock and we would just chat for half an hour, often not even about the film, but just about whatever. I think we had maybe fourteen weeks set aside for the edit, and I had moved out of my home before we went to America.

My mum had died in June 2018, and then we went to America in about October, and my family home was going to be sold, the one I grew up in, just in the week when we got home. I was getting home to be at the auction from America, having filmed Wanita, and then it didn't sell. All the siblings decided that we needed to renovate the place, give it a complete overhaul. The idea came out that I would stay there, and be with the tradesmen because no one lived there anymore. I'd man the house while the tradesmen worked and edit in my childhood bedroom. So, I found myself back in the bedroom that I was in until about six years of age, with the computer in Newcastle.

The first thing I did was I went through all the rushes and I typed them all up and ended up with a 140,000-word document describing all the rushes. That took me a couple of months. Then Nikki came on and she worked remotely in Sydney. We worked for fourteen weeks, and it was just very, very hard, it was very difficult to get the story working. And [when] she finished her tenure we hadn't managed to get it to rough cut, we were still pre-rough cut. And then I took over for a while editing. I had some funding money, but I didn't have income, so I lived with my sister in her spare bedroom and I edited and finally got it to rough cut after a few months.

Then Carolina, as producers do, went, "Right we're going to get another editor to bring this home" and pulled out some money from somewhere.

And Pete O'Donoghue came on who was a good friend of mine, and from that point on, it was just a beautiful, brilliant process where I rocked up to his edit suite every morning, and we talked through what was the problem with this part of the film, and then he stood up and went to his edit desk and I sat at the other one with transcripts and rushes, with a coffee in the morning, beer in the evening, and we finished it in about ten weeks. We had a great time.

Then we did the ABC one hour cut down in a few weeks, which we changed quite a lot because we were really concerned that they might want to put voiceover into it, so I went and did more audio interviews with Gleny Rae so that we filled up that space where voiceover might go with Gleny Rae speculating and hypothesising. We put in quite a few different scenes in there as well. Carolina didn't panic at once, even though we'd gone triple over-schedule, she just backed us and stayed with it, like a very patient midwife and just waited for it. That was just brilliant. There was a lot of pressure. I mean, I was freaking out, totally freaking out but not once I got with Pete because I could feel it was coming together. We made something that we liked, and Carolina and Clare, and everyone ended up being really happy. Finally Screen Australia and ABC and all those people gave us a thumbs up and then COVID hit just as we finished the edit.

Then I was in a room doing the beautiful music with Jonathan Dower because he'd done the music for the short film as well, so we used a lot of his old songs in the new cut, and we were getting him to do certain things. We started using this particular big chord, it's an A minor seven. It's that big 'brrrum' that we started using as a punctuation, and it was from a track he had done called *Ratty Nostalgia*. I was ringing him up and say "Okay, get the *Ratty Nostalgia* band back together, put them on acid and get them to jam for ten minutes." The next day he sent through this ten-minute jam of the old *Ratty Nostalgia* thing from the short film and we'd end up using this tiny little bit. The score is just beautiful. I just love it. I told him, *Pure Imagination*, from *Willy Wonka*, and spooky Beatles was the other thing, *Strawberry Fields* kind of thing. And instruments falling over, guitars getting knocked over with reverb on them, people searching for things down the back of pianos and whatnot. And he took all these 'directions' and just made this beautiful score. Then Luke Mynott did the sound, which is also quite radical in its own way, it's quite ramshackle, and at times, things are out of kilter with how loud they should be, at times it's very un-naturalistic.

It's nice to hear that how you approach things is reflective of Wanita as a person; the edit, the score, everything is feeding into the narrative of who she is as person, it's showing the respect, it's showing the dedication to her story. At what point did the end credit sequence come about? Was that always in mind to give her this grand concert hall sequence?

MW: You get notes, whether it's the funding bodies or it's other people, but they weren't excessive, it was more like "Keep going, it's not there yet, keep going it's not there yet." Being a first-time director as well, there wasn't a whole lot of confidence in me out there. I wasn't hearing that directly, but I was certainly imagining it, so I really took this idea of absorbing people's notes, rather than pushing back or conflicting with the notes. I was like, "Okay, bring in the notes, what are they, okay, let's take them on in some kind of unlikely way." If you have to change the whole film to absorb the spirit of the notes, then that's what I was trying to do, without screwing up my original vision.

Wanita Blanche, Matthew Walker, Hugh Miller
Photo Credit: Patrick Boland; Courtesy of People Productions. Used with permission.

I was trying to be very... like a plant. If a plant's growing, and you stick something next to it, it grows around it. I was trying to do it like that. Notes started coming through from Tait, somewhere around rough cut, that the film didn't have an ending. And he was saying this, even though we hadn't finished the cut, "The film didn't have an ending." And so I started thinking about this problem, and then one day, on Hunter Street in Newcastle, I just had the idea that her life is her art. Therefore, showing the journey through the house as the perfect rendition of her life, everyone's happy and shiny, and everyone's a character doing the right thing that she likes most. The idea that here she is in her full glory, her band is made up of all the bit-characters in her life, a lot of the musicians are characters who were in their film quite a lot who didn't end up in that in the final film. It's like this perfect version of Wanita.

I sent Carolina a text, "I've got an idea for the ending," and she rang me up and said, "Okay, what is it?" and I said, "Blah, blah, blah," she said, "Right, we can go for the regional film funding. We'll go to Screen New South Wales with regional funding. And I'm pretty sure Hugh Miller lives up in Mullumbimby now, who's one of the most beautiful cinematographers in Australia, so we could possibly get him," and she just launched into it and made it happen. In the next minute, we're up there with a bloody Steadicam operator, and the whole shebang. I think it was a one-day shoot, we did the house in the morning and the concert in the afternoon.

It is a perfect ending. It wraps up the narrative in a very satisfying way. In my review, I compared it to Wild Rose, which I think is just a magnificent film equally about country music and the importance of it in people's lives, and that in itself also has a concert hall sequence where it wraps up in a very satisfying way.

MW: That film came out in the middle when we were in the early stages, when we're shooting, and I remember, we just sent the link around to each other just going "Whoa, there's a red headed country singer film." Everybody just went "We can't think about that now, just keep going." I've never actually seen the film.

It's good. It is very different from I'm Wanita, obviously the narrative has a very similar theme, but the character [Jessie Buckley] is very, very different and the style of country music that she's singing is modern country music. It's not the traditional Honky Tonk style country music. For me, I'm Wanita cemented the notion of what home is to people, and the notion of home being in a song, and being in music, it's something that you can take away with you. There are moments here where Wanita is sitting on the streets of Nashville with the street drunks and just talking about her music, her life, her love. And then you've got the moment of her with the cat, which is... you can't write this stuff?

MW: That was always my favourite thing we got.

You can't shake that moment, it's so genuine, and heartfelt.

MW: It was thanks to Clare Lewis. I was with Kathryn [Milliss], the cinematographer, and we were filming cutaways of Loretta Lynn's house, and Clare suddenly came up and said urgently in my ear, "She's talking to Loretta's cat," we spun around, and there was this beautiful framed silhouette shot of the tour guide, Wanita, and Loretta's cat. And then Wanita said, "I want to get around to the front gates." So we took her around to the front gates, and she walked up and there was the cat. It was right around the other side of the house. And it was just such a powerful moment.

I get a little bit choked up hearing you talk about it. It's the emotion of it all.

Now, the film has been out in the world, and it will continue to be out there, what has your journey been like now that it's completed? It's out there, you're doing interviews like this, you're talking about it, you're getting audience reactions. What's that been like for you?

MW: The first thing that happened was we didn't know if it was going to get into any festivals or anything. And then finally, we heard that it had been shortlisted for Hot Docs. We heard that it was like the start of December, and we didn't hear back from them at all. I'd actually given up; I'd totally given up. But then I spoke to Carolina, because I thought it was dead in the water, and she said, "Well, no, just wait," and then we got this message from Hot Docs that we got in. I was so relieved at that point that it had got into something substantial.

And I guess at the start, because [I'm a] white male, [Wanita is a] sex worker, this is a female story, all that stuff. I wasn't sure whether people were going to come at me for that, because it was something that I was very, very aware of during the whole edit. I did my very, very best to navigate and to do it properly without ripping the guts out of it by being too paranoid or something. I read books and tried to know that I was not screwing this up. And we showed cuts of the film to Scarlet Alliance and Autism Spectrum Australia. But then people started responding to the film in the way that I hoped people would respond to the film. That was really quite startling at first, surprising, you know?

I've just been trying to work out how to do interviews. It's a strange thing. People hit you with questions, and you have to come up with something. Sometimes I can't even remember what the hell it was all about. You can when you're sitting by yourself, but it's quite a different thing being put on the spot and trying to talk and then you kick yourself afterwards for something you've said or something you didn't say. I've actually found that experience to be quite an interesting process in a learning progress kind of way. I've just been amazed that the film's connected with people. And very grateful for that, because it's not an infrequent thing for lots and lots of people to put your heart and soul and lots and lots of work into something and put it out whatever it is, and it just falls silently and disappears and maybe you get a shrug of the shoulders or two or something.

It's resonated. The awards attention as well as got to be good too. Does that matter to you at all?

MW: It's certainly not a bad thing. And it certainly has been helpful immediately, after we got the Sydney Film Festival Award, some cinemas that were holding out, have rolled over and said, "Yeah, okay, let's put it on." I think it's just been great for everyone's confidence, and it's also helped us to hopefully make another film, because I've joined Clare and Carolina's production company now.

Congratulations.

MW: They asked me to at some point, just after the edit, and I said, "Yes, bloody oath." It's brilliant having collaborators that you actually click with, and everyone's got different skills, and you harmonise really well.

Do you have an idea of what you want your catalogue of films to look like, as an editor, director or whatever capacity you decide to work in as a filmmaker?

MW: I love stories that are genuinely, genuinely weird, but also very, very human. Stuff that unravels in a way that's totally unexpected, but not in a written way. Stuff that gently unfolds in a peculiarly human way. I like shooting without an agenda, and finding the story as you go along, and particularly in the edit and just following your instincts and your fascinations. It's always going to be character stuff. And I daresay music will play a significant role in it all. We referenced *Grey Gardens* and *Grizzly Man* and *Some Kind of Monster* and *DIG!* and *The Devil and Daniel Johnston* and Mike Leigh films, *Career Girls* by Mike Leigh, this is the stuff that I love.

Rattling off those names of documentaries that you can feel the influences in your work here. I think that's really important to be able to embrace what you love and be able to see what made those films work and then implement it in your own language in your own style. And you've done that so well.

MW: Absolutely. Yes. Thank you. It's so much easier if you're doing something that resonates with you that you love doing, that you're doing it in the way you want to do it. It makes everything so much easier, and you know what decisions to make. I've had a lot of experiences as an editor where you're trying to put someone else's vision together, which is very interesting in itself, but it's so much less confusing when you're doing it the way you want to do it.

SPORTS FILMS

When talking about Australian culture, sports are often integral and intwined in our identity. Being sports-obsessed has become synonymous with being Australian, so much so that in 1962 *Sports Illustrated* magazine noted that Australia was the most sports-obsessed country in the world. Australian culture and its identity has changed a lot since in the 1960s, but our fascination and love with sports of all kind has been a constant throughout the years.

As the pandemic hit the world, sports were one of the first full contact events that were given the nix. Through fortune and early planning, Australia managed to minimise the impact of COVID-19, and as such, sports were able to stay alive through their own variety of 'bubbles' that helped keep players, coaches, and staff safe, albeit excluded from family and friends as the sports season rolled on. Australia's national sport, the AFL, managed to keep its truncated season alive, and filmmaker Nicole Miller was along for the journey to document South Australian club Port Adelaide as they celebrated their 150th anniversary with *This is Port Adelaide*.

While monumental anniversaries and COVID were captured in that film, the AFL took an interesting turn to combat the growing instances of racism and racial abuse within the league by hiring filmmaker Peter Dickson to direct *The Ripple Effect*. Starting with the racism that league legend Nicky Winmar endured as one of the iconic players, *The Ripple Effect* then moves throughout the different sporting codes within Australia and looks at how athletes have been impacted by racism, as well as exploring what practices are being put in place to reduce the presence of racism in sporting Australia. Operating in unison is Larissa Behrendt's *Araatika: Rise Up!*, a powerful film that displays the act and importance for Indigenous Australian rugby league players to engage in a pre-game 'unity dance'. Inspired by the Maori Haka, a group of Indigenous players join up to create a dance that will change rugby's perspective when it comes to Aboriginal players. This film celebrates culture, and highlights how putting culture forward can help combat racism within the league as well as within the supporter base.

Elsewhere, legendary and hidden sporting icons like Cathy Freeman and Poppy Starr Olsen were honoured with films focusing on their respective sporting efforts. For Cathy, Laurence Billiet's *Freeman* allowed the Olympian to reflect on one of Australia's greatest global sporting achievements, whereas for Poppy, Justine Moyle's *Tall Poppy: A Skater's Story* saw her legacy being cemented as an emerging legend in the skateboarding scene. *Tall Poppy* shows how at the age of 14, Poppy became the world number one female bowl skater in Australia, and with skateboarding being added as an official Olympic sport, her hopes of becoming an Olympic legend also come with the added pressure of being a professional athlete. But when COVID hits, and the Tokyo Olympics are delayed, Poppy's focus shifts to a cross-continent relationship, and staying fitness fit for future games.

Equally so, the pressure that surfing legends Jodie Cooper, Frieda Zamba, Pauline Menczer, and more found themselves in as they pushed against the male dominated international surfing circuit is explored in Christopher Nelius' *Girls Can't Surf*. Putting you in the thick of the action – both on the waves and in the protests – *Girls Can't Surf* is enlightening in ways you hope it wouldn't be.

Finally, thrusting you in the mix of the action was Cameron Brunt's addition to the burgeoning motorbike doc genre with *Wide of the Mark*. Here, Brunt follows six riders as they tackle some of Tasmania's most treacherous and difficult off-road terrain with their hand build road bikes.

Sports documentaries are represented here with interviews with *This is Port Adelaide* director Nicole Miller and *Girls Can't Surf* director Christopher Nelius.

INTERVIEW
THIS IS PORT ADELAIDE - DIRECTOR
NICOLE MILLER

Presented in stunning black and white with cinematography by Isaac Walgos, Nicole Miller's *This is Port Adelaide* follows the Power's 150-year journey to become one of Australia's most successful footy clubs. In 2020, they sought Premiership glory, all the while battling a raging pandemic. Within *This is Port Adelaide*, challenge after challenge is presented, with Miller by the teams' side to put it all on film. This is a rare portrait of a football team in full flight.

Nicole Miller's connection to AFL comes after directing and producing *The AFL Show* for the Port Adelaide Football Club in 2016, a 25-episode series that introduced the team and the sport to Chinese audiences. Her connection with Port Adelaide continued with the short documentary *Power Dreaming* in 2016, which presented the connection the club has with Aboriginal role models and programs. *This is Port Adelaide* feels like a natural progression for Nicole as a producer and documentarian, and as someone connected deeply with the club.

This is Port Adelaide received a theatrical release around Australia with Q&A sessions as well.

Interview conducted April 2021.

▶▷▶

I was fairly ignorant of the fact that Port Adelaide had been around for 150 years. Which is sad, because as you show in the film, there is so much history to them. Were there surprises for you when it came to tfilming the Port Adelaide history and their journey?

Nicole Miller: 150 years of history is such a long history that there's always going to be surprises in there when you start really delving in. But, even some of the stories we couldn't include in the doco around what happened during the wartime period and what happened to football in the state during that time with some amalgamated teams and leagues and obviously a lot of war veterans coming back and then going on to play back in Port Adelaide for the team. There are decorated war heroes playing as part of their team during that period of time. From 1870 is this endless story of so many individuals over so long a period of time.

It's humbling to know that a team like Port Adelaide has been around for so long. I know that your journey to football has been a bit interest-

ing because you weren't originally a football fan and then brought on to do The AFL Show. Can you talk about that journey for you into football and into bringing football to Chinese audiences?

NM: I grew up in Australia and in the western suburbs of Adelaide which is a bit Port Adelaide mad. Somehow I managed to go through my life without knowing too much about football at all. I started being quite ignorant about the sport, but for what we were trying to achieve with communicating it to Chinese audiences that were totally unfamiliar with the sport as well, that worked to my advantage in terms of actually having to explain things and not taking anything for granted as to what would be understood in the gameplay or anything like that. I don't think you can get a better learning experience than that in terms of actually explaining the rules to someone else. That got me started.

But that also got me started in terms of understanding and appreciating Port Adelaide and their history, so that was where the journey began for me. I got to know this club and started getting more and more invested and I thought, "Oh wow, this is quite exciting. And I really believe in these guys, and I want them to achieve their dreams." I think as soon as you're emotionally invested, it will start from there.

I'm a Freo fan and it's hard not to get emotionally involved in not only the 2020 season but also the whole entire club's history. It's hard to not feel passionate about it. For you, what's that's that like, having that feeling wash over you for the first time and realising that maybe I love this football club?

NM: I think that with this documentary and the journey we started with, this is where I really got to understand the depth of their history and the people that have contributed to it over time. And how much it means to everyone. We delve into not just the player side or the administration which is often the focus of these sorts of documentaries, but we spoke with the community and what that means to them to see their team up there and achieve and how that gives them a sense of pride even though they're a spectator. But they still take on some of that, it's your tribe out there winning. With so many people, with so much at stake, and then I'm making a documentary about them, so of course I want them to do well, but also I've been talking to so many people about that history and what it means to them to win. And, I can't probably overstate how invested I was at that point. I wanted it to go well, for everyone.

Did you have a map planned out for how you wanted the narrative to go? You're not just telling the history of the club, but you're following a sea-

son of football as well, the rise and fall and the unexpected mishaps. And unfortunately, the tragedy at the end of the year, they didn't get the flag.

NM: We certainly did in terms of establishing what we wanted from it thematically and what we wanted to be able to capture, and what was important to us in those moments. But we're lucky in that sport has natural drama to it, so no matter which way it goes, you just pivot with it, and it feeds into the highs and lows of football. It's even more to themes about what it means to people, and you want to put people in the perspective of being a fan of this football club and feel those highs and lows with people. When COVID happened and the season was upended, we just had to be adaptive and pivot with whatever happened. We couldn't really write the ending. It was something that was happening before us. We just had to look at the events and how each game was going and think, "Okay, well, what's important to the story that we're telling here?" And try and pull out those parts.

There is a lot of archival footage and historical footage, and you're blending it in with the recent events. What was the editing and curating process like?

NM: We did a lot of exploring through our lives and for a lot of that, there's no shortcut. You just have to sit down and watch a lot of archival material and then you flag which moment seemed to speak to your themes. We've got timelines and timelines of things that are really interesting but didn't end up fitting where the narrative was going. I don't think there's a shortcut when it comes to archival material, you just have to sit there. And really, it's a process of being able to fully immerse yourself, though.

Where did you access the archival footage? Is it kept it at the NFSA, or is there a local place in Port Adelaide that has it?

NM: It came from such a variety of sources, some from Port Adelaide Football Club. They had some archival material, old VHS's that we had to digitise. We got a lot from The State Library, particularly of the actual community in the area. We went through some film reels there and VHS and DVD and all sorts of formats. It went really far back because Port Adelaide is a commercial hub in Adelaide. It has quite a well-documented history which was to our advantage. And then there's the Port Adelaide Historical Society. And then we had some news interviews through our archivist. He captured anything that has a topic of Port Adelaide in recent history for us to look through.

Wow.

NM: Yeah. It was a lot.

One of the discussions lately about Australian film history and Australian cultural history is the conservation of it all and the importance of it. And it's easy to forget the importance and the value of having a great archive to be able to dip into for these kinds of reasons. For you as a documentarian what kind of importance is it for you in going ahead into future projects that you can have these kinds of deep archives just sitting there ready and available to dip into?

NM: That would be incredible. I think our State Library and museums and the National Film and Sound Archive do a good job of archiving some material. If, as a documentary filmmaker, I think when you find the archival gold, there's something in visuals that can talk to an era better than you can ever have a talking head describe what it was like then. If you can see it, that's so much more valuable. If there was a database where you can easily access that sort of stuff, I think that would save a lot of low budget filmmakers from having to use a lot of precious post-production time to be poring through everything that they can possibly find from multiple sources. It'd be awesome if it was a central source that you could go to.

How much time is spent doing the archival researching? Is it 50/50, or does it depend on what the narrative needs?

NM: I think it does depend what the narrative needs. Our archival material did play a larger part on the front portion of the film and establishing that history. We went out and filmed a lot of current footage as well which does make up the majority of the film. There's a balance there. But in terms of how long you spend looking, it's a few weeks and it's a lot of trying to reach out to who might have a copy of this particular moment, it does take a lot of legwork.

Yes, it comes back to that community aspect. And that's one of the most enduring things about this is, it's all about community. With a different aspect about This is Port Adelaide is that because so much of Australia was denied the chance to go and watch football, there's something that brings everybody together at the end of this film that celebrates that community aspect of football. It's been years since I've been to the football, unfortunately. I tend to sit at home and watch it but I forgot what the communal aspect is like sitting in a stadium surrounded by thousands of other people cheering for your team to win. And that's a tangible thing that's felt in the actual film itself.

NM: Kind of [a] virtual crowd.

But reminding us why we enjoy football. It's important.

NM: I think it is. I'm glad that that came across, because that was some-thing that we really did try and capture. We were there in the stands, filming people. Particularly that season it felt like there was so much at stake and with COVID, it felt like it brought those themes out more than ever, and that it was more important than ever that people were together and sharing something, sharing this event all at once. It's hard to describe the energy that you feel when you are in a crowd like that, when you hear thousands of other voices chanting a chorus or cheering, it's so contagious. There's a certain feeling that you don't get when you watch it on TV. If you're sitting there in the stands, there's an energy that you feed into.

One of the things which threw me is how the teams had to move around Australia. And there was the threat of being locked down in different places. How did you go about moving with them? I didn't take a proper look at their fixtures for last year but was Port Adelaide mostly staged in Adelaide last year for the teams? Or did they had to move to the hub in Queensland?

NM: It certainly was complex. They spent probably a majority of the sea-son in Queensland. And the AFL had implemented some strict COVID protocol so they were in what was called 'the COVID bubble'. There were certain people within their team that were either in or out of the bubble. Even within their own organisation, they couldn't necessarily interact with each other in person.

There were people that were quarantined and people that weren't. For us, as filmmakers, we were just lucky that we had a good relationship with Port Adelaide. They've got some of their own media people there on the ground all the time, so we tapped into that resource and we said, "These are the sorts of things we'd like you to capture while you're there. And make sure you get this moment and this moment." We had to be resourceful and adaptive as well and just work collaboratively with the clutter to get those moments. But it's reflective of that moment in history as well that we could get in the bubble via their team as well.

Coming back to the longevity of Port Adelaide, they've been around for 150 years and there's no challenge that they can't take on board. And certainly for football, playing during a pandemic is probably the biggest challenge that you might ever get. It's overwhelming. How do you prepare yourself for that challenge as a documentarian?

NM: That's what we figured, as things were really dramatically shifting, we thought, "Oh, what's going to happen here? Do we follow this storyline?"

And we thought pretty quickly, "Well, this is history happening right now in front of us, and we're documentary filmmakers so we better capture it." It was how much more significant could you get, on the 150th year to have this COVID pandemic take over the season? And what would that mean for them and the longevity of their club? It did speak to that, to their resilience and history even more.

I don't think there was any way anyone could prepare for what happened with COVID. That was the world turned upside down. What did inform me from that point on, and the creative team, was the fact that I had spent already a lot of time going through that archival [footage], I was very familiar with the history. We already started piecing together the community and what that meant to people there, what football means to people, those bigger picture things. I think knowing that that was our foundation or the core of our theme or what we were trying to explore here, we just had to use that to help guide our decisions as to what we did next. It was lots of conversations with our editor and producer about, "Okay, do we capture this moment? It feels like that kind of feeds into what we're trying to say here." And I'm not sure how much you can prepare for something like that, but just trying to be as adaptive as possible. And make sure you don't lose sight of what the core of your story is there.

We don't have that many documentaries about our football teams. There's a Collingwood documentary which came out a couple of years ago and that's quite interesting [Collingwood: From the Inside Out]. But there seems to be, on the theatrical front, less of these explorations into the teams themselves. I hope that this kind of film does spawn a change and we get more documentaries about different teams because again there was so little I knew about Port Adelaide that now I'm even more informed and I understand what drives the players as they run out onto the field. As a filmmaker, what's it like bringing that vitality to such a mammoth entity that is the Australian Football League?

NM: It was incredible to me. Like you said, there's not that many documentaries out there that either explore the full history or the people behind certain clubs. And considering it's our national sport and it means so much to so many of us, that is pretty incredible how untapped it is. I think now people are starting to become aware of [how] in the past, people used to watch the games again or there'd be reruns of Grand Finals. But I think we're starting to get a greater appreciation of history and the people involved in making things happen. I'm glad that the documentary can be part of that national conversation, but I think it's something that's already been starting. I personally came at it with a little bit of an outsider point of view, in that I'm just really interested in people as well, organisations, how people have contributed to those organisations to make them what they are today. It was a story of all the individuals over the different eras of Port Adelaide that really captured me, how much people loved and cared for that club and how they built it up. And by doing so, built up that area and built up the state. I think through football, it tells this bigger story of us as Australians.

I haven't seen [your previous film] Power Dreaming but reading about the role that the Port Adelaide Football Club has with Indigenous kids in Australia and getting them excited with football, it's not just about the football, it's about building communities. It's about the people who helped make it happen, who helped bring communities together. It's what film can do as well, bring people together. It is a community in itself. It's wonderful to see. Could you talk about Power Dreaming just a little bit as well? What went into making that and telling the story in the pilot program?

NM: With *Power Dreaming*, all those programs, they're all about Port Adelaide. That's just by virtue of we were always interested in telling that community story and Port Adelaide have a lot of community programs. It's always been the way that they see themselves as part of that community. And, part of their mission statement is to give back and make their community proud. They do invest in a lot of different programs to reach out to young kids or in particular, this one is focused on their Indigenous programs. That was headed by Pauly Vandenbergh at the time. And the amount that they go out and support kids from rural settings, education programs that they put out there as well as role modelling, how they then support young talented kids wanting to explore football or come through their club. They have programs there that still focus on making sure that they get an education, that they're getting good life experiences, and carry them kind of into football if that's going to be their career, [or] into other careers. That definitely resonated with me. And I think other clubs are definitely stepping up in terms of having some more programs. Port Adelaide particularly, at that time, were definitely the most advanced with their community programs. I think that spoke a lot to their personality or the way they kind of interact with the community as a club.

INTERVIEW
GIRLS CAN'T SURF - DIRECTOR
CHRISTOPHER NELIUS

Just like every sport in Australia, the sport of surfing is rife with issues of ine-quality, misogyny, and actively excluding women from participating. Christopher Nelius' documentary, *Girls Can't Surf*, takes a look at the many women of the Australian surf scene who have tackled the bloke-heavy world of surfing and cut a line in the waves for themselves, and the women who would come after them.

Featuring a wide array of interviews with icons like Layne Beachley, Wendy Botha, Pam Burridge, Jodie Cooper, Pauline Menczer, and Lisa Andersen, this fascinating documentary dives deep into the world of surfing with the help of stunning archival footage and imagery.

Christopher is a documentarian who has a filmography stacked with films focused on the waves of the world, with the successful *Storm Surfers* series (2008-2012), through to the TV series *Focus: What Drives the World's Top Athletes* (2013-2015). He also directed the 2018 short *Don't Believe in Never* which followed Richmond Football Club on the lead up to their 2017 Grand Final win. Addressing difficult subjects has become part of his later filmography, as he toured around Australia with Henry Rollins in 2018 to film *Tough Conversations*.

Interview conducted March 2021.

▶▷▶

I want to find out what drew you to this story of trying to find equality in a male dominated industry?

Christopher Nelius: To be honest, coming into it, that wasn't my goal. I didn't quite realise that it was an equality story. And I know that sounds odd, because I'm talking about women's surfing in particular. Through the dichotomy of that, and men's surfing is what you expect it to be, I knew the sexism would be part of the story.

But I was mostly attracted to it because of the characters, these individuals. How the hell did these women do it? I've always been a fan of that 1980s surf world, just because it's so wild. It's pre-social media, even the guys were scrabbling to become superstars. There always looked like there was more money than there actually was. I knew that because I've got a couple of close friends who were pro-surfers in the 1980s, so I'd heard all those stories on the male side.

And somewhere along there, I thought, if they were scrapping for [the limited money], how the hell did the women do it?

That sent me on a journey to ask: who is Pam Burridge? Where she now? Who is Pauline Menczer? Who is she now? When I did that initial dig, and started talking to them, 'hi would you talk to me for an hour about your story', that's when I was like, "Wow, all of these women have their own powerful stories on their own."

That's what really drew me into it. It wasn't until I started to hear all of their stories as a group, and they talk about the industry and the institutional angle on the story, and things like the Roxy revolution, and all of those types of things. Why was it that women weren't being given decent waves to surf in? All of those questions, that's when it started to become: This is a story about equality.

This is actually what's wonderful for me is that *Girls Can't Surf* is about these women, but it's also genuinely about equality, and why equality is important. And that was probably something I didn't truly discover, with my co-writer Julie-Anne De Ruvo until we were starting to put the edit together, and starting to put their stories together. When I was interviewing them as well, I asked, "Did you realise you had this fight on your hands? Coming into it?" They're all like, "No, no, we just wanted to be stars and make money and beat the other girls..."

...at the competition...

CN: Exactly. Like any athlete would, male or female, except, because they're women, they discovered that there's actually this whole other thing that they had to do, which was promote and try and get the sport off the ground because no one wanted to help them do it. They would realise that was up to them.

As you're discovering this story, as you're directing, and co-writing, was there any moment where you had a question of yourself whether you're the right person to tell this story? I know that one of the main things [being discussed) in Australian film and international film at the moment, is equality behind the screen, and the ownership of stories. Was that something that you felt challenged by yourself as you're making this film?

CN: Yeah, in the very early beginning, I did. Yes.

So, it was my idea, I had the nose for it. I thought, I think there could be a film in this. And then I did very quickly think, am I the person to make it?

I probably had a few months there where I wondered if I can find the right woman to direct this story. I kept doing the research in the meantime, and I just started falling in love with it. And I started building a really good rapport with the four main surfers, and I just felt in my heart that I could do it, and that I could do it really well.

The next thing that was very important to me was that if I'm going to be a guy telling the story, that I need to surround myself with the right women in significant roles in order to do it. So I knew I wanted a female producer [Michaela Perske]. I knew I wanted a female editor [Julie-Anne De Ruvo]. And I was lucky enough to know my editor Julianne for 20 years, we're mates we've worked together before. And she's also really brilliant writer as well. She agreed very early on to cut it.

Wendy Botha
Photo Credit: Peter 'Joli' Wilson © 2020 The Side Show Movie Pty Ltd. Used with permission.

So I felt a bit more like I wasn't just being a dickhead bloke by wanting to direct it by surrounding myself with the right people. You know, our cinematographer was a woman [Anna Howard], production manager [Kiki Dillon], woman, researcher, a woman. That's not really for the optics of it. They were the best people for the job.

We often forget that there are so many other people working on a film. And we often look at a film and go, well, Girls Can't Surf is directed by this guy Chris Nelius, who is a man. Well, yeah, okay, but look at everybody else that's behind the scenes as well. I think that, certainly for critics and for the media, we tend to forget that there are so many other people who are behind the scenes of these kinds of stories.

CN: I don't mind answering that question. I don't mind being asked that question, either. I think it's a totally valid question to ask, even if it was a pretty male focused story, we should just be asking the question: could it be a woman in this role here, right now? Let's just ask it. Could we do it this way? And, it doesn't have to be every single time and we don't have to crucify ourselves over it either. But it's healthy if we ask those questions.

I want to talk about the editing process of the film, because what impressed me the most, besides hearing all these powerful stories, is the quality of the footage and the photos that you've got. How how did you go about collating all of that imagery?

CN: The archive research on this one was an Everest. In itself, it was a mountain climbing expedition. And you didn't always feel like you could even see the summit, or whether you'd gotten off base camp. It was rough.

I was lucky enough to have a team around me. But that team was driven to the edge in the process of doing it. We always knew it would be hard, because you're talking about women in the 1980s, and coming into the 90s, where there just weren't many photographers – who were all men – there weren't many of them that stuck around when the women went out because the crowds didn't stick around. There was just not many shooters who stuck around, so we knew we were going to have to try and find them and then also lean on more traditional sources like ABC TV and ESPN in the US or whatever and then we were really lucky with the women themselves.

They've had all these beautiful personal archives, and videos, and they were just so generous in opening up those old crates of photos. It was then up to us to, as you say collate it all and say, "Oh God, what year is this? And where are you here?" It was it always felt like a detective thing. Sometimes Julianne and I were going, "Hey Jodie[Cooper], what era's this?" She was like, "I don't know!"

We were like, "Oh god, this is someone in a jersey, does that say 1983 on it?" We'd have to piece it together there. It was really hard. There was one or two times where I wondered whether we had enough. But in the end, we did.

It works out so well, it is really quite impressive. It adds to the history of everything. It feels like as the film wraps up, and all of these decades of fighting for change take place, it's informed by all of these images that just feel almost like they've been held aside for this exact moment for this exact film. It's really brilliant. Congratulations.

CN: Thank you.

I want to talk as well about your work in relation to Pauline and getting a statue set up because I think that is really fantastic. It shows that there is life outside of this film for this recognition of the women surfers. Can you talk about that a little bit as well?

CN: I've lived in the Sydney's East my whole life and been up around Bondi my whole life and still live around there. I think that's why that idea came to me. I think every woman in this film should have a statue. That's why the Pauline one jumped out at me.

I was looking at this footage of her in the 1980s, this little grommet paddling out in South Bondi. Which was a heavy scene back then, it's not like it is today. They used to call Bondi 'Scum Valley'. It was different, it was really different. Not many people realise that, especially the some of the people swanning around Bondi these days. I've seen over the last twenty years, the numbers of women change in the water to go from one or two here or there, to today where you can go surfing, and there'll be 50/50, and have all different ages and abilities. And I would sometimes look at them in the water and go, I wonder if you even know who Pauline Menczer is?

You have time to meditate with the story in the edit suite, and it dawned on me that there's only ever been one world title winner in surfing to come out of the Bronte/Bondi area. And there has been a lot of incredible surfers to come out there out of there and go on the pro tour, male and female, but she's the only one that's won a world title. And that's where one day I was just like, "Oh, there should be a statue of her at Bondi." Why not?

Why don't we lionise this little grommet girl who was not going to take no for an answer. Who got told to get out of the water. Who paddled out at a time where there was hardly anyone else. We have a Wally Lewis statue outside Suncorp Stadium. How cool would it be to have a statue of a woman surfer? And for them to be a world title holder. Why aren't we doing that? What's stopping us from doing that?

And then I pitched the idea to someone I know, she's an editor of Marie Claire. And she said, "You know, I happen to have researched the statistics on statues in Australia." And I can't quite remember that exact stat, but it was somewhere between three and seven per cent of statues in Australia are women[30].

Wow. That's absurd. That's crazy.

CN: And most of those royalty. The Queen Victoria, Queen, whoever, they're mostly queens. It's back to the equality again. Why don't we put in a statue of a woman at Bondi? She earned it. She's an inspirational figure. Why shouldn't every surfer that runs down to the beach, walk past that statue and know who she is?

QUEER
CINEMA

5

When approaching queer cinema, it's important to keep in mind that it is not a genre unto itself. Like the rainbow Pride flag that represents diversity within the LGBTIQA+ community, queer cinema is a section of cinema that is embraced by all genres. In the early 90s, academic B. Ruby Rich coined the term 'new Queer cinema'[31], with the notion that queer cinema would focus on the "positive" image of queer relationships. As time has progressed, and queer cinema has become more prevalent, the definition of what constitutes modern queer cinema is best attributed to João Ferreira in Little White Lies[32]:

> *Queer characters are no more, no less than any other character.*
> *Queer Cinema is an expression of freedom.*

It is through that prism that we look at the queer Australian films of 2021, witnessing a wave of emerging queer artists and filmmakers who together add to the growing modern identity of queer Australian cinema. In 2021 alone, Aussie queer cinema was seen within the romance genre, in documentaries, fantasy, hyper-realism, and more.

A wealth of short films embraced the notion of queer cinema: Christopher Elena's furious and passionate short film, *Refused Classification*, takes aim at ratings groups and film censorship boards around the world who actively tear out any sign of queer relationships from films, mainstream or otherwise, ultimately highlighting the absurdity and hypocrisy of these archaic and cruel decisions to erase queer figures from culture.

Jacqueline Pelczar guided Tina Fielding's glitter-soaked *Sparkles* into existence with spectacular direction that gave Fielding her on screen debut. Here, the story of Courtney (Fielding), a queer woman living with Down Syndrome in rural WA, is given a splash of vibrancy amongst a pub karaoke event with Gary Cooper's extravagant Diamond. Being queer in the outback can be hard, let alone living with a disability, and it's Tina's lived experience script that helps reinforce the need for a community to feel alive and at home. *Sparkles* earned Tina the award for Outstanding Achievement in Writing at the West Australian Screen Culture Awards in 2021.

Madeleine Gottlieb's *You and Me, Before and After* showed Yael Stone and Emily Barclay's sisters mending fresh-wounds and bonding over the experience of getting tattoos, reinforcing what is a powerful story about reconnecting with family members at a later stage in life. For Stone's Hannah, the pain of Barclay's Rachel not being supportive of her coming out experience lingers well into her thirties, while Rachel is dealing with her own pain of going through a double mastectomy. Both Yael Stone and Emily Barclay deliver compassionate and supportive performances that should once again remind viewers that some of the best filmmaking can be found in the world of short films.

You and Me, Before and After was nominated for an AACTA award for Best Short Film at the 2021 awards, an honour which it shared with fellow queer cinema nominees, Adrian Chiarella's *Dwarf Planet* and Cloudy Rhodes *Beautiful They*. In both of these shorts, the emerging queer identities of their main protagonists as they discover their own sexuality are what makes them important moments of short film cinema.

Within *Dwarf Planet*, Adrian Chiarella pulls from Andy Boreham's short story *Concealer* to craft a deep and complex script for his two leads, Jaxon Graham-Wilson and Alex Rowe, to lose themselves within. Jaxon Graham-Wilson's space-fascinated Eddie is a teenager who seeks out the company of Alex Rowe's sex worker Greg, with Eddie convinced that he won't be able to find true love or companionship. As Eddie explains the emotionality attached to the demotion of Pluto from being a planet into a dwarf planet, we get a glimpse into his life, where he recognises that his coming out feels similar to act of being 'othered'. Eddie is no different than he was, but because of words and society, he *feels* different. Graham-Wilson's performance is masterful here, quiet and conscious of the weight of the words he's saying, imbued with an informed perspective that is sensitively depicted.

Non-binary photographer and filmmaker Cloudy Rhodes brought queer relationships to the surf with *Beautiful They*. Impressive, almost silent performances from Sariah Saibu as Violet and Morgan Davies as Blue, and golden hour cinematography from Stewart Arnott, help make *Beautiful They* a compassionate presentation of what it means to feel safe with someone else. The comfort of the privacy of a bedroom is given space to breathe here, with Cloudy's direction and script allowing Saibu and Davies to present non-binary and transgender characters free of trauma and pain. The presentation of two people simply discovering and understanding who they are as people, *together*, is beautiful in its simplicity.

Cloudy Rhodes became the first open non-binary director to be nominated for an AACTA award for a short film. Elsewhere, Zoe Terakes became the first non-binary actor in contention for the Best Lead Actor in a Feature Film award for their work in Monica Zanetti's Best Indie Film winning *Ellie & Abbie (& Ellie's Dead Aunt)* [33] which presented Julia Billington as a spectral lesbian 'dead aunt' who dolled out advice to her well-and-truly alive niece, Ellie (Sophie Hawkshaw), as how best to invite her beau-in-waiting Abbie (Zoe Terakas) to the school dance.

Also receiving AACTA award nominations for the Best Indie Film category was David O'Donnell's gender fluid drama *Under My Skin*, and Katie Found's lesbian romance drama *My First Summer*. With three of the six films nominated for Best Indie Film being part of the new Queer cinema canon at the AACTA awards, it's clear that a new wave is emerging.

Queer films flourished on streaming services, with *Under My Skin* and *My First Summer* both finding homes on Stan., with Christopher Amos' Australian Directors Guild nominated documentary *Hating Peter Tatchell* finding a home on Netflix. Ian Watson and Ally Burnham's *Unsound* received a theatrical release, before also finding a home on Netflix alongside Thomas Wilson-White's Queer fantasy *The Greenhouse*.

Instead of the LGBTIQA+ characters being relegated to the background, these films embraced their queer narratives. In the case of *Hating Peter Tatchell*, a figurehead in the queer community is lionised and revered, showcasing the lengths that he goes as a human rights campaigner around the globe to protect and help queer communities, while also shaking down the establishment and the structures that actively harm and destroy queer lives. Some may say that Peter Tatchell is a controversial figure for the way he uses uncommon acts of protest to disrupt society and make his cause know, while others, like interviewer Sir Ian McKellen who questions and listens to Tatchell as he retells his life's journey, might call him a hero as he fights for equality. Either way, *Hating Peter Tatchell* is a powerful essay of a figure who has dedicated his life to making the lives of others fairer, championing and putting his life on the line for their rights to freedom.

Over the next pages, we take a critical look at Katie Found's *My First Summer*, *Under My Skin* director David O'Donnell writes about producing his ground-breaking film, Tina Fielding, Jacqueline Pelczar, and Cody Greenwood talk about the production of *Sparkles*, Chris Elena shakes the roof with *Refused Classification*, and Thomas Wilson-White talks about the personal journey that he went on with *The Greenhouse*.

REVIEW
MY FIRST SUMMER

KATIE FOUND'S FEATURE DEBUT HERALDS THE ARRIVAL
OF A VITAL NEW TALENT IN AUSSIE QUEER CINEMA

The notion of freedom runs through every frame of Katie Found's feature debut *My First Summer*, with golden hues and candy chains imbuing the burgeoning relationship between orphaned Claudia (Markella Kavenagh) and Grace (Maiah Stewardson). Initially, *My First Summer* suggests that it will be a tale tinged with sadness and looming heartbreak, after Grace witnesses Claudia's mother take her own life in a lake near their house. Knowing that there is a girl, alone, needing comfort and support, Grace rides over on her bike and sees a desolate teen embracing her dog, Tilly. With Grace's support, Claudia learns of the possibilities of life after growing up with a reclusive mother, and together a friendship, and more, develops.

Katie Found's script reveals itself as a tender portrayal of the precipice of youthful romance, where the moments of hoping that the crush you have wants to kiss you too. There is a keen understanding of the hope of youth, where carefree actions can happen on a whim, and the oncoming pain of adulthood where responsibilities slam into every waking moment feels like an eternity away. *My First Summer* is a film that lives in the moment, that recognises the power of learning about someone, and gradually falling in love with them.

Sometimes films feel like secrets, created for a group of people to hold onto, to covet, to embrace as if it were a piece of their own, and *My First Summer* feels like that exact experience. This is the power of having women tell stories about women, for women to see themselves on screen. Claudia's bond with her bitsa dog Tilly is akin to this relationship, where the pup knows all of her secrets, understands who she is, and receives the wealth of love that thrives within Claudia that she may otherwise not know where to put. There is a power to seeing a Queer relationship like this on screen, one that will hopefully act as a touchstone for future generations of emerging Queer women and non-binary folk.

When Matthew Chuang's cinematography is paired with Nicholas Hower's colourist post-production work, the two create a truly warm and tender visual styling that feels pronounced in a way that sets *My First Summer* apart from many Australian films. The colour yellow transforms from a sombre tone after Claudia's mother dies, to being a source of warmth, with her home being soaked in golden rays. Within the blue tones of Grace's home, where she's constantly barraged with questions and heated moments, it's clear this is a cold house that is not a home. As Claudia and Grace spend more time with each other, a wistful nostalgic silk sheen covers the frame, as if we're watching unforgettable memories being seared into these girls' minds.

At the close of its brisk eighty-minute runtime, *My First Summer* reminds viewers that the safety of a queer relationship is not always secure, and that the only certainty is the time we have with each other, making the future feel even more precious. Katie Found's arrival feels like the herald of a grand new talent, someone who hopefully will amass a catalogue of queer cinema for the youth of Australia to look to for their stories to be reflected back at them.

CONTRIBUTION
UNDER MY SKIN - DIRECTOR
DAVID O'DONNELL

The world tries to teach us that we must be tougher, harsher, we must have thicker skin. That we should press and impact with just a bit more force. Under My Skin is a film that seeks to inspire a measure of empathy and love – the true commodity needed in today's climate.

Under My Skin follows Denny (they/them), a free spirit and artist who falls for Ryan, a strait-laced lawyer. When Denny questions their gender identity, they are not only met with the internal and societal pressures associated with a journey to self-realisation, but also a partner largely ignorant that such a journey could exist. Tensions escalate, and Denny attempts to navigate the shifting sands, grappling with their own needs and the varied textures of their relationship with Ryan.

Denny, is played by four different actors who identify as non-binary, or trans non-binary: Liv Hewson *(Santa Clarita Diet, Bombshell)*, Bobbi Salvor Menuez (*Nocturnal Animals, Transparent*) and newcomers Lex Ryan, Chloe Freeman. Given we were making a film with a gender non-conforming lead, it felt like a natural choice to utilise a non-conforming narrative structure that would challenge an audience to question conventional (and often defunct) approaches.

Liv Hewson
Photo © David O'Donnell. Used with permission.

Producer Raynen O'Keefe (they/them) comments on the casting "The ensemble of actors playing Denny feels very intuitive to me and my understandings. These change points of actors are entirely redirections of internal compass for Denny. Simultaneously, the ensemble cast brings a multitude of perspectives to the experience of being non-binary."

"At this point in history, the casting of trans, gender-diverse and non-binary characters with people of lived experience, is not only a social responsibility of film-making, but is also a moral imperative in the task of uplifting trans and gender-diverse stories, voices, and representation," said Raynen.

Raynen considers much of the strength of this film to be in the efforts that were made towards clarifying, supporting, and re-centering trans voices and experience - where possible - from within this narrative.

"When we move towards greater trans and gender-diverse authorship," said Raynen, "we move towards authenticity, belonging, and a valuing of the differences, similarities and intricacies that make up trans experiences. The ensemble cast structure for Denny was a step in this direction, one that intuits a vast and often under-appreciated resource - that is the knowledge, expertise, and wisdom that is inseparable from lived experience."

"Much can be said for the communities and individuals from which these stories arise, and have always arisen. When we consider the theoretical, social and embodied manifestations of what it takes to navigate such experiences within the world and current climate, we begin to acknowledge the great erasure, and over-sighting of what it means to bring such presence, grace and fearlessness into the living, loving and continuing knowing of each another, and also ourselves."

INTERVIEW
SPARKLES - WRITER/ACTOR TINA FIELDING, DIRECTOR JACQUELINE PELCZAR, AND PRODUCER CODY GREENWOOD

Sparkles is an award-winning short film that champions the arrival of three vital and important voices in Australian cinema: Tina Fielding. Jacqueline Pelczar. Cody Greenwood. *Sparkles* has screened at many festivals around Australia, from Perth's Revelation Film Festival to the prestigious Flickerfest.

With Tina's script and performance, Jacqueline is given a glorious gem of a story to work with, which producer Cody helped shape into a stunning beauty of a film called *Sparkles*.

Tina plays Courtney, a 30-something Down Syndrome woman who lives in country WA who is bullied by her mother's partner on a job site. Frustrated and hurt, she makes for Perth, seeking a place where she'll be accepted for who she is. Along the way, she encounters drag queen Diamond (a larger-than-life Gary Cooper), who helps Courtney celebrate who she really is: a karaoke singing, dancing Queen named Sparkles.

Interview conducted January 2021.

▶▷▶

Could you all introduce yourselves?

Cody Greenwood: You're here with Cody Greenwood. And I am the producer.

Jacqueline Pelczar: I'm Jacqueline Pelczar. I'm the director.

Tina Fielding: And I'm Tina, the writer, co-producer, and I star in *Sparkles*.

I saw Sparkles when it was up for AACTA consideration, and I really liked it a lot. I watched it a couple of times and really just found it a beautiful short film. It's great to see that you guys are gonna have a fantastic journey ahead this year, because I know that people are gonna love it.

CG: I hope so. We can't wait for it. It's always that weird time when you make something and then you start putting it out in the first couple of festivals and you're waiting for that momentum to kick in and you're like what's going to happen?

JP: Yeah, it's such a long time. You make it and then a year or two later, you finish it. And it's usually like almost a year worth of releasing it.

When did you start making it?

TF: About 2019.

CG: We shot it in July 2019.

JP: July 2019 we shot it, but I was working with Tina since June of 2018. And we spent about six months working on the script and at the end of it, because Tina wanted to learn how to write screenplays and DADAA [Disability in the Arts, Disadvantages in the Arts] is like awesome organisation. She has cupboards upon cupboards of filing cabinets of fifty-to-hundred-page handwritten scripts because she never thought she'd have the opportunity to have any training, and they taught her how to write a screenplay, and this is the story she wanted to tell and it just got better and better. I remember saying "And what happens next?" And she was like, "She meets a drag queen." I'm like, "Brilliant." It just kept getting more fun and more colourful.

Tina, I want to ask you where did this story come from? Where did the idea come from? Because it's so beautiful. It's so wonderful.

TF: It's from the life around where I'm from and that's in Rockingham in WA. And my family and friends I love so much. And I think that because of them, we made *Sparkles*.

JP: Her family were incredibly supportive with her screenwriting career. Do you want to tell him the story about Universal?

TF: I went to LA to give them my very first script that I had ever done. It was a bit before making *Sparkles*. And I went originally to Universal Studio. I would star in everything I had done. It was on a USB, and then I told him, "Is there any director that can call me or text me." But when I got back, I had nothing back from them.

JP: Still waiting.

After this I'm certain they're gonna be in touch with you.

JP: She just turned up at the front office or reception with this USB and was just like, "When you read it, call me." Brilliant. Anyway, sorry, go on with your [answer]. Your family was super supportive.

TF: Very supportive of me.

JP: I think when we first started working together, we were brainstorming because there were a couple ideas that you had that you might want to write about. You mentioned *Star of the Night*. But we brainstormed what Tina wanted to tell a story about, so just keywords. And I think the main keywords were 'home' and 'acceptance'. And she really wanted to represent the LGBTQIA+ community. And whilst the story touches on a lot of Tina's experience, it's told through a different character. Tina's had an incredibly supportive upbringing, but related to that small town feel being from Rockingham and not living directly in the city, would you say?

TF: Yeah, definitely. I was going to say it's from a small town to the city. And sometimes I go to Perth sometimes at night to go to nightclubs and pubs.

JP: When you first came out, you went to The Court, and that's where your first experience was of drag queens?

TF: No, it was-

JP: Connections?

TF: Yes.

JP: Sorry, Connections, not The Court. Connections was the first time you experienced that world and you loved it.

It's so wonderfully presented in the film as well. The relationship between the two characters is just so beautiful and tender, and it feels so completely Australian as well. Jacqueline, what was it like directing Tina and her script and bringing it to life? It's a pretty big task to be trusted to bring somebody's story to life on the screen.

JP: Initially I said to Tina when she finished the script, it was in a really good state, and I said we should put it up for funding. And I had been introduced to Tina as a director, and it was blurry lines there for a little bit. And I said, "I'll set you up with whatever director you want to go for." I made some suggestions. She suggested that she did some research, and then she asked me to direct it. But I think she knew that we had worked together for so long, that I think it was a natural yes. Obviously, I loved the story, but I just really enjoyed working with Tina. I think we work together really well.

We like to tell stories about the same kinds of things, about belonging and stories that encourage more kindness and awareness.

Directing her was honestly probably my best experience directing an actor because we put in a lot of work, and it was Tina's first time on screen. But to work with an actor - and maybe other actors might hate me for saying this - but she came at it with no ego and was so happy to be there. To experience that was epic, because we were both super vulnerable, and that was a really awesome experience. It's to date, it's my favourite experience directing an actor. It was a challenge for me at times because obviously I had to put myself in someone else's shoes. Not that that was a challenging thing. But I think all in all, whenever you work with a new actor, you have to figure out how they work and adapt. It's only my third, fourth short film so I'm still figuring it out. But it was epic. It was a match made in heaven.

And you, Cody, as well. I know you've done a lot of producing work. I really liked Mystic Pines, too. I thought that was really great. What was the challenge coming on board with Sparkles? And how did you bring your producing hat to a film like this?

CG: I had done quite a few short films beforehand. The team was really great, I wasn't worried about that, but the only challenge with this was more the location because we'd always thought about shooting it out in Kalgoorlie or Southern Cross. And, even though it was a short film, we still had a fairly large film crew to take out there with us. And then outside of that, it's also finding locations that we could shoot in Perth as interiors and then shoot the rest of the exteriors in Southern Cross.

JP: Yeah, we spent ages.

CG: Locations were the hardest part of this film by far. Because I think everybody that was involved in it was so excited to be involved in it. The crew and the cast and all that was just wonderful. But it was just trying to bring Tina's vision of a country town to life on a short film budget, which is always a bit tricky.

JP: One of our main actors lives in Kalgoorlie, and so bringing him down during rehearsals and also factoring - I said to Cody, "I want two weeks' worth of rehearsals or three weeks, as much time as possible." And it's the best thing when you have a producer that says "Yeah, sure, no problem," and then they just do the sweating. [laughs]

CG: It was fun. But Gary, poor thing, we dragged him from Kalgoorlie to Perth, back to Kalgoorlie to Perth to Southern Cross. He was sort of all over WA but he didn't mind.

How did you find him as well? Because he's really great. He's wonderful.

JP: Simone Flavelle who worked at DADAA at the time - she was the one that matchmade Tina and I, and she suggested him. I think she'd known him from theatre and knew that he had done film, but like not since the Nineties. He hadn't been on screen for a long time, or like early 2000s. But she recommended him and honestly, I saw a picture and we had a phone call. And that was it. I cast him over the phone call and he was like "You don't even know what I look like." And I was like "I've got a photo of you, obviously!" I hadn't seen him perform or anything, but I just thought he had the right energy and again was so willing. It's great to find people that are excited by the story and are so willing, because I think the biggest thing when you're stepping into a directing role is like feeling a lot of imposter syndrome, so to have people that are willing to figure it out with you is really a good thing and a privilege.

There's a touch of Muriel's Wedding with the singing and the dancing and stuff like that in here. Was that an inspiration?

TF: Not for me, no. I do love the movie *Muriel's Wedding*, but the real love for me is karaoke. I think karaoke is one of the things really get me to sing, not the only thing, I often sing all the time. But I really like to play karaoke in *Sparkles* to realise that I love karaoke.

JP: A karaoke lover. Just doing that I'm never not doing a film with a dance number. You don't even hear it but that was a full routine and I'm just the biggest dance mum. It's just so much fun. But I think that scene in particular shows a huge part of Tina's personality because she is-

TF: A performer.

JP: -and loves karaoke. And it has an energy about her that I think is pretty similar to Courtney, in terms of it excites people about life and brings the best out of people and Tina has taught me about embracing myself more than anyone else in terms of just sheer confidence and funk and groove. It's great.

I definitely think that Australian cinema does need a lot more dancing. And I was thinking that the other day. There's so much more dancing that needs to take place. So please, yes, Jacqueline, do that for us in the future.

JP: Yeah, even if it doesn't make sense, a real Ferris Bueller moment in every film.

It's like Slumdog Millionaire, the very last scene in that film is a dance scene and it feels kind of out of nowhere. I want more out of nowhere dancing. But it feels very organic in this one. With that in mind, what are your karaoke songs that you choose? What do you sing when you go to karaoke?

CG: I mean, I actually don't do karaoke because I've got such a terrible singing voice, but I'd probably do like Tina Turner. Simply The Best or something.

JP: Yeah! Mine is always Womack and Womack's Teardrops. I mean I'll sing anything but that's definitely at the top of the list.

TF: For me, it would be Celine Dion's My Heart Will Go On.

CG: You're doing singing and everything. You're good at pretty much everything.

JP: Triple threat.

TF: Yeah.

JP: Yeah, she can dance as well, she can really dance. There were a lot of dance-offs in the Southern Cross pub. What it's like walking into the Southern Cross footage, I've got this photo on my phone of a Swan beer can and we were cleaning out and that was just like pink feathers everywhere and all these Swan beer bottles on the ground, and it was like we left our mark, like there was pink and glitter everywhere.

CG: Everywhere that we did shoot really embraced the film like Southern Cross pub - I haven't spoken to you guys about it but they want to do a screening at the pub.

JP: Oh yeah.

CG: The manager wrote to me yesterday and I've got to get back to her today. Everywhere that we shot everyone's been - there's a scene at the end in a gas station, and Maz whose gas station it is - Karragullen, she came to the premiere and she always writes to me. You don't often have that when you're shooting. Most of the time as a film crew, you're more annoying if anything. They just want to get rid of you. But everyone really loved having us around to shoot.

TF: Oh cool.

That's fantastic. Tina, what was it like stepping on set for the first time with your story? What was it like being there and being able to tell this particular story?

TF: It was exciting to go and feel the mood for me. It's not my story but at that moment, it is my story, it is me. And I don't know if you've seen *The Greatest Showman* it's where Keala Settle is singing 'This is Me' on the big circle, and I feel like I am her in that circle. So it's wonderful with all of the crew and all of the cast, they just came down, and this is for you because of your story and that meant so much.

JP: It was really special. I think when we were filming, you get caught up in the heat of the moment. But like Frankie would often - who is our continuity person - she would often pull me aside and - the kerb scene and the karaoke scene - she would whisper, "I've never seen this before. Like, I've never actually seen this on screen before." And that wasn't to dust off our shoulders or anything. That was a great moment where I could get out of the fuzziness of directing and just pull myself back and be like, "Oh, this is actually a bigger moment than that." It doesn't even matter how the film turns out for Tina, this is just such a big moment. And it was epic to be a part of it was such a thrill.

What stories do you have from production that kind of stick out? What are the main moments that in years to come you'll think of when making this film?

CG: I think for me, watching the relationship between Jacq and Tina really sticks out. I remember on the last night of filming when it was - always the last day of filming, people are really exhausted – and just watching the two of you and how you worked together in those last moments where you were exhausted, we were all exhausted. I mean, for us as a team, it was really important that the story was authentic and the way that the production was run was authentic, all that kind of stuff. And watching you two was probably the highlight, I think, especially on that last day when things were getting a bit tough and it was 9pm at night. They've got a very, very strong working relationship, which is really admirable. And then my other highlight which Jacq touched on before is her turning into a dance mum during the dance routine because we actually did that close to dawn. Wasn't it?

TF: Yeah, yeah.

JP: Yeah, it was 'Delta Dawn' by Helen Reddy.

TF: I was getting ready to dance.

JP: There are so many videos of me having my water bottle up, being like, "All right now, big smiles! And hands! And three, two, one, go!" Loving it, it was so much fun. But that routine we made up on the first day of rehearsals because, to be honest, I had a day. Tina and Gary had just met that day, but we only had three weekends with them. I knew I had to hustle. But that day, I just couldn't find the groove, the exercises that I was wanting weren't really working. I was like, "Let's make up the dance" because we all knew what was coming. And it was a way that we bonded really quickly, because we all came up with moves and came up with the song together. And we did that dance routine so many times over, because there's so many logistics to that. Poor Gary and his boots as well. What was your highlight?

Tina Fielding, Gary Cooper
Photo © Rush Films. Used with permission.

TF: I'd say, first day on set to the last is all my dreams coming true. To see my story coming alive. And I was waiting for that moment to make certain that I actually doing this for a long time. So all of it.

JP: That was pretty epic. When I first met Tina, I was twenty-three and she was thirty-seven. And I think that really hit home in terms of this was the first opportunity she was getting to live out her dream. And you had done community theatre and stuff with DADAA, and this is the first time that you got to put stepping stones to make it a reality. And I think that just really hit home because it shows, yes, how far we've come but it shows how much of time we have to make up for and how many stories were not told during that time. So that really hit home.

I imagine this is not going to be like the first and last time that we'll see you guys working together then.

TF: No.

CG: No, we've just put in another funding application for something the other day.

Great.

JP: We hope that *Sparkles* can keep going and hopefully we can turn it into a series or a feature down the line, that would be an ultimate dream. Because it changed so much. Originally when we wrote it, it was a train journey across the peninsula.

CG: Oh, yeah, that's what I'm talking about. When you said earlier about, having my producer hat on, I think the first script was on a train. And I was like, "How are we gonna travel across Australia on a train?" And it kind of morphed over time.

JP: But, if we got the opportunity to in the future, I think it'd be great to combine those two scripts and stories and make a larger thing out of it. Because there's so much that we didn't go into. A few short films?

Well, there seems to be a lot more focus and a lot more celebration on making films in Perth lately. Certainly, last year, there has been a lot more discussions about the fertile ground and scene that we've currently got here. I'm hopeful and I'm sure that you're hopeful too that that will carry on and snowball from here, because there seems to be a lot of interest, both domestically and internationally, in making films here. Are you all excited for whatever's to come?

CG: I personally think that WA was already starting to, there's a tonne of films being made here. But I think with news of the studio that's potentially coming here and all the rest of it, that it's going to become a real focus within Australian cinema, which is really exciting. I think it's great that Screenwest are putting out initiatives like the Out Now[34] which they've just done which is shining a light on the films that we all need to be making and watching. I'm really excited about it at the moment. I think there's a lot of opportunity here.

JP: Also, Screenwest is the first organisation to roll out diversity and inclusion plans. I'm pretty sure they were the first, if not one of the first. Like an actual action plan to engage practitioners and funding streamlined towards that. I'm really excited about it. I think WA has always been a great incubator. And I think in recent years, it's showing that we have capacity as well. So hopefully, all the crew that have gone east will come back.

Definitely. I'm a huge fan of this film, and I'm a huge fan of what you're all doing and working with, and I'm really excited to see what comes forward. One of the last questions I want to ask is about the costumes. The costumes are so vibrant and exciting. How did you organise that? And is that from your own closet, Tina? Did you get to keep them?

TF: I would have loved it if they were my own costume but no. We got the best costume designer in Texx Montana. She was asking me about what costumes I want, and I said, "Okay, we're going to need double denim. Maybe adding diamonds to our costume, and she said she would look into it.

JP: Texx has come to be a really close friend of mine. I think on initial meeting, you just know that she's - okay, she's got the capability and the know-how, but she's actually got talent, real talent as a costume designer. And she was the one - I'll give her full credit - she was the one - I remember it so vividly because originally in the karaoke scene, there wasn't two worlds. There wasn't a dream sequence and reality. And Texx is one of those people that I can give my little vision bible to and she'll be like, "Great." And she'll just go off that and she'll know exactly what I'm after.

But she called me and she was like, "I think if we're gonna do this, if we're gonna have that pay-off moment, we're going to need to actually drag them off." And she was like, "What if you intercut that?" and I was like, "Well, I actually was thinking about that, but I don't know if logistically, we have the time for that." And she [said] "I just think that if you want to create this kind of dreamy nostalgic world, you're going to have to go there, Jacqueline. The movie wouldn't pay off otherwise." Even though it's not the end of the film, it's a real point that highlights what the story is about. I'll give her full credit.

I think I got really lucky with the people that are around me in terms of I had these people that do their roles but bring so much. It wouldn't be *Sparkles* without Texx, it wouldn't be *Sparkles* without our makeup [Tess Rowe]. It wouldn't be *Sparkles* without Gemma [Hall, first assistant director] or all these people - you know, Mick. I think when you find people that can do the job but also add production value, that's a real special quality.

CG: Yeah, we got really lucky.

Well, you've done a great job. What's the one thing that you want people to take away from this film going into it?

TF: What is really important for me is acceptance for who they are and what they are. I really like to think that I created this film. And I feel like this was happening to myself so I really hope it helps others.

JP: I think it's a film that just makes people feel good. I think that was when we had the cast and crew screening, that was the big - I just could not stop smiling that night. If we can bring joy whilst showing people that haven't typically historically been on screen before have their moment. It's a very joyful film, which I really love about it.

CONTRIBUTION
REFUSED CLASSIFICATION -DIRECTOR
CHRIS ELENA

There were two things I was made to believe when growing up and discovering my love for films: 1) Australian films are bad, and 2) Violence on screen is ok but sex is not. Both things I quickly realised (and at an early age too) were very incorrect. But I also worked out why people had these ideas about Australian films and sex on screen: they both had a very real honesty about them, one that most want to ignore when watching films purely to be entertained.

Australian films have some of the most honest depictions of human behaviour I've seen. Characters will say 'fuck' and 'cunt' and with such sincerity that it made me understand why most Australians believe our films are bad, because they don't want to see themselves. I did. From seeing *Noise* to *Bad Boy Bubby* to *Welcome to Woop Woop* to *The Proposition*, these were all films that revelled in the rough, brutish nature of how people think and feel. But always with affection for its characters and location. It's seeing Australian films and most people's reaction to them that convinced me that I want to make Australian films until the day I die.

Sam O'Sullivan, Bernie Van Tiel, Gabrielle Scawthorn
Photo Credit: Kym Vaitiekus. © Rogue Projects. Used with permission.

Sex on screen was similar, people would rather see and show their kids violence because it never resembled their lives or any recognisable human behaviour. The thought of sex scenes and honest dialogue between characters about sex being more detrimental to a young me compared to characters being shot and stabbed repeatedly is lunacy. I learnt more about sex and gender through films than I did in school or from the grown-ups around me. Especially queer cinema. It's when I knew I had to make *Refused Classification*.

The film is a love letter to Australian cinema and queer cinema and ho' both have always had to fight to be seen purely because they told the truth – Australians love profanities and sex is fun. Having an American censor challenge an Australian relationship with a rating system that doesn't exist in Australia was so important to me, because it's how we think Australian films are perceived by the rest of the world and especially Americans, the number one high power when it comes to film and television, yet they use a system so dated, archaic and borderline homophobic and misogynist to censor stories before they even reach us.

Censorship and more importantly calculated censorship to appease a certain type of conservative person exists to remove the honesty from storytelling. To remove the honesty is to remove voices that we don't often get to hear, if at all. It's a practice that excludes the stories we're meant to be hearing, the one's that tell us about ourselves but give us hope and fulfilment. Fuck censorship and long live Australian and queer cinema.

INTERVIEW
THE GREENHOUSE - WRITER/DIRECTOR
THOMAS WILSON-WHITE

With a decade of short films under his belt, writer/director Thomas Wilson-White was more than prepared to tackle a feature film. With acclaimed short films *St. Augustine* and *Only Different* in his filmography, he continues building his experience and talent with his deeply personal queer time-travel fairy tale *The Greenhouse*. Thomas' work can also be seen as a writer on the 2022 Netflix revival of *Heartbreak High*.

The Greenhouse tells the story of Beth (Jane Watt), a young woman grieving the death of her mother Lillian (Rhondda Findleton). Staying at her mother's house in a remote home, Beth wakes one night and discovers a fog that transports her into the past where her siblings and her two loving Mums exist. Yearning for their presence, yet unaware of the dangers that lay ahead, Beth continues to visit the past and spend time with Lillian. *The Greenhouse* utilises its low budget to great effect, creating a familial fantasy that feels profoundly real and full of grand emotions.

Interview conducted February 2022.

▶▷▶

I watched The Greenhouse on AACTA TV, and I was blown away by it. And I kept waiting for the announcement of when it was going to come out to a wider audience, and now of course, it's hitting Netflix. It's super exciting. I didn't know what to expect going into it, but I was moved and I felt just so comforted by it. And it is clear that everything that you had intended to tell with the film you've managed to do quite brilliantly. Congratulations.

Thomas Wilson-White: It's crazy. It's surreal to – I've never had this part of the process, particularly something of long form – to actually get to interact with people who have watched the film and are picking up what I was putting down.

I think in short films, you really don't have that sort of breadth of conversation afterwards. I poured myself into *The Greenhouse*; my experience and my upbringing. I am constantly blown away that people enjoyed it. It's crazy to me, because it's so personal. I lost perspective I think by the end of the edit-because we were in post-production for two years, almost two and a half years, I was like 'I know it has a consistent emotional landscape. I know that it feels a certain way.' I've lost perspective on everything else in terms of performance and comedy and drama. I just have to trust that I've made the best film that I can with the resources I have available.

And at the end of the day, if it's making me feel something while I'm watching it for the 300th time, hopefully there'll be people who receive that as well.

Definitely, that was the case. And it's there. It's all on the screen.

TWW: Thanks, Andrew.

It's sad to hear those short films don't get the same respect that feature films do. They have equal the amount of emotional impact as a feature length film. What's been your journey to being a feature filmmaker? Working on shorts, did you ever conceive short films as being their own entity? Or were they a path to getting a feature made?

TWW: I always felt short films were a really great way to say one singular thing and to nurture my creative voice and my approach as a director. I feel like I broke my back on short films in film school that no one can watch, thankfully. But around 2014-2015, I made a bunch of short films, and the last one that I made, it's actually unreleased, but it was a four-day shoot, and the first cut was fifty minutes long. And I remember going "Okay, so we shot for four days and we have a fifty-minute film." And the short film ended up being twenty minutes-ish.

I remember thinking "So, all I'd have to do is shoot for twelve days, sixteen days, twenty days if I could, and I'd have a feature film." And I think because my voice really lends itself to longer form and scenes that can be a bit longer and (the) character arc and character journey that can be a little bit more extrapolated, I just went, 'Let's just do a feature, I think I'm ready'. I now look at that person and I'm like 'Wow, so naïve'. It took guts, I think, and I really respect that in my former self who went, 'Yeah, okay, let's make a feature film'.

Ironically, I made *The Greenhouse* and then I went away and I made *St Augustine*, my most recent short film afterwards. Because I was writing what I thought would be my second feature and I couldn't crack the concept and the theme. And so I went, 'I'm going to turn it into a short and I'm going to go away'. I kind of had said to myself, 'I don't care if the short film is never seen, if it doesn't go to any festivals. I'm going to do this as a process tool to find the kernel and the heart of the next film that I want to make'. So, I went back to short films after the feature, which was really beautiful. *St Augustine* went to festivals and did all of this stuff and has really helped me figure out what my next film is, which is cool.

How do you know when you're ready for a feature? Or what's ready for a short? Is it just instinct?

TWW: I think it's instinct. I've often found that it's really useful. I'm really lucky because I've been making films with Lizzie [Cater] who produced *The Greenhouse*. We've been making films together since 2015. And she will often look at my concepts and go, 'That's a TV show', or 'That's a feature'. I'm getting better at it myself now. I think for a while there, I was developing so many TV concepts because it gives you so much flexibility and variety. I love the freedom of creating ten characters and really drawing a story out and being able to play.

But recently, I've really come back to features because I think what I love about cinema and feature films particularly is they really have to earn themselves. The story has to be deserving of being a film, and that's quite different to TV. With TV, you can throw everything at the wall and see what works. But with features, it has to be very singular, I find. Feature films feel more like the domain of the artists still, in my mind, and TV is definitely another beast. But yeah, I think it's instinct. I felt ready to make a feature film.

And now ironically, I'm dreading doing it again. Because this is the fun part, coming up with the idea and writing it and sitting in my room and romanticising it all is so much fun. The real hard yakka is on the horizon.

Obviously, these are completely different beasts, directing and making a feature film as opposed to writing a book, but there is this romantic notion of creating. As you say, you're sitting in your bedroom and you go, 'Ah, I can think about this, and I can do that', and you build it up in your mind. And then when you sit down and actually go to the process of it, there are days where you just go, 'What are you doing? How are you even doing this?' How do you deal with that?

TWW: Look, from one writer to another, I promise you, you will break through and you'll come out the other side. I think I had probably been dissociating for a couple of years there. I look back on *The Greenhouse* and I don't ever remember making the choices I made. How did I convince forty people to go away with me and make a movie? Like, how did we get here?

But I think on those hard days, I have often held on really tightly to a couple of other filmmakers and artists who went and did things similar to me before me, and who did interviews or wrote books, started podcasts or anything. I would go back to those people and listen to them talk about how they found resilience and galvanised and got through. It really was harder than anyone could ever have prepared me for, to get the film to where it is now. But it's those people that I admire and respect so much who did it before me that became the example and would get me through.

Part of my joy of being on Netflix is that I can now be that for other people in Australia and be a reference point when they're pitching their films and say, 'Well, look at what *The Greenhouse* did and look at where it ended up.' And hopefully I can be that person for another Queer filmmaker somewhere.

Who are those people that you look up to?

TWW: It's quite a long list, but the main ones for me with *The Greenhouse* were Jill Soloway who created *Transparent* and Michaela Coel [*I May Destroy You*] was a huge one as well. Cate Shortland, Jane Campion, the filmmakers who really hustled at the beginning of their careers and moved mountains to make their first film. I really held on tight to those sorts of anecdotes of how crazy it is. I feel like we're similar in the way that I feel very romantically about filmmakers who just go, 'Let's make a movie.' And I kind of indoctrinated myself with all of these writer-directors who just went run and gun and just made a movie.

I think often about Christopher Nolan's beginnings and these filmmakers who in twenty years are directing the biggest movies in the world, but who just started by shooting things with their friends, ultimately. I really wanted to walk in those shoes and just rip the band-aid off and do the first one. That was always kind of my mantra.

I'm glad you mentioned Cate Shortland, because that was the feeling when I watched The Greenhouse. I felt real Somersault vibes from it. Not so much the narrative, but the vibe and the visuals of the film gave me this feeling of that particular film, I just feel it is in the blood of this film, too. The thing which I love about The Greenhouse is that it encapsulates what it feels like to be silent in a Queer identity. And that is really something that is hard to translate on-screen because it's often so internalised. It's a feeling that's universal as well. Can you talk about how you managed to write that into the script?

TWW: I felt really passionate about the tone of the film being melancholic and this reflective malaise is the way that I kept on saying it. For me, the greenhouse is born from Beth's melancholy and grief, and dictated by her emotions and connected to her identity. For me, the film is about finding the courage to come out as the person you are, no matter what that is.

And for me, the really big important moment which many people probably don't realise is that she finally gets to sleep at the end of the movie, in the car. She's spent the whole film having her sleep disturbed by the greenhouse, and to give her rest at the end of this film. It's probably my favourite part of the film because she has just been running from herself for so long.

I was raised by two mums, and when I came out, it was not the celebration that I thought it was going to be. They were really worried and they said, "Are you sure? You know, it's not a walk of life that we would want for you. It's really hard." And I think that's the reality of the rainbow family or any family that's different, it isn't a cliché or a stereotype, there's a lot of complexity there. I really wanted to reflect that in the film, and use the other siblings who are maybe more expressive and more confident with who they are, to show that there is nuance inside of these families. And that it is not just, you know, 'I came out and my mums made me a rainbow cake and were like "Yay, we always knew"'. They were really worried. And that was really sobering, you know?

In relation to the first part of the question, I guess, the film is a really niche family Queer story that doesn't maybe tick the boxes people associate with Queer cinema. And I'm really proud of it landing on Netflix and of us getting it to where it is because I hope it opens doors for filmmakers to have variety in their stories and to be able to say, '*The Greenhouse* found its audience and so can my story', you know? I definitely held on to a couple of those examples. But honestly, particularly with the Queer Australian cinema, it was very limited when I was pitching the film or in rooms trying to sell it or whatever. I was flying by the seat of my pants, just going like, 'Trust me, trust me. I know we can have a festival run, I know that we can find an audience'.

You're right about Queer Australian cinema being quite limited. There's Drown, Teenage Kicks, Sequin in a Blue Room. These are all great films but the audience for them is often a little bit limited. And that's disappointing – and it's not because of the subject matter. It's just because of where they end up in the grand scheme of things, that they're either on a festival or they get buried as a video on demand offering. And it's great to have them available that way, but the mentality of people is still, 'well, I've got a Netflix subscription, so therefore, Netflix has everything'. And that's the benefit of having The Greenhouse on there.

I'm looking at my notes that I had written as soon as I finished watching it, and what I love is something that you've touched on already, which is that this is a film about confronting memories, and it's the Rubik's cube of trying to make sense of the past and the present. And just when you think you've got it all figured out, the colours change, and that's reflected in your coming out. There's often a belief, at least in media, that families are going to have that rainbow cake ready and go, 'It's gonna be okay'. But your mums were concerned for you. And then your life changes at that point, and I feel that reflected so deeply in the film itself. That we think that we're heading in the right direction and then things just change. I found that really powerful, really emotional, and the way that it's presented here is fascinating and reflective of so many different people's experiences and reflective of my experience, at least. I'm appreciative for that quite a bit.

TWW: Thank you. I find the hardest thing [is when] the thing that I can't really handle in life has changed, I'm so opposed to it and so exposed when I have to really face it. And when I was writing the film, my mum had just been diagnosed with cancer, and told 'Your treatment's not going to work and you will die'.

And the whole family was crossing this threshold into the unknown and looking forward at a really scary reality. I became fixated on the past and how good we had it and when we had no idea. Ultimately, it feels like a snapshot of time where everything was simpatico and calm, and we were just living our lives. And then these things happen to you that completely redirect your life. And I think all of my work is probably going to be thematically in there somewhere and tied to that, because it really exposes me, and I'm a big believer that if it makes you feel really vulnerable, you should write about it and put it in front of as many people as possible. [laughs]

Is there a comfort for you in being exposed, in being vulnerable in your work?

TWW: No. I've been grappling with this. My next film, I want to write a love story and write about love and how scary it is and how scared I am of it and how much I crave it. And it's not easier. I thought it would be easier now that I've done *The Greenhouse*, but it's just always really exposing.

Yes, I definitely have more resilience. I know it's not going to matter to me if it doesn't matter to me. So it has to. And that comes with the turf now. But I also seem to have been lucky enough to have a couple of our projects that are comedies or, this movie over here – someone's asked me to write but it's like a band-aid because it's just so joyous or something different. So I can balance it out a little bit.

Do you have a body of work in mind or a theme running through your work? Do you have that in mind as something that you want to achieve as a filmmaker?

TWW: Absolutely. Yeah.

I think there's a couple of tenets that I'll take through with my body of work. And one of those would be centring Queer characters in genre films and putting them into stories that aren't driven by their sexuality. I think for me, I really craved that as a teenager. I saw everything, I watched every movie and I constantly was projecting myself into these heterosexual roles. And when I started to see cinema or TV that centred Queer people doing things that I had not seen them do before, it actually was healing and empowering. And I went, "Oh, maybe this is what everyone else feels all the time with film and TV."

I really want to push the potential for what we're used to seeing with Queer narratives. But I always think there will be a magic realist angle or sort of genre angle on my work. I'm taking it away from reality a step, I find it really exciting. It's the stuff I grew up watching that I loved. At the end of the day, I think you should be putting something into the world that you would want to watch as well.

Have you revisited The Greenhouse much?

TWW: I'm about to watch it this week at some point. But that's probably the first time in a few months. I haven't watched it since maybe the last festival we did, which would have been maybe June last year (2021), something like that. I definitely need to watch it again. Because I think in the periods where I don't watch it, it turns into something else. You know, I'll read this review or I'll read that thing, and the movie changes, and then I watch it again, and it's kind of like coming home, you know? I'm so proud of it.

I just love it.

You should be. I can hear it in your voice as well. It's quite beautiful. It's great to hear because often Australian filmmakers – and I've talked to a lot of them – can often feel like they have to almost defend their work or be a little bit defensive of their work. And there is this denial of being proud about their work. So it's really comforting to hear that you are very proud of it.

One of the enduring conversations that I had with people last year was about genre in Australian film. And this film doesn't really on the surface feel like it's going to be a genre film, but then it skews into that magical realism. Do you consider it a genre film because of that?

TWW: I don't know. I didn't really realise this until we were trying to pitch the film to people or sell the film, but genre exists mostly for marketing. If you think about the films that you love the most – and I find this with myself – yes, it says science fiction on the cover, but the film inside is a love story or is not science fiction, really, it's fantasy. Films kind of get shoe-horned into genres.

And I understand why. I mean, a lot of people have called it fantasy. I just would never have set out to make a fantasy film. It doesn't feel anywhere close to what I thought I was making. Other people have called it science fiction. Other people have called it a psychological thriller. I've been calling it a fairy-tale, because we got labelled as a fairy tale about a year ago in a review, and I was like, 'I'll take that'. That's the closest thing, because I mean, she goes down to the woods. It's got a sort of ethereal nature to it. I don't know what to label it. I just say drama. I say a time-travel drama.

Yeah. I think that works. Because fantasy makes it feel like, 'oh we're gonna go down to Rivendell and there's going to be elves and stuff.'

TWW: [laughs]

No, this is not that. And that's what I love about The Greenhouse as well, is it pushes against genre. It's pushing against the norms. And I think that's again something that Australian filmmakers have been a little bit afraid of doing, about pushing against what has already been established, afraid of trying to change it and shake it up. And I see you as a really powerful new voice in Australian cinema and very excited to see where you go from here. Because you know exactly what you're doing. And it's clear. It's great.

TWW: It was a lonely path to tread. I think I now understand. I've read so much by people who have done similar things – and I would never compare myself to those people – but who have gone, 'All right, I'm going to do this thing, and everyone's telling me no, and I'm going to try and prove them wrong and commit to my vision'. And, it was really daunting because there were very few films that I could say, 'It feels like this film', or 'It looks like this film', or 'It's that film meets this film'. It doesn't really lend itself to those sorts of comparisons.

But often in the film industry, that's the comparison that sells the script to someone. It's been bizarre. I'm trying not to overthink it for my next film. I'm trying to just intuit where I want it to go and then listen to it. What story do I want to write? What scene do I want to write? Why do I want it to go there? I'm not necessarily going to interrogate it until I've got a script. Because I think that's kind of where the magic is actually.

It feels like you are really comfortable with your own work. And that's really nice to see as well. Oh, I'm so excited.

TWW: Somebody said to me once – I mean, this is specific, like the exact moment in my life. I was prefacing a short film I'd made and I was like, 'Oh, it's not very good. Blah blah, blah, blah, blah.' And the person was like, 'Why would I want to watch it if you tell me it's not good? You can just be proud of it. It doesn't matter. You can be happy with what you did.'

And it just like blew my whole worldview apart. Going into all of this for *The Greenhouse* and knowing it was going to go to press and that I'd do things like this [interview], I went 'I'm just going to love it and be proud of it. I'm not going to defend it or feel like I have to.'

That is so comforting. Because I think that we all do that. It's taken me a while to feel proud about my work that I do. And it's a hard step to get to there. It can sometimes be just having somebody go, 'Well, why would I want to watch that? Why would I want to pay attention to it?' It's as simple as having confidence in yourself. And that can sometimes be external. And sometimes it's an internal thing. And I think that we all need to take that away and learn a bit of that.

TWW: It's very Australian, right?

We inherit this from the culture we grew up in. But I think there's a really nice balance that we can strike where – because if you're too Hollywood, people will be like, 'Oh, no way. I'm not listening to you.'... I try and do everything with love. I try and speak from my heart. But it's a fine balance.

Oh, it is.

Where was it filmed?

TWW: So other than the train station and the driving scenes – they were shot in Berry in New South Wales – we shot the whole film in Jervis Bay at a friend's farm like just off the water. It was a five-minute drive to the beach. And the family knew my mums and knew my family, I grew up with them. They were really passionate about hosting us and letting us shoot. I mean, they were literally eating dinner in the living room, and we'd be shooting this super emotional scene in the kitchen. We just took over their house. And by the end of it, it was like clockwork. I'd be like, 'Okay, so we'll be shooting here, here, and here today.' They'd be like, 'cool. We'll just go out for the day or whatever.' They're amazing. So yeah, that's their property.

GENRE
FILMMAKING

6

Right, let's get a little messy for a moment.
When we talk about genre cinema, we get into a complicated field of discussion. Trying to navigate exactly what constitutes a 'genre' is creates a mighty contentious topic, the kind that would have you arguing in the pub all night long, getting shuffled out right on closing time while you're still blue in the face ranting and raving about whether a thriller is a horror film or not.

Take Luke Sparke's *Occupation: Rainfall* for example. This big-budget indie flick (yes, they exist) falls comfortably into the hybrid field of action/sci-fi. Easy. But maybe you're pinning string on the wall trying to figure out which genre-box Josh Lawson's *Long Story Short* fits into. Is it straight up drama? Or maybe it's romance? Or is it comedy? Or is it just a good old fantasy film? The truth is, it's a bit of everything in between. How about Thomas Wilson-White's *The Greenhouse*? That slips into the drama field quite comfortably, but it's also a fantasy film too, and there's a touch of romance as well, and there's a thriller element too. Another genre mash-up.

I told you it would get messy.

Unsurprisingly, the dominant genre in Australian cinema right now is that of the dramatic. Given its cultural dominance, especially within the Australian film landscape, drama often gets pushed into its own box, syphoned away from its genre brethren by being shoved into the air lock and jettisoned into space far away from the sci-fi films, laughed out of the room like a joke in the comedies of the world, and dispatched as the first victim in the blood-soaked gore fests that make up horror films.

Keeping track of what is and what isn't a drama becomes a mammoth task in itself. Screen Australia states that between 2008/09-2020/21 37% of the films shot within Australia fell into the drama category[35], followed by the burgeoning thriller genre at 17%, with the remaining 46% making up a genre-fluid group of films. Outside of feature films, it gets even messier, with TV and online productions all being classified as 'TV dramas' or 'online dramas'.

For Screen Australia funded feature films, there is a distinct preference to support drama productions over horror or sci-fi films, given the domestic box office dominance for drama productions. However, if we look abroad, the appetite for genre fare leans away from drama productions, and more towards, well, genre fare. The success of Jennifer Kent's *The Babadook* (2014) on an international front showed that there was a distinct global appetite for horror films that skewed a little bit differently than most.

For the sake of simplicity, over the next chapter, 'genre' cinema is the catch-all phrase that we'll apply for anything and everything that *isn't* a drama film.

We explore far-off worlds within the field of science-fiction from Seth Larney's *2067* to Richard De Carvalho's fan film *A Blaster in the Right Hands: A Star Wars Story*. Indie filmmakers find comfort in the realm of horror with everything from Jon Bell's *The Moogai* to Sam Curtain's gristly *The Slaughterhouse Killer*. 2021 curiously saw the once dormant romantic-comedy bounce back, with a tall stack of romance-focused films like Christopher Weekes *Christmas on the Farm* and Tori Garrett's *Sit. Stay. Love.* Kids films got a look in too with Netflix's *Back to the Outback* by Harry Cripps and Claire Knight, and *Tales From Sanctuary City* continued with Ricard Cussó's *Daisy Quokka: World's Scariest Animal*. Finally, the world of queer cinema exploded with David O'Donnell's *Under My Skin* and Katie Found's *My First Summer*.

So, let's get messy with genre films.

SCIENCE-FICTION AND FANTASY

When you think 'big budget filmmaking', two of the prominent genres come to mind: Sci-Fi and Fantasy. Fighting against the $100m and beyond budget Hollywood blockbusters for attention at the box office means that Aussie films often struggle to get the financial backing to make expensive looking films. In 2021 alone, we saw that budgetary limitations weren't a problem for filmmakers like Luke Sparke, Richard de Carvalho, Antaine Furlong, Aaron McJames, Seth Larney, Andrew Jaksch, and Josh Lawson.

For indie filmmaker Luke Sparke, the drive to make an expensive looking sci-fi action film was in his blood, and with a growing fanbase with the first *Occupation* film, he was able to turn around and produce *Occupation: Rainfall* – again, independently – with a budget of $25 million. Featuring a cast that included Dan Ewing, Temeura Morrison, Ken Jeong, Vince Colosimo, and Jason Isaacs, the global scope of the *Occupation* series was immediately broadened. Sparke put every cent to work on screen from the very first frame, never letting up with explosion after explosion, interesting creative and spaceship designs, and the promise of a grander sci-fi legacy to come. After limited screenings at MonsterFest 2020, *Occupation: Rainfall* received a domestic release at the beginning of 2021, but like many of the sci-fi films featured here, it truly found its audience with a global release on Netflix.

On the polar opposite of the action sci-fi spectrum is Richard de Carvalho's impressive love letter to the biggest sci-fi series of them all, *A Blaster in the Right Hands – A Star Wars Story*. It's every *Star Wars* fans dream to play in that universe, and within the strict guidelines of 'fan-films', Richard was able to realise that dream. This is a passion project, and as such Richard will not make any money from. With that said, Richard's dedication to the *Star Wars* mythology is right there on screen in every frame, making it hard to believe that this was shot just outside of Sydney. As Richard told Filmink: "Let's not forget that George Lucas was one of the great indie filmmakers a long, long time ago and had also championed fan-films and indie filmmakers."[36]

Working upon that ideology is *Astro Loco* director Aaron McJames, a filmmaker echoes the early work of John Carpenter (*Dark Star*) and throws in a bit of *Alien* and *Red Dwarf* too, to make an endearing and slightly goofy blue-collar story of a spaceship that shows a ship full of workers trying to solve the problem of being, well, a little bit bored with their situation. Working on a truly micro-budget, McJames clearly delights in the genre trappings, and loves spending time with his characters. Like many microbudget filmmakers, McJames found an audience for *Astro Loco* on user-submitted streaming platform Tubi, which has become a haven for indie genre filmmakers eager to reach an audience with a low-cost entry point (at time of publication, that cost is 100% free).

Working within a contained environment for a sci-fi film can sometimes be allow for unexpected creativity within a story. Case in point: Antaine Furlong's *Ascendant*, which puts viewers in the elevator ride from hell. When environmentalist Aria Wolf (*Home and Away* and *Puberty Blues* star Charlotte Best) finds herself kidnapped and trapped in an elevator of a super high-rise building, it isn't long before she realises who put her in there, and what they want. With stunt work that puts Best through the wringer, *Ascendant* shows what's possible within a small space.

For filmmakers, the urgency to deal with the world around them can come through in the films they create, case in point: Seth Larney's *2067*. Continuing on the environmentalist thread of *Ascendant*, *2067* finds Kodi Smith-McPhee's Ethan Whyte being sent into the future to solve humanities biggest environmental crisis yet. It's within these genre films that filmmakers can try and instil hope by solving the world's problems, and time travel is often one of the great playground equipment tools they could use. *2067* launched on Netflix around the world, with director Seth Larney receiving a Best Direction in a Feature Film (Budget $1m or Over) nomination at the Australian Directors Guild Awards, while Jacinta Leong received a nomination for Best Production Design in Film at the AACTA Awards.

Blending the two concepts of a contained environment and addressing the issues of the world at large is Andrew Jaksch's short film *Today*, pushing the sci-fi genre into darker territory with a story that's steeped in domestic abuse, asking the question of how does a victim break out of the isolation caused by her abuser? At 21-minutes long, *Today* resonates with urgency and a genuine interest in creating discussion and change. Creative producer Melanie Killingsworth and director Andrew Jaksch provide their insight into creating *Today* on the following pages.

Also joining them is Rafe Spall, lead actor of Josh Lawson's fantasy-romance-drama-comedy film *Long Story Short*. Teddy (Spall) is a bumbling man child who struggles to learn to grow up, that is until he wakes on the morning after his wedding to find that he's jumped forward a year in his life. Doomed to leap forward a full year after each startling time jump – the leaps from seeing his child as an infant to a grown teen carry the biggest weight – Teddy has to figure out how to break the curse he finds himself in. Lawson's use of a fantasy trope to tell a grounded story is done without a huge budget or special effects, instead *Long Story Short* relies on pure storytelling to explore the realm of fantasy.

Then, if we keep our gaze momentarily on the imports, both *Mortal Kombat* and *Peter Rabbit 2* gleefully delight in making the best out of their respective fantasy genre trappings. But more on those later on.

If this group of sci-fi and fantasy films have shown, it's clear that Australian filmmakers enjoy exploring the possibilities of the genres, regardless of whether they have the budget to back them or not.

CONTRIBUTION
TODAY - CREATIVE PRODUCER MELANIE KILLINGSWORTH AND DIRECTOR ANDREW JAKSCH

Today started from a desire to create a simple 'period sci-fi' contained to one location with a small cast, and over the course of three years morphed and encompassed so much more. Being set in 1969, I wanted to give the film a *Twilight-Zone* feel whilst blending in contemporary elements to conflate the time period in the viewers mind, rather than a straightforward realistic period piece.

Once the story idea had solidified – originally titled "The Loop" for its repeating motifs – the first thing to find its way in thematically was domestic abuse; it became evident this story was suited to how domestic abuse often involves isolation and repeated, escalating events. I approached Philip Cristian Claassen, who previously wrote two successful shorts around this subject. Philip's familiarity and detailed research were fleshed out by a few key personal experiences, great advice and feedback from a friend who worked for 20 years with survivors of domestic abuse, and the insightful book "See What You Made Me Do" by Australian author Jess Hill.

Philip and I were confident the science fiction genre would take our challenging subject matter and not only make it immediately recognisable and accessible in a short runtime – the film ended up at 21 minutes – but enable audience members to understand and sympathise with both characters caught in the story's warped loop.

The second surprising tie-in with the story's themes was production itself. DP Mark Kenfield notes "With a film about characters stuck in a constantly looping time warp, nothing was going to be more important to the production than establishing complete control of the lighting, so that we could quickly and easily rotate through the various times-of-day that we kept re-visiting within the story. It was one of the first issues that Andrew, Melanie and I discussed. And moving ahead with a complete tenting of the house (effectively turning our location into a studio space) really was key to our success."

Tenting the house was initially a practical necessity because of our tight 3-day shoot, but the studio-like setting it created suited our 'isolation' and 'of the era' themes perfectly, even when outside the shoot many of us had started to experience those things in new and different ways in daily life . . . because the last thing to bring surprising parallels to the concept was, of course, COVID. Not much point talking details of pandemic life in what turned into one of the most locked-down cities in the world. But when we lucked into our shoot timing, we felt very fortunate to have something to work on, and then from lockdown we were able to edit, colour, and score the film remotely.

The last touch was from our composer, Leon Ross, who did a lot of research on the film's topic as well as late 1960s scores. He notes "our focus was to not create a time-period focused score, but instead create an internal psychological score that actually pulls modernistic techniques [which] created an interesting narrative resonance [while remaining] faithful and sensitive to the themes the film covers. The score became an extension of the films characters, an inner dialogue."

We were incredibly proud to finish our film under these challenging circumstances and have our Australian premiere at St Kilda Film Festival 2021. Our hope is that the viewer gets a sense of the confusion and despair of our protagonist, and insight to the way it feels to be isolated by a partners controlling actions enough to lose track of time and place, even when she finally starts to recognise the patterns of abuse unfolding before her. Ultimately in addition conveying many types off loss – of time, of innocence, of love, of hope, of self – the film also shows a way out of the void and a way forward after it, though acknowledging it is difficult and may take many attempts. Nothing seems to suit the theme of the year in which we made this film more.

Onward we go, living for *Today*.

INTERVIEW
LONG STORY SHORT - ACTOR
RAFE SPALL

Multi-threat talent Josh Lawson (wearing writer, director, actor, and executive producer hats here) returns to feature films with *Long Story Short* after receiving an Academy Award nomination for the short film *The Eleven O'Clock* in 2018. Taking a more down-to-earth tone than his previous outrageous comedy, *The Little Death* (2014), Lawson leans into the 'what if' mode of fantasy filmmaking to tell the story of Rafe Spall's Teddy, a man-child who struggles to mature with his fiancée Leanne (Zahra Newman).

While Rafe Spall has worked with many of Australia's finest actors (Rose Byrne, Russell Crowe, Chris Hemsworth) on previous films, *Long Story Short* marks his first Australian feature film.

Interview conducted March 2021.

▶▷▶

It was a little bit a while ago that you filmed Long Story Short.

Rafe Spall: Last September (2019).

Matching with the theme of the film, time goes quickly, doesn't it? I imagine there's the experience of stepping on set for the first day and now, here we are, a year and a bit later on, and you're talking about it doing promotion. What does that do to your mind as an actor?

RS: It's like a dream. It's like a dream. It's like almost like a thing that's happened to someone else. Sometimes you have to question: did I even do that? Because that sort of Halcyon period of Bronte beach of 2019 feels like a different world in many, many ways. And it's always a strange thing to think back on something that when you're doing it, it's so intense and involving. And then it finishes, just like that, and you've made bonds with people, you've made a connection to a place to project to material. And it just finishes. And as sad as that is, it's also part of the thrill and joy of my job, that I get to experience so many different people, places and things.

You've had the solo relationships with people like Josh, who is done a fantastic job throughout his career as both an actor and as a director, and then you've had the continued relationships with directors like Edgar

Wright, what's the difference between those kinds of directing relation-ships? How do you maintain a strong bond between those two differences?

RS: Well, you hope to get invited back when you work with people, espe-cially if they're as successful as Edgar Wright as a bonus. And, in many ways, I have a lot to thank Edgar for because he gave me a break really, in *Shaun of the Dead* even though I had a small bit in it. And, I still get rec-ognised for that, even though I was 19 when I did it. And so, I think really, to get invited back and to work with people, again, more important than being talented, it's just being a nice person is just being the sort of person what people want to have about. You're not a dick, that's a pretty central tenant of my professional life. Don't be a dick.

And it pays off. It pays off sometimes most of the time. And then in terms of working with new people, that's what you want. One of the great joys of my job is that you could get something in your inbox, which is some-one who never heard of like Josh. I watched his film *The Little Death* and thought it was fantastic. Read the script. And I was like, "Yeah, come on, kids. We're going to Bronte beach." Simple as that, really. It was an adven-ture. And I really, really loved making this film.

And, it is a thing, "Is this film gonna be a success?" I have no power over that. I'll turn up, show up, do my best. But the most important thing is, is it a good time? I get to dress up and mess about for a living and get to make other people's lives better sometimes in terms of I might give someone an hour and a half to watch a film that *Long Story Short*, they forget their life for a minute, they have a laugh that gets them endorphins. Lovely. That's what I'm in it for. But whether that happens or not, is for the gods. But what I do have control over is my enjoyment and doing it and the connection that I make to people. That's what life's all about.

I want to talk about your connection with Zara as well, who's so brilliant in the film, and obviously for your character, you're living essentially a week and change in a row. And yet she's going through 10 years and there's still this real connection and bond together even through all the difficult stuff that you're going through. How do you maintain that? And did Josh giving you pointers as to what had happened in between those years that you would skip forward?

RS: He was pretty up on that he because he's such a smart quick guy, that he was really brilliant. A pretty brilliant guide and help with that sort of thing. So much of it's in the writing that makes it easy. You can't you can't polish a turd if the scripts bad then you you've got no you've got no hope really in the script. Fantastic.

Zara Newman is extremely talented and very easy to act with. You're only as good as the person acting opposite you. And she's really clever. So that that was a really positive experience.

I imagined after this as well, she's already done a great job on Wentworth but hopefully her career will continue to blossom after this as well.

RS: I think so mate. I think she's so good. And so real. And excellent. And she's been doing a lot of theatre for a long time in in in Australia. She's extremely talented. And that that will come to the fore. And hopefully this is a good outlet for her

Speaking of theatre, obviously, you started off in that kind of realm as well. What was the what were the challenges for you growing up, you know, transferring from theatre to film?

RS: I still do theatre. It's funny because I don't know if it's the same in Australia, but actually, in some ways, it's almost harder to break into theatre than it is than it is film.

I think it is.

RS: It's a closed shop in UK theatre, from what I understand about Australia, it's similar, you're either in or you're out. And if you're on the outside of it's quite difficult to break into. And if you're not considered a theatre actor, it's quite difficult to get a break. Luckily, I started early, as you say, and got some lucky breaks early on, was able to work at some fantastic theatres.

And really, it's the thing I'm most proud of my theatrical career. I equate theatre as being the sort of test cricket of the entertainment industry. It's difficult, and it really tests your testicular fortitude as it were to deliver in front of 1000 people. I did a one person show last year, where I had to learn 13 and a half thousand words on my own for an hour and a half at the National Theatre. Now, that's tough.

How do you prepare for that?

RS: There's no easy way, man, you've just got to sit there and jam all the words into your head. And really, try really hard and work really, really hard, which is difficult when you've got young kids because it can be to the detriment of the family life sometimes, but that's what you've gotta weigh up. And it's like, certain parts that you take on where you go, "Man, if I take this on, it means all I can do is this" and it is quite difficult to have a family life at the same time. I might not do something like that again, for a while. But something like *Long Story Short*, I was able to bring the kids over, you know, we stayed on Bronte Beach, and I had a really a really, really wonderful time. And that definitely has a bearing on things for me now is my family can join me in

That's completely understandable. What was the differences of working in Australia as opposed to UK or the US? I get to talk to Australian filmmakers about how they make films here. But it's, it's rare that I get the opportunity to talk to somebody who's from outside of Australia getting to make a film here.

RS: Yeah, listen, mate, it's more or less the same. Wherever you are, there's a few technical differences in terms of how the lighting department might work and that sort of thing in terms of— I won't go into the boring details or I'll bore you silly but really, you know, it's very familiar.

I've got a big connection with Australia, my sister lives in Sydney, now my oldest sister lived there for 10 years, I spent a lot of my lifetime Australia. I love it. And what I love most about it is that I don't have to - if I go to America, I have to tailor the way I speak a little bit I you know, I have to tailor my vernacular to make me understandable to people - but I don't have to do that in Australia, you guys are down. We have the same sense of humour, literally the same sense of humour, which is really great. You love a laugh as do the British so we get on, as much as we sort of rivalry rivals in sport and stuff. I love Australia and Australians and I can't I can't wait to come back again and do something else.

We're doing pretty well with getting external productions and domestic productions here, so fingers crossed, it won't be long before you're back.

RS: I'd love to come because I was only there for six weeks. I'd love to come and spend a couple of months in Australia. It'd be a real dream come true.

It was the start of summertime as well for years, wasn't it?

RS: It was beautiful mate, just beautiful. Down there just swimming in the sea every day. Just gorgeous and lovely.

The film is about balance of life. And you touched on that, especially learning massive plays solo person plays and raising kids and the like. How do you manage that balance of life now, especially given everything that's going on?

RS: I've been away a lot from my kids more than I would like, and although this is now a difficult period in the world history, specifically in the UK, you've got to look for the positives, and one of the positives is that I'm around my kids all the time, which is something I want to do more of. The message of the film is 'life's too short', and you can get very caught up in the accumulation of money, success, status, all the stuff that you do that you're geared up towards.

And I've been really lucky. By any measure of my 15-year-old self-expectations, I've made it, right? I get asked to do work, I don't have to audition that much anymore. And I make a good living. And thank God for that. I'm extremely privileged and lucky to have that. But really, you realise that the answers don't lie there, you realise that no matter how much success you get, you garner, you achieve, there's really, when you get to the end of that rainbow, there's no pot of gold.

It doesn't make it doesn't make you go, "Oh, wow, now I'm that level of success. Shit, I feel better." And as humans, we get caught in this loop of going, "If I just get that. I'll be okay. If I just get that job. If I just make that amount of money. If I just lose that amount of weight, I get that body. If I get that affirmation, I'll be okay." And what I'm learning now at the age of 38 is that really, none of those answers exist on the outside man. And all that matters in life is connection with family, friends, people, nothing else matters.

I completely agree with that. And given everything going on, I think this is a perfect film for the time that we're living in. Because it does suggest 'don't take everyday for granted. You have got to make everyday count.' Which can sound a little bit silly on paper sometimes, but in practice in the film, it's really emotional, that those final scenes are really emotional, and I think that's what will make this film stick with people.

RS: It's the passing of time. I think that the passing of time is a really difficult thing to deal with. When I think back to when my kids were really little, it was so hard at the time, but I think back on it now and I'm like, "Oh, shit, I'd have that back." I'd go back to that now, but it's difficult to stay present. It's a difficult thing to do. If it was easy to be present, everyone would do it. But it ain't easy. But you've got to try. You've got to try.

Does that inform your decision as to what kind of films do you take on board? Do you say, "Alright, I can take my family to Australia for six weeks and make a film there?"

RS: Yeah, of course, you have to weigh it up. There's first and foremost, I'm going "Is this the sort of story I want to tell? Is this a force for good? Is this the thing that the world needs right now?" At the moment, I don't want to play people murdering, I've been offered parts to play murderers and all that I'm just not interested. I don't want to. I don't want to tell horrible stories at a moment, I want to tell important stories. I want to tell stories that make a difference. Stories that reflect people's stories, entertain stories that make people think, make them laugh. That's my first requisite when it comes to choosing what I do.

Yeah, I have to consider how long I'll be away for if my family can come with me. But I'm also aware, as I'm saying that it's a huge liberty and a huge privilege that I get to have those choices, because a lot of people want to do my job, and they don't have the luck I do. So you got to keep reminding yourself of the luck. Which I try to do every day.

What do you do to ground yourself?

RS: I'm trying to meditate every day, exercise, get outside man, that's just my advice if ever you feel shitty, or you feel low or you feel bad: get outside and you feel good within half an hour, that makes me feel good. I'm lucky enough to live in the English countryside and it's beautiful, even though it's pissing with rain right now. Reading a lot and trying to nourish myself, not just sit there reading prophecies of doom on Twitter or the news or whatever, because it's human nature, you see a car crash and slow down have a look, and this is a massive version of that. You can't help it, you want to have a look, if you if you read a headline saying the vaccine doesn't work, you're going to click on it, because that's a human thing. And then you click on the article and you see it some fringe academic who says that and it's been quoted and it's been used to as clickbait. Understand us how the media works. But I think it's really affecting everyone's mental health. And I think that we need to look after ourselves and maybe lay off a little bit.

HORROR AND THRILLERS

If there's one genre that indie filmmakers comfortably thrive in, it's in the realm of horror and thrillers. Armed with a bucket of fake blood, a whole bunch of atmospheric tension, little to no budget, and a stack of hope and dreams, it's within the horror genre that many of the great filmmakers of the world have made a name for themselves.

For Aussie filmmakers, they found horror audiences outside of the mainstream in film festivals like Monster Fest (which itself incorporated Trasharama a Go-Go into its run) and A Night of Horror International Film Festival. As with many other festivals, Monster Festival and A Night of Horror pivoted either online or to reduced screenings in 2021.

Monster Fest '21 celebrated Aussie horror with a slew of gore-drenched flicks, from preview screenings of Kiah Roache-Turner's 2022 zombie flick *Wyrmwood: Apocalypse*, to the Australian premiere of Josh Tardo's short *Button Mani,* to the debut of Samuel Galloway's dogsploitation film *Mutt,* the world premiere of Martin Copping's psychological thriller *The Dunes*, and even a look back at established genre classic *The Tunnel* with Adrian Nugent's making-of doc *The Tunnel: The Other Side of Darkness*, and Cameron McCulloch's lost early 2000's gem *Scam*, featuring Kestie Morassi.

A Night of Horror also celebrated Aussie horror shorts, with a slew of films dabbling in the depth of the genre. These were Noel Vinson's *Jane*, Ryan Cauchi's *Golem*, Jean-David Le Goullon's *Barnacle Face*, Margaret M. MacDonald's *The Writer*, Kenny Foo's *Corridor*, Natalie Simonov's *Smile*, Miguel Nieto Montenegro's *Remembrance*, Shaun Hume's *Would Never Die*, Alex Dona's *A Girl's Best Friend*, the multi-director *Exquisite Corpse* (with Amelia Foxton, Kirsty McKenzie, Rebekah Mowbray, Chiara Gizzi, Sylvia Keays, Erin Connor, Kya Stewart, Lauren Hamilton Neill all creating a short in COVID lockdown to find the heart of Lilac), Angus Middleton's *Prey School*, Alex Linder's *Anoxia,* Connor Clarke's *Effigy*, Jamie Zin's *The Strawman*, Millicent Malcolm's *The Familiars*, and Michael Anthony Kratochvil's *I Call Upon Thee*. Joining this sensational amount of shorts was Addison Heath and Jasmine Jakupi's black comedy slasher *My Cherry Pie*.

Lest we think that horror films only managed to play at horror-focused festivals, we find Jon Bell's award winning short *The Moogai* playing at Cinefest Oz, the Sydney Film Festival, and beyond, while Levon J. Polinelli's micro-budget slasher *Everybody Gets Stabbed* received a home-town screening at the WA Made Film Festival.

Outside of film festivals, horror films found audiences with limited run screenings, or by being released online to an audience that will eat up any slice of the genre. Here, Martin Wilson's *Great White* screened to receptive audiences who sought the tension that comes from nature with creature features, this one (naturally) focused around the titular shark. Mathew J. Wilkinson's Christmas-focused indie slasher comedy *Stuffings* turned to Amazon Prime to receive a global audience. Sam Curtain's bleak slasher *The Slaughterhouse Killer* conjured a new horror villain with Craig Ingham's threatening Box.

For indie filmmaker Robbie Studsor, he turned to the thriller genre to create the proof-of-concept short film *Shallow Breath*. Joining him in the short film field is Katherine Chediak Putnam's *Inferno*, which presents a sinister reality that comes with knocking down a family home. James Hunter's *Nest* pushed into the diminishing wilderness, with a timber feller haunted by the sound of an infant's cries.

Over the next pages, we hear from Jon Bell, Levon J. Polinelli, Robbie Studsor, Addison Heath & Jasmine Jakupi about their genre works.

INTERVIEW
THE MOOGAI - WRITER/DIRECTOR
JON BELL

Every so often, a horror film emerges that leaves you shaking and in tears. Not figuratively either. *The Moogai* quite literally left me shaken and weeping in my seat at its close. Writer/director Jon Bell has crafted an instant horror classic that unsettles as much as it interrogates the traumatic past of the Stolen Generation. As a white viewer, it forces an introspection that many other films addressing this part of Australian history have yet to reach.

With searing performances from Shari Sebbens and Meyne Wyatt, *The Moogai* further disturbs by its relatable and universal appeal. Shari leads as Sarah, a new mother bringing her child home with her new family, with Meyne's Fergus as the father. Together, they have hopes for a bright future, but a darkness exists in their home that they don't initially realise. As the fifteen-minute short unfurls, we grow to learn about a spirit in the house, the titular Moogai.

The Moogai screened at the 2020 Melbourne International Film Festival and at the 2021 Sydney Film Festival and Cinefest Oz.

Interview conducted October 2021.

Readers are advised that this interview discusses the Stolen Generation and intergenerational trauma.

▶▷▶

What a powerful film you've created. Congratulations.

Jon Bell: I wanted to do something more serious. [I'm] probably known for maybe for lighter fee, or just sort of episodic television [*Cleverman*]. But, filmmakers need to have something to say. It can be frustrating, where you got something to say, and you can't say because there's no room in that sort of environment, like comedy, or? Well, there is room in comedy, I guess, with sketch comedy, well any kind of comedy. But yeah, it was good to be able to say something about something serious.

As you're saying, you can investigate that in comedy, but it's maybe not given the same level of attention or care, as it might do in other genres. What I liked about the horror genre is that it is so clearly able to investigate and explore really serious themes, like what you're exploring here, the stolen generation, so well. I was left shaken at the end of it. It's one of the best films I've seen this year, and you manage it in about 15 minutes, the economy that you have with storytelling here is impressive. How did you manage to inject everything into such a short period of time? How did you know what to put in what to leave out from the script?

JB: I tried to make a try to really actually make a short film not a small film in or, like, it's still a film, and it's still got the journey of a feature film. And I think maybe that's like, what you're just saying, that's what makes it feel [complete], so there's still, there's still definitely beginning, middle and end, there's still a journey for the lead character, or for all the characters, but certainly for the lead character. And, when I was writing the short, – well, it's kind of a proof of concept – when I was writing that I was also writing the feature, so sketching out the biggest things, and then kind of trying to condense them, not condense the content. So it might be like, 'Oh, let's take this scene and make that.'

The little girl in the short, she's in a bigger part of it in the feature. So, her journey is the same. It was almost like adapting a book or something, where you take that longer version. I think it is important that we when we do make these short films - like we sort of got into a habit of making shorts that have a setup and a punch line, that are comedic - instead of, okay, this is still a film, you still got 15 minutes, 10 minutes, five minutes, to tell something, to tell a story that could easily be a feature. It is good for your discipline, in the sense, that when you do switch over the biggest canvases, you set up real quick.

You certainly have more time but the way that people have gotten now, if you don't grab them in the first 10 minutes, they just literally pick something new on a streaming service. That's important too, hooking them, but that doesn't mean fast paced stuff. That doesn't mean you got to cut and it's got to be action and all that. Because what I was trying to do was have a slow pace, just to get before audiences come in, if they would have seen in the cinema come in, sit down, they've had the sugar rush, popcorn, sugar, drinks, whatever, and then they just come down, and they just get into the film's rhythm. So that when we go up, that's okay, because they've, they've settled down and their heartbeats dropped, and they relaxed.

And it's also trying to get them into that state, so that when you do start showing things that are creepy, it genuinely unnerves them, because the audience is hopefully invested enough physiologically so that they are actually down instead of 'Ah, oh, that wasn't really scary', yeah, that's because you're up. So it was a combination of those things.

I like what you're saying about short films, I think that so often, we'll just see short films at a film festival, and that's the life for them. I've watched countless short films over the years and have found them to be much better than the feature length films that are out there. And people disregard them as being films, but they're still films. It's literally in their name: it's a Short. Film. We need to treat them with a little bit more respect. Is that something that you have found as a filmmaker?

Shari Sebbens
Photo credit: Tess Peni. © No Coincidence Media and Causeway Films. Used with permission.

JB: Yeah, absolutely. I really wanted to make a film that— Certainly, if the feature never gets made, you'd go back and go, "Oh, that holds up." Like, it feels a bit timeless, and it feels like, if you've got 15 minutes, "Hey, do you want to watch something a bit unnerving," the audiences would come back to it, in the same way that we might come back to longer films. I don't know about you, but I'm actually finding it a little bit harder these days to settle down and to commit, [that I] can actually commit to the storytelling. That's even as a filmmaker, you've got to watch other people's work, you've got to see what's out there, you've got to see the new things.

I think you're right, [short films] may have been sort of disrespected, or not disrespected, but maybe relegated to "Oh, that's that kind of storytelling." But I feel like they're still films [that are] in a way are coming into their own. To commit to a longer thing, who's got an hour and a half to scratch themselves really? Especially with kids at home, COVID, all that sort of stuff.

Exactly. And I've found that, a lot of the films nowadays, they feel a little bit bloated, like I went and saw The Last Duel the other day, and it's two and a half hours long. And I felt it could have been shorter, the economy of storytelling is just not there. But the short film, you've got to really get to the point.

Let's also talk about the meaning of the word 'Moogai', because I understand that there's two different meanings, two different countries have two different meanings for the particular term. Can you talk about that by any chance?

JB: For Bundjalung people, it's just a spirit, it just means spirit. So, we do use it in ways of saying to a kid, 'The boogey man will get you. Yeah, there's a Moogai over there, stay here,' but we also use it genuinely like "Nah, something felt wrong, I think there's a Moogai over there." That's the way Bundjalung people use it, but they use the same word for some somewhere else. I think it means elder or something. I'm not sure but here it just means spirits. In that sense, the Moogai in the film— yes, the Stolen Generation has transgenerational trauma and all that sort of stuff and postnatal depression and all that stuff's in there.

But it's also like the Moogai itself has its own point of view, in that, it just wants what it wants. A lot of traditional Aboriginal stories, they're not always like Aesop's Fables, where this is designed to teach you something, sometimes they're just the story that happened, and the people remember the story. And so in that sense, I think the Moogai isn't bad either. It just is, it just wants what it wants, which just happens to be your baby, in the world of the story. But in the world of the story, and in traditional Aboriginal stories, the Spirit, the agents of destruction aren't always evil.

It does carry a very clear, double meaning in the film, too, when you're writing the script was it 'I need to write about the stolen generation first,' and then postnatal depression, or were they both at the same time as you're writing the script?

JB: They were both the same time. I was raised by a single mother, and just had sisters and a wife, four daughters, more granddaughters than grandsons, just surrounded by women. I was just trying to tell the story of— certainly in my family, there have been close calls, my grandparents, when they were younger, white people came there to take them, but the property that they lived on the white people that owned the property, told him that they were not there at different times, but there white people that came to take them knew that they were there.

So there's been these close calls, but we pass that story down within the family as a cautionary tale, and like, 'You just gotta watch em, you just gotta watch em, because you never know'. So it was a boogeyman story, and it was like, "Ah just gotta watch these whitefellas because they'll try and take your kids ."

And even now, like my Mrs., she works with young mothers and stuff like that. And even now, there can be fear within the community, not an overt fear, but still a fear that if you do go to hospital, and people want to make a judgment call on you, not knowing your history or not knowing anything, doc's will be in and they'll try take your baby. So that ever-present boogeyman is ever present in our lives, and it sort of started from that, which is kind of a little bit Stolen Generation, a little bit horror film.

I had an uncle we used to make a ton of horror films when we were kids, and so I just wanted to get back to that sort of genre filmmaking where... something that's not just chock full of jump scares, like cheap scares, like things that a genuinely creepy that sit with you and you go, 'Oh, my God, see that! That really, that scares me when I think about it', those fears, those deep-seated fears, like the Stolen Generation, and someone taking your children, that's a universal fear. 'Am I really seeing what I think I'm seeing', we've all had those moments. Taking this specific of Aboriginal people and of women, and trying to make it universal, trying to get the universal in there. It started from the family stories.

Do you see filmmaking as kind of a continuation of carrying on these stories that have been going on for generations and generations?

JB: Good question. Yes and no? Yes, in the sense that absolutely there is a certain style of storytelling that Aboriginal people have. And that, once it's put on the screen, people will find it's quite different to— well, (it's) a different sub-genre of horror films. *The Moogai* is kind of a monster film and a psychological horror. There's also the little girl in there who feels a little bit like Japanese horror, or something like that. There's enough things in there that you go, "Oh, this feels like other things", but it definitely is its own thing, in that what I'm saying about The Moogai just having its own point of view.

"Come into my parlour said the spider to the fly", like, if flies all get around and tell horror stories, they're probably all about spiders. But spiders are just like— It's like us with cows. Cows be like, "Oh man, you got to watch them humans ." So, it is a continuation in that sense, but also, it just continues on regardless of film, or regardless of Western civilisation or anything like those stories still get told.

The story itself is something that has value, and I don't know if that can ever really be translated to the screen. Because maybe now because you've got phones and stuff, you can just make a film for yourself; nobody might ever see that film, it's just for yourself. Previously, because it took so much capital to make a film, it's like a film had to find an audience to be considered valid. And even if everybody says that's the worst film ever made that story still is a being in itself, almost, in Aboriginal culture. So that's what I mean. Yes, it is the latest expression of it, but no it isn't, because the stories just live.

That makes sense. I had been curious about how, because Aboriginal stories are so much for the Country that they come from, but films are a communal aspect. And, for me, as a white guy, it feels like I'm trespassing sometimes when I'm watching Aboriginal stories, like I shouldn't be part of this. And that was one of the things I really felt amplified with the Moogai, and I don't know if this is a conscious decision or not, but the way that you place the camera, from the perspective of the creature, (who) is behind the camera, and effectively, I'm sitting there feeling the characters staring at me going, "you, you're the guy that's going to steal our baby", it added this extra layer of 'you shouldn't be here, you shouldn't be here at all.' And it really felt like it put the spotlight on me, justifiably, which was a really unsettling experience. Was that a conscious decision at all?

JB: That was a conscious decision. Certainly budgetarily, we didn't have the money to see it [the Moogai]. But certainly, that was a conscious decision artistically to try and garner that exactly that kind of reaction. No, it was deliberate. And it's also, because it's a common technique in these kinds of films, it doesn't feel out of place, but it certainly was like that, I thought [that] white Australians might feel that way.

It's good. I'm glad that it made me feel uncomfortable, because I shouldn't feel comfortable at all. And, to have that desired effect is really is really something I think.

JB: That's the trick I reckon, like the real the creepiness, something's gotta be creepy. "There's something wrong with this, and I don't know quite what it is." You walk down a dark alley, and a bin gets knocked over, you know it's a cat. You know it's a cat. But because it's darkness, and because there's no answer, your brain just rushes in with all these answers. And, I think that's the key to creepiness, but that to really helps the metaphor for these kinds of things [to] play.

Certainly at different times Sarah's thinking, "Is that really a chicken foetus? Or was that just a egg? Hang on, what?" And it's gone before you really get the chance to sort of forensically examine what did you see? That's the trick of the trying to find the creepiness.

Let's talk about the casting as well, because both Shari and Meyne, they're always great, but I'm getting to see another level of who they are as actors. Did you always have them in mind when you when you had this written?

JB: Yeah, yeah, pretty much. I've worked with both of them before [*The Gods of Wheat Street, Black Comedy, Mystery Road, Redfern Now*]. And they really are such good actors. Because this was a still film all about stillness, they're good enough actors, and it's not like you have to tell them what to do, they get it. But just getting to see them as a viewer, just sitting there and just watching them, I think it just really helps you see sometimes just what people are capable of. I know what you mean, because I feel the same.

When Shari did the scene, just after the car accident, when she's on her back and the Moogai takes the baby, me, Sam [Jennings] and Kristina [Ceyton], two of the producers were on set as well, we were sitting behind the monitor and man, it was so emotional, like it was so confronting. Just sitting there and just hearing it and just trying to like... you know, it was 4am and we were out there at the at the back out near Penrith, and we're in the bush, and it's completely quiet.

And it's just this voice screaming out, "Give me back my baby."

Oh man, you know you're making a horror film, but we just had tears, like we were so full on. And there was there was a line that I'd forgotten that she remembered. "You're not listening to me" was the line she remembered, and in the midst of all that, we were feeling it, I was in tears, and then she can stop and say, "Oh, do you want this line?" I was just like, "What? How? What level of acting are you on?"

You're like, 'Hang on, I'm having an emotional moment over here because of what you're doing.'

JB: Yeah, it was like (imitating holding back tears), "Yeah, say it, say the line, say the line."

And then Meyne in that scene when he's got to come back in [to the house], Fergus has kind of brushed her off, he thinks, "Oh, I think you're going through something. I've got a shitload of work seriously. I don't need this aggravation right now." And then when he comes back in the room, and he sees it, and we talked about, if you walk back in a room, and you saw a tiger sitting in the corner, when you see a tiger in the flesh, you go, "Oh, my God, that is a massive animal ." And the way that it moves is so powerful.

It's almost like you can't of take your eyes off it, and you're just trying to be as silent as possible and get out. And where did it come from? You see all that stuff just moving around in his head, even though he's not playing all these things? And that's exactly it man. I'm a big believer in your hire good people, and you get out of the way really.

There's a moment of comedy that comes a little bit earlier as well, which I think is really pointed because it's a moment where Meyne, is like, "So there's a drunk white guy who's wanting to steal our baby", and his line delivery is both a little bit amusing, and it's this diffusion of the tension. Was that a pointed decision to be like "We've got a certain period of time we need to diffuse some tension somewhere so we can build it up again?"

JB: Yes, absolutely. Like the rhythm of, very slow in the beginning, even when they walk in, they're crossing a threshold, they're entering the space, they're walking through a doorway, with a child. They're not a couple anymore. They're family now. So they come into the space redefined.

Photo credit: Leo Baker. © No Coincidence Media and Causeway Films. Used with permission.

And that shot from the beginning is the Moogai's point of view. It's a series of family portraits, from the three of them, to the two of them, to just the Moogai wants the baby. And that rhythm there, leading up to the first jump, or the first scare, like the little girl in the room, and then reset, she comes back out, "I'm just gonna cook breakfast", and then we start to go up again. And it's just that rhythm of resetting, without consciously trying to show. For the audience, it's not obvious that it's a reset. It's not scare,

'Okay, now we're gonna cut to a whole different location or something,' it's trying to be more subtle and almost trying to craft it. You just take it out and try and not show people where the joins are.

But especially that moment, you're right, especially that moment in terms of a bit of a laugh, diffuse tension so that they can leave the shot, and then we can do zoom out, zoom in. Or zoom out, and then we and then we cut to night, so that when we come back to her on reverse, like she's in the middle of something, we didn't even start up again. We started up and started to come down, but then realised we're actually up here, because she's getting to a really manic place. But that's the rhythm, that's absolutely the rhythm. You're spot on there.

As you're retelling all this, my heart is starting to race again. Like just revisiting the images in my mind. That's how that's how good it is.

JB: Ah, thanks man. Yeah, yeah, yeah. The little girl is my Granddaughter.

It's a family affair!

JB: Yeah. Yeah. When I showed it to my other nephews and stuff, and they're older men, they still sort of jumped at it. It's like, you know her, you know that child, you know her. You see her all the time. When she's got her head down, they were like, "Oh, ok, what's he doing?" And yeah, just that visceral reaction to it.

What was it like having your family on set as well, especially your Grand-daughter in such a vital role?

JB: Oh, it was awesome. It was awesome. The lad who plays the gas station attendant, that's my cousin. And then the rest of them, all the kids, are like nephews, nieces and grandkids. And it was a real family affair, and it relaxed me, because I was working with children, that I'm used to reprimanding, so you can actually direct them like adults. [sternly] "No, that's not what I want to do it like this."

[laughs] Not that I do that, I'm a pretty soft touch. But it made it easier. And then it also set up the next generation, even though they're all young, they all watch stuff and then they turn around and say "Oh Pop is that person an extra? Is this a such and such?" And they use the terminology. So it's good to educate kids and just give them an experience and also let them know, when you watch something, there's been so much hard work put into that. But no, it was freeing.

I'm a bit surprised as well, like, Australia has got a lot of great horror films, for sure. But we don't have that many Aboriginal horror films. I think there's beDevil and maybe, gosh, maybe a couple of others that I'm not aware of. I've been tracking a list of the different horror films that we've got, and beDevil was the only one that really came to my mind, and then The Moogai. Is there a reason why there hasn't been that many Aboriginal horror films?

JB: There's been a few shorts, as well, that I'm aware of, but I think they haven't quite like... well, like what I was saying about Aboriginal stories just existing for their own sake, I think maybe because none of them have garnered attention, but I don't mean that there's anything better or anything worse. I just mean, Australia's a bit of an odd decision maker around those things anyway.

It really is.

JB: Because really, when something does well, it's not like we go back. We did *Mad Max*, and then it wasn't like we did 100 post-apocalyptic things. So I think there's also an element of, *dismissive tone* "Okay, Aboriginal people, you're gonna tell horror stories, what are they about? What are they going to be about?" I don't know if Australia is that interested in the answer? Because horror, you're going to talk about trauma, horror stories about trauma, and, the traumatic things [history], and nobody really wants to... Well, not nobody, but depends on how they presented.

I was gonna say, I disagree. I know there's an audience out there for Aboriginal stories and Aboriginal cinema, if it's not in Australia than it certainly is globally.

JB: Well, I think that's the difference, too. This market that we're in now, with streamers, and, certainly the streamers are probably still gatekeepers, in some respect, but there's not as many gatekeepers. People are interested in going, "Oh, well, what does this culture say about this thing?" "Boom, here you go."

Certainly on Netflix, at least, there's a lot of a lot of horror films that I didn't know existed or from different cultures, like, Under the Shadow (2016), for example, which is a great Persian horror film, and because it's on Netflix, it's accessible. And I would hope that that might be an avenue going forward. But we're in such a complicated time with Australian film. It's so frustrating at times. I was part of the Australian Film Summit the other day online, and there was a lot of people in the chat who were talking about the need for more support for horror films. And then the people who were doing the presentations were like, "Oh, there's no audience for horror films ." And it's like, well, there is an audience. There's an audience there. The people who are making them are saying that there is an audience, I know there's an audience.

JB: Oh, absolutely. Horror is probably, geez, is one of the, if not the genre, that always consistently sells. There's no period where it's gone away. People are always willing to watch something that scares them and gives them a jolt, so that they can feel scared while being safe. Horror is massive. The meetings that have happened off the back of *The Moogai,* which is a 15-minute film, didn't happen off *The Gods of Wheat Street,* and that was a six-hour miniseries that I wrote. A 15-minute piece, versus however many hours of TV and whatnot, and this is the one that gets meetings in the US. They know that it sells. Horror sells.

What's the future The Moogai? As soon as it ended, I remember back in the early 2000s, I used to be able to buy short films on DVD [Rubber Johnny, the BMW series], and they'd have director's commentary and stuff. And I remember buying them and giving them to friends, because I'd be like, "You've gotta see this short film, you've gotta watch this ." And, that was my immediate reaction when I finished watching, 'I need to have 10 copies so I can give it to all the people I know and say, "Here, watch this film ." Is there a life outside of the film festival circuit?

JB: So, NITV, they're going to screen it. I'm not total sure when, but after the first festival circuit. I've finished another draft of the feature. I really tried to make *The Moogai* itself make it feel original enough that it's something that we haven't seen. There's a little bit of a weight on this, the weight to make something that feels strong enough to prove that there is a market for Aboriginal horror films, like you're saying. Trying to make the monster in a monster film feel authentic enough and to sort of maybe lay the way for some more filmmakers to get opportunities in the genre. Maybe that's an avenue like putting it out on DVD or something like, even though it feels old school now, but I don't know how many people got DVD players, but there was something nice about going and buying it and having it, and having it there. And that's not a bad idea at all, man.

I've got The Babadook sitting right next to me, I have it sitting next to my computer because I like to look at it, and remember Essie Davis' performance in that. I watch it almost every year, because it's a great film, but just having the physical thing there, it brings everything back, just like you retelling the story about how you're making it earlier, it brings everything back. And it's funny, I was talking on the radio the other week about horror films, and the guy I was talking with was like, "Why do people want to be terrified? Why do they want to be scared?" Because there's no other feeling like it. And I think one of the things that you had mentioned [in an interview prior] was "You watch drama, but you feel horror." It's that feeling, the emotion that stays with you. It's a tangible thing. You can't get that really anything else.

JB: No, you can't. It's got to affect you physically. Like, comedy [is] a little bit as well. If it doesn't do what it's supposed to do, then it fails. And drama is so interpretable. You and I probably similar age, I had one uncle who was who was really into horror, and he's used to show me horror films when I was a kid. And I remember watching *The Evil Dead*, the original, when I was like, eight, or something. And it scarred me. And I still haven't watched it since. Because it was so — exactly what you're saying — it brings back that feeling. The relationship that you end up having with these films, yeah, it's exactly what you're saying. To own them, and then you've got them there. And it's not just in your head and then out your head, like everything else these days.

There are films that I haven't re-visited, but they're still some of the best I've ever seen, because of that feeling. Because I saw them at a certain point, like watching Child's Play, when I was younger, and just being terrified by that film. I've never revisited it because I don't need to, it's all in my mind. I can remember it all the time. Just like you can remember Evil Dead. And it's just like it sits there in your mind.

JB: Yeah, and when you look back on it now, it feels like what kind of childhood were we having to watch those films? So, but those in the 80s, I think horror films, maybe that was their heyday, the 70s, 80s, where they had these really disturbing films. I mean, they're disturbing. There's seriously something wrong with them. I don't know if we internalise that jump or that physical, that adrenaline rush, and so for a certain generation, we've just gone after it further, you know, we've kind of become addicted to it or something.

It's a formative thing. It really is. I liked what you were saying about having your grandkids and nieces and nephews on set to try and kind of give them the language and the idea of going forward, carrying on the generation of filmmaking as well. And I hope that that pairing of horror and filmmaking for them has sparked to a whole new generation within themselves for appreciating horror films and wanting to make them as well. So I look forward to seeing what they do in 10, 15 years' time.

JB: Well, certainly even when we when we do watch stuff, because they were right into *It*, and I was like "Oh, I don't know if you should watch this." "No, like it's alright, we know it's pretend, this, that and the other" and ok. So we watched it and they were like just pointing out little things, it takes the artifice off it. Except they just go "Okay, now I'm just going to look at the craft" and still the story and everything, but a bit of the craft, which is good for any kids to learn about craft in this day and age.

Without a doubt, especially something that's so practical too. I think that practical effects have kind of fallen by the wayside, which is a bit of a shame because there's nothing like having a tangible thing. And that's one of the things which is so effective in The Moogai is the hand just come in from out of frame and we don't need to see the whole creature because we've seen enough or we've at least built up an image of it in our mind of what it looks like and how terrifying it might be. And to just see its hand is just like... oh...

JB: Well, the hands and the chicken embryo.

Oh that chicken embryo, I won't forget that.

JB: They're both practical. You're right, you can't beat it. It just feels real. Like there's no other way to say it. It just feels real. Feels like it has weight feels. Feels real.

Jon, I appreciate your time, and being able to talk about The Moogai. I've been talking with a couple of friends about this over the weekend, and I'm so excited to be able to talk to you about this because it honestly is the best Australian film I've seen this year. That's a level of how much I love this film. I can't wait to get behind it and get people out to go and see it at Sydney Film Festival and be like, whenever it's screening on NITV, and be like, 'folks, you've got to stop everything and just watch this'. People need to learn from this film, about what you've done. It's great.

JB: Thanks bruz, I really appreciate that because so it's always good to speak to people who are as invested in horror as I am. And have the knowledge of horror. Like, you can actually have a good yarn.

I appreciate it.

JB: It's been a good yarn.

We just won [the] Brooklyn Horror Film Festival, Best Director. That's my first Best Director. New York City. You beauty.

Fantastic mate, that's really good.

JB: Thanks, man. Cheers. This film as well, the way the international audiences have embraced it, it really shows you that, exactly what you're saying before, the appetite for horror films and horror films that have a certain point of view, really is out there. It really is out there. It's not just Australia, where people just sort of have preconceived notions and then just sort of find stuff that reinforces their bias.

You're gonna go from strength to strength, I'm looking forward to catching the feature length film.

JB: There's stuff that I'd love to tell you about how, but I won't, I won't yet.

That's part of the joy of what I get to do, is to be able to talk to people like yourself, and then know that there is something in the future coming along. Because, so often, I'll talk to feature filmmakers and they only make one feature film, and then they kind of disappear, but I know, on the strength of everything that you've done, that we're gonna have a whole [lot more], there is so much more to come.

JB: Well, I'd certainly like to try and make a trilogy of Aboriginal horror films. So you know, if we're not going to be a movement or anything, but at least there's a group of films there.

Well, whatever happens, I'm there.

JB: Thanks man.

CONTRIBUTION
EVERYBODY GETS STABBED - WRITER/
DIRECTOR LEVON J. POLINELLI
EVERYBODY GETS STABBED, OR HOW I LEARNED TO
STOP WORRYING AND ENJOY BEING ROBBED

Everybody Gets Stabbed is a stupid movie I made, based on two stupid friends who start murdering their other friends because they believe the world owes them something, when it doesn't.

It was an idea that always makes me sensibly chuckle - take something that already exists, and think about how it came to be, and what it might look like from someone else's point of view. I looked at *Scream (1995)*, and thought it would be funny to see how those two assholes came to start murdering their friends, how they'd justify it, and also just how long you need to wait in someone's wardrobe for them to get home. Around the same time, I was properly developing this idea, Me Too hit. And I realised that toxic male entitlement is the perfect motivation for my two idiots.

I'd spent far too many years seeking permission to make a movie. Funding bodies. Private investors. Distributors. Producers, both scrupulous and scurrilous. And, to be honest, it's tiring, and it beats you down. I had a feature film finally ready to go with funding in place after four years of battling, only for it to disappear overnight during the 2007 Global Financial Crisis.

After a terrible 2017/2018, that broke me for so many different reasons, I thought "you know what'll pull me out of this deep dark hole? Making a movie with no money!" I'd initially planned the film to be mostly improvised, with each scene having a very detailed beginning, middle and end point (so, you know, it had a cohesive plot), but a few actors were stronger with scripted dialogue, so often the night before each shoot I'd write however many pages were needed for the next day. We shot fourteen days across September-December. I'd written and structured it knowing that on most of those days I'd be a crew of one, but with a few scenes and sequences that I'd need to call in some more experienced camera operators for (the great Sergio Zanello for some of the elaborate murder sequences, and Martin Dryg Lundmark for the opening six-minute single take shot).

As with most non-existent budget movies, post production took quite a while, and it was in January 2020, as a harbinger of things to come, just as I locked off the edit and was about to go into sound mixing, my laptop and the hard drives containing all the files for the film were stolen. At the same time, our cat Maddi went into liver failure; nursing her back to health was a welcome distraction, and she's giving me a contented squint from across the room while I write this.

When the lockdowns hit, I was left wondering what to do. I'd found a near-final edit I'd uploaded to YouTube, and found some amazing trial software that uses machine learning to upscale footage to 4K resolution, but that still left me with the problem of YouTube smushing all the audio down into a single stereo track. I fixed as much as a could, but I'm not an audio guy, and wasn't sure if that was as good as it gets or not. My composer, the inimitable Ash Gibson Greig, asked local film industry sound legend Ric Curtin to take a listen, and through some downright witchcraft, he managed to pull together a 5.1 surround sound mix.

Side note about Ash. We'd worked together on a number of projects, and at the time of making Stabbed he was on a feature, a doco series, and a TV series, so had absolutely no time for a no budget feature, but he'd recently developed a near-terminal case of synth addiction. Between us we came up with the idea that his nightly noodling to unwind would form the basis of the score for Stabbed, and he would do this without seeing a frame of the film. I'd nudge him a little in ways, like "I need something that feels tense," or "something for a chase", but that was it - to the point that when I dropped a trailer, Ash asked me who did the music for it, and I had to gently remind him that he did.

The film premiered at the 2021 WA Made Film Festival, and the sheer terror leading up to a film premiere is something very real. I was googling the specifications of the theatre's projector at 4am the night before, after panicking it might not be able to play the frame rate the film was encoded in. Then on top of that the worry that no one would be there, or no one would get it, and it would be ninety interminable minutes of stone-cold audience silence. You know, just normal stuff.

But... it worked. People laughed, people cheered, people were invested. The palpable relief of that first laugh is something else; like a fist you didn't know was clenching your heart suddenly letting go.

I didn't know what to do with the film after that festival screening; but then a few months later I got an email from a sales agent asking if I had anything unrepresented, and that he found me through IMDb. I figured I had nothing to lose, so sent him *Stabbed*, and within a week I had a world-wide distribution deal. It's still not on Amazon Prime here in Australia, but there are ways that don't involve air travel to watch it from the US or the UK (also please don't pirate it, I have cats and a pug to feed).

I learnt a lot from making Stabbed, like backing things up across multiple hard drives stored in different locations. But I also learned to stop asking for permission and waiting around for someone else to let you make a movie. You don't need millions of dollars (although that would help), you just need a good story, written with the resources you have in mind. Just do it. Go make the thing. And if it's not good, who cares? You can't learn from something you didn't do, or get better by not trying. It's all too easy to make excuses, and find reasons why you can't make a movie, and put yourself out there. I get it, it's scary (I have the empty valium boxes to prove it), but the main person stopping you, is you, and that's also the one person who's going to get stuff done for yourself.

So, go. Go make something. Be bad at it. Get better at it. Use your phone, use whatever you have around you. Make friends, ask for favours. Make your own future. Go get stabbed.

INTERVIEW
MY CHERRY PIE - CO-DIRECTORS
ADDISON HEATH AND JASMINE JAKUPI

My Cherry Pie is a gleefully bonkers love letter to many aspects of horror cinema. From giallo films to Ozploitation handlebar moustaches to seventies era eroticism, *My Cherry Pie* has it all, telling the story of three crims on the run who find themselves being hunted in an old hospital by a masked killer. Co-directed by genre-fiends Addison Heath and Jasmine Jakupi, this micro-budget film screened at the A Night of Horror International Film Festival. Interview conducted October 2021.

▶▷▶

Jasmine Jakupi: I'm Jasmine Jakupi. I'm co-director of *My Cherry Pie* along with-

Addison Heath: Addison Heath. I'm the co-director and writer of *My Cherry Pie.*

Congratulations on the film, guys. It's really good.

AH: Thank you.

It's a nice dive into a blend of different horror subgenres, the Seventies aesthetic, the giallo aesthetic, the brutal violence, the bleak humour. Where did the idea come from? Was it to kind of play with these different genres of horror?

AH: Definitely from the outset we went into it wanting to make a slasher movie but we could put all those elements into a blender and see what we came up with. There's a film from 1974 that was on the video nasties list called *Axe*, it's also called *Lisa Lisa* in some countries, and I hired it with Dylan Heath who plays Jack in the film. He's one of the main criminals in the film. We grew up together watching movies. We [also] hired a movie on VHS called *California Axe Massacre*. That's what it was called at my video store, at least, and I remember we hired it, being big fans of *Texas Chainsaw Massacre* we were like, "This movie's nothing like *Texas Chainsaw Massacre*. This is terrible."

And it was a film that when I watched it again, I was like, "Hang on, there's actually a really cool plot going on here which is sort of a similar thing, where it's basically a group of criminals are forced to flee the city. And they find themselves in a horror-centric location. It sort of starts as like a Seventies crime film and turns into a horror film. I was like, "Well, I love that idea." And I haven't really seen that done in Australia. We could do something that could be a nod to like Eighties Ozploitation crime cinema, and then it gets interrupted by an early Eighties slasher movie. That's kind of where the original idea came from.

JJ: We are no strangers to genre mashups. We love so many different elements of film, and we just think that it's a new way to kind of combine different things to get different results. And so definitely, the interruption was a really important kick off for us.

AH: Totally. In the original script for *My Cherry Pie*, it was the criminals show up at a farmhouse. We had written it as a farmhouse because we had no idea we could get that location. That came after. And then when we visited the location, we're like, "Oh, my", and I just started rewriting, because I was like, "This feels like something from like a Dario Argento movie, or a Lucio Fulci movie, like this is going to be cool. If we just blow this out in red lights and green lights and give it this otherworldly look at night", we knew that place could look like a giallo nightmare. We thought, "Well, that's totally the style that we'll lean into."

JJ: And it's a vast contrast too because we utilised grimy elements to the crime components. It's a nice kind of pairing.

AH: It's cool to do the neons and try to make that stuff look like a beautiful nightmare, the way that the giallo films of the Seventies would evoke.

I want to talk about the costume of the killer because that skews towards the whole giallo aspect, too. It's this brilliant kind of Halloween-ish costume. Where did the design come from? Where was the idea for that for?

JJ: We were really fortunate enough to work with our costume designer Noelle [Criminova]. She is just amazing to work with.

AH: Her and James. We had two people that basically helped us design that. In the script, it started as something much smaller and then when we got to the hospital, we started realising, well, the plague doctor aesthetic worked into it being an old hospital. We thought that would be cool.

JJ: James comes into play in terms of the mask quite heavily. He is a mask maker, a leather worker from Melbourne. We wanted to incorporate both of their skills that they have, and they worked together really well to create this character. It was really fun for us to have a vague idea, but then watch it take shape in terms of location influences and both Noelle and James' style.

AH: Like you said, the giallo aesthetic, the black leather gloves which is a really cool-

JJ: Sick.

AH: The wide brim hat is a box that you tick. It reminds me of some of those early Eighties slasher movies. *Pieces* was a big influence for us. To be honest with you, *Motel Hell, Pieces*, and *The Texas Chainsaw Massacre 2* were the biggest influences on us for this film. Definitely the killer's aesthetic in *Pieces* was hugely influential.

With My Cherry Pie, it's like the inspirations are there and it's clear, but the personality of both of you is so clear in the script and in the direction and in the performances that are drawn out. How do you find that balance? How do you manage to straddle that line comfortably?

AH: As far as the writing goes, we've made a lot of films together. I've worked on other films, so I've been able to go through genres a little bit, and that's really how I feel I was able to find my writing voice a lot on those other films. When it comes to tackling a new genre like the slasher giallo thing, it's like that voice comes naturally in a lot of ways. I pretty much always want things to be as funny as they can be.

JJ: I think that's where a lot of personality comes from.

AH: Jasmine and I love Australian comedy and the intricacies of Australian dialogue that can be just funny.

JJ: And because this film was a throwback as well, the 1980's were a huge influence for us in terms of dialogue. The slang of the times. And I find that just Australian slang itself is a form of humour.

AH: Political correctness didn't exist at that point in a lot of films of that era. So we never had to be too concerned about, "Oh, is this going to upset people?", all of those films would now. It felt like open border a little bit as far as not having to be too concerned about offending anybody, because that's sort of par for the course with this type of film.

The characters are relatively unlikable, they're all pricks or they're all, you know, killers, or they're all evil people, so it makes sense that they would say and do the things that they do. And it gives you a bit of that free rein to be able to do those unpopular things.

AH: 100%. I remember reading in screenwriters' books and things like that when I was studying years ago, the best stories are good versus evil, and they'll say things like that. We wanted to make a movie that was bad versus evil. We start you off with bad and then you meet something much sicker and darker the further you get into the film. That also puts you in a position of you can have so much fun with the writing of it because you're not trying to manipulate an audience into rooting for these guys. These guys are scumbags. I think that means that, as an audience, I think you can root for the movie more than you can for the characters. And that's sort of what we wanted to try to do.

JJ: Totally. I think that's kind of the fun element that we wanted to bring in too as a spectator. Who are you rooting for?

AH: And if we can manage to flip you and have you go, "Oh, now I kind of want these guys (to live)", that's a really cool place to try to put an audience as well. It's interesting to show characters doing the worst things to begin with, and can we flip that around and by the end of it actually have you wanting them to come through? That can be trickier, it's a wire walk of screenwriting. Can we do this without pushing it too far into one or the other? Again, that is just having fun writing it and making it.

What direction do you give the actors to ensure that they're meeting that script at that level as well?

JJ: We were lucky enough to have a lot of Zoom rehearsals, so particularly with the criminals, we would separate the elements of the film and work them separately. We would work with the main three criminals of the film and really get that natural banter, that vibe that there is a history with those characters. Once we had that base, it was really introducing them together.

AH: It also helps that those three actors [Sotiris Tzelios, Dylan Heath, Tim Jason Wicks] have known each other for so long that they do have a real friendship. They went into the film already friends, and have worked together on other shorts, and we were friends with all of them. When they got the script, it didn't take that much pushing with them to get them in the right place. Glenn Maynard who plays the uncle Edwin Crowe at the hospital, he was really fun to work with. I got to write a film that he did in 2012, *Chocolate Strawberry Vanilla*, so we'd worked together previously. He's the type of guy that is almost like a Nicolas Cage, you just bring him in and just let him go, and he will give you that crazy performance.

We just tried to make sure that anyone we cast were people that we knew would come in and totally get the material. It didn't take directing gymnastics to get anybody to that. The criminals knew we're living in the same world as *Chopper* here, this is kind of where we're going. And Glenn Maynard has such a great reference for Seventies and Eighties horror films, he knows exactly the type.

JJ: And Trudi Ranik is a big horror fanatic. So for her, it was just a matter of like-

AH: -the movie's called *My Cherry Pie*, she plays Cherry, she's the heart of the entire movie. We wanted to get the best actress for that role and the person that we knew would bring a real honesty and groundedness because everyone else is so big. You wanted a groundedness from her, and she was the perfect person for that.

JJ: We had worked with her previously on a film called *Good Girl Lola* during lockdown, that was an improv film, and that was really good to have that relationship built up there and to see how she works. We're very big on collaboration. If anyone has an idea, we're gonna explore it because you never know what you're going to get. I think a lot of the actors had a lot of fun with that.

AH: Trudi came into it not knowing us as well. We had worked together, but it was all virtually done, it wasn't the same as being onset. She had to come into a big group of people that knew each other and knew what they were doing, so it would have been intimidating. And then by the end of the shoot, she has a line in the film that for me, for my money, is one of the funniest lines in the film. It was totally improvised by her, made up by her onset. Everyone else comes in at eleven, and we actually have to make her wait a little bit to have her moment.

I want to talk about the look of Freddy - Sotiris is a delight in the film. The clear decision to base him on Roger Ward there is really impressive. Did you did you say to him, "Right, we're gonna make you look like Roger. Can you kind of meet his kind of acting level as well?"

AH: Sotiris already lends himself to that look anyway, the sort of brute male look. When we first were doing the read-throughs, at the start of the movie, you see Sotiris and his hair is longer. It starts with him coming out of prison and then we get to see him transform back into himself. When I think of the Eighties Aussie tough guy, it's Roger Ward. That is the quintessential Australian tough guy of that era. That's the best way to lean into it.

JJ: The boys had a lot of fun influencing each other in terms of what styling they should go for. I would throw out some really silly ideas because I knew that if I threw something out at 200%, I could rein it in to what I wanted initially. We would throw out these crazy ideas, and then after a few beers of courage, the boys were those characters. It was really funny. Once they got those haircuts and those trims, they just turned into those characters. It's really funny how little details like that can really bring out more elements as well.

AH: Sotiris is so great. He'd had smaller parts on our films, but I'd always been chatting to him, "One day, man. One day, I'm gonna write that film where you're the lead guy in the film and it's gonna be really fun." Finally, we got to do that. It was written to his strengths. Sotiris is a really funny, complex actor, he's a great actor. He can bring in an energy that was perfect for that role, this sort of violent energy.

JJ: It kept everyone on their toes, when you have that on top of this as well, you don't really know which way he's going to swing.

AH: And Glenn Maynard. I think if you place a couple of those actors in, these firecracker actors are gonna bring their own stuff and it's gonna be really interesting. It's cool to put them in with actors that are good with improv. When you put all those people together, you can mould it into what we needed it to be.

This is screening via the Night At Horror film festival online. What would you recommend for people who are going to be watching this at home? What's the ideal night to create around this film?

AH: Well, look, I'm not gonna lie, a little bit of devil's lettuce with this film is going to enhance it. A couple of beers. The main thing I would say is I'm so excited about A Night Of Horror, and Bryn [Tilly] has done a brilliant job. The only thing I would really ask is try your hardest not to watch it on your phone. It's easy to do. It is really a much better film to watch on the largest screen you can with the loud sound if you can. We had a great sound design created for the film.

JJ: Great music as well.

AH: I think it's got a really cool soundtrack. If any of the visuals have made you think "Oh, that's gonna be a giallo movie, just wait to hear the music." Try to watch it on the biggest screen you can and feel free to have a few drinks, and a bit of devil's lettuce is not going to be the worst thing for you.

JJ: We want to have fun and we want you to have fun watching how much fun we had making the film.

Let's talk about that score for a moment because it's really good. How did you come about creating it and what kind of direction did you give for the score?

JJ: In terms of soundtrack, we were really lucky to work with The Screaming Meanies [who is] Jesse Breckon-Thomas. We've got Puscha which is Jacob Richards. And then we also have the other featuring artists like Tim Jason Wicks.

AH: He's the actor who plays Green, he did some of the music.

JJ: Along with Damien Vennell who is also an actor in the film.

AH: He plays Jimmy the Fruit's partner. And we also had the two Eastern European backpackers at the end of the movie.

JJ: Sasha Cuha.

AH: Sasha also contributed music. It was a lot of people but with the main people being The Screaming Meemees and Jacob Richards. We were so excited to hear what these guys are gonna do. They know the genre, they're fans of giallo, especially the John Carpenter synth sort of wave sounding stuff. They knew what we wanted, and then they just delivered. They kept sending me stuff and I was like "This is amazing."

JJ: And they would bounce back and forth and sample each other's work and work it all in together. It was really interesting to see happen because again it's all virtual, and then you get these things sent to you "Oh, check this out." And you're just like "That's amazing."

AH: "Keep going with that." They were amazing with that. When you edit you typically will use temp music - I try my hardest not to because I know it's the bane of every sound designer's and sound composer's, it's the bane of their existence. Because they always go, "You're going to use Danny Elfman temp music." Well, that sounds amazing. A lot of directors can get stuck in that in feeling that "I'm never going to get something as good." We would use bits of temp music, and then the music they would supply would be so much better. "Oh, this brings it out even more." It was never a thing of "I hope they can give me something that's even half as good as the temp music." It was always better and stronger and would suit the visual aesthetic. It was just brilliant with those guys.

Did they did they have a film to score to? Or did you give them a vibe of what the scene was going to be and say, "Look, it's going to be about this long. We need music that fits this."

AH: Pretty much that's how it would go. Because the thing that's amazing about Jesse who's the Screaming Meanies, we've worked with him on everything, we made a movie a few years back called *Mondo Yakuza* that he did that almost had like a spaghetti western sort of sounding score.

JJ: He can handle it all. You start telling him, "Think about Lucio Fulci, think about Dario Argento and the Goblin scores", and he knows exactly where you're going with that. We just wanted to give those guys as much freedom as possible. And they would send us music while we were shooting the film. I would hear things and go, "Listen to how cool this is." And that would start to give ideas of how stylistically we could go. A lot of their stuff fed into the actual making of the film.

And I think also rhythmically too. Addison edits as well, and I handle some post-production too. We have a lot of foresight for when we're shooting and onset. And in terms of getting sound while we're shooting, we know now what rhythm we're needing and what things we might need to introduce with this style. It's really interesting to kind of see live editing and our brains as we're shooting.

AH: We're always thinking of the edit. And Jesse and Jacob just delivered some really unbelievably layered music.

You filmed this kind of during a lockdown-ish period, is that right?

AH: It was right in between. We filmed the bulk of the film up in Stawell, about three hours from Melbourne.

JJ: We were fortunate enough to have a completely enclosed location that was ours the entire time.

AH: But we also weren't in lockdown at that point. We got right in the sweet spot of-

JJ: -as soon as masks were a bit flexible.

AH: We went straight and did it, and any other pick-up day shots. We got it in that sweet spot, that was really lucky. When you start thinking about if we were halfway through it, what's going on [in locked down Melbourne 2021] right now we wouldn't be comfortable shooting anything. And we were fortunately in a position where things were opened back up by the time we shot.

JJ: We had to work real quick and get it done.

I can imagine. As indie filmmakers as well, does the indie landscape or the feeling of being an indie filmmaker kind of prepare you for that kind of environment of basically having to pivot on the go?

AH: 100%.

JJ: I think that was a massive advantage. At the time, a lot of big budget films were not shooting and were shut down.

AH: People were getting four or five days into their shoot and shutting down because the crews too big. And the thing about it is for us, this is the biggest crew we've ever worked with. We felt like it was huge because we really are used to having basically no one with you. And this one had a crew. For us it was a huge jump up. But I think having that background of doing a lot of the things yourself, it was a fortunate place to be now.

JJ: And we were really lucky to have everyone in our crew wearing multiple hats. Everyone was on the same page and really happy to be able to make something in this time. There were a lot of things that in many ways we were used to already battling an uphill battle.

AH: Even without coronavirus.

JJ: Besides the COVID protocols, it was like a new challenge, let's get it done.

As you mentioned, Australia doesn't really do slashers or giallo films all that often.

AH: Oh hey, look, I'll tell you right now, making *My Cherry Pie* has been the most fun and rewarding project we've ever been involved with. To be totally honest, I'd love to make a sequel to *My Cherry Pie*. Jasmine and I had discussions into the idea of making an Australian disco slasher. Can we do something like *Prom Night*, something in a high school that's like a disco. How about that? And I thought, "Oh we could have a disco ball killer head. That would be good!" It's so silly, it's just opening up that imagination. Australia in the current climate we're in, we're just not making movies like that. It's just not getting done.

JJ: I think in the current climate, in terms of audience, you want to see something that's a bit fun and exciting and takes your mind off everything that's going on right now. You don't really want to settle into something that's a total hard drama. I want to watch something really silly and fun and that's what relaxes me. And I know that there's people out there that are like me that want to watch movies like this.

AH: It's like a form of escapism. There's room for all of that stuff. And I don't feel we're getting enough on the other end of that. I love watching a drama that sucks me in and makes me feel the story and feel those emotions. And I also like watching *Halloween 4* and *Friday the 13th Part 6*. I love watching movies like that and just chucking them on and having a good time. And I just feel like Australia could do with a movie like that every now and then. It's not worse thing to do that.

INTERVIEW
SHALLOW BREATH - WRITER/DIRECTOR
ROBBIE STUDSOR

Robbie Studsor made an impact with his first feature film, *Burning Kiss* (2018), with eye-catching imagery that helped steep the film in its film noir vibes. Studsor returned in 2021 with the tense and taut short film, *Shallow Breath*, seeing him play with the thriller genre with the story of a drowning survivor who has grown a dangerous fixation on the woman who saved her. *Shallow Breath* acts as another entry in the promising filmography of an emerging genre-loving filmmaker.

Interview conducted December 2021.

▶▷▶

How did you manage to create the liminal space between living and death in the visual style of Shallow Breath?

Robbie Studsor: There is a real condition that can happen after swimming if somebody accidentally got water in their lungs known as secondary drowning whereby their body can experience the physical symptoms of drowning without being anywhere near water.

I basically fictionalised this to be a psychosomatic symptom for a drowning survivor whereby their body inexplicably imitates drowning itself everyday as a weird kind of repetition compulsion. The idea that a character could be revived from death only for their body to constantly try to relive or return to it has a kind of fatalistic noir tone which I found really exciting. If you add into the mix the weird intimacy of being saved by someone breathing life back into their body, and them wanting the same person to save them again to cure themselves, it becomes quite dark and obsessive!

The liminal space between the character being alive and her memories of drowning was absolutely crucial to the film and I tried to honour as much of her conflicted feelings about the accident as possible. I wanted the obvious motif of water to be always present in her everyday life [rain, dripping taps etc] and to have a liquid quality to the editing and the sound design. She unconsciously wants to return to whatever she experienced during her momentary death, so her desire to drown herself had to have an allure as well as a danger.

There is a brevity to the short that manages to encompass a deep chasm of obsession, fear, and trauma - how do you honour the short film format while also hinting at a grander scale?

RS: Short films and feature films are very different forms and although they can both say the same things and have the same power, the presentation is quite dissimilar. Short films only have a limited amount of real estate and often they are strongest when they depict a moment or glimpse of something bigger, but are self-contained and stand on their own. I felt that if we meet this character at the absolute terminal point of her condition and catch up on the plot through the letter she is writing and visually hint at things that have happened in the past it could capture the spectrum of feelings and states that the character is experiencing and make it quite intimate and immediate as every shot counts in a five-minute short.

Can you talk about the creative challenges that are faced with a short versus a feature, while also possibly talking about the creative choices you make with your visual style - what are your influences, do you storyboard/take photos?

RS: For me, the creative challenges are basically identical between a short and feature film, and are really the same problems filmmakers have faced since the silent era, such as how to tell a story visually, convey character, create tension or drama etc. The main difference between the two are the practical challenges, as a feature film has many more moving parts and logistics that need to be solved on a daily basis over weeks or months [which requires much more stamina and focus].

In terms of pre-visualisation and storyboards, for this film I only worked with shot-lists which were finessed on the day between myself, the Director of Photography, Garry Richards, and the actor [Belinda Lack, Casey Layne Mannix], as when you are dealing with low-budgets you don't always know exactly what kind of space you might be dealing with until the day you arrive and storyboards can actually hold you back from exciting new possibilities the space offers.

Two big influences on the film would be Nicolas Roeg for the way merges time in the edit and a filmmaker called Jene Painleve who made these really weird underwater Avant Garde films about jellyfish and seahorses and all kinds of strange creatures of the deep.

ROMANCE

2021 was a landmark year for Australian romance films with at a wealth of films that played within the genre. We've already touched on the Netflix romance *I Met a Girl* which, alongside Josh Lawson's *Long Story Short*, both of which are the more dramatic takes on the genre. Over on Stan., Katie Found's wonderful queer coming of age romance *My First Summer* gave a younger generation of emerging lesbians a new queer relationship to embrace, while Christopher Weekes brought Christmas film writer extraordinaire down under for *Christmas on the Farm*, delivering another summer Xmas film for the service. On the festival and cinema front, Joy Hopwood's landmark film *Rhapsody of Love* became the first Asian-Australian rom-com.

But if there was one company above them all that has been working hard over the years to establish family friendly and romance films as viable genre films within Australia, it's The Steve Jaggi Company. The Canadian-Australian producer has been working tirelessly since 2001 to bring diverse stories to the screen. Over the past five years or so, Jaggi and co have been strengthening the production houses work to be market ready for an international audience, delivering suitable family fare and romance cinema for the Disney and Hallmark adjacent audiences in the US. They've been pushing the Disney angle for years, so much so that there are honourable imitators following a similar format in the guise of Eric C. Nash's *Love You Like That*, which featured a co-lead performance from Disney star Mitchell Hope, alongside Allira Jacques

In 2021 alone, alongside their hugely popular Netflix series *Dive Club*, The Steve Jaggi Company released three romance films seeking a US audience. Christine Luby's *This Little Love of Mine* was the first film to go into production in Australia after COVID hit, making the best of the secluded beaches in North Queensland, and disguising the island local as an American retreat. Tori Garrett's *Sit. Stay. Love.* equally transformed Australia into America, this time utilising the Warner Bros. backlot on the Gold Coast to replicate the snow-kissed streets of winter in North Haven, Vermont. Finally, Rosie Lourde's *Romance on the Menu* (aka *Hearts Down Under*) allowed the Aussie cast to use their natural accents as it followed romance genre regular Cindy Busby's Caroline (a mainstay of Hallmark films) to Australia to run a café that she inherits.

While domestically these productions may not traditionally find an audience, they have been well received by the romance loving fans in America thanks to their easy availability on Netflix or the Hallmark channel. When it comes to a film like *This Little Love of Mine*, or even *I Met a Girl*, the stunning vistas, glorious aerial shots, and sun-soaked atmosphere are as much of an allure for the audience as the promise of a predictable love affair is. Sure, one could look at the glorious island beaches of Queensland in the film and think 'this is just a tourism ad, just without Lara Bingle', but the reality is, part of what makes the romance genre such a delight to lose yourself in is the enticement and intoxication of *desire*, no matter if that's the locations or the actual romance itself.

For *Sit. Stay. Love.*, that notion of desire came with the powerful combination of dogs, Christmas, family reconnection, and (of course) love. The carefree Christmas vibe manages to replicate that certain Hallmark-esque charm wonderfully here, ensuring that *Sit. Stay. Love.* will no doubt become part of the regular rotation of Christmas movie loving fans around the world. After all, Hallmark Christmas movies have spawned their own Comic Con-esque event called, appropriately, Christmas Con.

There's something otherworldly about a Christmas film set in America being made in Australia. The accent work by the predominantly Australian cast of *Sit. Stay. Love.* is impressive. Aspects of Australia shine through in the oddest ways, with everything from Australian-esque set design, to the Christmas slices that are served up in some scenes (these particularly feel like they've come from your local Aussie café). Whether American audiences will recognise that these are Australian films or not is another aspect altogether, and almost besides the point.

After all, the artifice of these kinds of romance films is unshakeable. Maintaining focus on *Sit. Stay. Love.*, the crisp, worry-free existence leans into the not-quite-real charm of these kinds of Christmas films, and while it can often feel more than a little plastic, it is always endearing and smile-inducing. Holly Hester's script even slips in a knowing sly joke about how 'a baking sale isn't going to cut it' when the inevitable trope of the town needing to raise funds for an unexpected urgent issue (that's not a big issue at all) arises. The community, naturally, comes together and the two will-be romantics, Annie (Georgia Flood) and Dylan (Ezekial Simat), fall in love.

Routine and formula are why the romance genre works, with audiences seeking that expected denouement that can often play like a warm hug or an unexpected kiss. While the aforementioned films don't shake up the formula in any new way, they do all play within the genres parameters in their own cheeky way, together revitalising romantic films in Australian cinema.

The romance genre has all but disappeared over the years, and thankfully films like Wayne Blair's *Top End Wedding* and Jon M. Chu's *Crazy Rich Asians* have helped usher in a new generation for the once booming genre. While we may never go back to the heights of the Nineties where the genre topped the box office every second week, it's comforting to see that there are filmmakers and production companies eager to cater for the audiences who crave a live bit of heart-warming romance in their lives.

Over the next pages, we hear from filmmaker Joy Hopwood about what the genre means to her and how *Crazy Rich Asians* inspired her to make *Rhapsody of Love* in 2021.

CONTRIBUTION
RHAPSODY OF LOVE - WRITER/DIRECTOR
JOY HOPWOOD

I had just finished filming my first feature as director, the romantic comedy *The Script of Life*, starring Erica Long and Callum Alexander. I wasn't brave enough to have an all-Asian cast at that stage, like *The Joy Luck Club*, but I'd experimented with having a mixed-race cast. To my surprise, the film won Best Drama at the Amsterdam International Film Festival and was picked up for distribution by Leomark Studios. Then in the same year, *Crazy Rich Asians* was released. It was only the second big feature that had an all-Asian cast; 25 years after *The Joy Luck Club* came out, finally there was another. I loved this film and every Asian I spoke to also enjoyed it, because it gave us a sense of identity and belonging.

On the last day of filming on *The Script of Life*, I recall sitting in the car talking to Kathy Luu, a supporting actress in the film. I said, "Wouldn't it be great to work together again on another project, but with you and another Asian actor as the leads?" Kathy agreed and replied, "It would be the first Asian-Australian rom-com – we'd be making history."

I was about to fly off to New York for break and I told Kathy I'd work on a script idea while I was away. The film I came up with was *Rhapsody of Love,* which follows the lives of couples at different stages of their relationships in four intertwined storylines. I wanted to make this romantic comedy about more than just falling in love, but also touch on the subject of mental health, looking at how anxiety can overtake how a person lives and is seen by others. I myself suffer from anxiety, as do many of my friends, and it's an issue that isn't tackled enough on screen.

I also chose to address the issue of body positivity in relation to Kathy Luu's character, Jessica Flowers, because at the beginning of my acting career, I was often told to lose weight. I recall on a shoot in Singapore, I was told I could only have two pieces of sushi, while everyone else on set could eat as much they wanted. Luckily, food and I have a good relationship and I decided from that point onward that no one would ever tell me what I could or could not eat. I want women to never feel ashamed of their bodies, but instead be proud of them.

These are some of the important choices I made whilst making *Rhapsody of Love* and I was lucky that my producer partner, Ana Tiwary, was on the page as I was. It was important to me to make a film that championed diversity with not only a strong Asian-Australian cast – Kathy Luu, Damien Sato, Jessica Niven and Benjamin Hanly – but also gave women in the crew opportunities they hadn't had before. Our cinematographer, Goldie Soetianto, who is

Asian Australian, got to shoot her first feature and Meret Hassanen, who has a disability, shone as an associate producer, alongside Kathy Luu. Our set designer, Jessie Singh, and sound recordist and post sound, Lara Cross, are also both Asian Australian.

I hope to continue to change the narrative of how Asians are represented on and off screen with my next film, *Get a Life, Alright*, again championing diversity and giving opportunities for women in order to create social change in the industry. All my films give people a sense of hope and are uplifting, they represent 25% of my real-life experiences. It warms my heart when cast and crew call and thank me for giving them their first feature credit as my films have been stepping stones for their careers, which I'm proud of.

FAMILY AND ANIMATED FILMS

From the Yoram Gross Films Studios production house, Flying Bark Productions, to the wealth of animal focused flicks that have proliferated across the watchful eyes of a young audience, the shadow of the animated work of Yoram Gross carries across the Australian animated film industry even now. While Aussie animated films don't often get the theatrical releases they might deserve, they do at least find a welcome home on streaming services and on demand where kids of all ages (this writer included) lose themselves in the unique and bright stylings of the genre.

The connection to the ocker icon Blinky Bill is clear in the *Tales from Sanctuary City* series, which director Ricard Cussó kicked off in 2020 with *The Wishmas Tree*, following it up in the same year with *Combat Wombat*, and then bringing the third entry in 2021, the Angourie Rice voiced *Daisy Quokka: World's Scariest Animal*. *Daisy Quokka* had its world premiere at the Children's International Film Festival in Australia on 28 November 2020, with its theatrical release being delayed into the new year due to the pandemic.

The direct connection Gross' work is seen with the Flying Bark Productions studio, which has helped bring the hugely successful *Maya the Bee* and *100% Wolf* series to life. In 2021, the third *Maya* film was also pushed from 2020 into 2021 due to the pandemic, with limited audiences able to see Noel Cleary's *Maya the Bee 3: The Golden Orb* in cinemas before it was released on streaming services.

Even though they were concerned about the "huggability of the animal cast"[37], Netflix opted to also get into the Aussie animated film game with Harry Cripps & Claire Knight's star-studded flick *Back to the Outback*. Featuring the vocal talents of Isla Fisher, Tim Minchin, Eric Bana, Guy Pearce, Miranda Tapsell, Keith Urban, Angus Imrie, and Jacki Weaver, *Back to the Outback* feels like the most direct imitation of Blinky Bill (albeit, a subversive take), with Tim Minchin's rude koala Pretty Boy thwarting the escape effort of the Australian Wildlife Park's animals. The film received a limited theatrical run before landing on the service right in time for school holidays in December 2021.

Somewhat unsurprisingly, given the success of the first film, it was Will Gluck's Aus-UK-US co-pro *Peter Rabbit 2: The Runaway* that triumphed at the domestic box office, making it the fourth highest grossing film of 2021, wedged between *Godzilla vs. Kong* and *F9 The Fast Saga* respectively[38]. The box office haul of $21,967,130 pushed Baz Luhrmann's *Strictly Ballroom* out of the top ten all time earners by $206,101 (unadjusted). *Peter Rabbit 2: The Runaway* joined *The Dry* (14), *Mortal Kombat* (38) and *Penguin Bloom* (53) in the all-time totals for Australian films, once again highlighting the landmark year that 2021 was for Australian cinema[39].

HOLLYWOOD COMES TO AUSTRALIA

7

One of the most curious and contentious discussions about Australian films arises from the basic question of 'what constitutes an Australian film?'

For the sake of simplicity, this writer will always point a finger at what Screen Australia considers "Significant Australian Content"[40]:

— The subject matter of the film
— The place where the film was made
— The nationalities and places of residence of the persons who took part in the making of the film
— The details of the production expenditure incurred in respect of the film, and
— Any other matters that we consider to be relevant.

Sure, that last clause feels awfully open-ended in the grand scheme of allocating the label "Australian film" to productions, so for further clarification, let's turn to the eligibility requirements for Australia's Oscars, the AACTAs[41]:

GENERAL ELIGIBILITY FOR ALL ENTRIES
(a) In order for a Production to be deemed eligible for entry (other than in relation to the International Awards), the Production must:
(i) contain "significant Australian content" for the purposes of section 37665(2) (a)(i) of the Income Tax Assessment Act 1997 regardless of whether the Production satisfies the thresholds for "qualifying Australian production expenditure" as set out in section 376-65(6) of the Income Tax Assessment Act 1997; OR

(ii) have at least 51% financing from Australian investors; OR
(iii) be an official co-production (as per a formal agreement with Australia and an international territory) or produced under the creative control of Australians if an international collaboration has occurred outside of a formal treaty; OR
(iv) otherwise satisfy the AFI and AACTA, in their sole and absolute discretion, that the Production is an eligible Production.
(b) A Program, Film, Episode or Season which has been previously entered into the Awards is ineligible for entry into the current or any future Awards.

For the sake of clarity, Screen Australia's statement "Any other matters that we consider to be relevant" and AACTAs section (a) (iv) are essentially the same statement. The determination of what constitutes an Australian film can then become almost liquid.

If we propose a case study of Jane Campion's *The Power of the Dog*, we can see the strength of international co-pros coming together to help finance a film that may have struggled to gain significant financing by itself. Here, the New Zealand Film Commission, Bad Girl Creek, Max Films, Cross City Films, BBC Film, See-Saw Films, and Brightstar Films came together to help bring Campion's vision to life. Screen Australia[42] provided 'development support'[43] to the film, and labels the production as an Australian/New Zealand Co-Production, even though there was significant support from the UK.

The Power of the Dog tells a deeply American tale with universal themes, and even though it was filmed in Aotearoa New Zealand, it feels at one with the American landscape and history. In front of the camera, Australian actor Kodi Smith-McPhee delivers a career best performance that earned him a well-deserved Academy Award nomination. Also nominated is Australian cinematographer Ari Wegner who transforms the New Zealand mountain scapes into a haunted Montana, conjuring an ethereal and unsettling experience that carries on the wind. For this point alone, it's clear that parts of the production crew, including Aussie producer Emile Sherman (who won an Oscar for the equally Australian-adjacent production *The King's Speech* in 2011), fits part of Screen Australia's remit for what constitutes an Australian film.

Curiously, AACTA had Jane Campion's film (which received a stunning twelve Oscar nominations) on the eligibility list for the 2021 award ceremony. A planned virtual screening for academy members was 'postponed' with the intention of offering in person cinema screenings for members. The film was then quietly removed from the domestic line-up, going on to receive AACTA International Award wins for Best Film, Best Actor, and Best Supporting Actor. Curiously, it competed against Justin Kurzel's *Nitram* for major awards.

So, is *The Power of the Dog* an Australian film?

Sort of.

That question is ultimately pushed aside by the more pertinent one: Does it matter?

Yes, it does.

Australia plays a major role in film production around the world, with some of the highest grossing Hollywood blockbusters and TV series being made here. On a television front, Nicole Kidman's choice to set up shop in rural NSW for the HBO series *Nine Perfect Strangers,* and the sci-fi series *La Brea* subbing in Melbourne for Los Angeles. Additionally, Tim Brown's *Buckley's Chance* was made possible thanks to being an Australian-Canadian co-pro.

Marvel production *Shang-Chi and the Legend of the Ten Rings* sought safety from COVID in Fox Studios Australia in Sydney (with the working title *Steamboat* to keep some anonymity), and keeping sections of the local film industry afloat by employing hundreds of crew members. The landmark bus action sequence that takes place in San Francisco had interiors shot in Sydney, with the exterior shots being filmed in San Francisco itself. COVID was unable to be kept at bay, with production being shut down mid-shoot due to positive cases on set.

Peter Rabbit 2: The Runaway had a 2019 shoot in both Australia and the UK. For its Australian leg, the locations of Centennial Parklands and Camden NSW were utilised for the country sequences. While Mostofa Sarwar Farooki's American-Bangladeshi-Indian drama *No Land's Man* used Australia as a location only while also employing Australian actress Megan Mitchell.

Heading up to Queensland, Michael Matthews shot the creature-romance flick *Love and Monsters* on the Gold Coast in 2019, with the film being delayed for a 2021 release by Netflix. Sticking in the North East is Adam Wingard's *Godzilla vs. Kong*, yet another monster mash flick which carried on the series penchant for turning the Aussie outback into a battleground for digital beasties. Alongside the series *Reef Break*, over 1,300 people were employed to work on *Godzilla vs. Kong*. With *Kong: Skull Island* (2017) and the upcoming fifth entry in the series also being made in some capacity in Queensland, it's clear that there's something about Australia that makes these massive productions find it an attractive place to shoot.

It's not hard to see what is so attractive about Australia for Hollywood productions, with the Federal Government's Location Incentive Program effectively purchasing the promise for productions to spend money within Australia. The Location Incentive[44] works alongside other financial incentives like the Location Offset[45] and the PDV Offset[46] to make film production in Australia an attractive proposal for international productions. This is why, if you sit through the credits of many American productions like *King Richard* or *The Whistleblower*, you might see the Screen Australia logo at the end. Each state's screen body can also opt to top up the Screen Australia funding, sweetening the deal and enticing productions to their location to secure employment for local industries.

In the case of Simon McQuoid's *Mortal Kombat*, the South Australian government fought hard and fiercely to ensure that the effects-heavy production put the state on the map as a great place to shoot international features. The state had already become a fertile place for productions to set up shop, but none as massive as *Mortal Kombat* had filmed there. In an interview Simon McQuoid talks about the strength of the local crews and the joy of being able to shoot in the South Australian landscape.

But while films like *Mortal Kombat* carry some Australian identity with certain characters, there is a key aspect to many of these Hollywood productions, and that is the threat of becoming the Vancouver of the Southern Hemisphere, with productions dominating the creative landscape and smothering the Australian identity. As mentioned in the last chapter, *Peter Rabbit 2: The Runaway*'s dominance at the box office secured its place in the top ten highest grossing films ever, joining the likes of *Happy Feet, The Great Gatsby, Moulin Rouge!*, and the first *Peter Rabbit* film as Australian films that are distinctly *not* Australian tales.

Which brings us to *Fist of Fury Noongar Daa*, a fascinating blend of International cinema and Indigenous languages. Kylie Bracknell and Dr Clint Bracknell worked together to create a Noongar-dub of Bruce Lee's iconic *Fist of Fury* for Perth Festival in 2021, recontextualising the notion of what Australian cinema can be.

Over the next pages, we explore that concept in an interview with Kylie Bracknell, before digesting the subject of the identity of Australia on screen and how it might be lost by these Hollywood productions, before swinging back to Simon McQuoid's blend of Australiana and Hollywood with *Mortal Kombat*, possibly paving a way forward for a symbiotic relationship between the two.

INTERVIEW
FIST OF FURY NOONGAR DAA - FILMMAKER
AND ARTIST KYLIE BRACKNELL
(KAARLJILBA KAARDN)

Kylie Bracknell's (Kaarljilba Kaardn)[47] work to strengthen and raise the aware-ness of Australia's Indigenous languages has led to the creation of some of the most exciting film and live theatre performances to come out of Perth in re-cent years. For the 2019-20 Perth Festival, Kylie adapted and directed (alongside husband Dr Clint Bracknell), the Shakespeare adaptation, *Hecate*, a transla-tion of *Macbeth*, performed entirely in Noongar. For the 2020-21 Perth Festival, Kylie presented a Noongar-dub of the Bruce Lee classic, *Fist of Fury Noongar Daa*, making it the first feature film to be dubbed in an Australian language.

Kylie's work extends from behind the screen, to on screen, with roles in *The Sapphires*, *The Gods of Wheat Street*, *I Met a Girl*, and the upcoming Peacock TV and Netflix Australia series, *Irreverent*.

Interview conducted October 2021.

▶▶▶

What are you doing in Queensland, if you don't mind me asking that is?

Kylie Bracknell: Oh that's fine. I landed a role in the US network Peacock TV and Netflix Australia's new series called *Irreverent*.

Congratulations!

KB: Thank you. I'm playing a lead role in that series, so I've got a fair bit of a workload, but it's exciting. It's nice to get back to wearing my actor hat. I haven't done it for a while, so I'm relishing in it and very grateful for the opportunity.

That's good! I can imagine it must be a nice place to be able to film. Queensland is such a beautiful place on screen.

KB: Oh my gosh, even just watching the split monitor one day – wow! I wasn't watching my work, because I'd rather not. It's just stunning the way that the DOP, Gary Phillips is like a God in the industry, is making the show look. It's incredible. It's definitely making this place in Djiru Country, this Djiru land here that we're on, just breathtaking, incredibly breathtaking. And it is!

Let's get started talking about Fist of Fury. Because it's so good. I saw it earlier in the year at Perth festival.

KB: Oh you did, great.

It was wonderful. It was quite an emotional experience. I'd seen Fist of Fury as a kid and I hadn't revisited in a long time. I had forgotten the narrative and watching it this way was just so brilliant. I know you've talked about this quite a bit in interviews in the past, but can you talk about how this came about and where the idea came from?

KB: I remember starting work at Perth Festival in 2019 as Artistic Associate and Tom Vincent, who's the curator of the film festival, came to me and said "Hey Kylie it's great work that you're doing with *Hecate*, and I'm really looking forward to seeing it. What do you think about the Navajo dubbed *Star Wars* and they're also currently working on *Finding Nemo* – do you think that type of language dub would be a cool prototype to do something in Noongar? Is that something you'd be interested in?"

My simple response to that was "Hell yes, but not *Star Wars*." He was like, "Oh, really why's that?" And I said, "Well *Star Wars* is written in English, right. and I've just come from adapting English, like the best English – I think – which is William Shakespeare [*Hecate*]. I want to work on different text and I just think, with *Star Wars*— well what's the point?"

For me, when I work on something creatively it has to have purpose and it has to have authentic drive to it, I think in terms of why you're doing it. I think any creative person should always ask themselves, "Why would you do that? What is the meaning behind it?"

I often get quite frustrated with how people can feel as though they can just translate something from one language to another, particularly with English to Noongar. It's not a simple task. I didn't want to translate from that language anymore. I thought, well, the obvious thing that people miss in language, in particularly First Peoples languages, is that our actions speak louder than our verbal dialogue, in metaphor, in principle, practically, so I wanted to focus on something more arthouse and give light to a film that was around before my time, that would also pay homage to that era and to anchor us in where we've come from.

Trust me – a lot of that depth, the contemplation went through my mind in that very brief five to ten minutes of conversation. I actually said to Tom, "Leave it with me." The film I'd love to do, my favourite film of all time, is *Coming to America*. But that would be absurd. That'd be ridiculous. Why would you do that, it would be ludicrous?

Why not?

KB: Well, it would be good for comedy. That's the parallel I guess, with our community. When I say 'our' I mean, Noongar, first and foremost, but also Aboriginal communities in the country, because we're doing it for them first and foremost, and then broader audiences in Australia. But why we wouldn't do *Coming to America...* because it wouldn't be great as a first one.

I felt as though Bruce Lee would be a really good first one. I mentioned that to Tom and said we need something that honours body language, physical expression. Who better to do that with from seeing the first non-Anglo film hero in this country in the drive-ins to a time where language really suffered in the Sixties, Seventies and Eighties. And even earlier, and I'm surprised that the 100 odd languages that have survived colonisation in this country are still here. It's a celebration, it's an amalgamation of celebration of all of that.

I'm glad that I landed on that choice, I think it was genius. I'm allowed to say that about my choice. [laughs]

[laughs] It really is genius and it works so well. It fits so well. I didn't realise at first that Fist of Fury had such a great response, through the drive-ins, through the Aboriginal communities around Australia when it first released. Did you know about that when you first came up with [the title] at the particular time?

KB: I didn't know about that when I first came up with it. To be honest a lot of decisions I make in life and creatively, I do with my first brain and that's my gut. I trusted my gut instincts with this one, purely because of the cinematography. That particular film has inspired the likes of Tarantino and many other well-known filmmakers, it was a breakthrough film. And when I mentioned this project to the Noongar Advisory Circle at Perth Festival, Senior Arts Leader, Barry McGuire, jumped out of his chair and said "Ohhh daughter, you know, we used to watch [it], this is the whole story about how we love Bruce Lee when I was a kid", and it just went *boom*, like I think his response to this creative idea sold it to the festival. And everyone was like, "Yep, okay Kylie we believe you. This is a great idea. That's fun." Yeah, so it's great to have that endorsement. It was really wonderful to hear those nostalgic moments from that particular era I had hoped we could focus on.

It's something that is really nice to be able to hear removed from the really quite terrible English dubs. I know that Monkey Magic had recently been re-released on Netflix as well and revisiting that, especially as a white kid it washes over you, and I didn't pay attention to that at all or realise. Revisiting it now – like holy shit this is just terrible. It's really, really quite comforting to be able to have that removed from a classic film. I think for a lot of people, especially for Fist of Fury, the dubbed version that they're still hearing is the one from the 70s.

KB: It's a fine line. I don't want to judge the quality of dubs because it's great that people can watch something in their own language to get the story. At the same time, how much obligation should there be in honouring the on-screen story and honouring the origin of where this plot-line is coming from and the people that essentially are acting this out on screen for us?

I don't rate the English version. Clint and I, we are **Boomerang and Spear**, we did the subtitles too, for our Noongar version. The subtitles were updated as well to honour a middle ground of the Noongar and the Cantonese.

How do you find that middle ground?

KB: Respectfully through lots of conversations and considerations, and experience, just having experience and depth of compassion and understanding and respect of language and your collaborators.

It makes for a much more entertaining film, that's for sure. The subtitles are... there's something – there's an energy to them, which I find really interesting.

KB: There is. Absolutely. And Clint and I had a lot of fun with subtitles because that was us using English maybe the way it should have been used originally when they dubbed it, to stick to the original Cantonese storyline.

It's very much for a Noongar audience – the subtitles, the laughs sit in the right place and I think also Noongar community when it was playing there and I think also like communities around Australia, Aboriginal communities will understand it especially that line like, "Oh this poxy bloke", you can tell that he is just annoying, he's not getting it right. We did have a lot of fun with the subtitles.

Most people know how stressful it is to put something like this together and the limitations you have, but also the constricted pockets of time to deliver things and get things ready so it can be mastered and it's not like a holiday.

It's hard work and we're representing a language that's endangered, only 2% of our community speak it and it is not smooth sailing, trying to keep your language humming, it is not smooth sailing at all.

How long did it take to prep?

KB: I think it got greenlit in early September [2020], so we had around three and a half months turn around.

Wow! That's intense!

KB: That was from translation process, editing process, refining process, finalizing process just a script. And then it was audition process, expression of interest callout for emergent speakers and then the final casting process and then the recording process, directing, final mix process, subtitle process, mastering process. So, a lot of sleepless nights and doing all of that with a toddler as well.

I can imagine for most people that would take a whole year, two years to do.

KB: It is a testament to my husband and I's ability now that we've been together for seven years. We've worked on translations before this having co-translated *Hecate*, the Macbeth adaptation in Noongar. I'm not sure if you caught that.

I wanted to lead into talking about that too. I did see that it was really something!

KB: Oh you did!? Thank you for seeing that. We've also co-translated two episodes of *Little J and Big Cuz*, the award-winning animation series. We've co-translated some songs and some covers, we know each other's rhythm and how to work efficiently. I have some colleagues of mine joke and say, "How the heck do you stay married? How do all that together and work together? How do you do that, I couldn't do that." [laughs]

Because of our love of our language and us really wanting to keep it strong.

We want to keep it in a neat pocket. We want to keep it in a place where it is revered, and not just tacked on to something, or just used as a response mechanism to translate English. You know, we're coming from a strength of language and that keeps us together that keeps us collaborating and challenging each other creatively.

So how do we do it? Well, we have Roma Yibiyung Winmar who is a stalwart champion and ambassador of our language. We are incredibly grateful for her support, her backing and endorsement. Also her wits and smarts around the Noongar language. She has taught Noongar language to children for years and that's often the hardest group to teach anything to. Having her there as a collaborator to edit our work is vital. It gives us the courage to do these ground-breaking world firsts.

Ching Ching Ho[48] was incredibly instrumental we could not have done this without her because her work was incredibly vital too. What she did for us was create an Excel spreadsheet that listed the Cantonese character dialogue and an extension of that was a column of the semantics of that. We also have the column for the not-so-great English dub. Then we had another column for the Noongar and then we had a column for the Noongar back into English which we call the Noonglish. It's tiring looking at all of those columns but necessary, of course.

Then what happens with that from the script section is, I take that into the studio and we're working with actors and we're trying to, in order for us to honour this work completely, make it a really classy dub. I strived to match the on-screen characters performance, mouth or verbal movements as much as possible without compromising on our language, because I would never do that. Often that meant reducing the line by a syllable or adding a syllable or switching the phrasing slightly, so that we're shifting a word around to suit the mouth movements a little better. That is really nerve wracking to do in the studio.

Some days I'd try to call Aunty Roma to consult a section or two, but she'd be teaching a class so I couldn't reach her. Often I would have to make executive decisions – "Okay, we're going to go with this and because we're on a tight timeframe and we need to get this wrapped." I would check with her later if I needed to do any ADR pick-ups but because we've worked together numerous times before she said, "No, that's okay. The way that you've shifted or edited it is good. You know what you're doing!" Did I digress too much? [laughs]

No, not at all. This is really interesting and something which had rolled through my mind a lot when I was watching Hecate, which was an experience, a really powerful performance and especially it came at a time pre-COVID, which we were on the cusp [of things locking down], and sitting in the theatre and just experiencing everything was just wonderful. Watching the actors come down aisles. It made it really made you feel part of the actual performance and part of the narrative that was going on. That was so, so exciting.

Is there a freedom to Perth Festival, giving you the ability to be able to put on something like both Fist of Fury Noongar Daa and Hecate and really presenting the Noongar language respectfully and powerfully to an audience that may otherwise not usually go and see it?

KB: Absolutely. The wonderful thing about Perth Festival and their current directorship is there's a smartness in heart about where we should be by this point in time. And there is a want and a willingness and a passionate advocacy for the maintenance, preservation and celebration of local, historical, current contemporary culture. And that means Noongar culture. And that means Noongar language. And that means amplifying Noongar voices in Noongar language. And it means collaborating with local artists and investing in the community and investing in the development of the community and development of future artists to maintain that. That's the other thing I really appreciate about being an Artistic Associate at Perth Festival is that the group understands that whatever investment we make now will have a ripple effect in years to come. It's an exemplary display of leadership in action, in my opinion.

It makes for a really powerful festival. It's called the Perth International Arts Festival, but it really actually focuses back on home, which is something that somebody who's lived in Perth almost all my life I was born here grew up a little bit in Queensland and came back here it's made me respect Perth a little bit more and love Perth a little bit more, which is nice to see because we're always looking afar like, you know, art festivals are often always looking afar and it's nice to have that focus back on home, and especially in this way as well.

I want to talk about how we can save an endangered language. What's the process? Is it through creating art like this? Are there other ways as well that we can get behind and make sure that we can save these dying languages?

KB: You cannot save a language like it is one exhibit item. A language can only be saved when the community whose language it is are supported to do that very act.

Saving a language is about acknowledging and recognizing that language is one component of a functioning community, how people connect with their culture. And often you'll find the language that is spoken is a celebration of how people view the world. It's a celebration of how people value life, and how that interconnects with nature, the very thing that provides us that life. Saving a language, I think people also need to realize that the question you ask is not simple. It's a little complex to respond to, but I'll do it in parts.

To help save a language it definitely needs to be embraced. So it's wonderful that the Western Australian government are contributing one hour a week to Aboriginal languages, it's not enough, but it's a start. I would say to community members who are passionate about supporting languages being kept alive that they should celebrate the local language with their children, and praise local Aboriginal groups for their positive optimistic display and use of their mother tongue. Continue to encourage arts bodies who are actively reclaiming language and working with the reclamation of language whether it be financially or in written form, or just whatever celebration you can offer that shows them encouragement. Because whatever language comes from the area that you live is a part of that air you breathe and a part of that that country that you live on and let you source your produce from for example.

I've said this a couple of times before in Noongar language, 'boodj' is the first stage of pregnancy add an extension to that word, 'boodj' will become 'boodjar' adding the 'ar' sound becomes land, the land or the Mother Earth. When you add a 'ee' sound on the end of that, so 'boodj', 'boodjar', 'boodjari'. 'Boodjari' is full term pregnancy. So your land or your Mother Earth, the provider of life, sits inside the first stage of creating life. And before the end stage of that fully formed life. That's how our language celebrates us as a people and it keeps us connected to our place. There is a lot of metaphor embedded in the way we sound out our language and the way that we speak our language.

The danger though, right now I see as a language activist is that it's becoming more fashionable to speak local languages, but a lot of people are speaking those local languages through an English lens. So the grammar in which people are using the local language is respecting English more than it is respecting their own natural language flow and meaning. And that makes me quite concerned and it makes me quite sad. There are lots of things to consider when you're wanting to celebrate and somehow help save a language. I think the most common thing to say would be tread carefully and tread lightly and ask the people who know about the language how to save it and what help you can offer them so that they can continue to do it in the best way they feel is most appropriate.

Thank you.

I know that you've travelled around Australia with Fist of Fury Noongar Daa. You were supposed to have at it MIFF, and now it's going to be at Sydney Film Festival. What's that journey been like with taking it to places other than Perth?

KB: Internally, it's been a bit conflicted because we haven't been able to be there personally and it's the first time that the film is going to play outside of Noongar country without us there to talk to it and hold it safely. When it toured Noongar country, we made it very obvious to Perth Festival, from us at Boomerang and Spear that it needs to travel with community. So it's about generating an opportunity for a couple of the voice cast to be paid to go and speak about them reclaiming their language in this wonderful art vehicle, for lack of a better phrase. With MIFF, they wanted it to go to MIFF play, we said no to that, because we're not ready for it to be streamed, because we don't want it to be a product per se. I do want it to be celebrated as a language reclamation dub and it's about bringing people together.

Even though it's not Noongar country, whatever language group that's there that either speak their language or are also reclaiming, restoring their language. Or if they've, if the language is going completely into sleeping mode, and then they can't access it or speak it anymore. Watching something like this can be triggering and so having some of us there to talk about that and having some of the local community feel comfortable enough to come up and have yarn with us and say 'that was solid what you mob did.'

Fist of Fury Noongar Daa Poster
Image Credit: Perth International Arts Festival. Used with permission

Most of our community in Noongar country were very teary, moved and emotional. So, I imagine it will have an equal sort of response in other areas where their languages is a missing part or a longing part or something that's still present but they're working and striving to connect to it. It's just wonderful to have us there in person wherever possible because it's about being with people. I think that's the thing that COVID has really made apparent to our communities is just how much it means to have people around us. You know, often Aboriginal people have been put-down for how many people they have in their houses or you know, in there's too many of them in that room, or whatever, it may be circumstantial, but we've always known the importance and the strength of having our mob with us and being together as one in appreciation of what's really important.

Not separate to that. Not taking each other's presence for granted. So we still apply that sort of togetherness in a cinema or an outdoor cinema and having everyone there to sharing that and celebrate it together. If you're celebrating it alone, how does that look, what is the point?

Having said that, I'm really excited. I'm nervous and excited. I don't know how it will be received. It's the first interstate festival where it will actually play. Because in Melbourne it didn't get to play in cinema and that was conditional for us. I'm actually keen to see how many people will actually go see it. Because, to be very honest, I don't think the hearts of some or most Australians take our languages seriously enough yet. And if you don't speak any other languages but English, you don't tend to really be drawn to non-English films where you have to read subtitles. So we'll see.

That's been my experience as well. I like to try and embrace as many different films as possible and watch as many different films as possible.

KB: Oh, but they'll go and see a French film—

That's what I was going to say it's like the French Film Festival. People go and they'd love it. And it's like, yeah, okay. All right. You kind of, see one French film, you know, I love them. I do but you've got to embrace local.

KB: Yeah, and it makes me sad. And I get to interviews. I'm like, "Well, how should I conduct myself in the interview today? Should I speak about all of the optimistic lovely, you know, glossy sort of beautiful glowing sunshine flower blossoming things", "Or should I actually just call people out and go 'what are you doing?'"

I mean, you just asked me the question, how can we help said languages? Go and see the film. Go and hear it.

Let 109 minutes of Noongar language wash over you, absorb it. Learn about it. Learn how you can connect with people. You've got to do the work, you've got to do the research.

How do you prepare for interviews as well? For me, I do the research, I read, I watch, I do all the reading and everything. But I've never actually asked the people who I do interview how they prepare for interviews. So how do you do that yourself?

KB: An interviewer hasn't asked me that.

I prepare for my interviews by meditating. And that meditation isn't long. It's a very short process of acknowledging where I am, at that present moment, speaking to my ancestors, asking them for guidance.

Knowing who I'm speaking to, and what they celebrate, or don't. And trusting that the way that I speak from my heart will always resonate. I don't need to research being me. But I do need to clock my growth and what I am advocating for, to ensure that the leadership of the project that I'm representing beams.

The interview is never about me. It's about what I'm working on, and about what my contribution is. So it's not even about nervousness or worry. It's a period of excitement where I go, "Okay, what can I celebrate in this interview that I perhaps haven't done in other interviews? What else can I offer the listening audience, or reading audience that they might not have heard about this project before?" So I meditate through those patterns of thought process, and it's always about giving, it's always about educating and opening new doors of understanding.

Thank you. Thank you for that answer. As I said, I've never actually asked it before, but I sit here and I feel what I do is a great privilege to be able to talk to people like yourself to be able to talk to filmmakers, who are sharing their stories and their work. It is a great privilege. And I don't take it lightly. And that's part of the reason I like to highlight and celebrate films like what you've done with Fist of Fury Noongar Daa, because and I believe in my core, that this is the kind of thing that we need more of that we need to be able to, as you were saying, people need to go along and see these films.

KB: I'm so grateful. And it's just serendipitous that you have been there in person for the Somerville premiere screening, and also that you've seen *Hecate* too. So you can, you really can write to the personal experience of being in the space and feeling it in person. And that that's makes me smile.

I felt at least as somebody who writes about the arts, who experiences and enjoys it and wants to support it, it would be disingenuous of me if I didn't actually go along and participate in these kinds of events. It's... what am I doing then? It's pointless. It would be dishonest, basically.

Then I go along and see it, and I'm like, 'oh, gosh, I want 10 more of these. I want 20 more of these.' That's the joy of being able to walk out of a cinema and, especially at Somerville, which is such a beautiful place, and there's a buzz, an excitement there.

KB: Traditionally, it was a very joyful area, ceremonies all about love and marriage. The marriage place is not far from there. So that particular area itself has a rich history of beautiful energy, and that permeates through that space.

I think you can feel that for sure. What are you going to do next? Are we going to see something else like this again, because I kind of want to see something else like this again, but I also want to see something that's unique and different. That's not based on pre-existing text.

KB: I'm currently a part of a writing team for a feature film. I can't say any more than that at the moment, announcements haven't been done. So that's what I'm doing at the moment. I'm looking at making my contribution to that project another first as well, something that we haven't seen on screen before. And Clint is working on a wonderful album of songs that will be celebrated in Perth Festival 21.

And there are tons of other ideas bubbling away that will eventually I think, take some really wonderful next steps.

We're juggling big projects at the moment. I mean, I'm working on this new series for Peacock TV and Netflix. And that's, that has to be my primary focus right now. But we are absolutely looking at what extended life *Fist of Fury Noongar Daa* can have before we immediately move on, but we are saying yes to a couple of other projects, and instigating a couple of other projects and creating space for our other ideas to be nurtured into development phase and, and beyond. And we always lift others with us. How I will tie that up in a nice little cute bow is by saying, I don't like to talk about what we're working on until it's ready to be celebrated with the world.

All I need to know is I've got things to look forward to. That's as a purely selfish thing. All I just need to know. It's like things on the horizon. They're coming.

KB: I love the selections [of Perth Festival] that are supporting female directors, as well as it's nice to see a new wave coming through.

I remember going to watch Portrait of a Lady on Fire in the press screening, and I don't think that anybody was expecting what we got to see there. And that was it was a little bit overwhelming. They do a really good job of supporting great, great work with the film festival. So that in itself is something that I love a lot.

KB: It's so good that Perth has that right? We've got to keep celebrating the good things about Perth to keep it hip, keep it smart.

THE AUSTRALIAN FILM INDUSTRY: ON BECOMING THE VANCOUVER OF THE SOUTHERN HEMISPHERE

Before embarking on this piece, I want you to ask yourself: what was the last Canadian film that you watched that didn't have either of the Cronenberg directors name attached to it?

Take your time. Keep those names in mind.

On we go:

Early in David Stratton's second book, *The Avocado Plantation*, he writes about the removal of the 10BA tax incentive[49], and the impact its dissolution might have on the Australian film industry. He rightfully criticises the incentive, highlighting how some 'production companies' manipulated it for personal gain, effectively creating filmic versions of unwatchable trash that would never receive a proper release platform, while also highlighting how important it was for sustaining the Australian film industry. Doing so, Stratton ties a line between the Australian film industry and the Canadian film industry, keenly sounding an alarm that the Australian film industry runs the risk of collapsing into anonymity, much like the Canadian film industry did.

He writes:

> *The destruction of the English-speaking Canadian film industry during the early 70s by just such a policy of tax concessions and an open go for foreign actors, had been well documented: Canada still has not recovered from that dreadful period.*

If we take that statement in isolation, remove it out of time, it feels applicable to the current Australian film landscape, where the notion of what constitutes an Australian film is gradually collapsing before our eyes.

If that sounds alarmist, then I assure you, it is.

I want to focus on the Canadian film industry for a moment, as it feels like the closest film industry to the currently amorphous Australian film industry. If we think of what a Canadian filmmaker is, we often come up with the same handful of names: David Cronenberg, Atom Egoyan, Guy Maddin, Xavier Dolan, Sarah Polley, and Denis Villeneuve. Out of that bunch, maybe Cronenberg and Villeneuve are considered 'household' names, as in, if you mentioned their filmography, people would be aware of *The Fly* or *Dune*. Sure, the others have #FilmTwitter cache, and are greatly appreciated by the broader film loving community, but their impact on the casual film loving community is rather muted.

If we then broaden our purview into how the Canadian film industry presents Canadian culture on screen, well, depending on your appreciation and experience with Canadian films, we find ourselves slightly lacking in this regard.

While films like *Goon* and its sequel, masterfully employ Canadian actors and talent to tell a narrative that's defiantly Canadian (after all, ice hockey is the AFL of Canada), and proudly so, we can't particularly glean the same appreciation of Canadian culture from films like *Antiviral* or *Hobo with a Shotgun*.

Xavier Dolan's filmography has long found fertile footing in Canadian culture and society, with *Mommy* in particular working as a critique of Canadian politics. Denis Villeneuve's *Incendies* delicately combines Canadian culture with a global refugee legacy, leaving a masterfully devastating impact on the viewer. Then there's Patricia Rozema's powerful drama, *Mouthpiece*, a film that appeared at TIFF in 2018, and in the year 2020 finally received global attention thanks to the exhaustive and impressive support from Canadian website, Seventh Row, whose in depth coverage[50] helped usher in a global appreciation for the indie film, leading to UK film critic Mark Kermode[51] helping champion it for a UK audience.

For a country that has one of the major film festivals that is used by Hollywood as the launching pad for Oscar-friendly fare, the Toronto International Film Festival (TIFF), it's a cruel shame that the global awareness of the output of the Canadian film industry feels deceptively muted around the world. We so often hear about how well films like *Three Billboards Outside Ebbing, Missouri* and *Jojo Rabbit* were received at TIFF, but outside of this, there's little awareness of Canadian films. As an Australian, I've grown to rely on independent websites like Seventh Row who have come into play with their tireless championing and support for smaller, independent Canadian films that we would otherwise not hear about.

Elsewhere in film festival land, in 2022, MIFF announced that they would launch the 'richest feature film competition in the Southern Hemisphere'[52]. The $140,000 award would be decided by a jury of prominent international and Australian guests from an array of films from directors' first-or-second-time-feature-length films that make their Australian premieres at the festival. Unlike Western Australian based festival, CinefestOz, which has an annual prize of $100,000 for competing Australian films, the MIFF prize is available for Australian and global films. This announcement further aligns the prestigious festival with TIFF as a location for international acclaim and attention. MIFF will continue to provide funding and support for Australian filmmakers through their MIFF Premiere Fund and Accelerator Lab.

On the Wikipedia entry for the 'Cinema of Canada'[53], the varied reasons behind why the Canadian film industry struggles to gain attention are laid bare. Two fields are worthwhile highlighting:

> *Films labelled as American films could often be better described as collaborations between Canada and the US. In addition, films which are sometimes designated as "American" productions often involve a higher-percentage of Canadian participation but the "American" designation is favoured for tax purposes. Also, unlike other countries who tend to have citi-*

zens with discernible accents, the American media too rarely highlights or identifies actors, directors or producers as Canadian in origin, leaving the false perception that few Canadians work in the industry.

In a phenomenon which can be likened to the theory of cultural cringe, a considerable number of Canadians reflexively dismiss all Canadian films as inherently inferior to Hollywood studio fare. This is not necessarily connected to reality, as many critically acclaimed films have been made in Canada, but the idea nevertheless presents a significant hurdle to Canadian filmmakers seeking to build an audience for their work.

If we sub-out the word Canadian, and insert the word Australian, then we're almost in line with what the current reality of Australian filmmaking looks like. The excellent web-series *Every Frame a Painting* covered the subject of international filmmaking in Canada in the creatively titled video, *Vancouver Never Plays Itself*[54], showcasing in surprising depth how the city of Vancouver subs in for cities around the world. Now, this isn't a new thing, as anyone familiar with the process of filmmaking would appreciate that cities all around the world have been substituted for other cities, with everywhere from Romania to England swapping out their home locations for (usually) American locales. But, as Tony Zhou explains, Vancouver is often presented in make-up, never allowing its true self to appear, and in turn, effectively nullifying Canadian culture on film.

With many of these American-Canadian co-productions (like the ironically-applicable-to-this-piece *Saw* film, made by Aussie filmmakers James Wan and Leigh Whannell) utilising Canadian crews to make American-facing productions, it's no wonder that the Canadian film industry struggles to pull itself out from underneath the behemoth of Hollywood and into its own deserving spotlight. Sure, we can easily point out the reality that French-Canadian films can sometimes 'backdoor' their way into public consciousness via the Francophiles of the world, with films like *Incendies* and *The Barbarian Invasions*, each receiving global acclaim and accolades as a (cringe) 'foreign language' film.

For film viewers, they see films like *Chicago*, *The Incredible Hulk*, *Mean Girls*, and *Good Will Hunting*, as being proudly American films. And while they are *technically* American stories, with American actors, set in *American* cities, these films were shot and made in Canada with Canadian crews. It may be great for the Canadian film industry to have these mammoth productions made there, but it leaves little for the Canadian identity, which leads into the heightened feeling of 'cultural cringe' for Canadian audiences.

As per that Wikipedia entry, *'this is not necessarily connected to reality'*, but that doesn't mean that it doesn't exist. Globally, we have become so attuned and accentuated to the American dialect and style of filmmaking, that when presented with our own countries fare, we often neglect it, thinking it to be inferior or lacking in the shadow of our Yankee friends. If I think of my knowledge and understanding of the Canadian identity on film, the first images that come to mind are Terence and Philip from *South Park* and the Canadian Mounties of *Due South*. I know full well that there is more to Canada than these characters, but additionally, I'm certain it's hard for international audiences to shake the leather-skinned ockerisms of Paul Hogan and a certain knife in New York.

In many ways, the American identity has become the default, much in the same way that the American film industry has become the default. Hollywood is not the originator of film – it was, and always has been, a global art form – yet, the manner that financial decisions are made about film seems to be predominantly focused on how far the US dollar will stretch. Where many countries like the UK, Canada, France, Australia, and New Zealand, have film industries established and supported by the government, America's film industry is one propped up by the balustrades of the studio system.

With behemoths like Disney and Warner Bros. that appear to have their own Smaug-protected money pits, it's understandable why they would look at the rather affordable options of filming 'internationally' (even if Canada is right across the border). Additionally, given the assured promise of Hollywood productions, and the guarantees that come with cash-loaded producers, it's understandable why countries like Canada and Australia would want to sidle up to Hollywood to ensure film production crews stay employed. It's pretty much guaranteed.

That's where we'll leave our Canadian friends for now, as we head down to Australia, the country that may as well forever be collectively known as the 'Vancouver of the Southern Hemisphere.'

In the year 2021, we've already seen a bunch of American films made in Australia with Australian talent, crew, and partially financed by Australia state and federal governments. First, we have *Godzilla VS Kong*, which, like a previous film in the series (*Kong: Skull Island*), utilised parts of Queensland for its production. Then there's the dystopian monster-romance flick, *Love and Monsters*, which was filmed in Queensland, and showcases a world that's overrun by giant monsters, leaving humanity threatened (jeeze, almost like we're seeing a narrative thread emerge here). And finally, we've got the South Australian made *Mortal Kombat*, which gave Perth director Simon McQuoid a fairly hefty project to tackle for his directorial debut, all the while utilising Australian crews as best as possible for all aspects of the production.

In a microcosm, you'd barely recognise these are being Australian 'made' films. Those inverted commas are important, because while the production crew behind the scenes might be Australian, and the financial support from the government makes a certain consistently wavering percentage of the film 'Australian', it's hard to definitely call these Australian made films. In some ways, it feels bizarre to even call them American-Australian co-productions, given how muted the Australian-ness of the films can be. And, if we were to grab out the abacus and start moving beans around, we'd be sitting here all day long trying to figure out exactly what percentage of each production is *actually* Australian.

But, while I'm no mathematician, I can at least look at these three co-productions and glean simply from watching them how 'Australian' they are. What I'm particularly looking for is how distinct the Australian identity emerges throughout these films.

For *Godzilla vs. Kong*, while the film itself is rather entertaining and enjoyable, and delivers impressively on its massive-scale destruction and big screen theatrics, it also struggles to showcase the Queensland outback for what it is. It's hard to tell exactly which sequences were shot in Queensland, but I would hazard a guess and say that it would be the Skull Island sequences, which transplant the iconic rainforest of the Cairns region into a remote, mythical island. There's something truly 'otherworldly' about the Daintree and its associated regions, and if you'll allow me to unleash my inner-tree hugger for a moment, I do wish the Queensland government would recognise the strength of the environment they have for cinematic ventures, as opposed to continually clearing it for farmland or mining space. (As an aside, it's moderately amusing that the rebooted *Godzilla* film in 2014 was predominantly shot in, you guessed it, Vancouver, Canada.)

Then we shift on to *Love and Monsters*, which also utilises the Queensland landscape to impressive effect, while also utilising the imagery of suburbia to highlight the destruction of what the 'normal world' looked like prior to the catastrophic event that brought the titular monsters to life. I want to focus on the imagery of Aussie suburbia momentarily, because while the numberplates have been changed, and people drive on different sides of the road, there's a distinct difference to the housing of Australia as opposed to that of America. It's hard to say exactly, but the tan bricked abodes and sea of sun-kissed lawns feels distinctly Australian. In a dystopian film like this, or even in Leigh Whannell's masterful *The Invisible Man*, this not-quite-American familiar imagery helps add an off-kilter, askew feel to the world.

In 2021, as more international productions sought sanctuary and safety in the relatively COVID-safe Australia, the suburban landscape was presented in different ways that hint at the Australiana of these productions (see the TV show *Nine Perfect Strangers*, or the 2022 film *Blacklight*). For Americans and other keen-eyed watchers, it's easy to see when a production that is set in New York is filmed in Los Angeles, so naturally this kind of difference would become even more accentuated when the common place imagery of American suburbia is replaced by that of Australia's varied houses.

Joining the lead character, Joel (Dylan O'Brien) on his journey in *Love and Monsters* is an expressive canine called Boy, played by Kelpie mastermind duo Hero and Dodge, who had previously played another iconic Kelpie mastermind, Koko, in the excellent flick *Koko: A Red Dog Story*. I'm not sure how prevalent the Kelpie breed is in America, but honestly, alongside the humble Blue Heeler, there's no more iconic Aussie breed of dog than a Kelpie.

Outside of the bush setting, the canine representation, and the brief imagery of suburbia in *Love and Monsters*, there's little else to suggest that this film was made in Australia as a whole, especially with precious few Aussie actors in the mix (tip of the hat to the always enjoyable Dan Ewing). Back in *The Avocado Plantation,* David Stratton mentions the appearance of Barry Otto and Todd Boyce in the Aussie based production of Dolph Lundgren's *The Punisher,* saying, as if they were lucky enough to be in the same space as Hollywood royalty as the Russian boxer from *Rocky IV.*

So, if we extrapolate from that just a little bit more, then we come to the most Aussie production of the bunch: *Mortal Kombat.*

Yeah, look, I'm as surprised as you are that they actually gave the role of Kano to a true-blue Aussie, given there's precedent for non-Aussies trying to tackle the 'Stralian accent (see *Pacific Rim* and *Rough Night* for appalling examples), but here we are, in the year 2021, with Oscar nominee Josh Lawson banging on as one heck of an obnoxious Aussie in this ultra-violent video game adaptation. Where Tom Hardy mumbled his way through *Mad Max: Fury Road,* somewhat muting the ocker personality of that flick even though the dialogue was full of Aussie slang, Josh Lawson slathers on the strine and embraces his inner evil-Steve Irwin with a proud kick to the crotch, making the most of his screen time and becoming one of the most memorable things about the film.

Lawson is joined by fellow Aussies Jessica McNamee as Sonya Blade, Angus Sampson as Goro, Damon Herriman as Kabal, with cameos from David Field and Kris McQuade helping bulk up the Aussie actor quota. While the diversity of talent is on full display in *Mortal Kombat,* the Aussie accent cuts through like a knife, ensuring that the brutal colloquialisms stick in the viewers mind powerfully. If we were to focus on the global awareness of Australian culture (represented here as a misogynistic Aussie bloke dialled up 200% to the point of absurdity), then *Mortal Kombat* takes the cake with a solid chunk of Australiana given screen time.

Good-o for dogs then.

Yet, *Mortal Kombat* is the exception, and not the norm, and while it's great to sit down and watch a Hollywood blockbuster and feel a little bit seen, it's becoming a rarity, and will likely continue to do so going forward. Sure, *Thor: Ragnarok* had a wealth of Australian imagery in the mix, with Valkyrie's spaceship being called 'the Commodore' and painted in the colours of the Aboriginal flag, but these are peripheral tokens that, if taken away from the film itself, would not effectively 'harm' the final product.

And that's what we're dealing with here: products.

American cinema and television is one of the grandest products around. It's easily exportable, transferrable across the globe, becoming the dominant force. Where we once rose up in anger at the Americanisation of Arnott's biscuits, Aeroplane Jelly, the staple Aussie food that is Vegemite, and even brands of matches, the Australian public carries an air of indifference when it comes to the Americanisation of Australian film and television culture. We, like Canadian audiences, have found ourselves wrapped up in a cultural cringe when it comes to Australian film and television.

This is not to say there aren't exceptions to the rule, with Robert Connolly's masterful *The Dry* and the family friendly *Penguin Bloom* showing that there is still an audience for a certain type of Australian cinema, but the dominant feeling about Australian films is that Australian audiences simply aren't interested in them. We recoil when a kitchen sink drama appears, and shudder at the notion that anyone would ever decide to make an Aussie comedy after *The Castle* (now 25 years old). Audiences still hold onto the rose-tinted notion that the hey-day of Australian film came with *Muriel's Wedding* and *Priscilla*.

And yet, as Australia entered part two of our COVID world in 2021 with expensive two-week staycations in quarantine hotels, and quarantine hubs on farms for the wealthy, we became a sanctuary for Hollywood to make films in the relative safety of a world without masks. With a triumphant announcement in early 2021, Marvel announced that they would transfer some of their film productions to Australia[55], transferring *Thor: Love and Thunder* from the hub in Atlanta, Georgia, after having turned Sydney into San Francisco with *Shang-Chi and the Legend of the Ten Rings*. Maybe as a duty of service to Australia, Marvel should finally introduce the Aussie hero Manifold into the mix.

It's not just Marvel calling Australia home, with countless other Hollywood productions[56] shifting location here, including Melissa McCarthy and husband Ben Falcone making Sydney their home-away-from-home, Liam Neeson in Canberra doing yet another action flick, and Nicole Kidman and her entourage filming the *Nine Perfect Strangers* TV series here. Sure, there's another *Mad Max*-associated film, *Furiosa*, coming along, this time the elements will hopefully allow to be actually filmed in Australia, but the slate of Aussie-focused Hollywood fare is slight, and with production crews being swallowed up by Hollywood productions, it's hard to see how Australian films and shows will emerge safely and securely from this sea of seppos.

In 2021, the Federal government threatened to scarper any chance of local post-production crews being utilised on Hollywood productions when it proposed to raise the minimum expenditure threshold to $1 million[57], double the current threshold of $500,000. Thankfully, through vociferous protests from the Australian film industry, sense saw reason and Minister for the Arts Paul Fletcher announced in late December 2021 that they would retain the $500,000 threshold[58]. The news came after a tense and fraught period for the Australian film community, with many practitioners out of work and failing to be covered by Jobkeeper payments due to the impermanency of their jobs, payments that were intended to keep workers financially stable during COVID times. (Although the Federal government announced that the Arts industries would be supported with payments, it's clear that even in 2022, many of those payments failed to appear[59].)

This is a pointed issue given how both state and federal governments continually champion the work opportunities for local industries, and how it will give them exposure to working on larger productions. There's an air of 'payment in exposure' here to the kind of announcements that are happening with greater frequency than usual, almost as if local production teams should be grateful that each government is working to ensure their job security. It's possible to be angered by this, and at the same time celebrate the employment of thousands of members of the film industry on major Hollywood productions.

Yet, closer to home for this writer (Western Australia), for all the bleating and baaing from the state government about a proposed studio being built smack bang in the middle of Freo harbour, which was subsequently abandoned in lieu of being built a cosy 30-minute drive away from the CBD in Whiteman Park, there's been precious little interest or investment in assisting locals in getting a foot into the film industry itself. If we're landing in such a fertile ground of Hollywood film production in Australia, then where's the splash back for the next FTI which will help foster the next generation of Aussie production designers, editors, visual effects artists, and more?

This leads us to the crossroads and the crux of the identity crisis that is looming over the Australian film industry:

Will the practitioners, artists, creatives, and production crews across Australia become rent-a-crowd workers for the factory line of Marvel and DC films that'll be made in Sydney, Melbourne, and the Gold Coast going forward? And, in the process of doing so, will the Australian cultural identity start to fade away into the miasma of digital trickery that is swallowing up film movements around the world?

While Australian films are supported through Screen Australia grants, it's on the small screen that Australian stories are allowed to thrive, with shows like *Wentworth, Mystery Road,* and *Please Like Me* all receiving welcome international audiences.

The Australian film industry has long championed and fought for the Australian cultural identity on screen, and yet, because of how our film industry is set up, with so many films relying solely on government grants and support, it's going to be harder to establish these Australian stories, and to maintain a wider, global audience appeal. And for those that are funded outside of government bodies, the filmmakers are often pushed into a deep financial sinkhole that they struggle to ever get themselves out of.

To be clear, the Canadian film industry continues and thrives, supporting Canadian stories and filmmakers, and embracing new waves of Canadian cinema. It's just stifled and smothered like so many other film movements around the globe by the unceasing, ever-pumping, enduring Hollywood fare that filters onto our screens. While Canadians and Australians alike are employed en masse to help bring these films to life, it occurs at the cost of their country's cultural identities.

It's not as if there isn't an audience for Australian films, with fare like *Lion, Hacksaw Ridge, and Mad Max: Fury Road* receiving Best Picture nominations (even if *Hacksaw Ridge* is an American story made in Australia), and Jennifer Kent's masterpiece, *The Babadook,* shaking the international horror community to its core. Additionally, Shannon Murphy's debut feature, *Babyteeth,* hit the right audience at the right time, becoming an underground success with fans around the globe.

But as we're seeing with films like *Peter Rabbit* or *The Invisible Man*, the 'Australian' identity simply isn't there. It's got the cast, it's got the crew, they've got the directors, but otherwise, the rissoles have been turned into meat loafs, and Mel Gibson's been dubbed by a yank.

It's not all doom and gloom though, as we look towards the horror community to find the dedication and affection the global gorehounds have for the macabre, and see the support for horror and exploitation films in Canada with the likes of *Hobo with a Shotgun*, *The Void*, and *Pyewacket*, all adding to the burgeoning and thriving horror genre in the decade. In Australia, *The Babadook*, *Relic*, *Little Monsters*, *Wyrmwood*, and *Lake Mungo*, all gained global audiences who lapped up the outback frights with utter delight.

On the back of *The Babadook*'s success, Jennifer Kent effectively established herself as one of the most vital and important directors of this generation, making each subsequent film she will make appointment viewing. This helped immensely when it came to promoting her follow-up film, *The Nightingale*, an excoriating and furious rape-revenge thriller that pulled no punches and demanded viewers witness the horrors and brutality of colonialism in Australia. It's a devastating film to endure, and if this were Kent's first film, it likely would have demolished any chance of an audience attending her second.

Sure, if we sequester a countries cultural identity into a genre that mainstream audiences rarely venture into unless they feel it's safe enough, it might help provide it with some kind of bizarre oasis of safety. Within the horror community, cultural identities remain safe and widely accepted, with the otherwise shunned affectations of a culture being allowed to grow freely within its terror-inducing boundaries. But that's also just one genre, when we all know that film genres are multitudinous.

This is cherry-picking an example, but it's an apt one to highlight how easily it is for a countries cultural identity to become a niche enterprise for the country alone to appreciate and enjoy. Australian culture can be great, and can be a wonderful thing to share with the world, so why shouldn't Australian governments – current or future – embrace who we are and champion Australian stories? Instead, the outward appearances seem to be open season for Hollywood to use our film industry as it pleases because 'this playground is safe'. (Of course, with the emergence of the Omicron strain of COVID, the sanctuary of filmmaking that Australia once offered became ruined, causing productions to halt and be delayed.[60])

It's even more frustrating and devastating as we're witnessing the emergence of a decade long creative streak from the Indigenous New Wave within Australia, with filmmakers like Warwick Thornton, Rachel Perkins, Wayne Blair, Ivan Sen, and Leah Purcell, all creating work that is redefining what Australian cinema is and should be. *Sweet Country*, *Top End Wedding*, *Jasper Jones*, and the 2022 film *Here Out West*, are all top tier films that should be embraced around the globe.

While it's easy to champion how Australian *Mortal Kombat* is and feels at times, it's also a Hollywood production that never truly embodies Australian culture. I'm happy and glad that South Australian creatives got to make one heck of a bloody, effects heavy film, and I'm stoked that it's a success too. Hopefully they get to hit for six for a sequel. But additionally, I hope that Warner Bros. and Marvel take a look at what we've got here and utilise our culture for their own stories. A bit of give and take. We can't allow the Australian film industry to be turned into parrots for the American film industry, imitating a lifestyle and culture that is distinctly different from our own.

Australian cinema like *Sweet Country, The Babadook, Mad Max, My Brilliant Career, Top End Wedding, Chopper, The Dry, I'm Wanita, My Name is Gulpilil,* and *The Adventures of Priscilla, Queen of the Desert,* are our Vegemite, our Tim Tams, our AFL. They flood through our veins and fill our guts like an ice cold tinny on a scorcher of a day. They are in the air we breathe like the hazy smell of distant smoke during a prescribed burn off. They are a sunset on Cottesloe beach with your feet in the sand, salt water spattering your face. They are distinctly *Australian.* This is what we're fighting for. We cannot lose this.

I want to leave you with versions of the question I opened this piece with, and for you to take these questions to everyone you talk to film about with:

What was the last Australian film that you watched that wasn't one of the fifteen rotating titles that always comes up in discussion? And who are the Australian directors that best explore Australian culture on screen? And, most importantly, what was the last Australian film that you recommended someone seek out?

INTERVIEW
MORTAL KOMBAT - DIRECTOR
SIMON MCQUOID

*M*ortal Kombat is director Simon McQuoid's feature film debut, having worked on commercials (notably the epic 2011 Playstation Love Live Play commercial, as well as for *Call of Duty*, Logitech, Samsung, Telstra, and more) and directing the 2014 short film *The Night-time Economy*. Born in Perth, Western Australia, Simon helped make waves when *Mortal Kombat* was filmed entirely in South Australia, utilising local crew and production facilities to bring the sci-fi action film to life.

Interview conducted April 2021

▶▷▶

Having made Mortal Kombat in Australia, can you talk about the production and what it was like to head to South Australia and film there?

Simon McQuoid: It was a wonderful experience shooting in South Australia, they treated us so well. The South Australian government were really, really gung-ho about getting us to come there. They really were very brave about the decisions they made to get us there. And it took an entrepreneurial spirit and the spirit of can-do, which those guys really have. I give a lot of credit to those guys for helping us make this happen.

And then getting to South Australia, they've got a really rich film history of shooting some pretty amazing films in South Australia. Often they don't get the credit they deserve, because some pretty incredible films have been made there. So I was really thrilled about knowing that, and then also knowing that there's some really amazing locations there. One of the early locations that I was really worried about trying to find in Australia, anywhere in Australia was the old growth pine forest that opens the film. That's about an hour's drive outside of Adelaide at this place called Mt Crawford, and it's just stunningly beautiful.

There's so much South Australia and Adelaide spread across the film, it's all there. And then finding all the other locations was wonderful. And then we had this international crew and cast mixed with A-level crew and cast from Australia, then the great joy and surprise for me was just the skill level of the local crew in South Australia was just amazing and indistinguishable between all of us. And we became this really big, rich, layered, interesting crew and cast that they just all got on really well. And it was so much fun to do that and we all learn from each other, we all we all got better as a result of helping each other out and working together.

I think that's what gets a little lost on people is that all the people that work on that film, they individually got better. And so the Australian Government in providing incentives and really getting us there, they'd really made the film industry there better as a result that's materially what they've done. Yes, they've employed a ton of people, and if you sit through the credits on the end, you're gonna see just who they are. And then add to that the visual effects companies that are in Adelaide. Rising Sun Pictures and Mr X. And the coupled with Method in Melbourne and Slate in Sydney. There's just so much talent there. It was just great. I mean, honestly, it was very hard to find any faults at all. Maybe that just made a new hotel and that's it.

Given how many of the productions are moving here to Australia, it seems to be becoming a destination place. Mortal Kombat feels like being on the cusp of a new movement of Hollywood-Australian films, which is really great to see. One of the things which was really impressive was you managed to bring that Australian-ness out in the character of Kano who is just so brilliantly performed by Josh Lawson. Can you talk about that process? Was that in the script or was it something that you developed along the way?

SMcQ: A combination. Greg Russo, the writer who's American, he did a pretty good job on writing in the Australian character, but also then when I signed on, he knew enough to say, "Hey, let's try and make this character more Australian." He said, "Obviously, there's things I'm not going to know." So then I added a few things, but then once Josh got hold of it, that's when it really took off.

Josh and I talked about doing an Australian character that feels truly Australian and doesn't feel like it's been compromised by trying to be a bit homogenised and for the worlds ears. The studio never put any pressure on us, they just loved him for who he was, they loved the Australian-ness of him and they loved how funny he was.

Every character we wanted to be authentic. Whether we were casting a Chinese person to play Chinese character, a Japanese person to play Japanese, (Tadanobu) Asano for Raiden, and Hiroyuki Sanada for Scorpion/Honzo, each of these characters needed to be authentic and Kano was no different.

So Josh, and I said to each other, just be really Australian. Much of the dialogue is Josh's improv. We had the skeleton of the script, and he knew what was the need of the scene and what he needed to be talking about, Josh is incredibly experienced and gifted and got such great comedic timing. He had never really played someone who was a psychopath and comedic so for him, he can be such a nice guy and such a sweet guy, so the psychopathic, aggressive, horrible, dreadful side of Kano was not Josh at all, but the comedic side is Josh and he's got that wonderful sense of timing. So I just let him go. I just said, "Go for it, mate." And it was just all Josh, he's a talent.

It really works so well. There's the Australian-ism and the ocker nature of being charming and nice and kind and that fine balance of being, Mick Taylor from Wolf Creek. It's a brilliant blend there, and the comedy works absolutely perfectly. Congratulations on that. Going forward for you, as more of these kinds of productions come into play, would you suggest or recommend that they be made in Australia? Is that your plan going forward as a filmmaker?

SMcQ: There's always many forces at play on how and where to make a film. One of them is what's creatively right for the script. One of them what's financially right for the budget. And then you've also got to look at where the talent lies to be able to bring and realize a vision to the screen. And at the moment, Australia has all three things going for it.

Depending upon what the script is that would that would inform it, that might be the only thing that would suggest going somewhere else but it's such a varied place Australia, there's so much we can get done here. And now that Perth is building a new soundstage, which is going to be fantastic. I've been a little bit of part of that process of helping those guys to work out the best way to want to put they're really going to bring Western Australia and Perth into the into the picture massively.

My goal is just to continue the harness what Australia has to offer. I think the Australian film industry at the moment has an incredibly bright next decade in front of it, and that's very exciting to me. I feel very lucky.

AUSTRALIAN FILMS OF 2021

AUSTRALIAN FILMS OF 2021

Over the next few pages are the credits for the Aussie Film Class of 2021.

All efforts have been made to include the Australian films released during 2021, however there may be instances where films have been missed.

Credits have been retrieved from IMDb. Films are made by more than the people credited below, so we urge you to seek out their entries on IMDb to see the full credits list of creatives on the film.

2067
Director: Seth Larney; Writer: Seth Larney; Cast: Kodi Smit-McPhee, Ryan Kwanten, Sana'a Shaik, Aaron Glenane, Leeanna Walsman, Deborah Mailman; Producers: Kate Croser, Lisa Shaunessy, Jason Taylor; Music: Kenneth Lampl, Kirsten Axelholm; Cinematography: Denson Baker; Editor: Sean Lahiff

A FIRE INSIDE
Directors: Justin Krook, Luke Mazzaferro; Writers: Justin Krook, Luke Mazzaferro, Nick Worthington; Featuring: Ian Aitken, Nathan Barnden, John Brogden, Shane Fitzsimmons, Victoria Herrera; Producers: Michael Hilliard, Camilla Mazzaferro, Casey Ventura; Music: Matteo Zingales; Cinematography: Josh Flavell; Editor: Scott Walmsley

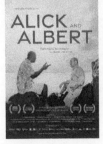

ALICK AND ALBERT
Director: Douglas Watkin; Writers: Trish Lake, Alick Tipoti, Douglas Watkin; Featuring: Prince Albert of Monaco, Alick Tipoti; Producers: Trish Lake, Meredith Garlick; Music: Glen Hunt, Will Kepa, Tane Matheson; Cinematography: Mark Broadbent, Richard Fitzpatrick, Sylvain Peroumal, Lucas Tomoana; Editors: Sue Schweikert, Scott Walton

AN IMPROBABLE COLLECTION

Director: Bruce Beresford; Writer: Bruce Beresford; Cinematography: Cordelia Beresford; Editor: Mark Warner; Music: George Ellis; Narrator: Nicholas Hammond

ARAATIKA: RISE UP

Director: Larissa Behrendt; Writer: Larissa Behrendt; Featuring: Adam Goodes, Stan Grant, Dean Widders, Preston Campbell; Producer: Sam Griffin; Cinematography: Anna Howard, Justine Kerrigan; Editor: Andrea Lang

ASCENDANT

Director: Antaine Furlong; Writers: Antaine Furlong, Kieron Holland; Cast: Charlotte Best, Jonny Pasvolsky, Andrew Jack, Susan Prior, Karelina Clarke; Producers: Drew Bailey, Antaine Furlong, James M. Vernon, Kristy Vernon; Music: David Hirschfelder; Cinematography: Frank Flick; Editor: Jonathan Tappin

ASTRO LOCO

Director: Aaron McJames; Writer: Aaron McJames; Cast: David Argue, Jon Reep, Hayley Dallimore, Frank Handrum, Dasha Naumova; Producers: Craig A. Kocinski, Kris Maric, Aaron McJames; Music: Matt Bissett-Johnson, Tim Johnson; Cinematography: Nick McLean; Editor: Patrick Troy

BACK TO THE OUTBACK

Directors: Harry Cripps, Claire Knight; Writers: Harry Cripps, Gregory Lessans; Voice Cast: Isla Fisher, Tim Minchin, Eric Bana, Guy Pearce, Miranda Tapsell, Keith Urban, Jack Charles; Producer: Daniela Mazzucato; Music: Rupert Gregson-Williams; Editor: Marcus Taylor

BATOOR: A REFUGEE JOURNEY
Director: Barat Ali Batoor; Writers: Gin Kai Chan, Justin Deimen, Ian White; Featuring: Barat Ali Batoor; Producers: Justin Deimen, Jeremy Sim; Cinematography: Barat Ali Batoor, Gwyn Lau; Editor: Oliver Jeyrald Lee

BEAUTIFUL THEY
Director: Cloudy Rhodes; Writer: Cloudy Rhodes; Cast: Sariah Saibu, Morgan Davies; Producer: Ella Millard; Music: Freya Berkhout; Cinematography: Jordan Maddocks; Editor: Stewart Arnott

BIG DEAL
Director: Craig Reucassel; Featuring: Christiaan Van Vuuren, Malcolm Turnbull, Katharine Murphy, Sam Dastyari; Producer: Aline Jacques; Music: Michael Allen, Cameron McKenzie; Cinematography: Toby Ralph; Editor: Philippa Rowlands

BIRTH TIME
Directors: Zoe Naylor, Jo Hunter, Jerusha Sutton; Writers: Jo Hunter, Zoe Naylor, Jerusha Sutton; Featuring: Zoe Naylor, Aaron Jeffrey, Jerusha Sutton, Jo Hunter; Producers: Zoe Naylor, Jo Hunter, Jerusha Sutton; Music: Paul Prestipino; Cinematography: Jerusha Sutton; Editors: Ryan Harrison, Jerusha Sutton

BRAZEN HUSSIES
Director: Catherine Dwyer; Writer: Catherine Dwyer; Featuring: Elizabeth Reid, Anne Summers, Pat O'Shane, Matha Ansara; Producers: Philippa Campey, Andrea Foxworthy; Music: Amanda Brown; Cinematography: Erika Addis, Sky Davies, Anna Howard; Editor: Rosie Jones

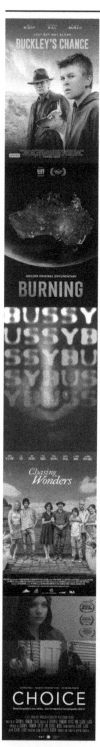

BUCKLEY'S CHANCE

Director: Tim Brown; Writers: Willem Wennekers, Tim Brown; Cast: Bill Nighy, Victoria Hill, Kelton Pell, Martin Sacks, Milan Burch; Producers: Gilbert Adler, Tim Brown, Scott Clayton, Todd Giroux, Andrew Mann; Music: Christopher Gordon; Cinematography: Ben Nott; Editors: Jon Anctil, John Scott

BURNING

Director: Eva Orner; Featuring: Mike Cannon-Brookes, Daisy Jeffrey, Michael Harrington, Tim Flannery, Scott Morrison; Producers: Jason Byrne, Eva Orner, Jonathan Schaerf; Music: Pascal Babare, Thomas Rouch, Cornel Wilczek; Cinematography: Greg Harrington; Editors: Forrest Borie, Kimberley Hassett, Dave Shulman

BUSSY

Directors: Morgan Davies, Felix Gerber, Stella Bennett; Writer: Alan Smithee; Cast: Felix Gerber, Morgan Davies, Stella Bennett, Kiki Smith; Producer: Kiki Smith; Music: Greyson Chance

CHASING WONDERS

Director: Paul Meins; Writer: Judy Morris; Cast: Paz Vega, Edward James Olmos, Jessica Marais, Carmen Maura, Antonio de la Torre; Producers: Stewart Le Marechal, Anna Mohr-Pietsch, Hilton Nathanson, Louise Nathanson, Anna Vincent; Music: Ilan Eshkeri, KT Tunstall; Cinematography: Denson Baker; Editor: Nicolas Gaster

CHOICE

Directors: Sharnya Yates, Claire Leach; Writer: Sharnya Yates; Cast: Sharnya Yates, Saffron Bell, Peter Bruderlin; Producers: Sharnya Yates, Carole McKee

CHOPPER

Director: Andrew Dominik; Writer: Andrew Dominik (based on the books by Mark Brandon Read); Cast: Eric Bana, Vince Colosimo, Kate Beahan, Simon Lyndon, David Field, Dan Wyllie, Renee Brack; Producers: Michele Bennett, Michael Gudinski; Music: Mick Harvey; Cinematography: Geoffrey Hall, Kevin Hayward; Editing: Ken Sallows

CHRISTMAS ON THE FARM

Christopher Weekes; Writer: Jennifer Notas Shapiro; Cast: Poppy Montgomery, Darren McMullen, Hugh Sheridan, Nicholas Brown, Jeanette Cronin; Producer: Nathan Mayfield, Tracey Robertson, Tracey Vieira; Music: Ack Kinmonth; Cinematography: Jason Hargreaves; Editor: Christopher Beeson

CROSSING PATHS

Director: JJ Winlove; Writer: JJ Winlove; Cast: Ariel Donoghue, Adam Dunn, Benedict Hardie, Johnny Lahoud, Zara Michaels; Producers: Emily Bull, Libby Hams, JJ Winlove; Music: Alison Cole, Dave Smith; Cinematography: Jonathan Tyler; Editor: Alexandre Guterres

CRY OF THE FORESTS

Director: Jane Hammond; Featuring: Kelton Pell

DAISY QUOKKA: WORLD'S SCARIEST ANIMAL

Director: Ricard Cussó; Writers: Ryan Greaves, Trudy Hellier; Voice Cast: Angourie Rice, Sam Neill, Frank Woodley, Richard Wilkins, Sharnee Tones; Producers: Nadine Bates, Kristen Souvlis; Music: Ack Kinmonth; Editor: Michelle McGilvray

DISCLOSURE

Director: Michael Bentham; Writer: Michael Bentham; Cast:
Geraldine Hakewill, Mark Leonard Winter, Matilda Ridgway, Tom
Wren; Producer: Donna Lyon; Music: Tony Dupé; Cinematography:
Mark Carey; Editor: Ryan Wade Howard

DRY WINTER

Director: Kyle Davis; Writer: Bridget McDonald; Cast: Courtney
Kelly, Andrew Phillips, Michael Harpas; Producer: Michael Harpas;
Cinematography: Gere Fuss; Editor: Gere Fuss

DWARF PLANET

Director: Adrian Chiarella; Writer: Adrian Chiarella; Cast: Jaxon
Graham-Wilson, Alex Rowe; Producers: Katie Amos, Bec Janek;
Music: Freya Berkhout; Cinematography: Michael Filocamo;
Editor: Danielle Boesenberg

EACH OTHER

Director: Oskar Weimar; Writer: Oskar Weimar; Cast: Jack Riley;
Producer: Oskar Weimar; Cinematography: Bernard Winter;
Editor: Oskar Weimar

EVERYBODY GETS STABBED

Director: Levon J. Polinelli; Writers: Daniel Buckle, Nick Pages-
Oliver, Levon J. Polinelli; Cast: Daniel Buckle, Nick Pages-Oliver,
Jayden Arts, Grace Johnson, Mikaela Johnson; Producers:
Tanya Dharmapala, Levon J. Polinelli; Music: Ash Gibson Greig;
Cinematography: Sergio Zanello; Editor: Levon J. Polinelli

FINDING JEDDA

Director: Tanitha Glynn-Maloney; Writer: Tanitha Glynn-Maloney; Cast: Siobhan Breaden, Amarlie Briscoe, Marta Dusseldorp, Benjamin Winspear, Teigan McCarty; Producers: Tanitha Glynn-Maloney, Meg O'Connell, Dan Lake; Music: Freya Berkhout; Cinematography: Tyson Perkins; Editor: Elliott Magen

FIRESTARTER: THE STORY OF BANGARRA

Directors: Wayne Blair, Nel Minchin; Writer: Nel Minchin; Featuring: David Page, Stephen Page, Russell Page; Producer: Ivan O'Mahoney; Cinematography: Andy Taylor; Editors: Karen Johnson, Nick Meyers

FIST OF FURY NOONGAR DAA

Directors: Wei Lo, Kylie Bracknell; Voices: Kyle J Morrison, Clint Bracknell, Kylie Bracknell, Shontane Farmer, Michael Fuller, Peter Humphries, Denzel Humphries

FREEDOM SWIMMERS

Director: Olivia Martin McGuire; Writer: Olivia Martin McGuire; Producer: Brooke Silcox

FREEMAN

Director: Laurence Billiet, Stephen Page; Writer: Laurence Billiet; Featuring: Cathy Freeman, Lillian Banks, Cecelia Barber, Peter Fortune, Bruce McAvaney; Producers: Helen Panckhurst, Laurence Billiet

FRIENDS AND STRANGERS

Director: James Vaughan; Writer: James Vaughan; Cast: Fergus Wilson, Emma Diaz, Amelia Conway, Malcolm Kennard, Greg Zimbulis; Producers: Rebecca Lamond, Lucy Rennick; Cinematography: Dimitri Zaunders; Editor: James Vaughan

GIRL LIKE YOU

Directors: Frances Elliott, Samantha Marlowe; Writers: Frances Elliott, Samantha Marlowe; Featuring: Lauren Black, Elloise Walsh; Producer: Cody Greenwood; Music: Ned Beckley; Cinematography: Toby Hoffman, Editors: Frances Elliott, Samantha Marlowe

GIRLS CAN'T SURF

Director: Christopher Nelius; Writers: Julie-Anne De Ruvo, Christopher Nelius; Featuring: Pam Burridge, Lisa Andersen, Rochelle Ballard, Pauline Menczer, Layne Beachley, Wendy Botha; Producers: Christopher Nelius, Michaela Perske; Music: Haydn Walker; Cinematography: Anna Howard; Editor: Julie-Anne De Ruvo

GODZILLA VS. KONG

Director: Adam Wingard; Writers: Terry Rossio, Michael Dougherty, Zach Shields; Cast: Alexander Skarsgård, Millie Bobby Brown, Rebecca Hall, Brian Tyree Henry; Producers: Alex Garcia, Jon Jashni, Eric McLeod, Mary Parent, Brian Rogers, Thomas Tull; Music: Junkie XL; Cinematography: Ben Seresin; Editor: Josh Schaeffer

GOOD FOR NOTHING BLUES

Director: Alexander Lorian, Writer: Alexander Lorian; Cast: Cody Brown, Andrea Lim, Bryce Myles Fenwick, Rhys Hyatt, Blake del Popolo, James Broadhurst; Producer: Elle Cahill; Cinematography: Alexander Lorian; Editor: Alexander Lorian

GOODY GOODY GUMDROPS

Directors: Tropical Fuck Storm, Nina Renee; Featuring: Gareth Liddiard, Fiona Kitschin, Lauren Hammel, Erica Dunn

GREAT WHITE

Director: Martin Wilson; Writer: Michael Boughen; Cast: Katrina Bowden, Aaron Jakubenko, Kimie Tsukakoshi, Tim Kano; Producers: Pam Collis, Neal Kingston, Michael Robertson; Music: Tim Count; Cinematography: Tony O'Loughlan; Editor: Lawrie Silvestrin

HATING PETER TATCHELL

Director: Christopher Amos; Writer: Christopher Amos; Featuring: Peter Tatchell, Sir Ian McKellen, Stephen Fry, George Carey; Producers: Christopher Amos, Veronica Fury, Lee Matthews; Music: Paul Arnold, Andrew Barnabas; Editor: Bergen O'Brien

HIGH GROUND

Director: Stephen Johnson; Writer: Chris Anastassiades; Cast: Sean Mununggurr, Jacob Junior Nayinggul, Simon Baker, Ryan Corr, Caren Pistorius, Jack Thompson, Aaron Pedersen, Callan Mulvey; Producers: David Jowsey, Maggie Miles, Greer Simpkin; Cinematography: Andrew Commis; Editors: Jill Bilcock, Hayley Miro Browne, Karryn de Cinque; Music: Miriam Ashley, Witiyana Marika, Arian Bambung Pearson, Jan Skubiszewski

HISTORY BITES BACK

Directors: Craig Anderson, Trisha Morton-Thomas; Writers: Craig Anderson, Trisha Morton-Thomas; Featuring: Clayton Bailey, Annette Bray, Elaine Crombie, Rachel Clements, Steven Oliver; Producers: Rachel Clements, Meredith Garlick, Bridget May, Trisha Morton-Thomas; Editor: Craig Anderson

I MET A GIRL

Director: Luke Eve; Writer: Glen Dolman; Cast: Brenton Thwaites, Joel Jackson, Lily Sullivan, Zahra Newman, Peter Rowsthorn, Kylie Bracknell; Producer: Adam Dolman; Music: Matteo Zingales; Cinematography: Patrick O'Sullivan; Editor: Melanie Annan

I'M WANITA

Director: Jonathan Alley; Writer: Jonathan Alley; Featuring: Jill Birt, D.B.C. Pierre, David McComb, Richard Kingsmill, Paul Kelly, Joanne Alach; Producers: Tait Brady, Danielle Karalus; Cinematography: Danielle Karalus; Editor: Tony Stevens

IN AUSTRALIA

Director: Miley Tunnecliffe; Writer: Miley Tunnecliffe; Cast: Karin Kowi, Ben Mortley, Gemma Sharpe, Michael Rainone, Michael Muntz; Producer: Emilia Jolakoska; Music: Stephen Callan; Cinematography: Jim Frater; Editor: Caitlan O'Connor

INCARCERATION NATION

Director: Dean Gibson; Writer: Dean Gibson; Featuring: Leetona Dungay, Karina Holden, Amy McQuire, Keenan Mundine, Chelsea Watego; Producers: Mitzi Goldman, Bronwyn Ketels, Helen Morrison, Kurt Roynan; Music: Tane Matheson, Peter Thornley, Glen Hunt; Cinematography: Mark Broadbent; Editor: Lindi Harrison

INFERNO

Director: Katherine Chediak Putnam; Writer: Katherine Chediak Putnam, Dean W. Law; Cast: Sam Cotton, Melinda Joan Reed, John McNeill, Keiran McGinlay, Karen Pudlyk

INFERNO WITHOUT BORDERS

Directors: Sandrine Charruyer, Sophie Lepowic; Writer: Sophie Lepowic; Producers: Laura Sivis, Sandrine Charruyer, Sophie Lepowic

IT'LL BE OVER SOON

Director: Benjamin Rigby; Writer: Benjamin Rigby; Cast: Benjamin Rigby, Robyn Rigby, Harry Thompson; Producer: Benjamin Rigby; Cinematography: Daren vinson crawford; Editor: Martin Sharpe

JAIMEN HUDSON: FROM SKY TO SEA

Director: Leighton De Barros; Writer: Leighton De Barros; Featuring: Jaimen Hudson, Jess Hudson, Leighton De Barros; Producers: Leighton De Barros, Jodie De Barros; Music: Sean Tinnion; Cinematography: Jaimen Hudson, Leighton De Barros; Editor: Jonathan Rowdon

JANE

Director: Noel Vinson; Writer: Noel Vinson; Cast: Roger Ward, Jacki Mison, Yasmin Polley; Producer: Noel Vinson; Music: Matthew Hamm; Cinematography: Robert C. Morton; Editors: Abel Robinson, Noel Vinson

JEANETTE IS THE DOG

Director: Pat Mooney; Writer: Pat Mooney; Featuring: Tamara Natt, Hannah Camilleri, Josh Glanc, Dianne Valente; Producer: Lucie McMahon; Music: Pat Mooney, Nathaniel Currie, Alexandrew Lourie; Cinematography: Thom Neal; Editor: Mitch Goldberg

JOHN FARROW: HOLLYWOOD'S MAN IN THE SHADOWS

Directors: Claude Gonzalez, Frans Vandenburg; Featuring: John Farrow, Phillip Noyce, David Stratton, Margaret Pomeranz; Producers: Claude Gonzalez, Frans Vandenburg; Music: Sam Petty; Cinematography: Susan Lumsdon; Editors: Antoinette Ford, Walter McIntosh

JUNE AGAIN

Director: JJ Winlove; Writer: JJ Winlove; Cast: Noni Hazlehurst, Claudia Karvan, Stephen Curry, Wayne Blair, Di Adams, Nash Edgerton; Producer: Drew Bailey, Jamie Hilton, Michael Pontin; Music: Christopher Gordon; Cinematography: Hugh Miller; Editor: Mark Warner

KIDNAPPED

Director: Vic Sarin; Writer: Shanrah Wakefield; Cast: Claire van der Boom, Lynn Gilmartin, Todd Lasance, Melina Vidler; Producers: Steve Jaggi, Spencer McLaren, Tina Pehme, Kim Roberts; Cinematography: Simon Harding; Editor: Trent Mitchell

LAURA'S CHOICE

Directors: Cathy Henkel, Sam Lara; Writers: Cathy Henkel, Sam Lara; Featuring: Laura Henkel, Cathy Henkel, Sam Lara; Producers: Cathy Henkel, Ryan Hodgson, Melissa Kelly, Sam Lara; Music: Nicolette Boaz; Cinematography: Cathy Henkel, Sam Lara, Mahmudul Raz, Patrick Wally; Editor: Nicholas Dunlop

LIKE THE WIND

Director: Ted McDonnell; Featuring: Christopher Doyle, Rain Li, Phillip Noyce; Producers: Nelson Khoury, Nelson Yap; Music: Jonny Driver; Editor: Notey Viriyarat

LONG STORY SHORT

Director: Josh Lawson; Writer: Josh Lawson; Cast: Rafe Spall, Zahra Newman, Ronny Chieng, Noni Hazlehurst, Josh Lawson, Dena Kaplan; Producer: Jamie Hilton, Michael Pontin, Isabel Stanfield; Music: Chiara Costanza; Cinematography: Matt Toll; Editor: Kasra Rassoulzadegan

LOVE AND MONSTERS

Director: Michael Matthews; Writers: Brian Duffield, Matthew Robinson; Cast: Dylan O'Brien, Jessica Henwick, Dan Ewing, Michael Rooker, Bruce Spence; Producers: Dan Cohen, Shawn Levy; Music: Marco Beltrami, Marcus Trumpp; Cinematography: Lachlan Milne; Editors: Debbie Berman, Nancy Richardson

LOVE IN BRIGHT LANDSCAPES

Director: Jonathan Alley; Writer: Jonathan Alley; Featuring: David McComb, Jill Birt, Dave Faulkner, D.B.C. Pierre, Paul Kelly; Producers: Tait Brady, Danielle Karalus; Cinematography: Danielle Karalus; Editor: Tony Stevens

LOVE YOU LIKE THAT

Director: Eric C. Nash; Writer: Eric C. Nash; Cast: Allia Jaques, Mitchell Hope, John Jarratt, Steph Tisdell, Chris Haywood; Producers: Sean Gannon, Patrick Kriz, Eric C. Nash; Music: Mark Smythe; Cinematography: Robert Draper; Editor: Paul Black

MAYA THE BEE: THE GOLDEN ORB

Directors: Noel Cleary, Writers: Adrian Bickenbach, Noel Clearly, Fin Edquist, Tess Meyer, Adam Rainford; Voice Cast: Coco Jack Gillies, Benson Jack Anthony, Tess Meyer, Justine Clarke, Jimmy James Eaton; Producers: Benjamin Ey, Tracy Lenon; Music: Ute Engelhardt; Editor: Adam Rainford

MEET THE WALLERS

Director: Jim Stevens; Featuring: Emily Waller, Jasmine Waller, Mark Waller, Nicola Waller; Producers: Lav Bodnaruk, Michael Mier, Gil Scrine, Jim Stevens; Cinematography: Jim Stevens; Editor: Michael Craft

MEASURE FOR MEASURE

Director: Paul Ireland; Writers: Damian Hill, Paul Ireland, (based on the play by William Shakespeare); Cast: Hugo Weaving, Daniel Henshall, Mark Leonard Winter, Doris Younane, Fayssal Bazzi, Malcolm Kennard, John Brumpton, Megan Smart; Producers: Damian Hill, Paul Ireland; Music: Tristan Dewey, Tai Jordan; Cinematography: Ian Jones: Editor: Gary Woodyard

MORTAL KOMBAT

Director: Simon McQuoid; Writers: Greg Russo, Dave Callaham, (Story by Oren Uziel, Greg Russo, based on the videogame by Ed Boon, John Tobias); Cast: Joe Taslim, Jessica McNamee, Josh Lawson, Lewis Tan, Mehcad Brooks, Tadanobu Asano, Hiroyuki Sanada; Producers: Simon McQuoid, E. Bennett Walsh, James Wans; Music: Benjamin Wallfisch; Cinematography: Germain McMicking; Editors: Scott Gray, Dan Lebental

MY CHERRY PIE

Directors: Addison Heath, Jasmine Jakupi; Writer: Addison Heath; Cast: Sotiris Tzelios, Trudi Ranik, Nadia Hunter, Cris Cochrane, Glenn Maynard, Anthony Lindsay; Producers: Addison Heath, Dylan Heath, Jasmine Jakupi; Music: Jesse Breckon-Thomas, Jacob Richards; Cinematography: Jasmie Jakupi; Editor: Addison Heath

MY FIRST SUMMER

Director: Katie Found; Writer: Katie Found; Cast: Markella Kavenagh, Maiah Stewardson, Arthur Angel, Katherine Tonkin, Edwina Wren; Producers: Jonathan auf der Heide, Alisha Hnatjuk; Music: Kyle Morton; Cinematography: Matthew Chuang; Editor: Annabelle Johnson

MY NAME IS GULPILIL

Director: Molly Reynolds; Writers: Molly Reynolds, Rolf de Heer; Featuring: David Gulpilil, Sara Bailey, Mary Reefed, Jack Thompson; Producers: David Gulpilil, Peter Djigirr, Rolf de Heer, Molly Reynolds; Music: Tom Heuzenroeder; Cinematography: Maxx Corkindale, Miles Rowland; Editor: Tania Nehme

NEST

Director: James Hunter; Writer: Steve Anthopoulos; Cast: Lasarus Ratuere, Ana Thu Nguyen, Kevin Ryan, Robbie Durrant; Producer: Faith Guoga; Music: Mitchell Sloan; Cinematography: Campbell Brown; Editors: James Hunter, Shannon Michaelas

NIGHT OF THE HUNSTMAN

Director: James Dudfield; Cast: Christopher Moro, Prea Cunningham, Vanessa Cobbs, Sebastian Smith, Jack Hopgood; Producer: Grace Stevenson; Music: Milo Paulus; Cinematography: Connor Fantasia-Serve, Nitzan Hanin

NIGHT SHIFT

Director: Joey Menzel; Writer: Joey Menzel; Cast: Jesse Morton, Georgia Walters, Anthony Winnick, Rueben Jacob, Louis Dickens; Producers: Michael Whyntie, Luke Woodhouse; Cinematography: Pedro D.T. Pinto; Editor: Joey Menzel

NITRAM

Director: Justin Kurzel; Writer: Shaun Grant; Cast: Caleb Landry Jones, Judy Davis, Anthony LaPaglia, Essie Davis; Producers: Nick Batzias, Shaun Grant, Justin Kurzel, Virginia Whitwell; Music: Jed Kurzel; Cinematography: Germain McMicking; Editor: Nick Fenton

OCCUPATION: RAINFALL

Luke Sparke; Writer: Luke Sparke; Cast: Dan Ewing, Temeura Morrison, Dan Gillies, Mark Coles Smith, Ken Jeong, Jason Isaacs; Producers: Carly Imrie, Carmel Imrie; Music: Frederik Wiedmann; Cinematography: Wade Muller; Editor: Luke Sparke

OFF COUNTRY

Directors: Rhian Skirving, John Harvey; Writers: Rhian Skirving, John Harvey; Producers: Rhian Skirving, John Harvey, Nick Batzias, Charlotte Wheaton

PALAZZO DI COZZO

Director: Madeleine Martiniello; Writer: Madeleine Martiniello; Featuring: Franco Cozzo, Don Lane; Producers: Philippa Campey, Samantha Dinning; Music: Antony Partos; Cinematography: Vincent Lamberti; Editors: Rosie Jones, Jane Usher

PAPER CITY

Adrian Francis; Producer: Melanie Brunt; Cinematography: Brett Ludeman; Editors: Luca Cappelli, Adrian Francis

PENGUIN BLOOM

Director: Glendyn Ivin; Writers: Shaun Grant, Harry Cripps; Cast: Naomi Watts, Griffin Murray-Johnston, Andrew Lincoln, Jacki Weaver, Rachel House; Producers: Emma Cooper, Steve Hutensky, Jodi Matterson, Bruna Papandrea, Naomi Watts; Music: Marcelo Zarvos; Cinematography: Sam Chiplin; Editor: Maria Papoutsis

PETER RABBIT 2: THE RUNAWAY

Director: Will Gluck; Writers: Will Gluck, Patrick Burleigh; Cast: Rose Byrne, Domhnall Gleeson, David Oyelowo, James Corden, Margot Robbie; Producers: Catherine Bishop, Will Gluck, Jodi Hildebrand, Zareh Nalbandian; Music: Dominic Lewis; Cinematography: Peter Menzies Jr.; Editor: Matt Villa

PLAYING WITH SHARKS

Director: Sally Aitken; Writer: Sally Aitken; Featuring: Valerie Taylor, Jeremiah S. Sullivan, Ron Taylor, Rodney Fox; Producer: Bettina Dalton; Music: Caitlin Yeo; Cinematography: Nathan Barlow, Michael Latham, Judd Overton, Toby Ralph, Ron Taylor; Editor: Adrian Rostirolla

PROM NIGHT

Director: Lydia Rui; Writer: Lydia Rui; Cast: Diane Gray; Producer: Lydia Rui; Cinematography: Lukáš Bistrickÿ; Editor: Mira Thu

PUFF: WONDERS OF THE REEF

Director: Nick Robinson; Writers: Peta Ayers, Nick Robinson; Voice: Rose Byrne; Producers: Peta Ayers, Nick Robinson, Daniel Stoupin, Pete West; Cinematography: Pete West

REFUSED CLASSIFICATION

Director: Chris Elena; Writers: Chris Elena, Bradford Elmore; Cast: Gabrielle Scawthorn, Bernie Van Tiel, David Whitney, Sam O'Sullivan, Angela Elmore; Cinematography: Kym Vaitiekus; Editor: Kym Vaitiekus

REPTILE

Director: Jordan Giusti; Writer: Jordan Giusti; Cast: Alex Prokos, Peter Krokos, Luka Rhoderick, Marcel Laidlaw; Producers: Chris Luscri, Hayley Surgenor; Music: Louis Marlo; Cinematography: Bonita Carzino; Editor: Jordan Giusti

RHAPSODY OF LOVE

Director: Joy Hopwood; Writer: Joy Hopwood; Cast: Amanda Benson, Jessica Niven, Khan Chittenden, Lily Stewart, Kathy Luu; Producer: Ana Tiwary; Music: Roy Nicolson; Cinematography: Goldie Soetianto; Editor: Jon Cohen

ROMANCE ON THE MENU

Director: Rosie Lourde; Writers: Alison Spuck McNeeley, Casie Tabanou; Cast: Cindy Busby, Tim Ross, Naomi Sequeira, Joey Vieria, Marita Wilcox; Producers: Steve Jaggi, Spencer McLaren; Music: Jazz D'Arcy; Cinematography: Jason Hargreaves; Editors: Charlotte Cutting, Adrian Powers

SAME TIME MONDAY

Director: Russell Wyatt Roberts; Writer: Russell Wyatt Roberts; Cast: Steve Bisley, Liv Richardson; Cinematography: Connor Fantasia-Serve

SHALLOW BREATH

Director: Robbie Studsor; Writer: Robbie Studsor; Cast: Belinda Lack, Casey Layne Mannix; Producer: Robbie Studsor; Music: Matt Adair, Nick Wilson; Cinematography: Garry Richards; Editor: Robbie Studsor

SHANG-CHI AND THE LEGEND OF THE TEN RINGS
Director: Destin Daniel Cretton; Writers: Dave Callaham, Destin Daniel Cretton, Andrew Lanham; Cast: Simu Liu, Awkwafina, Tony Leung, Ronny Chieng, Michelle Yeoh; Producers: Kevin Feige, Jonathan Schwartz; Music: Joel P West; Cinematography: Bill Pope; Editors: Elísabet Ronaldsdóttir, Nat Sanders, Harry Yoon

SHARK
Director: Nash Edgerton; Writers: Nash Edgerton, David Michôd; Cast: Nash Edgerton, Rose Byrne, Kieran Darcy-Smith, Brendan Donoghue, Krew Boylan; Producer: Michele Bennett; Cinematography: Aaron McLisky; Editor: David Whittaker

SIT. STAY. LOVE.
Director: Tori Garrett; Writer: Holly Hester; Cast: Georgia Flood, Ezekiel Simat, Kaushik Das, Anthony Phelan, Christine Amor; Producers: Steve Jaggi, Spencer McLaren, Kelly Son Hing; Music: Craig McConnell; Cinematography: HB Gibson; Editor: Charlotte Cutting

SPARKLES
Director: Jacqueline Pelczar; Writer: Tina Fielding; Cast: Tina Fielding, Gary Cooper, Chandra Wyatt, Siria Kickett; Producer: Cody Greenwood; Music: Sean Tinnion; Cinematography: Michael McDermott; Editor: Elaine Smith

STEP INTO PARADISE
Director: Amanda Blue; Writers: Amanda Blue, Jacob Hickey; Featuring: Anthea Donaldson, Emma Gore, Mali Alexiou, Yaya Deng, Rika Hamaguchi; Producers: Darren Dale, Fran Moore; Music: Amanda Brown, Nick Wales; Cinematography: Bonnie Elliott; Editor: Jane Usher

STREAMLINE

Director: Tyson Wade Johnston; Writer: Tyson Wade Johnston; Cast: Levi Miller, Jake Ryan, Laura Gordon, Jason Isaacs, Steve Bastoni, Tasia Zalar; Producers: Jay Douglas, Blake Northfield, Nathan Walker; Music: Angela Little; Cinematography: Michael Latham; Editor: Stephen Evans

STRONG FEMALE LEAD

Director: Tosca Looby; Editor: Rachel Grierson-Johns; Featuring: Julia Gillard; Music: Robert Davidson; Producers: Laura Grace, Karina Holden

STUFFINGS

Director: Mathew J. Wilkinson; Writer: Mathew J. Wilkinson; Cast: Kathleen Halligan, Daniel Moody, Isabella Robinson, Ognjen Trisic, Marcello D'Onofrio; Music: David Paul Saunders; Editor: Mathew J. Wilkinson

SUNBURN

Director: Jaslyn Mairs; Writer: Claudia Bailey; Cast: Brenna Harding, Zoe Terakes; Producers: Ben Bauchet, Lev Jutsen; Cinematography: Gabriel Morrison; Editor: Angus Roche

SUNSET COUNTRY

Director: Petra Leslie; Writer: Petra Leslie; Cast: Chris Davies, Raelee Hill, Trevor Hanna; Producer: Georgina Wills; Music: James Mountain; Cinematography: Peter Leslie; Editor: James Taylor

TALL POPPY: A SKATER'S STORY

Director: Justine Moyle; Writers: Justine Moyle, Emily O'Connell;
Featuring: Poppy Starr Olsen, Kameron Hood; Producer: Jo Austin;
Music: Ben Corbett, John Vella; Cinematography: Dane Howell;
Editor: Rolando Olalia

TELEVISION EVENT

Director: Jeff Daniels; Featuring: Nichola Meyer, Ted Koppel,
Stephanie Austin, Ellen Anthony, Stu Samuels; Producers:
Jeff Daniels, Ozzy Inguanzo, Amanda Spain; Music: T. Griffin;
Cinematography: Nick Albert, Bryan Donnell, Nick Higgins; Editors:
Eileen Meyer, Aaron Wickenden

THE BENDS

Director: Tom Campbell; Writers: Adam Spellicy, Tom Campbell,
Annie Thatcher; Cast: Annie Thatcher, Carter Mitchell, Thomas
Ruderman; Producer: Alexandra George; Music: Mikey Young;
Cinematography: Sam Chiplin; Editor: Maria Papoutsis

THE BOWRAVILLE MURDERS

Director: Allan Clarke; Producers: Adam Kay, Dan Goldberg, Stefan
Moore, Susan Lambert; Music: Anthony Partos; Cinematography:
Nathan Barlow; Editor: Mark Middis

THE CHILDREN IN THE PICTURES

Directors: Simon Nasht, Akhim Dev; Writers: Simon Nasht, Akhim
Dev; Producer: Tony Wright

THE DEPARTMENT

Director: Sascha Ettinger-Epstein; Producers: Ian Darlin, Mary Macrae, Majhid Heath, Hayley Johnson, Kate Hodges; Cinematography: Sascha Ettinger-Epstein; Editors: Sally Fryer, Mat Evans

THE DRY

Director: Robert Connolly; Writers: Harry Cripps, Robert Connolly, additional writing by Samantha Strauss, (based on the book by Jane Harper); Cast: Eric Bana, Genevieve O'Reilly, Keir O'Donnell, Matt Nable, BeBe Bettencourt, Miranda Tapsell, Bruce Spence, Julia Blake; Producers: Eric Bana, Robert Connolly, Steve Hutensky, Jodi Matterson, Bruna Papandrea, Music: Peter Raeburn; Cinematography: Stefan Duscio; Editors: Alexandre de Franceschi, Nick Meyes

THE GREENHOUSE

Director: Thomas Wilson-White; Writer: Thomas Wilson-White; Cast: Harriet Gordon-Anderson, Rhondda Findleton, Joel Horwood, Camilla Ah Kin, Kirsty Marillier, Shiv Palekar, Jane Watt; Producer: Lizzie Cater; Music: Freya Berkhout; Cinematography: Daniel Bolt; Editors: Kelly Cameron, Christine Cheung

THE LAST HORNS OF AFRICA

Director: Garth De Bruno Austin; Writer: Sean Viljoen; Featuiring: Don English, Petronel Nieuwoudt; Producer: Morgan Pelt; Music: Sean Tinnion; Cinematography: Garth De Bruno Austin

THE MOOGAI

Director: Jon Bell; Writer: Jon Bell; Cast: Shari Sebbens, Meyne Wyatt; Producers: Kristina Ceyton, Taylor Goddard, Samantha Jennings, Mitchell Stanley; Cinematography: Sean Ryan; Editor: Simon Njoo

THE NEON ACROSS THE OCEAN
Director: Matthew Victor Pastor; Writer: Matthew Victor Pastor; Cast: Chi Nguyen, Waiyee Rivera, Corey Reason, Rachel Javier, Gregory Pakis; Producer: Evangeline Yin; Music: Corey Reason; Editor: Matthew Victor Pastor

THE POWER OF THE DOG
Director: Jane Campion; Writer: Jane Campion; Cast; Benedict Cumberbatch, Kodi Smit-Mcphee, Kirsten Dunst, Jesse Plemons; Producers: Jane Campion, Iain Canning, Roger Frappier, Tanya Seghatchian, Emile Sherman; Music: Jonny Greenwood; Cinematography: Ari Wegner; Editor: Peter Sciberras

THE RECORDIST
Directors: Indianna Bell, Josiah Allen; Writer: Indianna Bell; Cast: Brendan Rock, Jordan Cowan, Nathan O'Keefe, Joel Coveney; Producer: Ashleigh Knott; Music: Jack Davis: Cinematography: Samuel Twidale; Editor: Josiah Allen

THE RIPPLE EFFECT
Director: Peter Dickson; Writer: Peter Dickson; Featuring: Nicky Winmar, Ben Long, Bachar Houli, Nova Peris; Producer: Peter Dickson; Editor: Peter Dickson

THE SERPENT'S NEST
Director: Alice Maio Mackay; Writers: Alice Maio Mackay, Ben Pahl Robinson; Cast: Jamila Main, Felicia Tassone, Brendan Cooney, James McCluskey-Garcia, Erin Moran; Producer: Alice Maio Mackay; Music: Christopher Doucet; Cinematography: Justin Eckert, Rebecca Duncker; Editor: David Castle

THE SLAUGHTERHOUSE KILLER

Director: Sam Curtain; Writers: Sam Curtain, Benjamin Jung-Clarke; Cast: Craig Ingham, James Mason, Kristen Condon, Dean Kirkright; Producer: Sam Curtain; Music: Caleb Jacobs; Cinematography: Leuke Marriott

THE WITCH OF KINGS CROSS

Director: Sonia Bible; Writer: Sonia Bible; Featuring: Kate Elizabeth Laxton, George Gittoes, Eileen Kramer, Jack Sargeant, Graham Yates; Producers: Sonia Bible, Peter Butt; Cinematography: Eddy Gill; Editor: Sonia Bible

THE XROSSING

Director: Steven J. Mihaljevich; Writers: Carl Maiorana, Steven J. Mihaljevich; Cast: Luke J. Morgan, Kelton Pell, Georgia Eyers, Steven J. Mihaljevich, Jamie Smith; Producers: Christine Kirkness, Jag Pannu; Music: James Tumilty Leadbitter, Desmond Richardson; Cinematography: Shane Piggott; Editors: Steven Kong Mun Liew, Steven J. Mihaljevich

THIS IS PORT ADELAIDE

Director: Nicole Miller; Featuring: Nathan Buckley, John Cahill, Ken Hinkley, Fos Williams, Russell Ebert; Producer: James Moody; Music: Benjamin Speed; Cinematography: Isaac Walgos; Editor: Matt Gierke

THIS LITTLE LOVE OF MINE

Director: Christine Luby; Writer: Georgia Harrison; Cast: Saskia Hampele, Liam McIntyre, Lynn Gilmartin, Craig Horner, Tiriel Mora; Producers: Steve Jaggi, Spencer McLaren, Kelly Son Hing; Music: Jazz D'Arcy; Cinematography: Simon Harding; Editor: Charlotte Cutting

TODAY
Director: Andrew Jaksch; Writer: Philip Cristian Claassen; Cast: Tim Clarke, Jessica Tanner, Tom Farrah; Producer: Melanie Killingsworth; Music: Leon Ross; Cinematography: Mark Kenfield; Editor: Shannon Michaelas

TOUGH
Director: Taylor Ferguson; Writer: Taylor Ferguson; Cast: Mark Leonard Winter, Alex Kis, Ariel Donoghue, Falilou Tall, Logan Reberger; Producer: Eddy Bell; Music: Boy & Bear; Cinematography: Aaron McLisky; Editor: Phoebe Taylor

TWO SANDS
Director: Poppy van Oorde-Grainger; Writers: Kook Manuer, Poppy van Oorde-Grainger; Cast: Atem Dau, Garang John Deng, John Deng Geu, Tyroe Muhafidin; Producers: Lauren Brunswick, David Kucha; Music: Ned Beckley; Cinematography: Lewis Potts; Editor: Dominic Pearce

UNDER MY SKIN
Director: David O'Donnell; Writer: David O'Donnell; Cast: Liv Hewson, Chloe Freeman, Lex Ryan, Bobbi Salvör Menuez, Alex Russell, Alexis Denisof; Producers: Paul F. Bernard, Rob Gibson, Chase B. Kenney, David O'Donnell, Raynen O'Keefe, Alex Russell, Carrie Finn; Music: Evelyn Ida Morris; Cinematography: Jac Fitzgerald; Editor: Kevin Ward

UNDER THE VOLCANO
Director: Gracie Otto; Writers: Cody Greenwood, Gracie Otto, Ian Shadwell, (Joseph Nizeti, Jennifer Peedom, story consultants); Featuring: Sting, Jimmy Buffett, Mark Knopfler, Stewart Copeland, Nick Rhodes; Producer: Cody Greenwood; Music: Piers Burbrook de Vere; Cinematography: Hugh Miller; Editor: Karen Johnson

UNE BELLE JOURNÉE

Director: Malo Hawkins; Writer: Malo Hawkins; Cast: Heloïse Trouvé, Barnabe Brokensha; Producer: Daniel Woods; Music: Ruby Schofield; Cinematography: Jack Donald-McDowall; Editor: Tyler Mace

UNSEEN SKIES

Director: Yaara Bou Melhem; Writer: Yaara Bou Melhem; Featuring: Trevor Paglen, Amanda Horn; Producer: Yaara Bou Melhem; Music: Helena Czajka; Cinematography: Tom Bannigan; Editor: Francisco Forbes

UNSOUND

Director: Ian Watson; Writer: Ally Burnham; Cast: Reece Noi, Anthony Brandon Wong, Yiana Pandelis, Paual Duncan, Christine Anu, Terry Serio, Todd McKenney; Producers: Tsu Shan Chambers; Music: Mark D'Angelo; Cinematography: Kent Marcus; Editor: Scott Walmsley

WE ARE CONJOLA

Director: Anthony Ash Brennan

WE DON'T DESERVE DOGS

Director: Matthew Salleh; Producer: Rose Tucker; Music: Blake Ewing

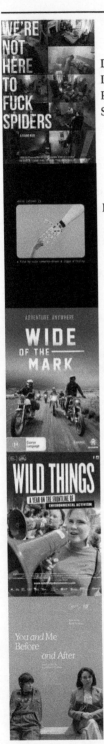

WE'RE NOT HERE TO FUCK SPIDERS

Director: Josh Reed, Writer: Josh Reed; Cast: Stephanie King, Lindsay Farris, Max Brown, Fayssal Bazzi, Anthony Taufa; Producers: Rob Gibson, Sarah-Jane McAllan; Cinematography: Steven Kirkby; Editors: Ben Nunney, Josh Reed

WHILE (ALIVE) {}

Directors: Cody Cameron-Brown, Ziggy O'Reilly

WIDE OF THE MARK

Director: Cameron Brunt; Featuring: Max Duff, Tom Gilroy, Justin Holmes, Emma Mcferran, Matty Mcferran; Producers: Cameron Brunt, Tom Gilroy; Cinematography: Jake Ashe; Editor: Jake Ashe

WILD THINGS

Director: Sally Ingleton; Producer: Sally Ingleton

YOU AND ME, BEFORE AND AFTER

Director: Madeleine Gottlieb; Writer: Madeleine Gottlieb; Cast: Yael Stone, Emily Barclay, Lily LaTorre; Producers: Liam Heyen, Cyna Strachan; Cinematography: Alex Cardy; Editor: Christine Cheung

2021 AACTA AWARDS NOMINEES AND WINNERS

BEST FILM

The Dry – Bruna Panadrea, Jodi Matterson, Steve Hutensky, Robert Connolly, Eric Bana; The Dry Film Production Pty Ltd

The Furnace – Timothy White, Tenille Kennedy; Southern Light Films & The Koop

High Ground – David Jowsey, Maggie Miles, Witiyana Marika, Greer Simpkin, Stephen Johnson; Maxo, Bunya Productions & Savage Films

***Nitram* – Nick Batzias, Virginia Whitwell, Justin Kurzel, Shaun Grant; GoodThing Productions**

Penguin Bloom – Bruna Papandrea, Steve Hutensky, Emma Cooper, Naomi Watts, Jodi Matterson; Penguin Bloom Film

Rams – Janelle Landers, Aidan O'Bryan; WBMC

BEST INDIE FILM

Disclosure – Michael Bentham (Dir.), Donna Lyon; Disclosure Films Pty Ltd

***Ellie and Abbie (& Ellie's Dead Aunt)* – Monica Zanetti (Dir.), MahVeen Shahraki, Patrick James; Brazen Lot formerly Cobbstar Productions**

Lone Wolf – Jonathan Ogilvie (Dir.), Mat Govoni, Adam White, Lee Hubber; Future Pictures & Black Frame

Moon Rock for Monday – Kurt Martin (Dir.), Jim Robison, Agnieska Switala, Aron Walker, David Bradley; Lunar Pictures

My First Summer – Katie Found (Dir.), Jonathan Auf Der Heide, Alisha Hnatjuk; Noise & Light

Under My Skin – David O'Donnell (Dir.), Raynen O'Keefe, Alex Russell, Rob Gibson; Five Lip Films

BEST DOCUMENTARY

Girls Can't Surf – Christopher Nelius (Dir.), Michaela Perske; Pursekey Productions & Finch

I'm Wanita – Matthew Walker (Dir.), Carolina Sorensen, Clare Lewis, Tait Brady; People Productions

***My Name is Gulpilil* – Molly Reynolds (Dir.), Rolf de Heer, Peter Djigirr, David Gulpilil; Vertigo Productions**

Playing With Sharks – Sally Aitken (Dir.), Bettina Dalton; WildBear Entertainment

Strong Female Lead – Tosca Looby (Dir.), Karina Holden

When the Camera Stopped Rolling – Jane Castle (Dir.), Pat Fiske; Bower Bird Films & Freckled Duck Films

BEST SHORT FORM DRAMA
Beautiful They – Cloudy Rhodes, Ella Millard; Boobook Media
The Bends – Tom Campbell, Alexandra George, Adam Spellicy, Annie Thatcher
Dwarf Planet – Adrian Chiarella, Bec Janek; Brick Road
Grace – Darren McFarlane, Brian Patto, Aaron Farrugia, Christopher Gillingham; Disturbing Notions
***The Tailings* – Liz Doran, Richard Kelly, Stephen Thomas, Stevie Cruz-Martin, Caitlin Richardson; Good Lark Pty Ltd, The Two Jons & Roar Film**
You and Me, Before and After – Madeleine Gottlieb, Liam Heyen, Cyna Strachan; Mad Ones Film

BEST SHORT FORM COMEDY
A Life in Questions: Wisdom School with Aaron Chen – Aaron Chen, Henry Stone, Joshua Duncan; West Street Sports
***All My Friends Are Racist* – Enoch Mailangi, Kodie Bedford, Bjorn Stewart, Liliana Munoz; Maximo Entertainment & Hoodlum Entertainment**
Celebration Nation – Molly Daniels, Jenny Zhou, Gaby Seow; Satellite Pictures Pty Ltd
Hug the Sun – Aaron McCann, Sam Lingham; Haven't You Done Well & Johnny Ma Studios
Jimmy Rees – Jimmy Rees, David Gillett
Samantha Andrew – Samantha Andrew

BEST DIRECTION IN FILM
The Dry – Robert Connolly
The Furnace – Roderick MacKay
High Ground – Stephen Maxwell Johnson
***Nitram* – Justin Kurzel**
Penguin Bloom – Glendyn Ivin

BEST LEAD ACTOR IN FILM
High Ground – Simon Baker
The Dry – Eric Bana
***Nitram* – Caleb Landry Jones**
The Furnace – Ahmed Malek
High Ground – Jacob Junior Nayinggul

BEST LEAD ACTRESS IN FILM
Peter Rabbit 2 – Rose Byrne
***Nitram* – Judy Davis**
June Again – Noni Hazlehurst
The Dry – Genevieve O'Reilly
Penguin Bloom – Naomi Watts

BEST SUPPORTING ACTOR IN FILM
Rams – Michael Caton
The Furnace – Baykali Ganambarr
Nitram – Anthony LaPaglia
High Ground Sean Mununggurr
High Ground – Jack Thompson

BEST SUPPORTING ACTRESS IN FILM
Nitram – Essie Davis
June Again – Claudia Karvan
High Ground – Esmerelda Marimowa
The Dry – Miranda Tapsell
Penguin Bloom – Jacki Weaver

BEST ORIGINAL SCREENPLAY IN FILM
Ellie and Abbie (& Ellie's Dead Aunt) – Monica Zanetti
The Furnace – Roderick MacKay
High Ground – Chris Anastassiades
June Again – JJ Winlove
Nitram – Shaun Grant

BEST ADAPTED SCREENPLAY IN FILM
***The Dry* – Rob Connolly, Harry Cripps, based on the book by Jane Harper**
Penguin Bloom - Shaun Grant, Harry Cripps, based on the book by Cameron Bloom and Bradley Trevor Grieve
Peter Rabbit 2 – Will Gluck, Patrick Burleigh, based on the characters by Beatrix Potter
Rams – Jules Duncan, based on the film by Grímur Hákonarson

BEST CINEMATOGRAPHY IN FILM
***The Dry* – Stefan Duscio**
High Ground – Andrew Commis
Mortal Kombat – Germain McMicking
Nitram – Germain McMicking
Penguin Bloom – Sam Chiplin

BEST CINEMATOGRAPHY IN A DOCUMENTARY
After the Night – Episode 1: *The End of Innocence* – Jim Frater
***The Beach* – Episode 1: *Too Mad Too Shy* – Dylan River**
The Bowraville Murders – Nathan Barlow
FREEMAN Bonnie Elliott
Step into Paradise – Bonnie Elliott

BEST EDITING IN FILM
The Dry - Nick Meyers, Alexandre de Franceschi
Friends and Strangers - James Vaughan
High Ground - Jill Bilcock, Karryn de Cinque, Hayley Miro Browne
Nitram - Nick Fenton
Peter Rabbit 2 - Matt Villa

BEST EDITING IN A DOCUMENTARY
FREEMAN - Daniel Wieckmann
My Name is Gulpilil - Tania M. Nehme
Playing With Sharks - Adrian Rostirolla
Under the Volcano - Karen Johnson
When the Camera Stopped Rolling - Ray Thomas

BEST COSTUME DESIGN IN FILM
The Dry - Cappi Ireland
High Ground - Erin Roche
Mortal Kombat - Cappi Ireland
Nitram - Alice Babidge
Rams - Tess Schofield

BEST PRODUCTION DESIGN IN FILM
2067 - Jacinta Leong
Mortal Kombat - Naaman Marshall
Nitram - Alice Babidge
Penguin Bloom - Annie Beauchamp
Peter Rabbit 2 - Roger Ford

BEST ORIGINAL SCORE IN FILM
The Dry - Peter Raeburn
June Again - Christopher Gordon
Nitram - Jed Kurzel
Penguin Bloom - Marcelo Zarvos
Rams - Antony Partos

BEST ORIGINAL SCORE IN A DOCUMENTARY
FREEMAN - James Henry
Playing With Sharks - Caitlin Yeo
Step into Paradise - Amanda Brown, Nick Wales
The Beach - Episode 1: Too Mad Too Shy - Megan Washington, Kristin Rule
When the Camera Stopped Rolling - Kyls Burtland

BEST SOUND IN FILM

Ascendant - Angus Robertson, Peter Purcell, Phil Heywood, Scott Mulready
The Dry - Chris Goodes, Ann Aucote, Glenn Newnham
Mortal Kombat - Robert Mackenzie, James Ashton, Des Kenneally, Adrian Medhurst, Jed Dodge, Phil Heywood
Nitram - Steve Single, Dean Ryan, James Ashton
Peter Rabbit 2 - Kevin O'Connell, Robert Mackenzie, Andy Wright, Ben Osmo

BEST SOUND IN A DOCUMENTARY

The Bowraville Murders - Richard Boxhall
FREEMAN - Byron Scullin
Life in Colour with David Attenborough - Episode 1: Seeing in Colour - Wayne Pashley
My Name is Gulpilil - Tom Heuzenroeder
When the Camera Stopped Rolling - Sam Petty

BEST HAIR AND MAKEUP

Australian Gangster - Sheldon Wade, Helen Magelaki, Mariel McClorey, Donna Kennedy
Mortal Kombat - Nikki Gooley
Ms Fisher's Modern Murder Mysteries - Lynn Wheeler
New Gold Mountain - Helen Magelaki, Cheryl Williams, Ian Loughnan
Nitam - Fiona Rees-Jones

BEST CASTING

The Dry - Jane Norris
High Ground - Anousha Zarkesh
The Newsreader - Nathan Lloyd
Nitram - Nikki Barrett, Alison Telford, Kate Leonard
Wakefield - Marianne Jade

BEST VISUAL EFFECTS OR ANIMATION

Jungle Cruise - Jim Berney, Jake Morrison, J.D. Schwalm, Jamie Macdougall, Marla Henshaw, Maite Sarnes; Rising Sun Pictures
Mortal Kombat - Chris Godfrey, Prue Fletcher, Avi Goodman, Nick Tripodi; Method Studios
Mortal Kombat - Dennis Jones, Dan Bethell, Chris Godfrey, Prue Fletcher, Peter Stubbs; Rising Sun Pictures
Peter Rabbit 2 - Will Reichelt, Simon Pickard, Simon Whiteley, Fiona Chilton, Jason Bath, Matt Middleton; Animal Logic
Shang-Chi and the Legend of the Ten Rings - Christopher Townsend, Damien Carr, Josh Simmonds, Nathan Ortiz; Method Studios

GLOSSARY

10BA – A tax incentive that allowed investors to claim a 150 per cent tax concession and to pay tax on only half of any income earned from the investment

AACTA – Australian Academy of Cinema and Television Arts

ABC – Australian Broadcast Commission

ADR – Automated dialogue replacement

AFI – Australian Film Institute

AFL – Australian Football League

AFTRS – Australian Film, Television and Radio School

AIDC – Australian International Documentary Conference

Antenna – Antenna Film Festival, an international documentary film festival

ANZAC – Australia and New Zealand Army Corps

APRA-AGSC – Australasian Performing Rights Association, Australian Guild of Screen Composers

ATOM – Australian Teachers of Media

Avid – Editing software

Bitsa – Mixed breed dog

Co-pro – Co-productions

DADAA – Disability in the Arts, Disadvantage in the Arts

DOP – Director of Photography

EMDR – Eye Movement Desensitisation and Reprocessing

Hot Docs – The Hot Docs Canadian International Documentary Festival the largest documentary festival in North America

IF – Inside Film, a print and online magazine focused on the Australian Film Industry

IMDb – Internet Movie Database

Gender Matters - the umbrella name of Screen Australia's efforts to address the underutilisation of female talent in key creative roles in the Australian screen industry

LGBTQIA+ - Lesbian, Gay, Bisexual, Transgender, Queer/Questioning, Intersex, Asexual

MIFF – Melbourne International Film Festival

NFSA – National Film and Sound Archive

NSW – New South Wales

obdoc – Observational Documentary

PDV – Post, Digital and Visual Effects; usually associated with the Post, Digital and Visual Effects offset guidelines which allows for post-production in Australia to be offset by tax incentives

recce – reconnaissance

SBS – Special Broadcasting Service

Scarlet Alliance – Sex Workers Association Australia

VOD – Video on Demand

WA – Western Australia

BIBLIOGRAPHY

CHAPTER 1

1. www.c21ch.newcastle.edu.au/colonialmassacres/map.php
2. www.abc.net.au/news/2020-06-09/meyne-wyatt-delivers-powerful-monologue-on-racism/12333854
3. www.paytherent.net.au/
4. www.indigenousx.com.au/
5. www.youtube.com/watch?v=knkYoT_11OY

CHAPTER 2

6. https://www.theguardian.com/culture/2021/sep/26/i-was-incredibly-scared-of-it-justin-kurzel-on-making-port-arthur-massacre-film-nitram
7. www.deadline.com/2021/07/nitram-justin-kurzel-shaun-grant-port-arthur-massacre-australia-gun-reform-1234787379/

CHAPTER 3

8. https://www.imdb.com/title/tt13370156/plotsummary
9. www.theconversation.com/why-young-women-say-no-to-rural-australia-100760
10. www.sbs.com.au/language/english/audio/stories-inspired-by-and -filmed-during-the-pandemic
11. www.telethonkids.org.au/projects/past/trans-pathways/

CHAPTER 4

12. www.mediaweek.com.au/documentary-sector-asks-government-to-keep-film-funding-changes-on-cutting-room-floor/
13. www.if.com.au/offset-reform-passes-qape-threshold-to-remain-at-500k/
14. www.screenaustralia.gov.au/sa/screen-news/2021/10-27-gender-matters-update-2020-21
15. www.theguardian.com/australia-news/audio/2021/jul/10/julia-banks-on-barriers-and-boys-clubs-in-parliament-house
16. https://www.theguardian.com/australia-news/2022/mar/29/scott-morrison-labelled-an-autocrat-and-bully-with-no-moral-compass-by-liberal-senator-concetta-fierravanti-wells
17. https://www.news.com.au/finance/work/leaders/julie-bishop-is-most-popular-liberal-leadership-contender/news-story/e489fcfcbad39e43563809aa64587656
18. www.en.wikipedia.org/

wiki/2021_Australian_Parliament_House_sexual_misconduct_allegations

19. Covering black deaths in Australia led me to a breakdown, but that's the position this country puts Aboriginal journalists in - ABC News

20. www.theguardian.com/australia-news/2021/sep/14/christian-porter-reveals-part-of-legal-fees-paid-by-blind-trust-with-funds-from-unknown-source

21. https://www.abc.net.au/radionational/programs/partyroom/auukus-nuclear-christian-porter-labor-diversity/13544432

22. www.makeitabigdeal.org/

23. www.theguardian.com/news/2019/jul/15/euthanasia-and-assisted-dying-rates-are-soaring-but-where-are-they-legal

24. https://www.mamamia.com.au/voluntary-assisted-dying-wa/

25. https://www.rogerebert.com/roger-ebert/eberts-walk-of-fame-remarks

26. www.lauraskitchentable.circle.so/c/welcome

27. www.batoor.com/the-dancing-boys-of-afghanistan

28. www.theguardian.com/environment/2020/jul/01/bunnings-stops-selling-timber-logged-vicforests-court-ruling

29. www.taslabor.com/libs-divided-over-dangerous-and-illegal-video-content/

30. www.smh.com.au/lifestyle/tracey-spicer-why-arent-more-women-immortalised-in-stone-20170928-gyqm59.html

CHAPTER 5

31. https://www2.bfi.org.uk/news-opinion/sight-sound-magazine/features/new-queer-cinema-b-ruby-rich

32. www.lwlies.com/articles/finding-a-definition-queer-cinema/

33. "It's not an easy decision. I'm not a woman, but I also don't feel entirely like a man. I'm a boy human. A human boy. And so, until there is an awards system that accommodates for genderqueer/trans folks, we're gonna have to make the system work for us. I'm an actor, not an actress. I definitely feel more aligned with "male" identifiers. And I don't want to be nominated for the gender of the character I'm playing. Yes, 'Abbie' in the film is female. But Eddie Redmayne wasn't nominated for Best Actress at the Oscars when he did The Danish Girl.
"So, listen. It's all a bit confusing and feels a bit, to quote Missy Higgins, "triangle trying to squeeze through a circle" but until we de-gender awards ceremonies altogether, I'll be up for nomination in the category that most aligns with my gender; best male actor." In a group statement AACTA said: "While AACTA have had other non-binary entrants and nominees in the past, this is the first time a non-binary actor has engaged in the conversation and exercised their right to choose which award suited them. To the best of AACTA's knowledge, Zoe is also the first person to enter a gendered award for a role portraying a different gender character."
www.filmink.com.au/public-notice/ellie-and-abbie-star-zoe-terakes-becomes-first-non-binary-actor-in-consideration-for-all-male-category-at-aacta-awards/

34. www.screenwest.com.au/funding-incentives/production-funding/#section-out-now

CHAPTER 6

35. www.screenaustralia.gov.au/fact-finders/production-trends/feature-production/australian-feature-films/genres-produced
36. www.filmink.com.au/richard-de-carvalho-a-blaster-in-the-right-hands-a-star-wars-story/
37. www.thewrap.com/back-to-the-outback-netflix-trailer/
38. www.screendaily.com/news/australian-films-reach-35-year-high-at-the-local-box-office-in-2021/5166951.article
39. www.screenaustralia.gov.au/fact-finders/cinema/australian-films/top-films-at-the-box-office

CHAPTER 7

40. www.screenaustralia.gov.au/funding-and-support/producer-offset/guidelines/eligibility/significant-australian-content
41. www.aacta.org/aacta-awards/entries/ - Quote taken from the 2021 AACTA Awards Rule Book. This rule book is updated annually.
42. www.screenaustralia.gov.au/the-screen-guide/t/the-power-of-the-dog-2021/38093
43. www.screenaustralia.gov.au/funding-and-support/feature-films/development
44. The **Location Incentive** is a grant of up to 13.5% of the production's QAPE. It is a merit assessed grant which complements the 16.5% Location Offset. It provides funding of AUD$140 million over four years ($35 million per annum) from 1 July 2019 to 30 June 2023. In July 2020 the Federal Government announced a further $400 million in funding for the Location Incentive Program over the next seven years. To be eligible, the production must also be eligible for the Location Offset. Note that the Producer Offset, the Location Offset, the Location Incentive and the PDV Offset are mutually exclusive. Therefore, a company is not eligible to claim the Producer Offset for a project if that project has received a final certificate for the Location or PDV Offset.
www.screenaustralia.gov.au/funding-and-support/producer-offset/location-and-pdv-offsets
45. The **Location Offset**, a 16.5 per cent offset on qualifying Australian production expenditure (QAPE) for film and television projects filmed in Australia with an Australian spend of over $15 million.
www.screenaustralia.gov.au/funding-and-support/producer-offset/location-and-pdv-offsets
46. The **PDV Offset,** a 30 per cent offset on the QAPE that relates to post, digital and visual effects production for a film.
www.screenaustralia.gov.au/funding-and-support/producer-offset/location-and-pdv-offsets
47. www.boomerangandspear.com/about-us/
48. www.chambermade.org/people/ching-ching-ho/
49. www.screenaustralia.gov.au/fact-finders/people-and-businesses/production-businesses/in-the-archive/operation-of-10ba
50. www.seventh-row.com/tag/mouthpiece/
51. "Patricia Rozema's Mouthpiece is the kind of brilliantly experimental, engaging and empathetic film that Charlie Kaufman could only DREAM of making."
www.twitter.com/kermodemovie/status/1370685416819597312
52. www.if.com.au/miff-announces-140000-best-film-award/
53. www.en.wikipedia.org/wiki/Cinema_of_Canada

54. Vancouver Never Plays Itself – Every Frame a Painting (A sly nod to Thomas Andersen's influential and impactful video essay *Los Angeles Plays Itself*) www.youtube.com/watch?v=ojm74VGsZBU

55. www.dailymail.co.uk/tvshowbiz/article-9282707/Marvel-movies-filmed-Australia-foreseeable-future.html

56. www.abc.net.au/news/2021-01-24/from-matt-damon-to-zac-efron-why-celebrities-flock-to-australia/13078358

57. www.if.com.au/post-and-vfx-companies-fear-pdv-offset-threshold-change-is-short-sighted/

58. www.if.com.au/offset-reform-passes-qape-threshold-to-remain-at-500k/

59. www.theconversation.com/no-the-federal-government-didnt-spend-4-billion-on-covid-support-for-culture-and-the-arts-177443

60. www.deadline.com/2022/01/julia-roberts-george-clooney-rom-com-ticket-to-paradise-delayed-australia-covid-1234914259/

Printed in Australia
AUHW021431010722
365773AU00001B/1

9 780645 429602